marketing

marketing

2ND EDITION

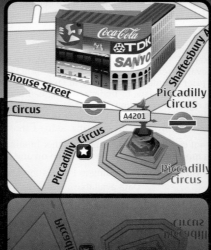

Paul Baines, Chris Fill,
and Kelly Page

OXFORD
UNIVERSITY PRESS

OXFORD
UNIVERSITY PRESS

Great Clarendon Street, Oxford OX2 6DP

Oxford University Press is a department of the University of Oxford.
It furthers the University's objective of excellence in research, scholarship,
and education by publishing worldwide in

Oxford New York

Auckland Cape Town Dar es Salaam Hong Kong Karachi
Kuala Lumpur Madrid Melbourne Mexico City Nairobi
New Delhi Shanghai Taipei Toronto

With offices in

Argentina Austria Brazil Chile Czech Republic France Greece
Guatemala Hungary Italy Japan Poland Portugal Singapore
South Korea Switzerland Thailand Turkey Ukraine Vietnam

Oxford is a registered trade mark of Oxford University Press
in the UK and in certain other countries

Published in the United States
by Oxford University Press Inc., New York

© Oxford University Press 2011

The moral rights of the authors have been asserted
Database right Oxford University Press (maker)

First published 2008
This edition 2011

British Library Cataloguing in Publication Data
Data available

Library of Congress Cataloguing in Publication Data
Data available

Typeset in 9.7/13pt Slimbach by TechType, Abingdon

ISBN 978-0-19-957961-7

5 7 9 10 8 6 4

Printed by Bell & Bain Ltd Glasgow

$ 25.00

'To my wife, Ning, my best friend and constant companion'

Paul Baines

'To Karen, our boys and LvB'

Chris Fill

'To Mum and Dad, for showing me the road less travelled
and believing in me on every path'

Kelly Page

Brief Contents

Detailed Contents

> **Additional lecturer material**
>
> **Online Case Study**
> Written by Dr Paul Baines, Cranfield School of Management, Cranfield University
> *CIM: The Problem of 'Marketing' Marketing*
>
> **Academic Insight**
> Guest Lecture by Professor Michael Saren, School of Management, University of Leicester
> *Why is it Important to be Critical in Marketing?*

> **Additional lecturer material**
>
> **Online Case Study**
> Written by Professor Phil Harris, University of Otago, New Zealand
> *The Self-Regulation and Development of the Chemical Industry in Europe*
>
> **Academic Insight**
> Dr Paul Baines, Cranfield School of Management, Cranfield University
> *Why Analysing the Marketing Environment is the Key to Marketing Success*

Additional lecturer material

Online Case Study
Written by Lorna Stevens, University of Ulster
Red Magazine: Women Consumers, Lifestyle Trends and the New Zeitgeist

Academic Insight
Professor Jagdish Sheth, Emory University, USA
The Consumer Buying Psyche

Additional lecturer material

Online Case Study
Written by Nigel Bradley, Westminster Business School, University of Westminster
Research projects: Insight at Mary Holidays

Written by Dr Paul Baines, Cranfield School of Management, Cranfield University
Writing Research Proposals: The Case of PolMedia

Academic Insight
Nigel Bradley, Westminster Business School, University of Westminster
The Marketing Research Mix

Dr Kelly Page, Cardiff Business School
How the world's best companies use market research effectively

Additional lecturer material
Online Case Study
Written by Dr Paul Hughes, Loughborough University and Professor Robert Morgan, Cardiff Business School
Blackberry: Lessons in Strategic Positioning

Written by Dr Charles Denis, Brunel University
Promoting the Promoters: Outdoor Advertising of JC Decaux

Academic Insight
Professor Nigel Piercy, Warwick Business School
The Rhetoric and Realities of Marketing Strategy
Professor Malcolm McDonald, Cranfield School of Management, Cranfield University
Why Some Marketing Programmes Fail and Others Do Not

Additional lecturer material

Online Case Study

Written by Professor Emeritus Malcolm McDonald, Cranfield School of Management, Cranfield University

Globaltech: How Market Segmentation Improved Profitability in a Global Company's Aftersales Service Operations

Academic Insight

Gareth Smith, Loughborough University Business School

Market Positioning and the UK Automobile Industry

Additional lecturer material

Online Case Study

Written by Dr Kelly Page, Cardiff Business School

Cargill: Localization in the Chinese Food Market

Academic Insight

Professor Stan Paliwoda, University of Strathclyde

Do Global Consumers Really Exist?

Additional lecturer material

Online Case Study
Written by Professor Simon Knox, Dr Paul Baines, Cranfield School of Management, Cranfield University and Gary Smith, Rolls Royce
Building the 7E7: NPD at Boeing

Academic Insight
Dr Stuart Roper, Manchester Business School
A Brief History of Branding

Additional lecturer material

Online Case Study
Written by Tom Chapman, University of Portsmouth
Apple Inc — the Significance of 'iPricing'

Academic Insight
Tom Chapman, University of Portsmouth
Pricing: Marketing's Forgotten Holy Grail

Additional lecturer material

Online Case Study
Written by Martin Evans, Cardiff Business School
Dr and the Ghostly Persuaders: Multi-step Flows of Communication in Medical Markets

Academic Insight
Chris Fill, Managing Director of Fill Associates, formerly Principal Lecturer at the University of Portsmouth.
The Changing Nature of Marketing Communications
Chris Fill, Managing Director of Fill Associates, formerly Principal Lecturer at the University of Portsmouth.
The Role of Marketing Communications in Relationship Marketing

Additional lecturer material

Online Case Study

Written by Dr Yasmin Sekhon, University of Bournemouth

Talking to Heidi: Choosing the Right Communications Mix

Written by Dr Yasmin Sekhon, University of Bournemouth

Planning to Sell Waterbeds: Aqua Style Waterbeds' Strategic Planning

Academic Insight

Beth Rogers, University of Portsmouth

Issues in Sales Management and Planning

Professor Denis Sadler, Pace University, USA

Planning and Implementing a Marketing and Communications Campaign (Ambush Marketing)

John Egan, Middlesex University Business School

To Integrate or not to Integrate your Marketing Communications?

Additional lecturer material

Online Case Study

Written by Professor Leigh Sparks, University of Stirling

Seven-Eleven Japan: 'Life Infrastructure'

Academic Insight

Dr Fiona Ellis-Chadwick, Loughborough

How IT Has Transformed Retail Marketing

Additional lecturer material

Online Case Study
Written by Dr Steve Oakes, University of Liverpool
Lewington's: Designing the Department Store Musicscape By Zone—How Music Influences Consumers in Service Environments

Academic Insight
Professor Christine Ennew, Nottingham University Business School
The Importance of Quality and Experience in Services Marketing

> **Additional lecturer material**
>
> **Online Case Study**
> Written by Beth Rogers, University of Portsmouth
> *The Personal Touch: How Dal Maschio Sales Engineers Deliver Value to Customers*
>
> **Academic Insight**
> Professor Caroline Tynan, Nottingham University Business School
> *Managing Buyer–Seller Interactions to Achieve Marketing Success*

> **Additional lecturer material**
>
> **Online Case Study**
> Written by Dr John Egan, Middlesex University Business School
> *When the Relationship is Over: the Case of Disney*
>
> **Academic Insight**
> Professor Hugh Wilson, Cranfield School of Marketing, Cranfield University
> *Actioning Customer Insight: the 6 Is of CRM*

Additional lecturer material

Online Case Study

Written by Professor Stephen Brown, University of Ulster

Titanic: The Unsinkable Brand

Academic Insight

Dr Pamela Odih, Goldsmiths, University of London

Advertising and Postmodern Consumer Culture

Additional lecturer material

Online Case Study

Written by Dr Iain Davies, Cranfield School of Management, Cranfield University

Who to Work With: Ethical Dilemmas at Day Chocolate Company

Academic Insight

Chris Fill, Managing Director of Fill Associates, formerly Principal Lecturer at the University of Portsmouth

Why Ethics in Marketing is More Important Than Ever Before

Case Insights

▶ **Chapter 1: Systembolaget**
Systembolaget is the world's first alcohol monopoly and remains the only retailer of alcohol in Sweden. We speak to Fredrik Thor, to find out how a state alcohol monopoly with a prohibition remit can possibly market itself.

▶ **Chapter 2: Michelin Tyres**
Michelin Tyres has been established for over a century and is now active in more than 170 countries. We speak to Helen Tattersall to find out how it keeps abreast of the marketing environment.

▶ **Chapter 3: BRAND sense agency**
BRAND sense agency is involved with developing a holistic understanding of a brand's sensory impact. We speak to CEO Simon Harrop to find out how they go about this.

▶ **Chapter 4: i to i research**
The i to i research agency conducted market research into public support during the bid process for London to hold the Olympic Games in 2012. We speak to CEO, Claire Spencer, to find out more.

▶ **Chapter 5: Innocent Drinks**
Innocent Drinks market their smoothies in a highly innovative way. We speak to Dan Germain, Head of Creative, to find out what strategies they will use to market their new water/juice drinks.

▶ **Chapter 6: Stagecoach**
Stagecoach Group Plc, operates bus services across the UK. We speak to Elaine Rosscraig to find out how it knows who its customers are and where they want to access its services.

▶ **Chapter 7: Orange**
We talk to Sue Wilmot, Head of Customer Strategy Delivery in the customer marketing team at Orange, to find out how they set about retaining large numbers of international customers.

▶ **Chapter 8: 3M**
3M is well known for brands including Scotch, Post-it, and Thinsulate. We speak to Andrew Hicks, European Market Development Manager, to find out how the company developed an innovative, new product, the Visual Attention Service 3M VAS.

▶ **Chapter 9: P&O Ferries**
P&O Ferries now operates in competition with low-cost airlines, as well as low-cost ferry operators. We speak to Simon Johnson to find out how it makes its pricing decisions.

▶ **Chapter 10: London Eye**
The British Airways London Eye has become the UK's most popular visitor attraction. We speak to Helen Bull to find out how it uses marketing communications in a number of interesting ways.

▶ **Chapter 11: ZSL London Zoo**
London Zoo, located in Regent's Park in the centre of London, has changed its name to ZSL London Zoo. We speak to James Bailey to find out why.

▶ **Chapter 12: HMV**

HMV opened its first store in Oxford Street, London, and today is more of a multiple entertainment hub than a pure music retailer. We speak to Gennaro Castaldo to find out how HMV is adapting to changing customer and market expectations.

▶ **Chapter 13: MOLLY MAID**

MOLLY MAID provides a professional and personalized home cleaning service, undertaken by a team of two people. We speak to Pam Bader to find out more.

▶ **Chapter 14: Reed Smith**

Reed Smith is a major global law firm that represents many of the world's leading companies in high-stakes disputes, strategic transactions, and crucial regulatory matters. We speak to Victoria Gregory to find out more.

▶ **Chapter 15: RAKBANK**

RAKBANK is the highly successful National Bank of Ras Al-Khaimahin, in the United Arab Emirates. We speak to Banali Malhotra, Head of Marketing, to find out how they sought to improve relationships with their customers.

▶ **Chapter 16: Oxfam**

Oxfam opened one of the world's first charity shop chains in 1948. We speak to Nick Futcher, Brand Manager, to find out how this world-renowned charity has kept pace given major changes in the world since then.

▶ **Chapter 17: Rage Against the X-Factor**

We talk to Jon and Tracey Morter from Essex who launched a Facebook campaign in December 2009 aimed at using the power of social networks to prevent the X-Factor single from topping the UK single charts.

▶ **Chapter 18: Livity**

Livity is a youth marketing agency set up with the core aim to be socially responsible. We speak to Michelle Clothier and Sam Conniff to find out how it communicates sensitive messages to hard-to-reach audiences.

▶ **Chapter 19: The Co-operative Bank**

The Co-operative Bank was the first and remains the only UK high street bank with a customer-led Ethical Policy, which gives customers a say in how their money is used. We speak to Kelvin Collins to find out more.

Author Profiles

 **Paul Baines** is Reader in Marketing at Cranfield School of Management and Course Director, MSc Strategic Marketing. Paul is Managing Editor, Europe of the *Journal of Political Marketing*. He is author/co-author of more than eighty published articles, book chapters and books, concentrating particularly on political marketing issues. Paul is an experienced author whose publications include books on PR, marketing research and strategy. Paul's marketing consultancy projects have included work for a variety of large public and private organisations including a high-profile football club, a large aerospace maintenance company, a national charity, an advertising agency, an awarding body, government departments, and a private jet start-up company. He was a board director of the sub-regional development agency, North London Limited from October 2005-April 2008, and operates his own strategic marketing / research consultancy, Baines Associates Limited.

 **Chris Fill** is the founder and Managing Director of Fill Associates. The company develops, supplies, and evaluates resources for marketing communications and related topics. Formerly a Principal Lecturer at the University of Portsmouth, Chris now works for a variety of organisations, including private and not-for-profit organisations plus several publishers. He is a Visiting Professor at the Grenoble Graduate School of Business and a Fellow of the Chartered Institute of Marketing where he is the Senior Examiner responsible for designing, writing and managing the Professional Postgraduate Diploma module, *Managing Corporate Reputation*. In addition to numerous papers published in a range of academic journals, he has written a series of books, including his internationally recognised textbook, *Marketing Communications*. Other titles include *Managing Corporate Reputation*, *Business-to-Business Marketing* and the most recently published *Essentials of Marketing Communications*.

Fill Associates develops learning materials related to marketing and corporate communications, some of which can be found online at www.MarketingMentor.net, and provides training, evaluation and consultancy for organisations wishing to manage their reputation. Chris speaks regularly on marketing and corporate communication issues.

 **Kelly Page** is Lecturer in Digital Media Marketing at Cardiff Business School. Her research explores digital media knowledge, literacy and participation in digital media marketing. She has a PhD on Consumer Web Knowledge from the University of New South Wales (UNSW) in Sydney Australia. Her publications have appeared in peer-reviewed journals in the fields of Psychology, Marketing and Digital Media/IT and her work involves partnerships with organisations in the digital media, web design and Internet marketing sectors. Kelly is a visiting fellow in Digital Marketing at Cranfield School of Management (UK) and Grenoble Graduate School of Business (GGSB) (France) and currently a board member of the Academy of Marketing Research Committee (AMRC). Before she relocated to the UK, Kelly worked in Australia for APESMA Management Education (now Chiefly Business School), UNSW and worked as a consultant with The Leading Edge (TLE) Research Group.

Acknowledgements

As we discovered when writing the first edition, course textbooks are substantial projects, resulting from the sweat and toil of many people not just in their design, development, and production, but in the sales, marketing and distribution of them. The production of a text is only a small aspect of what is now an integrated package including website, book and audio-visual components. So, there have been a great many people who have contributed to the 2nd edition of this particular book, and its Online Resource Centre and DVD; some of those people we outline below and many others we don't, but whose contributions should be acknowledged anonymously nonetheless.

We would like to thank our colleagues at Cranfield School of Management, Cardiff Business School and the Portsmouth Business School for their support, discussions, and general input over the years. We would especially like to thank Robert Ormrod of Aarhus University, Denmark, Ning Baines, and Mark Wilson for their contributions to the online resources for this second edition.

As with any large textbook project, this work is the result of a co-production between the academic authors and Oxford University Press editors and staff. We would particularly like to thank Sacha Cook, Editor-in-Chief, for persuading us to take on such a gargantuan project in the first instance and organising us to develop a second edition so quickly after the success of the first edition. The contributions of the Development Editors have been fundamental; thanks to Helen Cook and Sarah Lodge for their work on the chapter development and the book's associated online resources. We would also like to thank Francesca Griffin, our publishing manager, for keeping a watchful eye over the text in the second edition and helping with the development of the DVD and the Online Resource Centre. Many thanks to Fiona Goodall for her work as web editor, given its fundamental importance as a book's success increasingly focuses on its online resources.

We would like to thank Angela Butterworth, Production Editor, for her role in shaping the final design of the book and bringing it out on schedule with the help of the design team, Gemma Barber and Simon Witter, and our freelance picture researcher Sophie Hartley, who worked so hard to find us such fitting photographs. Thanks also to James Tomalin, and the team at Oxford Digital Media, for their continuing excellent video production work. James' easy-going style makes him a pleasure to work with.

Finally, as marketers we know unless our customers, students and lecturers want to use this book, there's no use in producing it so we recognise the efforts of the marketing team, Marianne Lightowler, Marketing Director, and Katy Duff, Marketing Manager, in developing and implementing an innovative sales and marketing plan for this second edition.

The original design for the book – going back to the first edition - was initially developed from six anonymous university lecturer participants of a focus group, who kindly agreed to meet at OUP offices to discuss what was needed in a new marketing textbook. We would particularly like to thank them again for their support and hope this second edition stays true to, and advances, their original concept.

The authors and publishers would like to thank the following people, for their comments and reviews throughout the process of developing the text and the Online Resource Centre:

Geraldine Cohen, *Brunel University*

John Egan, *Middlesex University*

Fiona Ellis-Chadwick, *Loughborough University*
Malcolm Goodman, *Durham University*
Michael Harker, *University of Strathclyde*
Nnamdi Madichie, *University of East London Business School*
Alice Maltby, *University of the West of England, Bristol*
Tony McGuinness, *Aberystwyth University*
Richard Meek, *Lancaster University*
Nina Michaelidou, *University of Birmingham*
Janice Moorhouse, *Thames Valley University*
Chris Rock, *University of Greenwich*
Lorna Stevens, *University of Ulster*
Paul Trott, *University of Portsmouth*
Prakash Vel, *University of Wollongong, Dubai*
Peter Waterhouse, *University of Bedfordshire*
Peter Williams, *Leeds Metropolitan University*
Matthew Wood, *University of Brighton*
Helen Woodruffe-Burton, *University of Cumbria*
Andrea Prothero, *University College Dublin*
George Masikunas, *Kingston University*
Connie Nolan, *Canterbury Christ Church University*
Neil Richardson, *Leeds Metropolitan University*
Heléne Lundberg, *Mid Sweden University*
Mike Flynn, *University of Gloucestershire*
Jennie White, *Bournemouth*
Ann Torres, *National University of Ireland Galway*
Mikael Gidhagen, *Uppsala University*
Charles Graham, *London South Bank University*
Liz Algar-Soanders, *University of Essex*
Dr Patrick McCole, *Queen's University Management School*
Dr Elizabeth Jackson, *Newcastle University*

Thanks also to those reviewers who chose to remain anonymous. The publishers would be pleased to clear permission with any copyright holders that we have inadvertently failed, or been unable to, contact.

Preface

Welcome to the 2nd edition of *Marketing*. You may be wondering **"why should I buy this marketing textbook?"** The simple answer is that your marketing lecturers told us you needed a new one! In our first edition, we were the first truly integrated print and electronic learning package for introductory marketing modules And for this second edition, we've gone further. Before we started writing the 2nd edition we went back to marketing lecturers, building on our research for the 1st edition, to identify how we could further tailor the book to meet your learning needs. We discovered that you needed;

▶ more concise coverage of marketing communications

▶ greater integration between the wealth of material online and the textbook

▶ coverage of advances in new technology and the social web and how to take advantage of these in a marketing context

▶ information on how to get your first job in marketing and what skills employers look for

▶ A chapter dedicated to not for profit and social marketing

▶ A shorter textbook to better fit your module's coverage

▶ More examples from Europe and the Middle East to understand marketing in an international context

As with the first edition, the purpose of this package remains to bring contemporary marketing perspectives to life for students new to the concept of marketing, and for it to be motivational, creative, applied, and highly relevant to you. We've included brand new examples from organisations including Oxfam, HMV and Orange to help illustrate how real life practitioners tackle marketing problems.

Marketing starts with the basic concepts from classical marketing perspectives and contrasts these with newer views from the relational and service-based schools of marketing, helping you develop your knowledge and understanding of marketing. On the Online Resource Centre we also provide you with web-based research activities, abstracts from seminal papers, study guidelines, multiple-choice questions, and a flashcard glossary to help you broaden and reinforce your own learning.

We aim to provide powerful learning insights into marketing theory and practice, through a series of 'Insight' features – Case, Market, and Research Insights. *Marketing* is for life, purchased at level 1 or 2 or as reference reading for postgraduate marketing courses but retained and referred to throughout the course of your marketing or business degree. We sincerely hope you enjoy learning more about marketing!

Who Should Use This Book?

The main audiences for this book are:

▶ Undergraduate students in universities and colleges of Higher and Further Education, who are taught in English, around the world. The case material and the examples within the text are deliberately global and international in scale so that international students can benefit from the text.

▶ Postgraduate students on MBA and MSc/MA courses with a strong marketing component will find this text useful for pre-course and background reading, particularly because of the real-life case problems presented at the beginning of each chapter accompanied by an instructor DVD containing material presenting the solution.

New to this Edition:

▶ Now more concise and shorter in length.

▶ Features a new chapter on not-for-profit and social marketing, and condensed coverage of marketing communications, all in keeping with market recommendations.

▶ Includes a fantastic new feature presenting the skills marketing practitioners really look for in graduates, and what past students have found useful through both written quotes and online tips.

▶ Downloadable author podcasts summarising each chapter.

▶ Additional online learning material, including worksheets, exercises, and further reading, is now all clearly signposted throughout the textbook.

▶ More examples from Europe and the Middle East.

▶ Brand new case insights and associated DVD material featuring well-known companies including HMV, Orange and Oxfam.

How To Use This Textbook

This text aims to enhance your learning as part of an undergraduate or introductory course in marketing or as pre-reading for your postgraduate course. It can, however, also act as a 'book for life' in the sense that it will also operate as a reference book for you on marketing matters,during your initial career in marketing and business.

Generally, we only learn what is meaningful to us. Consequently, we have tried to make your learning fun and meaningful by including a multitude of real-life cases. If there is a seminal article associated with a particular concept, try to get hold of the article through your university's electronic library resources and read it. Reflect on your own experience if possible around the concept you are studying.

Above all, recognise that you are not on your own in your learning. You have your tutor, your classmates and us to help you learn more about marketing.

This textbook includes not only explanatory material and examples on the nature of marketing concepts, but also a holistic learning system designed to aid you, as part of your university course, to develop your understanding through reading the text. Work through the examples in the text and the review questions; read the seminal articles that have defined a particular sub-discipline in marketing; and use the learning material on the website. This textbook aims to be reader-focused, designed to help you learn marketing for yourself.

Most of you will operate either a surface or a deep approach to learning. With the former, you memorise lists of information, whereas with the latter you are actively assimilating, theorising about, and *understanding* the information. With a surface learning approach, you can run into trouble when example problems learnt are presented in different contexts. You may have simply memorised the procedure without understanding the actual problem.

Deep approaches to learning are related to higher quality educational outcomes and better grades, and the process is more enjoyable. To help you pursue a deep approach to learning, we strongly suggest that you complete the exercises and worksheets at the end of each chapter and on the Online Resource Centre to improve your understanding and your course performance.

Honey And Mumford's Learning Style Questionnaire

Honey and Mumford (1986) developed a learning style questionnaire that divides learners into four categories based on which aspect of Kolb's learning process they perform best at. Completion of the questionnaire, available at a reasonable price as a 40-item questionnaire at www.peterhoney.com, provides you with scores on each of the following four categories to allow you to determine your dominant learning style. The four styles are:

1 **Activists** – Where this style is dominant, you learn better through involvement in new experiences through concrete experience. You learn better by doing.

2 **Reflectors** – Where this style is dominant, you are more likely to consider experiences in hindsight and from a variety of perspectives and rationalise these experiences. You learn better by reflecting.

3 **Theorists** – Where this style is dominant, you develop understanding of situations and information by developing an abstract theoretical framework for understanding. You learn better by theorising.

4 **Pragmatists** – Where this style is dominant, you learn best by understanding what works best in what circumstances in practice. You learn through practice.

Analysis of your learning style will allow you to determine how you learn best at the moment, and give you pointers as to what other approaches to learning you might adopt to balance how you develop. You may already have completed a learning style questionnaire at the beginning of your course and so know which learning styles you need to develop.

We believe most textbooks are designed to particularly develop the theorist learning style. Review type questions also enhance the reflector learning style. However, in this text, we also aim to develop the pragmatist component of your learning style by providing you with Case Insights, by showing you material in which marketing practitioners discuss real-life problems with which they had to deal. Finally, we ask end of chapter discussion questions which require you to work in teams and on your own to develop your activist learning style.

We aim to enhance your learning by providing an integrated marketing learning system, incorporating the key components that you need to understand the core marketing principles. In this respect, we hope not only that this text and its associated website will facilitate and enhance your learning, making it fun along the way, but that you will find it useful to use this text and, refer back to it, throughout your student and life experiences of marketing.

Remember, learning should be fun as well as challenging. Good luck with your learning and in your career!

How To Use This Book

Learning Outcomes

A bulleted outline of the main concepts and ideas indicates what you can expect to learn from each chapter.

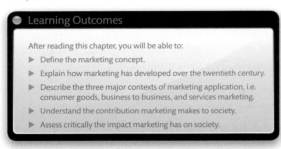

Learning Outcomes

After reading this chapter, you will be able to:

▶ Define the marketing concept.

▶ Explain how marketing has developed over the twentieth century.

▶ Describe the three major contexts of marketing application, i.e. consumer goods, business to business, and services marketing.

▶ Understand the contribution marketing makes to society.

▶ Assess critically the impact marketing has on society.

Case Insights

Learn from real-life situations and discover what top marketers from organizations including Innocent, Orange, HMV and Oxfam actually do and the challenges they face. Once you've read about the dilemma facing the marketer you'll have the opportunity to think about how you would go about tackling the problem.

Market Insights

Topical and lively examples will help you to apply the marketing theory to a well known brand or product. Questions accompany each Market Insight to enhance your critical thinking skills.

Research Insights

Seminal journal articles and books are signposted to broaden your understanding of the chapter topics.

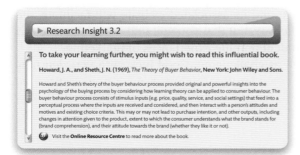

▶ Research Insight 3.2

To take your learning further, you might wish to read this influential book.

Howard, J. A., and Sheth, J. N. (1969), *The Theory of Buyer Behavior*, New York: John Wiley and Sons.

Howard and Sheth's theory of the buyer behaviour process provided original and powerful insights into the psychology of the buying process by considering how learning theory can be applied to consumer behaviour. The buyer behaviour process consists of stimulus inputs (e.g. price, quality, service, and social settings) that feed into a perceptual process where the inputs are received and considered, and then interact with a person's attitudes and motives and existing choice criteria. This may or may not lead to purchase intention, and other outputs, including changes in attention given to the product, extent to which the consumer understands what the brand stands for (brand comprehension), and their attitude towards the brand (whether they like it or not).

Visit the **Online Resource Centre** to read more about the book.

▶ Case Insight 3.1

BRAND sense agency helps clients build brands that enjoy deeper emotional connections with their consumers both through communications and the customer experience to arrive at a holistic understanding of the brand's sensory impact. We talk to CEO, Simon Harrop, to find out more.

Imagine you are walking through a supermarket, surrounded by products in aisles and point-of-sale material all vying for your attention, when you suddenly become aware of the smell of bread, which captures your senses and sends you off in a hurry to the supermarket's boulangerie. If smell has such power in a supermarket could it be used for advertising or enhancing the customer experience in other ways? In such a vision- and sound-cluttered promotional world, could other senses be used instead?

BRAND sense agency was set up because of a belief that brands and marketers rely too heavily on vision and words to communicate with and engage consumers. Our intuition and experience was confirmed when we carried out one of the largest ever studies into the relationship between brands and consumers across all the senses. There is a serious imbalance between how, as humans, we experience brands and how marketers seek to communicate brand propositions. Our mission is to address this imbalance, make marketing more effective, and build a business that we enjoy in the process!

Consumer behaviour is the sum of our rational and conscious relationship to the products or services that we buy but also the emotional and non-conscious influences. Consumer behaviour is the sum of

This bank smells as good as it looks!

▶ Market Insight 3.1

Volvo Deals for Anxious Buyers

The Volvo website showroom presents its S40
Volvo Car Uk

In 2007, car manufacturer Volvo, headquartered in Göteborg, Sweden, sold 30,100 new cars in Britain, taking a 1.3% share of the market, behind more popular UK brands such as Peugeot, Renault, Audi/VW, GM/Vauxhall, Ford, Toyota/Lexus, BMW, and Honda. Sales were down 0.3% between 2002 and 2006 in a difficult trading environment. Since 2007, the car market has suffered further with the 'credit crunch' and declining consumer confidence. In May 2009, because new car registrations were at an all-time low and to re-energize the car market, the British government introduced a new scrappage scheme whereby £2,000 would be paid to buyers who scrapped a car that was at least ten years old when buying a new one.

Vehicle manufacturers and dealership sales personnel understand the psychological anxiety car buyers feel when purchasing a new car. The buyer's key consideration is ensuring they have obtained value for money and not feeling that they have been 'ripped off'. The problem is particularly acute when customers are buying new cars, because new cars are so much more expensive than second-hand cars. When we consider that cars lose 20–30% of their value in depreciation the moment they leave the showroom, we see why new car buyers feel particularly vulnerable. Of course, there are benefits: new cars look better, incorporate the latest design features, and have reduced maintenance costs.

Car dealers work hard to reinforce the decision made by new car buyers by sending customers newsletters and offering efficient (or free three-year warranty)

Skills for employment

▶▶ When recruiting great marketers, I look for stro
creative thinking in any walk of life. Have you solve

Skills for employment

Hear from top marketers on what skills and attributes they look for in new recruits, and how to stand out in today's competitive job market.

go online

conabiting. (See Chapter 6 for more on lifecycle segmentation.
Visit the **Online Resource Centre** and complete Internet Act
how VW uses the family lifecycle to communicate its brand va
Most market research agencies routinely measure attitudes a
on lifecycle stage to determine differences among groups. Tab
difference in the type of goods and services purchased as a res

Go Online

The Online Resource Centre contains a wealth of material and activities to expand and test your knowledge. In each chapter you'll find helpful links to online resources including internet activities, web links and worksheets.

Review Questions

1 What is the process consumers go through when buying goods and ser
2 What is cognitive dissonance and how does it relate to consumer beha
3 How are the psychological concepts of perception, learning, and mem

Review Questions

Test your understanding of the chapter's central themes.

Worksheet summary

Visit the Online Resource Centre and complete Worksheet 3.1. This will help yo
between consumer behaviour in each of the National Readership Survey's soci
D and E.

Worksheet Summary

This summary gives you a flavour of the worksheet you can complete online in your own time. The worksheets encourage you to apply your learning to the marketing of real products and brands.

Discussion Questions

1 Having read Case Insight 3.1 at the beginning of this chapter, how
agency to develop a sensory marketing campaign for its retail ba
smell not only for the brand itself but also for the retail environm

Discussion Questions

Stimulating questions are provided to help you develop skills in analysis and debate.

gical influences—our debt to **social anthropology** increases
litative market research approaches such as **ethnography** .
nsumer behaviour (see Chapters 4 and 19), particularly th

social anthropology the scientific discipline of observing and recording the way humans behave in their different social groupings.

Key Terms and Glossary

Key terms are highlighted in blue where they first appear in each chapter and are also collated with their definitions in the glossary at the back of the book.

The Online Resource Centre

www.oxfordtextbooks.co.uk/orc/baines2e/

The Online Resource Centre (ORC) comprises resources for both lecturers and students, including:

Lecturer Resources Free for all registered adopters of the textbook

Case Insight: Rage Against the X-Factor

- How could an online community use social networks to oppose an international music franchise and make British music history?
- In 2009, Jon and Tracey Morter from Essex showed Simon Cowell they have much more than the X-Factor.
- Having dominated the Christmas No. 1 Charts for 4-years, they started a campaign through a Facebook Group, promoting for Christmas No. 1 a non-X-factor single.
- The single 'Killing in the Name' by artists Rage Against the Machine (RATM), was first released 17 years earlier in 1992.

PowerPoint slides

Accompanying each chapter is a suite of customizable slides to be used in lecture presentations.

Tutorial activities

Full of interactive activities that reinforce practical marketing skills, the tutorial activities have been designed for in-class seminars and tutorials. The activities link directly to the wealth of resources on the Marketing Resource Bank DVD providing lecturers with an array of ideas for integrating the textbook and its resources into their teaching.

Pointers on answering discussion questions

For each chapter there are suggested answer guides to the end of chapter discussion questions.

Online case studies

The book is accompanied by online cases for each chapter. These cases are designed to reinforce students' understanding of particular chapter themes and to encourage them to undertake more involved situational analyses of marketing scenarios. Each case study is accompanied by critical thinking questions and solutions.

Essay questions

For each chapter stimulating essay questions are provided for lecturers to set students.

Branding resource

This valuable resource provides additional branding material, linked to and supplementing that which appears here in the textbook. As well as presenting students with the core theory they will need when developing their knowledge of this area, this resource also provides them with examples, and annotated links to help consolidate their learning.

Test bank

This ready-made electronic testing resource, which is fully customizable and contains feedback for students, will help lecturers to save time creating assessments.

Marketing planning resource

This practical guide is designed to offer students additional support while studying their marketing module. The theory on the development of the marketing plan is balanced alongside useful practical tips on implementation, and advice on core skills such as presenting and negotiating.

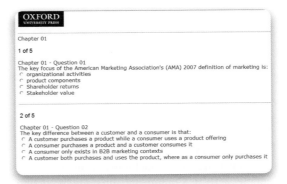

Don't forget that all of these resources can be uploaded to your institution's Virtual Learning Environment to allow students to access them directly!

Student Resources   Free and open-access material available

Internet activities

Arranged by chapter, the internet activities encourage you to undertake web based research and enhance your understanding of key marketing concepts.

Web links

These annotated web links provide pointers towards important marketing related sites.

Student worksheets

These task focused worksheets can be completed in class or independently. They provide you with the opportunity to enhance your understanding of marketing frameworks and theories.

Multiple choice questions

With 20 interactive multiple-choice questions per chapter this bank of questions gives you instant feedback and page references to help you focus on areas that need further study.

Seminal paper links

Throughout the textbook you'll find references to seminal academic papers. This resource provides links to these papers, available on the types of electronic databases subscribed to by most universities worldwide.

YouTube library of links

For each chapter there are links to YouTube videos on marketing and marketing practice.

Skills corner

Hear from other students and graduates about the skills they've developed and how these have helped them in the world of work. You'll also find links to lots of helpful advice on enhancing your employability.

Podcasts

The authors have provided audio podcasts summarizing the key learning objectives for each chapter. You can listen to these on the go, to help you revise and to give you a quick overview of each chapter.

Walkthrough of the DVD Resource

DVD

Marketing comes with an extraordinary suite of additional materials including your exclusive adopter's DVD. Comprising three DVDs: practitioner videos, academic videos and a marketing resource bank, all linked back to the textbook, the DVD package ensures that you'll never need to search anywhere else for resources for your teaching.

Contact your local OUP representative (*please see* **http://www.oup.co.uk/contactus/academic/ sales/hecontact**/) for a tour of the complete DVD package and the opportunity to trial the DVD for yourself.

Marketing Resource Bank

The Marketing Resource Bank contains a suite of interactive and multi-media marketing tools, and examples of marketing practice that have been sourced from a wide range of businesses, industries, and country contexts. The bank of resources has grown with this edition and new interactive tools have been added for each chapter. These include, but are not restricted to, examples of integrated marketing communications campaigns, TV and magazine advertisements, podcasts, websites, viral marketing campaigns, corporate marketing, direct marketing, online games, and educational tools.

The purpose of the Marketing Resource Bank is to provide lecturers with a diverse repository of marketing illustrations and practical examples that can be dropped into lecturers, seminars, and/ or online discussions that can inspire and educate students on marketing in practice. The Marketing Resource Bank has been designed to illustrate and contextualize key theoretical concepts throughout each chapter, with each resource accompanied by a paragraph of commentary, making them easy to drop into your teaching.

Academic Insights

In these short guest lectures, leading academics provide their perspective on every chapter topic. Show these in class to introduce your students to a particular topic in marketing and enthuse them about the subject you are about to cover. PowerPoint slides are interspersed with the 'talking heads' to ensure students grasp the key points.

Practitioner Insights (practitioner interviews to accompany the chapter Case Insights)

In these short interviews, the practitioners explain how they actually dealt with the marketing challenge outlined in the Case Insights. Once students have read each Case Insight and chapter, and formulated a strategy for dealing with the marketing challenge themselves, the lecturer can show them the video in class: thus completing the learning loop, and really bringing marketing to life for the students.

Marketing fundamentals

1 | Marketing Principles and Society

Learning Outcomes

After reading this chapter, you will be able to:

▶ Define the marketing concept

▶ Explain how marketing has developed over the twentieth century

▶ Describe the three major contexts of marketing application, i.e. consumer goods, business-to-business, and services marketing

▶ Understand the contribution marketing makes to society

▶ Assess critically the impact marketing has on society

▶ Case Insight 1.1

Systembolaget AB was the world's first alcohol monopoly and remains the only retailer of alcohol in Sweden. It has a government mandate to limit the harm that might come to Swedish society from alcohol consumption. We speak to Fredrik Thor, to find out how a state alcohol monopoly with a prohibition remit can possibly market itself.

It all started in 1850 with the formation in Dalarna, Sweden, of a company that was granted exclusive rights to operate outlets for the sale and serving of alcoholic drinks. This was the world's first ever alcohol monopoly and it worked so well that the model spread nationwide. In 1955, the various local monopolies were merged to form a single one—Systemaktiebolaget.

Systembolaget's mandate is to help limit the medical and social harm caused by alcohol and thereby improve public health. It aims to do this by limiting alcohol availability through: the number of retail outlets (opening hours and selling rules); not endeavouring to maximize profits; not promoting additional sales; being brand-neutral; providing good customer service; and being financially efficient. But if the company is essentially designed to limit societal harm from alcohol—in effect, implementing and ensuring compliance with the government's alcohol policy—how can it market alcoholic products responsibly?

The company's marketing communication is steered by legislation, such as the Swedish Marketing Practices Act and the Swedish Alcohol Act, by Systembolaget's agreement with the State, and by the company's own internal guidelines for marketing communication in relation to alcohol products.

So, the monopoly exists to ensure alcohol-related problems are, as far as possible, minimized. If it were abolished, it is generally believed that people would drink more and social problems would increase. But the monopoly isn't a given. It will only continue to

exist as long as it has public support. Therefore, the company does everything it can to ensure that when you visit us, you like what you get.

The goal of all our communication measures has been to persuade more Swedes to support the monopoly. Or at least to ensure more people understand why it exists. The problem was in 2002, only 48% of Swedes actually supported the monopoly—a risky proportion of the public in other words didn't. As Systembolaget's President said, "If everyone knows why it exists, and people still don't want it, we shouldn't have an alcohol monopoly. But it would be awful if it were to be abolished because no one understood why it existed".

The company therefore defined a concrete goal in its strategic plan to boost support for the monopoly to 54% over the course of two years.

The question is how does an alcohol monopoly increase public support for its existence without promoting alcohol consumption?

Refreshing lack of promotional material at Systembolaget

Introduction

How have companies marketed their products to you in the past? Consider the drinks you buy, the sports teams you follow, the music you listen to, and the holidays you take. Why did you decide to buy these products? Each one has been marketed to you to cater for a particular need that you have at a particular time. Consider how the product was distributed to you. What component parts is it made of? What contribution does each of these products make to society? How useful are these products really? Are other versions of these products available that meet your needs and the needs of society better? These are just some of the questions that marketers might ask themselves when designing, developing, and delivering products to the **customer** and determining whether or not the customer's wants and needs have been met.

In this chapter, we develop our understanding of marketing principles and marketing's impact upon society by defining marketing, comparing and contrasting definitions from the American, British, and French contexts. We consider the origins and development of marketing, throughout the twentieth century. We explore how marketing is different in the consumer (B2C), business-to-business (B2B), and services marketing sectors. The core principles of marketing, incorporating the marketing mix, the principle of marketing exchange, **market orientation**, and **relationship marketing**, are all considered. How marketing impacts upon society is also detailed and, finally, we explore the need to reflect on marketing critically, as both marketers and consumers, by considering its impact on society from both positive and negative perspectives. In short, in this chapter, we cover the basics of marketing, providing a thorough grounding in the principles, in order to understand the rest of the book!

What is Marketing?

Consider your own already fairly vast experience of being marketed to throughout your own life. So far, you have probably been subjected to millions of marketing communications messages, bought many hundreds of thousands of products and services, been involved in thousands of customer service telephone calls, and visited tens of thousands of shops, supermarkets, and retail outlets. You're already a pretty experienced customer, so you've experienced one side of the marketing exchange already. Our role as authors is to explain how professionals do the other side of marketing. In other words, how to market products to customers. Remember most customers are just like you and will be just as discriminating as you are when buying goods. If they don't like the product, they won't buy it.

In order to explain how we go about marketing goods and services to customers, we must first describe exactly what marketing is. There are numerous definitions of marketing, but we present three of these for easy reference in Table 1.1.

▶ **Table 1.1** Definitions of marketing

Defining institution/author	Definition
The Chartered Institute of Marketing (CIM)	'The management process of anticipating, identifying and satisfying customer requirements profitably' (CIM, 2001).
The American Marketing Association (AMA)	'Marketing is the activity, set of institutions, and processes for creating communicating, delivering, and exchanging offerings that have value for customers, clients, partners, and society at large' (AMA, 2007).
A French perspective	*'Le marketing est l'effort d'adaptation des organisations à des marchés concurrentiels, pour influencer en leur faveur le comportement de leurs publics, par une offre dont la valeur perçue est durablement supérieure à celle des concurrents'*, which broadly translates as 'Marketing is the endeavour of adapting organizations to their competitive markets in order to influence, in their favour, the behaviour of their publics, with an offer whose perceived value is durably superior to that of the competition' (Lendrevie, Lévy, and Lindon, 2006).

go online

Visit the **Online Resource Centre** and follow the weblinks to the CIM and AMA websites to read more about their views on 'What is Marketing?'.

The **CIM** and **AMA** definitions recognize marketing as a 'management process' and an 'activity', although many firms organize marketing as a discrete department rather than across all departments (Sheth and Sisodia, 2005). The CIM and AMA definitions are similar as they stress the importance of considering the customer, of determining their requirements, or needs. The CIM definition refers to customer 'requirements' and the AMA to 'delivering value'. The French definition by contrast refers to developing an offer of superior **value**. Neither the AMA nor CIM definition refers explicitly to products, whereas the French definition explicitly discusses an 'offer'.

The CIM definition discusses anticipating and identifying needs and the American Marketing Association discusses 'creating ... offerings that have value for customers'. Both definitions recognize the need for marketers to undertake environmental scanning activity (see Chapter 2) and marketing research (see Chapter 4) to satisfy customers, and in the long term, to anticipate customers' needs.

The French definition talks of influencing the behaviour of publics, rather than customers, recognizing the wider remit of marketing in modern society. The challenge, according to the French definition, is to develop an offering that is 'durably superior' to that of the competition. This definition, therefore, explicitly recognizes the importance of market segmentation and **positioning** concepts (see Chapter 6).

The CIM definition recognizes that marketing is a process with a profit motive, although it does not explicitly state whether or not this is for financial profit, or some other form of profit, e.g. of gain in society, as in the case of a charity.

The AMA definition is clearer, by arguing that marketing is a process undertaken to benefit 'clients, partners, and society at large' as targets for marketing activity.

What we can clearly see with these definitions is how the concept of marketing has changed over the years, from transactional concepts like pricing, promotion, and distribution, to relationship concepts such as the importance of customer trust, risk, and commitment.

However, marketing is increasingly being used by not-for-profit organizations. Because the nature of the relationship between customers in not-for-profit and for-profit organizations are different, because the products/services are different and because the missions of the organizations concerned are different, how marketing is used in the not-for-profit context is somewhat different from the way it is used in the commercial context. Nevertheless, the broad principles of how marketing is used are the same. (For more on not-for-profit marketing, see Chapter 16.)

Visit the **Online Resource Centre** and complete Internet Activity 1.1 to learn more about the two leading professional marketing associations.

go online

What's the Difference Between Customers and Consumers?

We've discussed that you probably have lots of experience as a customer already. But what is a customer? And what is the difference between a customer and a **consumer**?

A customer is a buyer, a purchaser, a patron, a client, or a shopper. A customer is someone who buys from a shop, a website, a business, and, increasingly, another customer, e.g. Ebay or Amazon exchange. The difference between a customer and a consumer is that whereas a customer purchases or obtains a product, service, or idea, a consumer uses it (or eats it in the case of food).

To illustrate the example, consider the marketing degree or marketing course you are enrolled on, assuming you are using this book as an aid to learning on the course. Did you pay your course fees yourself? Or did your parents pay them for you? Or did someone else pay for them? If you did pay the fees yourself, you are the customer. If someone else paid for them, they are the customer. But you make use of, and study for, the degree or course. So you are the consumer.

Another example is Yoplait's Frubes, the fruity yoghurt tubes product-designed to make fruit and yoghurt more accessible to children. In this case, the customer is the chief shopper,

Frubes: flavoured yoghurt for kids
Source: Yoplait Dairy Crest.

the mother/father, or guardian, and the consumer is the child. The customer and consumer can be the same person, e.g. the girl buying the cinema tickets for herself and her boyfriend online to see the next big blockbuster movie is both the customer and consumer, but her boyfriend is only a consumer, unless she was with him and they bought the tickets at a kiosk.

Market Orientation

How close to the customer should a company aim to be? This is the principle of market orientation. The concept lies at the heart of what marketing is concerned with. Developing a market orientation is argued to make organizations more profitable, especially when there is limited competition, unchanging customer wants and needs, fast-paced technological change, and strong economies in operation (Kohli and Jaworski, 1990).

But developing a **market orientation** is not the same as developing a marketing orientation. So what's the difference? A company with a marketing orientation would be a company that increases the importance of marketing within the organization, e.g. by appointing a marketing person to its board of directors, or trustees in the case of a charity, or part of the executive team in a limited company or partnership.

Developing a **market orientation** refers to 'the organisationwide generation of market intelligence pertaining to current and future customer needs, dissemination of the intelligence across the departments, and organisationwide responsiveness to it' (Kohli and Jaworski, 1990). So a market orientation doesn't just involve marketing, it involves all aspects of a company, gathering and responding to market intelligence (i.e. customers' verbalized needs and preferences, data from customer surveys, sales data, and information gleaned informally from discussions with customers and trade partners). Developing a market orientation means developing the following:

▶ Customer orientation—concerned with creating superior value by continuously developing and redeveloping product and service offerings to meet customer needs. To do so we must measure customer satisfaction on a continuous basis and train and develop front-line service staff accordingly.

▶ A competitor orientation—requires an organization to develop an understanding of its competitors' short-term strengths and weaknesses and its long-term capabilities and strategies (Slater and Narver, 1994).

▶ Interfunctional coordination—requiring all the functions of an organization to work together to achieve the above foci for long-term profit (as shown in Figure 1.1).

Achieving a market orientation so that an organization is internally responsive to changes in the marketplace can take an organization four years or more to develop and requires top senior management support, the development of teams to gather the necessary market intelligence data and design appropriate market-based reward systems, and management to implement the recommendations made as a result (Kohli and Jaworski, 1990).

Developing a market orientation within a company is a capability, something that not all companies can do. Organizations that manage to develop a market orientation are better at **market sensing**, i.e. understanding the strategic implications of the market for a particular organization, and acting on the information collected through **environmental scanning**. (This topic is covered fully in Chapter 2.) Colgate-Palmolive, the fast-moving consumer goods

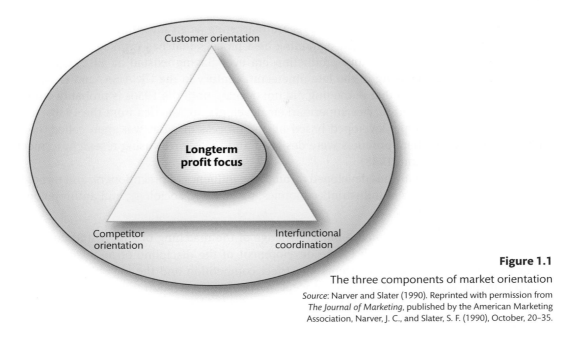

Figure 1.1

The three components of market orientation

Source: Narver and Slater (1990). Reprinted with permission from *The Journal of Marketing*, published by the American Marketing Association, Narver, J. C., and Slater, S. F. (1990), October, 20–35.

company, developed a high market orientation by aligning their entire company to the task of promoting trade satisfaction, measuring the number of orders delivered on time, and number of orders completed (Day, 1994).

Marketing: Ancient or Brand New?

So far it sounds as if marketing is a relatively new technique, but it might be surprising to learn that marketing as a coherent approach to business has been around since the early 1920s. However, it is difficult to pinpoint exactly when marketing was born! Most marketing texts present the development of marketing as a four-stage sequence in the twentieth century, as follows:

1 Production period, 1890s–1920s—characterized by a focus on physical production and supply, where demand exceeded supply, there was little competition, and the range of products was limited. This phase took place after the industrial revolution.

2 Sales period, 1920s–1950s—characterized by a focus on personal selling supported by market research and advertising. This phase took place after the First World War.

3 Marketing period, 1950s–1980s—characterized by a more advanced focus on the customer's needs. This phase took place after the Second World War.

4 Societal marketing period, 1980s to present—characterized by a stronger focus on social and ethical concerns in marketing. This phase is taking place during the 'information revolution' of the late twentieth century (Enright, 2002).

Enright (2002) criticizes the above timeline, arguing that there was good evidence of mass consumption in England in the seventeenth and eighteenth centuries, and of the operations of guildsmen and entrepreneurs in the sixteenth- and eighteenth-century markets, as well as a strong market for insurance from the early eighteenth century.

So whereas some marketing historians regard marketing as an invention of the twentieth century (Keith, 1960), others regard marketing as a process that has evolved over a much longer period of time, without any production era ever having existed at all. Soap firms, for example, were **advertising** in the late nineteenth century in the UK, USA, and Germany (Fullerton, 1988). The idea that marketing did not develop until the 1950s is probably wrong when we consider that self-service supermarkets developed in America from the 1930s, and products were increasingly developed based on the process of what was then called 'consumer engineering', where products were designed and redesigned, using research, to meet customer needs (Fullerton, 1988).

Marketing as a discipline has developed through the influence of practitioners, and through developments in the areas of industrial economics, psychology, sociology, and anthropology, as follows:

▶ *Industrial economics influences*—our knowledge of the matching of supply and demand, within industries, owes much to the development of the discipline of microeconomics. For instance, the economic concepts of perfect competition and the matching of supply and demand underlie the marketing concept, particularly in relation to the concepts of the price at which goods are sold and the quantity distributed (see Chapter 9) and the nature of business-to-business marketing (see Chapter 14). Theories of income distribution, scale of operation, monopoly, competition, and finance facilities all come from economics (Bartels, 1951). Nevertheless, the influence of economics over marketing is declining over time (Howard *et al.*, 1991).

▶ *Psychological influences*—our knowledge of consumer behaviour comes principally from psychology, particularly motivational research (see Chapter 4) in relation to consumer attitudes, perceptions, motivations, and information processing (Holden and Holden, 1998), as well as our understanding of persuasion, consumer personality, and customer satisfaction (Bartels, 1951). Understanding buyer psychology is of fundamental importance to the marketing function. As marketing is about understanding customers' needs, we must place ourselves in the mindset of our customer if we are to properly understand their needs.

▶ *Sociological influences*—our knowledge of how groups of people behave comes mainly from sociology, with insights into areas such as how people from similar gender and age groups behave (demographics), how people in different social positions within society behave (class), why we do things in the way that we do (motivation), general ways that groups behave (customs), and culture (Bartels, 1951, 1959). Our understanding of what society thinks as a whole (i.e. public opinion), and how we influence the way people think and to adopt our perspective (propaganda), have all informed market research practice.

▶ *Anthropological influences*—our debt to **social anthropology** increases more and more as we use qualitative market research approaches such as **ethnography** and **observation** to research consumer behaviour (see Chapters 4 and 18), particularly the behaviour of sub-groups (e.g. beer drinkers or motorcyclists).

Differences Between Sales and Marketing

When we are new to marketing, we may well ask: what is the difference between selling and marketing? If we consider the four stages in the development of marketing as outlined above, we would say that marketing has developed from sales.

But perhaps a more comprehensive answer is that sales emphasizes the process of 'product push', by creating distribution incentives for both salespeople and customers to make exchanges that may or may not benefit the customer in the long term (see Chapter 14 for more on sales management).

Marketing on the other hand is more focused on creating 'product pull', or demand, among customers and consumers, and the offering is designed and redesigned through customer and consumer input, through research, to meet their longer term needs. Marketing activity is geared around understanding and communicating to the customer to design, develop, deliver, and determine the value in the product offering, whereas sales is organized principally around enhancing the distribution of the companies' products once the product offering has already been designed. Sales departments are mostly concerned with the delivery part of the value creation process. However, sales as a function does and should have inputs to the design phase (through information from sales representatives), the development phase (particularly in test marketing, see Chapter 4), and the determination phase, where their often informal knowledge of customers' needs is important in the marketing process (as we saw earlier in the section on market orientation).

Whereas marketing activities principally act to stimulate demand, sales activities are designed to principally stimulate supply. In this sense, marketing is clearly a more sustainable approach to business, if we assume that keeping customers and consumers happy leads to business profitability or organizational success. Table 1.2 provides a basic summary of these differences.

▶ **Table 1.2** Differences between marketing and sales

Marketing	Sales
Tends towards long-term satisfaction of customer needs	Tends towards short-term satisfaction of customer needs; part of the value delivery process as opposed to designing and development of customer value processes
Tends to greater input into customer design of offering (co-creation)	Tends to lesser input into customer design of offering (co-creation)
Tends to high focus on stimulation of demand	Tends to low focus on stimulation of demand, more focused on meeting existing demand

What Do Marketers Do?

To answer this question, the British government set up the Marketing and Sales Standards Setting Body (MSSSB) to work with relevant stakeholders to map out how the marketing function operates.

go online

Visit the **Online Resource Centre** and follow the weblink to the MSSSB website to learn more about why and how the MSSSB was established.

Their consultation indicated that the job covered eight function areas as indicated in Figure 1.2, each of which is interlinked with stakeholder requirements. Marketers at different levels within the organization will undertake different components of these functions at different levels. Generally, the senior marketer or marketing director will guide and direct these functions, while the marketing manager will manage them, the marketing executive will undertake the actions necessary to fulfil these functions, and the marketing assistant will support the marketing executive.

Just as society is constantly changing, so the marketing profession is constantly changing, and marketing's place within the business profession and society more generally is often criticized. Whereas doctors, teachers, and judges are generally held in high respect (Worcester, Mortimore, and Baines, 2005: 277), marketing practitioners tend to be held in low respect (Bartels, 1983; Kotler, 2006). According to renowned US scholars Jagdish Sheth and Rajendra Sisodia, to reform marketing practice we need to:

▶ Make marketing a corporate staff function so that it operates across departments, and is strategic, as are the finance, information technology, legal, and human resource management functions.

▶ Ensure that the head of the marketing function reports directly to the chief executive officer (CEO).

▶ Rename the head of corporate marketing the chief customer officer (CCO).

▶ Provide marketing with capital expenditure budgets in addition to operating expenditure budgets so that the marketing function can make major capital investments, e.g. in customer acquisition and retention technologies (e.g. CRM projects), building and plant, and other capital items.

▶ Ensure that the marketing function controls the functions of branding, key account management, and business development.

Figure 1.2

A functional map for marketing

Source: The Marketing and Sales Standards Setting Body (2010). Reproduced with the kind permission of Dr Chahid Fourali, Head of MSSSB.

▶ Ensure that the marketing function manages external suppliers such as market research, advertising, and public relations agencies.

▶ Set up, within the public limited company, a board-level standing committee, on which senior marketers sit, comparable to audit, compensation, and governance committees (Sheth and Sisodia, 2006).

The Principal Principles of Marketing

Despite around a hundred years of study and thousands of years of practice, there are few true scientific principles of marketing. Nevertheless, we do still know an awful lot about marketing in general. Over 60 years ago, Robert Bartels said, 'there exists neither a clearly identified body of marketing principles nor general agreement as to what a principle is' (Bartels, 1944). Since then surprisingly little has changed. Bartels (1951) stated in a discussion of whether or not marketing is an art or science that only two marketing generalizations exist as follows:

1 As [a consumer's] income increases, the percentage of income spent for food decreases; for rent, fuel, and light remains the same; for clothing remains the same; and for sundries [miscellaneous items] increases (Engels' Law).

2 Two cities attract retail trade from an intermediary city or town in the vicinity of the breaking point (the 50% point), approximately in direct proportion to the populations of the two cities and in inverse proportion to the square of the distance from these two cities to the intermediate town (Reilly's Law of Retail Gravitation).

Clearly, things have changed since Engels produced his 'Law', especially as we now tend to buy our accommodation rather than renting it, and food is relatively less expensive than it was 60–80 years ago, so it is debatable as to whether or not the first 'Law' still applies. On the second 'Law', the point is that when we are locating our store, for example, if we are working in the site location department for a major supermarket, we should locate our store near the larger of the major population centres, and as close to them as possible. Again this might sound obvious as a general principle, but Reilly's Law allows retailers to determine with some degree of precision exactly where that location might be. Nowadays multiple retail grocers, such as Carrefour in France, Tesco in the UK, Coles in Australia, and Lotus in Thailand, might use complex mathematical formulae (e.g. algorithms) to determine where to locate their supermarkets, often purchasing land and developing suitable properties rather than converting existing business premises where they find a particularly valuable location.

In the race for a scientific approach to marketing, several prominent US academics became strong proponents for developing a 'General Theory of Marketing' (Bartels, 1968; Hunt, 1971, 1983). Currently, we are still searching for this Holy Grail of marketing theory, although we have moved a little closer to achieving it. To understand the phenomenon of marketing more completely, we must first understand the following:

▶ The behaviour of buyers—why do which buyers purchase what they do, where they do, when they do, and how they do?

▶ The behaviour of sellers—why do which sellers price, promote, and distribute what they do, where they do, when they do, and how they do?

▶ The institutional framework (e.g. government, society, and so on) around selling/buying— why do which kinds of institutions develop to engage in what kinds of functions or activities to consummate and/or facilitate exchanges, when will these institutions develop, where will they develop, and how will they develop?

▶ The consequences for society of buying/selling—why do which kinds of buyers, behaviours of buyers, behaviour of sellers, and institutions have what kinds of consequences on society, when they do, where they do, and how they do (Hunt, 1983)?

The listing above indicates how marketing involves a series of highly complex interactions between individuals, organizations, society, and government, and that we know relatively little about how marketing works in theory. But, we can make some more generalizations about marketing. According to Leone and Shultz (1980), these include the following:

▶ Generalization 1—advertising has a direct and positive influence on total industry (market) sales, i.e. all advertising done at industry level serves to increase sales within that industry.

▶ Generalization 2—selective advertising has a direct and positive influence on individual company (brand) sales, i.e. advertising undertaken by a company tends to increase the sales of the particular brand for which it was spent.

▶ Generalization 3—the **elasticity** of selective advertising on company (brand) sales is low (inelastic), i.e. for frequently purchased goods, advertising has only a very limited effect in raising sales.

▶ Generalization 4—increasing store shelf space (display) has a positive impact on sales of **non-staple** grocery items. For example, products bought on impulse (e.g. ice cream, chocolate bars) rather than those that are planned purchases, less important but perhaps more luxurious types of goods (e.g. gravy mixes, cooking sauces), i.e. for impulse goods, the more shelf space you give an item the more likely you are to sell it.

▶ Generalization 5—distribution, defined by the number of outlets, has a positive influence on company sales (market share), i.e. setting up more retail locations has a positive influence on sales.

As we are beginning to see, marketing techniques are not generally developed in a scientific sense. We cannot accurately describe in a scientific sense, or predict, the behaviour of consumers, customers, and producers according to some pre-defined formulae. At least, not yet anyway.

However, there are some general concepts that help managers frame their actions as they develop their marketing plans and undertake marketing tactics. We cover these concepts next in the chronological order in which they were developed including the marketing mix for products (4Ps) in the 1950s–1960s, the concept of exchange in marketing in the 1970s, the marketing mix for services (7Ps) in the 1980s, market orientation developed in the 1990s, and **relationship marketing** developed mainly in the 1990s.

> ▶ Research Insight 1.1
>
>
>
> **To take your learning further, you might wish to read this influential paper.**
>
> **Borden, N. H. (1964), 'The concept of the marketing mix',** *Journal of Advertising Research*, 4, 2–7.
>
> Perhaps the most famous concept in marketing, this easy-to-read early article explains how marketing managers act as 'mixers of ingredients' in developing their brand policies and programmes. The concept of the marketing mix, popularized as the 4Ps, remains very popular even today, although the advent of relationship marketing has challenged the impersonal notion of marketers as manipulators of marketing policies, and focused more on the need to develop long-term interpersonal relationships with customers (see Chapter 15).
>
> @ Visit the **Online Resource Centre** to read the abstract and access the full paper.

The Marketing Mix and the 4Ps

What are the responsibilities of the marketing manager? To outline these, Neil Borden developed the concept of the **marketing mix** in his teaching at Harvard University in the 1950s, although he did not formally write the theory up until 1964. The idea came from the notion that the marketing manager was a 'mixer of ingredients', a chef who concocted a unique marketing recipe to fit the requirements of the customers' needs at any particular time.

The emphasis was on the creative fashioning of a mix of marketing procedures and policies to produce the profitable enterprise. He composed a 12-item list of elements (with sub-items, not reproduced here), which the manufacturer should consider when developing marketing mix policies and procedures, as follows (Borden, 1964):

1 product planning;

2 pricing;

3 branding;

4 channels of distribution;

5 personal selling;

6 advertising;

7 promotions;

8 packaging;

9 display;

10 servicing;

11 physical handling; and

12 fact finding and analysis.

This useful, although not exhaustive, list was simplified and amended by Eugene McCarthy (1960), to the more memorable but rigid 4Ps as follows (see Figure 1.3):

1 **product**—e.g. the offering and how it meets the customer's need, its packaging and labelling (see Chapter 8);

2 **place** (distribution)—e.g. the way in which the product meets customers' needs (see Chapter 12);

3 **price**—e.g. the cost to the customer, and the cost plus profit to the seller (see Chapter 9); and

4 **promotion**—e.g. how the product's benefits and features are conveyed to the potential buyer (see Chapters 10–11).

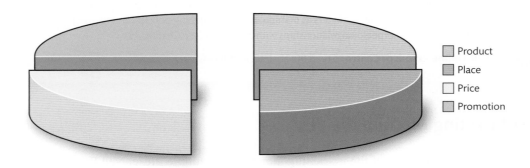

□ Product
□ Place
□ Price
□ Promotion

Figure 1.3
The 4Ps of the marketing mix

The intention was to create a simpler framework around which managers could develop their planning. Although there was some recognition that all of these elements might be interlinked (e.g. promotion based on the price paid by the consumer), such interplay between these mix components was not taken into account by McCarthy's framework. (See Market Insight 1.1 for an example of why the flavoured alcoholic beverages (FABs) product needs redeveloping.)

Although some commentators have argued that the 4Ps framework is of very limited use, we include it here because managers still use the framework extensively when devising their product plans.

▶ Market Insight 1.1

Have FABs Lost their Fizz?

The UK market for flavoured alcoholic beverages (FABs) has been in strong decline over the period between 2002 and 2007, from £1.485bn to £801m, a double digit decline of 46% over six years. This downward spiral is forecast to continue, with the market reaching £513m by 2012 at 2007 prices. The problem is that customers are getting older, meaning there are fewer 18–34 year olds, they are trading up to the more expensively priced cocktails, made in situ rather than pre-packed, and flavoured alcoholic beverages are perhaps simply no longer 'cool'.

The competition is on among the drinks manufacturers to develop the next generation of FABs to spice up the nightlives of their target audience. The question is what new products will they have to develop to keep the punters drinking?

1 Alcoholic beverage companies are not allowed to promote youth lifestyles in their advertising promotions or suggest that alcohol enhances sexual prowess, or that alcoholic drinks are key to social success. Why do you think this is?

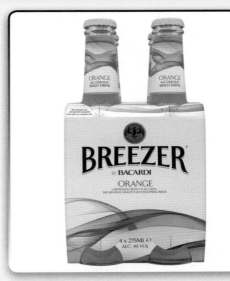

Barcardi's FAB Breezer drink
Source: Mintel (2007).

2 There has been increasing concern by government that young people are binge-drinking. Should alcoholic beverage manufacturers do more to ensure responsible drinking? How do they do this?

3 How can alcoholic beverage manufacturers use the 4Ps to revive the market for FABs?

Marketing as Exchange

Marketing is a two-way process. It's not just about the marketing organization doing all the work. The customer also has a strong input. In fact, not only must they specify how we might satisfy their needs as marketers, because marketers are not mind-readers, but also they must pay for the product or service.

Around the middle of the 1970s, there was increasing belief that the underlying phenomenon in marketing related to the exchange process between buyers and sellers and associated **supply chain** intermediaries. Exchange relationships might not only be economic, e.g. a consumer buying groceries, but also social, e.g. the service undertaken by the social worker on behalf of society paid for by government (Bagozzi, 1975). This recognition of the importance of the underlying relationship within marketing has led to the broadening of the concept of marketing and the relationship marketing school of marketing (which we consider in more detail in Chapter 15).

There are three main types of buyer–seller exchanges in marketing. Figure 1.4 outlines these two-way (**dyadic**) exchanges as follows:

1 In the first exchange type, the exchange takes place between the fire service who protect the general public from fire and provide emergency planning activity and services, and the public who support them in return, sometimes politically through signing petitions to keep them in service in a particular locale, and especially through their national and local taxes, depending on the country.

2 In the second exchange type, the one we are probably more familiar with as consumers, we enter a shop, say H&M—the Swedish fashion outlet—and purchase the necessary goods by paying for these with money or by credit/debit card.

3 In the third type of exchange, we have a manufacturer, and a retailer. Here, the retailer (e.g. London's Hamley's toyshop) purchases goods from the manufacturer (e.g. Mattel) through a credit facility, e.g. payment in 30 days, and expects any damaged goods to be returnable, and wants the goods delivered on certain types of pallets at a certain height, within a particular time limit. In return, the retailer undertakes to pay a wholesale (i.e. trade discounted) price.

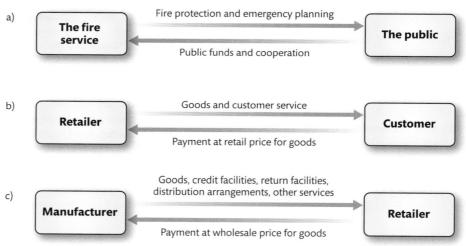

Figure 1.4
Simple marketing exchange processes

However, few exchanges in marketing are really this simple. They might well involve lots of other individual transactions and may involve multiple combinations. For example, (2) and (3) can be combined to indicate a simple supply chain for, say, a toy manufacturer selling through to shops that sell on to the general public, their customers. Understanding exactly how our exchanges take place between the various members of the supply chain allows us to understand where we are, and are not, adding value to the customer experience.

We can imagine from the discussion above about marketing exchanges that what is exchanged in a service context (e.g. purchasing a holiday) is different from a product context (e.g. buying a DVD). By the end of the 1970s, it was recognized that the traditional 4Ps approach to marketing planning based on physical products, e.g. salt, CDs, alcoholic drinks, was not particularly useful for either the physical product offering with a strong service component, e.g. laptop computers with extended warranty, or services with little or no physical component, e.g. spa and massage, hairdressing, sports spectatorship. (We consider the differences between services and physical goods marketing in greater detail in Chapter 13.)

To illustrate how marketing needed to market services differently, two American scholars, Booms and Bitner (1981), incorporated a further 3Ps into the marketing mix as follows (see Figure 1.6):

1 Physical evidence—to emphasize that the tangible components of services were strategically important, e.g. potential university students often assess whether or not they want to attend a university and a particular course by requesting a copy of brochures and course outlines or by visiting the campus.

2 Process—to emphasize the importance of the service delivery. When processes are standardized, it is easier to manage customer expectations, e.g. DHL International GmbH, the German international express, overland transport, and air freight company, is a master at producing a standardized menu of service options, e.g. track and trace delivery services, which are remarkably consistent around the world.

3 People—to emphasize the importance of customer service personnel, sometimes experts and often professionals interacting with the customer. How they interact with customers, and how satisfied customers are as a result, is of strategic importance.

Consider how the extended marketing mix is used in the airline industry. For instance, the process component of the services marketing mix within the airline sector has been revolutionized through internet ticket booking and web check-in services. The traditional middleman, the travel agency, has had to radically alter its customer proposition as the major national carriers (e.g. Air France, American Airlines, British Airways) offer their services directly by internet to compete with a new class of lower cost airlines also offering their services direct to the public via the internet at substantially lower prices (see Market Insight 1.2). The travel agencies have put their own services online, customizing their holiday offerings in a bid to differentiate their services from the airlines and add value for the customer, offering better deals on insurance, identifying best flight connections, providing advice on best airlines, and offering affiliate hotel deals (Saren, 2006).

▶ Market Insight 1.2

Low-Cost Airlines: Cutting out the Middlemen

In the European low-cost airline market, airlines (e.g. Ryanair and EasyJet as the pioneers) recognized that they could cut out the travel agents, who acted to 'collect' customers in large volumes for the airlines,

if the low-cost carriers could deal with the airline passengers directly themselves in sufficient volumes. To do this, they decided to:

▶ reach passengers through the internet;

▶ fly to airports with lower landing charges and directly to specific points, rather than flying out to

▶ Market Insight 1.2   (continued)

hubs, e.g. Chicago O'Hare or London Heathrow, and then onward elsewhere;

▶ lower the baggage allowance to reduce weight carried to increase fuel efficiency; and

▶ limit the food stored and the number of cabin crew required to service the passengers. (See Figure 1.5.)

The first model (Figure 1.5a) represents the national airline carriers, mainly pre-2001 before they started to sell their own tickets online, trim their services, and reduce their number of routes, e.g. Lufthansa, Air France, and British Airways. The second model (Figure 1.5b) represents the low-cost carriers, e.g. EasyJet, Wizzair. What would this model look like for the airline you are most familiar with?

By analysing these kinds of marketing exchanges we can see where the value might lie in the transaction. For example, a problem could arise if the airline

passengers are not provided with the kind of service that they expect to receive in both of the above cases. If passengers believe that they receive a poor-quality service, this has an effect on the airline brand and on whether or not customers repurchase tickets. The key consideration for the low-cost airlines is ensuring that in cutting out the middlemen (i.e. the travel agents), they don't also cut out all the value that the middlemen once provided to the airline passenger (e.g. choice of levels of service).

1   Do you think low-cost airlines provide a valued service for the airline passenger or do you think they have taken the no-frills concept too far?

2   As the third party (or middleman), how should travel agents try to reclaim their relationships with holidaymakers flying by air? What other services do they need to offer to lure us back?

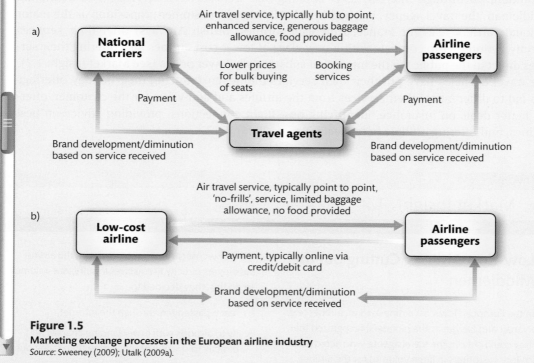

Figure 1.5
Marketing exchange processes in the European airline industry
Source: Sweeney (2009); Utalk (2009a).

▶ Market Insight 1.2

Low-cost airlines ditch the middleman
Source: © Wizz Air.

3 Think of as many other products or services where we use a third party (middleman) to deliver products or services to us as you can.

Do you think it would be advantageous for those companies to deal with us directly?

▶ Research Insight 1.2

To take your learning further, you might wish to read this influential paper.

Bagozzi, R. P. (1975), 'Marketing as exchange', *Journal of Marketing*, 39 (October), 32–9.

An important article that outlined how the key consideration in marketing is the satisfaction of exchange relationships, setting the scene for widespread acceptance of social marketing methods and accelerating the search for a general theory of marketing, particularly through marketing relationships. Bagozzi wanted to answer such questions as: how do people and organizations satisfy their needs through exchange? Why do some marketing exchanges last and others fail? What is an equitable exchange? How should we go about analysing marketing exchanges? And is the exchange concept equally applicable to all societies around the world?

 Visit the **Online Resource Centre** to read the abstract and access the full paper.

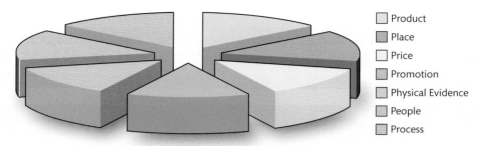

Figure 1.6
The amended marketing mix for services: the 7Ps

The people, process, and physical evidence components of the service marketing mix are fundamental in the development of the overall airline service offering. Of course, we should recognize that airlines do not offer everyone the same level of service. Most airlines offer an economy service, an economy plus service (with slightly more seating space), and a business-class service (with even more seating space, a better meal, personalized cabin crew service, fast-track service through passport control, and often a limousine service to and from the airport), whereas first-class with Malaysia Airlines, for instance, offers all this and even more together with a helicopter service to and from the airport on selected routes. Table 1.3 provides a summary of the marketing mix for the airline industry.

▶ **Table 1.3** The marketing mix: the airline industry

Marketing aspect	Airline industry
Basic customer need	Safe long- and short-haul transportation, domestic and international
Target market	Mass consumer market (economy class), businesspeople (business class), and high-net-worth individuals (first class)
Product offering	Typically, differentiated based on class of passenger, with seat size increasing, check-in and boarding times reducing, quality of food increasing and levels of ancillary services (e.g. limousine service) increasing as we move from economy through business- to first-class. Some carriers focus on 'no-frills', basic services (e.g. EasyJet, Ryanair, Air Asia)
Price	Substantial difference depending on class of service, type of carrier, and purchasing approach (e.g. via internet tends to be cheaper)
Principal promotional tools	(1) press, magazine and radio advertising, (2) the internet, (3) billboards
Distribution	Increasingly purchased via the internet, including third-party brokerages, such as Expedia, as well as through travel agents, the once-dominant now increasingly redundant medium

Marketing aspect	Airline industry
Process	Self-service via internet or aided by travel agent in retail location. Travel options increasingly customized to the customer's needs, including size of baggage allowance, class of travel, increasing availability of alternative locations
Physical evidence	Airline loyalty cards and souvenirs, in-flight magazines, in-flight entertainment services, food and snack meals, grooming and toiletry products provided
People	Combination of check-in staff, customer service personnel, and cabin crew/pilot teams, all of whom interface with the customer at different points in the experience

Relationship Marketing

If marketing is about exchange, as we outlined earlier, shouldn't marketing also be concerned with relationships between those parties that are exchanging value? This was the principal idea behind the development of relationship marketing. It is really an evolution of the marketing concept, as there is a shift in focus from the need to engage in transactions towards the need to develop long-term customer relationships (see Market Insight 1.3). Relationship marketing concerns not only the development of longer lasting relationships with customers, but also the development of stronger relationships with other external markets including:

▶ suppliers;

▶ potential employees;

▶ recruiters;

▶ referral markets—where they exist, e.g. retail banks partly relying on professional services organizations including estate agents for mortgage referrals;

▶ influence markets—e.g. government bodies for companies and organizations in the public sector, regulatory authorities, and so on; and

▶ internal markets, e.g. existing employees (see Chapter 15).

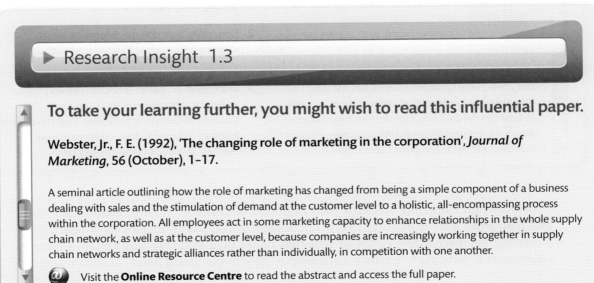

▶ Research Insight 1.3

To take your learning further, you might wish to read this influential paper.

Webster, Jr., F. E. (1992), 'The changing role of marketing in the corporation', *Journal of Marketing***, 56 (October), 1–17.**

A seminal article outlining how the role of marketing has changed from being a simple component of a business dealing with sales and the stimulation of demand at the customer level to a holistic, all-encompassing process within the corporation. All employees act in some marketing capacity to enhance relationships in the whole supply chain network, as well as at the customer level, because companies are increasingly working together in supply chain networks and strategic alliances rather than individually, in competition with one another.

@ Visit the **Online Resource Centre** to read the abstract and access the full paper.

> ## ▶ Market Insight 1.3

The Body Shop Sold to L'Oréal: Did its Customers Mind?

When French cosmetics giant L'Oréal bought the global high street ethical retailer The Body Shop for £652m (nearly €1bn) in 2006, it obtained more than 2,000 stores in 53 countries. L'Oréal immediately announced its intention to let The Body Shop continue as a stand-alone brand. At the time of purchase, L'Oréal paid around a 12% premium over the share price for The Body Shop brand, recognizing the goodwill that founder Dame Anita Roddick had built up in the brand in over 30 years of trading. By 2010, it had a network of 2,550 stores in 64 countries but its market share of the beauty sector had dropped by 2008 to 7% from 7.5% in 2007.

A potential problem in 2006 was whether customers of The Body Shop minded that the retailer had been taken over by the cosmetics giant. Many of its customers prided themselves on the company's ethical trading credentials, which they could now see compromised, feeling that the company had 'sold out'. Clearly, others did not. The question for L'Oréal is did the original Body Shop customers continue to purchase from The Body Shop after the L'Oréal takeover and how do they win back those who switched to another brand, such as Lush, for example?

Although The Body Shop, under L'Oréal, might have lost some brand fanatics (heavy buyers who buy frequently) as a result of the takeover, has it managed to broaden the base of customers (less heavy buyers now buying more frequently) through more efficient management of the company's operations, more

Bodyshop's first community trade supplier

Source: Bodyshop's first community trade supplier, Courtesy The Body Shop International plc.

new products, and a more experienced approach to product development? It seems that L'Oréal has adopted a 'light touch' strategy so far so as not to alienate existing customers, but some reorganization of The Body Shop brand will be necessary if L'Oréal is to realize its substantial investment.

Sources: BBC News (2006); L'Oréal (2010); Mintel (2010).

1 Do you think L'Oréal has changed the way in which The Body Shop is now marketed? Why do you think this?

2 Generally, how do you determine which customers you want to have a relationship with and which you do not?

3 In a similar scenario, Innocent Drinks sold a minority proportion of its company to The Coca-Cola Company for £30m. Visit Innocent's blogs to determine how customers have reacted at www.innocentdrinks.co.uk

Relationship marketing concerns the integration of customer service, quality assurance, and marketing activity (Payne, 1993). Consequently, companies employing a relationship marketing approach stress customer retention rather than customer acquisition. Customer retention is a particularly important strategic activity in marketing mass consumer services.

Research has demonstrated that when a company retains loyal customers it is more likely to be profitable compared with competitors who do not, because customers:

▶ will increase their purchases over time;

▶ are cheaper to promote to;

▶ who are happy with their relationship with a company are happy to refer it to others; and

▶ are prepared to pay a (small) price premium if they are loyal (Reichheld and Sasser, 1990).

This can be demonstrated by the fact that mobile telecommunication providers in Europe, e.g. Vodafone, Orange, now focus on retaining customers and getting them to spend more, to reduce so-called 'churn' rates, rather than persuading potential customers who haven't got a mobile phone to buy one. Retention programmes focus marketing activity on enhanced customer service satisfaction, rewarding loyalty, CRM (**customer relationship management**), and sales promotion activities in areas such as utilities and telecommunications, the travel industry, and retail banking.

Companies have been urged to develop long-term interactive relationships before (Gummesson, 1987). However, the idea that we need to rethink the way marketing activity is organized is a good one and suggests moving away from simply adopting the 4Ps to adopting an **interactive marketing** approach, paying more attention to the customer base rather than simply market share (Grönroos, 1994). We consider relationship marketing in greater detail in Chapter 15.

Marketing in Context

Does the practice of marketing change if we are marketing goods compared with services, and to consumers compared to businesses? Most textbooks on marketing focus on the marketing offering being essentially a product, rather than a service, experience, or an idea. Yet we've known since the 1960s that services were making important contributions to the US economy (Regan, 1963), and no doubt other major economies. Although the product has been the focus of marketing practice and theory, it should no longer be so. Figure 1.7 shows clearly how important services are to a wide variety of economies around the world, including those in the developed world (e.g. Sweden), the developing world (e.g. Thailand), and in the lesser developed countries (e.g. Namibia). Even in China and the United Arab Emirates (UAE), services make up more than 35% of the economy; a substantial contribution.

Marketing techniques need to be adapted to the specific sector in which they are used (Blois, 1974). The context, whether it is industrial (e.g. business-to-business), consumer (e.g. retail), or services based (e.g. either business-to-business services like accountancy or business-to-business products like component manufacturers), or used in the not-for-profit context, has an impact on the marketing tools and techniques that we need to use. Whether products are business-to-business or business-to-consumer, they may principally be either product or service, but all offerings combine some elements of the two. (We discuss the intangible nature of services further in Chapter 13 and not-for-profit marketing in Chapter 16.)

Having identified three unique contexts of marketing: consumer goods, industrial (business-to-business), and services, we briefly discuss how each of these contexts affects how we undertake marketing activity.

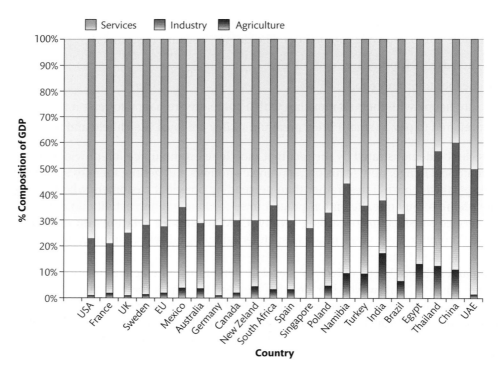

Figure 1.7

Estimated GDP % composition by sector for selected countries (year)

Note: GDP = gross domestic product. All data for 2008

Source: Data taken from CIA World Factbook, www.cia.gov. Reproduced with the kind permission of CIA World Factbook.

The Consumer Goods Perspective

Bucklin (1963) defined consumer goods as convenience goods (purchased frequently with minimum effort), shopping goods (purchased selectively based on suitability, quality, price, and style), or speciality goods (purchased highly selectively because only that product was capable of meeting a specific need). Examples of consumer goods industries might include the retail car market, the luxury goods market, and multiple retail groceries. Examples of companies operating in these industries might include car manufacturer Ford, French fashion house Louis Vuitton Moët Hennessey (LVMH), and Wal-Mart, the American supermarket chain.

The consumer goods perspective of marketing has been dominant in the history and study of marketing. The concept is concerned with ideas of the 'marketing mix' and the 4Ps. The consumer goods perspective, borrowing heavily from neoclassical economics, assumes there are comparatively few suppliers within a particular industry, all rivals for the **aggregated demand** (i.e. demand totalled at the population level rather than at the individual level). In fast-moving consumer goods markets (FMCG), the price at which a good is sold is clearly defined. The product exchanged is tangible (i.e. has physical form) and exchanged between buyer and seller through retail distribution outlets. Consumption takes place at a later and different point in time, with demand stimulated through the **promotional mix**, i.e. advertising, personal selling, direct marketing, and public relations (see Chapter 11).

The focus of marketing in this context is how to facilitate the rapid exchange of goods, the effectiveness of the marketing in determining the match between supplier offering and customer demand, and efficiency in managing the distribution of the product through the supply chain. Of particular importance in the consumer goods marketing context are the principles and practice of channel management and retailing (see Chapter 12), as this is the main way in which customers acquire their consumer goods.

Because of the need to stimulate demand from consumers, focus is placed on the importance of advertising (see Chapter 10) to stimulate demand and market research (see Chapter 4) to determine how to develop appropriate consumer products and how they are received by the consumers once they've launched into the marketplace. More recently, the internet and other digital mechanisms have greatly increased the way in which customers receive information about their goods and by which retailers reorder goods and services from their suppliers. (We cover the impact of new technologies on marketing in further detail in Chapter 17.)

The Consumer Services Perspective

The services perspective in marketing is organized around the idea that markets are increasingly characterized not by physical goods but by intangible services. Around the late 1970s and early 1980s, there was recognition that the standard goods marketing approach was ill-suited to the marketing of services. Services marketing thinkers suggested that the intangible, performance-dependent, nature of services substantially affected the way they should be marketed (Shostack, 1977). There was a focus on the quality of service offered as a result (Grönroos, 1984), as well as a focus on the difference between customer perceptions of actual service quality and their expectations of service quality (Parasuraman, Zeithaml, and Berry, 1985).

Some commentators have questioned the use of the product analogy altogether in services marketing (Grönroos, 1998; Vargo and Lusch, 2004). Quite simply, they argue that there are significant differences and similarities between goods and services as follows. Services:

▶ cannot be protected by patent;

▶ do not make use of packaging;

▶ lack a physical display; and

▶ cannot be demonstrated in the same way.

Others have argued that there are major similarities (Judd, 1968), including the need to:

▶ work at full capacity;

▶ develop trade and service marks;

▶ use promotional media;

▶ use personal selling techniques; and

▶ use an approach to pricing based on cost and value.

The Business-to-Business Perspective

Many marketing textbooks over-emphasize consumer goods marketing, paying inadequate attention to industrial/organizational marketing. Business-to-business marketing is essentially different from consumer marketing because the customer is a business rather than an individual household, or chief shopper, for example. Business-to-business marketing requires that marketers deal with more sophisticated customers who may buy in volume, as part of a decision-making unit (with other buyers and technicians), who are trained to buy/procure professionally, and who are rewarded for buying the right products and services at the right price (see Chapter 14).

Much business-to-business marketing activity revolves around the need to develop strong prospects for a company's products and services, and to ensure effective supply chain management operations to develop the market for a business-to-business product and to ensure it is delivered appropriately. Because buyers typically purchase in large volumes of product or complex 'bundles' of services (e.g. customized IT software solutions sold by the German company SAP), tight specifications are usually produced with which suppliers must comply. Buyers try to ensure they obtain the best supplier possible by offering suppliers a contract to supply for a set period of time through a bidding process.

In public sector markets, the **procurement** process (i.e. purchasing) is bound by strict legal guidelines for product and service contracts valued over a set amount. This process creates substantial rivalry, with firms often submitting bids they cannot then fulfil either because they've underpriced themselves, or because they've over-promised what they can deliver; a phenomenon known as the **winner's curse** as the winning company ends up servicing an unprofitable contract (Fleisher and Bensoussan, 2004).

The emphasis in business-to-business markets is strongly focused on the development and building of mutually satisfying relationships based on commitment and trust (Morgan and Hunt, 1994) to win the contract in the first place and then to deliver it to the customer's specifications. Whether or not a firm meets these specifications is in part linked to the **logistics** function (i.e. warehousing, inventory management, delivery) of the firm, be it product or service focused. Consequently, business-to-business marketers can create a competitive advantage if they develop a strong linkage between the marketing and logistics functions, developing a strong customer service proposition through (Christopher, 1986):

▶ cycle time order reduction;

▶ accurate invoicing procedures;

▶ reliable delivery;

▶ effective claims procedures;

▶ inventory availability;

▶ good condition of goods/effective service delivery;

▶ few order size constraints or limited customization of services;

▶ effective/planned salesperson visits;

▶ convenient ordering systems/provision of order status information;

▶ flexible delivery times; and

▶ strong after-sales support.

What Impact Does Marketing Have on Society?

If we consider how much the marketing industry contributes to society in any one country, we will probably be amazed. Wilkie and Moore (1999) describe the complexities of how the 'aggregate marketing system' works using the example of how marketing brings all the ingredients of a breakfast to households in America.

Consider the individual ingredients of a typical American breakfast, for example, coffee or tea, together with pancakes and syrup (and the necessary ingredients required here), the cups and plates to contain the food, the hotplate or grill to heat the food, and so on. The aggregate marketing system is awesome when reflected on in this way. We should remember that there are over 270m people in the USA, with over 100m households (Wilkie and Moore, 1999), each of which is brought its own unique mixture of products and services which come together to form an individual breakfast for any one particular person. Broadly, the system in most countries around the world works reasonably well. We're not all generally starving and we don't have to ration our food to preserve the amount we eat to be fair to others. Of course, there are certain countries in Africa, North Korea, and parts of China, for example, where people are dying of hunger, but these countries often experience imperfections in supply and demand because of political (e.g. war, dictatorship, famine) and environmental circumstances (e.g. drought). Marketing plays an important role in developing and transforming society. Consider how some of the products outlined in Table 1.4 have affected your own life (see also Market Insights 1.4 and 1.5).

▶ **Table 1.4** Some modern consumer products and their dates of invention

Consumer product	Product attribute	Consumer need	Inventors/ pioneers[a]	Year of invention
Tin can (for storing food)	Metallic food storage device	Allowed traditionally perishable food to be stored for longer periods of time	Hall and Dorkin, UK	1810
Ketchup (from the Chinese word *ketsiap*)	A food condiment, derived from the Chinese fish-based sauce, *ketsiap*, but adapted for Western taste, using tomatoes	Designed to improve the consumer's enjoyment of their food by improving the taste, and reducing the dryness of some foodstuffs	F. & J. Heinz Co., USA	1876
Diesel-fuelled internal combustion engine	An engine with an efficiency of 75% (meaning that 75% of the energy produced was used to power the engine) as opposed to 10% for the steam engines of the day	Enabled independent craftsmen to compete with large industry	Rudolph Diesel, Germany	1892
Breakfast cereals	Cereals, which, when added to milk, provide a healthy meal	Quick and easy to prepare foodstuff, which was rapidly adopted as a breakfast meal	W. K. Kellogg Foundation, USA	1906

Consumer product	Product attribute	Consumer need	Inventors/ pioneers[a]	Year of invention
Television	Transmission of moving images	Information, entertainment, and education	Baird Television Development Company, UK/ Telefunken, Germany	1929/1932
Microwave oven	Heating device for use in kitchen	Allows rapid heating of foodstuffs, saving time and labour. Particularly useful for frozen food meals	Raytheon Company, USA	1946
Consumer credit card	Allowed user to purchase products and services without paying in cash at time of original purchase	Convenience of not having to pay immediately and provision of credit for a set period of time	Diner's Club, USA	1950
Velcro fasteners	An ingenious hook and fastening device inspired by the technology used for transport by seed pods in nature. Named based on French velour (velvet) and crochet (small hook)	A simple means to fasten two items together, without permanently fastening, and that allows easy separation	George de Mestral/Velcro Industries, Switzerland	1955
Artificial sweeteners	Xylitol, as the sweetener is known, is used to sweeten food products such as sugar-free chewing gum and toothpastes	It sweetens food products without damaging teeth	Cultor, Finland	1969
Karaoke sing-along system	A TV system linked to music player, with words of music tracks displayed on screen, allows a person with a microphone to sing to a track's musical background	Designed to entertain small groups in house parties and large groups of individuals at venues who typically enjoy singing themselves and listening to others, or laughing at their friends' efforts	Roberto del Rosario/ Trebel Music Corporation, The Philippines	1975
Personal computer	Machine that allows users to play electronic games, perform calculations, and write word-processed documents and other applications	Time-saving device simplifying complex writing/ arithmetic tasks, offering recreational possibilities, i.e. game playing	IBM, USA	1980

Consumer product	Product attribute	Consumer need	Inventors/ pioneers[a]	Year of invention
Mobile phone	A hand held device for making telephone calls while in motion	The ability to stay in telephone contact with others regardless of one's location	NTT, Japan	1979
Portable digital music player	A device for storing and playing digital music files	The ability to listen to high-quality music wherever and whenever, by carrying a small portable device	Apple Computer, USA	2001
Social networking	A website designed for personal interaction between friends and acquaintances	Provides easy and instantaneous communication between two or more people in multiple locations around the world	Facebook, Inc. USA	2004

[a]The named companies are not always the inventors per se; often they acquired the patents from the inventor and were so licensed to produce and distribute the invention.

Sources: Various including: www.inventors.about.com, manufacturers' websites.

▶ Research Insight 1.4

To take your learning further, you might wish to read this influential paper.

Wilkie, W. L., and Moore, E. S. (1999), 'Marketing's contributions to society', *Journal of Marketing*, **63 (Special Issue), 198–218.**

This is a ground-breaking article, describing how marketing operates as an aggregated system within society. The article explains how marketing impacts on, and contributes to, society by considering how products and services flow through society, contributing both positively and negatively to individual well-being and the economy. The article concludes that the marketing system not only adapts and changes to the needs of modern society, but also broadly contributes greatly to it.

 Visit the **Online Resource Centre** to read the abstract and access the full paper.

▶ Market Insight 1.4

Back to the Future: Bringing Electric Cars to the Masses

The race is now well and truly on to produce the Wünderkind of the car industry, an all-singing, all-dancing, good-looking electric car. Silent and pollution-free, with engineering underpinned by green technologies, the car must not compromise on performance, looks, or handling. The change has come about because of greater public concern, and the need for European legislation concerning vehicle fuel emissions, to combat global warming. As car drivers are collectively a major user of oil, to power their cars, a shift to electric seems obvious. Problems with oil supply in the Middle East, since the OPEC crises of the 1970s, have worsened the situation.

But battery-powered cars have had a poor history. In Britain in 1984, Sir Clive Sinclair launched a battery-assisted tricycle, the Sinclair C5, with a top speed of 15 mph, but was met with public contempt. Sinclair Vehicles, which developed the concept in partnership with Lotus and Hoover, collapsed after sales of only 17,000 vehicles. Electric wasn't cool enough.

Then Toyota Motor introduced a new concept in green car technology, the hybrid Prius in 1997, combining a petrol engine with an electric battery and other manufacturers (e.g. Honda, Ford, and Chevrolet) in the industry swiftly followed. The car performed at similar speeds to a traditional car, but with greater fuel economy. It used the petrol engine when it needed high performance and the battery when it did not.

Now Renault promises to bring us a new breed of electric car from 2011–2012 (in hatchback, city car, saloon, and van formats), to minimize the impact of global warming, pollution, and urban noise. What is interesting is that the business model will change. Instead of buying petrol at a station, the purchaser of a Renault electric vehicle will either be able to lease the battery with a subscription to an energy supplier or own the whole car outright and charge-up the battery separately as necessary. The critical questions will be: will there be a large enough network of recharging stations, will the time/price taken to recharge offset the time/price to fill up with unleaded

Cars of the future? Renault's ZE range

Source: © Renault SA.

▶ Market Insight 1.4

fuel, will the car perform as well as any hybrid/non electric vehicle? Only time will tell....

(See Market Insight 17.4 for more on the launch of Renault's Zero Emission (ZE) electric vehicle.)

Sources: Dale (1985); Toyota (2006); Renault (2009)

1 Why do you think it has taken so long to develop the clean electric car?

2 What might be a further advancement on the electric car in 10 years time?

3 Can you think of other well-known products or services which have taken advantage of society's movement towards stronger environmental values? What are they?

What would we do without these products in today's world? In each case, we enjoy these products because innovative individuals and companies brought these products to us, as consumers. Take the tin can for storing food, for example. We couldn't conceive of not having this device now and yet it is only around 200 years old. Prior to that, food was stored in earthenware pots and was spoilt at a much faster rate. Could you imagine ketchup not existing? It was brought to us by Heinz but based on an ancient Chinese fish sauce recipe called ketsiap! Of course, in each of these cases, the invention outlined has been an extraordinary success. But the aggregate marketing system not only serves to bring consumers those products and services that truly meet their needs, it also serves to stop the failures from getting through as well (see Chapter 8). The aggregate marketing system serves to impede products because they don't meet consumer needs. So, it serves a number of benefits to society including the following:

▶ the promotion and delivery of desired products and services;

▶ the provision of a forum for market learning (we can see what does and what doesn't get through the system);

▶ the stimulation of market demand;

▶ the offering of a wide scope for choice of products and services by offering a close/customized fit with consumer needs;

▶ facilitates purchases (or acquisitions generally, e.g. if no payment is made directly as in the case of public services);

▶ saves times and promotes efficiency in customer requirement matching;

▶ brings new products and services, and improvements, to market to meet latent and unserved needs; and

▶ seeks customer satisfaction for repeat purchases (Wilkie and Moore, 1999).

Nevertheless, the marketing function within society does not always serve the good (see Chapter 19). Marketing is frequently criticized for doing precisely the opposite. Marketing is charged with being unethical in nature, and manipulative, and creating wants and needs where none previously existed (Packard, 1960).

The Critical Marketing Perspective

Because marketing's contributions to society are not necessarily all good, it is important that we develop a critical approach to understanding marketing. This allows us to constantly evaluate and re-evaluate marketing, to improve it, so that marketing continues to operate in a desirable manner within society. Although the aggregate marketing system distributes life-saving medicines, food, and important utilities, e.g. heat and light, it also distributes alcohol, tobacco, and gambling products, for example, products we might regard as dangerous to our health and well-being. Of course, in many cultures around the world, people enjoy drinking, smoking, and gambling. However, we are fooling ourselves, especially if we use these to excess, if we think we are really satisfying our own needs and not causing ourselves harm.

Unless told otherwise by government, the aggregate marketing system would distribute anything. Were prostitution and soft drugs, such as cannabis, made legal in Britain, the aggregate marketing system would distribute them. It already does this in the Netherlands, for instance, where these practices are no longer illegal. In that sense the aggregate marketing system in itself is inherently amoral, i.e. without morals. Not immoral, i.e. designed to harm, but amoral, designed without any care as to whether it harms or not. The system is only made moral by the decisions made by government and other institutional actors who may act upon and regulate the aggregate marketing system.

Some might consider the very ideology of marketing to be rooted in big business, mass consumer sovereignty, and excess supply over demand and ever-increasing consumption (Brownlie and Saren, 1992). In other words, we consume far too much and marketing companies are to blame for it! This argument, mooted at the very start of the 1990s, was far-sighted for its time, and has developed some considerable backing in the 2000s, with governments around the world working to regulate, for example, the fast food industry to ensure that they deliver a healthy product to the marketplace (see Chapter 19 for further discussion of the concept of **sustainable marketing**). Consider: what else are we over-consuming because of marketers? There are many other controversies in marketing, some of which include the following:

▶ What is a fair price for companies and organizations in wealthier countries to pay suppliers in poorer countries (see Market Insight 1.5)?

▶ Where is the line between persuading customers and manipulating customers to purchase products, services, and ideas? Is some marketing promotion really corporate propaganda?

▶ To what extent should the goods, services, and ideas of one country be marketed over the goods, services, and ideas of another country? What are the cultural implications?

▶ How much should we consume of any one particular good, service, or idea? When should governments step in to limit consumption?

▶ Are some groups more susceptible than others to certain types of marketing promotion? If they are, at what point and how should they be protected?

▶ Are some producers or buyer groups more powerful than others, and what impact, if any, does this have upon society?

▶ Does the aggregate marketing system itself advantage some groups over others and what are the implications for society?

A critical approach to marketing can help us to understand the nature of marketing knowledge. 'Marketing can then be learned from the many varieties of market that exist rather than concentrating on branded, mass consumption products in developed economies' (Easton,

2002), as marketing is so often portrayed. Adopting a critical approach to understanding marketing serves us well, and is in keeping with how managers actually learn the discipline in practice (Easton, 2002). Critiquing marketing helps to consider:

▶ How marketing knowledge is developed and the extent to which this is based on our contemporary social world. For example, much of current marketing knowledge is based on American practice and research. What implications does this have for the rest of the world?

▶ How do the historical and cultural conditions in which we operate, as consumers, and as students of marketing, impact on how we see marketing as a discipline?

▶ The need for continuous re-examination of the categories and frameworks that we use to understand marketing.

▶ How marketing can benefit from other intellectual perspectives, e.g. social anthropology, social psychology (see Burton, 2001).

In this chapter, we have aimed to explore marketing from the perspective of how it interacts and has developed in society. We see marketing as a force within society in itself, as a form of virus because of the way in which it replicates itself (Gladwell, 2002). We consider marketing as a management process, operating as an holistic process, within and outside the firm or organization that is using it. Of course, it is currently fashionable, and perhaps always was, to criticize marketing, and **capitalism** in particular (Packard, 1960; Klein, 1999). But the move from a production-led to a consumer-led society within many societies has undoubtedly arisen because of marketing, as the following quote illustrates: 'The power of market forces and that of marketing to virtually shape every aspect of a society's mores [customs], attitudes and culture should not be underestimated. Used wisely and with restraint, marketing can harness and channel the vast energies of the free market system for the good of consumers, corporations and for society as a whole. Used recklessly, it can cause significant harm to all those entities. Thus, marketing is like a potent drug with potentially serious side effects' (Sheth and Sisodia, 2005).

▶ Market Insight 1.5

Fairtrade: Clean Conscience for Consumers and Fair Deal for Farmers?

Fairtrade Labelling Organisations International (FLO) is an umbrella organization of 20 labelling initiatives and producer networks that represents Fairtrade-certified producer organizations in Africa, Asia, and South America. In the UK, the Fairtrade Foundation is the labelling initiative that licenses the Fairtrade mark to products that meet international Fairtrade standards. The mission of FLO is to ensure the economic independence and empowerment of producer organizations and their members, through Fairtrade certification by:

▶ setting international standards in Fairtrade certification;

▶ supporting producers in using Fairtrade product labelling as effectively as possible; and

▶ raising awareness for the Fairtrade movement generally.

▶ Market Insight 1.5   (continued)

Fairtrade products taste as good as their principles
Source: © Sue Atkinson.

Through long-term trading relationships, Fairtrade-certified producers benefit from economic stability and improved livelihoods. The additional Fairtrade social premium payment is used by producers to invest in social, economic, or environmental development projects such as technical assistance for infrastructure development, communication system development, improved healthcare and education, and skill development for their cooperative members and families.

The Fairtrade certification system has been applied to a variety of agricultural commodity items, including fruits, honey, cotton, nuts, tea, and wine. The scheme operates across 15 European countries, as well as in Australasia, North America, Mexico, and Japan. And, clearly, the consumer also approves because, by 2008, global sales in Fairtrade products totalled around €2.9bn, growing at an average of 40% over the previous five years (FLO International, 2009). The question is: are consumers prepared to pay the generally higher prices that they have to pay for products with the Fairtrade mark than non-labelled products?
Source: www.fairtrade.net.

1   **Why has the Fairtrade mark become so important in recent times?**

2   **Are consumers really prepared to pay the higher prices for a cleaner conscience? Why do you think this is?**

3   **Have you bought a Fairtrade-labelled product recently? If not, why haven't you purchased such an item?**

go online

Visit the **Online Resource Centre** and complete Internet Activity 1.2 to learn more about the positive impact marketing and the FLO can have on society.

Skills for Employment

▶▶ I believe it is also crucial to tailor your CV and covering letter to the job you are applying for—don't send in a standardized CV because we can tell and this lacks care and attention to detail. Make your CV professional but personal—for example, don't simply state that you like to read books, include the last book you read and what your thoughts were about it; or if you like sport, which sports and what is it about them that you like. It is these personal aspects that will make your CV stand out from the pack. ◀◀

Victoria Gregory, CRM Systems Manager, Reed Smith

 Visit the **Online Resource Centre** to discover more tips and advice on skills for the workplace.

Chapter Summary

To consolidate your learning, the key points from this chapter are summarized below:

■ **Define the marketing concept.**

Marketing is the process by which organizations anticipate and satisfy their customers' needs to both parties' benefit. It involves mutual exchange of benefits. Over the last 20 years, the marketing concept has been altered to recognize the importance of the long-term customer relationship to organizations.

■ **Explain how marketing has developed over the twentieth century.**

Whereas some writers have suggested a simple production era, sales era, marketing era development for marketing over the twentieth century, others recognize that marketing has existed in different forms in different countries. Nevertheless, there is an increasing recognition that marketing is a more systematic organizational activity through market research, and sophisticated promotional activity, than before. There is a move towards recognizing the need for companies and organizations to behave responsibly in relation to society.

■ **Describe the three major contexts of marketing application, i.e. consumer goods, business-to-business, and services marketing.**

Marketing divides into three types, recognizing that marketing activities are designed based on the context in which an organization operates. The consumer goods marketing approach has been dominant stressing the 4Ps and the marketing mix. Business-to-business marketing focuses more on principles of relationship marketing, particularly those required in coordinating supply chain members. Services marketing stresses the intangible nature of the product, the need to manage customer expectations, and levels of service quality.

■ **Understand the contribution marketing makes to society.**

The aggregate marketing system delivers to us a wide array of products and services, either directly, or indirectly through business markets, to serve our needs and wants. There is much that is positive about the aggregate marketing system and it has served to improve the standard of living for many people around the world.

■ **Assess critically the impact marketing has on society.**

The aggregate marketing system also has its faults, by also allowing the promotion and distribution of products and services that could be bad for us, and the over-consumption of products, which in moderation are good for us. We propose adopting a critical marketing perspective as a natural approach to learning marketing. As society is changing, new critical approaches to marketing are increasingly developing (e.g. the Fairtrade movement).

Review Questions

1 How do we define the marketing concept?

2 How do the American Marketing Association and the Chartered Institute of Marketing definitions of marketing differ?

3 How has marketing developed over the twentieth century?

4 What is the marketing mix?

5 How does Bagozzi define marketing exchange?

6 What is the difference between sales and marketing?

7 What are the three major contexts of marketing application?

8 What are the five characteristics of services marketing?

9 What contribution does marketing make to society?

10 How should the aggregate marketing system operate within society?

Worksheet Summary

Visit the **Online Resource Centre** and complete Worksheet 1.1. This will help you learn about how managers can use McCarthy's 4Ps framework to market goods and Bitner and Boom's 7Ps framework to market services.

Discussion Questions

1 Having read the Case Insight at the beginning of this chapter, how would you advise Systembolaget to use marketing in the future to: a) maintain public support for the Swedish alcohol monopoly? b) ensure that customers drink responsibly?

2 Read the section on the marketing mix within the chapter and draw up marketing mixes for the following organizations:

A A Hollywood movie studio releasing a blockbuster film and the cinema audience.

B A travel agency specializing in luxury holidays and their wealthy clientele.

C Apple, as makers of the iPod, its network of distribution outlets, and the end user.

D A chemical company supplying fertilizers to farmers.

3 **Outline simple marketing exchange processes for the following buyer–seller relationships:**

  A The relationship between a toy company salesperson and the owner of a retail outlet.

  B The relationship between a pop band of your choice and its audience.

  C The relationship between an online dating agency and its subscribers.

4 **What are the attributes of the product offer, and consumer needs associated with those attributes, for the following product offers:**

  A Retail bank current accounts?

  B A spa offering massage, facial treatment, aromatherapy, and detox services?

  C The Mont Blanc pen?

  D A celebrity magazine like *Hello!* (*Ola*, etc.) or *OK*?

  E Watching a football match live in a sports stadium?

go online

Visit the **Online Resource Centre** and complete the Multiple Choice Questions to assess your knowledge of Chapter 1.

References

American Marketing Association (AMA) (2007), 'Definition of marketing', retrieve from www.marketingpower.com/Community/ARC/Pages/Additional/Definition/default.aspx?sq=definition+of+marketing, accessed 17 April 2010.

Bagozzi, R. P. (1975), 'Marketing as exchange', *Journal of Marketing*, 39, 4 (October), 32–9.

Bartels, R. D. W. (1944), 'Marketing principles', *Journal of Marketing*, 9, 2 (October), 151–8.

—(1951), 'Can marketing be a science?', *Journal of Marketing*, 15, 3, 319–28.

—(1959), 'Sociologists and marketologists', *Journal of Marketing*, October, 37–40.

—(1968), 'The general theory of marketing', *Journal of Marketing*, 32 (January), 29–33.

—(1983), 'Is marketing defaulting its responsibilities?', *Journal of Marketing*, 47 (Fall), 32–5.

BBC News (2006), 'Body Shop agrees L'Oréal takeover', 17 March, retrieve from: http://news.bbc.co.uk/1/hi/business/4815776.stm, accessed 17 April 2010.

Blois, K. J. (1974), 'The marketing of services: an approach', *European Journal of Marketing*, 8, 2, 137–45.

Booms, B. H., and Bitner, M. J. (1981), 'Marketing strategies and organisation structures for service firms', in J. H. Donnelly and W. R. George (eds), *Marketing of Services*, Chicago: AMA Proceedings Series, 48.

Borden, N. H. (1964), 'The concept of the marketing mix', *Journal of Advertising Research*, 4, 2–7.

Brownlie, D., and Saren, M. (1992), 'The four Ps of the marketing concept: prescriptive, polemical, permanent, and problematic', *European Journal of Marketing*, 26, 4, 34–47.

Bucklin, L. P. (1963), 'Retail strategy and the classification of consumer goods', *Journal of Marketing*, January, 51–6.

Burton, D. (2001), 'Critical marketing theory: the blueprint?', *European Journal of Marketing*, 35, 5/6, 722–43.

Christopher, M. (1986), 'Reaching the customer: strategies for marketing and customer service', *Journal of Marketing Management*, 2, 1, 63–71.

Chartered Institute of Marketing (CIM) (2001), 'Marketing', Glossary, available at www.cim.co.uk, accessed 17 April 2010.

Dale, R. (1985), *The Sinclair Story*, Ely: Fern House Books.

Day, G. S (1994), 'The capabilities of market-driven organisations', *Journal of Marketing*, 58, 3, 37–52.

Easton, G. (2002), 'Marketing: a critical realist approach', *Journal of Business Research*, 55, 103–9.

Enright, M. (2002), 'Marketing and conflicting dates for its emergence: Hotchkiss, Bartels and the fifties school of alternative accounts', *Journal of Marketing Management*, 18, 445–61.

Fleisher, C. S., and Bensoussan, B. E. (2002), *Strategic and Competitive Analysis*, Englewood Cliffs, NJ: Prentice-Hall.

FLO International (2009), *Annual Reports 2008–2009*, Bonn: Fairtrade Labelling Organisations, retrieve from www.fairtrade.net/fileadmin/user_upload/content/FT_ANNUAL_REPORT_08-09.pdf, accessed 17 April 2010.

Fullerton, R. A. (1988), 'How modern is modern marketing? Marketing's evolution and the myth of the "Production Era"', *Journal of Marketing*, 52 (January), 108–25.

Gladwell, M. (2002), *The Tipping Point: How Little Things Can Make a Big Difference*, London: Abacus Books.

Grönroos, C. (1984), 'A service quality model and its marketing implications', *European Journal of Marketing*, 18, 4, 36–44.

—(1994), 'From marketing mix to relationship marketing: towards a paradigm shift in marketing', *Management Decision*, 32, 2, 4–20.

—(1998), 'Marketing services: a case of a missing product', *Journal of Business and Industrial Marketing*, 13, 4/5, 322–38.

Gummesson, E. (1987), 'The new marketing: developing long term interactive relationships', *Long Range Planning*, 20, 4, 10–20.

Holden, A. C., and Holden, L. (1998), 'Marketing history: illuminating marketing's clandestine subdiscipline', *Psychology and Marketing*, 15, 2, 117–23.

Howard, D. G., Savins, D. M., Howell, W., and Ryans, J. K., Jr (1991), 'The evolution of marketing theory in the United States and Europe', *European Journal of Marketing*, 25, 2, 7–16.

Hunt, S. D. (1971), 'The morphology of theory and the general theory of marketing', *Journal of Marketing*, April, 65–8.

—(1983), 'General theories and fundamental explananda of marketing', *Journal of Marketing*, 47, 4 (Fall), 9–17.

Judd, R. C. (1968), 'Similarities and differences in product and service retailing', *Journal of Retailing*, 43, 4, 1–9.

Keith, R. J. (1960), 'The marketing revolution', *Journal of Marketing*, 24 (January), 35–8.

Klein, N. (1999), *No Logo*, London: Flamingo.

Kohli, A. K., and Jaworski, B. J. (1990), 'Market orientation: the construct, research propositions and managerial implications', *Journal of Marketing*, 54 (April), 1–18.

Kotler, P. (2006), 'Ethical lapses of marketers', in J. N. Sheth and R. J. Sisodia (eds.), *Does Marketing Need Reform: Fresh Perspectives on the Future*, Armonk, NY: M. E. Sharpe, chapter 17.

Lendrevie, J., Lévy, J., and Lindon, D. (2006), *Mercator: Théorie et pratique du marketing*, 8th edn, Paris: Dunod.

Leone, R. P., and Shultz, R. L. (1980), 'A study of marketing generalisations', *Journal of Marketing*, 44 (Winter), 10–18.

L'Oréal (2010), 'Brands', retrieve from www.loreal-finance.com/site/us/marques/marque5.asp#, accessed 2 May 2010.

McCarthy, E. J. (1960), *Basic Marketing*, Homewood, Ill.: Irwin.

Marketing and Sales Standards Setting Body (2010), *Developing World-Class Standards for the Marketing Profession*, March, retrieve from www.msssb.org/marketing.htm, accessed 17 September 2010.

Mintel (2007), *Flavoured Alcoholic Beverages—UK—October 2007*, London: Mintel, retrieve from www.mintel.com.

—(2010), *Beauty Retailing —UK—January 2010*, London: Mintel, retrieve from www.mintel.com.

Morgan. R. M., and Hunt, S. D. (1994), 'The commitment-trust theory of relationship marketing', *Journal of Marketing*, 58, 3 (July), 20–38.

Narver, J. C., and Slater, S. F. (1990), 'The effect of a market orientation on business profitability', *Journal of Marketing*, October, 20–35.

Packard, V. O. (1960), *The Hidden Persuaders*, Harmondsworth: Penguin Books.

Parasuraman, A., Berry, L. L., and Zeithaml, V. A. (1985), 'A conceptual model of service quality and its implications for further research', *Journal of Marketing*, 49 (Fall), 41–50.

Payne, A. (1993), *The Essence of Services Marketing*, Hemel Hempstead: Prentice-Hall.

Regan, W. J. (1963), 'The service revolution', *Journal of Marketing*, 27, 57–62.

Reichheld, F. F., and Sasser Jr., W. E. (1990), 'Zero defections: quality comes to services', *Harvard Business Review*, September–October, 105–11.

Renault (2009), *Drive the Change*, retrieve from: www.renault-ze.com/uk/, accessed 17 April 2010.

Saren, M. (2006), *Marketing Graffiti: The View from the Street*, Oxford: Butterworth-Heinemann.

Sheth, J. N., and Sisodia, R. J. (2005), 'A dangerous divergence: marketing and society', *Journal of Public Policy and Marketing*, 24, 1, 160–2.

—(2006), 'How to reform marketing', in J. N. Sheth and R. J. Sisodia (eds), *Does Marketing Need Reform: Fresh Perspectives on the Future*, Armonk, NY: M. E. Sharpe, chapter 20.

Shostack, G. L. (1977), 'Breaking free from product marketing', *Journal of Marketing*, 41 (April), 73–8.

Slater, S. F., and Narver, J. C. (1994), 'Market orientation, customer value and superior performance', *Business Horizons*, March–April, 22–7.

Toyota (2006), *Hybrid Synergy Drive*, retrieve from www.hybridsynergydrive.com/en/top.html, accessed 17 April 2010.

Vargo, S. L., and Lusch, R. F. (2004), 'Evolving to a new service dominant logic for marketing', *Journal of Marketing*, 68 (January), 1–17.

Webster, F. E., Jr. (1992), 'The changing role of marketing in the corporation', *Journal of Marketing*, 56 (October), 1–17.

Wilkie, W. L., and Moore, E. S. (1999), 'Marketing's contributions to society', *Journal of Marketing*, 63 (Special Issue), 198–218.

Worcester, R. M.; Mortimore, R. and Baines, P. (2005), *Explaining Labour's Landslip*, London: Politicos Publishing.

2 The Marketing Environment

Learning Outcomes

After reading this chapter, you will be able to:

▶ Identify and define the three key areas of the marketing environment

▶ Describe the key characteristics associated with the marketing environment

▶ Explain PESTLE analysis and show how it is used to understand the external environment

▶ Explain the environmental scanning process

▶ Analyse the performance environment using an appropriate model

▶ Understand the importance of analysing an organization's internal environment and identify the key resources and capabilities

▶ Case Insight 2.1

Michelin Tyres has been established for over a century and is now active in more than 170 countries. How does it keep abreast of the marketing environment? We speak to Helen Tattersall to find out more.

Helen Tattersall for
Michelin Tyres

The Michelin Tyre Company Ltd, first incorporated in 1905, was set up in 1889 by two brothers, André and Edouard Michelin. Now active in more than 170 countries, Michelin operates across all continents of the world, manufacturing and selling tyres for all kinds of vehicles, publishing maps and guides, and operating specialist digital services. Most people recognize our world famous mascot, Bibendum, 'the Michelin man', looking good considering his age! My own division is concerned with tyres made for heavy goods vehicles over 3.5 tonnes, including trucks, coaches, and buses. In the UK and the Republic of Ireland, we have an extensive sales force supporting thousands of tyre distributors, from tyres used in cars and trucks, to those used in specialist industrial and earthmoving equipment.

To conduct environmental scanning, we adopt several approaches. We use joint panels with key national and regional trade journals, conducting telephone questionnaires with customers on challenges, issues, and developments in the haulage industry. Our sales force in the UK and Ireland is responsible for collecting market intelligence, especially on competitors' actions and products.

Bibendum, helping drivers for more than 100 years

We work with the Road Haulage Association and the Freight Transport Association, which offers us a chance to mix with customers in a non-selling environment, and we belong to the EuroPool organization, an independent body that acts on behalf of all European tyre manufacturers. Here, we declare our sales on a monthly basis and they send back to us details of our market share. In addition, we conduct our own annual surveys with distribution partners (including ATS Euromaster—a Michelin group company—and independent tyre dealers). We use the results of these surveys to track industry market shares with sales revenues. Finally, we analyse and test competitors' tyre products at our research and development centre.

Our scanning activity has picked up lots of challenges, for example rising fuel costs, changes in haulage patterns due to an increase in internet shopping, new legislation around driving and emission standards, and changing patterns of labour with the increase in Eastern European drivers (often bringing with them their cheaper fuel). However, the biggest challenge that we have experienced in the last four or five years is the strong competition from cheap imported tyre manufacturers from emerging economies in the East, including India, China, and Korea. These new tyre brands sell very cheaply because of the low manufacturing and labour costs in these countries. Although we knew these brands were coming, we were very surprised by how rapidly customers adopted them.

If you were faced with unexpected competition of this type, what would you do?

Introduction

Have you ever wondered how organizations adapt to the changing business environment? How do companies keep up with the many changes that occur in politics, markets, and economics? What processes do they use to try to anticipate changes in technologies? How do they know which factors will impact on their businesses and which won't? We consider such questions in this chapter.

The operating environment for all organizations, whether they are commercial, charitable, governmental, or in the public sector more generally, is never static and seldom entirely predictable, and can therefore profoundly affect a company's course of action. In this chapter, we examine the nature of the marketing environment, determine environment-related issues, and provide a context for developing marketing strategies (see Chapter 5).

Consider the degree to which an organization can influence the various environmental forces acting on it. The external environment, for example, consists of the political, social, and technological influences, and organizations usually have very limited influence on each of these. The performance environment consists of competitors, suppliers, and indirect service providers who shape the way an organization achieves its objectives. Here, organizations have a much stronger level of influence. The internal environment concerns the resources, processes, and policies an organization manages in order to achieve its goals. These elements can be influenced directly by an organization. Each of these three marketing environments is discussed in this chapter (see Figure 2.1).

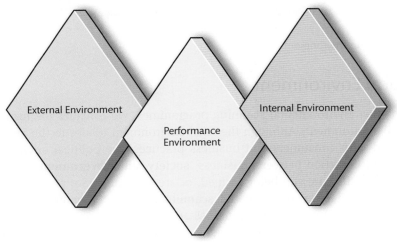

Figure 2.1
The three marketing environments

Understanding the External Environment

The external environment is characterized in two main ways. In the first, the elements do not have an immediate impact on the performance of an organization, although they might do in the longer term. In the second, although the elements can influence an organization, it is not possible to control them. This suggests that the level of risk attached to the external environment is potentially high. To make sense of the external environment, we use the well-known acronym, **PESTLE**. This is by far the easiest and one of the most popular frameworks with which to examine the external environment. PESTLE stands for the Political, Economic, Socio-cultural, Technological, Legal, and Ecological environments, as shown in Figure 2.2.

Figure 2.2
The external marketing environment

The Political Environment

When we conduct environmental scanning programmes, we consider the firm or organization's political environment. Although the legal environment relates to the laws and regulations associated with consumers and business practices, the political environment relates to the period of interaction between business, **society**, and **government** before those laws are enacted, when they are still being formed, or are in dispute. So, political environmental analysis is a critical phase in environmental scanning because companies can detect potential legal and regulatory changes in their industries and have a chance to impede, influence, and alter that legislation. Most marketing strategy textbooks teach that the **political environment** is largely uncontrollable. However, this is not always the case. There are circumstances when an organization, or an industry coalition, can affect legislation in its own favour, or at least respond more flexibly to changes in legislation than its competitors. There is increasingly an understanding that business–government relations, properly undertaken, can be a source of **sustainable competitive advantage**. In other words, organizations can outperform other organizations over time if they can manage their relationships with government and regulatory bodies better than their competitors (Hillman, Keim, and Schuler, 2004). (See Market Insight 2.1 for an example of a business–government relations campaign.)

Because legislation is such a technical area, and often written in technical legal language, few firms have the capability to understand and influence legislation without employing specialists. In such circumstances, special industry lobbyists are hired for the following reasons (Moloney and Jordan, 1996):

▶ to represent clients to government decision-makers;

▶ to provide strategic advice to clients on how to design their campaigns; and

▶ to provide administrative support for their clients.

▶ Market Insight 2.1

Air Tanker Contract Fuels Fight of the Lobbyists

When the US Pentagon put out a tender for an order for KC-30 advanced multirole tanker transport planes worth \$35–40bn, it created something of a dogfight between aerospace companies Boeing and European Aeronautic Defence and Space company (EADS)/ Northrop Grumman. European Aeronautic Defence and Space company, the parent of Airbus and Northrop Grumman, an American aerospace company, decided to collaborate in an attempt to rival Boeing's bid. In fact, the contract was high stakes because it was the first of three such deals likely to be worth over \$100bn over 30 years. The contract was originally won by Boeing in 2003, but was cancelled after a corruption scandal involving a US Air Force official. Then the contract was awarded to EADS/Northrop Grumman in February 2008 but Boeing contested the decision, lodging a protest with the US Government Accountability Office (GAO), the oversight arm of Congress, arguing that the deal would damage the US industrial base and cost American jobs.

Boeing took out full-page newspaper adverts protesting and pointing out the impact of the potential loss of American jobs to the American public, despite the fact that EADS/Northrop had intended to assemble the planes in Alabama. Meanwhile, Northrop hired a lobbying firm run by former Senators Trent Lott and John Breaux and

EADS hired Washington DC firms Hill and Knowlton, Quinn and Gillespie and Public Strategies to challenge Boeing's challenge. European Aeronautic Defence and Space company/Northrop were urging Congress not to interfere with the initial decision made by the Pentagon but there had been substantial opposition to the EADS/Northrop bid in Washington DC, particularly over the involvement of EADS in the bid—the parent of Boeing's arch-rival Airbus.

The GAO then issued a statement in June 2008 explaining that the competition should be re-run, citing errors in the awarding of the tender to EADS/ Northrop, namely that the US Air Force:

▶ Did not assess the relative merits of the tanker contract in accordance with its own criteria.

▶ Gave the EADS/Northrop bid extra credit for offering a larger tanker, even though the Boeing tanker was perceived to be adequate for the job.

▶ 'Unreasonably' favoured EADS/Northrop after the company declined to set up maintenance depots within two years of delivery of the planes.

▶ Miscalculated the Boeing lifecycle costs and incorrectly calculated that EADS/Northrop costs would be lower.

▶ Conducted 'misleading and unequal' discussions with Boeing telling them that they had met a key performance indicator, but then stated later that they had only partially met that key performance indicator.

Two years later, in March 2008, EADS/Northrop Grumman withdrew from the bid, two months prior to the revised bid date of May 2010, because they believed the revised air tanker requirements were

▶ Market Insight 2.1   (continued)

unfairly geared towards Boeing's smaller tanker aircraft. The European Union issued the following statement that: 'it would be extremely concerned if it were to emerge that the terms of the tender were such as to inhibit open competition for the contract'. Nevertheless, EADS decided to submit a solo bid. So, it seems that whoever finally wins the contract, seven years later, will only win after the intervention of Washington DC's finest lobbyists.

Sources: BBC (2010); Madslien (2010); Sevastopulo (2008); Wallace (2008).

1 Why do you think Boeing was ultimately successful in gaining the award of the contract?

2 How did both Boeing and EADS/Northrop Grumman try to influence the GAO's decision?

3 Do you think it is ethical to try and influence government defence policy in this way? Why do you think this?

Companies or organizations often make the decision to influence governments in collaboration with other organizations, either through industry or trade bodies or together with other large companies in their industry. For example, Japanese automotive manufacturers Nissan and Honda lobbied the EU to recognize cars assembled in the UK largely from Japanese parts to be European in the early 1990s to offset import quotas on certain Japanese goods (see Kewley, 2002). There have been many successful examples of other lobbying campaigns, for instance, that of the Shopping Hours Reform Council (SHRC), consisting mainly of large supermarket chains, who managed to lobby the then Conservative government to make Sunday trading legal in July 1994 (Harris, Gardner, and Vetter, 1999). Generally, there are several ways in which marketers might conduct business–government relations in various countries as shown below:

▶ Lobbyist firms, with key industry knowledge, can be engaged either permanently or as needed.

▶ **Public relations** consultancies, e.g. Weber Shandwick, can be commissioned for their political services, often having MPs or others with a high degree of political influence serving as directors and/or advisers.

▶ A politician may be paid a fee to give political advice on matters of importance to an organization, where this is legal within that particular jurisdiction, and that politician is not serving directly within the government in question on the same portfolio as that on which they are advising.

▶ An in-house public relations manager might handle government relations directly.

▶ An industry association might be contacted to lobby on behalf of members (e.g. in the European financial services industry, groups include the Banking Federation of the EU, the European Savings Bank Group, and the European Association of Co-operative Banks).

▶ A politician may be invited directly to join the board of directors, board of trustees, or board of advisers of an organization to aid the company in developing its business–government relations.

Working with parliaments, civil servants, and governments in different countries provides serious difficulties, particularly where a company or organization has limited knowledge of the market. In addition, successive governments seldom work in the same way as their predecessors, so there is usually a learning curve at the beginning of each electoral cycle in any jurisdiction. Generally, when conducting a public affairs campaign, it is important to:

▶ Identify and prioritize the issues at hand (commercial and political).

▶ Develop contacts with the appropriate officials in the relevant government, commission, or parliamentary departments.

▶ Design a planning and contacts 'grid' that outlines which **stakeholders** need to be contacted over what issues by which dates.

▶ Identify key politicians and other interested parties—what Décaudin and Malaval (2008) call the deciders (key politicians who can affect regulation), the prescribers (technical experts, usually civil servants), industrial actors (e.g. other member companies in an industry body), and the general public.

▶ Read, and try to influence, the press over the campaigning issues (Morris, 2001).

It is important not only to try to change or influence the political environment, but also to understand how changes in it might affect specific business. A case study by Melewar *et al.* (2008) showed the impact of the newly enlarged European Union on Fjord Seafood, a Norwegian company, and one of the world's largest salmon producers. When 10 new countries joined the EU, those structural changes were likely to have profound effects on Fjord Seafood's export sales, the nature of its international marketing strategy, and indeed all aspects of its marketing mix. A key consideration was whether or not it could sell a standardized product across the EU or whether it would need to tailor the product to individual countries (see Chapter 7).

The Economic Environment

Companies and organizations must develop an understanding of the economic environment because a country's economic circumstances have an impact on what economists term factor prices within a particular industry for a particular firm or organization. These factors could include raw material, labour, building and other capital costs, or any other input to a business. The external environment of a firm is affected by the following items:

▶ Wage inflation—annual wage increases in a particular sector will depend on the supply of labour in that sector. Where there is scarcity of supply, wages usually increase (e.g. doctors).

▶ Price inflation—how much consumers pay for goods and services depends on the rate of supply of those goods and services. If supply is scarce, there is usually an increase in the price of that consumer good or service (e.g. petrol).

▶ **Gross domestic product (GDP)** per capita—the combined output of goods and services in a particular nation is a useful measure for determining relative wealth between countries when comparisons are calculated per member of the population (GDP per capita at **purchasing power parity**, see paragraph below).

▶ Income, sales, and corporation taxes—these taxes, typically operating in all countries around the world usually at different levels, substantially affect how we market goods and services.

▶ Exchange rates—the relative value of a currency vis-à-vis another currency is an important calculation for those businesses operating in foreign markets or holding financial reserves in other currencies.

▶ Export quota controls and duties—there are often restrictions placed on the amounts (quotas) of goods and services that any particular firm or industry can import into a country, depending on to which trading bloc or country a company or firm is exporting. In addition, countries sometimes charge a form of tax on particular items as well to discourage or encourage imports and to protect their own economies.

When operating in other countries, we should understand how exchange rates and living standards operate. We might also need to understand how prices or labour costs change if we are importing our goods and services, or components of them, from another country, i.e. our factor prices. This is known as the rate of price or wage inflation. The difficulty comes in comparing prices from one country to another. Should we just compare costs (what is paid for a proposition as a company) and prices of goods (at what price a good is sold, or what is paid as a consumer) through the exchange rate at any one particular time? Apparently not, as this is itself subject to political and other pressures. What economists tend to do is calculate prices for a particular basket of goods—a fixed list of common items—and compare the costs in one country versus another. This is known as the **purchasing power parity exchange rate**. This rate then allows us to compare directly the relative costs between two countries for a given item.

Firms usually have little impact on the macroeconomic environment as they have little control over macroeconomic variables, e.g. oil prices, which might affect their business, e.g. stock prices if they are multinationals listed on a major stock exchange (e.g. NYSE, FTSE, or Euronext). The challenge when examining the macroeconomic environment is to foresee changes in the environment that might affect the firm's activities. If a computer company in Sweden imports silicon chips from Japan, and pays for them in Swedish Kronor, but the exchange rate for yen is rising against the Swedish Kronor (in other words, you get more yen per Kronor perhaps because of strong Japanese export sales to Europe generally), then you might source your silicon chips from another country to ensure that your own prices are relatively unaffected.

Similarly, if **inflation** drives consumer prices higher in a particularly country, it may mean that the price of your goods becomes more expensive and this may force a drop in sales. Typically, during a **recession**, consumers tend to purchase fewer goods and increase their savings, and prices fall further as producers attempt to stimulate demand. But prices can also increase during a recession. It is important to understand general economic trends in the macroeconomy and the firm's marketplace. Surveys of consumer expectations of inflation, forecasts of foreign exchange rates, wage forecasts, and lots of other financial information are frequently available from government central banks.

go online

Visit the **Online Resource Centre** and complete Internet Activity 2.1 to learn more about how the contribution of service industries to the UK's national economy has changed over the last 10 years.

The Socio-Cultural Environment

Lifestyles are constantly changing and consumers are constantly shifting their preferences over time. Companies that fail to recognize changes in the socio-cultural environment, and change their goods/service mix accordingly, typically fail. Levi-Strauss, the jeans company, has lost its way since its heyday in the 1990s when the brand alone was reputedly worth nearly $7bn, yet was worth only around $1.4bn in 2008 (Millward Brown, 2008) as new generations of consumers turned away from the brand. When considering the socio-cultural environment, companies must consider the changing nature of households, demographics, lifestyles and family structures, and changing **values** in society.

Demographics and Lifestyles

Changes in population proportions have an impact on a company's marketing activity. In the UK, immigration from Poland after EU enlargement has substantially increased the Polish component of the population, with some supermarkets specifically targeting the Polish population using adverts in Polish and by stocking Polish products such as borsch, meatballs, pickled vegetables, and sauerkraut soup (BBC, 2006). Off licences in Britain have also seen increased sales of vodka, particularly Polish vodkas such as Wyborowa (Neate, 2008). According to the UN Population Division (2005), by 2050, India's population is set to reach around 1.6bn, China is set to reach 1.4bn, America is due to reach 395m, and the UK only 72m. Notably, some countries' populations are set to fall (e.g. Japan and Russia). What implications will these changes have for different consumer and industrial sectors? But it is not just the absolute number of people within a population that matters to the marketer, we are also concerned with the ages of those different people. Figure 2.3 illustrates the relative differences in age structure in a variety of selected countries.

The figure shows clearly the relatively large proportion of people in the 65-year-old-plus age bracket (the 'silver' or 'grey' market, so-called because of the colour of the hair of this group). Those countries with comparatively younger citizens include African and Middle Eastern countries, such as Namibia, South Africa, and Egypt. The changes and relative differences in age structure in different countries correspond to different sized markets for brand propositions relevant to these particular communities of citizens. Clearly, the market for private pensions in Europe is likely to increase substantially as national governments and the EU move towards developing appropriate schemes, which should bode well for insurance and pension groups. But this is just one example; there are a whole host of goods and services that might be targeted at these different groups.

People's lifestyles are also changing. In Europe, the trend is towards marrying later and a greater tendency to divorce than in previous generations. In some countries, citizens are increasingly living alone, for example, in single-person households. There is a rise in industrialized nations of same-sex civil marriages or partnerships, and some countries and states within countries have legitimized these more than others (e.g. UK, and California in the USA). Marketers dub the homosexual segment the 'pink' market. Up to 10% of the American population identifies itself as gay/lesbian, with marketing activity increasingly targeted at this population by companies such as Coors Brewing, Volvo, and Absolut Vodka (Valdiserri, 2002). Specific destinations, particularly during gay festivals, are targeted at the pink consumer such as Manchester in the UK, San Francisco in the USA, Sydney in Australia, and Rio de Janeiro in Brazil. There are obvious opportunities for the hotel and leisure industry, which can offer

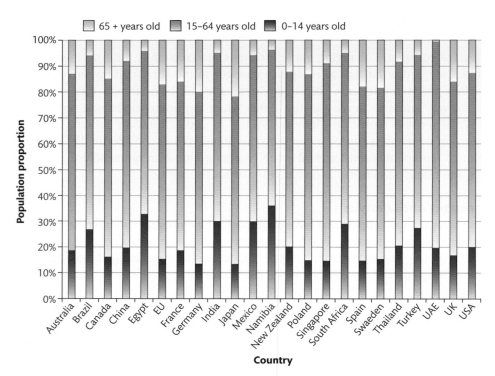

Figure 2.3

Population proportion estimates by age in selected countries

Source: CIA World Factbook (2009 estimates, row totals may not add up to 100% due to rounding).

pink honeymoons, weekends, and travel facilities. Gay people have also been shown to differ from their straight counterparts by more readily adopting new technology, showing greater brand loyalty, taking more city breaks, and spending twice as much tending their appearance, favouring **brands** such as Sony, Gillette, Virgin, and Nivea (Snoddy, 2006). According to the Out Now 2008 Millivres Gay Market Study, collectively, the estimated 3,000,000 gay men and women in the UK earned around £81bn (Anon., 2008). There is comparatively little research, however, showing the difference in consumption behaviour, if there is any, between gay men and gay women. So, we can see the change in values in these societies.

Societal changes, however, need not necessarily be demographic, or lifestyle-oriented, to have an impact on marketing. There are also changes taking place within society that affect the way that consumers now interact with an organization's marketing activity. Customers are increasingly happy to work with companies and organizations to solve problems. Howe (2006) refers to this phenomenon as **crowdsourcing**. Whitla (2009) suggests that the role and process of crowdsourcing is to identify a task or group of tasks currently conducted in-house, and then release the task(s) to a 'crowd' of outsiders who are invited to perform the task(s) on behalf of the company (for a fee or prize). This invite might either be truly open to everyone or restricted in some way to ensure that those who respond are only those qualified to undertake the task. This new approach can help marketers gain insights into both new product/service development and marketing communications. (See Market Insight 2.2 for examples of this activity.)

▶ Market Insight 2.2

The Wisdom of Crowdsourcing

The following three examples outline different uses of crowdsourcing for market ideas and solutions, including the development of a political billboard advert, a name for a newly developed product, and creative ideas for a print and TV advert campaign.

When the UK Labour Party developed its first ad for the General Election campaign in April 2010, it used the talents of its own supporters to design the ad. The party's advertising agency, Saatchi and Saatchi invited supporters to respond to an online brief to design their first election billboard poster and received around 1,000 responses. The winning entry parodied the leader of the Conservatives, David Cameron, as the politically incorrect Gene Hunt, the character from 'Ashes to Ashes', a BBC TV show set during the Thatcher years, sitting on the bonnet of an Audi Quattro. Ironically, the Conservatives felt that the advert was so positive that they developed their own version of it, replacing the Labour words, 'Don't let him take Britain back to the 1980s' with 'Fire up the Quattro, it's time for a change'. The development of a successful beer for women in Britain has been a difficult marketing challenge. Only 13% of beer is drunk by women in Britain compared to 36% of beer in Ireland. Previous attempts to produce a female-friendly beer incorporating tastes of fruit and green tea failed so Molson Coors have now developed a clear low-calorie beer after undertaking a survey of 30,000 female drinkers. But what do you call a clear light beer for women? That's where Molson Coors think women can help again, by giving them the chance to name it.

Unilever offered $10,000 in a competition to develop ideas for its next Peperami print and TV advert campaign, based on its quirky character Animal, a living representation of the pork salami snack (see also Market Insight 2.3). Using a crowdsourcing website, www.ideabounty.com and its production house SmartWorks, Unilever asked for an 'unapologetic, unexpected, and incredibly memorable piece of communication'. The Unilever team were so impressed with the submissions they received that instead of picking one winning idea they actually selected two!

Sources: BBC (2010b); Robinson (2010); Sweney (2009); Taylor (2010); www.ideabounty.com/blog/post/2485/peperami.-picks-two-winning-ideas.

1 **When do you think crowdsourcing is most useful?**

2 **When do you think crowdsourcing might not be an appropriate technique to use?**

3 **Do you know of any other companies that have used crowdsourcing approaches? What did they use it for?**

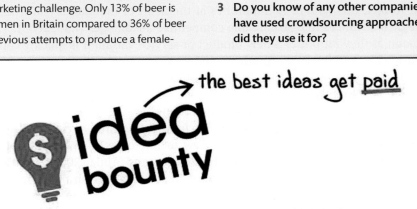

Submit your marketing ideas and win cash prizes!
Source: Courtesy of Idea Bounty.

The Technological Environment

The emergence of new technologies can substantially affect not only high-technology businesses but also non-technology businesses. Examples include those aspects of technology that impact on productivity and business efficiency (e.g. changes in energy, transportation, information, and communication technologies). New technology is increasingly changing the way that companies go to market through moves towards more email and web-based marketing and greater efficiency in direct and database marketing techniques (Sclater, 2005). Shifts in major technologies such as nanotechnology, biotechnology, and artificial intelligence also have implications for marketers. Nanotechnology has been used to develop stain-resistant clothes, self-cleaning windows, and super-strong materials. Biotechnological applications include genetically modified organisms and biomedicines. Advances in artificial intelligence have particularly large societal implications as increases in computer processing power allow computers to learn from previous experience and think for themselves (Ling, 2006). Changes in technology particularly affect high-technology industries, where firms must decide whether they wish to dominate that market by pushing their own particular technology standards, and especially where new technology renders existing standards obsolete (e.g. cloud computing and digital music files, the MP3 player and the tape and vinyl record manufacturing industries).

As marketers scanning the technological environment, we are particularly interested in research and development trends, particularly those of our competitors. Strategies to ascertain these can involve regular searches of patent registration, trademarks, and copyright assignations as well as maintaining a general interest in technological and scientific advances to determine their potential impact on product and service redesign. Firms' actions vis-à-vis one another are shaped by technological opportunity within the technological environment (Wilson, 1977). For example, in the pharmaceutical and chemical industries, companies have for a long time developed new compounds based on modifications of compounds registered for patents by their competitors in a process known as '**reverse engineering**'.

But the reverse engineering principle does not solely operate within these industries. Companies in other industries frequently develop new product and service formulations based on their competitors' products and services, through 'me-too' or imitation marketing strategy. In fact, this kind of imitation lies at the heart of the inability of firms to turn their technological advances into sustainable competitive advantages (Rao, 2005). The problem is that as soon as they introduce a new product or service variant it is quickly copied. The trick is to continually introduce new products and services, and to stay as close to the consumer as possible. Many companies also indulge in technology forecasting, an attempt to identify future technology trends.

The difficulty for most firms is how to determine whether or not to invest in radical new technologies, as the potential benefits are far from clear at the outset. Fear of obsolescence is usually a greater incentive to invest in new technologies than the lure of enhancement of existing products and services (Chandy, Prabhu, and Antia, 2003). Companies are particularly concerned about the impact of technological changes on their product and service lifecycles. However, innovation becomes a necessary condition in the strategic marketing decision-making of high-technology firms. For less technology-intensive firms, innovation of some form, whether it is process- or product/service-focused, or at least rapid adoption of new product/service variants based on competitors' offerings, is still usually necessary to stay ahead of the competition.

The Legal Environment

The legal environment covers every aspect of an organization's business. Laws and regulation are enacted in most countries ranging from the transparency of pricing, the prevention of restrictive trade practices, product safety, good practice in packaging and labelling, and the abuse of a dominant market position, to codes of practice in advertising, to take just a small selection.

Product Safety, Packaging, and Labelling

In the European Union, product safety is covered by the General Product Safety Directive to protect consumer health and safety both for member states within the EU, and importers from third-party countries to the EU or their EU agent representatives (see Chapter 8 for more on product decisions). Where products pose serious risks to consumer health, the European Commission can take action, imposing fines and criminal sentences for those contravening the Directive. The General Product Safety Directive does not cover food safety; this is subject to another EU Directive, which has established a European Food Safety Authority, and a set of regulations covering food safety. As a company operating in these sectors, it is important to keep up with changes in legislation. Failure to do so could jeopardize the business.

In the pharmaceutical industry, regulations govern testing, approval, manufacturing, labelling, and the marketing of drugs. Most countries also place restrictions on the prices that pharmaceutical companies can charge for drugs, and so, in Japan, price regulations are stipulated for individual products, whereas, in the UK, strict controls are placed on the overall profitability of products supplied by a specific company to the National Health Service, under the Pharmaceutical Price Regulation Scheme until 2014. Companies that develop cosmetics and fragrances are required to comply with legislative measures designed to protect the cosmetic user and so need to ensure that products remain cosmetics and are not reclassified under different regulations, for instance, those related to medicines, which makes innovation within the cosmetic industry more difficult (Gower, 2005).

Generally, in the EU, product labelling regulation tends to relate to recycling of packaging and waste to ensure it complies with environmental regulations, whereas in the USA, for example, packaging and labelling regulations are more concerned with fair practice and ensuring that packaging does not contain misleading advertising statements.

Codes of Practice in Advertising

Advertising standards differ around the world. In some countries, for example, the UK, advertising is self-regulated, i.e. by the advertising industry itself. In other countries, advertising is restricted by government legislation. In the UK, advertising is regulated by the Advertising Standards Authority (ASA), which has a mission to apply codes of practice in advertising and uphold advertising standards for consumers, business, and the general public (see Market Insight 2.3). Such self-regulatory agencies operate in other countries, e.g. the Bureau de Vérification de la Publicité in France, and the Federal Communications Commission in the USA. In the EU, the European Advertising Standards Alliance oversees both statutory and self-regulatory provision in most European countries and even non-European countries covering Russia, Canada, USA, New Zealand, and Turkey (see Chapter 11 for a more general discussion of advertising).

▶ Market Insight 2.3

Regulating Advertising in the UK: Peperami Salad

Codes of advertising are divided into broadcast and non-broadcast practice. In the UK, the British Code of Advertising, Sales Promotion and Direct Marketing provides regulations for non-broadcast advertisements, sales promotions, and direct marketing communications. This Code covers the content of marketing communications, the administration of sales promotions and the suitability of promotional items, the delivery of products ordered through an advertisement, and the use of personal information in direct marketing, but does not consider editorial content. The Committee of Advertising Practice (CAP) creates, revises, and enforces this Code and comprises organizations that represent the advertising, sales promotion, direct marketing, and media industries.

The Code of Practice aims to ensure that advertising is legal, decent, honest, and truthful to ensure consumer confidence in the advertising industry. In the UK, the ASA receives complaints from members of the public and adjudicates these.

In one example a complaint was not upheld against Unilever UK Ltd for an internet banner advert for Peperami salad, which appeared on the Brand Republic website. The advert stated '$10,000 TO KILL ME IN THE MOST CREATIVE WAY'. A cartoon Peperami was shown holding up a sign that stated 'ASSISTED SUICIDE'. The idea was that members of the public would submit their ideas for a TV and print ad to a formal brief and the individuals who submitted the successful ideas would receive a bounty of $10,000.

The complainant stated that the advert was likely to cause distress and serious offence, particularly to those with personal experience of assisted suicide, given public debates on the issue. In their response, Unilever argued that the advert appeared in specific media likely to reach a highly creative audience. They stated that visitors to the Brand Republic website would know the history of Peperami advertising and the 'Peperami Animal'—a sadistic cartoon character—and would understand the humorous approach.

In their judgment, the ASA acknowledged assisted suicide as a sensitive issue. They noted that the ad was targeted specifically at those who might want to enter the competition and considered that most members of the public who saw it would understand that the ad used a play on words intended to refer to the competition. They considered viewers would find the concept of assisting the suicide of an item of food ridiculous as opposed to offensive or distressing. Because it was not deemed to be distressing, the complaint was not upheld.

Source: ASA (2010).

1 **Do you think the advertising industry in your home country should regulate itself or be regulated by government? Why do you say this?**

2 **In the above example, do you agree with the judgment of the ASA? What did you think about the wording of the claim?**

3 **Can you remember an advert you've seen recently that made particularly wild claims or an advert you've seen that seriously offended you? What was it?**

In the UK, for broadcast advertising communications, codes of practice exist for both radio and TV typically with specific regulations for alcohol advertising, specifying that claims cannot be made in relation to sexual prowess, fitness or health, courage or strength. Restrictions on advertising exist for the advertising of alcohol products in most parts of the world, e.g. alcohol products cannot be advertised before 10 p.m. in Thailand. In France, as a result of the Evin Act, which restricts advertising for alcoholic beverages, manufacturers are obliged to show a government health warning on all advertisements using the following wording: 'L'abus d'alcool est dangereux pour la santé. Consommez avec modération', which translates into English as 'The abuse of alcohol is dangerous for your health. Consume with moderation'. In the UK, many breweries and distillers have been voluntarily placing the message 'drink responsibly' in the copy of their adverts for several years.

Government health warnings also apply to tobacco products, and tobacco advertising is now virtually banned in all marketing communication forms in many countries around the world. In most Western countries, consumers are dissuaded from smoking not only through high taxes placed on tobacco to reduce consumption, and through public restrictions on where people can smoke (e.g. Ireland, UK, California), but also through legislation banning and restricting advertising and requiring the placing of government health warnings on packages. In some countries, these government health warnings provide stark warning and graphic pictures. In Canada, in 1999, research into tobacco products and health warning labels found that there was a relationship between the size of a health warning message and its influence on stopping smoking, particularly among those stopping or starting smoking (Health Canada, 1999).

The Ecological Environment

In the 1990s, companies became concerned with the concept of 'green' marketing, and later in the 2000s with the concept of marketing sustainability (see Chapter 19). Increasingly, consumers are worried about the impact of companies on their ecological environments. They are demanding more 'organic' food, incorporating principles of better welfare for the animals they consume as food products and less interference with the natural processes of growing fruit and vegetables (e.g. the use of pesticides and chemical fertilizers).

BP's Helios logo
Source: BP.

▶ Market Insight 2.4

Who Ate All the Bars?

Weaning children off chocolate isn't easy!
Food and beverage companies, like their fast food counterparts, are facing increasing pressure from governments as child obesity rates increase in major Western nations. In England, obesity in children 2–15 years of age is expected to rise. In 2010, 19–23% of boys are estimated to be obese—up from 17% in 2003—whereas obesity in girls is expected to be

21–22%—up from 16% in 2003. The UK Government began to scrutinize public health policies in the 2004 White Paper on Public Health, which set out intentions to work across departments, with industry and other stakeholders, to support healthier life choices for citizens with specific requirements for food and beverage industry companies. They were particularly concerned about providing consumers with clearer information on labels about food ingredients; promoting healthy eating and drinking lifestyles; improving the nutritional quality of food

▶ Market Insight 2.4   (continued)

▶ **Table 2.1** Manufacturers' value shares in the UK chocolate market

Manufacturer	2005		2007		Change 2005–2007
	£m	%	£m	%	%
Cadbury Trebor Bassett	1,101	34.9	1,189	35.3	8.0
Masterfoods	953	30.2	1,010	30.0	6.0
Nestlé	470	14.9	494	14.7	5.0
Kraft Foods	63	2.0	61	1.8	–3.0
Ferrero	126	4.0	134	4.0	6.0
Own-label	189	6.0	217	6.5	15.0
Others	252	8.0	260	7.7	3.3
Total	3,154	100.0	3,365	100.0	6.7

Source: Mintel (2008, 2009a). Reproduced with the kind permission of Mintel.

products; and placing restrictions on certain food, alcohol, and tobacco marketing and promotion to protect children and young people's health through self-regulation or imposing some form of government legislation. In 2009, the Department of Health began an ambitious social marketing campaign called Change4Life aimed at preventing people from becoming overweight by encouraging them to eat better and move more.

The chocolate confectionery business is, therefore, a potential target for government regulation as it attempts to wean kids off chocolate snacks at schools and tries to introduce 'five-a-day' (portions) of fruit and vegetables instead, given the likely future cost to the government public health budget of dealing with obesity-related health problems. Children are beginning to eat more healthily, as nearly 40% of children now avoid products with artificial additives (Mintel, 2009a). Table 2.1 illustrates the size of the chocolate market in Great Britain, dominated by the trinity of chocolate makers Cadbury Schweppes (now owned by Kraft), Mars Inc. (which trades as Masterfoods Europe in Europe), and Nestlé. The

total market has grown only slightly, by around 1% between 2004 and 2005, with some of the major brands' sales falling by as much as 24% (e.g. Kit Kat). Nevertheless, Britain does seem to have a love affair with chocolate. The question is whether or not it expands our waistlines.

Sources: DoH (2004, 2010); Jotangia *et al.* (2006); Zaninotto *et al.* (2006).

1 **If you were CEO of Britain's largest chocolate manufacturer, Cadbury Schweppes, how would you develop the market for chocolate treats and continue to act as a socially responsible company?**

2 **How likely do you think it is that the UK government will bring in legislation to ban advertising on certain food products like chocolate?**

3 **How do you reconcile the fact that carbon labelling inherently suggests reduced consumption whereas advertising in itself suggests increased consumption?**

▶ Market Insight 2.4

Eat healthily or the vegetables get it!

Source: Crown Copyright material. Reproduced with the permission of the HMSO Controller.

Consumers are equally concerned with ensuring that products are not sourced from countries with poor and coercive labour policies, e.g. in parts of Latin America, the Far East, and Africa, a charge levelled at Nike in the 1990s. They are also keen to ensure that companies are not damaging the environment themselves or causing harm to consumers. There is a rise in 'Fairtrade' products. In Britain, for example, the Fairtrade Foundation trademarks all goods as a guarantee to indicate that that particular good has been sourced from disadvantaged producers in a developing country at a decent price to the producer. Sales of Fairtrade products include coffee, tea, banana, cocoa, flowers, wine, cotton, honey, and many others. The value of Fairtrade sales in the UK was £799m in 2009, a massive 467% on sales in 2004 (Fairtrade Foundation, 2010). Nevertheless, despite the good intentions of these companies, consumers remain confused over whether a particular product is organic, fairly traded, and/or ethically sourced (Murray, 2006).

One important question for marketers is how should a company incorporate the changing trend in sustainability into its organizational processes? To answer this question, Orsato (2006) suggests that a company can adopt one of the following four different green marketing strategies:

▶ Eco-efficiency—developing lower costs through organizational processes such as the promotion of resource productivity (e.g. energy efficiency) and better utilization of by-products. This approach should be adopted by firms that need to focus on reducing the cost and environmental impact of their organizational processes. Supermarket chains in Norway, and other Scandinavian countries, have for a long time encouraged recycling.

▶ Beyond compliance leadership—the adoption of a differentiation strategy through organizational processes such as certified schemes to demonstrate their ecological credentials, their environmental excellence, for example, the adoption of the UN Global Compact principles or other Environmental Management System (EMS) schemes and codes such as ISO14001. This approach should be adopted by firms that supply industrial markets, such as car manufacturers.

▶ Eco-branding—the differentiation of a firm's products or services to promote environmental responsibility. Examples include Duchy Originals, the British Prince of Wales' food brand, the Thai King Bhumipol's Golden Place brand, or the Toyota Prius labelled as 'mean but green'. Another example is BP—formerly British Petroleum—who changed their logo to make it green and yellow in a flower petal and sun synthesis, which they call the Helios, and slogan to 'beyond petroleum' to reflect their intended shift in meeting the world's energy requirements to more sustainable sources.

▶ Environmental cost leadership—the offering of products and services that give greater environmental benefits at a lower price. This strategy particularly suits firms operating in price-sensitive ecologically sensitive markets, such as the packaging and chemical industries.

Whatever the company and industry, ecological trends in marketing look set to stay and further develop as the sustainability debate rages on and companies use it to develop their own competitive strategies. It is important to assess how this movement towards greener and sustainable marketing is affecting a particular industry to ensure a company within that industry is either not adversely affected by these changes (e.g. by non-compliance with regulatory change such as packaging) or can take advantage of the opportunities (e.g. a haulage company taking advantage of hybrid lorries using engines that run on a combination of energy produced by petrol combustion and electricity production to lower energy costs).

Information about each of these sub-environments needs to be gathered in order for an assessment to be made about the potential impact on the organization. All organizations need to monitor all PESTLE elements, but some may be of particular importance to particular organizations. For example, pharmaceutical organizations such as GlaxoSmithKline monitor legal and regulatory developments (e.g. labelling, patents, and testing), the Environment Agency monitors political and ecological changes (e.g. flood plains for housing developments), road haulage companies should watch for any changes that impact on transport development (e.g. congestion charging, diesel duty, toll roads), whereas music distributors should monitor changes in technology and associated social and cultural developments (e.g. downloading trends and cloud computing).

Environmental Scanning

To understand how the external environment is changing, organizations need to put in place methods and processes to inform them of developments. The process of doing this is known as environmental scanning. **Environmental scanning** is the process of gathering information about a company's external events and relationships, to assist top management in its decision-making, and so develop its future course of action (Aguilar, 1967). It is the internal communication of external information about issues that may potentially influence an organization's decision-making process, focusing on the identification of emerging issues, situations, and potential threats in the external environment (Albright, 2004). Environmental scanning is an important component of the strategic marketing planning process (see Chapter 5). The development of an organization's strategic options is dependent on first determining the opportunities and threats in the environment and auditing an organization's resources.

We can gather information in environmental scanning exercises using company reports, newspapers, industry reports and magazines, government reports, and marketing intelligence reports (e.g. those published by Datamonitor, Euromonitor, and Mintel).

go online

Visit the **Online Resource Centre** and follow the weblinks to learn more about the information and services offered provided by Datamonitor, Euromonitor, and Mintel.

'Soft' personal sources of information obtained through networking are also important, such as contacts at trade fairs, particularly for competitive, and legal and regulatory information. Such verbal, personal sources of information can be critical in fast-changing environments (May, Stewart, and Sweo, 2000) when reports from government, industry, or specific businesses have yet to be written and disseminated.

Conversely, small manufacturing companies, for example, tend to scan three important areas of information in environmental scanning activities, which, according to Beal (2000) include:

▶ *Customer and competitor information*—including competitors' prices, competitors' new product introductions, competitors' advertising/promotional programmes, competitors' entry into new markets and new product technologies, customers' buying habits, customers' product preferences, customers' demands and desires.

▶ *Company resources and capabilities*—including company's R&D capabilities and resources, company's advertising and promotions resources, company's sales capabilities/resources, company's financial capabilities/resources, company's management capabilities/resources.

▶ *Suppliers of labour and funds*—including availability of external financing, availability of labour, and new manufacturing technologies.

For larger companies, or small companies operating in global environments, because of the increased complexity, there is an even greater need to undertake effective environmental scanning exercises. Thus, firms successfully operating in international markets were more likely to find information on export opportunities through information from secondary sources and from market research exercises. They tended to monitor their competitors' export performance, involvement in exporting, and their export intention, and they were more likely to monitor changes in technology, in products, in economic conditions, and in socio-political conditions (Lim, Sharkey, and Kim, 1996). A study on Thai small-to-medium-sized food processing companies has indicated that environmental scanning is a key factor in the new product development success in sectors with high technological turbulence (Ngamkroeckjoti and Speece, 2008).

The process through which companies scan the marketing environment typically involves three stages (see Figure 2.4). In Stage 1, the focus is principally, but not exclusively, on data gathering.

go online

Visit the **Online Resource Centre** and complete Internet Activity 2.2 to learn more about a number of sources that can be useful when conducting a scan of the marketing environment.

In Stage 2, the focus is principally, but not exclusively, on interpreting the data gathered in a process of environmental interpretation/analysis, and in the final stage, the focus is principally, but not exclusively, on strategy formulation.

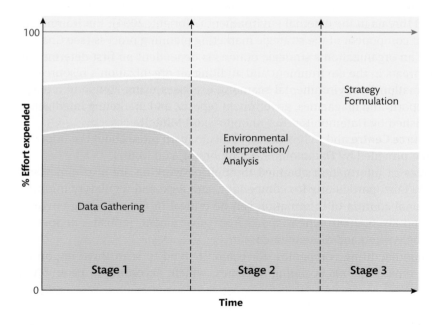

Figure 2.4

The environmental scanning process

Source: Adapted from O'Connell and Zimmerman (1979). Reproduced with the kind permission of *California Management Review*.

During each of the key scanning stages, there is also some activity in each of the other two areas so that each of the three processes dominates a particular stage but is also present at the other stages. So, in Stage 1, we might spend 60% of our time gathering data, 20% of our time undertaking environmental analysis/evaluation, and the remaining 20% of our time on strategy formulation. In Stage 2, we spend more time relatively on undertaking the environment analysis/evaluation, and in Stage 3, we spend more time relatively on strategy formulation. Environmental scanning is an activity that must be built into the strategy development and formulation process if it is to impact on company decision-making and help firms outperform their competitors by better adapting to their environment.

Although the process seems relatively straightforward, and simply a matter of collecting the 'right' information, barriers to effective environmental scanning occur because it is difficult to determine what the 'right' information actually is. In addition, data gathering can be time-consuming. In such cases, the information gathered ceases to provide a useful input to strategic marketing decision-making. In addition, multinational corporations may see opportunities and desire organizational change, and collect the right data, to take advantage of those opportunities, but fail to actually undertake such opportunities because of **switching costs** and organizational inertia related to production, sourcing, and other business operations. In a transatlantic survey of European and American companies in the late 1970s (O'Connell and Zimmerman, 1979), American executives reported a number of frustrations in their environmental scanning exercises including the inability to move faster; managerial inhibitions related to pessimistic discussions; conflict between the desire for stability and the reality of constant change; missed opportunities due to poor timing; and problems motivating the management team to discuss the issues. European executives reported frustrations including: the inability to organize for environmental scanning; difficulty matching individual executive beliefs with detectable trends; a delay between external developments and their interpretation of them; difficulty in applying a systematic approach; and problems finding relevant information.

Most commentators on environmental scanning assume that managers take advantage of environmental changes in a reactive manner rather than actually bringing about environmental change for their own gain. There are competing views on how organizations interact and react with their environment and their adaptability to it. Managers of a firm cannot stand outside the structure of their industries and adjust themselves to the trends they observe there; their actions make the trends (Brownlie, 1994). What is interesting is that managers frequently deliberately manage the information coming into a company surrounding the nature of uncertainty so as to advance their own positions and careers (Brownlie, 2009).

Some companies, however, have developed a proactive approach to determining how their operating environments are changing by considering potential future **scenarios** facing their company. For example, Shell, the multinational energy company, in its analysis of the world energy market to 2050, identifies two possible future energy scenarios based on how governments and companies respond to the energy production and sustainability challenge. In its 'scramble' scenario, there is energy price volatility, no effective carbon pricing, coal and biofuels are emphasized and renewables forced in by legislation, with a patchwork of national standards. In the 'blueprints' scenario, effective carbon pricing is established early, energy efficiency standards are put in place, the transport sector is electrified, and new energy infrastructure develops (Royal Dutch Shell, 2008). These two scenarios help Shell to plan for alternate realities in its strategic planning until it becomes clear if one or the other, or neither, of the scenarios is likely to occur.

▶ Research Insight 2.1

To take your learning further, you might wish to read this influential paper.

Levitt, T. (1960), 'Marketing myopia', *Harvard Business Review*, July–August, 45–56.

This is, perhaps the most famous and celebrated article ever written on marketing. It has twice been reprinted in the *Harvard Business Review*. The central thesis of the article, as true today as it was in the 1960s, is that companies must monitor change in the external environment and keep abreast of their customers' needs or they risk decline.

@ Visit the **Online Resource Centre** to read the abstract and access the full paper.

Understanding the Performance Environment

The **performance environment**, often called the microenvironment, consists of those organizations that either directly or indirectly influence an organization's operational performance. There are three main types:

1 Those companies that compete against the organization in the pursuit of its objectives.

2 Those companies that supply raw materials, goods, and services and those that add value as distributors, dealers, and retailers, further down the marketing channel. These organizations have the potential to directly influence the performance of the organization by adding value through production, assembly, and distribution of products prior to reaching the end user.

3 Those companies that have the potential to *indirectly* influence the performance of the organization in the pursuit of its objectives. These organizations often supply services such as consultancy, financial services, or marketing research or communication agencies.

Analysis of the performance environment is undertaken so organizations can adapt to better positions, relative to those of their stakeholders and competitors. These adjustments are made as circumstances develop and/or in anticipation of environmental and performance conditions. The performance environment encompasses not only competitors but also suppliers and other organizations such as distributors, who all contribute to the industry value chain.

Knowledge about the performance arena allows organizations to choose how and where to operate and compete, given limited resources. Knowledge allows adaption and development in complex and increasingly turbulent markets. Conditions vary from industry to industry. Some are full of potential and growth opportunities, such as cruise holidays, Fairtrade food, and the online travel and gaming industries, whereas others are in decline or at best stagnating, for example high street music stores and car manufacturing. Rivalry may be on an international, national, regional, or local basis. The source and strength of competitive forces will vary so that a strong organization operating in an 'unattractive' industry may have difficulty in achieving an acceptable performance. Weaker organizations, however, operating in 'attractive' environments, may record consistently good performances.

Analysing Industries

An industry is composed of various firms that market similar products and services. According to Porter (1979), we should review the 'competitive' environment within an industry to identify the major competitive forces as this can help assess their impact on an organization's present and future competitive positions. There are a number of variables that help determine how attractive an industry is and shape the longer term profitability for the different companies that make up the industry. Think of industries such as shipbuilding, cars, coal, and steel, where levels of profitability have been weak and hence unattractive to prospective new entrants. Now think of industries such as new media, oil, banking, and supermarkets, where levels of profitability have been astonishingly high. The competitive pressures in all these markets vary quite considerably but there are enough similarities to establish an analytical framework to gauge the nature and intensity of competition. Porter suggests that competition in an industry is a composite of five main competitive forces. These are the level of threat that new competitors will enter the market, the threat posed by substitute products, and the bargaining power of both buyers and suppliers. These, in turn, affect the fifth force, the intensity of rivalry between the current competitors. Porter called these variables the Five Forces of Competitive Industry Analysis (see Figure 2.5).

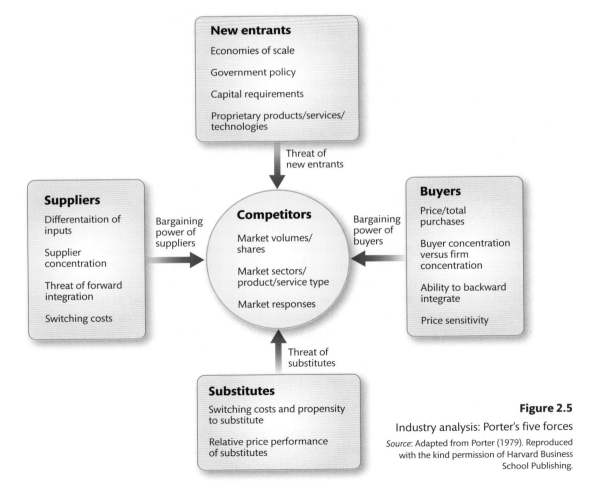

Figure 2.5

Industry analysis: Porter's five forces

Source: Adapted from Porter (1979). Reproduced with the kind permission of Harvard Business School Publishing.

As a general rule, the more intense the rivalry between the industry players, the lower their overall performance. On the other hand, the lower the rivalry the greater will be the performance of the industry players. Porter's model is useful because it exposes the competitive forces in operation in an industry and can lead to an assessment of the strength of each of the forces. The collective impact determines what competition is like in the market. As a general rule, the stronger the competitive forces the lower the profitability in a market. An organization needs to determine a competitive approach that will allow it to influence the industry's competitive rules, protect it from competitive forces as much as possible, and give it a strong position from which to compete.

New Entrants

Industries are seldom static. Companies and brands enter and exit industries all the time. Consider the UK beverage industry: it has witnessed the entrance of energy drink manufacturers such as Red Bull and fruit smoothie makers PJ Smoothies (since bought by Pepsi in 2006 and now retired) and Innocent Drinks. These companies had been competing head-on with industry stalwarts Pepsico, Coca-Cola, and GlaxoSmithKline's Lucozade, probably the original energy drink in the UK beverage market. Supermarkets have also begun to develop own-label smoothies.

When examining an industry, we should consider whether economies of scale are required to operate successfully within it. For instance, motor manufacturing in the UK requires significant investment in plant and machinery. Unfortunately, as British labour costs are also high and foreign direct investment incentives (e.g. government development grants) are not as lucrative as they once were, many British-based motor manufacturers have moved their manufacturing facilities to Eastern Europe and Far Eastern countries. New entrants may be restricted through government and regulatory policy or they may well be frozen out of an industry because of the capital requirements necessary to set up business. For example, in the oil and gas industry, huge sums of capital are required not only to fund exploration activities but also to fund the extraction and refining operations.

Companies may be locked out of a market because companies within that market are operating using proprietary products/services or technologies, e.g. the pharmaceutical industry where patents protect companies' investments in new medicines. The cost of a typical new patented drug at the turn of the twenty-first century was around $800 million in R&D costs alone (DiMasi, Hansen, and Grabowski, 2003)—before marketing and other commercial costs—taking on average around 12 years from invention through to commercial launch (Wall Street Journal, 2001). Few companies can compete in such a market as the set-up and ongoing R&D costs are very large. One strategic response in the industry has been a wave of consolidation (i.e. mergers and alliances) as pharmaceutical companies tried to build critical mass in R&D, marketing, and distribution. Examples have included GSK, from the merger of Glaxo Wellcome plc and SmithKline Beecham plc in 2000, and AstraZeneca from the merger of Sweden's Astra AB and Britain's Zeneca plc in 1999. In 2009, pharmaceutical industry giants Pfizer and GlaxoSmithKline agreed to set up a joint company to develop and market their HIV/AIDS drugs in a bid to share risk and development costs (Ruddick, 2009).

Substitutes

In any industry, there are usually substitute products and services that perform the same function or meet similar customer needs. Levitt (1960) warned that many companies fail to recognize the competitive threat from newly developing products and services. He cites the

American railroad industry's refusal to see the competitive threat arising from the development of the automobile and airline industries in the transport sector.

Consider the telecommunications sector. As telecommunications markets continue to converge (i.e. move together) with the development of broadband internet services, we now see a variety of different companies operating in the same competitive marketspace e.g. Orange, BT, AOL Time Warner, and many others. With the development of VOIP (voice over internet protocol), internet telecommunication voice transmission standard, fixed line telecommunications is already becoming a commodity and firms operating in the area will increasingly look to develop value-added services such as online TV (content-on-demand), interactive gaming, and web-conferencing services.

At the moment, most countries' fixed line operators are still holding on to the vast majority of their subscribers even though much cheaper alternatives are beginning to appear in the market (e.g. cable, internet, fusion telephone plans incorporating mobile and fixed lines). It takes time for consumers to become aware of new product and service possibilities and obtain the necessary information to allow them to make a decision over whether or not to switch to an alternative offering. Consumers consider the switching costs associated with such a decision, which, in turn, affects their propensity to substitute the product or service for another offering. They consider the relative price performance of one offering over another. For example, if we decide we wish to travel from Amsterdam to Paris, we can fly from Schipol airport to Charles de Gaulle airport, take the train, or drive (or hire a car and drive if we don't have one). We would consider the relative price differences (the flight is likely to be the most expensive, but not always) and we would also factor into this decision how comfortable and convenient these different journeys were hypothetically before we finally make our choice. In analysing our place within an industry, it is fundamental that we consider what alternative product and service offerings exist in the marketplace, which also meet, to a greater or lesser extent, our customers' needs.

Buyers

Companies should ask themselves how much of their sales go to one individual company. This is an important question because if one buying company purchases a large volume of product from the supplying company, as car manufacturers do from steel suppliers, it is likely to be able to demand price concessions (price/total purchases) when there are lots of competing suppliers in the marketplace relative to the proportion of buyers (buyer concentration versus firm concentration). Buyers may also decide to increase their bargaining power through **backward integration**. For instance, a company is said to have backward integrated when it moves into manufacturing the products or services it previously bought from its suppliers. Tesco—the British multiple retail grocer operating in 14 markets outside the UK in 2009—also sells financial services including debt and credit services to its customers, which it previously would have purchased from Visa and MasterCard **merchant** operators. As customers have tended to pay for many years now using credit/debit cards rather than cash, Tesco has lowered its transaction costs by setting up its own credit/debit services. Nevertheless, for the other suppliers in a market, it means that they effectively have a new entrant into the market and hence a new competitor. Another factor impacting on a buyer's bargaining power is how price sensitive that particular company is (see Chapter 9). Depending on their trading circumstances, some companies might be more sensitive to price than other buyers. If such companies are more price sensitive and yet there are lots of competing suppliers for their business, they are likely to display less loyalty to their suppliers. Most companies try to enhance other factors associated with an offering (e.g. after-sales service, product/service customization) to try to reduce a client company's **price sensitivity**. When analysing an industry, we should understand the bargaining power that buyers have with their suppliers as this can impact on the price charged and the volumes sold or total revenue earned.

Suppliers

In analysing a particular industry, we should determine how suppliers operate and the extent of their bargaining power. For instance, if a small number of suppliers operate within an industry with a large number of competitors, the suppliers have the stronger bargaining advantage. Conversely, in an industry where there is a large number of suppliers with few competing companies, the buying companies have the bargaining advantage. We should also consider whether or not the suppliers are providing unique components, products, services that may enhance their bargaining situation. In some industries, suppliers increase their market dominance by forward integrating (e.g. a toy manufacturer setting up a retail outlet to sell its own products). Forward integration not only allows a company to control its own supply chains better but also allows it to sell at lower prices, thereby increasing sales vis-à-vis competitors and profit from increased retail sales as well. Equally, if companies face high switching costs, economic, resource, and time costs associated with using another supplier, then a supplier has stronger bargaining power as a result with that particular company.

Competitors

To analyse an industry, we develop an outline of which companies are operating within that particular industry. For example, in the UK cosmetic sector, the market leading cosmetic manufacturers include: Avon European Holdings Ltd, Estée Lauder Cosmetics Ltd, L'Oréal (UK) Ltd, Procter & Gamble Ltd, the Unilever Group, and large retailers such as Boots Group plc, The Body Shop International plc, and Superdrug Stores plc. In undertaking a competitor analysis we outline each company's structure (e.g. details of the main holding company, the individual business unit, any changes in ownership), current and future developments (these can often be gleaned from reading company prospectuses, websites and industry reports), and the company's latest financial results. We would be interested in calculating the market volumes and shares for each competitor, as market share is a key indication of company profitability and return on investment (Buzzell, Gale, and Sultan, 1975).

In analysing the competitors within an industry, we are interested in different types of goods and services that competitors offer in different market sectors. Clark and Montgomery (1999) call this process of identification of competitors the supply-based approach because it considers those firms who supply the same sorts of goods and services as your own firm. However, they identify another approach to competitor identification, which they term the demand-based approach, identifying competitors based on customer attitudes and behaviour. Firms with similar offerings, as perceived by the customer, are regarded as competitors.

We are also interested in measuring market responses to any new strategy developments that our company initiates. Although this might seem obvious, research indicates that companies do not tend to consider their competitors' strategies (what the authors call 'strategic competitive reasoning'), except occasionally in relation to pricing strategy, perhaps because they do not feel it is worth the effort (Montgomery, Moore, and Urbany, 2005). Generally, managers tended to name relatively few competitors and need to focus more on competitors as determined by customer requirements (Clark and Montgomery, 1999).

▶ Research Insight 2.2

To take your learning further, you might wish to read this influential paper.

Porter, M. E. (1979), 'How competitive forces shape strategy', _Harvard Business Review_, 57, 2 (March–April), 137–45.

This paper was Porter's first public presentation of his ideas about industry analysis. They were subsequently reproduced in his book _Competitive Strategy: Techniques for Analysing Industries and Competitors_, published the following year by The Free Press of New York, and which has become the seminal work on industry analysis.

 Visit the **Online Resource Centre** to read the abstract and access the full paper.

Understanding the Internal Environment

An analysis of the internal environment of an organization is concerned with understanding and evaluating the capabilities and potential of the products, systems, human, marketing, and financial resources. An analysis of an organization's resources should not focus on the relative strength and weakness of a particular resource, but look at the absolute nature of the resource itself. As Thompson (1990) suggests, 'resources are not strong or weak merely because they exist ... their value depends upon how they are being managed, controlled and used.' Attention here is given to two main elements, products and finance.

Product Portfolio Analysis

When managing a collection or portfolio of products, we should appreciate that understanding the performance of an individual product can often fail to give the appropriate insight. What is really important is an understanding about the relative performance of products. By creating a balance of old, mature, established, growing, and very new products, there is a better chance of delivering profits now and at some point in the future, when the current products cease to be attractive and profitable. One of the popular methods for assessing the variety of businesses/products that an organization has, involves the creation of a two-dimensional graphical picture of the comparative strategic positions. This technique is referred to as a product portfolio or portfolio matrix. The Boston Consulting Group (BCG) developed the original idea and their matrix—the **Boston Box**, shown in Figure 2.6—is based on two key variables, market growth and relative market share (i.e. market share as a percentage of the share of the product's largest competitor, expressed as a fraction). Thus, a relative share of 0.8 means that the product achieves 80% of the sales of the market leader's sales volume (or value, depending on which measure is used). This is not the strongest competitive position but not a weak position either. A relative market share of 1 means that the company shares market leadership with a competitor with an equal share. A relative market share of 2 means that the company has twice the market share of the nearest competitor.

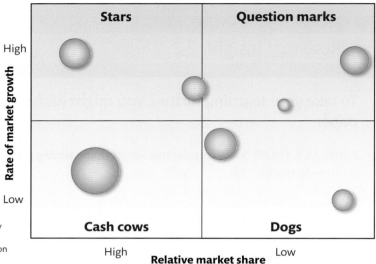

Figure 2.6

The Boston Box

Source: Reprinted from B. Hedley, 'Strategy and the business portfolio', *Long Range Planning*, 10, 1, 12. © 1977, with permission from Elsevier.

In Figure 2.7, the vertical axis refers to the rate of market growth and the horizontal axis refers to a product's market strength, as measured by relative market share (as described above). The size of the circles represents the sales revenue generated by the product. Relative market share is generally regarded as high when you are the market leader (i.e. the relative market share is 1 or greater). Determining whether or not market growth rate is high or low is more problematic and depends on the industry to some extent. In some industries, a market growth rate of 5% might be regarded as high, whereas in others this might be 10%. The benchmark between high and low is, however, often taken to be 10%. This lack of clarity on what is regarded definitively as high and low rates of market growth is a key criticism of the approach.

Question marks (also known as 'problem children') are products that exist in growing markets but have low market share. As a result there is negative cash flow and they are

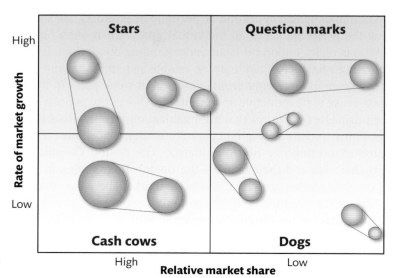

Figure 2.7

Present and future positions in the BCG matrix

Source: Reprinted from B. Hedley, 'Strategy and the business portfolio', *Long Range Planning*, 10, 1, 12. © 1977, with permission from Elsevier.

unprofitable. Stars are most probably market leaders but their growth has to be financed through fairly heavy levels of investment. Cash cows on the other hand exist in fairly stable, low-growth markets and require little ongoing investment. Their high market share draws both positive cash flows and high levels of profitability. Dogs experience low growth, low market share, and generate negative cash flows. These indicators suggest that many of them are operating in declining markets and they have no real long-term future. Divestment need not occur just because of low share. In March 2007, Procter & Gamble decided to leave the paper business, and this involved selling off Bounty, their kitchen roll brand, and Charmin, their toilet tissue brand. They sold the business because of falling performance and because they did not see how they could achieve number 1 or 2 position in the different paper markets. Instead, they sold the business to their main rivals, SCA (Godsell, 2007). From a reverse perspective, in 2009, Coca-Cola bought a £30m stake in Innocent drinks, in an attempt to give it access to the smoothie market; a market that prior to 2008 (and the recession) had grown rapidly over the previous ten years and in which it had no presence whatsoever. By buying a minority 18% stake in Innocent (which it increased to a 40% majority stake in 2010), Coca-Cola bypassed the set-up costs of developing their own 'question mark' smoothie product, thereby gaining a market presence at a relatively modest cost (see Fernandez, 2010).

Portfolio analysis is an important analytical tool as it draws attention to the cash flow and investment characteristics of each of a firm's products and indicates how financial resources can be manoeuvred to attain optimal strategic performance over the long term. Essentially, excess cash generated by cash cows should be utilized to develop question marks and stars, which are unable to support themselves. This enables stars to become cash cows and self-supporting. Dogs should only be retained as long as they contribute to positive cash flow and do not restrict the use of assets and resources elsewhere in the business. Once they do they should be divested or ejected from the portfolio.

By plotting all of a company's products onto the grid it becomes visually easy to appreciate just how well balanced the product portfolio is. An unbalanced portfolio would be one that has too many products clustered in one or two quadrants. Where products are distributed equally, or at least are not clustered in any one area, and where market shares and cash flows equate with their market position, it is said that the portfolio is financially healthy and well balanced. By analysing the product portfolio in this way it becomes possible to project possible strategies and their outcomes. These are shown in Figure 2.7.

Portfolio Issues

Portfolio analysis is an important guide to strategic development, if only because it forces answers to questions such as:

▶ How fast will the market grow?

▶ What will be our market share?

▶ What investment will be required?

▶ How can a balanced portfolio be created from this point? (See also Market Insight 2.5.)

▶ Research Insight 2.3

To take your learning further, you might wish to read this influential paper.

Day, G. (1977), 'Diagnosing the product portfolio', *Journal of Marketing,* **April, 29–38.**

Day outlines in this very readable article how managers should evaluate the relative performance of products within a portfolio in order to develop appropriate marketing strategies. He concludes that portfolio analysis is a useful guide—but not substitute—for strategy development.

@ Visit the **Online Resource Centre** to read the abstract and access the full paper.

▶ Market Insight 2.5

Drinking the Fruits of a Balanced Portfolio

Britvic is the UK's second biggest soft drinks manufacturer with many of its brands positioned as number 1 or 2 in their respective sub-categories.

Britvic's product portfolio includes still and carbonate brands, including Robinson's, Pepsi, 7 Up, Drench, Tango, J₂O, Britvic, Fruit Shoot, R. White's, and Pennine Spring to name a few. Britvic has tried to develop the breadth and depth of its portfolio so that it can target consumer demand in all the major soft drinks categories, through all relevant distribution channels, and across a wide range of consumption occasions.

Britvic has a successful long-standing relationship with Pepsico that was renewed in 2004 for a further fifteen years. This relationship gives Britvic the exclusive right to distribute the Pepsi and 7 Up brands in Great Britain, and access to all new carbonated drinks developed by Pepsico for distribution in Great Britain.

The breadth of Britvic's 'balanced' portfolio of market-leading brands, the existing customer relationships, and its scale of operations provide Britvic with a solid base for growth. Britvic believes that in order

Tango, the zesty brand from Britvic
Source: Courtesy of Britvic Drinks Ltd.

▶ Market Insight 2.5

to achieve the company's objectives it places great emphasis on the portfolio and the need to develop it through innovation to meet evolving consumer preferences. Its marketing strategy will continue to focus on driving brand awareness around its major growth products through advertising and promotion and using its distribution network to further increase availability of its products.

1 How might Britvic maintain its portfolio in the light of strong competition from its rivals? Are there other types of soft drink brands that it could acquire?

2 How might use of the internet help Britvic achieve its marketing goals?

3 The phrase 'consumption occasions' was used in the Market Insight. Can you think of three different occasions when Robinson's or Pepsi might be the preferred drink?

However, the questions posed and the answers generated through use of the Boston Box do not produce marketing strategies in themselves. As with all analytical tools and methodologies, the BCG provides strategic indicators, not solutions. It is management's task to consider information from a variety of sources and then make decisions based on their judgment. The Boston Box has been criticized for providing rigid solutions to product portfolio evaluation when exceptions to the rule might exist, e.g. proposing that 'cash cow' products should not be invested in, when a company may rely solely on its 'cash cow' products to provide profits and not necessarily have new products/services in the pipeline to replace them. Equally, the Boston Box proposes that 'dog' products should be divested, when, in fact, they may actually be returning a profit to the company. Finding the necessary and objective data to plot the positions of products or SBUs on the two axes of relative market share and market growth rate can also be problematic. Reliable industry data may not actually always be available. Finally, it is not always easy to determine what market we are concerned with. For example, if we consider the smoothie market, does this include fruit-based milkshakes, or fruit juices more generally?

Marketing Audit

To make sense of all the information that has been collected, considered, and analysed during the strategic market analysis part of the marketing strategy process, a marketing audit is normally undertaken. Just as a financial audit considers the financial health of an organization, so the marketing audit considers its marketing health. In particular, it brings together views about the three environments. First, it considers the external opportunities and threats, where management have little or no control. Second, it considers the nature, characteristics, and any changes occurring within the performance environment, where management have partial influence. Third, the audit reviews the quality and potential of the organization's products, marketing systems, resources, and capabilities, as part of the internal environment, where there is full control. The topics normally undertaken as part of the marketing audit are shown in Figure 2.8.

Environmental Audit—external and performance environments

Marketing Strategy Audit—mission, goals, strategy

Marketing Organization Audit—structure, personnel

Marketing Systems Audit—information, planning, and control systems

Marketing Function Audits—products, services, prices, distribution, promotion

Figure 2.8
Dimensions of a marketing audit

The audit covers the marketing environment, an organization's objectives and strategies, its marketing programmes and performance, plus the organization itself and the relevant marketing systems and procedures. We undertake marketing audits because they bring together critical information, identify weaknesses in order that they can be corrected, and provide a platform to build marketing strategy.

The marketing audit can be undertaken either by an internal team, led by a senior manager, or if a more objective interpretation is desired, an outside consultant can be used. Whoever conducts the audit it should be undertaken on a regular, annual basis and be regarded as a positive activity that can feed into marketing strategy. Marketing audits should not be instigated in response to a crisis but undertaken on a regular, annual basis.

Skills for Employment

▶▶ A new recruit should be able to present him or herself in a credible, professional, and confident manner. They also need to demonstrate an awareness of our competitors' marketing campaigns and be able to critically assess the effectiveness of such campaigns. ◀◀

Banali L Malhotra, Head of Marketing, **RAKBANK**

 Visit the **Online Resource Centre** to discover more tips and advice on skills for the workplace.

Chapter Summary

To consolidate your learning, the key points from this chapter are summarized below:

■ **Identify and define the three key areas of the marketing environment.**

The marketing environment incorporates the external environment, the performance environment, and the internal environment. The external environment incorporates macroenvironmental factors, which are largely uncontrollable and which an organization generally cannot influence. The performance environment incorporates key factors within an industry, which impact on strategic decision-making. The internal environment is controllable and is the principal means, through its resource base, by which an organization influences its strategy.

■ **Describe the key characteristics associated with the marketing environment.**

The external environment consists of the political, social, and technological influences, and organizations have relatively little influence on each of these. The performance environment consists of the competitors, suppliers, and indirect service providers who shape the way an organization achieves its objectives. Here, organizations have a much stronger level of influence. The internal environment concerns the resources, processes, and policies an organization manages in order to attempt to achieve its goals. These elements can be influenced directly by an organization.

■ **Explain PESTLE analysis and show how it is used to understand the external environment.**

We considered the various components of the external marketing environment in detail using the PESTLE acronym, which includes the following factors: political, economic, socio-cultural, technological, legal, and ecological. It is important to note that some of these factors are more important than others in any particular industry. We use the acronym to identify possible factors that may impact on any particular organization.

■ **Explain the environmental scanning process.**

The environmental scanning process consists of the data-gathering phase, the environmental interpretation/analysis phase, and the strategy formulation phase. The three processes are interlinked, but, over time, more attention is focused on each one more than the others so that at the end of the process, greater effort is expended on using knowledge gleaned from the external and competitive environments to formulate strategy.

■ **Analyse the performance environment using an appropriate model.**

The most common technique used to analyse the performance environment is Porter's Five Forces Model of Competitive Analysis. He concludes that the more intense the rivalry between the industry players, the lower will be their overall performance. On the other hand, the lower the rivalry the greater will be the performance of the industry players. Porter's Five Forces comprise (1) suppliers, (2) buyers, (3) new entrants, (4) competitors, and (5) substitutes.

■ **Understand the importance of analysing an organization's internal environment and identify the key resources and capabilities.**

An organization's principal resources relate to the product portfolio that it carries and the financial resources at its disposal. We use product portfolio analysis, specifically the Boston Box, to help us determine whether products are stars, dogs, question marks, or cash cows, each category of which provides differing levels of cash flow and resource requirements to develop. It is important to undertake a marketing audit as a preliminary measure in order to allow proper development of marketing strategy.

Review Questions

1 What are the three main marketing environments?
2 What are the three stages of the environmental scanning process?
3 How might changes in the political environment affect marketing strategy?
4 How might changes in the economic environment affect marketing strategy?
5 How might changes in the socio-cultural environment affect marketing strategy?
6 How might changes in the technological environment affect marketing strategy?
7 How might changes in the legal environment affect marketing strategy?
8 How might changes in the ecological environment affect marketing strategy?
9 What are Porter's Five Forces?
10 What is product portfolio analysis and why is it useful?

Worksheet Summary

Visit the **Online Resource Centre** and complete Worksheet 2.1. This will help you learn how the PESTLE framework, Five Forces model, and BCG Matrix can be used to analyse the marketing environment. It will also help you understand how the internal, external, and performance environments interact.

Discussion Questions

1 Having read the Case Insight at the beginning of this chapter, how would you advise Michelin Tyres to react to the rapid uptake of cheap imported Indian, Korean and Chinese tyres in the UK market? What strategy would you recommend?

2 Read the Market Insight 2.4 Who Ate All the Bars? example. Search the internet for further information on the obesity debate, and answer the following questions:
   A What changes have taken place in the external environment to bring about the obesity debate?
   B How should Kraft, Cadbury's new owner, ensure that they keep up to date with trends in consumer lifestyles, government legislation, and competitor new product development?
   C What strategies in relation to product development and promotion could Kraft adopt to ensure that they maintain their market dominance in the chocolate countline market?
   D Why do you think Kraft acquired Cadbury's?

3 Undertake an environmental analysis using PESTLE, by surfing the internet for appropriate information and by using available market research reports, for each of the following markets:
   A The automotive market (e.g. you might be Renault, BMW, Ford, or Toyota).
   B The global multiple retail grocery market (e.g. you might be Walmart, Carrefour, or Tesco).
   C The beer industry (e.g. you might be InBev, Carlsberg, Heineken, Miller Brands, or Budweiser Budvar).

4 Analyse the ecological marketing environment for the cosmetics industry in a country of your choice. Look specifically at socio-cultural patterns and trends in habits, particularly in relation to male versus female grooming. You may surf the internet for appropriate documents and market intelligence material to help you develop your arguments.

5   Using the data in Table 2.2 below identify the relative market shares of the various brands in UK lager market. Use the market growth rate figure as the difference in total sales between 2007 and 2009. Then draw up a Boston Box to illustrate the product portfolio for each of the key companies and their brands.

▶ **Table 2.2** UK Lager Market

Brand	Brewer	2007 £m	2007 %	2009 (est) £m	2009 (est) %	2007–2009 % change
Stella Artois	AB InBev	520	17.7	510	18.0	–2
Carling	Molson Coors	360	12.2	383	13.5	+6
Foster's	Heineken UK	325	11.1	312	11.0	–4
Carlsberg	Carlsberg UK	220	7.5	255	9.0	+16
Budweiser	AB InBev	150	5.1	128	4.5	–15
Carlsberg Export	Heineken UK	135	4.6	119	4.2	–12
Kronenbourg 1664	Heineken UK	125	4.3	88	3.1	–27
Beck's	AB InBev	80	2.7	108	3.8	+35
Grolsch	Molson Coors	100	3.4	79	2.8	–21
Tennent's	C&C[a]	72	2.4	65	2.3	–9
Own-label	NA	85	2.9	85	3.0	–
Others	NA	768	26.1	704	24.8	–8
Totals		**2,940**	**100**	**2,837**	**100**	**–4**

[a]Formerly AB Inbev.

Source: Mintel, 2009b.

Visit the **Online Resource Centre** and complete the Multiple Choice Questions to assess your knowledge of Chapter 2.

go online

References

Aguilar, F. Y. (1967), *Scanning the Business Environment*, New York: Macmillan.

Albright, K. S. (2004), 'Environmental scanning: radar for success', *Information Management Journal*, May–June, 38–45.

Anon. (2008), 'Why target the gay marketing pink pound? 81 billion good reasons', *PRWeb*, 15 May, retrieve from www.prweb.com/releases/gay/marketing/prweb945134.htm, accessed 11 April 2010.

ASA (2010), 'ASA Adjudication on Unilever UK Ltd', London: Advertising Standards Authority, retrieve from www.asa.org.uk/Complaints-and-ASA-action/Adjudications/2010/2/Unilever-UK-Ltd/TF_ADJ_48085.aspx, accessed 11 April 2010.

BBC (2006), 'Supermarkets covet Polish spend', 10 September, *BBC News*, retrieve from http://news.bbc.co.uk/1/hi/business/5332024.stm, accessed 11 April 2010.

— (2010a), 'EADS-Northrop tanker contract exit prompts EU fears', 9 March, *BBC News*, retrieve from www.news.bbc.co.uk/1/hi/business/8557769.stm, accessed 11 April 2010.

— (2010b), 'Gene Hunt poster sparks propaganda battle', 3 April 2010, *BBC News*, retrieve from http://news.bbc.co.uk/1/hi/uk/8601781.stm, accessed 17 April 2010.

Beal, R. M. (2000), 'Competing effectively: environmental scanning, competitive strategy, and organisational performance in small manufacturing firms', *Journal of Small Business Administration*, January, 27–47.

— (1994), 'Organising for environmental scanning: orthodoxies and reformations', *Journal of Marketing Management*, 10, 703–22.

— (2009), 'Tales of prospects past: on strategic fallacies and uncertainty in technology forecasting', *Journal of Marketing Management*, 25, 5/6, 401– 429.

Buzzell, R. D., Gale, B. T., and Sultan, R. G. M (1975), 'Market share—a key to profitability', *Harvard Business Review*, January–February, 97–106.

Chandy, R. K., Prabhu, J. C., and Antia, K. D. (2003), 'What will the future bring? Dominance, technology expectations and radical innovation', *Journal of Marketing*, 67 (July), 1–18.

Clark, B. H., and Montgomery, D. B. (1999), 'Managerial identification of competitors', *Journal of Marketing*, July, 67–83.

Décaudin, J-M. and Malaval, P. (2008), 'Le lobbying: techniques, intérêt et limites', *Décisions Marketing*, 50 (Apr–Jun), 59–69.

DiMasi, J.A.; Hansen, R.W., and Grabowski, H.G. (2003), 'The price of innovation: new estimates of drug development costs', *Journal of Health Economics*, 22, 151–85.

DoH (2004), 'Choosing Health: Making Healthy Choices Easier', *White Paper, Cm 6374*, London: The Stationery Office.

— (2010), 'Change4Life', retrieve from www.dh.gov.uk/en/MediaCentre/Currentcampaigns/Change4Life/index.htm, accessed 11 April 2010.

Fairtrade Foundation (2010), 'Sales of Fairtrade certified products in the UK', retrieve from www.fairtrade.org.uk/what_is_fairtrade/facts_and_figures.aspx, accessed 11 April 2010.

Fernandez, J. (2010), 'Coca-cola becomes majority shareholder in Innocent', *Marketing Week*, 9 April, retrieve from www.marketingweek.co.uk/news/coca-cola-becomes-majority-shareholder-in-innocent/3012101.article, accessed 22 April 2010.

Godsell, M. (2007), 'Not number one, not interested', *Marketing*, 21 March, 18.

Gower, I. (ed.) (2005), *Cosmetics and Fragrances Market Report 2005*, London: Keynote Limited.

Harris, P., Gardner, H., and Vetter, N. (1999), "Goods over God" lobbying and political marketing: a case study of the campaign by the Shopping Hours Reform Council to change Sunday trading laws in Britain', in

B. I. Newman (ed.), *Handbook of Political Marketing*, London: Sage Publications.

Health Canada (1999), *Information Research on Labelling*, Quebec, retrieve from www.hc-sc.gc.ca.

Hillman, A., Keim, G. D., and Schuler, D. (2004), 'Corporate political activity: a review and research agenda', *Journal of Management*, 30, 6, 837–57.

Howe, J. (2006), 'The rise of crowdsourcing', *Wired*, Issue 14.06 (June), retrieve from www.wired.com/wired/archive/14.06/crowds.html, accessed 17 April 2010.

Jotangia, D.; Moody, A.; Stamtakis, E and Wardle, H. (2006), *Obesity Among Children Under 11*, London: NatCen/UCL, retrieve from www.dh.gov.uk/prod_consum_dh/groups/dh_digitalassets/@dh/@en/documents/digitalasset/dh_065358.pdf, accessed 11 April 2010.

Kewley, S. (2002), 'Japanese lobbying in the EU', in R. Pedler (ed.), *European Union Lobbying*, Basingstoke: Palgrave Press.

Levitt, T. (1960), 'Marketing myopia', *Harvard Business Review*, July–August, 45–56.

Lim, J.-S., Sharkey, T. W., and Kim, K. I. (1996), 'Competitive environmental scanning and export involvement: an initial enquiry', *International Marketing Review*, 13, 1, 65–80.

Ling, J. (2006), 'Going anywhere exotic?', *The Marketer*, July–August, 25.

Madslien, J. (2010), 'Boeing wins as EADS gives up mid-air refuelling battle', BBC News, 9 March, retrieve from www.news.bbc.co.uk/go/pr/fr/-/1/hi/business/8557293.stm, accessed 11 April 2010.

May, R. C., Stewart, W. H. Jr., and Sweo, R. (2000), 'Environmental scanning behaviour in a transitional economy: evidence from Russia', *Academy of Management Journal*, 43, 3, 403–27.

Melewar T.C.; Mui, H.; Gupta, S. and Knight, J. (2008), 'The impact of the current expansion of the European Union on international marketing strategies on Norwegian multinational farmed salmon producers', *Marketing Intelligence and Planning*, 26, 4, 405–15.

Millward Brown (2008), 'Top 100 Most Powerful Brands', Millward Brown Optimor, retrieve from www.brandz.com/upload/BrandZ-2008-RankingReport.pdf, accessed 11 April 2010.

Mintel (2008), *Chocolate Confectionery – UK – April 2008*, London: Mintel International Group, retrieve from www.mintel.com, accessed 11 April 2010.

— (2009a), *Children's Eating Habits – UK – November 2009*, London: Mintel International Group, retrieve from www.mintel.com, accessed 11 April 2010.

— (2009b), *Lager – UK – November 2009*, London: Mintel International Group, retrieve from www.mintel.com, accessed 11 April 2010.

Moloney, K., and Jordan, G. (1996), 'Why companies hire lobbyists', *Service Industries Journal*, 16, 2, 242–58.

Montgomery, D. B., Moore, M. C., and Urbany, J. E. (2005), 'Reasoning about competitive reactions: evidence from executives', *Marketing Science*, 24, 1, 138–49.

Morris, P. (2001), 'Dealing with Whitehall and Westminster', Hawkesmere Seminar on Lobbying, Berners Hotel, London, 4 April.

Murray, S. (2006), 'Confusion reigns over labelling', *Financial Times*, Special Report on Responsible Business, 2.

Neate, R. (2008), 'Vodka overtakes Scotch after Polish influx', *The Telegraph*, 12 June, retrieve from www.telegraph.co.uk/news/uknews/2119735/Vodka-overtakes-Scotch-after-Polish-influx.html, accessed 11 April 2010.

Ngamkroeckjoti, C. and Speece, M. (2008), 'Technology turbulence and environmental scanning in Thai food new product development', *Asia Pacific Journal of Marketing and Logistics*, 20, 4, 413–32.

O'Connell, J. J., and Zimmerman, J. W. (1979), 'Scanning the international environment', *California Management Review*, 22, 2, 15–23.

Orsato, R. J. (2006), 'Competitive environmental strategies: when does it pay to be green?', *California Management Review*, 48, 2 (Winter), 127–43.

Porter, M. (1979), 'How competitive forces shape strategy', *Harvard Business Review*, March–April.

Rao, P. M. (2005), 'Sustaining competitive advantage in a high-technology environment: a strategic marketing perspective', *Advances in Competitiveness Research*, 13, 1, 33–47.

Robinson, J. (2010), 'David Cameron depicted as Gene Hunt in Labour poster', 2 April, *The Guardian*, retrieve from www.guardian.co.uk/politics/2010/apr/02/david-cameron-gene-hunt-labour-poster, accessed 17 April 2010.

Royal Dutch Shell (2008), 'Shell energy scenarios to 2050: an era of revolutionary change', *Internal Corporate Presentation*, 20 March, London: Royal Dutch Shell.

Ruddick, G. (2009), 'Glaxo-Pfizer tie-up opens new era in AIDS battle', *The Telegraph*, 31 October, retrieve from www.telegraph.co.uk/finance/newsbysector/pharmaceuticalsandchemicals/6474678/Glaxo-Pfizer-tie-up-opens-new-era-in-Aids-battle.html, accessed 18 April 2010.

Sclater, I. (2005), 'The digital dimension', *The Marketer*, May, 22–3.

Sevastopulo, D. (2008), 'Dogfight over dollars 35bn air force contract grows more intense', *Financial Times*, 17 March, p.18.

Snoddy, R. (2006), 'Brands face £70bn pink conundrum', *Marketing* (UK), 15 February.

Sweney, M. (2009), 'Unilever goes crowdsourcing to spice up Peperami's TV ads', *The Guardian*, 25 August, retrieve from www.guardian.co.uk/media/blog/2009/aug/25/unilever-peperami-advertising-crowdsourcing, accessed 17 April 2010.

Taylor, J. (2010), 'A new lager that's clearly for ladies', *Metro*, 15 April, p.35.

Thompson, K. M. (1990), *The Employee Revolution: Corporate Internal Marketing*, London: Pitman.

UN Population Division (2005), *World Population Prospects: The 2004 Revision*, retrieve from www.un.org/esa/population/publications/WPP2004/wpp2004.htm, accessed 11 April 2010.

Valdiserri, T. (2002), 'Pink market needs respect', *Precision Marketing*, 8 March.

Wallace, J. (2008), 'Boeing back in tanker running', Seattle Pi, 19 June, retrieve from www.seattlepi.com/business/367462_tanker19.html, accessed 11 April 2010.

Wall Street Journal (2001), 'Cost of developing drugs found to rise', 3 December.

Whitla, P. (2009), 'Crowdsourcing and its application in marketing activities', *Contemporary Management Research*, 5, 1, 15–28.

Wilson, R. W. (1977), 'The effect of technological environment and product rivalry on R&D effort and licensing of inventions', *Review of Economics and Statistics*, 59, 2 (May), 171–9.

Zaninotto, P.; Wardle, H.; Stamatakis, E.; Mindell, J. and Head, J. (2006), 'Forecasting Obesity to 2010', London: NatCen/UCL, retrieve from www.dh.gov.uk/prod_consum_dh/groups/dh_digitalassets/documents/digitalasset/dh_073033.pdf, accessed 11 April 2010.

3 Consumer Buying Behaviour

Learning Outcomes

After reading this chapter, you will be able to:

▶ Explain the consumer product acquisition process

▶ Explain the processes involved in human perception, learning, and memory in relation to consumer choice

▶ Understand the importance of personality and motivation in consumer behaviour

▶ Describe opinions, attitudes, and values and how they relate to consumer behaviour

▶ Explain how reference groups influence consumer behaviour

▶ Case Insight 3.1

BRAND sense agency helps clients build brands that enjoy deeper emotional connections with their consumers both through communications and the customer experience to arrive at a holistic understanding of the brand's sensory impact. We talk to CEO, Simon Harrop, to find out more.

Imagine you are walking through a supermarket, surrounded by products in aisles and point-of-sale material all vying for your attention, when you suddenly become aware of the smell of bread, which captures your senses and sends you off in a hurry to the supermarket's boulangerie. If smell has such power in a supermarket could it be used for advertising or enhancing the customer experience in other ways? In such a vision- and sound-cluttered promotional world, could other senses be used instead?

BRAND sense agency was set up because of a belief that brands and marketers rely too heavily on vision and words to communicate with and

engage consumers. Our intuition and experience was confirmed when we carried out one of the largest ever studies into the relationship between brands and consumers across all the senses. There is a serious imbalance between how, as humans, we experience brands and how marketers seek to communicate brand propositions. Our mission is to address this imbalance, make marketing more effective, and build a business that we enjoy in the process!

Consumer behaviour is the sum of our rational and conscious relationship to the products or services that we buy but also the emotional and non-conscious influences. Consumer behaviour is the sum of

This bank smells as good as it looks!

> ▶ Case Insight 3.1   (continued)

experience, intention, perception, and conception of all that we buy. In the modern world with so much choice and so much information to process, we are increasingly relying on habit and non-conscious associations to make our choices.

A sensory approach involves breaking down the key elements of the emotional relationship with brands in a category and identifying differentiated emotional space that a particular brand in that category can own. We then link this emotional space to key sensory attributes. When these attributes are aligned to this emotional space, you have a strong brand. If there is dissonance between experience and brand expectation we work with our clients to create a development programme to bring these elements into line. This has a positive influence on consumer perception and behaviour.

Our research highlighted the fact that consumers value all senses in their relationship with brand fairly much in balance. However, for certain brands in particular categories, some senses will clearly be more important than others, e.g. smell for shampoo. However, it is our contention that a multisensory approach should take a holistic view across each sense. In practice, most brands are already considering words and pictures as we have seen, so most of our work involves help with smell, taste, sound, and to a certain extent touch.

When BRAND sense agency was approached by a major Colombian bank, a bank beset with problems in developing a differentiated proposition from other banks in the marketplace, particularly in the interior and exterior design of the branches, it wanted to make a difference, not with the common approach to branding but with a multisensory approach emphasizing sound and smell, as well as sight. Colombian banks had all tended to offer the same financial service products and even looked the same.

If you were trying to create a multisensory brand communication approach to help the Colombian bank differentiate itself in the marketplace through sight, sound, and smell, what would you do?

Introduction

What selection process did you go through when deciding which university course you were going to study? How do you decide which restaurant to go to, or which movie to see? Have you ever considered why people buy certain things? After reading this chapter, we want to understand the difference between sympathy and empathy and its relation to marketing. With sympathy, we look at how people feel from our perspective. With empathy we look at how people feel from their perspective. Having high levels of customer empathy is a key reason why world class brands have become world class: their marketers have a profound understanding of their customers' needs/wants and behaviour. In this chapter we explore consumer behaviour (we will look at business-to-business buying behaviour in Chapter 14). We consider cognitions (thoughts), **perceptions** (how we see things), and learning (how we memorize techniques and knowledge). These are processes that are fundamental in explaining how consumers think and learn about products and brands. As consumers, we are always perceiving and learning. Learning about goods and services is no different from learning about concepts in general. Consider how we find out about a new product launch, e.g. the

Apple's iPad tablet computer. We don't just know about it intuitively, we have to learn about how it differs from existing music player systems; its relative benefits and disadvantages in terms of product features, price, and where it is available.

We discuss the concepts of personality and motivation to help understand how these psychological concepts affect how we buy. We also discuss opinions, attitudes, and values, to give an understanding of how we are persuaded by **reference groups**, i.e. groups who have an influence over our decision-making. These are important considerations in marketing because goods and services are often designed to appeal to particular types of people. Banks target their personal accounts at us based on our personalities and motivations. Fast-moving consumer goods companies constantly bombard us with images of celebrity endorsers, who act as our reference groups for a wide variety of goods and services. Marketing comes alive when it is interlinked into the fabric of our social lives so we also consider how **social class**, lifecycles and lifestyles influence consumer behaviour.

Consumer Behaviour: Rational or Emotional?

Consumption rose shortly after the 1950s, as citizens in countries around the world began to prosper in relative peace after the Second World War, and the industrial companies turned their attention from producing military equipment and supplies to producing consumer and industrial goods. At this time, consumers were generally thought to act rationally, according to **neoclassical economics** theory, individually maximizing their satisfaction (what economists call **utility**), based on a cost–benefit analysis of price and product scarcity (or availability). The consumer was thought to carefully measure whether or not the functional benefits of a good/service outweighed its costs.

Consider an example from the Soviet Union (Russia, pre-1990). In such a strictly regulated, planned economy, products were produced to meet basic functional needs. Nevertheless, consumers sought out televisions with specific factory numbers, produced in certain factories in certain regions or countries, because they were more reliable and produced better pictures. So, even when a country's government squeezes out human desires, the desire to possess the best of what is available continues anyway. Such rational purchasing decisions are based on the physical performance of the product (Udell, 1964).

By contrast, in the modern world, people are more likely to indulge socio-psychological buying or emotional buying motives. These motives stem from a buyer's social and psychological interpretation of the product and its performance. Consider our motivations to purchase particular types of music, for example. Let's take the example of Lady Gaga's debut album, The Fame. An album is not bought because of what it is, i.e. CD or download. Nor is the box in which the CD comes particularly useful, except to provide us with information about the disc when we are deciding to buy it or not. The insert on the other hand may be useful once the item is bought because it may contain some details about our favourite popstar and the tracks on the album. Instead, we are likely to buy her album not because of what it is, but what the music represents to us. In other words, we buy the music because of how it makes us feel (e.g. happy, powerful, elated).

go online

Visit the **Online Resource Centre** and follow the weblink to the Psychology Matters website to learn more about the application and value of psychology in our everyday lives.

▶ Research Insight 3.1

To take your learning further, you might wish to read this influential paper.

Holbrook, M. B., and Hirschman, E. C. (1982), 'The experiential aspects of consumption: consumer fantasies, feelings and fun', *Journal of Consumer Research*, 9, 132–40.

This influential article reconsidered how we perceive consumer behaviour, moving marketing thought away from the idea that customer behaviour is purely rational and towards a greater understanding of the irrational content of consumer decision-making, including the importance of our feelings and fantasies, and whether or not we are having fun. The authors developed a useful model contrasting the differences between the information-processing (i.e. rational) and the experiential view (i.e. irrational) perspectives of consumer behaviour.

 Visit the **Online Resource Centre** to read the abstract and access the full paper.

Proposition Acquisition

What is going on in consumers' minds, individually, when they decide whether or not to buy—or in the case of a not-for-profit consumer acquire—a particular offering? To answer this question, we first need to know how products (i.e. both goods and services) move from producers to consumers? For example, consider luxury-brand Hermes' controversial crocodile skin handbags, retailing for more than €35,000 (Shears, 2009). In a simplified process, the skin is sold by a crocodile farmer to the manufacturer who dries, cures, and tans it, before stitching it, and sending it on to the major brand owner who stocks and retails it. At any of these stages, a different supply chain partner could be involved (see Chapter 12 for more on this topic).

In the above Hermes example, there are a variety of transactions, the individual relationships between various buyers and sellers as the raw materials are transformed into a product, and **transvections**, the sequence of transactions seen from the seller's perspective all the way through the supply chain process (Alderson and Martin, 1965). Understanding transactions and transvections in distribution management (what we now call supply chain management) is important because this charts how propositions are developed and move from suppliers through companies to their end users. In the next section, we consider the end user component of the buyer–seller relationship, the perspective of the consumer buyer. (We consider the buyer–seller relationship again in Chapters 14 and 15.)

The Consumer Proposition Acquisition Process

The consumer proposition acquisition process consists of six distinct stages (see Figure 3.1). The model is useful because it highlights the importance and distinctiveness of proposition selection and re-evaluation phases in the process. In Figure 3.1, the buying process is iterative, because each stage can lead back to any of the previous stages in the process or move forward to the next stage in the process.

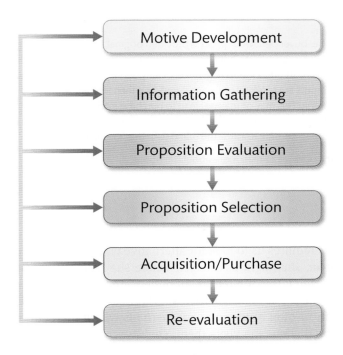

Figure 3.1

The consumer proposition acquisition process

Motive Development

The model begins when we decide we need to acquire a product. This involves the initial recognition that some sort of problem needs solving. To begin to solve the problem, we must become aware of it. So, an example might be a female consumer who decides that she needs to buy a new dress for a party, or because she's grown tired of the old one, or because she thinks it's out of fashion, or to cheer herself up, or for a special occasion (e.g. engagement or hen party), or a whole host of other reasons.

▶ Research Insight 3.2

To take your learning further, you might wish to read this influential book.

Howard, J. A., and Sheth, J. N. (1969), *The Theory of Buyer Behavior*, New York: John Wiley and Sons.

Howard and Sheth's theory of the buyer behaviour process provided original and powerful insights into the psychology of the buying process by considering how learning theory can be applied to consumer behaviour. The buyer behaviour process consists of stimulus inputs (e.g. price, quality, service, and social settings) that feed into a perceptual process where the inputs are received and considered, and then interact with a person's attitudes and motives and existing choice criteria. This may or may not lead to purchase intention, and other outputs, including changes in attention given to the product, extent to which the consumer understands what the brand stands for (**brand comprehension**), and their attitude towards the brand (whether they like it or not).

 Visit the **Online Resource Centre** to read more about the book.

Information Gathering

The next stage in the process requires us to look for alternative ways of solving our problems. In the case of the dress buyer, she might ask herself where she bought her last dress, how much dresses generally cost, what the different retail outlets are that sell dresses, and where they are located. She might also ask herself where she normally buys party dresses, what kinds of party dresses are in fashion at the moment, perhaps where there are sales on and which store staff treat her well when she visits them. Our search for a solution to solve our problem may be active, an **overt search**, or passive, in other words, we are open to ways of solving our problem but we are not actively looking for information to help us (Howard and Sheth, 1969). The search for information may be internal in that we consider what we already know about the problem we have and the products we might buy to solve our problem. Or, it could be external where we don't know enough about our problem and so we seek advice or supplementary information to help us decide.

Proposition Evaluation

Once we feel that we have all the information that we need to make a decision, we evaluate the proposition. But first we must determine the criteria we will use to rank the various products. These might be rational (e.g. based on cost) or irrational (e.g. based on desire). For example, the lady buying the party dress might ask herself which shop is the best value for money and which is the most fashionable retailer. A consumer is said to have an **evoked set** of products in mind when he/she comes to evaluate which particular product, brand, or service he/she wants to solve a particular problem. So an evoked set for a consumer looking for a party dress might include Zara, Monsoon, Jigsaw, H&M, Mango (MNG elsewhere in the world), or Mexx, for instance. The more affluent buyer might visit Anne Klein, DKNY, or Gucci, for example.

Proposition Selection

In most cases, the proposition that we eventually select is the one that we evaluate as fitting our needs best beforehand. However, we might decide on a particular proposition away from where we buy or acquire it. For example, the lady buying a party dress may have checked the stock of a shop online and made her selection but when she turned up at the retailer to try it on, the dress she wanted was not available, and so she decides on an alternative there and then at the point of purchase. Proposition selection is, therefore, a separate stage in the proposition acquisition process, distinct from proposition evaluation, because there are times when we must re-evaluate what we buy or acquire because what we want is not available, e.g. buying a cinema ticket for a different film because the tickets for a particular film are sold out.

Acquisition/Purchase

Once selection has taken place, different approaches to proposition acquisition might exist. For example, our dress buyer may make a routine purchase, a dress for work. A routine purchase is a purchase that we make regularly. Because the purchase is regular we do not become particularly involved in the decision-making process. We simply buy the proposition again that we bought previously unless there are new circumstances. The purchase may be a specialized purchase, conducted on a one-off or infrequent basis, e.g. a ball-gown for a ball or formal event. In this case, we may need to become much more involved in the decision-making process, to ensure that we understand what we are buying and that we are happy that it will satisfy our needs. For routine purchases, we tend to use cash and debit cards, whereas for infrequent purchases we tend to use credit cards. With infrequent purchases, it is important for the marketer to ease the pain of payment, for example, by extending credit. The lady buying a dress would purchase—acquire—the dress, but the store's policy on returns (i.e. whether they allow this or not) may have an impact on whether or not she actually buys a dress from a particular shop.

Re-evaluation

The theory of **cognitive dissonance** (Festinger, 1957) suggests that we are motivated to re-evaluate our beliefs, attitudes, opinions, or values if the position we hold on them at one point in time is not the same as the position we held at an earlier period due to some intervening event, circumstance, or action. This difference in evaluations, termed cognitive dissonance, is psychologically uncomfortable for us and causes anxiety. For example, we may feel foolish or regretful about a purchasing decision we have made. So, we are motivated to reduce our anxiety by redefining our beliefs, attitudes, opinions, or values to make them consistent with our circumstances. We will also actively avoid situations that might increase our feeling of dissonance. To reduce dissonance we might:

▶ selectively forget information;

▶ minimize the importance of an issue, decision, or act;

▶ selectively expose ourselves only to new information that agrees with our existing view (rather than information which doesn't); or

▶ reverse a purchase decision, for instance, by taking a product back or selling it for what it was worth.

The lady buying a dress might not be happy with her purchase because, although it seemed to fit her in the shop, when she tried it on at home she felt it was too tight or ill-fitting, or it did not flatter her as much as she thought when she was in the shop.

The concept of cognitive dissonance has significant application in marketing. Purchasers of goods and/or services, industrial or consumer, are likely to feel cognitive dissonance if their expectations of product or service performance are not met in reality. This feeling of dissonance may be particularly acute when we are highly involved in a high-involvement purchase (e.g. cars, houses, or high-value investment products). We are also likely to search out information to reinforce our choice of good or service. (See Market Insight 3.1 for Volvo's approach to minimizing cognitive dissonance.)

Model wears a Primark dress
Source: © Primark.

▶ Research Insight 3.3

To take your learning further, you might wish to read this influential book.

Festinger, L. (1957), *A Theory of Cognitive Dissonance*, Palo Alto, Calif: Stanford University Press.

A hugely influential development in psychological theory that explains how we resolve two sets of inconsistent opinions, attitudes, values, and behaviour, held at two different points, arising after we receive new information forcing us to change our initial position, e.g. on brands purchased. The theory proposed that we would change our existing opinions, attitudes, values, and behaviour to the new position to stop us from feeling the psychological discomfort associated with the inconsistent positions we hold.

@ Visit the **Online Resource Centre** to read more about the book.

▶ Market Insight 3.1

Volvo Deals for Anxious Buyers

The Volvo website showroom presents its S40
Source: Volvo Car UK.

In 2007, car manufacturer Volvo, headquartered in Göteborg, Sweden, sold 30,100 new cars in Britain, taking a 1.3% share of the market, behind more popular UK brands such as Peugeot, Renault, Audi/VW, GM/Vauxhall, Ford, Toyota/Lexus, BMW, and Honda. Sales were down 0.3% between 2002 and 2006 in a difficult trading environment. Since 2007, the car market has suffered further with the **credit crunch** and declining consumer confidence. In May 2009, because new car registrations were at an all-time low and to re-energize the car market, the British government introduced a new scrappage scheme whereby £2,000 would be paid to buyers who scrapped a car that was at least 10 years old when buying a new one.

Vehicle manufacturers and dealership sales personnel understand the psychological anxiety car buyers feel when purchasing a new car. The buyer's key consideration is ensuring they have obtained value for money and not feeling that they have been 'ripped off'. The problem is particularly acute when customers are buying new cars, because new cars are so much more expensive than second-hand cars. When we consider that cars lose 20–30% of their value in depreciation the moment they leave the showroom, we see why new car buyers feel particularly vulnerable. Of course, there are benefits: new cars look better, incorporate the latest design features, and have reduced maintenance costs.

Car dealers work hard to reinforce the decision made by new car buyers by sending customers newsletters and offering efficient (or free three-year warranty)

▶ Market Insight 3.1   (continued)

---

after-sales service to ensure that there are no or few maintenance problems. In many cases, new vehicles are also sold with free insurance, 0% finance deals, or buy-now-pay-later schemes, all of which are designed to reduce the post-purchase cognitive dissonance that many car buyers naturally feel after their purchase.

At Volvo, although the idea was that £1,000 came from the manufacturer and the other £1,000 came from government, they went a step further by offering a £3,500 discount instead of £1,000 for scrappage buyers. They sweetened the deal further by offering one year's complimentary insurance and three years servicing for £100 on purchases of their new S40 models, regardless of whether or not customers were scrapping their old cars, to help customers ease the pain of their new purchase.

But with many other, more popular car manufacturers offering so many different attractive promotions, will the promotion turn the tide of negative growth and result in an increase in market share for Volvo?

Sources: Mintel (2008a); www.volvocars.com/uk.

1 **What else could Volvo do to reduce the cognitive dissonance felt by customers?**

2 **Do you think cognitive dissonance would increase or decrease during a recession?**

3 **Consider a time when you purchased a good or service that left you feeling anxious. What product/service were you purchasing?**

In Figure 3.1, the buying process is iterative but particularly so at the re-evaluation phase of the acquisition process as the re-evaluation of the product may lead us back to any or all of the previous phases in the product acquisition process as a result of experiencing cognitive dissonance. For example, we may have bought a games console (Wii, PlayStation 3, etc.) but we are not completely happy with it (e.g. poor picture/sound). If it was covered under warranty, this would lead us to the acquisition phase, where a new, perfect product should be provided by the retailer. If the product was delivered in perfect working order but we simply didn't enjoy using it, we might go back to the original alternatives we selected (e.g. Xbox), and pick one of the other alternatives (e.g. which might offer a larger variety of games). If we are really not sure about which games console to buy after this initial purchase, we might re-evaluate the alternatives we originally selected and then decide. If we really disliked our original purchase, and this shook our belief in what we thought was important in selecting a games console, we might go back to the information-gathering phase to get more of an idea about the products available. Finally, if we were extremely disappointed with the product, we might decide that our original motive—the need to play, to relax, and have fun—can be best solved by purchasing something else other than a games console, which will still meet the same need, e.g. a multimedia computer or even participation in sport.

Perceptions, Learning, and Memory

Often consumers do not understand the messages that marketers are trying to get them to understand either because they have not received, or comprehended, or remembered those messages or because the messages were unclear in the first place. Consumer understanding very much depends on how effectively the message is both transmitted and perceived. In this section, we are concerned with how messages are perceived and remembered. (Consideration of how the marketer communicates the message is undertaken in Chapter 10.) In any one day, consumers receive thousands of messages.

Consider, for instance, a typical working woman in Paris, France, who might well be awoken by her clock radio, blaring out adverts for the local shopping centre. While she eats her breakfast, she may encounter audio-visual advertisements on her television. She will pick up visual advertisements in the magazine she is reading, say Paris Match, and when she opens her post, which may include direct mail from charities (e.g. Médecins Sans Frontières) and financial service organizations (BNP Paribas, etc.). On her way to the Métro station, she might encounter billboards, advertising, among other things, L'Oréal, for instance. On the Métro, she will probably encounter more visual adverts on the train itself. When she finally arrives at work, she has been subjected to hundreds of auditory, visual, and audio-visual marketing messages demanding her attention. When she retires to bed, this could literally have extended to thousands. If we consider that consumers are recipients of social and interpersonal messages as well—particularly through word of mouth—we can begin to realize how sophisticated the human perception, learning, and memory processes must be to attend to, filter, and store so many messages.

Perceptions

The American Marketing Association (AMA, 2009) defines perceptions as follows: 'based on prior attitudes, beliefs, needs, stimulus factors, and situational determinants [i.e. factors specific to the situation], individuals perceive objects, events, or people in the world about them. Perception is the cognitive impression that is formed of "reality" which in turn influences the individual's actions and behaviour toward that object.' If we paid attention to all the messages we receive, rather than filtering out those we find meaningful, we would probably become overloaded, just as a computer does when it crashes. The process of screening meaningful from non-meaningful information is known as **selective exposure** (Dubois, 2000).

As consumers, we are interested in certain types of products and services that are relevant to us at the moment we receive marketing messages, so men would not usually be interested in adverts about handbags unless they wanted to buy one for a present for an anniversary, birthday, or travel gift. Equally, young people are not usually interested in advertising messages for pensions. If you were looking to book a flight, you would suddenly become interested in messages from airline companies and travel agents. Even washing machine adverts become interesting if you need a washing machine! The messages we choose to ignore and forget are removed from our perceptual processes so that we can process those messages and items we do wish to consider more effectively. The brain selectively processes information and makes approximations based on that limited information. So, we avoid exposure to certain messages and actively seek out others. We may also selectively expose ourselves to particular messages through the media we choose to read, e.g. certain newspapers, magazines, internet websites, or watch, e.g. certain terrestrial, cable, satellite, or internet TV channels. Many people do not read a daily newspaper and, therefore, will not see press advertisements, although they may see banner advertising on internet websites or read and respond to blogs. Some people do not listen to the radio often or at all. The implication for marketers is the importance of determining which **media** channels their customers use.

Advertisers label this concept representing the personal importance a person attaches to a given communication message, **involvement**. This is an important construct because it explains a person's receptivity to communications. We are interested in their receptivity as marketers because we are interested in changing or altering their perceptions of particular products/services. We know, from earlier in the chapter, that products can be characterized on the basis of whether we as consumers use rational or emotional thinking to evaluate their relative appeal. Figure 3.2 illustrates a variety of common products and how they are generally viewed by US consumers (see Ratchford, 1987).

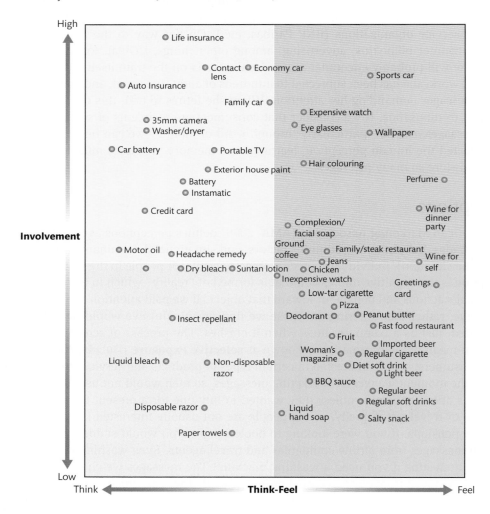

Figure 3.2

Involvement/think-feel dimension plot for common products

Source: Adapted from Ratchford (1987).

We should note that the position for a particular product is an average of all consumers and may not represent a particular individual's decision-making well. So, for example, the purchase of life insurance was generally regarded as being in the high involvement/thinking quadrant. The positioning of this type of product suggests the need for more informative advertising/promotion. An expensive watch, however, residing in the high involvement/feeling quadrant suggests a need for emotional advertising. Products in the low involvement/thinking quadrant, such as liquid bleach, suggest the use of advertising/promotion, which creates and reinforces habitual buying. Finally, products in the low involvement/feeling quadrant, such as women's magazines, should be promoted on the basis of personal satisfaction (Ratchford, 1987).

Another way of displaying how people think about particular products/services uses perceptual mapping, a technique with a long history of use since at least the early 1960s (Mindak, 1961). Figure 3.3 indicates how customers view different champagne and sparkling wine brands in the UK by comparing the brands on dimensions of differentiation versus trust. The diagram clearly shows that LVMH's Moët et Chandon is perceived as the most trusted and most highly differentiated brand in the UK. (We consider this brand differentiation further in Chapter 6.)

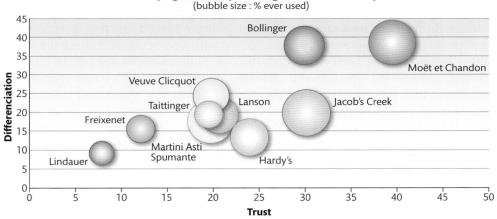

Figure 3.3

Example of a perceptual map

Source: Mintel (2008b), Reproduced with the kind permission of Mintel.

Learning and Memory

How do consumers continually learn about new product and service characteristics, their relative performance, and new trends? Learning is defined as the process by which we acquire new knowledge and skills, attitudes and values, through study, experience, or modelling others' behaviour. There are various theories of human learning, which include **classical conditioning**, **operant conditioning**, and **social learning** as outlined below:

▶ Classical Conditioning—Russian Nobel Laureate, Ivan Pavlov, investigated the digestive and nervous system of dogs, measuring the amount of saliva produced in response to food under certain conditions. He realized that his dog tended to salivate before food was actually served, and set out to investigate why. By carrying out a series of experiments and manipulating stimuli before the presentation of food using a bell, he realized that if he rang the bell before serving food, the dogs would associate the sound of the bell (the conditioned stimulus) with the presentation of food (the unconditioned stimulus), and begin salivating. So, classical conditioning occurs when the unconditioned stimulus becomes associated with the conditioned stimulus. In other words, we learn by associating one thing with another, in this case the sound of the bell with the arrival of food. This approach to learning has been frequently used in marketing through the use of: 1) jingles in advertising, e.g. using Marvin Gaye's 'Heard it Through the Grapevine' with Levis 501s in the 1990s; 2) supermarket layout designers include bakery sections to cause consumers to buy more products as they associate the smell of warm bread with eating!; and 3) perfume and aftershave manufacturers (e.g. L'Oréal) place free samples of products in sachets in magazines so that whenever a reader sees an advert for a particular brand of perfume/ aftershave they associate the image they see with the smell, and so are more likely to purchase the product when they see its image in the future.

▶ Operant Conditioning—B. F. Skinner (1954) was one of the pioneers of the behaviourist school of learning. He argued that learning was the result of operant conditioning whereby subjects would act on a stimulus from the environment. The resulting behaviour was much more likely to occur if this behaviour was reinforced. In other words, operant conditioning is learning through behavioural reinforcement. Skinner termed this reinforcement as the behaviour would occur more readily in connection with a particular stimulus if the required resulting behaviour had been reinforced, through punishment or reward. In relation to marketing, consider the typical in-store sales promotion. Perhaps it's a new yoghurt brand being offered in a supermarket. If we don't normally eat this brand, and we're curious, we might try it, because there are no costs in terms of time, effort, or money in acquiring a taste. The sales promotion provides the stimulus, the trial behaviour therefore occurs, and if the yoghurt is liked and perhaps the consumer rewarded with a money-off coupon, the behaviour of purchasing that particular yoghurt brand is reinforced (for more on sales promotion, see Chapter 11). Supermarkets reinforce our loyalty by providing reward cards and points for purchasing particular items from their stores. The Nectar card in Britain, a reward card that links a supermarket, selected retailers, and petrol retailers, to a points system, or the card and stamps system used by the Japanese retailer 7-Eleven, in their convenience stores throughout the world, are cases in point.

▶ Social Learning—this theory was first proposed by psychologist, Albert Bandura, who suggested that humans are less animalistic than the Skinnerian behaviourist school of learning suggests. Bandura (1977) argued that we can delay gratification and dispense our own rewards or punishment. So, we have more choice over how we react to stimuli than Skinner proposed, who felt that we blindly followed our instinctual drives. We can reflect on our own actions and change our future behaviour. This led on to the idea that we could learn not only from how we responded to situations but also from how others respond to situations. Bandura called this modelling. In social learning, we learn by observing the behaviour of others. The implications for marketing are profound. For adolescents, role models include both parents and famous athletes and entertainers, but, of these groups, parents are the more influential (Martin and Bush, 2000). Parents socialize their children into purchasing and consuming the same brands they buy, actively teaching them consumer skills—materialistic values and consumption attitudes in their teenage years. Interaction with peers also makes adolescents more aware of different products and services (Moschis and Churchill, 1978).

But what happens once consumers have learnt information? How do they retain it in their memories and what stops them from forgetting such information? Consumers do not necessarily have the same experience and, therefore, knowledge of particular products or services. Knowledge develops with familiarity, repetition of marketing messages, and a consumer's acquisition of product/service information. Marketing messages need to be repeated often as people can forget them over time, particularly the specific arguments or message presented. The general substance or conclusion of the message is marginally more likely to be remembered (Bettinghaus and Cody, 1994: 67).

We can enhance memorization through the use of symbols, such as corporate identity logos, badges, and signs. Shapes, creatures, and people carry significant meanings, as seen in badges, trademarks, and logos. Airlines around the world have adopted symbols, for example, the kangaroo of Australian airline, Qantas. Well-recognized symbols worldwide include the McDonald's 'Golden Arches' symbol, the Intel symbol, the Olympic movement's 'five rings' symbol, Apple's bitten apple logo, and the Microsoft Windows symbol.

Qantas A380 over Sydney
Source: Courtesy of Qantas.

Source: © International Olympics Committee.

Source: ©2010 McDonald's.

Some of the world's most recognizable logos

Our memories, as a system for storing perceptions, experience, and knowledge, are highly complex (Bettman, 1979). A variety of memorization processes can affect consumer choice, including the following:

▶ Factors affecting **recognition** and **recall**—less frequently used words in advertising are recognized more and recalled less. The information-processing task in transferring data from short-term to long-term memory differs for recognition (two to five seconds) and recall (five to ten seconds). Under high states of arousal, e.g. where the consumer is subject to time pressure, recognition speeds are increased whereas recall speeds are hindered. In practical terms, the more unique a campaign's message, the better it is recognized but the worse it is recalled.

▶ The importance of context—memorization is strongly associated with the context of the stimulus, so information available in memory will be inaccessible in the wrong context. For example, washing machine manufacturers advertising in car magazines are unlikely to be remembered.

▶ Form of object coding and storage—we store information in the form it is presented to us, either by object (brand) or dimension (product/service attribute) but there is no evidence that one form is organized into memory more quickly, or more accurately than the other (see Johnson and Russo, 1978).

▶ Load processing effects—we are likely to find it more difficult to process information into our short- and long-term memories when we are presented with a great deal of information at once.

▶ Input mode effects—short-term recall of sound input is stronger than short-term recall of visual input where the two compete for attention, e.g. in television and internet advertising.

▶ Repetition effects—recall and recognition of marketing messages/information increase the more a consumer is exposed to them, although later exposures add less and less to memory performance.

Evidence suggests that where consumers have little experience or knowledge of a product/ service brand, provision of in-store point-of-purchase information is more successful than general advertising (Bettman, 1979). This is why brand manufacturers frequently conduct product trials in-store, offering consumers the opportunity to try a product without expending time, money, and effort in purchasing the item (see Chapter 11 for more on sales promotion). This approach also places the brand in the consumer's evoked set, and helps the consumer contextualize the particular product and remember it when they shop next time. Consumer knowledge of products and services can be incomplete and/or inaccurate as consumers frequently think they know something about a product or service that is not accurate and believe this strongly (Alba and Hutchinson, 2000).

Personality

How and what we buy is also based on our personalities. **Personality** can be defined as that aspect of our psyche that determines the way in which we respond to our environment in a relatively stable way over time. There are various theories of personality. Here, we consider three main approaches as follows:

1 the psychoanalytic approach, which stresses self-reported unconscious desires;

2 trait theory, which stresses the classification of personality types; and

3 the self-concept approach, which is concerned with how we perceive ourselves as consumers.

The Psychoanalytic Approach

Sigmund Freud devised a theory of motivation that considered us as irrational beings. According to Freud (1927), a person's personality is determined by their sexual development through what he termed the oral, anal, phallic, latent, and genital stages. These stages emphasized development from an infant beginning with breastfeeding, to toilet training, to discovery of the genitals, through a stage of the development of hidden sexual desires from the age of about 5 until adolescence, and then in adolescence the individual is said to discover a sexual interest for persons of the opposite sex. Freud stated that an adult's personality is developed according to how well they cope with crises that occur during these five phases.

As an individual, Freud outlined how we are motivated by our subconscious drives, which he saw as a system comprising three interrelated components, comprising the id, the ego, and the superego. These are outlined below:

▶ **Id**—this part of our psyche harbours our instinctual drives and urges, a kind of seething mass of needs, which require instant gratification.

▶ **Ego**—this part of the psyche attempts to find outlets for the urges in our id and acts as a planning centre to determine the opportunities for gratification of our urges. According to Freud, the ego is moderated by the superego.

▶ **Superego**—this part of our psyche controls how we motivate ourselves to behave to respond to our instincts and urges, so that we do so in a socially acceptable manner and avoid any feelings of guilt or shame. It acts as a social conscience.

Psychoanalytic ideas of human personality and development have been applied to the marketing of mass consumer goods by the public relations specialist Edward Bernays, Sigmund's nephew, in America, and many others. The application of psychoanalytic methods and concepts to the understanding of consumer behaviour became known as motivation research and was used to understand consumers in an increasingly competitive market with high relative consumer affluence (Collins and Montgomery, 1969). Motivation research aimed to understand people's motivations to purchase and was undertaken extensively in the 1960s and 1970s, using focus groups and qualitative research methods, particularly projective techniques of interpretation, to identify subconscious desires (see Chapter 4). Such research techniques are still in use today. According to some motivation researchers, people buy the following goods for the following reasons (Dichter, 1964; Kotler, 1965):

▶ Train travel—was regarded as safer than airline travel by male passengers who felt less guilty about what might happen to their wives and families if there was an accident.

▶ Cigars—the strong smell is associated by males with virility.

▶ A convertible/cabriolet car—a substitute 'mistress' for the male buyer.

▶ Fur coats—demonstrates the financial prestige of the buyer and the sexual prowess of the wearer.

The Trait Approach

This approach to personality categorizes people into different personality types or so-called traits (pronounced 'trays'). Researchers characterize personalities according to bipolar scales, which have included the following traits:

- ▶ sociable–timid;
- ▶ action-oriented–reflection-oriented;
- ▶ stable–nervous;
- ▶ serious–frivolous;
- ▶ tolerant–suspicious; and

- ▶ dominant–submissive;
- ▶ friendly–hostile;
- ▶ hard–sensitive;
- ▶ quick–slow;
- ▶ masculine–feminine.

Researchers frequently also talk about the 'big five' personality dimensions including: extraversion (sociable fun-loving, affectionate, friendly, talkative), openness (original, imaginative, creative and daring), conscientiousness (careful, reliable, well-organized, hard-working), neuroticism (worrying, nervous, high-strung, self-conscious, vulnerable), and agreeableness (soft-hearted, sympathetic, forgiving, acquiescent) (McRae and Costa, 1987). An understanding of personality types helps marketers to segment customer groups (see Chapter 6) on the basis of a particular personality trait.

Car manufacturers might market products on the basis of personality types related to particular car attributes, for example, safety features versus aesthetic design or handling versus social prestige of owning a particular vehicle and so on. Matzler, Bidmon, and Grabner-kräuter (2006) argue that marketers of running shoes and mobile phones should be interested in two personality traits in particular, extraversion and openness to experience, because these traits are linked to how consumers form their view of brands and their attitudinal and purchase loyalty to those brands.

go online

Visit the **Online Resource Centre** and complete Internet Activity 3.1, an online quiz, to learn more about your own personality across a number of key personality traits.

Self-Concept Approach

There is an increasing belief among marketing researchers that people buy goods and services for the brand that they represent and its relation to the buyers' perception of their own self-concept or personality. In other words, we buy brands we feel resemble how we perceive ourselves. In a study of the luxury goods market, Dubois and Duquesne (1993) demonstrated how buyers of luxury goods typically divided into one of two categories, as follows:

1 Those that made their purchases based on product quality, aesthetic design, and excellence of service, motivated by the desire to impress others, ability to pay high prices, and the ostentatious display of their wealth.

2 Those that bought luxury goods based on what they symbolize, purchasing luxury goods representing an extreme form of the expression of their own values.

Consumers buy products based on self-concept through self-giving behaviour (Mick and DeMoss, 1990). Gift-giving is a common phenomenon, particularly among family, friends, and work colleagues. It is highly symbolic connoting love (e.g. Valentine's and Mother's/Father's Days), congratulations (e.g. wedding presents), regret (e.g. a card after offending a loved one), and dominance (e.g. clothes bought by a girl to change the look of her boyfriend). Self-giving arises from different motivations, e.g. to reward oneself, to be nice to oneself, to cheer oneself up, to fulfil a need, and to celebrate. There is a link between the purchase of clothing as a self-gift, i.e. a special purchase, rather than a typical purchase, and a consumer's self-concept (see Market Insight 3.2 for the expanding market in men's cosmetics). An extreme example of when people purchase products to build their self-concept, although it tends to work in the short term and damages longer term self-concept perceptions, occurs in compulsive consumer behaviour (e.g. shopping, gambling, excessive drinking).

▶ Market Insight 3.2

L'Oréal: Is He Worth It?

L'Oréal Paris, the French cosmetic giant, has long understood the importance of selling cosmetics as a form of self-gift. The company is involved in developing many cosmetic beauty care products, ranging from skincare, haircare, and hair colouring to make-up and styling products, marketed under famous brand names including Elsève, Studio-Line, and Dermo-Expertise. Famous for its 'Because I'm worth it' tagline originally invented by McCann Erickson in 1967, L'Oréal has recently changed its tagline to 'Because you're worth it'. The company emphasizes its self-indulgence advertising theme embodying Parisian beauty by using some of the world's most glamorous women, including Andie MacDowell, Eva Longoria, Milla Jovovich, and Oscar-winning actress Charlize Theron. Women are therefore purchasing the L'Oréal Paris brand because they want to feel glamorous and special themselves. But L'Oréal (with Men Expert and Lancôme Homme), Procter & Gamble (with Boss Skin), and Clarins (with Clarins Men) have all recognized that women may not be the only gender that want to pamper and preen themselves. A group of 'metrosexual' men exist who are quite prepared to buy and use cosmetic products. Their habits seem to differ based on age and nationality. Younger men are the most likely to buy L'Oréal's 'Men Expert' product range. However, in Britain, only about one-third of men use skincare products. In Japan and South Korea, significantly more young men use them. With a UK male grooming market that is forecast to be worth £940m

Male grooming is a growing market

▶ Market Insight 3.2   (continued)

by 2011, it's no wonder L'Oréal Paris thinks he's worth it, even if he doesn't himself.

Sources: Manning-Schaffel (2006); Mintel (2007a); Baines, Egan, and Jefkins (2004).

1 Why do you think younger men are most likely to use skincare products?

2 How do you think companies like L'Oréal need to position their men's skincare ranges better? How do male non-users perceive the category?

3 Consider your own perceptions of men's skincare products. If you are a man: have you ever bought any male skincare products in the past? Why? If you are a woman: have you ever bought a male friend or partner skincare products in the past or does your friend/ partner buy his own? If he buys his own, what are your perceptions of this behaviour? If you bought skincare products for him, why do you think he doesn't buy these products for himself?

Motivation

The most celebrated work on human motivation is that of Abraham Maslow (1943), who suggested a hierarchical order of human needs, as outlined in Figure 3.3. According to Maslow, we seek to satisfy our lower order physiological needs first, before our safety needs, before our belongingness needs, our esteem needs, and finally our need for self-actualization. There is little research evidence to confirm Maslow's hierarchy, but the concept does possess logical simplicity, making it a useful tool to understand how we prioritize our own needs. In contemporary societies, products/services tend to be focused on solving consumer needs in the esteem and self-actualization categories, as the needs in other categories are already provided for. However, in the poorer parts of sub-Saharan Africa, products and services may well operate for many citizens at the level of solving safety and belongingness needs. The implications for marketers are that products and services aimed at the mass market in Africa for products and services in the self-actualization category (e.g. higher education, long-haul travel) are likely to fail. Note, however, that this does not mean there are no market segments with this need. Quite the opposite: there are groups of people in sub-Saharan Africa whose income allows them to enjoy these very products and services.

There is still debate about whether a buyer of products and services is primarily motivated by rational (as outlined by Howard and Sheth, 1969) or irrational motives. Holbrook, Lehman, and O'Shaughnessy (1986) started to consider irrational motives when they suggested our wants could be latent, passive, or active, and were related to both intrinsic and extrinsic reasons, as follows:

▶ latent—needs are hidden, our subject is unaware of his or her need;

▶ passive—the costs of acquisition exceed, for the moment, the expected satisfaction derived from acquisition; and

▶ active—the subject is both aware of their needs and expects perceived benefits to exceed the likely costs of acquisition.

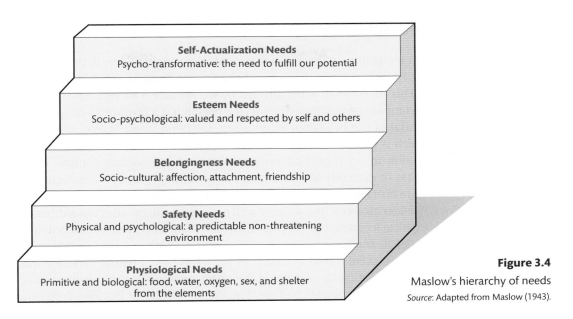

Figure 3.4

Maslow's hierarchy of needs

Source: Adapted from Maslow (1943).

According to Holbrook, Lehman, and O'Shaughnessy (1986), when our needs are active they can arise either through **habit**, or through a process of choosing a brand, which the authors call **picking**. Picking is the process of deliberative selection of a product or service from among a repertoire of acceptable alternatives, even though the consumer believes the alternatives to be essentially identical in their ability to satisfy his or her need. It can be motivated by intrinsic or extrinsic evaluations or both. Intrinsic evaluation occurs because a consumer likes a product, perhaps because of anticipated pleasure from using the product. Alternatively, an extrinsic evaluation might occur because a friend mentioned that it was a great product. Extrinsic evaluations can also entail explicit cost–benefit analyses. Extrinsic reasons for purchase can be subdivided into five categories including the following:

1   Economic—concerned with expenditure of money, time, and effort spent in purchasing and consuming a product or service. Economists refer to the concept of **price elasticity** of demand to determine how demand is affected when price is increased or decreased.

2   Technical—concerned with the product's perceived quality of performance in the anticipated usage situation.

3   Social—concerned with the extent to which a purchase will enhance a person's feelings of esteem, personal worth in relation to others (cf. Maslow's hierarchy), including the keeping up with the Joneses effect and general adherence to group norms and effects (see next section).

4   Legalistic—concerned with what are perceived to be the legitimate demands of others (e.g. buying on behalf of a company, or for a child or spouse).

5   Adaptive—(a form of social learning) concerned with imitating others, seeking expert advice (e.g. from consumer websites or industry or consumer magazines), or by relying on a particular company or brand's reputation in cases of uncertain or limited purchasing information.

Theory of Planned Behaviour

Theories of motivation in marketing can help us understand why people behave in the way they do. The Theory of Planned Behaviour outlines how behaviour is brought about by **intention** to act in a certain way. This intention to act is affected by the attitude a subject has towards a particular behaviour, encompassing the degree to which a person has a favourable or unfavourable evaluation or appraisal of the behaviour in question. Intention to act is also affected by the subjective norm, which is perceived social pressure to perform or not perform a particular behaviour. Finally, intention to act is also affected by perceived behavioural control, which refers to the perceived ease or difficulty of performing the behaviour, based on a reflection on past experience and future obstacles. Figure 3.4 provides a graphical illustration of the theory.

For example, if we consider cigarette use, we may well have different attitudes towards smoking based on our geographical location, e.g. whether we live in France or China versus Britain or New Zealand. Equally, we will also consider the opinions significant others have towards smoking cigarettes. For example, a recent advert launched by the UK National Health Service (NHS) tries to encourage smoking cessation by promoting the effect smoking has in causing anxiety in smokers' children who fear their parents will die. Finally, the Theory of Planned Behaviour considers whether we believe we have the capacity to bring about our desired behaviour. For example, we might think we can't give up smoking because we need a cigarette to calm our nerves (maybe we have a stressful job). As a social marketer trying to encourage smoking cessation, we could either a) try to alter subjects' attitudes towards smoking, b) change their views on how others see them as smokers, or c) change their perceptions of how they perceive their own ability to give up (see Chapter 16 for a wider discussion of social marketing).

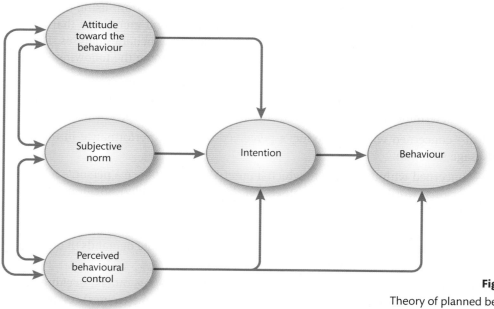

Figure 3.5

Theory of planned behaviour

Source: Azjen (1991).

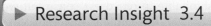

▶ Research Insight 3.4

To take your learning further, you might wish to read this influential article.

Azjen, I. (1991), 'The theory of planned behaviour', *Organisational Behaviour and Human Decision Processes*, **50, 179–211.**

In this highly cited, seminal article, the author outlines how behaviour and behavioural intention to act in a certain way, are affected by the attitude the subject has towards a particular behaviour, the subjective norm, and perceived behavioural control. The author developed our understanding of the fact that how humans intend to act may not be how they end up acting in a given situation. Intention, perception of behavioural control, attitude toward the behaviour, and subjective norm all reveal different aspects of the target behaviour and serve as possible directions for attack in attempts to alter particular behaviours, making this a powerful motivational theory in marketing.

 Visit the **Online Resource Centre** to read the abstract and access the full paper.

The Importance of Social Contexts

Although our own personality and other characteristics have an impact on how we think about and choose to consume products, the opinions, attitudes, and values of others also affect how we consume, as we discovered using the Theory of Planned Behaviour. Our own internal perspective is, therefore, not only determined by our own thoughts and personality structures but also by the input of others. So, other people have an effect on our opinions, attitudes, and values. We consider these three psychological constructs next.

Opinions, Attitudes, and Values

Opinions can be described as the quick responses we might give to opinion poll questions about current issues or instant responses to questions from friends. They are held with limited conviction because we have often not yet formed or fully developed an underlying attitude on this issue or item. An opinion might be what we think of the latest advertising campaign, for instance, for a high-profile brand. **Attitudes**, by comparison, are held with a greater degree of conviction, over a longer duration, and are much more likely to influence behaviour. **Values** are held even more strongly than attitudes and underpin our attitudinal and behavioural systems. Values tend to be linked to our conscience, developed through the familial socialization process, through cultures and subcultures, our religious influences, and are frequently formed in early childhood.

The marketer needs to understand the difference between these three different mental states. Opinions are **cognitive** (i.e. based on thoughts). Attitudes are what psychologists call **affective**, in that they are linked to our emotional states. Values are **conative**, i.e. they are linked to our motivations and behaviour. It is important to recognize that, although we sometimes have a specific attitude towards something, we do not always follow it in terms of our behaviour. In other words, we may want to be more fashionable in our dress sense but we don't bother trying new styles! VALs™ is framework that is used to segment consumers into differing types as based on their opinions, attitudes, values and behaviours

go online

Visit the **Online Resource Centre** and follow the weblink to the VALs™ online survey to identify which VAL type you fall into.

Group Influence

Consumers learn through imitation (i.e. social learning). We've learnt, for instance, by observing and copying our parents, and friends. As consumers we may consider our opinions, attitudes, values, and behaviour patterns in relation to those of our reference groups. Reference groups are those groups 'that the individual tends to use as an anchor point for evaluating his/her own beliefs and attitudes. A reference group may be positive; i.e. the individual patterns his or her own beliefs and behaviour to be congruent with those of the group, or it can be negative' (AMA, 2009). However, if a consumer feels his or her freedom to choose is being threatened, they may react against this intervention. So, a consumer whose decision alternative is blocked, partially or wholly, will become increasingly motivated to go against that specific decision alternative through rebellious behaviour (Clee and Wicklund, 1980). For example, the 'tweenage' daughter (aged between 10 and 12 years old) who is told by her father not to buy short skirts may very well continue to do so while the rebellious teenage son continues drinking against his mother's advice. This form of negative group influence occurs because of **psychological reactance**.

With reference to how we perceive and use products and services, consumers' assumptions about an individual's behaviour, based on identified group membership, become automated if they are frequently and consistently made (Bargh and Chartrand, 1999). This represents a form of social learning. For instance, a Swedish male consumer might continue to purchase Abba-branded herring because this was the brand his parents ate at the breakfast table, whereas a French female beverage consumer might drink Orangina religiously because that is what her parents provided for her as a child. The link between a consumer and a particular reference group depends on how closely the consumer associates with the particular reference group. Where we do associate closely, the attachment to the brand is also often assumed. For example, consumers identifying with the skateboarding genre might wear Vans trainers because the skateboarding crowd generally wear Vans trainers.

Message receipt is also affected by peer group pressure, through word of mouth whether intended or not. Members of groups tend to conform to a group norm, enhancing the self-image of the recipient and increasing the feeling of group identity and belongingness. Consumers, therefore, may have their own cultures and sub-cultures, which impact on how a particular marketing message may be received (see Chapter 18 for more discussion of how marketing and culture interact). Some marketing messages might incorporate **celebrity endorsement** appeals, e.g. through popular culture role models, who have influence over the target consumer group. H&M, the Swedish fashion retailer, has made use of major pop artists over the years, including Madonna and Kylie Minogue, to advertise its brands, particularly to young people, its target market. (See Market Insight 3.3 for an example of a successful celebrity endorsement campaign.) Marketing campaigns frequently leverage the persuasive power of reference group membership through word-of-mouth campaigns, particularly in the internet age, where consumers discuss product and service experiences in chatrooms and on blogs. The producers of the Hollywood film *The Blair Witch Project* initially marketed the film at minimal cost through their website, using only viral marketing techniques. Word-of-mouth communication is powerful because we trust our friends' and colleagues' opinions. For example, in the British funeral business (Mintel, 2007b), the key reasons for how people identify a funeral director when a loved one dies is because of: a recommendation from friends/family (24%); they are well-known and reputable (22%); the location of the premises (20%); and cost (14%). Many, therefore, rely on friends and family because of their own inexperience in funeral planning. In the next section, we consider how consumer behaviour is affected by social class, lifecycle, and lifestyle.

▶ Market Insight 3.3

The Naked Chef Endorses Sainsbury's

Sainsbury's, the UK's third-largest supermarket behind Tesco and Asda, signed celebrity chef, Jamie Oliver, the man behind the successful television programme, *The Naked Chef*, to promote their brand in 2000. Up until 2005, Oliver's celebrity presence in Sainsbury's adverts is thought to have added a cool £1.2bn to the company's bottom line over that period. In 2005, in a campaign that was said to have cost the supermarket £10m (Oliver's fee was £1m), he was rehired to work his magic on culinary consumers again. Within six months, Sainsbury's had recorded a 2.8% increase in second-quarter sales (Woodward, 2006). Jamie Oliver has been a passionate campaigner to improve the quality of

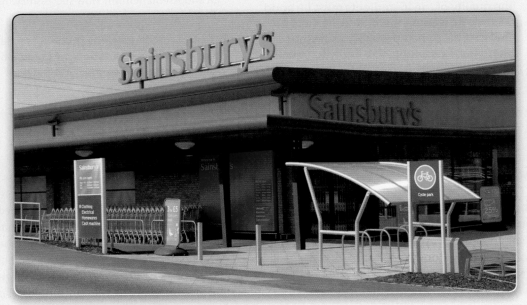

Sainsbury's, the naked chef's favourite supermarket

▶ Market Insight 3.3 (continued)

school meals, at one point signing up so many people that when his petition was presented to the Prime Minister he actually managed to change government policy (no more turkey twizzlers for kids, he argued, among other things). By 2009, Oliver was still promoting Sainsbury's, this time with the 'feed your family for a fiver campaign' (Benady, 2009). An executive at Abbott Mead Vickers (the agency behind the original campaign) stated the brand strategy was 'to re-emphasise the brand's focus on quality ... using Jamie Oliver who is renowned for quality would help us reposition on quality and that is what the adverts are conveying to the customer. In essence, what we are doing is borrowing his values and transposing them to the brand' (Byrne, Whitehead, and Breen, 2003: 293–4). Typical comments from focus groups indicate the message of quality was directly transferred with such comments as: 'Well Jamie Oliver advertises quality meals', 'the quality of the ingredients must be good because he is using them', and 'he's a top chef isn't he, so he's probably using the brand for his cooking, you know top quality at cheaper prices' (Byrne, Whitehead, and Breen, 2003: 294).

Nevertheless, celebrity endorsement deals are not without problems. Jamie Oliver publicly fell out with Sainsbury's over its policy on battery farming of chickens. Other celebrity endorsers have been sacked because brands were frightened the celebrity endorsement deal might damage their brands because of something the celebrity did wrong. Supermodel Kate Moss was sacked as the face of H&M after pictures were published of her taking cocaine in 2005, although, ironically, the extra publicity she gained from this episode made her even more marketable and she won other endorsement deals once the heat had died down. The question for Sainsbury's is how long will Jamie's appeal last and could another celebrity influence its target market more?

(See also Market Insight 11.1 for more on the promotional tools and techniques used in the Sainsbury's campaigns.)

1 Why do you think Jamie Oliver's endorsement of Sainsbury's has been so effective?

2 Who else might the supermarket have sought an endorsement from? How successful would this campaign have been?

3 Think of another celebrity endorsement deal that you are aware of. Who is the brand, who is the endorser and do you think that this campaign was effective?

Social Grade

In marketing, the term 'social grade' refers to a system of classification of consumers based on their socio-economic grouping. **Social grade** was originally developed for the IPA National Readership Survey (NRS) in the 1950s, and was subsequently adopted by JICNARS (the Joint Industry Committee for National Readership Surveys) on its formation in 1968. Social grade is a means of classifying the population by the type of work they do. This was originally based on the occupation of the head of household (the member of the household who owns the accommodation or is responsible for the rent), but since 1992 it has been based on the occupation of the chief income earner (the member of the household with the largest income). NRS Ltd (the successor to JICNARS) continues to provide social grade population estimates, not only for the National Readership Survey, but also for a number of other major industry surveys. These population estimates are obtained from the Survey's interviews with a representative sample of some 36,000 adults every year, and are based on detailed information about the occupation of the chief income earner (see Table 3.1). There is a widely held belief that consumers make purchases based on their socio-economic position within society. (Market Insight 3.4 looks at champagne drinking and social class.)

▶ **Table 3.1** Social grading scale

Social grade	Social status	Occupational status	Population estimate, Great Britain, age 15+ (1979) (%)	Population estimate, Great Britain, age 15+ (2009) (%)
A	Upper middle class	Professionals, chief executives, and senior managers with a large number of dependent staff	3.2	4.0
B	Middle class	Intermediate, managerial, administrative, or professional	13.4	22.6
C1	Lower middle class	Supervisory, clerical and non-manual administrative, lower managerial or early professional (e.g. junior white-collar workers based in offices)	22.2	29.1
C2	Skilled working class	Skilled manual workers	31.7	21.1
D	Working class	Semi- and unskilled manual workers	20.9	15.2
E	Those at lowest levels of subsistence	Unemployed and casual workers, pensioners or widowers with no income other than that provided by the state	8.6	8.0

Source: National Readership Survey. Reproduced with the kind permission of the National Readership Survey.

▶ Market Insight 3.4

Champagne: The Social Drink

Champagne, the sparkling wine from the Champagne region of France, has long been the drink of choice at weddings and on special occasions but is most often drunk at home by Britons and occasionally in restaurants and at the more upmarket pubs. Six brands account for 60% of total sales by value in the UK market including Moët et Chandon, Lanson, Veuve Clicquot, Laurent-Perrier, Bollinger and supermarket own-label.

Because of its relatively high cost, champagne drinkers can be easily analysed using social grading scales. The level of champagne drinking by the different social classes is distinct. A large proportion of the professional and managerial class (AB) are champagne drinkers (44%), drinking in moderation and at home, whereas 37% of clerical and administrative workers drink champagne (C1). By contrast, 22% of skilled manual workers (C2) tend to drink champagne. Only 19% of non-skilled manual workers (D), and 14% of the unemployed, and those on benefits (E) are champagne drinkers (see Table 3.2). There is, therefore, a marked decrease in champagne consumption as we move down the socio-economic scale.

Around 29% of British adults drink champagne, representing a significant market by volume, although a higher proportion of women than men drink it

Champagne, the party drink

(33% compared to 27%). Nevertheless, consumers are increasingly warming to sparkling wine, particularly the Spanish Cava and Australian sparkling wines such as Hardy's, which generated sales of £385m on 42.1m litres in 2007. Given the increasing switch to alternatives, and the downturn in the UK economy and other heavy champagne-drinking economies worldwide such as the USA, will consumers continue to pop their champagne corks?

Source: Mintel (2008b).

1 Why does champagne consumption differ by social class?

2 Do you think there is any difference by social class between those who drink champagne and those who drink sparkling wine? Why?

3 How do you think the recession in the late 2000s might have affected champagne consumption by social class?

▶ **Table 3.2** UK champagne consumers by usage type and social class

Social class	Heavy users (%)	Medium users (%)	Light users (%)
AB	11	21	11
C1	7	16	14
C2	5	8	9
D	3	9	7
E	2	5	7

Source: Mintel (2008). Reproduced with the kind permission of Mintel.

Social grading scales indicate a particular consumer's position in society. The NRS classification approach is widely used by market research agencies in Britain because of its simplicity. Social grade provides an effective demographic tool for advertising planning, and it is still extensively used by advertisers, advertising agencies, and media owners. Frequently, researchers combine the grades into two, ABC1 and C2DE, and three categories, AB and C1/C2 and DE. Segmenting consumers using class grading has been criticized, because Britain, and most other Western nations, have moved from manufacturing-based to service-based economies (see Chapter 1). More and more people in Britain, therefore, work in office-based environments (ABC1) rather than in manual or unskilled professions (C2DE). As a result, the social-class segmentation approach is becoming less able to discriminate between different group behaviours (see Chapter 6 on market segmentation). Although there are clearly differences in type of job conducted and the material wealth of each group, Martineau (1958) has suggested that there are also psychological differences between the middle, i.e. ABC1, and the lower classes, i.e. C2DE (see Table 3.3).

▶ **Table 3.3** Martineau's class differences by psychological outlook

Middle class	Lower class
1 Pointed to the future	Pointed to the present and the past
2 Viewpoint embraces a long expanse of time	Lives and thinks in a short expanse of time
3 More urban identification	More rural in identification
4 Stresses rationality	Non-rational essentially
5 Has a well-structured sense of the universe	Vague and unclear structuring of the world
6 Horizons vastly extended or not limited	Horizons sharply defined and limited
7 Greater sense of choice-making	Limited sense of choice-making
8 Self-confident, willing to take risks	Very much concerned with security and insecurity
9 Immaterial and abstract in thinking	Concrete and perceptive in thinking
10 See themselves as part of national happenings	World revolves around family and body

Source: Martineau (1958).

Lifestyle

Marketers are increasingly targeting consumers on the basis of lifestyle. The AMA define lifestyle as 'the manner in which the individual copes and deals with his/her psychological and physical environment on a day-to-day basis', 'as a phrase describing the values, attitudes, opinions, and behaviour patterns of the consumer', and 'the manner in which people conduct their lives, including their activities, interests, and opinions' (AMA, 2009). Todd and Lawson (2001) outline seven different lifestyle types among those who visit museums and galleries in New Zealand. These include the following lifestyle types:

▶ Active 'family values' people (15.5% of the population)—interested in the community with a traditional and positive outlook.

▶ Conservative quiet-lifers (13.5% of the population)—people who like to stay at home, who have conservative views, and are reflective and nostalgic.

▶ Educated liberals (9.7% of the population)—socially concerned, progressive, egalitarian types, who enjoy variety and diversity.

▶ Accepting mid-lifers (17.1% of the population)—observers rather than participants, who accept the status quo and are generally content.

▶ Success-driven extraverts (16.4% of the population)—self-oriented, actively ambitious people who are interested in free enterprise.

▶ Pragmatic strugglers (14.7% of the population)—focused on family survival, politically conservative and determined.

▶ Social strivers (13.0% of the population)—outer-directed and conformist people who feel life is a struggle.

In order to generate clusters of consumers according to different lifestyle types, marketers typically ask consumers questions around their activities, interests and opinions (AIO). The general idea is that if marketers fit around a consumer's lifestyle, consumers are more likely to benefit from, and appreciate, the proposition offered. (We cover the topic of lifestyle segmentation further in Chapter 6.)

Lifecycle

We hypothesize that people in the same stages of life purchase and consume similar kinds of products and, to some extent, this is the case. In research undertaken in America in the 1960s, Wells and Gubar (1966) determined that there were nine categories of lifecycle stage in a consumer's life, from leaving home to living as a solitary survivor, i.e. without a spouse. In contemporary society, the lifecycle concept has needed a degree of readjustment to take into account that fewer people are getting married, and at a later age, than they were in the 1960s, that there are singles with children, and increasingly there is a move by couples towards cohabiting. (See Chapter 6 for more on lifecycle segmentation.)

go online

Visit the **Online Resource Centre** and complete Internet Activity 3.2 to learn more about how VW uses the family lifecycle to communicate its brand values to its target audience.

Most market research agencies routinely measure attitudes and purchasing patterns based on lifecycle stage to determine differences among groups. Table 3.4 indicates that there is a difference in the type of goods and services purchased as a result, with solitary survivors far more likely to purchase funeral plans, nursing home care, and cruise holidays, and bachelors more likely to spend their income on package and long-haul holidays and educational service products, for instance. Club 18–30, a part of the Thomas Cook Group, caused controversy when it used blatant sexual appeals in its advertising campaigns aimed at young people in

▶ **Table 3.4** The lifecycle concept

Bachelor stage; young single people not living with parents/ guardians	Newly married or long-term co-habiting; young, no children	Full nest I; youngest children under 6	Full nest II; youngest children 6 or over	Full nest III; older married couples with dependent children	Empty nest I; older married couples, no children living at home, chief income earner or both in work	Empty nest II; older married couples, no children living at home, chief income earner or both retired	Solitary survivor, in work	Solitary survivor, retired
Few financial burdens. Fashion opinion leaders. Recreation oriented. Buy: basic kitchen equipment, basic furniture, cars, package and long-haul holidays, education.	Better off financially because of dual wages. High purchase rate of consumer durables. Buy: cars, refrigerators, package holidays.	Home purchasing at peak. Low level of savings. Buy: washer dryers, TV, baby food and related products, vitamins, toys.	Financial position better. Sometimes both parents in work. Buy: larger sized family food packages, cleaning materials, pianos, child-minding services.	Financial position better still. Both parents more likely to be in work. Some children will have part-time jobs. High average purchase of consumer durables. Buy: better homeware and furniture products, magazines, and non-essential home appliances.	Home ownership at peak. Most satisfied with savings and financial position. Interested in travel, recreation, self-education. More likely to give gifts and make charitable contributions. Less interested in new products. Buy: luxurious holidays, eating out, home improvements.	Drastic cut in household income. More likely to stay at home. Buy: medical appliances and private healthcare, products, which help sleep, digestion.	Financial position reasonable, likely to have paid off mortgage. Buy: individual food packages, entertainment, healthcare products and services.	Same medical needs as other retired group; drastic cut in income. Buy: household staples, cruise holidays, nursing home services, funeral plans.

Source: Adapted from Wells and Gubar (1966). Published by American Marketing Association.

1995. The company's campaign, which used a series of adverts to promote the chance for holiday-makers to meet sexual partners, was banned by the Advertising Standards Authority, because although it probably did not offend its target market, it certainly offended everyone else. Other tour operators, like Saga, target the older traveller, typically with more sedate appeals.

Ethnic Groups

In a globalized society, marketers are increasingly interested in how we market goods and services to ethnic groups within particular populations. These groups can be quite large and have their own unique customs, so they represent an opportunity either to build a niche (ethnic) market or to consolidate an existing market, i.e. by appealing to a new set of consumers in addition to the old. In the USA, the Hispanic population—principally, but not solely, immigrants from Mexico—and the Black population together represent a sizeable proportion of the total population. European countries have sizeable ethnic populations: for example, in France there is a large Black African population and in Germany a large Turkish community. France and Britain both have large Muslim populations. In Dubai, in the United Arab Emirates, a large community of expatriates exists, particularly from India. These groups within a country represent a potential opportunity for the marketer, if they are sizeable enough to be profitable and have similar needs. (See Market Insight 3.5.) Cui (1997) proposes that in any country where there are ethnic marketing opportunities a company has four options in deciding its strategic approach, as follows:

1 Total standardization—use the existing marketing mix (see Chapter 1) without modification to the ethnic market. This is actually very difficult to do. Even McDonald's, well known for their ardent approach to standardization, adapt their burgers in India to cater for local tastes and religious customs.

2 Product adaptation—use the existing marketing mix but adapt the product to the ethnic market in question, e.g. Nivea's Skin Whitening Lotion sells particularly well in Southeast Asian markets.

3 Advertising adaptation—use current marketing mix but adapt the advertising, particularly the use of foreign languages, to the target ethnic market by promoting the product using different associations more resonant with ethnic audiences (e.g. Tesco have used point of sale promotions written in the Polish language to target the large influx of Polish citizens who have come to Britain since EU enlargement in 2004). Companies frequently market goods and services in Spanish to the Hispanic population in the USA, although there is evidence that doing so, particularly for high-involvement service brands, is of limited effect (Torres and Briggs, 2005).

4 Ethnic marketing—use a totally new marketing mix, e.g. Bollywood cinema is aimed at audiences in the Indian sub-continent and at diaspora around the world, using strong love and ethical themes, and a musical format.

▶ Market Insight 3.5

Ethnic Brands in Britain: How Names Mean Business

In the UK, Muslims represent around 2% of the population or around 1 million people. Increasingly, we are beginning to see brands aimed more at Muslim customers. For example, GlaxoSmithKline, the pharmaceutical giant, announced that Ribena—the juice drink—is **halal** and HSBC, the British-based banking group, offers Islamic (Sharia-law compliant) insurance. The Qibla brand of cola was launched in the UK by a group of Muslim entrepreneurs as an alternative to Coca-Cola, in a deliberate attempt to gain customers among Muslims disaffected with America as a result of the war in Iraq, using the strapline 'Liberate your taste'. L'Oréal quickly recognized the development of the ethnic trend, launching the Dark and Lovely personal care brand for Afro-Caribbeans. With accession to the EU, the fastest growing, and second-largest, immigrant group in Britain is the Polish. Lloyds Banking Group has even opened a special bank account for them called the Silver account.

Part of the problem is that ethnic groups are relatively hard to research, and, although they sometimes cluster in particular residential locations, they are also more difficult to reach by traditional marketing media. One data management company, Experian, has launched a software package called Ethnic Origins, developed in association with ACORN developer Richard Webber (see Chapter 6 for more on ACORN), which allows the ethnic origin of an individual to be determined on the basis of their name (see below).

Ribena, now Halal

Source: Courtesy of GlaxoSmithKline.

▶ Market Insight 3.5 (continued)

▶ **Table 3.5** Text strings indicative of country or region of origins

Text string	Example	Likely origin	Text string	Example	Likely origin
...son	Watson	England	...elli	Martinelli	Italy
...ie	Farlie	Scotland	...ides	Economides	Greece/Greek Cypriot
O'...	O'Sullivan	Ireland	...oglu	Demiroglu	Turkey
...sma	Boersma	Netherlands	...ian	Aphrahamian	Armenia
...burger	Regensburger	Germany	El...	El Mahmoud	Middle East
...dahl	Lindahl	Sweden	...singh	Kpur-Singh	India—Sikh
...es	Fernandes	Portugal	...nathan	Swaminathan	India—Hindu
...ez	Fernandez	Spain	Ade...	Adebayo	Nigeria

Source: Webber (2006).

With over 2.9 million Asians, 1.4 million Black African and Afro-Caribbeans, and over 400,000 Chinese in the UK population, it is little wonder that companies are starting to wake up to the ethnic marketing opportunities

Other sources: Jenkins (2002); Stones (2004); Kleinmann (2003); Charles (2007); Tiltman (2007); Mintel (2009).

1 Do you think that targeting ethnic products exclusively to ethnic groups could cause racial tensions with the non-ethnic population within a country?

2 What kinds of goods and services do you think are best developed for an ethnic audience?

3 What goods and services could be offered specifically to the UK Chinese population?

Skills for Employment

▶▶ When recruiting great marketers, I look for strong evidence of creative thinking in any walk of life. Have you solved a problem? Do you fill your time with interesting or unusual activities? Have you started some interest or group and 'seen it through to the end'? We need sound marketing theory aligned with creativity, opportunism and leftfield thinking. Leaders not followers. ◀◀

Simon Harrop CEO, BRAND sense agency

 Visit the **Online Resource Centre** to discover more tips and advice on skills for the workplace.

Chapter Summary

To consolidate your learning, the key points from this chapter are summarized below:

- **Explain the consumer product acquisition process.**

Consumer buying behaviour has both rational and irrational components, although rational theories have dominated the marketing literature until now. Although there are a variety of models of consumer buying behaviour, the consumer product acquisition model is perhaps the simplest to understand, stressing how the consumer goes through six key stages in the product acquisition process including motive development, information gathering, product evaluation, product selection, acquisition, and re-evaluation.

- **Explain the processes involved in human perception, learning, and memory in relation to consumer choice.**

The human perception, learning, and memory processes involved in consumer choice are complex. Marketers should ensure when designing advertising, when developing distribution strategies, when designing new goods and services, and other marketing tactics, that they (repeatedly) explain this information to consumers in order for them to engage with the information and then subsequently retain it, if it is to influence their buying decisions.

- **Understand the importance of personality and motivation in consumer behaviour.**

Consumers are motivated differently in their purchasing behaviour dependent on their personalities and, to some extent, how they feel their personality fits with a particular brand of product or service. Maslow's (1943) seminal work on human needs helps us understand how we are motivated to satisfy five key human desires. From the Theory of Planned Behaviour (Azjen, 1991), we know that how we intend to behave is not always how we actually behave, because this is affected by our attitudes towards the behaviour in question, a subjective norm (how we think others perceive that behaviour) and our own perceptions of how we can control our behaviour.

- **Describe opinions, attitudes, and values and how they relate to consumer behaviour.**

Opinions are relatively unstable positions that people take in relation to an issue or assessment of something. Attitudes are more strongly held and are more likely to be linked to our behaviour. Values are more strongly held still and are linked to our conscience. Marketers are interested in all three because they help us understand consumers better and develop lifestyle marketing approaches.

- **Explain how reference groups influence consumer behaviour.**

Reference groups including such role models as parents, entertainers, and athletes have an important socializing influence on our consumption behaviour, particularly in adolescence. However, where we live, what social class we come from, what lifestyle we lead, what stage of the lifecycle we are in, and which ethnic group we belong to, all have an impact on our behaviour as consumers. Celebrity endorsers are particularly powerful influencers in this regard, especially as fame is becoming an increasingly attractive quality to many consumers in modern life.

Review Questions

1. What is the process consumers go through when buying goods and services?
2. What is cognitive dissonance and how does it relate to consumer behaviour?
3. How are the psychological concepts of perception, learning, and memory relevant to our understanding of consumer choice?
4. How are concepts of personality relevant to our understanding of consumer behaviour?

5 How are concepts of motivation relevant to our understanding of consumer behaviour?

6 What is the Theory of Planned Behaviour?

7 What are opinions, attitudes, and values and how do they relate to consumer behaviour?

8 How do reference groups influence how we behave?

9 What is celebrity endorsement?

10 How does lifestyle influence how we buy?

11 What are the four strategies available to ethnic marketers?

Worksheet Summary

Visit the **Online Resource Centre** and complete Worksheet 3.1. This will help you learn about consumer behaviour related to the National Readership Survey's social grading system (A, B, C1, C2, D, and E).

Discussion Questions

1 Having read Case Insight 3.1 at the beginning of this chapter, how would you advise BRAND sense agency to develop a sensory marketing campaign for its retail bank client? Consider sight, sound and smell not only for the brand itself but also for the retail environment of the bank.

2 Describe the process you might go through to obtain the following products in terms of the consumer product acquisition model shown in Figure 3.1.

A chocolate bar, e.g. Snickers or Cadbury's Dairy Milk; Plopp in Sweden;

B long-haul flight to an exotic destination from your home country;

C laptop to help you write the essays and group work for your marketing course;

D washing machine;

E a householder receiving refuse collection services from the local council (paid for indirectly through local council taxes).

3 Use the Theory of Planned Behaviour to explain consumer motivations to pursue the following behaviours:

A purchase of a hotel room at the Burj al Arab in Dubai, UAE;

B a visit to the Resistance Museum in Oslo, Norway;

C voting during an election in Afghanistan;

D bungee jumping in New Zealand.

4 What kinds of celebrity endorsers have you noticed companies using in their advertising to persuade you to adopt the following products?

A sports apparel (e.g. Nike or Adidas);

B luxury watches (e.g. Omega);

C beverages (e.g. Coca-Cola or Pepsi);

D sunglasses (e.g. Police).

5 Use PowerPoint to develop a short presentation on ethnic marketing highlighting some examples of how different companies are targeting ethnic groups.

Visit the **Online Resource Centre** and complete the Multiple Choice Questions to assess your knowledge of Chapter 3.

go online

References

Alba, J. W., and Hutchinson, J. W. (2000), 'Knowledge calibration: what consumers know and what they think they know', *Journal of Consumer Research*, 27, 123–56.

Alderson, W., and Martin, M. W. (1965), 'Toward a formal theory of transactions and transvections', *Journal of Marketing Research*, 2 (May), 117–27.

AMA (2009), *Dictionary of Marketing Terms*, retrieve from www.marketingpower.com, accessed 1 November 2009.

Azjen, I. (1991), 'The theory of planned behaviour', *Organisational Behaviour and Human Decision Processes*, 50, 179-211.

Baines, P., Egan, J., and Jefkins, F. (2004), *Public Relations: Contemporary Issues and Techniques*, Oxford: Butterworth-Heinemann.

Bandura, A. (1977), *Social Learning Theory*, Englewood Cliffs, NJ: Prentice-Hall.

Bargh, J. A., and Chartrand, T. L. (1999), 'The unbearable automaticity of being', *American Psychologist*, 57, 7 (July), 462–79.

Benady, D. (2009), 'Sainsbury's: King sets sights on crown', *Marketing Week*, 29 January, 20.

Bettinghaus, E. P., and Cody, M. J. (1994), *Persuasive Communication*, 5th edn, London: Harcourt Brace Publishers.

Bettman, J. R. (1979), 'Memory factors in consumer choice: a review', *Journal of Marketing*, 43 (Spring), 37–53.

Byrne, A.; Whitehead, M., and Breen, S. (2003), 'The naked truth of celebrity endorsement', *British Food Journal*, 105, 4/5, 288–96.

Charles, G. (2007), 'In pursuit of the Polish pound', *Marketing*, 2 May, 16.

Clee, M. A., and Wicklund, R. A. (1980), 'Consumer behaviour and psychological reactance', *Journal of Consumer Research*, 6, 389–405.

Collins, L., and Montgomery, C. (1969), 'The origins of motivational research', *British Journal of Marketing*, 13, 2 (Summer), 103–13.

Cui, G. (1997), 'Marketing strategies in a multi-ethnic environment', *Journal of Marketing Theory and Practice*, 5, 1, 122–35.

Dichter, E. (1964), *The Handbook of Consumer Motivation: The Psychology of the World of Objects*, London: McGraw-Hill.

Dubois, B. (2000), *Understanding the Consumer: A European Perspective*, London: FT/Prentice-Hall.

— and Duquesne, P. (1993), 'The market for luxury goods: income versus culture', *European Journal of Marketing*, 27, 1, 35–44.

Festinger, L. (1957), *A Theory of Cognitive Dissonance*, Palo Alto, Calif.: Stanford University Press.

Freud, S. (1927), *The Ego and the Id*, Richmond: Hogarth Press.

Holbrook, M. B., and Hirschmann, E. C. (1982), 'The experiential aspects of consumption: consumer fantasies, feelings and fun', *Journal of Consumer Research*, 9 (September), 132–40.

— Lehmann, D. R., and O'Shaughnessy, J. (1986), 'Using versus choosing: the relationship of the consumption experience to reasons for purchasing', *European Journal of Marketing*, 20, 8, 49–62.

Howard, J. A., and Sheth, J. N. (1969), *The Theory of Buyer Behavior*, New York: John Wiley and Sons.

Jenkins, P. (2002), *The Next Christendom: The Coming of Global Christianity*, Oxford: Oxford University Press, 94–104.

Johnson, E. J., and Russo, J. E. (1978), 'The organisation of product information in memory identified by recall times', in K. Hunt (ed.), *Advances in Consumer Research*, vol. V, Chicago: Association for Consumer Research, 79–86.

Kleinmann, M. (2003), 'Qibla-Cola backs anti-Western UK launch with £2m', *Marketing*, 24 April.

Kotler, P. (1965), 'Behavioral models for analyzing buyers', *Journal of Marketing*, 29 (October), 37–45.

McCrae, R. R., & Costa, P. T. (1987), 'Validation of the five-factor model of personality across instruments and observers', *Journal of Personality and Social Psychology*, 52, 81–90.

Manning-Schaffel, V. (2006), 'Metrosexuals: a well-groomed market?', 22 May, retrieve from www.brandchannel.com/features_effect.asp?pf_id=315, accessed 25 October 2009.

Martin, C. A., and Bush, A. J. (2000), 'Do role models influence teenagers' purchase intentions and behavior?', *Journal of Consumer Marketing*, 17, 5, 441–54.

Martineau, P. (1958), 'Social classes and spending behaviour', *Journal of Marketing*, October, 121–30.

Maslow, A. H. (1943), 'A theory of motivation', *Psychological Review*, 50, 370–96.

Matzler, K.; Bidmon, S., and Grabner-Kräuter, S. (2006), 'Individual determinants of brand affect: the role of the personality traits of extraversion and openness to experience', *Journal of Product and Brand Management*, 15, 7, 427–34.

Mick, D. G., and DeMoss, M. (1990), 'To me from me: a descriptive phenomenology of self-gifts', *Advances in Consumer Research*, 17, 677–82.

Mindak, W. A. (1961), 'Fitting the semantic differential to the marketing problem', *Journal of Marketing*, 25 (April), 29–33.

Mintel (2007a), 'Men's Grooming Habits—UK', March, London: Mintel International Group Ltd, retrieve from www.mintel.com, accessed 25 October 2009.

— (2007b), 'Funerals—UK', January, London: Mintel International Group Ltd, retrieve from www.mintel.com, accessed November 2009.

— (2008a), 'Car Retailing—UK', August, London: Mintel International Group Ltd, retrieve from www.mintel.com, accessed 25 October 2009.

— (2008b), 'Champagne and Sparkling Wines—UK', March, London: Mintel International Group Ltd, retrieve from www.mintel.com, accessed 1 November 2009.

— (2009), 'Ethnic Fashion Shopping Habits – UK', July, London: Mintel International Group Ltd, retrieve from www.mintel.com, accessed 25 October 2009.

Moschis, G. P., and Churchill, G. A., Jr. (1978), 'Consumer socialisation: a theoretical and empirical analysis', *Journal of Marketing Research*, 15 (November), 599–609.

Ratchford, B.T. (1987), 'New insights about the FCB grid', *Journal of Advertising Research*, 27, 4, 24–38.

Shears, R. (2009), 'Crocs of gold; they claim to be appalled by fur. So why do stars flaunt €35,000 designer bags that exploit the brutal trade in crocodile skin?', *Daily Mail*, 11 July, 50.

Skinner, B. F. (1954), 'The science of learning and the art of teaching', *Harvard Educational Review*, 24, 88–97.

Stones, J. (2004), 'Are companies set to embrace Islam?', *Marketing Week*, 19 August, 22.

Tiltman, D. (2007), 'Ethnic Britain', *Marketing*, 18 April.

Todd, S. and Lawson, R. (2001), 'Lifestyle segmentation and museum/gallery visiting behaviour', *International Journal of Nonprofit and Voluntary Sector Marketing*, 6, 3, 269–77.

Torres, I. M., and Briggs, E. (2005), 'Does Hispanic targeted advertising work for services?', *Journal of Services Marketing*, 19, 3, 150–7.

Udell, J. G. (1964), 'A new approach to consumer motivation', *Journal of Retailing*, Winter, 6–10.

Webber, R. (2006), 'The use of personal and family names to target consumers of particular cultural, ethnic or linguistic origins'. Presented at the *MRS Census and Geodemographics Group seminar on Geography and People: How Academic Theory has Evolved into Business Benefit*, 27 November 2006, Society of Chemical Industry, London, retrieve from www.mrs.org.uk/networking/cgg/downloads/richardwebber.pdf, accessed 26 October 2009.

Wells, W. D., and Gubar, G. (1966), 'Life cycle concept in marketing research', *Journal of Marketing Research*, 3 (November), 355–63.

Woodward, D. (2006), 'You're a celebrity, get me out of this', *Director*, 59, 6, 58–61.

4 Marketing Research

Learning Outcomes

After reading this chapter, you will be able to:

▶ Define the terms market research and marketing research

▶ Explain the use of marketing information systems

▶ Explain the role marketing research plays in the decision-making process of a business and the range of research approaches that might be used

▶ Recognize the importance of ethics and the adoption of a Code of Conduct when undertaking marketing research

▶ Understand the concept of equivalence in relation to obtaining comparable data

▶ Describe the problems arising when coordinating international marketing research

▶ Case Insight 4.1

The i to i research agency conducted market research to help the London Organising Committee of the Olympic Games (LOCOG) win public support during the bid process for London to hold the Games in 2012. We speak to CEO, Claire Spencer, to find out more.

Claire Spencer for i to i research

Since the creation of the Olympic Movement in 1894, Britain has been a strong protagonist, playing host to the Games in 1908 and 1948, and sending hundreds of British Olympians to compete. In the intervening years, Britain made two unsuccessful bids before London was nominated Official Candidate City for the 2012 Games in May 2004. In 2004 and 2005, the London organization produced a compelling case for London to host the 2012 Olympic Games in what Mike Lee, Director of Communications, called the 'most competitive ever bidding procedure mounted by the IOC'.

It was crucial that the London 2012 team convinced the 117-strong International Olympic Committee (IOC) voting members that London had the potential to deliver on the five selection criteria: i) the best Olympic Plan; ii) low-risk delivery; iii) an enthusiastic country; iv) clear benefits of holding the Games in London; v) a professional, likeable, and trustworthy team. In order to persuade the 117 IOC members that London met the five selection criteria, the London 2012 organization embarked

on a large-scale communications programme both internationally and within the UK.

However, London was challenged with one particular selection criterion: the games had to be held by an 'enthusiastic country', which, quite frankly, it had not been. Compared to the level of public support for the games in competing cities (Paris, Moscow, New York, and Madrid), London's enthusiasm was low. With public support hovering around the 60–70% mark, there was always the question of what did the other 30–40% think? LOCOG felt that there was a need to commission marketing research to help them develop a communication campaign to generate a more enthusiastic public, partly by encouraging the public to register their support for the bid by petition. Specifically, the research would need to aid evaluation of LOCOG's communication campaign in terms of: 1) were the right messages being communicated to engender support and registration for London to host the Games? 2) which part of the campaign was working/not working in terms of, for example, advertising (which media), and PR (which stories)?

i to i research
brand communications evaluation

i to i research logo

If you were creating the research programme for bid team of the London Organising Committee of the Olympic Games to help them improve London's support for the bid, how would you design the research programme?

Introduction

What's the most persuasive ad you've seen recently? How do companies make such useful products? Most of us take it for granted that great companies make great products, using their intuition, and that's why they're great. But, more often than not, companies develop extraordinary goods and services through rigorous research programmes designed to identify customers' constantly changing needs. These goods and services don't design themselves. They are made in the light of the knowledge that market research can bring to our understanding of customers' needs and wants. We start this chapter with an outline of the origins of market research beginning at the start of the twentieth century. Along with advertising, market research is one of the key sub-disciplines of marketing practice and a fundamental component of the marketing philosophy. In fact, we cannot really implement the marketing concept without it.

Marketing research is affected by the rate of change of technology, affecting how, where, and when we ask questions (see Chapter 17). We have chosen to call this chapter 'Marketing research' rather than 'Market research' because whereas market research is conducted with a view to understanding markets—customers, competitors, and industries—marketing research is conducted to determine the impact of marketing strategies and tactics in addition to determining information on customers, competitors, and industries. Marketing research subsumes (i.e. includes) market research. In this chapter, we provide a definition of what marketing research is, before proceeding to outline the research process including how and why it is conducted and commissioned. We outline how research is conducted and commissioned. In this chapter, we discuss **marketing information systems**, including a discussion of the development of the field of **competitive intelligence**, where companies obtain information legally on their competitors' trading activities to inform their marketing strategies. We discuss the problems and challenges of conducting international marketing research, a complex field because of the need to ensure that data obtained from one country are comparable to that from another if it is to be used properly in organizational decision-making. Finally, we discuss the problems inherent in conducting international marketing research.

The exact genesis of market research is unknown but we could probably state that the first systematic data-collection exercise began with the census of the Chinese people around AD 2. In Britain, the first serious survey was by William the Conqueror, who commissioned the Doomsday Book in AD 1085 to discover the extent of land and resources to determine suitable tax rates. However, the first official census of people, rather than land, took place in Britain in AD 1801 (Anon., 1989). Techniques used to collect large-scale demographic information have informed the techniques used later to understand consumer tastes. Determining when the first marketing research department was established is difficult to determine. One former Procter & Gamble (P&G) executive suggests that it was the economic research department established at P&G to 'help anticipate fluctuations in the commodity market'. Dr Paul Smelser, within this unit, then very shortly afterwards established the company's first Market Research Department in 1924 (Stevens, 2003). But 'serious research into consumer tastes, habits and buying patterns took off in the years following World War I' (Arvidsson, 2004). One of the best-known figures in the development of marketing research was George Gallup (1901–84), the American public opinion analyst who invented the Gallup opinion poll and founded the American Institute for Public Opinion in 1936 (Anon., 1989). His work used statistics to measure reader interest in magazine and newspaper advertisements. Another pioneer was Arthur Charles Nielson, Sr., who established A. C. Nielson in Chicago in 1923, a large international company best known for its broadcast measurement systems for television audience ratings (A. C. Nielson, 2007).

Definitions of Marketing Research

Marketing research is used to obtain information that provides the management of a company or organization with sufficient insight to make more informed decisions on future activities. It follows the philosophical premise of marketing that for a business or organization to be successful, an organization must understand the motivations, desires, and behaviour of its customers and consumers. However, there is sometimes confusion between the terms market and marketing research. The International Chamber of Commerce (ICC)/European Society for Opinion and Market Research (ESOMAR) multipart definition of marketing research stresses that:

> Marketing research is a key element within the total field of marketing information. It links the consumer, customer and the public to the marketer through information which is used to identify and define marketing opportunities and problems; generate, refine and evaluate marketing actions; improve understanding of marketing as a process and of the ways in which specific marketing activities can be made more effective. Marketing research specifies the information required to address these issues; designs the method for collecting information; manages and implements the data-collection process; analyses the results; and communicates the findings and their implications (ESOMAR, 1995).

This definition of marketing research has also been adopted, with modifications, by the American Marketing Association (AMA, 2009), who add that marketing research is used to monitor marketing performance. The Market Research Society (MRS), in the UK, defines market research as:

> The collection and analysis of data from a sample or census of individuals or organisations relating to their characteristics, behaviour, attitudes, opinions or possessions. It includes all forms of market, opinion and social research such as consumer and industrial surveys, psychological investigations, qualitative interviews and group discussions, observational, ethnographic and **panel studies** (MRS, 2010).

So, market research is work undertaken to determine either structural characteristics of the industry of concern (e.g. demand, market share, market volumes, customer characteristics, and segmentation), whereas marketing research is work undertaken to understand how to make specific marketing strategy decisions such as for pricing, sales forecasting, product testing, and promotion research (Chisnall, 1992).

go online

Visit the **Online Resource Centre** and follow the weblinks to the MRS and ESOMAR to learn more about these professional marketing research associations.

Even though marketing research is the foundational element of modern marketing practice, market research is valued by some companies more than others. For example, companies tend to spend between 0.5% and 1% of their revenues on research when they would be better off spending more to use the research to fine-tune their advertising and promotion (Kotler,

2005). The difficulty is that it is not always easy to interpret what the research is trying to say (see Market Insight 4.1).

▶ Market Insight 4.1

Dyson: What to Do When the Research Sucks!

In 2008, in Sweden, there were 97 vacuum cleaners per 100 households, 99 per 100 households in the United Arab Emirates, 98 vacuum cleaners per 100 households in the USA, 26 per 100 households in China, excluding Hong Kong, where there are around 84 per 100 households, and 30 per 100 households in India. Clearly, in most Western and many Eastern markets, the vacuum cleaner is a household accessory. By 2008, the West European market for vacuum cleaners was worth US$5.2bn and had grown 74% over the period 2003–8. The world market for vacuum cleaners by contrast was worth US$14.6bn and had grown 60% over the same period. But the vacuum cleaner wasn't always so common.

The growth in the market is at least partly based on the success of the Dyson vacuum cleaner and its innovative bagless machines. When James Dyson decided to reinvent the vacuum cleaner using a clear bagless bin on the front of his machine, the DC01, market research indicated that customers would not buy it because they did not want to see the dirt being sucked up the tube! Despite hawking his design around numerous major names in the vacuum cleaner business, no one was interested. But customer inertia around new products is common with revolutionary products and services: they do not test well because we are measuring the new product or service against what consumers are currently familiar with rather than how they might behave in the future.

In other words, consumers don't always know what they want, so it's a good job inventors sometimes do!

The bagless vacuum cleaner from Dyson

In 1993, James Dyson launched his Dual Cyclone™ vacuum cleaner, and became the UK market leader within two years and market leader in Western Europe shortly after. So much for the negative research then; it's a good job James Dyson ignored it!

Source: Euromonitor, 2009.

1 In this case, Dyson was wise to disregard the research. Under what circumstances should you do this?

2 How would you go about researching people's needs for high-technology products? What questions do you ask when people don't know what they want?

3 Can you think of any products/services that you didn't like initially but changed your mind after use? How would you go about designing research to determine whether or not people would be likely to adopt a new product/service?

Marketing Information Systems

The purpose of using marketing information is to provide us with timely information on a continuous basis, to support our decision-making. But what kind of information do we actually need as marketers? Typically, we might have the following information needs:

▶ aggregated marketing information in quarterly, annual summaries;

▶ aggregated marketing information around product/markets (e.g. sales data);

▶ analytical information for decision models (e.g. SWOT, segmentation analyses);

▶ internally focused marketing information (e.g. sales, costs, marketing performance indicators);

▶ externally focused marketing information (e.g. macro and industry trends);

▶ historical information (e.g. sales, profitability, market trends);

▶ future-oriented marketing information (e.g. environmental scanning information);

▶ quantitative marketing information (e.g. costs, profit, market share); and

▶ qualitative marketing information (e.g. buyer behaviour, competitor strategy information) (Ashill and Jobber, 2001).

Such information as outlined above could be provided on both a continuous and an ad hoc basis. Continuous information on industry trends can be gleaned from Mintel reports and other secondary data sources. However, the market research manager needs to remember to both buy the reports and input the data into a suitable marketing information system (MkIS). Other information may be obtained on an ad-hoc basis through commissioning specialist market research projects such as for pricing or segmentation research. This also needs to be fed into the MkIS to provide the company with an up-to-date picture of its marketing environment and customer base. The qualitative information related to competitor strategy information might be gleaned from sales reports or reports from overseas agents, for example. The key difficulty for the marketing manager is to obtain and customize the marketing information system to fit their company's specific needs (as the needs will probably change according to their industry), and to ensure that the data is input on a timely and continuous basis. Axelrod (1970) suggests adherence to the following 14 basic rules for building a MkIS:

1 get the top management involved;

2 set the objective for the system carefully;

3 figure out what decisions your MkIS will influence;

4 communicate the benefits of the system to users;

5 hire and motivate the right people;

6 free the MkIS from accounting domination;

7 develop the system on a gradual and systematic basis;

8 run a new MkIS in parallel with existing procedures;

9 provide results from the system to users quickly after its initiation;

10 provide information on a fast turnaround basis;

11 tie the MkIS with existing data-collection procedures;

12 balance the work of the MkIS between development and operations;

13 feed valid meaningful data into the system not useless information; and

14 design a security system to ensure different groups get different access to the information.

More recently, there has been a strong trend towards using customer relationship management (CRM) systems (see Chapter 15), to mine customer data, particularly when undertaking research into characterizing customer groups and their product/service usage. Britain's largest supermarket group Tesco, has for a long time used dunnhumby—a customer analytics agency—to analyse its customer and point-of-sale data. dunnhumby processes around 5 billion items of information per week for Tesco (McCawley, 2006) or about 156 items of information per week for every household in Britain. Each customer has a unique profile of past purchase transactions linked to lifestyle data derived from their address details. This information allows Tesco to determine the importance and use of price promotions, the degree of promotional cherry-picking (i.e. buying a product only when it is on special offer), the portfolio of products a customer purchases, how much they spend on their groceries, and other issues using a process it calls 'basket analysis' (Humby, 2007). In this situation, data and use of data become a strategic asset to the firm, allowing Tesco to differentiate itself from competitors through highly effective loyalty marketing programmes designed to reward customers for shopping at Tesco stores, providing them with coupons and offers on items of specific interest to them, in addition to a full range of the types of goods that they know the customer likes, in a store format they know the customer appreciates.

▶ Research Insight 4.1

To take your learning further, you might wish to read this influential paper.

Montgomery, D. B., and Weinberg, C. B. (1992), 'Toward strategic intelligence systems', *Journal of Marketing*, 43, 4 (Autumn), 41–52.

This article was written in the pre-computer era, nevertheless the authors provide amazing insights into the process of setting up a strategic intelligence system, outlining what data should be collected, the procedures to be used to collect the data, and how data are transformed into intelligence. Sources of intelligence include government, competitors, suppliers, customers, professional associations, company personnel, and other sources. The authors argue that data can be turned into intelligence through any of the following processes: by movement from outside the organization to another form within the organization, by accumulation, by aggregation (with other data), through analysis, and by being mixed into the organization's activities to provide intelligence.

 Visit the **Online Resource Centre** to read the abstract and access the full paper.

Companies are frequently swimming in data but have no means to convert the data into competitive intelligence or no means to store the data and provide it to end users at the appropriate point. One area of research that has become more prevalent in the last ten years is that of competitive intelligence. Competitive intelligence is defined as 'the organised, professional approach to collection, analysis, and distribution of timely, accurate, and useful information as intelligence products—intelligence that contributes materially to the achievement of strategic and tactical business objectives, as defined by the leadership of an enterprise' (Nolan, 1999). We outline it here because it provides useful information in strategic decision-making in addition to standard market research information. There are various techniques used, which include:

▶ using remote psychological assessment tools to build profiles of business opponents;

▶ collecting competitive intelligence at trade shows and conferences;

▶ collecting information on rivals from their customers and suppliers using **elicitation techniques**; and

▶ collecting intelligence on rivals from third parties using elicitation techniques.

Commissioning Marketing Research

Whether or not an organization conducts its own market research or commissions it externally depends largely on the size of the organization and the type of products/services it handles. Many large companies employ market research agencies to conduct their research for them, although equally very large companies often do much of their own. Those companies that do have their own departments either have a small group in charge of commissioning the research from agencies or a larger department that has the facilities to undertake its own research.

Depending on the ability and experience of the executives within the department, they may carry out some functions themselves, e.g. writing the questionnaire and/or the report, while leaving the sampling, and the fieldwork, **coding**, and data analysis, to an agency; the latter is called 'field and tab' (short for tabulation) in market research industry jargon. These executives will have responsibility for selecting the agency and controlling the quality of their work, including keeping the time schedule.

The main advantage of using agencies is that it is relatively cheap compared with undertaking the research in-house and collecting the data independently. The fixed cost of recruiting, training, and maintaining a large panel of interviewers and specialist staff is considerable, as is the effort expended. Agencies spread these costs over numerous projects throughout the year. Many agencies also specialize in a particular technique and excel in these niches.

An important difference is the fact that they stand independently from the client's own staff in the research design and reporting and so can be more objective. The main disadvantage of using agencies is that the agency sometimes cannot achieve the depth of knowledge of the client's problems, product or market, unless it offers a niche specialism in this area. In many syndicated surveys (e.g. **retail audits** and **omnibus surveys**), several rival organizations buy the same data from the agency, so that a cost-effective survey can be carried out.

In order to commission market research, the client must determine whether or not he or she wants to commission an agency, a consultant, a field and tabulation agency, or a data preparation and analysis agency (who unlike field and tab do not undertake the fieldwork). Typically, a consultant might be used for a small job that does not require extensive fieldwork, a field and tab agency when the organization can design its own research but not undertake the data collection, a data preparation and analysis agency when it can both design and collect the data but does not have the expertise to analyse it, and a **full-service agency** when it does not have the expertise to design the research, and collect or analyse the data.

Agencies are usually shortlisted according to some criteria and then asked to make a presentation of their services. Visits are made to their premises to check the quality of their staff and facilities, and previous reports may be considered to assess the quality of the organization's work. Permission to interview or obtain references from some of their other clients may also be requested. Each agency would be evaluated on its ability to carry out work of an acceptable quality at an appropriate price. The criteria used to evaluate the agencies' suitability, once they have submitted a proposal, might include the following:

▶ the agency's reputation;

▶ the agency's perceived expertise;

▶ whether the study offers value for money;

▶ the time taken to complete the study; and

▶ the likelihood that the research design will provide insights into the **management problem**.

Shortlisted agencies are given a preliminary outline of the client's needs in a **research brief** and asked to provide proposals on research methodology, timing, and costs. After this, we would then select an agency to do the market research work required.

▶ Research Insight 4.2

To take your learning further, you might wish to read this influential paper.

Moorman, C., Zaltmann, G., and Desphandé, R. (1992), 'Relationships between providers and users of market research: the dynamics of trust within and between organisations', *Journal of Marketing Research*, **29, 3, 314–28.**

In this highly cited article, the authors investigate the role of trust between market research users and providers, developing a theory of user–provider relationships focused on personal trust. The authors indicate that trust and perceived quality of interaction between the research user and the provider contribute most to the research findings actually being implemented. In other words, use market researchers that you think are highly reputable and develop a good working relationship with them because this will ensure the research is more operationalizable.

 Visit the **Online Resource Centre** to read the abstract and access the full paper.

The Marketing Research Brief

The research brief is a formal document prepared by a client organization submitted to the marketing research agency. When marketing research is conducted in-house, the department manager who requires the research prepares a brief for the marketing research manager. The brief should outline a management problem to be investigated (see Market Insight 4.2 for an example). The typical contents of a research brief might include the following:

▶ Background summary—providing a brief introduction and details about the company and its products and/or services that the organization offers.

▶ The management problem—a clear statement of why the research should be undertaken and what business decisions are dependent upon its outcome.

▶ The marketing research questions—a detailed list of the information necessary in order to make the decisions outlined above.

▶ The intended scope of the research—the areas to be covered, which industries, type of customer, etc. should be provided. The brief should give an indication of when the information is required and explain why that date is important (e.g. pricing research required for a sales forecast meeting).

▶ Tendering procedures—the client organization should outline how agencies are to be selected as a result of the tendering process. Specific information may be required such as CVs from agency personnel to be involved in the study, and referee contact addresses. The number of copies of the report required and preferences with regard to layout are usually also outlined.

▶ Market Insight 4.2

Private Jet Service Insight: The Brief

Hank Sopel is the managing director of TaxiJet, a start-up private jet company, operating out of London Luton airport. He has managed to obtain around £30m of private equity and investor funding to launch a new private jet airline service, principally operating from the UK to Europe at the customer's choice of time and locations (inbound and outbound). However, before he launches he wants to know much more about the type of service his potential customers want so that he can:

1 Understand how current private jet users and European business class flyers use existing airline services at present and their purchasing motives.

2 Understand how he should develop his promotional approach to generate awareness of the new service to existing private jet users and potential switcher clients prepared to upgrade from flying European business class with commercial scheduled airlines.

3 Determine how to custom-design the service to meet his potential clients' needs.

An important feature of the new service is that the private jets Hank intends to use are based on a new breed of very light jets (VLJs), typified by the Cessna Citation Mustang, which are cheaper to purchase, maintain, and operate, not least because they fly at a higher altitude, use less fuel and are made of lighter

▶ Market Insight 4.2

Private jet: the ultimate flying experience

material. These jets, however, are smaller than many existing private jets, providing seating for only six persons, (including two pilots), with a flying range of up to three hours, potentially taking clients to most parts of Europe reaching up to Turkey in the East and Moscow in Russia. Because of the lower costs of operation and the smaller size of the plane, there is a feeling that this new breed of jet could open the market up for private jet travel, positioning it somewhere just above first class (in flexibility, comfort and convenience) and around business class (in terms of in-flight services such as meals and entertainment) when compared to existing scheduled airline services. Hank also recognizes that the economic situation in the UK is not strong, given the unwelcome media attention displayed on the reportage of the use of private jets by companies in financial difficulties (e.g. General Motors in the USA). He wants to understand more about his potential clients' purchasing motives in the current market environment. There is also a

feeling that, despite the economic difficulties, there is still a profitable market for private jet use, especially among high net worth individuals travelling for business and leisure purposes. He also wants to know whether there is a need for other specific add-on services including limousines to and from London, for example. Sopel invites in representatives of Dynamic Research Limited (DRL) and spends two hours briefing them before asking them to prepare a proposal.

Source: Market Research Society (MRS). Reproduced with kind permission.

1 Do you think this brief has clear research objectives? Why do you say this?

2 Does the research brief indicate or imply that a specific methodology should be used? If so, which method does it imply?

3 Do you think the research objectives are feasible given the budget requirements? Why do you say this?

The Marketing Research Process

There are a number of basic stages in the process that should guide any marketing research project. These are outlined in Figure 4.1. The first, and most crucial, stage of the process involves problem definition, and setting the information needs of the decision-makers. The client organization explains the basis of the problem(s) it faces to the market research agency/consultant/internal company research department. This might be the need to understand market volumes in a potential new market or the reason for an unexpected, sudden increase in uptake of a product. Problem definition does not always imply threats facing the organization. The initial stage allows the organization to assess its current position, to define its information needs, and to make informed decisions about its future.

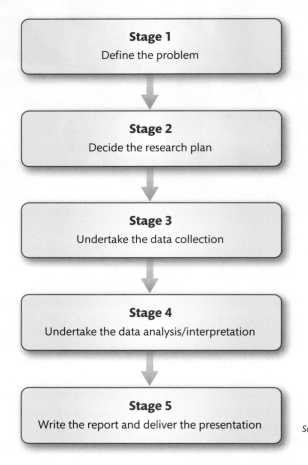

Figure 4.1

Marketing research process

Source: Adapted from Baines and Chansarkar (2002). © John Wiley & Sons. Reproduced with permission.

Stage 1. Problem Definition

This process occurs when an organization provides a marketing research brief defining the management problem. Typically, but not always, the problem is described in vague terms as organizations are not always sure what information they are looking for. An example might be the Carrefour supermarket chain explaining that sales are not as strong as expected in

Carrefour, the iconic French supermarket group, Czech Republic
Source: Carrefour.

one of their new stores in the Czech Republic and wondering whether or not this is due to the emergence of a new competitor supermarket nearby. This problem is shown in Figure 4.2. The marketing researcher then needs to translate the management problem into a marketing research question. This subsequent description of the problem provides the market researcher with relatively little depth of understanding of the situation in which the supermarket finds itself, so, the market researcher then needs to discuss the problem with the staff commissioning the study to shed further light on the situation. This leads to the development of a marketing research question. This question may include a number of sub-questions for further exploration. A possible, very general, marketing research question and a number of more specific sub-questions are shown in Figure 4.3.

Figure 4.2

Example of a management problem

> ### Management problem
>
> Sales at the new store have not met management expectations, possibly due to the emergence of a new competitor

The marketing research question transforms the management problem into a question while trying to remove any assumptions made by the management of the organization. Sometimes, the management problem is clear. The organization needs a customer profile, an industry profile, an understanding of buyer behaviour, or to test advertising concepts for its next TV advertising campaign and so on. The more clearly the commissioning organization defines the management problem, the easier it will be to design the research to solve that problem. Once the agency has discussed the brief with the client, the agency provides a detailed outline of how they intend to investigate the problem. This document is called the research proposal. Figure 4.4 briefly outlines a typical marketing **research proposal** and Market Insight 4.3 provides an example.

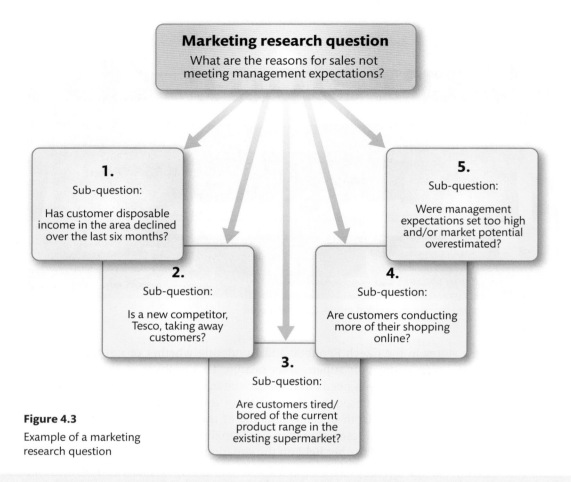

Figure 4.3

Example of a marketing research question

▶ Market Insight 4.3

Private Jet Service Insight: The Proposal

Client's information needs

The client, TaxiJet, a start-up airline company is looking to exploit new technologies in aircraft structure and design (the very light jet, VLJ) in the airline market, which potentially could create a new market for private jet services that might appeal to both existing private jet consumers and airline business class users. TaxiJet wish to understand its customers' primary motivations for selecting a scheduled airline or private jet provider, what decision-making process do they follow and what services do they desire?

Research objectives

The research objectives are to determine:

1   What are the benefit attributes, real and perceived, when/where existing private airline services are sourced and bought and how might the customer base be segmented?

2   What are competing alternatives at present?

3   How are airline services are generally sourced?

4   What are the deciding and relevant factor(s) when choosing a particular supplier?

5   What promotional methods do existing and potential private jet users respond to most?

▶ Market Insight 4.3

6 What features do current and potential private jet users desire in the service offered by private jet operators?

7 When do private jet users fly for leisure and when do they fly for business and what are their service requirements?

Research programme proposed

Initially, a two-stage research programme is recommended, involving qualitative and quantitative research aimed principally at current and potential private jet users (rather than at companies' procurement departments). We recommend that the qualitative research be carried out before the quantitative stage so that the findings can inform the design of the quantitative phase and include the testing of the questionnaire (with respondents who allow further contact for research purposes to be followed up for pre-testing).

Qualitative phase
Sampling

We propose to undertake 20 in-depth telephone interviews (at a pre-arranged time at the respondents' convenience). The respondents will be current or potential users of private jet services from the UK to the EU (i.e. the target group). Current users should have flown by private jet at least once in the last 12 months. The potential customer group will be identified as those who flew business class to European destinations more than once in the last six months. The sampling is illustrated below.

Group	No. to be interviewed
Existing European business class customers	10
Existing private jet customers	10

The sample will be identified in association with the client but it is envisaged that a snowball sampling approach will be used where high net worth respondents are selected initially through the company's contact database and then further respondents are selected through referral from the initial set of respondents. To encourage respondents to take part in the study, they will be offered the inducement of a £20 gift to a charity of their choice.

Data analysis

The qualitative data will be fully transcribed before analysis. The analysis will particularly focus around the customer purchase process, motivations for purchase and benefits sought when flying with a view to identifying potential market segments for later testing in the quantitative phase. This phase of the research will particularly focus on identifying the answers to research questions 1–3, and 6–7.

Quantitative research

For this stage, we propose to conduct a postal survey of very high net worth individuals. Although this group are not necessarily users of private jet services, they are able to afford private jet services, and are most likely to use them and be interested in using them in future.

Sampling

We would target high net worth individuals who live in houses (with a council tax band value of more than £1m) within a 40-mile catchment area of Luton airport.

Data are available from the civil aviation authority on numbers of people flying leisure and business class within specific local authority areas, allowing us to target areas with the highest numbers of business class travellers. We would select specific areas within the catchment area initially on a simple random basis. Our sample frame will be built using data purchased from a private list provider (classified using postcode data to identify differing lifestyle segments) cross-referenced with lists of named high net worth individuals in identified areas. We propose to send out questionnaires (with postage paid reply envelopes) to a simple random sample of 12,500 from our sample frame (anticipating a 4% response) offering an inducement of entry into a competition for a free two-hour private jet flight card (worth around £3,000) for five respondents selected at random. A second wave of questionnaires will be sent out if we fail to achieve our expected sample of 500 respondents. We

▶ Market Insight 4.3 (continued)

would send out a further batch of questionnaires to respondents in other local authority catchment areas not included in the original sample (but still within the 40-mile radius of Luton airport). A covering letter explaining who should complete the survey and explaining the eligibility criteria will be included.

Data analysis

The quantitative data will be analysed using SPSS software. This phase of the research will particularly focus on identifying the answers to research questions 1, 4, and 5. Key choice criteria will be identified for specific flyer segments, including existing and potential private jet users. In the event that we need to conduct a second wave of fieldwork, we would compare respondents in the first and second waves on key demographics and attitudinal dimensions to determine whether or not there are any differences.

Reporting

A full debrief on the qualitative stage will be available three weeks after the end of the field work. A Powerpoint presentation and topline report of the findings of the quantitative stage will be made six weeks after the end of the fieldwork period.

Costing and schedule

Qualitative phase (20 in-depth
interviews @ £750 each)   = £15,000

Quantitative phase (500 interviews
@ £65 per interview)   = £32,500

Total = £47,500 + value added tax

We suggest the study is undertaken over a six-week period beginning in September 2010, prior to the January 2011 launch of the new service.

Source: The authors wish to thank the Market Research Society for permission to publish this material.

1 **How does the proposal compare with the brief in Market Insight 4.2?**

2 **Do you think a postal survey is the most appropriate way of reaching high net worth individuals? What other approach might you select?**

3 **Do you think the research objectives are feasible given the budget requirements? Why do you say this?**

The basic structure and contents of a typical research proposal should include the following:

▶ **Executive Summary**—a brief summary of the research project including the major outcomes and findings. Rarely more than one page in length. It allows the reader to obtain a summary of the main points of the project without having to read the full report.

▶ **Background to the Research**—an outline of the problem or situation and the issues surrounding this problem. This section demonstrates the researcher's understanding of the management problem.

▶ **Research Objectives**—an outline of the objectives of the research project including the data to be generated and how this will be used to address the management problem.

▶ **Research Design**—a clear non-technical description of the research type adopted and the specific techniques to be used to gather the required information. This will include details on data-collection instruments, sampling procedures and analytical techniques.

▶ **Personnel Specification**—the details of the people involved in the collection and analysis of the data, providing a named liaison person and outlining the company's credibility in undertaking the work.

▶ **Time Schedule**—an outline of the time requirements with dates for the various stages to completion and presentation of results.

▶ **Costs**—a detailed analysis of the costs involved in the project is usually included for large projects or simply a total cost for the project.

▶ **References**—typically three references are outlined so that a client can be sure that an agency has the requisite capability to do the job in hand.

Figure 4.4

A marketing research proposal outline

Stage 2. Decide the Research Plan

At this stage, we decide whether or not to undertake primary or secondary research or both. Often, we might undertake an initial phase of secondary research to see whether someone has considered the same research question we now encounter. So, if we had recently bought a new cinema and wanted to know the types of people that lived in the local area, we could consult secondary data sources, which could tell us more about the characteristics of people living in the area (e.g. gender, age, population size). However, if we wanted to know what types of films they prefer, we might resort to a survey of a sample of the population.

Primary versus Secondary Research

Primary research is research conducted for the first time, involving the collection of data for the purpose of a particular project. Secondary data is second-hand data, collected for someone else's purposes. **Secondary research**, known also as **desk research**, involves gaining access to the results or outcomes of previous research projects, which is useful if someone else has carried out a project that already provides answers to the client's management problem. This method can be a cheaper and more efficient process of data collection. We can do a large amount of secondary research free by visiting a business library or searching the internet. Other sources of secondary data include the following:

▶ Government sources: including export databases, government statistical offices, social trend databases, and other resources.

▶ The internet: including sources identified using search engines, blogs, and discussion groups.

▶ Company internal records: including information housed in a marketing information/CRM system (see Chapter 15) or published reports. Where no formal marketing information system exists, we would identify sales reports, marketing plans, and research reports previously commissioned.

▶ Professional bodies and trade associations: these organizations frequently have databases available for research purposes, online, which may include industry magazine articles, and research reports.

▶ Market research companies: these organizations frequently undertake research into industry sectors or specific product groups and can be highly specialized. Examples include Mintel, Euromonitor, and ICC Keynote.

go online

Visit the **Online Resource Centre** and follow the weblinks to learn more about these market research organizations.

In practice, most research projects involve a combination of secondary and primary research, with a desk research phase occurring at the beginning to ensure that a company is not wasting its money on research that has already been conducted. Thus, primary research is undertaken to cover the gaps in a company's knowledge once all available secondary data has been evaluated. Once this initial insight is gleaned, we determine whether or not to commission a primary data study. Assuming primary research needs to be undertaken, researchers usually design their research by considering what type of research to employ. Marketing directors need to have some understanding of the different types of study that can be conducted because this has an impact on the type of information to be collected, and hence, the data that they receive to help them solve their management problem.

Categories of Research Design

Generally speaking, we define three categories of research design: exploratory, descriptive, and causal. These categories specify the procedure adopted for collection and analysis of the data necessary to identify a management problem.

1 **Exploratory research** is used when little is known about a particular management problem and to discover the general nature of the questions that might relate to it. Exploratory designs enable the development of hypotheses. We tend to adopt qualitative methods, e.g. focus groups, in-depth interviews, **projective techniques**, and **observational studies**. Exploratory research also makes use of secondary data, **non-probability** (subjective) **samples**, case analyses, and subjective evaluation of the resultant data.

2 **Descriptive research** focuses on accurately describing the variables being considered. It uses quantitative methods, particularly questionnaire surveys (on- and offline), for example, in consumer profile studies, product usage studies, price surveys, attitude surveys, sales analyses, and media research.

3 **Causal research** is used when there is a need to determine whether one variable causes an effect in another variable. For example, if we were interested in determining whether temperature increases cause Coca-Cola sales to increase we might use this method. Studies into the determination of advertising effectiveness and customer attitude changes are other examples. Causal designs make use of control variables or groups to allow meaningful comparisons between the outcomes of the treatment group (where a variable is manipulated) and the control group (where it is not). An example might be to use slight manipulations of price increases to determine their effect, if any, on sales. The difficulty arises in determining whether or not the sales effect was caused by the price increase, or some other unmeasured variable, e.g. an increase in compensation for the salespeople.

Qualitative Versus Quantitative Research

At the beginning of a research project, we might consider whether to use qualitative research or quantitative research or some combination of the two. The two main forms of research are outlined in Figure 4.5, along with the techniques associated with each main form of research. Whereas quantitative research techniques, such as surveys, emphasize theory testing, qualitative techniques are used to identify meaning and understanding. The client, or the in-house marketing research manager, may have specific budget constraints or an idea of which particular approach they wish to adopt. However, the choice really depends on the circumstances of the research project and its objectives. If a lot is known about the management problem either from past research or experience, then it may be more appropriate to use quantitative research to understand the problem further and determine the full extent of the problem. If there is little pre-understanding of the management problem, the researcher may wish to explore the problem further using qualitative research to gather insights.

Quantitative research methods, e.g. the survey questionnaire, are designed to elicit responses to pre-determined, standardized questions from a large number of respondents. This involves collecting information from many people, quantifying the responses as frequencies or percentages, and descriptive statistics, and statistically analysing them. Other quantitative research methods include mass observation techniques and experiments. Experiments are designed to determine cause and effect relationships, particularly in psychological studies. More recently, structural equation modelling has become a common technique to identify how variables interact and relate to each other. **Mystery shopping** is a common research technique, used particularly in retailing (on- and offline), where consumers are recruited by researchers to act as anonymous buyers in order to evaluate customer satisfaction, service quality, and the customer's own evaluation of their experiences. In contrast, **qualitative research** techniques are typically used at the preliminary stages of a research project to identify the basic factors affecting the management problem. The most common forms of qualitative research are discussion groups and in-depth interviews. Projective techniques can also be used in both forms. Qualitative research techniques attempt to uncover the underlying motivations behind consumers' opinions, attitudes, perceptions, and behaviour. Consequently, they adopt unstructured methods to elicit information from respondents. We would use a number of basic issues to guide the research but we would not use a structured set of questions for each respondent, as done with surveys.

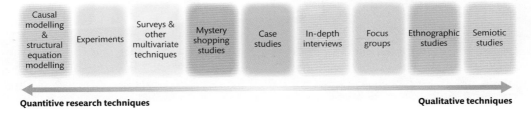

Figure 4.5
A continuum of research techniques

   In the market research industry, the most familiar qualitative techniques are **in-depth interviews**, **focus groups**, and **consumer juries**. The objective is to uncover feelings, attitudes, memories, and interpretations. They can range in form from an informal conversation to highly structured interviews. They might be used to seek an interviewee's perspective on a new campaign or to develop customer profiles covering a wide range of needs and preferences. Focus groups, or **group discussions** as they are more commonly referred to, have been used extensively in the marketing communications industry for many years. They normally consist of a small number of target consumers brought together to discuss elements from the initial concept stage to post-production stage. At the concept stage, the target sample is presented with rough outlines or storyboards (see Chapter 10) giving an idea of the campaign or campaigns under consideration. A professional moderator aims to understand the thoughts, feelings, and attitudes of the group towards a product or service, media, or message. Consumer juries consist, as do focus groups, of a collection of target consumers who are asked to rank in order ideas or concepts put to them and to explain their choices. In addition to these common qualitative techniques there is growing use of more creative qualitative techniques. For example Goulding (2002: 10) describes Semiotic Solutions as a company that 'specializes in cultural qualitative research, drawing upon techniques borrowed from linguistic philosophy, cultural anthropology and the systematic study of signs and codes' (see Chapter 18). The company's research has formed the basis of many national and international television campaigns and brand repositioning exercises for organizations such as British Telecommunications (BT), Tesco, and Coca-Cola. **Ethnographic studies**, which tend

Observational research, big brother or big insight?

to use in-depth interviewing methods and/or observational methods, are currently in vogue, although it is unlikely that many research agencies submerge themselves in consumer culture as deeply as perhaps they should (see Market Insight 4.4). **Semiotic** research is another qualitative research approach aimed at understanding consumer culture, which, instead of interviewing or observing people, analyses the content of advertisements and other texts to identify the meaning of the signs and symbols contained. (See Chapter 18 for a more detailed treatment of the topic of semiotics.)

▶ Market Insight 4.4

Guinness Drinking: The Irish Way?

Context-Based Research Group is a specialist research agency, set up in 1999, which focuses on providing clients with insights and meaning from ethnographic research, based in Baltimore in the USA. Its research uses the participant observation methodology, which involves spending time watching people as they go about their lives, observing what they do, in a natural setting. Ethnographic research findings are then delivered in the participants' own words from the perspective of how whatever is being researched fits into their lives (Context Research Group, 2009).

▶ Market Insight 4.4

Worshipping the stout god, Guinness
Source: Courtesy of Diageo Plc.

Context-Based Research Group undertook work for Guinness UDV, the Irish stout producer, by focusing on the Guinness experience in Ireland. Context felt it was fundamental to employ a team of Irish anthropologists who live, work, and study Irish culture in Ireland. Drawing on their proprietary network of professional ethnographers around the world, they assembled a team of Irish ethnographers, who acted as cultural insiders, to conduct a series of participatory research programmes. Working closely with Guinness UDV, Context's anthropologists in the USA directed and led the analysis of the data, while also making field trips to Dublin pubs for additional participant observation with Guinness customers.

The research helped Guinness UDV to understand trends in consumer attitudes and behaviour around the Guinness brand better, and provided numerous recommendations to help Guinness strengthen their long-term relationships with customers within their domestic market. As the Guinness brand is based on its Irish heritage, getting the experience right for its home customers is a first step to satisfying its international customers. So, it must have been a tough programme of research to conduct! (See also Market Insight 18.5 for details of how Guinness use semiotic analysis in their research.)

Source: Context Research Group (2009).

1 **How would an ethnographic study help us understand Irish Guinness drinking?**

2 **How do you determine marketing implications from data generated from watching a group of Irish Guinness drinkers?**

3 **How difficult do you think it would be to watch the subjects interact and behave without affecting their actions?**

Qualitative techniques generally involve a small number of respondents. The emphasis is on obtaining rich, detailed information from a small group of people rather than short, specific answers from a large group of respondents, as with survey questionnaires. The major characteristics of qualitative and quantitative marketing research techniques are outlined in Table 4.1. Case studies can be qualitative or quantitative depending on the number of case studies used, e.g. the analysis of a number of different markets to develop product lifecycles, for instance, and to note the impact of advertising. So Colgate-Palmolive might well research the product lifecycle of a particular toothpaste brand in Pakistan, India, Turkey, and the UAE, before launching a new brand in India.

Qualitative research is used to uncover underlying motivations for people's behaviour, attitudes, opinions, and perceptions, but because the research approach uses small samples, the results derived from this form of research are not generalizable to the wider population of interest and are used to generate insights only. Group discussions are reliant on the skill of the moderator in generating group interaction.

Quantitative research techniques are used to obtain representative samples to enable generalizability and are based on larger respondent samples, selected either randomly or to match the population. The researcher establishes the level at which the results will reflect the entire population by choosing the number and type of respondents required. One disadvantage of quantitative research is that we typically pre-determine the answers, so there is a chance that respondents do not fully express their true opinions.

▶ **Table 4.1** Qualitative and quantitative research methods compared

Characteristic	Qualitative	Quantitative
Purpose	To identify and understand underlying motivations, memories, attitudes, opinions, perceptions, and behaviours	To determine the representativeness of the sample to the population, i.e. how similar is the sample to the population?
Size of sample	Involves a small number of respondents, typically less than 30	Involves a large number of respondents, more than 30
Type of information generated	Provides detailed information	Provides narrowly defined descriptive information
Degree of structuring	Uses an unstructured approach typically using open questions	Uses a structured questioning process and frequently closed, multiple fixed response questions
Type of data analysis	Uses a non-statistical word (content-based) analysis, e.g. using the NVivo qualitative analysis software	Statistical analysis e.g. using SPSS software
Sampling approach	Uses non-probability sampling methods	Uses probability sampling techniques

Designing the Research Project

When we know what type of research to conduct and if we need secondary data or not to understand the management problem, we should consider the following:

▶ Who to question and how (the sampling plan and procedures to be used)?

▶ What methods to use (e.g. discussion groups or an experiment)?

▶ Which types of questions are required (open questions for qualitative research or closed questions for a survey)?

▶ How should the data be analysed and interpreted (e.g. what approach to data analysis)?

Research methods describe the techniques and procedures we adopt to obtain the necessary information. We could use a survey or a series of in-depth interviews. We might use observation to see how consumers purchase goods online, or how employees greet consumers when they enter a particular shop, i.e. mystery shopping. We could use consumer panels where respondents record their weekly purchases or their TV viewing habits over a specified time period. Fact Finders, an A. C. Nielson company, requests that consumers use specially developed barcode readers (hand-held 'wands') to record their supermarket purchases in return for points, which are redeemed for household goods.

Figure 4.6 indicates the key components we need to consider when designing both qualitative and quantitative research projects. The design of marketing research projects involves determining how each of these components interrelates with the others. The components comprise the following:

▶ research objectives;

▶ the sampling method;

▶ the interviewing method to be used;

▶ the research type and methods undertaken;

▶ the question and questionnaire design;

▶ data analysis.

Each of these components impacts on the others. When designing research projects we must first determine the type of approach to use for a given management problem (e.g. exploratory, descriptive, or causal). Then we would determine which techniques are most capable of producing the desired data at the least cost and in the minimum time period.

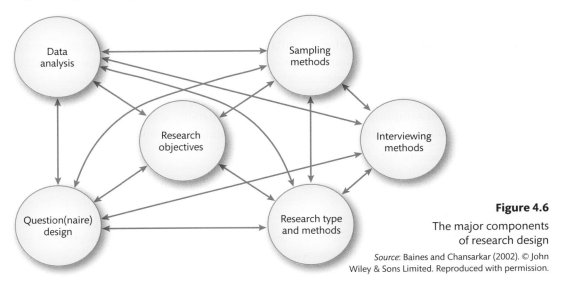

Figure 4.6

The major components of research design

Source: Baines and Chansarkar (2002). © John Wiley & Sons Limited. Reproduced with permission.

In order to determine whether or not we've got the 'right' data, we measure its value by measuring its validity, i.e. do the data correctly describe the phenomenon they are attempting to measure?, and reliability, i.e. would the data be replicated in a future repeat study of the same type? Generally, certain types of research (e.g. exploratory, descriptive, causal) use certain methods and techniques. For instance, exploratory research studies use qualitative research methods, non-probability sampling methods, and non-statistical data analysis methods. Descriptive research projects usually adopt survey interviews using quota or random sampling methods and statistical analysis techniques. Causal researchers use experimental research designs using convenience or **probability sampling** methods and statistical data analysis procedures.

Stage 3. Data Collection and Sampling

This stage involves the conduct of the fieldwork and the collection of the required data. At this stage, we send out questionnaires, or run the focus group sessions or conduct telephone surveys, depending on the decisions taken in the first design stage of the fieldwork. The procedures undertaken when conducting the fieldwork might relate to how to ask the questions of the respondents—whether this be using the telephone, mail, or in person, and how to select an appropriate sample, how to **pre-code** the answers to a questionnaire (quantitative research), or how to code the answers arising out of open-ended questions (particularly with qualitative research).

The market research manager might be concerned about whether or not to conduct the research in-company or commission a field and tab agency. Other issues concern how to ensure high data quality. When market research companies undertake shopping mall intercept interviews, they usually re-contact a proportion of the respondents to check their answers to ensure that the interviews have been conducted properly.

In qualitative research, samples are often selected on a convenience or judgmental basis. In quantitative research, we might use either probability or non-probability methods. Probability methods include:

▶ **Simple random sampling**, where the population elements are accorded a number and a sample is selected by generating random numbers, which correspond to the individual population elements.

▶ **Systematic random sampling**, where population elements are known and the first sample unit is selected using random number generation but after that each of the succeeding sample units is then selected systematically on the basis of an nth number, where n is determined by dividing the population size by the sample size.

▶ **Stratified random sampling**, where a specific characteristic(s) is used (e.g. gender, age) to design homogeneous sub-groups from which a representative sample is then drawn.

Non-random methods include:

▶ **Quota sampling**, where criteria like gender, ethnicity, or some other customer characteristic are used to restrict the sample, but the selection of the sample unit is left to the judgment of the researcher.

▶ **Convenience sampling**, where no such restrictions are placed on the selection of the respondents and anybody can be selected.

▶ **Snowball sampling**, a technique where respondents are selected from rare populations (e.g. high performance car buyers). Respondents might initially be selected from responses to newspaper adverts and then further respondents are identified using referrals from the initial respondents, thereby 'snowballing' the sample.

Stage 4. Data Analysis and Interpretation

This stage of the market research process comprises data input, analysis, and interpretation. How the data is input usually depends on the type of data collected. Qualitative data, usually alpha-numeric, i.e. words and numbers, are often entered into word-processed documents as interview transcripts from audio or videotape or entered directly into computer software applications (e.g. NVivo) as video or sound files for content analysis. Quantitative data analysis uses statistical analysis packages (e.g. **SPSS**). In these cases, data are usually numeric and are first entered into spreadsheet packages (e.g. Microsoft Excel) or entered directly into the statistical computer application itself. Online questionnaires are particularly useful in this regard because the data are automatically entered into a database, saving significant periods of data input time and ensuring a higher level of data quality. If **CAPI** or **CATI** methods are used, analysis can also occur instantaneously as the interviews are undertaken. Computer-assisted **web interviewing techniques (CAWI)** allow the researcher to read the questions from a computer screen and directly enter the responses of the respondents. Using the internet, computer-aided web interviewing techniques are also commonly used, allowing playback of video and audio files.

Market research methods are used to aid managerial decision-making. Information obtained needs to be valid and reliable as company resources are deployed on the basis of the information gleaned. **Validity** and **reliability** are important concepts in quantitative market research. They aid researchers in understanding the extent to which the data obtained from the study represent reality and 'truth'. Quantitative research methods rely on the degree to which the data elicited might be reproduced in a later study (i.e. reliability) and the extent to which the data generated are bias-free (i.e. valid). Validity is defined as 'a criterion for evaluating measurement scales; it represents the extent to which a scale is a true reflection of the underlying variable or construct it is attempting to measure' (Parasuraman, 1991: 441). One way of measuring validity is the use of the researcher's subjective judgment to ascertain whether or not an instrument is measuring what it is supposed to measure (content validity). For instance, a question asked about job satisfaction does not necessarily infer loyalty to the organization.

Reliability is defined as 'a criterion for evaluating measurement scales; it represents how consistent or stable the ratings generated by a scale are' (Parasuraman, 1991: 443). Reliability is affected by concepts of time, analytical bias, and questioning error. We can also distinguish between two types of reliability, i.e. internal and external reliability (Bryman, 1989). To determine how reliable the data are, we conduct the study again over two or more time periods to evaluate the consistency of the data. This is known as the test–retest method. This measures external reliability. Another method used involves dividing the responses into two random sets and testing both sets independently using **t-tests** or **z-tests**. This would illustrate internal reliability. The two different sets of results are then correlated. This method is known as split-half reliability testing. These methods are more suited to testing the reliability of rating scales than data generated from qualitative research procedures. The results of a quantitative marketing research project are reliable if we conduct a similar research project within a short time period and the same or similar results are obtained in the second study. For example, if the marketing department of a travel agency chain interviewed 500 of its customers and discovered that 25% were in favour of a particular resort (e.g. a particular Greek island), then repeated the study the following year and discovered only 10% of the sample were interested in the same resort, then the results of the first study can be said to be unreliable in comparison and the procurement department should not base its purchase of package holidays purely on the previous year's finding.

In qualitative research, concepts of **validity** and **reliability** are generally less important, because the data are not used to imply representativeness. Many practitioners believe that qualitative data are highly subjective anyway, so there is little need to measure reliability and validity. Qualitative data are more about the generation of ideas and the formulation of hypotheses. Validity may be assured by sending out transcripts to respondents and/or clients for checking, to ensure that what they have said in in-depth interviews or focus groups was properly reproduced for analysis. When the analyst reads the data from a critical perspective to determine whether or not this fits with their expectations, this constitutes what is termed a **face validity** test. Reliability is often achieved by checking that similar statements are made by the range of respondents, across and within the interview transcripts. Interviewees' transcripts are checked to assess whether or not the same respondent, or other respondents, have made the discussion point. Such detailed content analysis tends to be conducted using computer applications (e.g. NVivo).

Stage 5. Report Preparation and Presentation

The final stage of a research project involves reporting the results and the presentation of the findings of the study to the external or in-house client. The results should be presented free from bias. Marketing research data are of little use unless they can be translated into a format that is meaningful to the manager or client who initially demanded the data. Presentations are often attended by senior people within the commissioning organization who may or may not have been involved in commissioning the work. Usually, agencies and consultants write their reports using a basic pre-written template, which corresponds to a 'house style', although the content placed within that template is obviously different for each individual project.

Market Research Online

The internet has had a strong effect on marketing research and will continue to do so into the future. Many companies have switched their telephone and personal interviewing research approaches towards use of online methods instead. By 2008, online research was the most common method of research used in Europe (25% of all market research expenditure). The method is particularly common in Australia, Finland, and Canada, where 33%, 33%, and 31%, respectively, of market research expenditure adopted this approach (ESOMAR, 2008). There are two types of panel used in online research (Miles, 2004). Access panels provide samples for survey-style information and are made up of targets who have been invited by email to take part with a link to the web survey, an example of which includes the online pollster YouGov. Proprietary panels are set up or commissioned by a client firm and are usually made up of that company's customers. To encourage participation in these surveys, the researchers often use incentives such as the chance to win a prize. But there are pros and cons involved with undertaking online research. For more online research, see Bradley (2010). These are shown in Table 4.2. (For more on how technology affects marketing, see Chapter 17.)

▶ **Research Insight 4.3**

To take your learning further, you might wish to read this influential paper.

Ilieva, J., Baron, S., and Healey, N. M. (2002), 'Online surveys in marketing research: pros and cons', *International Journal of Market Research*, **44, 3, 361–82.**

This article evaluated the use of online research surveys in 2002 as they started to become widely used in place of mail and self-completion surveys, and particularly in international marketing research. The authors conclude that online surveys have more pros than cons, particularly as the internet evolves, in terms of page download speeds and data transfer rates, and users become more representative of the mainstream population. They cite the benefits of online research as including very low financial resource implications, short response times, the ability to control the sample, and the fact that data can be loaded directly into analysis software (removing the need for data processing).

@ Visit the **Online Resource Centre** to read the abstract and access the full paper.

▶ **Table 4.2** Advantages and disadvantages of online research

The pros of online research	The cons of online research
1 Clients and analysts can see results being compiled in real time	**1** Online panels' demographic profile can differ from that of the general population
2 Online surveys save time and money compared with face-to-face interviews	**2** If questionnaires take longer than 20 minutes to fill in quality can suffer and they may go uncompleted
3 Consumers welcome surveys they can fill in when they want to and often need no incentive to do so	**3** Poor recruitment and badly managed panels can damage the data
4 A more relaxed environment leads to better quality, honest, and reasoned responses	**4** Technical problems, such as browser incompatibility, can mean panellists give up
5 Panellist background data allow immediate access to key target audiences unrestricted by geography	**5** Programming costs are higher than for offline questionnaires

Source: Miles (2004): 40. Reproduced with the kind permission of Haymarket Media Group Limited.

go online

Visit the **Online Resource Centre** and complete Internet Activity 4.2 to learn more about the Market Research Portal, a useful source of online research resources.

Market and Advertisement Testing

Marketing research is used to reveal attitudes, to a campaign, brand, or some other aspect of the exchange process, whereas market testing, by comparison, measures actual behaviour. There is a difference, as attitudes do not always determine action (see Chapter 3). For instance, a consumer may respond very positively to the launch of a new, top of the range TV set in surveys but family circumstances or lack of funds may mean the TV is never purchased. Market testing studies use **test markets** to carry out controlled experiments in specific TV or radio regions, where specific adverts can be shown, before exposing the 'new feature' (product, service, campaign, distribution, etc.) to a full national or even international launch. (See Market Insight 4.5 for test-screening of the film Final Destination.) Depending on the feature involved, another region or the rest of the market may act as the **control group** against which results can be measured. As an example, films are often test-screened before they are released. As they represent multimillion-dollar enterprises in their own right, getting them right is an important consideration.

▶ Market Insight 4.5

Testing Horror to Death

Final Destination, the Hollywood hit directed by James Wong and released by New Line Cinema was a surprise hit in 2000, cast with a group of virtual 'nobodies' and a production budget of US$23m. It went on to gross US$53m at the US box office alone. The film was so successful that it has so far spawned three sequels in 2003, 2006, and 2009. *Final Destination II* took US$46 m at the US box office and *Final Destination III* took US$54 m at the US box office. The latest instalment, *The Final Destination*, released in 3D in 2009, took $28m in its debut weekend, making $66m domestically and is estimated to make $125m internationally. The studio earned considerably more income from VHS and DVD rental and sales for the four films.

What was the secret of the film's success? By test-screening the film before release, questioning audiences on everything from scenes and characters to their general interest in films, they identified alternative scenes to replace those scenes that tested

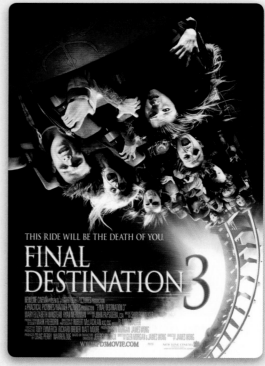

The film series Final Destination
Source: NEW LINE/THE KOBAL COLLECTION.

▶ Market Insight 4.5

badly. In fact, the original ending scene in the first film was hated by most audience members, who were visibly deflated afterwards. So, James Wong recast and reshot a spectacular new bloodlust-satisfying ending, paving the way for the sequels. By test-screening the film several times with different audiences, the producers were able to distil the essence of a thrilling horror film—scenes that contain something totally unexpected, but build up your anticipation of something terrifying and grisly about to happen.

See a trailer of *The Final Destination 3D* for yourself at: http://thefinaldestinationmovie.com/.

Sources: Goldstein (2009); IMDB (2007); Newline Cinema (2000); Rotten Tomatoes (2009); Vary (2009).

1   **Do you think it is always advisable to test-screen a film prior to release?**

2   **Why do you think some producers never test a film prior to release?**

3   **Why do you think the film-makers only wanted to understand the opinions of horror film lovers? Are there other types of audience member whose opinions you might want to gauge?**

Marketing research is frequently used to test advertisements, whether these are in print, online, or broadcast via radio or TV. The research company, Millward Brown International, is particularly well known for this type of research. There are a variety of methods used to test adverts. Typically, quantitative research is undertaken to test customer attitudes before and after exposure to the advertisement to see whether or not the advert has had a positive impact or not. In addition, research occurring after exposure to the ad would also test the extent to which audiences can either recognize a particular advert (e.g. by showing customers a copy of a TV advert still, a print advert or a photo online) or recall an advert without being shown a picture (we call this aided and unaided recall). Qualitative research is also used to identify and test specific themes that might be used in the adverts and to test **storyboards** and **cuts** of adverts (before they are properly produced). More recently, revolutionary advances in technology allow us to evaluate visual imagery more objectively, without relying on the opinion of the respondent (see Market Insight 4.6). For a useful discussion of audience and advertising research, see Bradley (2010).

▶ Market Insight 4.6

Eyecatching: The 3M Informatics Service

Imagine you're the marketing director of a hotel group. You want to know whether or not the digital messages displayed in your reception are persuading your customers. Perhaps you use messages such as 'upgrade your room for only £20 extra', or 'visit the bar for happy hour between 5 and 7 p.m.', or 'enjoy a his and hers massage in the Spa for only £60'. Whatever the message, how do you know it's working,

> ### ▶ Market Insight 4.6   (continued)

and which message provides the most income? Such questions have previously required months of painstaking trial and error to evaluate which message works best—until now.

In the USA, 3M have launched a solution that can quickly and accurately measure the true impact of digital communications in store, together with an optimization routine that ensures the most effective content plays at the most effective time. Using a revolutionary new approach, the 3M Informatics system takes a company's promotional content and marketing objectives, creates a playback media schedule, and then links the media to point-of-sale data to quickly and accurately determine the effect of in-store communication. As the system learns what messages are most effective, it continually optimizes the schedule to maximize performance (or revenue).

But what is particularly unique about the system is that using sophisticated machine-learning algorithms, taken together with the company's business objectives and content, 3M Informatics can automatically reallocate content to optimize a company's business performance. To take one example, Wendy's the US burger chain used the service to redesign the content of their point-of-sale advertising material to promote their burger products more effectively at the food counter. Never before have marketers been able to determine the effects of their promotional messages in such a short time. The question is: will the technology catch on in the USA, and particularly in Europe?

Sources: 3M (2009).

1   How successful do you think the 3M Informatics service is going to be in the USA and in Europe? Why?

2   What do you think the research limitations of the 3M Informatics service are?

3   How is technology affecting the development of other types of market research? (Hint: google the term 'neuromarketing'.)

Marketing Research and Ethics

Many supermarkets and high street retailers have adopted customer loyalty schemes to ensure the loyalty of their customers. In exchange for their continued custom, they provide customers with loyalty points, which may be cashed in for prizes or discounts on future purchases. Nevertheless, the major value of such schemes is the provision of consumer data. Typically, these data are collected at the point-of-sale (e.g. store and supermarket tills) and are analysed by a third party agency and sold back to the retailer to provide them with outlines of patterns and trends in consumption behaviour to inform their procurement, promotion, merchandising, and further research strategies. What we sometimes forget is that marketing research is based on the willing cooperation of individuals or organizations that provide the answers to our questions, for example, by filling in questionnaires, scanning home shopping or by attending focus groups.

Marketing research should be carried out in an objective, unobtrusive, and honest manner. Researchers are concerned about the public's increased unwillingness to participate in marketing research and the problem of recruiting suitable interviewers. The apathy among interviewees is probably associated with the growing, perhaps excessive, amount of research conducted, particularly through intrusive telephone interviewing, which is increasing, and door-to-door type survey interviewing, which is declining. Marketing research is increasingly conducted online. This has created its own set of ethical concerns. How can we verify that someone online is who they say they are? Is it acceptable to observe and analyse customer blogs and social networking site conversations, for example?

Generally, marketing research neither attempts to induce sales of a product or service nor influence customer attitudes, intentions, or behaviours. The MRS key principles outline that researchers shall (MRS, 2010: 4):

1 Ensure that participation in their activities is based on voluntary informed consent.

2 Be straightforward and honest in all their professional and business relationships.

3 Be transparent as to the subject and purpose of data collection.

4 Respect the confidentiality of information collected in their professional activities.

5 Respect the rights and well-being of all individuals.

6 Ensure that their respondents are not harmed or adversely affected by their professionl activities.

7 Balance the needs of individuals, clients, and their professional activities.

8 Exercise independent professional judgment in the design, conduct, and reporting of their professional activities.

9 Ensure that their professional activities are conducted by persons with appropriate training, qualifications, and experience.

10 Protect the reputation and integrity of the profession.

The MRS Code of Conduct—which is based on the ESOMAR Code—is binding on all members of the MRS. The general public and other interested parties are entitled to assurances that no information collected in a research survey, will be used to identify them, or be disclosed to a third party without their consent. In that respect, data in European countries are also subject to an EU data protection directive. Respondents must be informed as to the purpose of the research and the length of time they will be involved in it. Research findings must also be reported accurately and not used to mislead, in any way. In conducting marketing research, researchers have responsibility for themselves, their clients and the respondents from whom the information is being gathered.

The results of marketing research studies should remain confidential unless agreed by the client and agency, and the agency should provide detailed accounts of the methods employed to carry out the research project where this is requested by their clients.

go online

Visit the **Online Resource Centre** and complete Internet Activity 4.1 to learn more about the Marketing Research Code of Practice adopted by ESOMAR.

International Marketing Research

Marketing researchers often find it challenging to understand how culture operates in international markets and, therefore, how it affects research design. Complexity in the international business environment makes international marketing research more complex because it affects the research process and design. The main decision is whether or not to customize international marketing research to each of the separate countries in a study using differing scales, sampling methods, and sizes, or try to use one single method for all countries, adopting an international **sampling frame**. In many ways, this debate mirrors the standardization–customization dilemma common in international marketing generally and considered in more detail in Chapter 7.

International researchers try to ensure comparable data are collected despite differences in **sampling frames**, technological developments, and availability of interviewers. Western approaches to marketing research, data collection, and culture might be inappropriate in some research environments because of variations in economic development and consumption patterns. How comparable are the data related to the consumption of McDonald's products collected through personal interviews in the UAE, telephone interviews in France, and shopping mall intercept questionnaires in Sweden? Similarly, we could ask the question is the use of Unilever's Timotei shampoo by consumers in Latvia satisfying the same consumer needs as those consumers in the UK? Ensuring comparability of data in research studies of multiple markets is not simple. Concepts could be regarded differently, the same products and services could have different functions, language may be used differently—even within a country, products and services might be measured differently, the samples (the people who consume a particular product or service) might be different, and finally the data-collection methods adopted may be different because of different country infrastructures. Table 4.3 outlines three types of equivalence: conceptual, functional, and **translation equivalence**. All these types of equivalence impact on the semantics (i.e. meaning) of words used in different countries, e.g. in developing the wording for questionnaires or in focus groups. Getting the language right is important because it affects how respondents perceive the questions and structure their answers.

When designing international research programmes it is important to consider how the meaning of words is different and how the data need to be collected. Different cultures have different ways of measuring concepts. They also live their lives differently, meaning that it may be necessary to collect the same or similar data in a different way. Table 4.4 outlines how measurement, sampling, and data collection equivalence impacts on international research.

As we can see in Table 4.4, achieving comparability of data when conducting international surveys is difficult. Usually, the more countries included in an international study, the more likely it is that errors will be introduced and the results and findings will be inaccurate and liable to misinterpretation. International research requires local and international input, so the extent to which one can internationalize certain operations of the research process depends on the objectives of the research.

▶ **Table 4.3** Types of semantic equivalence in international marketing research

Type of equivalence	Explanation	Example
Conceptual equivalence	When interpretation of behaviour, or objects, is similar across countries, conceptual equivalence exists	Conceptual equivalence should be considered when defining the research problem, in wording the questionnaire, and determining the sample unit, e.g. there would be less need to investigate 'brand loyalty' in a country where competition is restricted and product choice limited

▶ **Table 4.3** (continued)

Type of equivalence	Explanation	Example
Functional equivalence	Functional equivalence relates to whether a concept has a similar function in different countries	Using a bicycle in India where it might be used for transport to and from work, or France where it might be used for shopping, is a different concept from purchasing a bike in Norway, where it might be used for mountain biking. Functional differences can be determined using focus groups before finalizing the research design by ensuring the constructs used in the research measure what they are supposed to measure
Translation equivalence	Translation equivalence is an important aspect of the international research process. Words in some languages have no real equivalent in other languages	The meaning associated with different words is important in questionnaire design as words can connote a different meaning from that intended when directly translated into another language. To avoid translation errors of these kinds, the researcher can adopt one of the following two methods: 1. Back translation—a translator fluent in the language in which the questionnaire is to be translated is used and then another translator whose native language was the original language is used to translate back again. Differences in wording can be identified and resolved 2. Parallel translation—a questionnaire is translated using a different translator fluent in the language the questionnaire is to be translated into, as well as from, until a final version is agreed upon (Malhotra, 1999: 814)

▶ **Table 4.4** Types of measurement and data collection equivalence

Type of equivalence	Explanation	Example
Measurement equivalence	The extent to which measurement scales are comparable across countries	Surveys are conducted in the USA using imperial systems of measurement, whereas the metric system is used in Europe. Clothing sizes adopt different measurement systems in Europe, North America, or South-East Asia. Multi-item scales present challenges for international researchers as dissatisfaction might not be expressed in the same way in one country compared to another. Some cultures are more open in expressing opinions or describing their behaviour than others
Sampling equivalence	Determining the appropriate sample to question may provide difficulties when conducting international marketing research projects	The respondent profile for the same survey could vary from country to country, e.g. different classification systems are in existence for censorship of films shown at the cinema in France compared with Britain

Type of equivalence	Explanation	Example
Data collection equivalence	When conducting research studies in different countries, it may be appropriate to adopt different data-collection strategies	Typically, data-collection methods include (e)mail, personal (or CAPI), or telephone (or CATI) ▶ Mail or email—Used more where literacy or internet access is high and where the (e)mail system operates efficiently. Sampling frames are compiled from electoral registers, although it is now illegal in some countries to use these lists. European survey respondents can be targeted efficiently and accurately as international sampling frames do exist ▶ Telephone/**CATI**—In many countries, telephone penetration may be limited and computer-assisted telephone interviewing software, using **random digit dialling**, more limited still. Telephone penetration is around 95% in America, although the European average figure is lower after the introduction of new East European economies ▶ Personal interviews/**CAPI**—Used most widely in European countries favouring the door-to-door and shopping mall intercept variants. Shopping mall intercept interviews are not appropriate in Arabic countries where women under Sharia law are not to be approached in the street. Here, comparability is achieved using door-to-door interviews. In countries where it is rude to openly disagree with someone, e.g. China, it's best to use in-depth interviews

▶ Research Insight 4.4

To take your learning further, you might wish to read this influential paper.

Craig, C. S., and Douglas, S. P (2001), 'Conducting international marketing research in the twenty-first century', *International Marketing Review*, 18, 1, 80–90.

This article indicates how international marketing research practice should adapt to support firms in the twenty-first century in four key areas. First, international marketing research must focus on market growth opportunities outside industrialized nations. Second, researchers need to develop the capability to conduct and coordinate research in these diverse research environments. Third, there is a need to develop new creative approaches to probe cultural underpinnings in these countries. Finally, there is a need to incorporate technological changes, including the internet, into the process of conducting and disseminating international research.

 Visit the **Online Resource Centre** to read the abstract and access the full paper.

With international projects, the key decision is to determine how much to centralize and how much to delegate work to local agencies. There is, throughout this process, ample opportunity for misunderstandings, errors, and lack of cultural sensitivity. To proceed effectively, the central agency should identify a number of trusted local market research providers on a variety of continents. Typically, an international agency will have a network of trusted affiliates who provide such a service and are monitored on a continual basis.

Skills for Employment

> ▶▶ We look for someone who shows a curiosity over and above the job they are applying for. The candidate should show an energy and enthusiasm to learn and grow. ◀◀

Claire Spencer, CEO, i to i research

 Visit the **Online Resource Centre** to discover more tips and advice on skills for the workplace.

Chapter Summary

To consolidate your learning, the key points from this chapter are summarized below.

■ **Define the terms market research and marketing research.**

Market research originated around the time of the First World War with the first market research department possibly being set up at Procter & Gamble. As a process, market research is intended to provide useful information for the company or organization to design, develop, and implement its decision-making in relation to marketing strategy and tactics.

■ **Explain the use of marketing information systems.**

Marketing information systems and customer information (CRM) systems are commonly used in companies to collect, store, and analyse data, in order to generate and disseminate marketing intelligence and generate effective marketing programmes. Increasingly, companies are recognizing the importance of mining customer data and the competitive advantages such strong customer understanding can bring. Competitive intelligence has evolved into a distinct sub-discipline with its own professional society and code of conduct. It comprises information obtained often through informal means from sales force personnel, suppliers, competitors, and customers.

■ **Explain the role marketing research plays in the decision-making process of a business and the range of research approaches that might be used.**

Marketing research plays an important role in the decision-making process of a business and tends to contribute through ad-hoc studies as well as continuous data collection, through industry reports and from secondary data sources, as well as through competitive intelligence either commissioned through agencies or conducted internally with data gathered informally through sales forces, customers, and suppliers.

- **Recognize the importance of ethics and the adoption of a Code of Conduct when undertaking marketing research.**

  Ethics is an important consideration in marketing research because consumers and customers provide personal information about themselves. Their privacy needs to be protected through the strict observance of a professional Code of Ethics and the relevant laws in the country where the research is conducted.

- **Understand the concept of equivalence in relation to obtaining comparable data.**

  International market research is complex because of the differences in language, culture, infrastructure, and other factors, which intervene in the data-collection process and ensure that obtaining comparable, equivalent data is more difficult.

- **Describe the problems arising when coordinating international marketing research.**

  International marketing research is more complex because it is difficult to obtain semantic equivalence (i.e. concepts mean different things in different countries). Similarly, obtaining equivalence in measurement, sampling, and data collection can be difficult because of local variations. International research therefore requires a strong mix of central coordination with local input in order to be effective.

Review Questions

1. What are the origins of market research?
2. How do we define market research?
3. How do we define marketing research?
4. What role does marketing research play in the decision-making process of a business?
5. What are the main different types of research that are conducted in marketing?
6. Why is a code of conduct important when conducting marketing research?
7. What is the importance of competitive intelligence and how is it used in a marketing information system?
8. What is the concept of equivalence in relation to obtaining comparable data from different countries?
9. How are the different aspects of the research process affected by differences in equivalence between countries?

Worksheet Summary

Visit the **Online Resource Centre** and complete Worksheet 4.1. This will help you learn about defining a Marketing Research problem for a low-price airline; designing a research plan and the selecting most appropriate method for data collection.

Discussion Questions

1. Having read Case Insight 4.1, how would you advise i to i research to develop a suitable research proposal for the London Organising Committee of the Olympic Games to measure and track public support for the bid? Use the outline proposal in Figure 4.4 to help you with this task.

2 **Orange, the telecommunications company, wants to conduct a market research study aimed particularly at discovering what market segments exist across Europe and how customers and potential customers view the Orange brand. Advise them on the following key components:**

   A Write a market research question and a number of sub-questions for the study.
   B How would you go about selecting the particular countries in which to conduct the fieldwork?
   C What process would you use when conducting the fieldwork for this multi-country study?

3 **What type of research (i.e. causal, descriptive, or exploratory) should be commissioned in the following contexts? Explain why.**

   A By the management of the Burj al Arab hotel in the United Arab Emirates when it wants to determine guest satisfaction with the hotel's luxury facilities, layout, location, room quality, and range of services.

   B By Nintendo when it wants new ideas for new online games for a youth audience.

   C By H&M the Swedish fashion retailer when it wants to know what levels of customer service are being offered at its flagship stores.

   D By Procter & Gamble, makers of Ariel detergent when it wants to test a new packaging design for six months to see if it is more effective than the existing version. Fifty supermarkets are selected from one key P&G account. In 25 of them the new design is used, in the other 25 the existing version is used.

4 **You've recently won the research contract to evaluate customer satisfaction for Pret A Manger, the worldwide chain of food retail outlets, specializing in delicious sandwiches, soups, and coffee. Your key account manager wants to increase customer satisfaction further using the knowledge gained from the study and identify potential new food offerings. Suggest a suitable research design (hint: you can advise more than one type of study) for:**

   A Collecting information about levels of customer satisfaction.

   B Deciding what new food offerings customers might like to see.
   In addition, your account manager asks you to:

   C Outline what secondary data you can find in the area, detailing market shares, market structure, and other industry information, suggesting specific secondary data sources and reports.

5 **The following questions are concerned with international marketing research.**

   A How should Unilever coordinate international marketing research to determine how to increase sales of its best-selling toothpaste in different parts of the EMEA (Europe, Middle East, and Africa) market?
   B Why is it difficult to achieve comparability of data across countries?

Visit the **Online Resource Centre** and complete the Multiple Choice Questions to assess your knowledge of Chapter 4.

go online

References

3M (2009), 'Winning the first glance', 18 November, retrieve from: http://solutions.3m.co.uk/wps/portal/3M/en_GB/about-3M/information/more-info/press-room/?PC_7_RJH9U5230ONQ6027DTROJH2482_assetId=1258557435277, accessed 21 November 2009.

AMA (2009), 'Marketing Research', Dictionary of Marketing Terms, retrieve from: www.marketingpower.com, accessed 15 November 2009.

Anon. (1989), *The Hutchinson Concise Encyclopaedia*, 2nd edn, London: BCA.

A. C. Nielson (2007), 'Our History', retrieve from http://uk.nielsen.com/company/history.shtml, accessed 15 November 2009.

Arvidsson, A. (2004), 'On the "pre-history of the panoptic sort": mobility in market research', *Surveillance and Society*, 4, 1, 456–74.

Ashill, N. J., and Jobber, D. (2001), 'Defining the information needs of senior marketing executives: an exploratory study', *Qualitative Market Research: An International Journal*, 4, 1, 52–60.

Axelrod, J. N. (1970), '14 Rules for building an MIS', *Journal of Advertising Research*, 10, 3, 3–12.

Baines, P., and Chansarkar, B. (2002), *Introducing Marketing Research*, Chichester: John Wiley and Sons.

Bradley, N. (2010), *Marketing Research: Tools and Techniques*, 2nd edn, Oxford: Oxford University Press.

Bryman, A. (1989), *Research Methods and Organisation Studies*, London: Unwin Hyman.

Chisnall P. M. (1992),. *Marketing Research*, 4th edn, Maidenhead: McGraw-Hill.

Context Research Group (2009), 'An ethnography of the Guinness experience across key market segments', retrieve from www.contextresearch.com/context/clients/clients_case_guiness.cfm, accessed 15 November 2009.

ESOMAR (1995), *ICC/ESOMAR International Code of Marketing and Social Research Practice*, 6, retrieve from www.esomar.org, accessed 17 June 2007.

— (2008), Global Market Research Report 2008, available for purchase at www.esomar.org, accessed 21 November 2009.

Euromonitor (2009), Vacuum Cleaner Possession, Retail Sales and Volumes, *Global Market Information Database*, retrieve from www.euromonitor.com, accessed 15 November 2009.

Goldstein, P. (2009), 'Cracking the case: the mysterious success of "The Final Destination"', 13 October 2009, *Los Angeles Times*, retrieve from: http://latimesblogs.latimes.com/the_big_picture/2009/10/cracking-the-case-the-mysterious-success-of-the-final-destination.html, accessed 15 November 2009.

Goulding, C. (2002), *Grounded Theory*, London: Sage Publications.

Humby, C. (2007), *R is for relevance, An antidote to CRM hype*. Paper presented to the Return on Marketing Investment (ROMI) Club, May, Cranfield: Cranfield University.

IMDB (2007), *DVD Details for Final Destination, I, II, III*, retrieve from www.imdb.com, accessed 17 June 2007.

Kotler, P. (2005), *FAQs on Marketing: Answered by the Guru of Marketing*, London: Cyan Books.

Malhotra, N. K. (1999), *Marketing Research: An Applied Approach*, 3rd edn, Englewood Cliffs, NJ: Prentice-Hall.

McCawley, I. (2006), 'Analysis: dunnhumby — Department of Tesco', *Marketing Week*, 8 June, 13.

Miles, L. (2004), 'Online, on tap', *Marketing*, 16 June, 39–40.

Newline Cinema (2000), 'A look at test screening', in *Final Destination*, DVD edn, New Line Home Cinema.

MRS (2010), Code of Conduct, London: Market Research Society, retrieve from www.mrs.org.uk/standards/codeconduct.htm, accessed 10 April 2010.

Nolan, J. (1999), *Confidential: Uncover your Competitors' Top Business Secrets Legally and Quickly—and Protect your Own*, New York: HarperBusiness.

Parasuraman, A. (1991), *Marketing Research*, 2nd edn, Wokingham: Addison-Wesley, 280–309.

Rotten Tomatoes (2009), *Final Destination (2000) Final Destination II (2003) Final Destination III (2006)* retrieve from www.rottentomatoes.com, accessed 15 November 2009.

Stevens, R. E. (2003), 'Views from the hills', 'Genesis II: The Second Beginning', retrieve from www.popsg.org/views/27oct03.html, accessed 2 December 2007.

Vary, A.B. (2009), '"Final Destination" No.1 at the Box Office', Entertainment Weekly, 30 August 2009, retrieve from http://edition.cnn.com/2009/SHOWBIZ/Movies/08/30/boxoffice.ew/index.html?eref=rss_mostpopular, accessed 8 November 2009.

Principles of marketing management

☆ Heineken®

5 Marketing Strategy

After studying this chapter you should be able to:

▶ Describe the strategic planning process
▶ Explain the key influences that impact on and shape marketing strategy
▶ Develop a SWOT analysis and set out how it can help strategic marketing decision-making
▶ Explain how understanding competitors can assist the development of marketing strategy
▶ Identify the characteristics of strategic marketing goals and explain the nature of the associated growth strategies
▶ Describe different approaches and concepts associated with strategic marketing action, including the implementation issues
▶ Understand the principles of marketing metrics and how these can contribute to the implementation and control of the marketing planning process
▶ Outline the key elements of a marketing plan

▶ Case Insight 5.1

Innocent Drinks market their smoothies in a highly innovative way. What strategies will they use to market their new water/juice drinks? We speak to Dan Germain, Head of Creative at Innocent, to find out more.

Innocent Drinks make smoothies, drinks made from pure whole crushed fruit, with no preservatives, colouring, or nasty additives. They're sold in little bottles and big cartons, all of which feature trademark innocent fun and games on the back of the pack. Innocent effectively developed a whole new drinks sector, one that many experts at the start said could not be done. Innocent is now a £100m business.

In 1999, Innocent's three co-founders had a great product and lots of enthusiasm, but no experience of running a business, no customers, and no turnover. To help get started we made a few smoothies and sold them at a small music festival. We asked our customers to place their empty cups in a 'yes' or 'no' bin to vote whether the three of us should give up our jobs and make smoothies full-time. At the end of the weekend, the 'yes' bin was full and so we quit our jobs the next day, spent several months finding the necessary finance and started a company that is now doubling its profits every year.

It has not all been plain sailing, as initially distributors refused to stock our drinks. Innocent's response was to load up a van and take the drinks to delicatessens and health food shops in Notting Hill. As a form of introduction we said, 'we're a local juice company that's just started up, here's four boxes for free, stick them on your shelves and if they sell give us a ring'. Out of the 50 shops reached, 45 wanted more. We then went back to the distributors, told them the story about the delis, and gave them a pallet for free. Now Innocent drinks are sold in over 7,000 outlets—a big change from those early days.

Innocent's water, as 'good' as its smoothies
Source: Innocent.

However, with growth and success questions arose about how we should develop the company and the Innocent brand. There are lots of opportunities to move into a number of health-related sectors. The strong ethical and health credentials associated with the brand provide opportunities for development, but these beliefs can constrain and limit the scope of the areas we can move into. For example, one area with great potential is drinks made from fruit juice and spring water.

But there are plenty of these types of products already in the market so could Innocent branded fruit/water juice be successful, and would such a product harm the Innocent brand?

Introduction

Have you ever thought about how organizations organize themselves so that they can make sales, achieve profits, and keep all their stakeholders satisfied? As you can imagine this does not happen accidentally and a great deal of thought, discussion, planning, and action needs to occur. This involves getting answers to questions such as which markets the organization should be operating in, what resources are necessary in order to be successful in these markets, who are the key competitors and what strategies are they using, how can we develop and sustain an advantage over these competitors, and what is happening in the wider world that might affect our organization? These questions refer to issues that represent the strategic context in which organizations operate. These contextual issues can be considered in terms of four main elements, namely: the organization (and its resources, skills, and capabilities), the target customers, a firm's competitors, and the wider environment. These are set out in Figure 5.1.

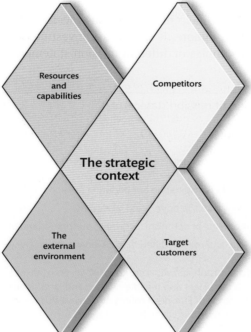

Figure 5.1

The four elements of the strategic context

Motorola's strategic context is shaped by its communications expertise and leading-edge technology skills, customers who expect a stream of added value communication-related products, and Nokia and Apple, its main competitors and market leader in the mobile phone handset market. In addition, the wider environment is becoming politically more sensitive to climatic change issues, terrorism anxieties, social change, the economic crisis, and surges in technological development. By understanding and managing these four elements it is possible to develop a coherent strategic marketing plan through which products or services have a greater chance of success than if no analysis or planning is undertaken. In order that a marketing strategy be developed successfully, first it is necessary to understand an organization's strategic context and to then fit the marketing strategy so that it matches the strategic context. Many organizations articulate their strategic context and their intended performance in the markets they have targeted, in terms of a framework that defines their vision, mission, values, organizational goals, and organizational strategy.

The **vision** sets out an organization's future. A vision is a statement about what an organization wants to become. It should give shape and direction to an organization's future. A vision should stretch an organization in terms of its current position and performance, yet at the same time it should help employees feel involved and motivated to want to be part of the organization's future. ASB Bank's vision statement is 'To be the best bank and financial services provider in New Zealand, excelling in customer service'.

The **mission** represents what the organization wishes to achieve in the long term. It should be a broad statement of intention as it sets out an organization's purpose and direction. It should be oriented to particular markets and customers served. A mission applies to all parts of an organization and in that sense serves to bind the many parts of an organization together. However, above all else, the mission should provide a reference point for its managers and employees. The mission should help managers make decisions concerning which opportunities to pursue and which to ignore. It should aid investment and development decision-making. See Table 5.1 for examples of different mission statements.

▶ **Table 5.1** A selection of mission statements

Organization	Mission statement
Tesco	To create value for customers to earn their lifetime loyalty
Coca-Cola	Everything we do is inspired by our enduring mission:
	To refresh the world ... in body, mind, and spirit
	To inspire moments of optimism ... through our brands and our actions
	To create value and make a difference ... everywhere we engage
EasyJet	To provide our customers with safe, good-value, point-to-point air services. To effect and to offer a consistent and reliable product and fares appealing to leisure and business markets on a range of European routes. To achieve this we will develop our people and establish lasting relationships with our suppliers
Oxfam	Oxfam works with others to overcome poverty and suffering
IBM	At IBM, we strive to lead in the invention, development, and manufacture of the industry's most advanced information technologies, including computer systems, software, storage systems, and microelectronics. We translate these advanced technologies into value for our customers through our professional solutions, services, and consulting businesses worldwide
JCB	Our mission is to grow our company by providing innovative, strong, and high-performance products and solutions to meet our global customers' needs

Source: Company websites.

Mission statements are sometimes prepared as a public relations exercise or are so generic that they fail to provide sufficient guidelines or inspiration. Some are just not realistic and are to be avoided. For example, to expect an airport such as Adelaide or Hong Kong to become the largest airport in the world is totally infeasible. Good mission statements are market- not product-oriented. For example, the product-oriented approach 'we make and sell lorries and trucks' is too general and runs the risk of becoming outdated and redundant. By focusing on the needs of the customers that the organization is seeking to serve, the mission can be more realistic and have a much longer lifespan. So, 'we transport your products quickly and safely to your customers', or 'logistical solutions for your company' provides a market approach to the mission statement. Amazon.com does not sell books, videos, and DVDs (product approach): much better to say that Amazon.com provides a 'friendly, safe and entertaining online buying environment'. Similarly, Haier, the leading Chinese manufacturer, do not make home appliances, 'they make lives more convenient and comfortable through innovative appliances'.

go online

Visit the **Online Resource Centre** and complete Internet Activity 5.1 to learn more about the use of mission and vision statements by differing organizations and their implications for marketing activities.

An **organization's values** must be in line with its vision and mission, if only because they define how people should behave with each other in the organization and help shape how the goals will be achieved. Organizational values define the acceptable interpersonal and operating standards of behaviour. They govern and guide the behaviour of individuals within the organization. Organizations that identify and develop a clear, concise, and shared meaning of values and beliefs shape the organizational culture and provide direction so that all participants can understand and contribute.

Organizational values are important because they can help to guide and constrain not only behaviour but also the recruitment and selection decisions. Without them, individuals tend to pursue behaviours that are in line with their own individual value systems, which may lead to inappropriate behaviours and a failure to achieve the overall goals.

Organizational goals at the strategic level represent what should be achieved, the outcomes of the organization's various activities. These may be articulated in terms of profit, market share, share value, return on investment, or numbers of customers served. In some cases the long term may not be a viable period and a short-term focus is absolutely essential. For example, should an organization's financial position become precarious then it may be necessary to focus on short-term cash strategies in order to remain solvent and so remove any threat arising from a takeover or administrators being called in prior to bankruptcy.

Organization or **corporate strategy** is the means by which the resources of the organization are matched with the needs of the environment in which the organization decides to operate. Corporate strategy involves bringing together the human resources, logistics, production, operations, marketing, IT, and financial parts of an organization into a coherent strategic plan that supports, reinforces, and helps accomplish the organizational goals, in the most effective and efficient way. In this chapter we are concerned with the make-up of the marketing strategy that should support and reinforce the corporate strategy.

▶ Market Insight 5.1

P&G Make the Consumer Boss

For a long time Procter & Gamble maintained a hierarchical structure, one in which decision-making was top-down and which restricted growth and the nature and form of its marketing strategies and operations. In 2000, a decision was made by the incoming CEO to transform the culture into one that focused on innovation. This has had a direct influence on corporate performance.

For example, in 2000 P&G's innovation success rate with new brands stood at 15–20% or as the CEO Lafley points out, 'for every six new product introductions, one would return our investment'. By 2008, this had changed to the target level of between 50 and 60%.

Another outcome is reflected in the business portfolio as they sold off most of P&G's food and beverage businesses. This enabled the company to concentrate on products that were driven by the kinds of innovation the organization knew best. With a narrower mix of businesses, the resources and attention needed to build an innovation culture can be targeted much more easily.

Back in 2000, P&G's employees were not oriented or unified by any common strategic purpose.

The corporate mission required that all activities should meaningfully improve the everyday lives of customers. Unfortunately this was not embraced by the majority of employees and innovation efforts suffered as a result. So, the mission was changed to encompass the notion that 'the consumer is boss'. This means that 'people who buy and use P&G products are valued not just for their money, but as a rich source of information and direction'. Lafley goes on to suggest that the mission is more likely to succeed if P&G find better ways of learning from customers, listening to them, observing them in their daily lives, and even living with them. 'The consumer is boss' became more than a slogan. It was a clear, simple, and inclusive cultural priority for both employees and external stakeholders, such as suppliers and retail partners.

Sources: Lafley (2008); Friscia (2008); www.pg.com.

1   **P&G changed to a culture driven by innovation. In which other ways might an organization drive its culture?**

2   **Go to the P&G website and find three ways in which the innovation culture is highlighted.**

3   **Find examples of purpose, values and principles (PVP), in two other organizations of your choice, which are operating in the same market. How do they compare?**

In some very large organizations the planning process is made complicated and difficult because the organization operates in a number of significantly different markets. In these cases the organization creates **strategic business units** or SBUs. Each SBU assumes the role of a separate company and creates its own strategies and plans in order to achieve its corporate goals and contribution to the overall organization. So, the Indian company Tata operates through seven SBUs, namely Information Technology and Communications, Engineering, Materials, Services, Energy, Consumer Products, and Chemicals. Each of these Tata companies operates independently. Royal Philips Electronics use four SBUs: Domestic Appliances and Personal Care, Lighting, Medical Systems, and Consumer Electronics. All of these represent significantly different markets, each with their own characteristics, customer needs, and competitors.

According to McDonald (2002: 37), who is referred to by many as the global guru of marketing planning, the Strategic Marketing Planning process consists of a series of logical steps that have to be worked through in order to arrive at a marketing plan. These steps can be aggregated into four phases. The first phase is concerned with setting the right mission and corporate goals. The second involves reviewing the current situation or context in which the organization is operating. The third phase is used to formulate strategy, and the final phase considers the allocation of resources necessary to implement and monitor the plan.

So, at a broad level, the strategic marketing planning process is as follows:

▶ At the corporate level the organization sets out its overall vision, mission, and values.

▶ Measurable corporate goals are established that apply to the whole organization.

▶ A series of analyses and audits are undertaken to understand the external situation in which the organization intends to operate and the resources available to be used.

▶ Strategies are formulated and probable outcomes estimated.

▶ Depending on the size of the organization, the range of businesses (SBUs) and/or products is determined, and resources are allocated to help and support each one.

▶ Each business and/or product then develops detailed functional and competitive strategies and plans, such as a marketing strategy and plan.

▶ The plan is implemented and the results measured and used to feed into the next planning cycle.

What arises from this is that marketing strategy and planning should support and contribute to the overall company strategy. However, it should also be understood that marketing strategy and planning can occur at the business, product, or market level.

▶ Research Insight 5.1

To take your learning further, you might wish to read this influential paper.

Mintzberg, H. (1987), 'The strategy concept: five Ps for strategy', *California Management Review*, 30, 1 (Fall), 11–26.

Mintzberg's paper made an important contribution because it argued that strategy should not be regarded just as a linear sequential planning process. He shows in this paper that strategy can also be interpreted as a plan ploy, pattern, perspective, and as a position.

 Visit the **Online Resource Centre** to read the abstract and access the full paper.

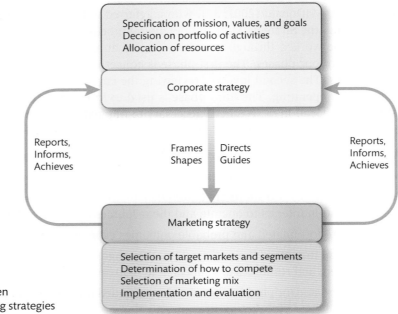

Figure 5.2

The relationship between corporate and marketing strategies

Influences on Strategic Marketing Planning

The development of a strategic marketing plan is a complex and involved process. It does not occur in linear logical steps as suggested earlier, but certain key aspects can be identified. These aspects concern three broad activities that are necessary when considering the development of marketing strategy and will form the framework through which we examine this topic.

Figure 5.3

Three key activities of marketing strategy development

These three elements are shown in Figure 5.3. Here it can be seen that it is necessary to first develop knowledge and understanding of the marketplace, referred to here as **strategic market analysis**. The second is to determine what the marketing strategy should achieve, in other words what are the strategic marketing goals that need to be accomplished. The third and final decision area concerns how the goals are to be achieved. This relates directly to strategic marketing action, that is, how the strategies are to be developed as plans and how these plans are to be implemented. These three activities form the basis of this chapter and are considered in turn.

Strategic Market Analysis

The starting point of the marketing strategy process is the development of knowledge and understanding about the target market(s) that have been identified as part of the corporate strategy. Different people in the organization will have varying levels of market knowledge and expertise, some of it accurate and up-to-date but some out-of-date and inaccurate. It is crucial that all people involved in the strategy process are well informed with accurate, pertinent, and up-to-date information.

In Chapter 2 we saw how use of PESTLE and environmental scanning processes can be used to understand and make sense of the external environment in which organizations operate. We also considered Porter's (1985) Five Forces model to understand industry dynamics and how firms should compete strategically if they are to be successful in the performance environment. We also gained an insight into the importance of understanding the internal environment and how a firm's resources need to complement the external and performance environments. The task is to now to assimilate this information, to bring it together in a form that can be easily understood, and consideration is given to **SWOT** analysis.

However, before these tools can be used, analysis of the performance environment, most notably our competitors and the industry's key suppliers and distributors, is required.

Analysing Competitors

The importance of understanding competitors cannot be overstated and as Noble, Sinha, and Kumar (2002) found, organizations that pay particular attention to their competitors generally perform better than those who do not. In order to undertake an analysis of a firm's competitors, five key questions must be answered. These are:

▶ Who are our competitors?

▶ What are their strengths and weaknesses?

▶ What are their strategic goals?

▶ Which strategies are they following?

▶ How are they likely to respond?

Who Are Our Competitors?

Competitors are those firms that offer products and services that attempt to meet the same market need as our own. There are several ways in which a need might be met, but essentially two approaches can be identified. Firms need to be aware of their direct and indirect competitors. Direct competitors are those who offer the same target market similar products and services, for example EasyJet, Flybe, and Ryanair. Direct competitors may also offer a product in the same category, but target different segments, for example, Haagen-Dazs, Walls, and Green and Black's offer a range of ice cream products for different target markets. Indirect competitors are those who address the same target market but offer a different product or service to satisfy the market need, for example, HMV, Sony, and Apple's iPod.

By understanding who the main competitors are, it becomes possible to make judgements about the nature and likely intensity of the competition plus who might represent a key

Green & Black's ice cream, targeting the ethical consumer
Source: Courtesy of Green & Blacks.

threat. This also provides a view about how a firm's own marketing strategy should evolve. For example, the strategy of a market leader, which identifies little competition, will be different from a small firm trying to establish a small market share. The former may try to dominate the whole market, whereas the latter may attack the leader or find a small, underserviced segment, called a **niche market**, and start to make it their own market.

What Are Their Strengths and Weaknesses?

Getting information about a competitor's range of products and their sales volumes and value, their profitability, prices, and discount structures, the nature of their relationships with suppliers and distributors, their communications campaigns and special offers, are all important. In some circumstances, getting information about new products that are either in development or about to be launched can be critical.

In addition to these marketing elements, however, it is important to obtain information about a whole range of other factors, not just their marketing activities. These factors include their production and manufacturing capabilities, their technical, management, and financial resources, and their processes, distribution channels, and relative success in meeting customer and market needs.

As this information accumulates and is updated through time, it is necessary to use the information in order to understand what a competitor's strengths and weaknesses might be and to then use this to either avoid the areas where competitors are strong or exploit the weaknesses. The overall task is to determine what **competitive advantage** a competitor might have and whether this advantage can be sustained, imitated, or undermined. Ideas about competitive advantage are explored in greater detail later in this chapter.

What Are Their Strategic Goals?

Contrary to what is often written in the popular press, profit is not the single, over-riding strategic goal for most organizations. Firms develop a range of goals, encompassing ambitions such as achieving a certain market share (which is quite common), market leadership, industry recognition for technological prowess or high-quality performance, or market reputation for innovation, environmental concern, or ethical trading.

Developing a full understanding of a competitor's strategic goals is not an easy task and this can usually only be inferred from a competitor's actions. Some firms try to recruit senior executives from their competitors in order to get real insight into their strategic intentions. Although this happens quite frequently, it is not an ethical way of operating and organizations can impose severe legal and financial constraints on employees in terms of who they can work for if they leave and the timescale in which they are not allowed to work in the industry.

Which Strategies Are They Following?

Once a competitor's goals are understood it becomes easier to predict what its marketing strategies are likely to be. These strategies can be considered through two main factors, competitive scope and positioning.

Competitive scope refers to the breadth of the market addressed. Is the competitor attempting to service the whole of a market, particular segments, or a single niche segment? If they are servicing a niche market, one of the key questions to be asked is whether they will want to stay and dominate the niche or are they simply using it as a trial before spring-boarding into other market segments?

Brands can be positioned in markets according to the particular attributes and benefits a brand offers. Cameras might be positioned according to their technical features, whereas cosmetics are often positioned on style and fashion, frequently with campaigns led by brand ambassadors who are considered to personify the brand values. Once this is understood it is possible to follow the marketing mix elements that are aligned to support the positioning strategy. Some brands are based on price and a low-cost strategy. This approach requires a focus on reducing costs and expenses rather than investing in heavy levels of marketing communications and/or product **research and development**. We will consider low-cost strategies in further detail later in this chapter.

How Are They Likely to Respond?

Understanding the strategies of competitors helps inform whether they are intent on outright attack or defence, and how they might react to particular strategies initiated by others. For example, a price cut might be met with a similar reduction, a larger reduction, or none at all. Changes in the levels of investment in advertising might produce a similar range of responses.

Some market leaders believe that an aggressive response to a challenger's actions is important otherwise their leadership position might be undermined. There are, of course, a range of responses that firms may use, reflecting organizational objectives, leadership styles, industry norms, and new strategies born of new owners. (See Market Insight 5.2 about how the main players compete in the games console market.)

▶ Market Insight 5.2

Playing Games in a Challenging Market

The games console market is intensely competitive, but, because of the severe upfront development and launch costs, the launch of a new system is often delayed. This is because of the experience curve effects, namely that as more units are sold and as a market matures a console becomes cheaper to make. Games are expensive to develop but manufacturing costs are very low, which means that successful consoles are extremely profitable, even though hardware is sold at a loss to build market share.

Sony's PlayStation brand has dominated the games console market in recent years. The main competition in the market comes from Microsoft, the market challenger, and the launch of Microsoft's Xbox 360 was an attempt to achieve market leadership. One of the reasons for Sony's success, which has continued with PS3, is that Sony had established the original PlayStation as a brand. This meant that a huge consumer base had been established and one of the key attributes of the PS2 was that it was backwards-compatible with PlayStation games, therefore enabling games developed for the first machine to be used on the PS2. In addition, it was able to play DVDs, unlike the competition, a major point of differentiation.

However, the market is dynamic and that means it is changing and that requires the competitors to update, differentiate, and launch as fast as is feasible. However, market leaders sometimes like to delay the launch of new products in order to capitalize on the revenue streams and margins associated with established brands. In this case, it appears that Sony delayed the launch of its next generation based on the logistical challenges it faced in producing sufficient stock to have a successful launch. Failing to fulfil market demand might have given the market

▶ Market Insight 5.2

challenger an opportunity to take share. The key challenger, Microsoft with their Xbox 360, sought to destabilize Sony by introducing new products with new attributes. Part of their strategy was to launch the Xbox 360 simultaneously in all major markets.

Another challenger, Nintendo, launched a radically new games console called Wii. The feature of this product was that the conventional key pad was replaced with an innovative motion-sensitive

controller. One of the key attributes of the market leader's response, the PS3, was to provide a built-in Blu-ray disc player, as it was believed this provided the best next-generation gaming experience, and had the added advantage of being able to play high-definition movies.

Competition has centred on the experience a games console generates for the participants. However, it likely that the definition of the games market is going to change as a wider remit emerges. For example, Xbox is focusing on streaming TV shows and connecting people to their social networking sites. The goal, according to McCormick (2009), is to position Xbox as an entertainment brand that ultimately will replace TVs as the centrepiece in people's homes.

Sources: Schofield (2005); Andrews (2006); Andrews (2006); Arthur (2007); McCormick (2009).

The console market, as challenging as the games!
Source: Courtesy of Sony Computer Entertainment UK Limited.

1 **What markets are the console manufacturers in, and, apart from using product attributes, what are the main ways in which they compete?**

2 **What do you believe are Sony and Microsoft's strategic goals?**

3 **What advantage do you think Nintendo thought they would achieve with the radically new product offering, Wii?**

Suppliers and Distributors

So far, analysis of the performance environment has tended to concentrate on the nature and characteristics of a firm's competitive behaviour. This is, of course, important, but Porter also realized that suppliers can influence competition and he built this into his Five Forces model. However, since he published his work there have been several significant supply side developments, most notably the development of outsourcing. Outsourcing concerns the transfer of non-core activities to an external organization that specializes in the activity or operation. For example, transport and delivery services are not core activities to most companies, although they constitute an important part of the value they offer their customers. In Japan, the Hitachi Transport System, a third-party logistics (3PL) service, is used by companies as an outsourced provider to transport their goods. Many suppliers, therefore, have become an integral part of a firm's capabilities. Rather than act aggressively they are more likely to be cooperative and work in support of the firm that has outsourced the work to them.

Similar changes have occurred downstream in terms of a manufacturer's marketing channel. Now it is common to find high levels of integration between a manufacturer and their distributors, dealers, and retailers. Account needs to be taken of the strength of these relationships and consideration needs to be given to how market performance might be strengthened or weakened by the capabilities of the channel intermediary. Suppliers and distributors have become central to the way in which firms can develop specific competitive advantages. It is important, therefore, that analysis of the performance environment incorporates a review of those organizations that are key suppliers and distributors to the firm under analysis.

SWOT Analysis

Perhaps the most common analytical tool is **SWOT analysis**. SWOT stands for Strengths, Weaknesses, Opportunities, and Threats. Essentially it is a series of checklists derived from the marketing audit and the PESTLE analysis, and is presented as internal strengths and weaknesses, and external opportunities or threats.

Strengths and weaknesses relate to the internal resources and capabilities of the organization, as perceived by customers (Piercy, 2002).

▶ A strength is something an organization is good at doing or something that gives it particular credibility and market advantage.

▶ A weakness is something an organization lacks or performs in an inferior way in comparison to others.

Opportunities and threats are externally oriented issues that can potentially influence the performance of an organization or product. Information about these elements is normally generated through PESTLE analysis.

▶ An opportunity is the potential to advance the organization by the development and satisfaction of an unfulfilled market need.

▶ A threat is something that at some time in the future may destabilize and/or reduce the potential performance of the organization.

SWOT analysis is a tool used to determine an overall view of an organization's strategic position. It highlights the need for a strategy to produce a strong fit between the internal capability (strengths and weaknesses) and the external situation (opportunities and threats). SWOT helps to sort through the information generated in the audit, it serves to identify the key issues, and then prompts thought about converting weaknesses into strengths and threats into opportunities, in other words generating conversion strategies. For example, some companies have developed and run call centres for their own internal use, but saw opportunities to use their strength to run call centres for other companies. It is said that a few years ago one major computer company only used its call centre during the day. An opportunity was spotted to run the call centre at night, routing calls for a nationwide pizza company.

SWOT in inexperienced hands often leads to long lists of items. Although the SWOT process may lead to the generation of these lists, the analyst should be attempting to identify the key strengths and weaknesses and the key opportunities and threats. These key elements should impact on strategy; if they don't then they should not be in the analysis. A strength is not a strength if it does not have strategic implications.

Once the three or four elements of each part of the SWOT matrix have been derived then a number of pertinent questions need to be asked.

1 Does the organization do something far better than its rivals? If it does, this is known as a competitive advantage (distinctive competence, differential advantage), and this can lead to a competitive edge.

2 Which of the organization's weaknesses does our strategy need to correct and is it competitively vulnerable?

3 Which opportunities can be pursued and are there the necessary resources and capabilities to exploit them?

4 Which strategies are necessary to defend against the key threats?

Figure 5.4 depicts a SWOT grid for a small digital media agency. The outcome of a successful SWOT analysis is a series of decisions that help develop and formulate strategy and goals.

Strengths	**Weaknesses**
Quick to respond to changes in the marketing environment	Too much work from a few clients and at non-premium rates
Flat management encourages fast decision-making	Few project-management skills
Use of contractors enables flexibility—lowers employment costs/finance and improves customers' perception of expertise	High office and finance costs
	Low customer base
Opportunities	**Threats**
Emerging markets such as Professional Services (e.g. dentists, lawyers, surveyors)	Larger media houses buying business
New distribution channels	Speed of technological advances
Tax incentives to encourage eCommerce	Contractors have low levels of loyalty

Figure 5.4

A SWOT analysis for a small digital media agency

Note that there are no more than four items in any one category, not a whole list of ten or so items. It is important to prioritize and make a judgment about what is really key rather than just an interesting point. The actions that follow the identification of the key issues should be based around matching opportunities with strengths and weaknesses with threats. In this example it may be possible to diversify into professional services, a niche market (an opportunity), using particular contractors who have knowledge and relevant expertise (a strength).

Weaknesses need to be addressed, not avoided. Some can be converted into strengths, others into opportunities. In this example, entering the professional services market would probably increase the number of customers and enable premium rates to be earned.

Threats need to be nullified. For example, by building relationships with key contractors (suppliers) and selected larger media houses, these threats might be dissipated, and even developed into strengths.

Strategic Marketing Goals

The purpose of strategic market analysis is to help managers understand the nature of the industry, the way firms behave competitively within the industry, and how competition is generally undertaken. From this information it becomes easier to determine exactly what the marketing strategy should actually achieve, in other words, what the strategic marketing goals should be.

There are several types of strategic objective but four main ones are considered here. These are niche, hold, harvest, and divest goals and are considered briefly. However, the section that follows considers a further objective, namely growth. Figure 5.5 sets out the content for this section.

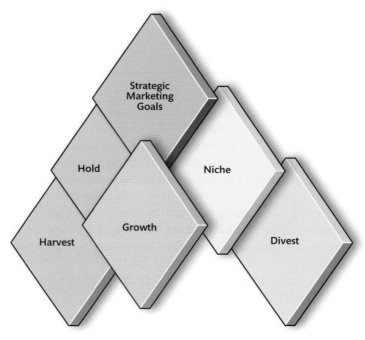

Figure 5.5

Five dimensions of strategic marketing goals

Niche objectives are often the most suitable when firms operate in a market dominated by a major competitor and where their financial resources are limited. A niche can either be a small segment or even a small part of a segment. Niche markets often arise because it is not economic for the leading competitors to enter this segment simply because these customers have special needs and the leading firm does not want to devote resources in this way. To be successful in niche markets it is important to have a strongly differentiated product offering, supported by a high level of service. The Australian government identified several niche markets when exploring ways in which it could develop its tourism business. It identified sports, cycling seniors, culture and the arts, backpackers, health, people with disabilities, caravanning and camping, food, wine, and agri-tourism as potential niche markets.

Hold objectives are concerned with defence. They are designed to prevent and fend off attack from aggressive competitors. Market leaders are the most likely to adopt a holding strategy as they are prone to attack from new entrants and their closest rivals as they strive for the most market share. Market leadership is important as it generally drives positive cash flows, confers privileges such as strong bargaining positions with suppliers, and enhances image and reputation. Holding strategies can take a number of forms, varying from 'doing nothing' in order to maintain market equilibrium, to implementing a counter-offensive defence, to withdrawing from a market completely.

Harvesting objectives are often employed in mature markets as firms/products enter a decline phase. The goal is to maximize short-term profits and stimulate a positive cash flow. By stripping out most of the marketing communications and R&D it becomes possible to generate cash that can be used elsewhere. These funds can be used to generate new products, support 'stars', or to turn 'question marks' into 'dogs' if it is realized that there will not be a long-term profit stream (see Chapter 2).

Divest objectives are sometimes necessary when products continue to incur losses and generate negative cash flows. Divestment can follow on naturally from a harvesting strategy. Typically low-share products in declining markets are prime candidates to be divested. Divestment may be actioned by selling off the product should a suitable buyer be available, or simply withdrawing from the market. For example, Procter & Gamble divested the Sunny Delight orange drink brand, General Motors sold off Saab to sports car manufacturer Spyker (Madslien, 2010), and Ford sold off Jaguar to the Indian company Tata, and have also been trying to sell Swedish brand Volvo to a Chinese company.

Growth

The vast majority of organizations consider growth to be a primary objective. However, there are different forms of growth and care needs to be taken to ensure that the right growth goals are selected. Growth can be intensive, integrated, or diversified.

▶ **Intensive** growth refers to concentrating activities on markets and/or products that are familiar. By increasing market share or by introducing new products to an established market, growth is achieved by intensifying activities.

▶ **Integrative** growth occurs where an organization continues to work with the same products and same markets but starts to perform some of the activities in the value chain that were previously undertaken by others. For example, Benetton moved from designing and manufacturing their clothing products into retailing.

▶ Growth through **diversification** refers to developments outside the current chain of value-adding activities. This type of growth brings new value chain activities because the firm is operating with new products and in new markets.

The idea that growth is allied to product/market relationships is important and Ansoff (1957) proposed that organizations should first consider whether new or established products are to be delivered in new or established markets. His product/market matrix (Figure 5.6), otherwise known as **Ansoff's matrix**, is an important first step in deciding what the marketing strategy should be. The product/market matrix is examined further in Chapter 7.

Figure 5.6

Ansoff's matrix

Source: Adapted from Ansoff (1957).

	Present Products	**New Products**
Present Markets	Market Penetration	Product Development
New Markets	Market Development	Diversification

▶ Market Insight 5.3

Vodafone: Talking Strategies

Vodafone Group plc is the world's leading mobile telecommunications company. Its vision is to be 'the communications leader in an increasingly connected world'. The company has created a significant global presence in Europe, the Middle East, Africa, Asia Pacific, and the USA. In most countries, its mobile subsidiaries operate under the brand name 'Vodafone'. In other countries, they use dual branding in cooperation with partner networks in the marketing of global services.

Vodafone's corporate strategy has been based on a number of dimensions, most notably growth through acquisition and geographic expansion, acquiring new and retaining existing customers, and increasing customer usage by developing new products that they find useful.

Vodafone's marketing strategy is based on the goal of retaining its market leadership position. This is achieved through a customer-oriented strategy based on delivering high-quality service and a stream of new products that are designed to utilize the latest technological advances. This recognizes that as

Source: Courtesy of Vodafone Group.

consumers become increasingly more sophisticated users of modern mobile technology, they seek added value through product improvements.

Vodafone's marketing objectives include:

▶ obtaining new customers;

▶ keeping the customers it already has;

▶ introducing new technologies and services (enabling the mobile internet, HSDPA/UPA and Mobile TV);

▶ continuing to develop the Vodafone brand.

Vodafone's results suggest that it is achieving these objectives and is continually updating its range of products and services to enable their customers to make the most of life's opportunities. In addition, Vodafone recognizes that customers are increasingly price-sensitive and has adapted highly competitive pricing strategies that offer true value.

The central brand idea reflects this customer obsession and focuses on how innovation can make their lives better. 'Power to you' is all about giving customers back the power and putting them at the heart of the organization.

Sources: www.vodafone.com/section_article/; www.thetimes100. co.uk/case_study; www.online.vodafone.co.uk/dispatch/Portal.

1 **To what degree do you think Vodafone's marketing strategy supports their corporate strategy?**

2 **Which of the different marketing objectives listed above do you feel Vodafone is using?**

3 **Visit the website of two organizations that operate in the same industry and try to compare their mission (or statements of purpose).**

Strategic Market Action

Having analysed the industry and the main competitors, determined suitable strategic marketing goals, and performed a SWOT analysis, the final set of marketing strategy activities concerns the identification of the most appropriate way of achieving the goals and then putting the plan into action, the implementation phase.

There is no proven formula or tool kit that managers can use simply because of the vast array of internal and external environmental factors. What we can draw upon is experience and a range of strategies that we know are more likely to be successful than others. In the following section we consider ideas about competitive advantage, generic strategies, competitive positioning, strategic intent, and marketing planning and implementation (see Figure 5.7).

Figure 5.7

Strategic marketing action

Competitive Advantage

Competitive advantage is achieved when an organization has a significant and sustainable edge over its competitors, when attracting buyers. Advantage can also be secured by coping with the competitive forces better than its rivals. Advantage can be developed in many different ways. Some organizations have an advantage simply because they are the best-known organization or brand in the market. Some achieve it by producing the best-quality product or having attributes that other products do not have. For example, some pharmaceutical brands have an advantage while patent protection exists. As soon as the patent expires and competitors can produce generic versions of the drug, the advantage is lost. Some organizations have the lowest price, whereas others provide the best support and service in the industry. However, whatever the advantage, the superiority has to be sustainable through time.

The conditions necessary for the achievement of sustainable competitive advantage (SCA) are, according to Porter (1985), as follows:

1 The customer consistently perceives a positive difference between the products and services offered by a company and its competitors.

2 The perceived difference results from the company's relatively greater capability.

3 The perceived difference persists for a reasonable period of time. SCA is only durable as long as it is not easily imitated.

▶ Research Insight 5.3

To take your learning further, you might wish to read this influential paper.

Day, G. S., and Wensley, R. (1988), 'Assessing advantage: a framework for diagnosing competitive superiority', *Journal of Marketing*, 52, 2 (April), 1–20.

As the title suggests this paper considers a framework for identifying competitive advantage. It achieves this by first considering the elements of competitive advantage and then brings together both competitor- and customer-focused elements in order to identify 'points of superiority'.

 Visit the **Online Resource Centre** to read the abstract and access the full paper.

Generic Strategies

If the importance of achieving a competitive advantage is accepted as a crucial aspect of a successful marketing strategy, then it is necessary to understand how strategies can lead to the development of sustainable competitive advantages. Porter (1985) proposed that there are two essential routes to achieving above average performance. These are to become the lowest cost producer or to differentiate the product/service to a degree that it is of superior value to the customer. These strategies can be implemented in either broad (mass) or narrow (focused) markets. Porter suggested that these give rise to three generic strategies; overall cost leadership, differentiation, and focus strategies.

Cost leadership does not mean a lower price, although lower prices are often used to attract customers. By having the lowest cost structure, an organization can offer standard products at acceptable levels of quality, yet still generate above-average profit margins. If attacked by a competitor using lower prices, the low-cost leader has a far bigger cushion than its competitors. It should be appreciated that charging a lower price than its rivals is not the critical point. The competitive advantage is derived from how the organization exploits its cost/price ratio. By reinvesting the profit, for example by improving product quality, investing more in product development, or building extra capacity, long-run superiority is more likely to be achieved.

A **differentiation** strategy requires that all value chain activities are geared to the creation of products that are valued by, and which satisfy, the needs of particular broad segments. By identifying particular customer groups, where each group has a discrete set of needs, a product can be differentiated from its competitors. The fashion brand Zara differentiated itself by reformulating their value chain so that they became the fastest high street brand to design, produce, distribute, and make fashion clothing available in their shops.

Customers are sometimes prepared to pay a higher price, a price premium, for products that deliver superior or extra value. For example, the Starbucks coffee brand is strongly differentiated and valued, as consumers are willing to pay higher prices to enjoy the Starbucks experience. However, differentiation can be achieved by low prices, as evidenced through the success of low-cost airlines, Ryanair and EasyJet.

Products can be differentiated using a variety of criteria, indeed each element of the marketing mix is capable of providing the means for successful, long-term differentiation. Differentiation can lead to greater levels of brand loyalty. For example, in contrast to low-cost ASDA, Waitrose provide a strongly differentiated supermarket service.

Focus strategies are used by organizations to seek gaps in broad market segments or find gaps in competitors' product ranges. In other words, focus strategies help to seek out unfulfilled market needs. The focused operator then concentrates all value chain activities on a narrow range of products and services.

Focus strategies can be oriented to being the lowest cost producer for the particular segment or offering a differentiated product for which the narrow target segment is willing to pay a higher price. This means that there are two options for a company wishing to follow a focus strategy. One is low cost and the other is differentiation, but both occur within a particular, narrow, segment. The difference between a broad differentiator and a focused differentiator is that the former bases its strategy on attributes valued across a number of markets, whereas the latter seeks to meet the needs of particular segments within a market.

Porter argues that, to achieve competitive advantage, organizations must achieve one of these three generic strategies. To fail to be strategically explicit results in organizations' being 'stuck in the middle'. This means that they achieve below-average returns and have no competitive advantage. It has been observed, however, that some organizations have been able to pursue low-cost and differentiated strategies simultaneously. For example, an organization that develops a large market share through differentiation and by creating very strong brands may well become the cost leader as well. Porter's contribution is very important; however, these generic strategies should not be treated as tablets of stone! It is a useful approach and one that has contributed to our understanding about the way in which markets operate.

Competitive Positioning

Having collected industry information, analysed competitors, and considered our resources, perhaps the single most important aspect of developing marketing strategy is to decide how to compete in the selected target markets. Two key decisions arise: what position do we want in the market, which is considered here, and what will be our strategic intent? This is examined in the following section.

The position that a product adopts in a market is a general reflection of its market share. Four positions can be identified; market leader, challenger, follower, and nicher, and each has particular characteristics, as set out in Table 5.2.

▶ **Table 5.2** Types of market position	
Market leader	The market leader has the single largest share of the market. Market leadership is important as it is these products and brands that can shape the nature of competition in the market, set out standards relating to price, quality, speed of innovation, and communications, as well as influencing the key distribution channels. For example, Tesco was an ordinary mid-ranking supermarket in the 1980s but has since grown to become the leading UK supermarket.
Market challengers	Products that aspire to the leadership position are referred to as market challengers. These may be positioned as number two, three, or even four in the market. They actively seek market share and use aggressive strategies to take share from all of their rivals. For example, Sainsbury's and ASDA are the two main market challengers in the UK supermarket sector.
Market followers	These firms have low market shares and do not have the resources to be serious competitors. They pose no threat to the market leader or challengers and often adopt me-too strategies when the market leader takes an initiative. If we extend the examples within the supermarket sector, then Morrisons might be deemed as a market follower.
Market nichers	Nichers are specialists. They select small segments within target markets that the larger companies do not want to exploit. They develop specialized marketing mixes designed to meet the needs of their customers. They are threatened by economic downturns when customers either cease buying that type of product or buy more competitively priced products. They are also vulnerable to changes in customer tastes and competitor innovation.

There are two main reasons to understand the competitive positions adopted by companies. The first is to understand the way the various firms are positioned in the market and from that deduce the strategies they are likely to follow and their most probable strategies when attacked by others. The other reason is to understand where the company is currently positioned and to decide where it wants to be positioned at some point in the future. This will shape the nature and quantity of the resources to be required and the strategies to be pursued. Some of these strategies are set out in Table 5.3.

▶ **Table 5.3** Prime strategy characteristics

Competitive position	Prime strategies
Market leader	Attack the market—create new uses, users, or increase frequency of use
	Defend the position—regular innovation, larger ranges, price cutting and discounts, increased promotion
Market challenger	Attack the market leader—use pricing, new product attributes, sharp increase in advertising spend
	Attack rivals—special offers and limited editions, offer superior competitive advantages
	Maintain 'status quo'
Market follower	Avoid hostile attacks on rivals
	Copy the market leader and provide good-quality products that are well differentiated
	Focus on differentiation and profits, not market share
Market nicher	Provide high level of specialization—geographic, product, service, customer group
	Provide tight fit between market needs and the organization's resources

▶ Market Insight 5.4

Developing New Programmable Space

Herman Miller (HM) is a major office furniture designer and manufacturer. Since 1923 the company has been renowned for selling high-quality, ergonomically designed, office chairs, desks, and storage facilities to major private companies, governments, and other leading organizations, around the world. However, in 2000, the company began to consider the future and soon reached the conclusion that growth in white-collar workers was going to slow, and so the demand for office furniture was also likely to fall. This represented a major threat to the company as its strategy was built around these main markets.

A new team of seven people was created. The team consisted of a mix of leading technologists, architects and engineers, some with no experience of the business. They were required to innovate, to identify new markets, and to guide HM to undeveloped areas of commercial potential. The team worked in relative isolation from other HM employees and outside contractors and experts.

The result was a raft of innovations, many of which served to redefine office interiors and the company itself. For example, HM launched a new company called Convia. Essentially, Convia offered an intelligent modular electrical system with a programmable data network, which is installed in a ceiling. It also provides an assembly that allows for the suspension of office interior devices. The result was a new market, one based on 'programmable workspace'.

▶ Market Insight 5.4   (continued)

Herman Miller's programable workspace concept

The value in this new approach can be seen in terms of the property development market. Buildings and offices can be reconfigured without disposing of wires, conduits, and other embedded materials. For facilities management companies, energy and light management issues can be managed more effectively. For users, space can be personalized, so that the levels of heat, light, and sound can be adjusted with a simple mouse click. HM now offered programmable workspace solutions and were the first to do so.

The company repositioned itself as a researcher, designer, manufacturer, and distributor of innovative office furniture. HM develop solutions for organizations so that they provide great places for people to learn and work. HM moved from a company that sold furniture to one that provides buildings with intelligent infrastructure and enables people to better manage their working environments.

Sources: Adapted from Birchard (2010); www.hermanmiller.co.uk/.

1   **Identify the type of strategy Herman Miller implemented.**

2   **To what extent is Herman Miller's response really strategic?**

3   **Apply Herman Miller's scenario to the Ansoff matrix. What other strategic options could the company have followed?**

Implementation

The implementation of any marketing plan is incomplete without methods to control and evaluate its performance. It is vitally important to monitor the results of the programme as it unfolds, not just when it is completed. Therefore, measures need to be stated in the plan about how the results of the plan will be recorded and disseminated throughout the team. Recording the performance of the marketing plan against targets enables managers to make adjustments should the plan not perform as expected, due possibly to unforeseen market events.

For ease of explanation the marketing planning process has been depicted as a linear, sequential series of management activities. This certainly helps to simplify understanding about how strategy can be developed and it also serves to show how various activities are linked together. However, it should be recognized that strategy development and planning, whether it be at corporate, business, or functional level, is not linear, does not evolve in preset ways, and is not always subject to a regular, pre-determined pattern of evolution. Indeed, politics, finance, and interpersonal conflicts all help shape the nature of an organization's marketing strategy.

Marketing implementation is a fundamental process in marketing because it is the actioning phase of the strategic marketing process. Whereas many of the concepts in this text help us to design marketing programmes, the implementation phase is about actually doing it. In reality, then, it is the most exciting part of marketing because it is the least predictable.

The problems identified in implementing marketing strategy are not particularly well researched. It seems likely that some companies are better at implementing marketing strategies than others. According to Piercy (1998), this may be because a company's marketing implementation capabilities are time-specific, culture-specific, partial, latent, internally consistent, strategy-specific, and person-specific, as outlined in Table 5.4.

▶ **Table 5.4** Characteristics of companies' marketing implementation capabilities

Characteristics	Explanation
Time-specific	Companies gain or lose the competencies necessary to implement a strategy based on time, e.g. senior executives or a dominant leader may retire. Company assets may be perishable, e.g. British Energy's nuclear reactors have a limited lifespan before needing to be decommissioned
Culture-specific	Strategy may be reliant on certain cultural conditions that do not exist in other cultures, e.g. customer service standards might on average be higher in some Western countries (e.g. the USA) than in developing countries (e.g. Russia) because people tend to work harder to take account of customer needs
Partial	Companies may be able to implement only parts of a strategy and so outsource other components, e.g. a pharmaceutical company developing a new drug with a ready customer base in Japan may not have the regulatory know-how to get the product formally and legally listed to comply with the relevant authorities
Latent	A company may have the actual knowledge required for the formulation of a particular strategy but not the knowledge to implement it either through poor deployment of resources of a lack of management understanding and experience
Internally consistent	Some parts of a company might be better able to execute a strategy than others
Strategy-specific	Companies develop capabilities to implement specific previously developed strategies but are not able to meet the needs of a new strategy, particularly where such strategies require significant organizational change
Person-specific	Companies' implementation capabilities may be dependent on a single person or a particular team (e.g. a new product development strategy may be reliant on a particular scientist or team, causing obvious problems if they then leave the company)

It is reasonable, therefore, to argue that the implementation of any marketing plan is far from straightforward. However, there are certain elements that impact on the implementation of most strategic marketing plans, and these are considered here.

▶ The structure and type of marketing function and the degree to which a marketing orientation prevails across the organization.

▶ The degree of team-working among co-workers associated with the implementation process. These can be internal (employees) and external (consultants, agencies or outsourced customer service representatives).

▶ The controls used to measure the effectiveness of the implementation process. These are referred to as **marketing metrics**.

go online

Visit the **Online Resource Centre** and complete Internet Activity 5.2 to learn more about the L'Oréal business simulation game designed to help students learn about developing effective brand strategies.

The Structures and Types of Marketing Organizations

How we organize ourselves to undertake the task of marketing has an impact on how effective we are. In addition, the way we organize the marketing function has an impact on how our colleagues in other professional disciplines view us and our effectiveness. According to a Chartered Institute of Marketing survey, only 10% of boardroom time is spent discussing marketing issues, whereas the number of CEOs with a marketing background appears to be falling (CIM, 2009a).

go online

Visit the **Online Resource Centre** and follow the weblink to the CIM to learn more about the role of marketing in organizations.

Despite the fact that brands account for 28% of companies' total intangible value on average, according to Brand Finance, boards of directors are not required to report to investors what they are doing with their most key assets, their brands. However, as Jack (2010) reports, investors appear to be more interested in how companies manage their brands. In addition, some financial analysts are beginning to accept that marketing and brand equity issues need to be taken more seriously.

So, it seems that marketing professionals are either less effective than their professional colleagues or they are underrated. The question is how do marketers organize a more effective function with their organization?

A further problem is that marketers do not always control all the elements of the marketing mix that are assumed to be under their control. For example, as O'Malley and Patterson (1998) indicate, marketers seldom control pricing, distribution, product development, and even promotion, as this is often outsourced to agencies, although they may exercise influence over all these activities and more. In addition, marketing may not necessarily be organized as a separate department but the ethos and influence of marketing philosophy may still be apparent and impact on an organization's decision-making (Harris and Ogbonna, 2003).

Marketing is present in all aspects of an organization, as all departments have some role to play with respect to creating, delivering, and satisfying customers. For example, employees in the R&D department designing new products to meet poorly met existing customer needs are performing a marketing role. Similarly, members of the procurement department buying components for a new product or service must purchase components of specific quality and at a certain cost that will meet customer needs. In fact, we can go through all departments of a company, and find that in each department, there is a marketing role to be played to some extent. In other words, marketing should be regarded as something that is distributed throughout an organization and all employees should be considered as part-time marketers (Gummesson, 1990). Marketing is not something that only people in the marketing department undertake (see Market Insight 5.5, which provides an interesting illustration of these issues).

▶ Market Insight 5.5

Pret A Manger: Marketing with a Smile

Pret A Manger was founded in 1986 by two university friends, Julian Metcalfe and Sinclair Beecham, in London. Offering sandwiches, soups, sushi boxes, and salads, the brand name literally means ready to eat in French. The two friends wanted to create a sophisticated sandwich chain, which dispensed with the preservatives and chemicals found in competitors' offerings, and provided good, clean, 'honest', but exciting, food at reasonable prices. Sandwich offerings include crayfish and avocado, brie, tomato, and basil, and pastrami wraps, as well as staples like tuna mayo and ham, cheese, and pickle. Soups such as carrot, ginger, and coriander, and pea, smoked bacon, and mint, add to the appeal.

The mechanism for delivery of the customer proposition involves making up the sandwiches in the morning every day before the shop opens, using fresh ingredients delivered and immediately refrigerated very early that morning. The sandwiches are served ready to eat in chilled display cabinets. Competitors tend to make the food in advance in central 'factories', using preservatives and plastic packaging, so that their sandwiches can be stored for several days.

Pret A Manger has enjoyed rapid success. In 2001, it sold a 33% non-controlling stake to the fast food burger chain McDonald's for £25m, principally to obtain the funding, and the know-how, necessary

Pret A Manger: good products, selling themselves
Source: Pret A Manger.

▶ Market Insight 5.5   (continued)

to develop the Pret concept around the world. By 2010, Pret had 225 outlets, mostly in the UK, but also in New York, and in Hong Kong, with a turnover of approximately £200m.

But what is remarkable about Pret, apart from its obvious success, is that it has no formal marketing, advertising, or public relations departments. It does centralize customer service and recruitment, but, incredibly, Pret does no formal customer service training. Instead, it relies on the shop employees to sell the company's enthusiasm for its food.

So, it's the shop employees who, as future co-workers, carefully select new recruits on the basis of their friendliness and ability to do the job well after the applicant has spent a day in a Pret outlet. Staff are encouraged to be nice to customers through the offer of a wage bonus, on top of a generous hourly pay rate, based on the results of extensive mystery shopping research.

So, with a business model like that, and fantastic tasting products, who needs full-time marketers?

Sources: Clark (2001); Anon (2007); Skapinker (2007); www.pret-com.

1 **Do you think the Pret A Manger business is held back because it does not employ marketing centrally? If yes, how is it held back?**

2 **Why do you think the Pret A Manger chain has been so successful until now? Will the fact that McDonald's owns a proportion of the chain and an option to buy more affect Pret's business in the future?**

3 **Are you aware of any other companies, either in this sector or another one, where a central marketing department is not employed?**

Types of Marketing Organization

Marketers have not always been able to highlight easily the performance of their departments against the return on investment made in paying marketing salaries and budgets by senior management. As a result, organizations have developed different ways of organizing their sales and marketing functions (see Figure 5.8).

In Figure 5.8a, marketing and sales are separate departments reporting to the manager in charge of a particular strategic business unit (SBU). In this situation, it is the job of the manager to coordinate the different departmental inputs into a coherent and complementary set of strategies. In Figure 5.8b, each sales and marketing department reports to a SBU manager, who will then report to a corporate headquarters. Corporate headquarters also have a corporate marketing group, which will tend to handle the marketing for the group as a whole (e.g. corporate identity, group market research). In Figure 5.8c, the marketing department still reports to a SBU manager, but the sales force is centralized and sells the products for other SBUs as well. In Figure 5.8d, sales and marketing operate for each individual SBU, but research and development (R&D) and manufacturing are undertaken centrally across the SBUs. Finally, in Figure 5.8e, manufacturing and R&D operate for each individual SBU, but sales and marketing are corporate functions.

Marketing organizations have changed in recent years. There is now an increased emphasis on key account management, where senior marketing personnel serve important accounts or customer segments, sometimes through cross-functional teams involving sales, marketing, and

(a) Marketing and Sales in a Functionally Organized Autonomous Business Unit

(b) Marketing and Sales in a Functionally Organized Business Unit with a Corporate Marketing Group

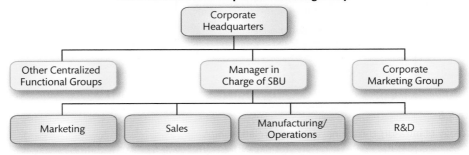

(c) Marketing in a Business Unit that Shares a Sales Force with Other Business Units

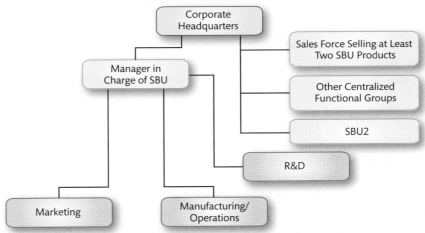

(d) Marketing and Sales in a 'Distribution Business Unit' with Few R&D or Production Capabilities

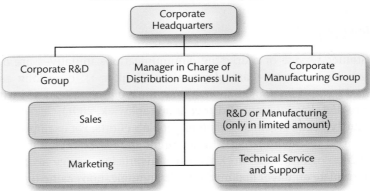

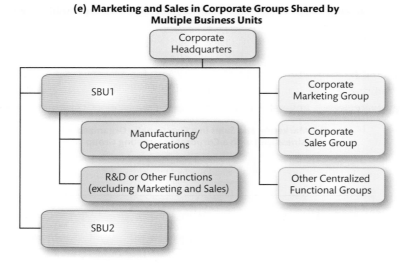

(e) Marketing and Sales in Corporate Groups Shared by Multiple Business Units

Figure 5.8

A typology of intra-organizational marketing relationships

Note: Support groups such as finance, human resources (HR), and legal are not shown here. R&D, research and development; SBU, strategic business unit.

Source: Reproduced with kind permission from the *Journal of Marketing* (American Marketing Association), Workman, Homburg, and Gruner (1998).

supply chain management personnel, particularly in sales and operations planning (S&OP) meetings, where detailed supply and demand plans are considered and reconciled (e.g. at AstraZeneca, the pharmaceutical giant). Where firms are operating in more than one country, the role of the country manager has been reduced. As companies have globalized (e.g. Nike), and their efforts spread across countries, senior managers now tend to operate across whole continental regions (e.g. Europe, Middle East, and Africa). In addition, product managers have lost their role as the primary marketing coordinator of sales, marketing, R&D, manufacturing, and other functions. This role has shifted to key account managers or category managers (e.g. Procter & Gamble), who oversee whole brand categories rather than individual products.

In addition, there has been an increasing shift towards outsourcing marketing activities. For example, advertising and market research have traditionally been outsourced to agencies by large multinational and many medium-sized firms. Recently, there has been an increasing shift towards outsourcing sales activities (e.g. health insurance), data warehousing (e.g. car and electrical goods manufacturers), and customer data analytics (supermarkets and financial services).

Team-Working

Whether customer service or marketing communications initiatives are outsourced or not, marketers have to be strong team players (see Chapter 1), especially as more and more departments take over functions that were once most closely associated with marketing, e.g. pricing and product development (Bristow and Frankwick, 2001).

Marketers are typically organizers of other people's efforts. For example, they may liaise with an in-house market research manager to determine the research plan for the year ahead for a particular product, or they may work with the advertising agency account planner and his/ her team to formulate an integrated marketing communications campaign. If they are involved in pricing and budgeting, it is frequently as a result of discussions with an executive from the finance department rather than undertaking the detailed costing work in their own capacity. Marketing personnel may have conversations with sales personnel over how to support the sales functions' objectives, but they do not get personally involved in selling. Similarly, marketing personnel should have an input into distribution of goods and services, particularly where service design might form a competitive advantage, but they would not actually undertake a service redesign exercise by themselves; this usually falls to the operations or supply chain management department instead. In less well-funded organizations, e.g. small to medium-sized enterprises, marketing executives may pick up some of these tasks themselves, e.g. undertaking market research and marketing communications activities in-house, to offset costs.

Marketing is an activity concerned with creating customer value and concerns most departments in an organization. Yet, despite the long recognized central importance of the customer (Levitt, 1960), marketers are all too often organized into silos as a line function, a department, rather than as a cross-departmental staff function, e.g. human resources or information technology (Sheth and Sisodia, 2006). This is still the case despite the fact that 'there is now increasing recognition that cross-functional working relationships have a key role to play in the successful implementation of marketing decisions' (Chimhanzi, 2002). In order to develop marketing's influence in a team setting, organizations must:

▶ Develop joint reward systems, which work across departments and reduce interdepartmental conflict (Chimhanzi, 2002). Successful marketing teams are appropriately rewarded. So, it is important that salespeople are evaluated and compensated not only for achieving sales volume targets but also for their contribution to the implementation of marketing programmes more generally, which may have wider objectives than short-term sales revenue increases (Strahle, Spiro, and Acito, 1996).

▶ Communicate the value of the marketing department to other teams—for example, firms that are market-oriented tend to show greater profitability (Wong and Saunders, 1993).

▶ Through their senior managers, encourage informal integration of departments and greater interfunctional coordination (Day, 1994).

Working successfully in teams requires participants to use a range of interpersonal skills from a variety of project management- and marketing-related skill sets. However, of the many reasons for marketing strategies and plans to underperform, two stand out; internal politics and budgeting.

Internal Politics and Negotiation

Part of the task of introducing a new marketing strategy into an organization is the process of persuading colleagues that the marketing strategy is the right strategy to adopt and implement. Sometimes marketing colleagues resist efforts to implement strategy. However, there has been a movement away from forms of organization that stress central coordination and multilevel hierarchies toward more flexible organizational forms where numerous organizations are tied together in cooperative supply chains (Achrol and Kotler, 1999).

Whether we are operating in networks of organizations or as part of a central marketing department within a company, it is important to overcome resistance to strategy implementation. Resistance to marketing implementation is known as **counter-implementation**. It is defined as encompassing 'a variety of different resistant behaviours that are motivated by anxiety on behalf of those tasked with or involved in the implementation process. Such behaviour may be motivated intentionally or unintentionally, but all may reduce the effectiveness of strategic implementation efforts' (Thomas, 2002). The main motivations for resisting strategic implementation efforts are outlined in Table 5.5.

▶ **Table 5.5** Motivations for passive and intentional counter-implementation

Passive counter-implementation	Intentional counter-implementation
Short-termism, failure to implement arises from managers continuing to pursue their existing strategies and/or the status quo	Politics (of change)
Poor quality administration of planning process	Power (to resist changes in power balances)
Insufficient information to do the implementation task properly	Psychological constraints: fear of uncertainty and fear of failure
Unclear expectations (of senior management)	Lack of trust (in either top management or implementation group)
Inappropriate timeframes provided (for the implementation process)	Betrayal and/or sabotage

Source: Based on Thomas (2002).

▶ **Market Insight 5.6**

Krafting Success

Kraft Foods became a highly centralized organization to the extent that senior managers at US corporate headquarters were required to make pricing decisions concerning brands in international and regional markets. Decisions were, therefore, being made by people who had little or no knowledge of the markets, whereas local staff had to spend time writing materials to support the case to be sent to head office rather than developing their understanding of the market dynamics and customer relationships. As a result Kraft's performance was less than optimal.

In 2007, Kraft introduced an initiative called 'Organising for Growth', which entailed restructuring the organization, decentralizing the decision-making to the people in the markets, and generating a culture of accountability. Teams were assembled to address the core change issues and each team had two members of the executive board in order to ensure consistency with the new business model. The key to Kraft's success was to build the new organization around the central business strategy, which was to move decision-making closer to the customer and their markets. Perhaps this approach led to the takeover of Cadbury in 2010?

Source: Rosenfield (2009); Paskin (2009); www.valuenetworks.com/public/item/241543.

1 **To what extent, if at all, do you think the use of teams to implement change is a good idea?**

2 **Why do you think Kraft became a centralized organization in the first place?**

3 **Can you find another organization that has radically changed its structure recently? Why did it do this? How did it do this? Was it successful?**

Budgeting

A marketing budget should indicate how much is to be spent on marketing activities and is an important aspect of a marketing manager's job. Yet, there are no hard and fast rules on how much should be allocated to marketing spend. A generally held view is that many companies lack a formal and proper budgeting process. When marketing budgets are properly determined, they are based on sales forecasts, often produced in association with the finance department of an organization, although usually with some input from the marketing department.

A marketing budget may be between 5% and 7% of sales revenues (excluding salaries), but exactly how much is spent on marketing activities is dependent on the particular industry, each firm and the overall economic climate. For example, the strongest companies to emerge from the previous recession were found to have invested 9% more in their marketing budgets than their least successful competitors (CIM, 2009b). The strongest advertisers tend to be companies in the food, beverages, and tobacco sector. Companies in the property sector spent the most on public relations. Financial services companies spent the most on sponsorship (e.g. Lloyds TSB's sponsorship of the 2012 London Olympics), retailers/wholesalers (e.g. supermarkets) on direct mail, surprisingly the public sector on email, utility companies (e.g. water, gas, and electricity companies) on promotions, business services (e.g. accountancy practices) spent most on telephone marketing, property companies spent most on **lead generation**, the consumer durables sector (e.g. stereos, TV manufacturers) spent the most on customer relationship management (CRM) programmes, whereas the food, beverages, and tobacco sector spent the most on branding. Interestingly, the utility companies spent the most on internal marketing activity.

There are differences in the pattern of expenditure, depending on the size of the company in the UK. The very large companies tended to spend more on every aspect of marketing, excluding email, telephone marketing, and lead generation activities. The smaller companies, unsurprisingly, invest the larger part of their budgets on relatively cheaper activities including direct mail, email, telephone marketing, and lead generation.

The marketing budgeting process is a political process of allocating marketing resources within a company. Clearly, where a company can demonstrate the effectiveness of the resources it has previously used, the more likely it is to receive an increase in the budget for the next year. Over the last 15 years or so, we have seen the rise in importance of measuring marketing effectiveness. As a consequence, marketers have become increasingly excited by the idea of using marketing **metrics** to determine the effectiveness of their organization's marketing activity.

Marketing Metrics

There is increased recognition of the need to determine efficiency and effectiveness in organizational marketing efforts. In the past, marketing control has been achieved through the annual marketing plan, through analysis of company profitability, some measure of efficiency (e.g. number of employees as a proportion of revenue or in retailing, net profit per square foot of retail space), or in terms of market share or some other strategic measure. But in the past, these measures have been focused towards financial or human resource measures. More recently, there has been a considerable shift in thinking towards the need for customer-based measurements (Kaplan and Norton, 1992). There has been a move towards setting key performance indicators, which companies set and measure their progress towards in order to determine whether or not they have improved or maintained their performance over a given period of time.

Research indicates that British companies are now using a variety of marketing metrics as key performance indicators in marketing. In a telephone study of 200 UK marketing and finance senior executives, nearly seven in ten respondents claimed to use the ten metrics identified in Table 5.6 (see Ambler, Kokkinaki, and Puntoni, 2004).

We discuss the benefits and limitations of using each of these key marketing performance metrics, as outlined in Figure 5.9, in the next section.

▶ **Table 5.6** Top ten marketing performance metrics

Rank	Metric	% Claiming to use measure	% Firms rating as very important
1	Profit/profitability	92	80
2	Sales, value, and/or volume	91	71
3	Gross margin	81	66
4	Awareness	78	28
5	Market share (volume or value)	78	37
6	Number of new products	73	18
7	Relative price	70	36
8	No. of consumer complaints or relative dissatisfaction	69	45
9	Consumer satisfaction	68	48
10	Distribution/availability	66	18

Source: Adapted from Ambler, Kokkinaki, and Puntoni (2004). Used with the kind permission of Westburn Publishers.

Profit/Profitability

Unsurprisingly, profit and profitability was the main key performance measure, where profit is broadly how much cash there is left in the business when all expenses are subtracted from all revenues generated. The benefit of this approach is that it indicates the 'bottom line'. It represents what is left over either for distribution to the shareholders of the business, whether that be a private or public business, or for reinvestment in the business.

However, the problem with profit/profitability as a marketing metric is that its link with marketing activity is not always clear. The process required to determine the link requires considerable input from the finance department to measure the contributions individual products/ services make towards the overall profit levels of a business. So, it can be difficult to determine whether or not the marketing activity itself has led to improved levels of profitability or whether some other factor led to it, e.g. the collapse of a competitor. Finally, we might have a very profitable business operating in the short term, e.g. with customers buying more of a low-value overpriced product, but in the long term, customers would defect and leave the business.

Figure 5.9

Key marketing performance metrics

Sales

Sales value or volume is a key performance measure, where sales value is determined by measuring how many units of a product or service are sold multiplied by the average unit price and sales volume is calculated by determining how many units of a product or service have been sold. The benefit of using this metric is that sales value and volume can be measured directly against individual product or services. Sales values and volumes are easier to determine and require limited input from the finance department, unlike in the determination of profit/profitability. Sales values and volumes may be linked to geographical sales territories and so when sales fall in a particular territory, and efforts have been made to increase sales, it is relatively easy to determine whether those efforts have been successful.

The use of sales volumes as a marketing metric is more problematic because with high-volume turnover products, particularly in brokerages where companies sell other companies' products and services, the profit may actually be disproportionately low. In such a situation, it would be wiser to measure profit/profitability, where the data are available. However, sales values may also hide the fact that a product or service is being sold at unprofitable levels. Rewarding a sales force for selling large quantities of product or service at unprofitable levels is a recipe for disaster, a recipe for the long-term decline and death of a company.

Gross Margin

Frequently, companies measure their performance based on the gross profit margins they can achieve in a particular industry. For example, the gross profit margin for supermarkets in the UK is around 5–8%, whereas in the USA gross profit margins are considerably lower at around 2–5%. However, supermarkets generally operate on very high-volume sales. Therefore, they can afford to operate on low-gross profit margins. For example, some restaurants operate a 200–300% gross margin on their wine. When gross margins for one company are compared with those of other companies in the industry, where the data are available, e.g. for publicly quoted companies, companies can determine whether or not they need to reduce their costs, or perhaps increase their prices.

The problem with using gross margins as a marketing metric is that they do not always provide an indication of how much the customer is actually willing to pay. For example, smoothie manufacturers (e.g. Innocent) generally operate higher gross margins (because they charge higher prices) than manufacturers in the fruit juice category (e.g. Del Monte, Minute Maid). However, if the smoothie manufacturers had set their initial prices based on typical fruit juice margins, they would never have been as successful as they have, especially when we consider that Innocent Drinks, for example, has achieved sales revenue of around £100m in its first ten years.

Awareness

Nearly eight in ten respondents mentioned (brand) awareness as an important marketing metric. However, although a customer may be aware of a brand, it does not mean they will buy that brand. Correspondingly, (brand) awareness is not a particularly good measure for determining the effectiveness of marketing activity, particularly in the short term, as it may take time for the increased awareness to lead to an increase in sales, if it does at all.

However, (brand) awareness is a very useful metric for determining whether your marketing communications activity is entering customer consciousness more generally (see Chapter 3). The more a target market recognizes a brand, the more likely they are to become purchasers of it. Nevertheless, building awareness may not necessarily build sales. As consumers we can become well aware of a brand, but not particularly like it, and therefore, not buy it. Brands can be marketed heavily but not achieve success; examples include Strand cigarettes, Ford Edsel and Tesco 'fresh and easy', in the USA, and the British retailer Marks and Spencer (M&S) in Far Eastern markets.

Market Share

One of the principal measures of market performance, the measurement of market share, is enshrined in many marketing strategy models such as the Boston Consulting Group's growth-share matrix (see Chapter 2). Measuring market share is particularly useful in determining a company's performance within the marketplace, particularly when measured relative to the market leader, because it gives an indication of how competitive a company is. Cadbury's, the confectionery company, use this metric, in conjunction with other marketing metrics such as brand awareness and advertising spend (Ambler, 2000).

A company's (company A) market share is determined by measuring that company's sales revenues, incorporating the sales of all companies within the industry including company A, as a proportion of total industry sales revenues as follows:

$$\text{Market share}_{(\text{company A, \%})} = \frac{\text{Sales Revenue}_{(\text{company A, £})}}{\text{Total Industry Sales Revenue}(£)} \times 100$$

Relative market share is determined by measuring the market share of company A against the market share of the market leader, or the nearest competitor (if company A is the market leader), as follows:

$$\text{Relative Market Share}_{(\text{company A, units})} = \frac{\text{Market Share}_{(\text{company A, \%})}}{\text{Market Share}_{(\text{market leader, \%})}}$$

Where company A is the market leader, relative market share is a value greater than one unit (see Chapter 2). Nevertheless, a company's market share, as determined by the value of the sales, does not necessarily point to a profitable company. Many a company has started a price war (see Chapter 9) in order to try to steal market share from a competitor, only to find prices fall generally in the industry, which inevitably leads to a decline in their own profitability.

Number of New Products

Most companies pride themselves on their capacity to innovate. However, in many industries, innovating new products and services is vital for the prosperity of the industry. For example, pharmaceutical companies must manage a pipeline of new drug compounds at various stages in the process of new product development. When they do finally develop a drug, they quickly patent it to protect their multibillion-dollar investments and to ensure that they can reap the financial rewards from the drug's development.

In 2006, pipeline problems occurred for global pharmaceutical manufacturers AstraZeneca and GlaxoSmithKline, when various high-profile compounds failed at the clinical trial stage, sending their share prices lower as a result (Griffiths, 2006). 3M (formerly the Minnesota Manufacturing and Mining Corporation), the company behind the Post-it note, among other innovations, uses the proportion of sales attributable to new products as one of its marketing metrics (Ambler, 2000) (see also the Case Insight 8.1).

Nevertheless, simply developing new products/services without measuring or predicting their impact on the sales of existing products can be problematic as the new product/service can take away sales from the existing sales without adding any new business (so-called cannibalization). In addition, this strategy may cause customer confusion as customers try to determine what they want from a variety of offers.

Mobile telephone companies quickly learned in the late 1990s and early 2000s that many consumers wanted a monthly charge service offering a limited range of telephone call packages, which included text message bundles and set levels of call time, or a pay-as-you-go plan with more limited options. What they didn't want was lots of different-priced telephone handset offers with many different call packages, offering different call charges for different times. Consumers wanted price transparency.

Relative Price

The price of a company's products/services can be indicative of how much they are valued in the marketplace. **Relative price** is determined by measuring the price of company A's

product/service against the price of the market leading company, or the nearest competitor (if company A is the market leader) as follows:

$$\text{Relative Price}_{(\text{company A's offering, units})} = \frac{\text{Price}_{(\text{company A's offering, } \pounds)}}{\text{Price}_{(\text{market leader's offering/nearest competitor, } \pounds)}}$$

Where company A is the market leader, relative price is a value greater than one unit.

There is increasing recognition that a company that can charge a price premium, vis-à-vis its competitors, has a competitive advantage over them. One approach to measuring brand equity actually uses relative price premiums (Ailawadi *et al.*, 2003).

The problem with measuring marketing effectiveness using relative price only is that a company may only obtain a proportion of the total revenue possible in a marketplace if the price it charges is too high. In other words, a higher relative price may lead to a smaller market share if customers do not value your offering more than the competitors' offerings.

Customer Satisfaction

Many companies operate on the principle of satisfying their customers. Companies in the travel and leisure industry, e.g. First Choice, Thomson, STA, Saga, work hard to satisfy their customers and to ensure an enjoyable experience. In the past, this meant measuring service quality levels (see Chapter 13) to determine whether companies were providing the level of quality of service that customers expected. In some industries, customer satisfaction is notoriously low but customers perceive the costs of switching their business to other providers to be too high. Retail banking services are a good example here as customers are reluctant to switch banks even when they are dissatisfied (Keaveney, 1995). Mobile phone companies (e.g. Orange, T-Mobile) measure the proportion of customers who fail to renew user contracts against the proportion of new customers acquired, termed 'churn rate' in the industry. Churn rate is a measure of disaffected customers as a proportion of new customers.

Some companies have gone beyond the concept of simply satisfying customers, e.g. the car maintenance company Kwik Fit operated the principle of '100% customer delight'. This is a principle that helped Scottish founder Sir Tom Farmer build a £1bn business empire before he eventually sold the business to Ford in 1999 (Bain, 2003).

Nevertheless, businesses may be spending too much serving those customers who are not necessarily either the most profitable or offer the most profit potential in the future. Generating very high levels of customer satisfaction or delight may ultimately reduce shareholder value in the longer term because the costs to generate such high levels of satisfaction produce lower levels of profitability. In other words, the extra costs of improving customer satisfaction from 95% to 99.5% of customers may not actually be worth it.

Distribution/Availability

The extent to which a product or service is distributed within the marketplace can also be an important marketing metric. For example, a Hollywood blockbuster film studio will want to ensure maximum take-up of its motion pictures through as many cinemas as possible as the more cinemas the film is shown in, the higher the box office takings are likely to be. In other businesses, it is not necessarily the quantity of locations within which a product is sold, but the quality of those locations. For example, Nokia sells its premium mobile phone

Film audiences enjoy films more in packed cinemas, distributors enjoy higher profits

brand, Vertu, through specialist retail outlets only, such as Selfridges and Harrods in London, Paragon in Singapore, Brusco Gioielli in Rome, and Vertu branded shops in such countries as Russia and Lebanon.

Cosmetics companies (e.g. French cosmetics giant L'Oréal) frequently distribute their new products initially through speciality cosmetics outlets and prestigious department stores, before stocking the products in supermarkets and other department stores later in the campaign.

Unilever, the world's biggest ice cream manufacturer, recognized the importance of providing confectioners, tobacconists, and newsagents (CTNs) with branded freezers to store its heartbrand ice cream products within the many overseas markets in which it operates, i.e. as Walls in the UK, Ola in the Netherlands, Algida in Hungary. Providing the freezers meant that CTNs could stock more of its ice cream products as opposed to those of their competitors, until an EU ruling in a case brought by Mars forced Unilever to allow CTNs to stock a small proportion of competing brands in the Unilever freezers.

In a wide range of diverse product and service industry sectors, distribution is critical so that customers can readily purchase a company's product/services. For this reason, companies often set up sophisticated systems designed to link their customers' purchasing needs with their own purchasing and distribution needs. Airline yield management systems, for example, reconcile customer pricing information with live seat availability, taking into account customers' price elasticities (see Chapter 9), in order to maximize total sales revenues. Measures of distribution and product/service availability are critical in this and many other industries.

Managing and Controlling Marketing Programmes

There is increasing debate in marketing about how we measure the performance of marketing programmes so that we can control them better. Most of the time, companies are not excellent at all marketing activities, e.g. the American crisp producer Frito-Lay has refined the functions of selling and distribution, whereas Gillette's Personal Care Division has mastered the power of advertising, but few companies master more than one or two specialist marketing functions excellently (Bonoma, 1984).

Companies often try to maximize marketing effectiveness, e.g. measured by market share growth, revenue growth, and market position, and marketing efficiency, e.g. measured by sales and marketing expenses as a proportion of gross revenue. However, there is some evidence that companies that succeed on one dimension, i.e. either marketing efficiency or effectiveness, succeed less on the other dimension (Vorhies and Morgan, 2003). But this makes sense because, to be effective at marketing, we have to spend more on marketing activity (which makes us marketing inefficient!). Nevertheless, this is an important finding. Firms that can be both marketing effective and marketing efficient probably do so by changing the 'rules of the game'. They do not spend on high-cost activities like advertising to achieve effectiveness, instead they consider new and innovative approaches, which make customers pay more attention.

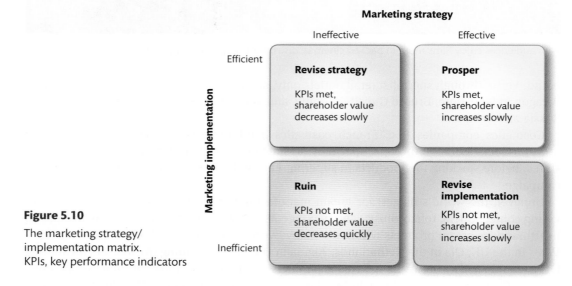

Figure 5.10

The marketing strategy/
implementation matrix.
KPIs, key performance indicators

One problem that arises is that marketers often consider strategy formulation to be problematic, but not strategy implementation. Managers frequently assume that implementation follows strategy as a sequential process. In fact, the two processes are often interlinked and run in parallel (Piercy, 1998). In other words, marketing strategy may be, and often is, formulated on the basis of implementation considerations in the same way implementation decisions are based on strategy formulation decisions.

In Figure 5.10 we can measure how effective and efficient our strategy has been, by using the metrics for efficiency and effectiveness outlined above. Where we consider that our marketing implementation has been efficient, but our marketing strategy has not been effective, we should reformulate our strategy as key performance indicators have not been met, otherwise we are likely to reduce shareholder value in the longer term. This situation means that we have spent marketing resources well in achieving what we set out as our strategy, but we employed the wrong strategy for what we really wanted to do. The control imperative is to intervene quickly to reformulate our marketing strategy.

The dream situation is that we operate an efficient implementation plan and an effective marketing strategy. In this situation, we prosper. There is no control imperative except to maintain a watching brief to see how competition might react, as this may force us to rethink our strategy.

Where we operate inefficient marketing implementation for an ineffective marketing strategy plan, we are likely to face rapid ruin! We are spending scarce resources badly on doing the wrong things. The control imperative requires a fundamental rethink of what we are doing and how we are doing it.

Finally, where we are operating an effective marketing strategy, but implementing it inefficiently, the control imperative is to reconsider how we implement marketing programmes. Although this situation may not be disastrous in the short term, where competition is adopting a more efficient approach, it could lead to mergers, sales, or takeovers in highly competitive industry sectors.

Marketing Planning

So far in this chapter we have considered the key activities associated with the strategic marketing planning process, essentially one of analysis, goals, and action. In order for organizations to be able to develop, implement, and control these activities at a product and brand level, marketing plans are derived. This final section of the chapter considers the characteristics of the marketing planning process, identifies the key activities, and considers some of the issues associated with the process.

Marketing planning is a sequential process involving a series of activities leading to the setting of marketing objectives and the formulation of plans for achieving them (McDonald, 2002: 27). A marketing plan is the key output from the overall strategic marketing planning process. It details a company's or brand's intended marketing activity.

Marketing plans can be developed for periods of one, two to five years, and anything up to 25 years. However, too many organizations regard marketing plans as a development of the annual round of setting sales targets that are then extrapolated into quasi-marketing plans. This is incorrect as it fails to account for the marketplace, customer needs, and resources. It is important that the strategic appraisal and evaluation phase of the planning process be undertaken first. This should cover a three- to five-year period and provides a strategic insight into the markets, competitors, and the organization's resources that shape the direction and nature of the way the firm has decided to compete. Once agreed, these should then be updated on an annual basis and modified to meet changing internal and external conditions. Only once the strategic marketing plan has been developed should detailed operational or functional marketing plans, covering a one-year period, be developed (McDonald, 2002). This makes marketing planning a continuous process, not something that is undertaken once a year, or worse, just when a product is launched.

A marketing plan designed to support a particular product consists of a series of activities that should be undertaken sequentially. These are presented in Table 5.7.

Many of the corporate level goals and strategies and internal and external environmental analyses that are established within the strategic marketing planning process can be replicated within each of the marketing plans written for individual products, product lines, markets, or even SBUs. As a general rule, only detail concerning products, competitors, and related support resources need change prior to the formulation of individual marketing mixes and their implementation, within functional level marketing plans.

▶ **Table 5.7** Key activities within a marketing plan

Activity	Explanation
Executive summary	Brief one-page summary of key points and outcomes
Overall objectives	Reference should be made to the organization's overall mission and corporate goals, the elements that underpin the strategy
Product/market background	A short summary of the product and/or market to clarify understanding about target markets, sales history, market trends, main competitors, and the organization's own product portfolio
Marketing analysis	This provides insight into the market, customers, and the competition. It should consider segment needs, current strategies, and key financial data. The marketing audit and SWOT analysis are used to support this section
Marketing strategies	This section should be used to state the market(s) to be targeted, the basis on which the firm will compete, the competitive advantages to be used, and the way in which the product is to be positioned in the market
Marketing goals	Here, the desired outcomes of the strategy should be expressed in terms of the volume of expected sales, the value of sales and market share gains, levels of product awareness, availability, profitability, and customer satisfaction
Marketing programmes	A marketing mix for each target market segment has to be developed, along with a specification of who is responsible for the various activities and actions and the resources that are to be made available
Implementation	This section sets out the: ▶ way in which the marketing plan is to be controlled and evaluated ▶ financial scope of the plan ▶ operational implications in terms of human resources, research, and development, and system and process needs
Supporting documentation	Marketing plans should contain relevant supporting documentation too bulky to be included in the plan itself but necessary for reference and detail. For example, the full PESTLE and SWOT analyses, marketing research data, and other market reports and information plus key correspondence

The strategic marketing planning process starts with a consideration of the organization's goals and resources and an analysis of the market and environmental context in which the organization seeks to achieve its goals. It culminates in a detailed plan, which, when implemented, is measured to determine how well the organization performs against the marketing plan.

Skills for Employment

> ▶▶ We like people who are inquisitive and entrepreneurial. People who don't need to be asked to do something once, let alone twice. So if you can show us that you possess the proactive gene, and got involved in projects and causes that were above and beyond the call of duty at uni or school, we'll always look upon that favourably. ◀◀

Dan Germain, Head of Creative, Innocent Drinks

 Visit the **Online Resource Centre** to discover more tips and advice on skills for the workplace.

Chapter Summary

To consolidate your learning, the key points from this chapter are summarized below:

■ **Describe the strategic planning process.**

The strategic planning process commences at corporate level. Here the organization sets out its overall mission, purpose, and values. These are then converted into measurable goals that apply to the whole organization. Then, depending upon the size of the organization, the range of businesses (SBUs) and/ or products is determined and resources allocated to help and support each one. Each business and/or product develops detailed functional and competitive strategies and plans, such as a marketing strategy and plan.

■ **Explain the key influences that impact on and shape marketing strategy.**

There are three key influences on marketing strategy. These are strategic market analysis, which is concerned with developing knowledge and understanding about the marketplace, strategic marketing goals, which are about what the strategy is intended to achieve, and strategic marketing action, which is about how the strategies are to be implemented.

■ **Develop a SWOT analysis and set out how it can help strategic marketing decision-making.**

SWOT analysis is a tool used to determine an overall view of the strategic position and highlights the need for a strategy to produce a strong fit between the internal capability (strengths and weaknesses) and the external situation (opportunities and threats). SWOT analysis serves to identify the key issues and then prompts thought about converting weaknesses into strengths and threats into opportunities.

■ **Explain how understanding competitors can assist the development of marketing strategy.**

An analysis of a firm's competitors involves answers to five key questions. These are: who are our competitors? What are their strengths and weaknesses? What are their strategic goals? Which strategies are they following? How are they likely to respond?

■ **Identify the characteristics of strategic marketing goals and explain the nature of the associated growth strategies.**

There are several types of strategic objective but the four main ones are niche, hold, harvest, and divest goals. However, the vast majority of organizations also consider growth to be a primary objective. Although there are different forms of growth, intensive, integrated, or diversified are generally accepted as the main forms.

■ **Describe different approaches and concepts associated with strategic marketing action, including implementation issues.**

Strategic marketing action is concerned with ways of implementing marketing strategies. Various concepts and frameworks have been proposed, and, of these, we considered ideas about competitive advantage, generic strategies, and competitive positioning.

■ **Understand the principles of marketing metrics and how these can contribute to the implementation and control of the strategic marketing planning process.**

There is increasing recognition of the importance of using marketing metrics in the control mechanism of the implementation phase of a marketing programme. Many companies now use some variant of the balanced scorecard (Kaplan and Norton, 1992). Recent research has highlighted widespread use of marketing metrics in firms, including metrics in the following areas: profit/profitability; sales, value, and volume; gross margin; awareness; market share; number of new products; relative price; number of customer complaints; consumer satisfaction; distribution/availability; total number of customers; marketing spend; perceived quality/esteem; loyalty/retention; and relative perceived quality (Ambler, Kokkinaki, and Puntoni, 2004).

■ **Outline the key elements of a marketing plan.**

The following represent the key elements associated with the structure of a marketing plan: overall objectives; product/market background; market analysis; marketing strategy and goals; marketing programmes; implementation, evaluation, and control. Although depicted as a linear process, many organizations either do not follow this process, do not include all these elements, or undertake many of these elements simultaneously.

Review Questions

1   What is the difference between vision and mission?

2   Draw a diagram that presents the four elements that make up the strategic context.

3   Make brief notes outlining the strategic planning process.

4   How might understanding a firm's competitors help develop marketing strategy?

5   Identify the key characteristics of SWOT analysis. What actions should be taken once the SWOT grid is prepared?

6   Describe the difference between intensive and diversified growth.

7   Porter argues that firms can differentiate themselves in one of two main ways. What are they and how do they work?

8   What are the key features of successful marketing teams?

9   Write brief notes explaining the principles of marketing metrics.

10   List the various parts of a marketing plan.

Worksheet Summary

Visit the **Online Resource Centre** and complete Worksheet 5.1. This will help you to learn about the differences between internal strength and weakness; external threats and opportunities, and how to conduct a SWOT analysis for Sony in the games console market (i.e. PS4).

Discussion Questions

1 Having read Case Insight 5.1, how would you advise Innocent Drinks to develop their brand?

2 Find three examples of mission statements and associated organizational goals. Then, using these examples, discuss the value of formulating a mission statement and the benefits that are likely to arise from setting organizational-level goals.

3 If the external environment is uncontrollable and markets are changing their shape and characteristics increasingly quickly, there seems little point in developing a strategic marketing plan. Discuss the value of formulating marketing strategies and plans in the light of these comments.

4 After a successful period of 20 years' trading, a bicycle manufacturer noticed that their sales, rather than increasing at a steady rate, were starting to decline. The company, Rapid Cycles, produced a range of bicycles to suit various segments and distributed them mainly through independent cycle shops. In recent years, however, the number of low-cost cycles entering the country had increased, with many distributed through supermarkets and national retail chains. The managing director of Rapid Cycles feels that he cannot compete with these low-cost imports and asks you for your opinion about what should be done. Discuss the situation facing Rapid Cycles and make recommendations regarding their marketing strategy.

5 Explain which marketing metric(s) might be used in the following circumstances:

A A newly themed Irish pub with a marketing objective to give customers the best pub experience in the immediate area in the first year of its operation.

B A large health and fitness organization wanting to expand its chain of gymnasiums to other countries across Europe within a five-year timescale.

C The manufacturers of a designer cosmetic, such as the Gucci Pour Homme II, wishing to determine how well distributed their product is.

D A pharmaceutical company wishing to find out whether its new asthma product will be better received in the marketplace in the next 12 months compared with competing brands and if it can hold its price premium.

Visit the **Online Resource Centre** and complete the **Multiple Choice Questions** to assess your knowledge of Chapter 5.

go online

References

Achrol, R. S., and Kotler, P. (1999) 'Marketing in the network economy', *Journal of Marketing*, 63, 146–63.

Ailawadi, K., Lehmann, D. R., and Neslin, S. A. (2003), 'Revenue premium as an outcome measure of brand equity', *Journal of Marketing*, 67 (October), 1–17.

Ambler, T. (2000), 'Marketing metrics', *Business Strategy Review*, 11, 2, 59–66.

—Ambler, T., Kokkinaki, F., and Puntoni, S. (2004), 'Assessing marketing performance: reasons for metrics selection', *Journal of Marketing Management*, 20, 475–98.

Andrews, S. (2006), 'Game on: the battle of the superconsoles begins', *Sunday Times*, 5 November, retrieve from www.driving.timesonline.co.uk/tol/life_and_style/driving/article624345.ece, accessed 25 February 2007.

Anon. (2007), 'Pret pair could have their cake and eat it', *Daily Mail*, 25 April, 73.

Ansoff, I. H. (1957), 'Strategies for diversification', *Harvard Business Review*, 35, 2, 113–24.

Arthur, C. (2007), 'Retailers suspiciously coy on PlayStation 3 pre-order figures', *The Guardian*, 22 February, retrieve from www.guardian.co.uk/technology/2007/feb/22/sonyplaystation.games.

Bain, S. (2003). 'Sir Tom Farmer: as if growing a £1bn business wasn't enough, he's nurturing the entrepreneurial spirit in others', *The Herald*, 20 December, 17.

Birchard, B. (2010) Herman Miller's design for growth, *Strategy & Business*, 59, 25 May 2010, retrieve from www.strategy–business.com/article, accessed 5 July 2010.

Bonoma, T. V. (1984), 'Making your marketing strategy work', *Harvard Business Review*, March–April, 69–76.

Bristow, D. N., and Frankwick, G. L. (2001), 'Product managers influence tactics in marketing strategy development and implementation', *Journal of Strategic Marketing*, 2, 211–27.

Chimhanzi, J. (2002), 'The impact of marketing/HR interactions on marketing strategy implementation', *European Journal of Marketing*, 38, 1–2, 73–98.

CIM (2009a), *The future of marketing*, White Paper—Chartered Institute of Marketing, May, retrieve from www.cim.co.uk/filestore/resources/agendapapers/futureofmarketing.pdf, accessed 6 April 2010.

—(2009b) *Keep calm and carry on marketing: Marketing in a Recession*, White Paper—Chartered Institute of Marketing, April, Retrieve from www.cim.co.uk/filestore/resources/agendapapers/keepcalm.pdf, accessed 6 April 2010.

Clark, A. (2001), 'Mine's a McLatte', *The Guardian*, 1 February.

Day, G. S. (1994), 'The capabilities of market-driven organisations', *Journal of Marketing*, 58, 3, 37–52.

—and Wensley, R. (1988), 'Assessing advantage: a framework for diagnosing competitive superiority', *Journal of Marketing*, 52, 2 (April), 1–20.

Friscia, T. (2008), A Conversation with Procter & Gamble CEO A. G. Lafley, 18 April, retrieve from www.amrresearch.com/Content/View.aspx?compURI=tcm:7-37226, accessed 25 March 2010.

Griffiths, K. (2006), 'Pharmaceuticals: UK drug giants hit by pipeline problems', *The Daily Telegraph*, 27 October, 3.

Gummesson, E. (1990), 'Marketing orientation revisited: the crucial role of the part-time marketer', *European Journal of Marketing*, 25, 2, 60–75.

Harris, L. C., and Ogbonna, E. (2003), 'The organisation of marketing: a study of decentralised, devolved and dispersed marketing activity', *Journal of Management Studies*, 40, 2, 483–512.

Jack, L. (2010), 'Building a bridge between marketing and boardroom', *Marketing Week*, 25 February, retrieve from www.marketingweek.co.uk/in-depth-analysis/cover-stories/building-a-bridge-between-marketing-and-boardroom/3010326.article, accessed 5 April 2010.

Kaplan, R. S., and Norton, D. P. (1992), 'The balanced scorecard: measures that drive performance', *Harvard Business Review*, January–February, 71–9.

Keaveney, S. M. (1995), 'Customer switching behavior in service industries: an exploratory study', *Journal of Marketing*, 59 (April), 71–82.

Lafley, A.G. (2008), 'P&G's Innovation Culture', *Strategy & Business*, 52, (Autumn), retrieve from www.strategy-business.com/article/08304?pg=all, accessed 12 January 2010.

Levitt, T. (1960), 'Marketing myopia', *Harvard Business Review*, July–August.

Madslien, J. (2010), Spyker boss outlines Saab plans, retrieve from www.news.bbc.co.uk/1/hi/business/8512224.stm, accessed 25 March 2010.

McCormick, A. (2009), 'Xbox strikes back', *Revolution*, December, 20–25.

McDonald, M. (2002), *Marketing Plans and How to Make Them*, 5th edn, Oxford: Butterworth-Heinemann.

Mintzberg, H. (1987), 'The strategy concept: five Ps for strategy', *California Management Review*, 30, 1 (Fall), 11–26.

Noble, C. H., Sinha, R. K., and Kumar, A. (2002), 'Market orientation and alternative strategic orientations: a longitudinal assessment of performance implications', *Journal of Marketing*, 66, 4, 25–40.

O'Malley, L., and Patterson, M. (1998), 'Vanishing point: the mix management paradigm reviewed', *Journal of Marketing Management*, 14, 8, 829–51.

Paskin, J. (2009), 'Kraft's Growth Plan: Q&A With CEO Rosenfeld', *SmartMoney Magazine*, 6 July, retrieve from http://bx.businessweek.com/consumer-packaged-goods/view?url=http%3A%2F%2Fwww.smartmoney.com%2Finvesting%2Fstocks%2Fkrafts-growth-plan-q-a-with-ceo-rosenfeld%2F%3Fcid%3D1108, accessed 19 October 2009.

Piercy, N. (1998), 'Marketing implementation: the implications of marketing paradigm weakness for the strategy execution process', *Journal of the Academy of Marketing Science*, 26, 3, 222–36.

— (2002), *Market-Led Strategic Change: Transforming the Process of Going to Market*, Oxford: Butterworth-Heinemann.

Porter, M. E. (1985), *The Competitive Advantage: Creating and Sustaining Superior Performance*, New York: Free Press.

Prahalad, C. K., and Hamel, G. (1990), 'The core competence of the organisation', *Harvard Business Review*, 68, 3 (May–June), 79–91.

Rosenfield, I. (2009), 'Inside the Kraft Foods Transformation,' *Strategy & Business*, 56, 27 August, retrieve from www.strategy-business.com/article/09307, accessed 12 January 2010.

Schofield, J. (2005), 'Console wars: challengers must force the pace to unseat the leader', *The Guardian*, 1 December, retrieve from www.guardian.co.uk/technology/2005/dec/01/microsoftbox.games1, accessed December 2007.

Sheth, S. N., and Sisodia, R. S. (2006), *Does Marketing Need Reform? Fresh Perspectives on the Future*, New York: M. E. Sharpe.

Skapinker, M. (2007), 'Interview: thinking outside the sandwich box', *Financial Times*, 19/20 May, Life and Arts Supplement, 3.

Strahle, W. M., Spiro, R. L., and Acito, F. (1996), 'Marketing and sales: strategic alignment and functional implementation', *Journal of Personal Selling and Sales Management*, 16, 1 (Winter), 1–20.

Thomas, L. C. (2002), 'The nature and dynamic of counter-implementation in strategic marketing: a propositional inventory', *Journal of Strategic Marketing*, 10, 189–204.

Vorhies, D. W., and Morgan, N. A. (2003), 'A configuration theory assessment of marketing organisation fit with business strategy and its relationship with marketing performance', *Journal of Marketing*, 67 (January), 100–15.

Wong, V., and Saunders, J. (1993), 'Business orientations and corporate success', *Journal of Strategic Marketing*, 1, 20–40.

Workman, J. P., Jr., Homburg, C., and Gruner, K. (1998), 'Marketing organisation: an integrative framework of dimensions and determinants', *Journal of Marketing*, 62 (July), 21–41.

▶ Case Insight 6.1   (continued)

An important target market for Stagecoach is the non-user segment. The customers contained within this segment demonstrate a propensity to switch the mode of transport to bus. We estimate that about 30% of existing non-bus users in the UK have a propensity to switch the mode of transport they are regularly using, given the appropriate incentives. In addition, it is essential that Stagecoach address the perceived barriers associated with bus travel among this group.

Through profiling our customers using geodemographic criteria, we have further identified microdemographic segments within each of the local areas that we serve, to whom specific barriers to bus use are an issue. This information has formed the basis of our segmentation strategy and how we subsequently tailor our communication with each of these prospect customer groups.

The major issue we need to consider is how public transport is perceived by these target segments. Public transport in general has a negative reputation in the UK. This is the result historically of limited customer communication, inadequate staff training, and poor customer relations within the industry.

Customer perception of Stagecoach is linked directly to the journey experience and customer satisfaction. In order of priority the following aspects of our service contribute to customer satisfaction: reliability/punctuality, staff attitude, comfort during the journey, cleanliness of the vehicle (interior and exterior), space for bags/pushchairs, and value for money.

Source: www.stagecoachbus.com/.

Given the primary research findings to date and the market segments identified, what would you recommend Stagecoach do to target and position their brand to the differing market segments to encourage customers to switch their mode of transport to Stagecoach's bus services?

Introduction

Ever wondered why we only target certain segments of a market and not everyone with our marketing activities or how these segments are identified? Think about universities for a moment: how do you think they identify which students to communicate with about degree programmes? What criteria do they use? Do they base it on where you live, your age, your gender, or is it just about your entrance scores? Do they market to postgraduate and undergraduate audiences differently? What about international and domestic student groups—is this difference important for the marketing of higher education services to prospective students?

In this chapter, we consider how organizations decide on which segments of a market to concentrate their commercial efforts. This process is referred to as **market segmentation** and is an integral part of marketing strategy, discussed in Chapter 5. After defining market segmentation, this chapter explores the differences between market segmentation and **product differentiation**, to clarify the underlying principles of segmentation. We also consider techniques and issues concerning market segmentation within consumer and business-to-business markets. The method by which whole markets are sub-divided into different segments is referred to as the **STP process**. STP refers to the three activities that should be undertaken, usually sequentially, if segmentation is to be successful. These are segmentation, targeting, and positioning, and this chapter is structured around these key elements.

The STP Process

The growing use of the STP process has occurred because of the increasing prevalence of mature markets, greater diversity in customer needs, and the ability to reach specialized, niche segments. Marketers segment markets and identify attractive segments (i.e. who to focus on and why), identify new product opportunities, develop suitable positioning and **communication** strategies (i.e. what message to communicate), and allocate resources to prioritized marketing activities (i.e. how much should we spend and where). Organizations commission segmentation research when they want to revise their marketing strategy, investigate a declining brand, launch a new product, or restructure their pricing policy. When operating in highly dynamic environments, segmentation research should be conducted at regular intervals in order to keep in touch with changes in the marketplace. STP refers to the three activities: segmentation, targeting, and positioning (Figure 6.1).

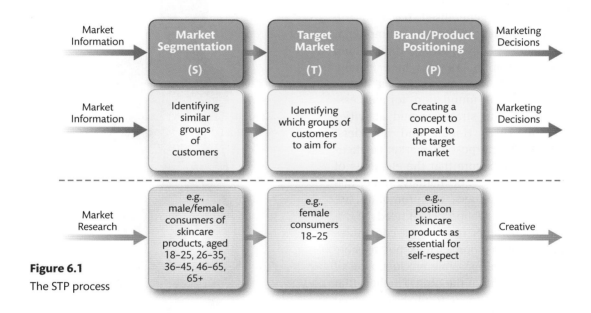

Figure 6.1
The STP process

The key benefits of the STP process include:

▶ Enhancing a company's competitive position, providing direction and focus for marketing strategies, including targeted advertising, new product development, and brand differentiation, e.g. Coca-Cola identified that Diet Coke (also marketed as Coca-Cola Lite) was regarded as 'girly' and 'feminine' by male consumers. The company therefore developed a new product, Coke Zero, targeted at the health-conscious male segment of the soft drinks market.

▶ Examining and identifying market growth opportunities through identification of new customers, growth segments, or product uses, e.g. Lucozade changed its original marketing strategy where it was positioned for people who were ill and rebranded as an energy drink.

▶ Effective and efficient matching of company resources to targeted market segments promises the greatest return on marketing investment (ROMI), e.g. HSBC, Barclays, Tesco, and ASDA

Wal-Mart use data-informed segmentation strategies to target direct marketing messages and rewards to customers they characterize as offering long-term value to the company.

The Concept of Market Segmentation

Market segmentation is the division of a market into different groups of customers with distinctly similar needs and product/service requirements. Or, to put it another way, market segmentation is the division of a mass market into identifiable and distinct groups or segments, each of which have common characteristics and needs, and display similar responses to marketing actions.

Market segmentation was first defined as 'a condition of growth when core markets have already been developed on a generalised basis to the point where additional promotional expenditures are yielding diminishing returns' (Smith, 1956). There is now widespread agreement that it forms an important foundation for successful marketing strategies and activities (Wind, 1978; Hooley and Saunders, 1993). The purpose of market segmentation is to ensure that the elements of the marketing mix, namely, price, distribution, products, and promotion, are designed to meet particular needs of different customer groups. As companies have finite resources it is not feasible to produce all possible products, for all the people, all of the time. The best that can be aimed for is to provide selected offerings for selected groups of people, most of the time. This enables the most effective use of an organization's scarce resources. As Beane and Ennis (1987) eloquently commented, 'a company with limited resources needs to pick only the best opportunities to pursue'.

Market segmentation is related to product differentiation. If you aim at different market segments, you might adapt different variations of your offering to satisfy those segments. Equally if you adapt different versions of your offering, this may appeal to different

The M&S Per Una range: designed to attract the young female shopper

Source: Courtesy of Marks & Spencer.

market segments. For example, in fashion retailing, if you adapt your clothing range so that your skirts are more colourful, use lighter fabrics, and have a very short hemline, this styling is more likely to appeal more to younger women. Alternatively, if you decide to target older women, then you might need to change the styling of your skirts to suit them by using darker, heavier fabrics, with a longer hemline. The former is product differentiation (focus on product offering), the latter market segmentation (focus on market segments). For example, in an attempt to attract younger female shoppers into their stores, Marks & Spencer, introduced the Per Una female clothing range. The fashion range has been a huge success, generating a significant proportion of the total womenswear sales at M&S. The difference between product differentiation and market segmentation is illustrated in Figure 6.2.

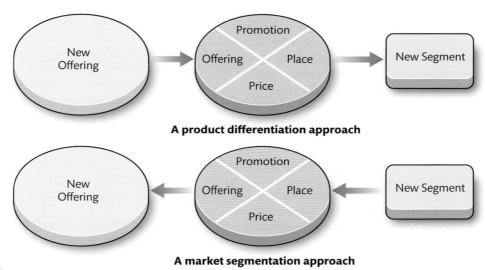

Figure 6.2

The difference between market segmentation and product differentiation

Market segmentation was first proposed as an alternative market development technique in markets where there are relatively few competitors selling an identical product—imperfectly competitive markets. Where there are lots of competitors selling identical products, market segmentation and product differentiation produce similar results. This is because competitors imitate each other's strategic approaches faster, and product differentiation approaches meet market segment needs more closely. With increasing proliferation of tastes in modern society, many consumers have an increased disposable income. As a result, marketers seek to design product and service offerings around consumer demand (market segments) rather than around their own production needs (product differentiation), and market research is used to inform the process (see Market Insight 6.1 and Chapter 4).

▶ Market Insight 6.1

A Tale of Two Approaches

Tale 1 is about Amway Global Plc., a global company that manufactures and distributes over 450 different consumer products contributing to worldwide sales of over US$8bn. Amway Global Plc. invests heavily in research and development in order to remain competitive and meet customer needs. For example, after several years of research and development, Amway produced a new range of products called Satinique, which used the 'Ceramide Infusion System'. The core attribute is that Satinique contains a moisturizing agent, which can restore the nutrients in hair. Once Amway had developed the product they then undertook market research to determine which group of consumers they should target. That segment was made up of professional women who always want to look their best, who want professional, salon-quality products, and who rely on recommendations from friends when making haircare purchase decisions. They then developed a marketing strategy and implemented a successful marketing plan.

Tale 2 is about NIVEA Sun, the leading suncare brand owned by Beiersdorf. There are three main usage segments in the suncare market: protection (from harmful rays), after sun (for relief and moisturizing after being in the sun), and self-tan (for those who want an all-year-round 'cosmetic' tan). Beiersdorf have developed their portfolio of NIVEA Sun brands around these usage segments, but, unlike Amway, have used innovation to develop products to meet customer needs identified through market research and segmentation analysis. For example, market research has shown that awareness of the need for protection from the sun does not necessarily lead to product purchase and usage. It was also found that women enjoy the luxurious nature of suncare products, men prefer convenience, and unsurprisingly children don't enjoy the suncream application process. As a result NIVEA Sun developed and introduced a spray application device, designed specifically to appeal to men and their preference for convenience. They also introduced a coloured formulation for children's sun products in order to make the application process more fun.

Sources: www.amway.com; www.nivea.com.

1 **Which of these two companies uses a product differentiation approach and which uses a market segmentation approach? Justify your selection.**

2 **Choose a beauty, fragrance, or grooming product that you like to use and determine likely segments to which it appeals.**

3 **Do you believe Amway or Beiersdorf should change their approach? Justify your decision.**

Nivea sun products: something for everyone?
Source: © NIVEA SUN, Courtesy of Beiersdorf UK Limited.

▶ Research Insight 6.1

To take your learning further, you might wish to read this influential paper.

Smith, W. R. (1956), 'Product differentiation and market segmentation as alternative marketing strategies', *Journal of Marketing,* July, 3–8.

A seminal article on market segmentation outlining the idea that neither supply nor demand in marketing was homogeneous (i.e. different groups wanted to produce *and* consume different things). Therefore, a product differentiation approach, concerned with bending demand to the will of supply, can also be accompanied by an alternative mechanism of bending supply to the will of demand. This alternative marketing strategy was termed market segmentation.

@ Visit the **Online Resource Centre** to read the abstract and access the full paper.

The Process of Market Segmentation

The market segmentation process is often problematic because an offering can have multiple applications (Griffith and Pol, 1994). There is also increasing customer variability and problems associated with the identification of the key differences between groups of customers. To aid the process, there are two main approaches to segmenting markets. The first adopts the view that the market consists of customers that are essentially the same, so the task is to identify groups that share particular differences. This is the **breakdown method**. The second approach considers a market to consist of customers that are all different, so the task is to find similarities. This is known as the **build-up method**.

The breakdown approach is the most established and is the main method used for segmenting consumer markets. The build-up approach seeks to move from the individual level where all customers are different, to a more general level of analysis based on the identification of similarities (Freytag and Clarke, 2001). The build-up method is customer-oriented, seeking to determine common customer needs. The aim of both methods is to identify market segments where identifiable differences exist between segments (segment heterogeneity) and similarities exist between members within each segment (member homogeneity). This is displayed in Figure 6.3.

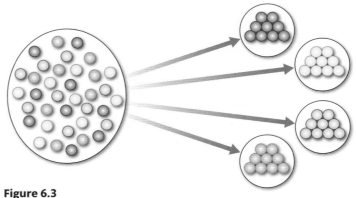

Figure 6.3

Segment heterogeneity and member homogeneity

Other segmentation researchers have distinguished between **a priori** or **post hoc** segmentation methods following a six- or seven-stage process of development as outlined in Table 6.1.

▶ **Table 6.1** A priori and post hoc segmentation approaches

Stage	A priori	Post hoc
1	Selection of the base (a priori) for segmentation (e.g. demographics, socio-economics)	Sample design—mostly using quota or random sampling approaches
2	Selection of segment descriptors (including hypotheses on the possible link between these descriptors and the basis for segmentation)	Identification of suitable statistical methods of analysis
3	Sample design—mostly using stratified sampling approaches and occasionally quota sampling	Data collection
4	Data collection	Data analysis—formation of distinct segments using multivariate statistical methods (e.g. cluster analysis, CHAID)
5	Formation of the segments based on a sorting of respondents into categories	Establishment of the profile of the segments using multivariate statistical methods (e.g. factor analysis) and selection of segment descriptors (based on the key aspects of the profile for each segment)
6	Establishment of the profile of the segments using multivariate statistical methods (e.g. multiple discriminant analysis, multiple regression analysis)	Translation of the findings about the segments' estimated size and profile into specific marketing strategies, including the selection of target segments and the design or modification of specific marketing strategy
7	Translation of the findings about the segments' estimated size and profile into specific marketing strategies, including the selection of target segments and the design or modification of specific marketing strategy	N/A

Note: N/A, stage not applicable

Source: Adapted from Green (1979) and Wind (1978).

In business markets, segmentation should reflect the relationship needs of the parties involved and not be based solely on the traditional consumer market approach such as the breakdown method. Through use of both approaches, a more accurate, in-depth, and potentially more profitable view of industrial markets can be achieved (Crittenden, Crittenden, and Muzyka, 2002). However, problems remain concerning the practical application and implementation of B2B segmentation. Managers often report that although the analytical processes are reasonably clear, it is not apparent how they should 'choose and evaluate between the market segments obtained (Naudé and Cheng, 2003).

Segmentation theory has developed during a period when transactional marketing was the principal approach to marketing, rather than the relational approaches prevalent in today's service-dominated environment. Under the transactional approach, the allocation of resources to achieve the designated marketing mix goals was of key importance. However, customers who make up the various segments have needs that may change, and, consequently, those customers may no longer remain members of the particular segment to which they originally belonged (Freytag and Clarke, 2001). Consequently, market segmentation programmes must use current customer data. The segmentation process will, therefore, vary according to prevailing conditions in the marketplace and the changing needs of the parties involved.

Market Segmentation in Consumer Markets

To segment consumer markets, we use market information collected based on certain key customer-, product-, or situation-related criteria (variables). These are classified as segmentation bases and include profile (e.g. who are my market and where are they?); behavioural (e.g. where, when, and how does my market behave?); and psychological criteria (e.g. why does my market behave that way?). These differing types of segmentation bases are depicted in Figure 6.4. A fourth segmentation criterion that can be added is contact data, a customer's name and full contact details beyond their postcode (e.g. postal address, email, mobile and home telephone number). Contact data are useful for tactical-level marketing activities such as addressable direct marketing (see Chapter 11).

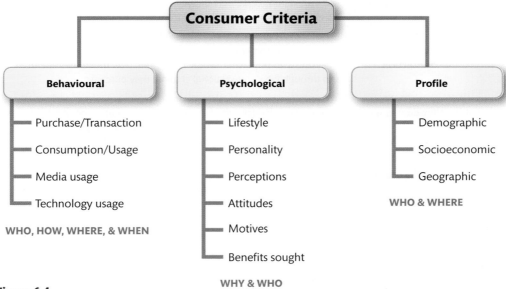

Figure 6.4

Segmentation criteria for consumer markets

Table 6.2 illustrates the key characteristics associated with each of the main approaches to consumer market segmentation.

▶ **Table 6.2** Segmenting criteria for goods and services markets

Base type	Segmentation criteria	Explanation
Profile	Demographic	Key variables concern age, sex, occupation, level of education, religion, social class, and income characteristics
	Lifestage	Based on the principle that people need different products and services at different stages in their lives (e.g. childhood, adulthood, young couples, retired)
	Geographic	The needs of potential customers in one geographic area are often different from those in another area, due to climate, custom, or tradition
	Geodemographic	There is a relationship between the type of housing and location that people live in and their purchasing behaviours
Psychological	Psychographic (lifestyles)	Analysing consumers' activities, interests, and opinions, we can understand individual lifestyles and patterns of behaviour, which affect their buying behaviour and decision-making processes. We can also identify similar product and/or media usage patterns
	Benefits sought	The motivations customers derive from their purchases provide an insight into the benefits they seek from product use
Behavioural	Purchase/ transaction	Data about customer purchases and transactions provide scope for analysing who buys what, when, how often, how much they spend, and through what transactional channel they purchase
	Product usage	Segments can be derived on the basis of customer usage of the product offering, brand, or product category. This may be in the form of usage frequency, time of usage, and usage situations
	Media usage	What media channels are used, by whom, when, where, and for how long provides useful insight into the reach potential for certain market segments through differing media channels, and also insight into their media lifestyle

When selecting different bases for segmentation, the trade-off between data acquisition costs and the ability of the data to indicate predictable customer choice behaviour needs to be considered. As depicted in Figure 6.5, demographic and **geodemographic** data are relatively easy to measure and obtain; however, these bases suffer from low levels of accurate consumer behaviour predictability. In contrast, behavioural data, what a customer does, their **product usage**, purchase history, and media usage, although more costly to acquire, provides a more accurate base on which to predict future behaviour. So, the brand of toothpaste you purchased on the last three occasions is more than likely going to be the brand of toothpaste you purchase next time. However, this is also influenced by a customer's susceptibility to marketing communications such as sales promotions (**media usage** and response behaviour) and market environment.

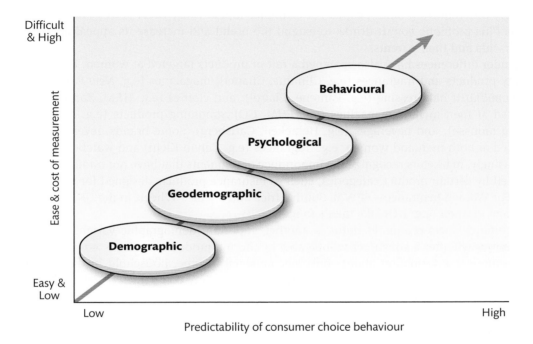

Figure 6.5

Considerations for segmentation criteria accessibility and use

Source: Integrated Marketing Communications in Advertising and Promotion (AISE; 7th edn. by Shimp, 2007). Reprinted with permission of South-Western, a division of Thomson Learning.

Profile Criteria

A core customer-related method of segmenting consumer goods and service markets is the use of profile criteria to determine who the market is and where they are. To do this, we use demographic methods (e.g. age, gender, race), socio-economics (e.g. determined by social class, or income levels) and **geographic** location (by postal code systems). For example, a utility company might segment households based on geographical area to assess brand penetration in certain regions; or a financial investment fund might segment the market based on age, employment, income, and asset net worth to identify attractive market segments for a new investment portfolio. These are all examples of segmentation based on profile criteria.

Demographic

Demographic variables relate to age, gender, family size and lifecycle, generation (e.g. baby boomers, Generation Y, Millenials), income, occupation, education, ethnicity, nationality, religion, and social class. They indicate the profile of a consumer and are particularly useful in assisting marketing communications and media planning, not least because media selection criteria are developed around these variables.

Age is a common way of segmenting markets and is often the first way in which a market is delineated. Children are targeted for confectionery and toys because their needs and tastes are very different from older people. For example, Yoplait Dairy Crest (YDC) launched Petits Filous Plus probiotic yogurt drinks to extend the brand and increase its appeal among 4 to 9-year-olds and their parents.

Gender differences have also spawned a raft of products targeted at women. For example, beauty products and fragrances (e.g. Clinique, Chanel); magazines (e.g. *New Woman, Cleo, Cosmopolitan*); hairdressing (e.g. Pantene, Clairol); and clothes (e.g. H&M, Zara). Products targeted at men include magazines (e.g. *FHM, GQ*); grooming products (e.g. hair gel and styling mousse); and beverages (e.g. Heineken, Carlsberg). Some brands develop products targeted at both men and women, e.g. fragrances (e.g. Calvin Klein) and watches (e.g. Tag). Increasingly, marketers recognize the importance of segments that have not traditionally been targeted by certain product categories, such as insurance products designed for women (e.g. First For Women Insurance—FFW in South Africa and Sheila's Wheels in the UK) and beauty products for men (e.g. L'Oréal's men's range).

Income or socio-economic status is another important demographic variable because it determines whether a consumer will be able to afford a product. As discussed in Chapter 3, this comprises information about consumer personal income, household income, employment status, disposable income, and asset net worth. Many companies target affluent consumers (e.g. Chanel, DKNY, Bentley) offering high-end exclusive product offerings. Targeting low-income earners can also be profitable. German discount supermarkets such as Aldi and Lidl make a considerable market impact by developing an offering for low-income market segments. The socio-economic distinction in marketing strategies is also increasingly apparent in the development of differing strategies for multinational retailers such as Carrefour and Tesco own-branded products. For example, at Tesco, Tesco Finest is developed for markets with more disposable income in contrast to Tesco Value, which is marketed to the more price-conscious and low-income market segment.

▶ **Table 6.3** Kantar Media—TGI lifestage segmentation groups

Lifestage group	Demographic description
Fledglings	15–34, not married and have no son or daughter; living with own parents
Flown the nest	15–34, not married, do not live with relations
Nest builders	15–34, married, do not live with son/daughter

Lifestage group	Demographic description
Mid-life independents	35–54, not married, do not live with relations
Unconstrained couples	35–54, married, do not live with son/daughter
Playschool parents	Live with son/daughter and youngest child 0–4
Primary school parents	Live with son/daughter and youngest child 5–9
Secondary school parents	Live with son/daughter and youngest child 10–15
Hotel parents	Live with son/daughter and have no child 0–15
Senior sole decision-makers	55+ not married and live alone
Empty nesters	55+, married, and do not live with son/daughter
Non-standard families	Not married, live with relations, do not live with son/daughter, and do not live with parents if 15–34
Unclassified	Not in any group

Source: Reproduced with the kind permission of Kantar Media.

Lifecycle

Lifestage analysis is based on the principle that people have varying amounts of disposable income and different needs at different stages in their lives. Their priorities for spending change at different points and these points or lifestages do not occur at the same time. Adolescents need different products from a single 26-year-old person, who in turn needs different products from a 26-year-old who is married with young children. For example, in the UK, Tesco, ASDA Wal-Mart, and Sainsbury's have all invested in the development of product lines targeted at singles with high disposable incomes and busy lifestyles with their 'meal for one' ranges in contrast with the 'family value' and 'multipacks' targeted at families. As families grow and children leave home so the needs of the parents change and their disposable income increases. Holidays (e.g. Euro Disney) and automobiles (e.g. people carriers) are key product categories that are influenced by the lifestage of the market.

Historically, the family lifecycle consisted of nine categories through which individuals and households would progress (see Chapter 3): single bachelor, newly married, married with children under 6 years old, married with children over 6 years old, older married couples with dependent children, empty nest household with or without employment, and solitary survivor in work or retired. However, since this classification was developed, society has changed and continues to change in terms of values, beliefs, and family lifecycle. A more modern lifecycle classification was developed with support from the British Market Research Bureau (BMRB) called the Target Group Index (TGI) or BMRB-TGI Lifestage Segmentation Product, which classifies 12–13 lifestage groups based on age, marital status, household composition, and children (e.g. if they have children and the child's age). These groups are presented in Table 6.3.

go online

Visit the **Online Resource Centre** and follow the weblink Kantar Media to learn more about the TGI.

Geographics

This approach is useful when there are clear locational differences in tastes, consumption, and preferences. For example, what do you put on your toast in the morning: Vegemite, Marmite, jam, or jelly? Or perhaps you don't east toast at all and prefer cold meats or rice dishes for your morning meal. Whereas the British often celebrate Christmas with turkey dishes, many Swedes eat fish. These consumption patterns provide an indication of preferences according to differing geographical regions. Markets can be considered by country or region, by size of city or town, postcode, or by population density such as urban, suburban, or rural. For example, it is often said that American beer drinkers prefer lighter beers, compared with their UK counterparts whereas German beer drinkers prefer a much stronger drink. In contrast, Australians prefer colder more carbonated beer than the UK or the USA. For more on international market differences see Chapter 7.

In addition to product selection and consumption, geographical segmentation is important for retail location, advertising and media selection, and recruitment. For example, recruitment to the armed forces draws people with similar demographic attributes from a variety of geographic areas. Low-cost retail formats might be used for retail outlets in low-income regions. Direct sales operations (e.g. catalogue sales) can use census information to develop better customer segmentation and predictive models.

Geodemographics

Geodemographics is a natural outcome when combining demographic and geographic variables. The marriage of geographics and **demographics** has become an indispensable tool for market analysis. Fusing census data with demographic information, especially socio-economic data, can lead to a rich mixture of who lives where and what they are like. Consumers can be classified by where they live, which is often dependent on their stage in life and their lifestyle (see Chapter 3).

go online

Visit the **Online Resource Centre** and complete Internet Activity 6.1 to learn more about how we use databases compiled with geodemographic data to profile market segments effectively.

Two of the best known UK geodemographic systems are ACORN and MOSAIC. Developed by the British market research group CACI, ACORN—A Classification of Residential Neighbourhoods—demonstrates how postcode areas are broken down into five lifestyle categories, 17 groups, and 56 types. The lifestyle categories include wealthy achievers, urban prosperity, comfortably off, moderate means, and hard pressed. ACORN is a geodemographic tool used to identify and understand the UK population and the demand for products and services. Marketers use this information to improve their understanding of customers and target markets, and to determine where to locate operations, field sales forces, retail outlets, and so on. ACORN can also be used to determine where to send direct marketing material and host billboard and other advertising campaigns. In total, ACORN categorizes all of Britain's 1.9m UK postcodes, using over 125 demographic statistics within England, Scotland, Wales,

There are clear locational differences in tastes: would you eat fish at Christmas?

go online

and Northern Ireland, and 287 lifestyle variables. The classification technique operates on the principle that people living in similar areas have the same needs and lifestyles.

Visit the **Online Resource Centre** and follow the weblink to CACI to learn more about the ACORN system.

MOSAIC is a geodemographic segmentation system developed by Experian and marketed in many countries worldwide. MOSAIC was originally constructed for the UK using the 1990 census, updated annually and overhauled after each census. The resulting segmentation system consists of 60 segments, presented as 12 separate groups. MOSAIC is based on the premise of assigning lifestyle groups to differing geographic catchment areas.

go online

Visit the **Online Resource Centre** and follow the weblink to Experian to learn more about the MOSAIC system.

Psychological Criteria

Psychological criteria used for segmenting consumer markets include attitudes and perceptions (e.g. negative feelings about fast food); **psychographics** or the lifestyles of customers (e.g. extrovert, fashion conscious, high achiever), and the types of **benefits sought** by customers from products and brands and their consumption choices.

Psychographics

Psychographic approaches rely on the analysis of consumers' activities, interests, and opinions to understand consumers' individual lifestyles and patterns of behaviour. Psychographic segmentation includes understanding the values that are important to different types of customers. A traditional form of lifestyle segmentation is AIO, based on customer Activities, Interests, and Opinions. These provide useful insight into what makes people tick. Taylor Nelson Sofres (TNS) developed a UK Lifestyle Typology based on lifestyles and classified the following types of lifestyle categories: belonger, survivor, experimentalist, conspicuous consumer, social resistor, self-explorer, and the aimless.

The Accor hotel group have used value-based segmentation to develop their brand. The Dorint-Novotel was repositioned to attract those who value personal efficiency. This involved changing the service offering by introducing efficiency-related facilities such as automated checkouts, car hire facility, 24-hour food, and wireless computing. The Dorint-Sofitel brand was repositioned by introducing fine art for the walls, real fires, fine wines, live piano in the reception, libraries, and more experienced concierge staff. This was designed to appeal to those who valued classical styling, customization, and passion (Howaldt and Mitchell, 2007). See Market Insight 6.2 about market segmentation based on demographic and psychographic criteria.

▶ Market Insight 6.2

Watch the Designer Gap!

Children might be smaller in size, but the market for childrenswear is large. The value of the UK market for childrenswear, covering all clothing for children up to the age of 10, was £5bn in 2009 Mintel (2010a). The Infant clothing segment (up to the age of four) outperformed all other segments with girlswear accounting for £2bn compared with boyswear's £1.5bn. However, both segments have fallen by about 3% in the past five years, with the strong performance in infantwear partly a result of higher birth rates and the trend for older, more affluent people to become parents. However, childrenswear is not just about segment age.

Kidswear: small people, big market

Consumer spending in childrenswear suffered due to the economic downturn. Mintel (2010a) predicts that the childrenswear category will only incur a modest value increase of 3% over the next five years. To stimulate fashion sales, European retailers are keeping entry-level price points low to encourage fashion shoppers. In the UK, consumers are switching from specialty high street fashion retailers to cheaper more convenient outlets for childrenswear. According to Mintel (2010b), UK supermarkets now have 29% of

the childrenswear market, clothing multiples 26%, and department stores 7%. Almost seven in 10 shoppers have reported that supermarkets were their most likely source of kids' clothing, with ASDA WalMart and Tesco the most popular.

However, leading global fashion retailer Gap Inc. offers clothing and accessories for children through its brand GapKids and for babies at BabyGap. In 2009, Gap decided to target a very different childrenswear

▶ Market Insight 6.2

segment—the fashion-conscious mummy. To appeal to this segment, Gap commissioned fashion designer Stella McCartney to design a new clothing collection for children and babies for Gap Inc. Launched in October 2009, the range is sold in select GapKids and BabyGap stores in the USA, Canada, the UK, France, Ireland, and Japan. It will also be sold online in the USA.

With 70 designs in the collection, consisting of both boyswear and girlswear, with pieces for newborn babies to 12-year-olds, the collection includes little replicas of McCartney's womenswear range. The range is targeted at fashion-conscious mums, who want to keep their children suitably attired in designer clothes. However, at a time of economic downturn and recovery, will the price tag keep many jumpers out of kids' reach?

Sources: Bainbridge (2010); Anon (2009a); Ramsey and Hargitay (2009); Berton and Foreman (2009); www.gap.com; Mintel (2010a, b).

1   **Which segmentation criteria should be used to segment the market for childrenswear?**

2   **How should the family lifecycle and psychographic criteria be used to segment the market for childrenswear?**

3   **How does the Gap Inc. segmentation strategy differ from that used by supermarket retailers for childrenswear?**

Benefits Sought

Rather than provide offerings based on design and style, the benefits sought approach is based on the principle that we should provide customers with exactly what they want, and on the benefits that they derive from use. This might sound obvious, but consider what the real benefits are, both rational and irrational (see Chapter 3), for the different offerings that people buy, such as mobile phones and sunglasses.

Major airlines often segment on the basis of the benefits passengers seek from transport by differentiating between the first class passenger (given extra luxury benefits in their travel experience), the business class passenger (who gets some of the luxury of the first class passenger), and the economy class passenger (who gets none of the luxury of the experience but enjoys the same flight). This segmentation approach is useful with respect to new and emerging technologies. Marketers can identify the key benefits and motivations of electronic technology adoption and use. For example, the benefits of convenience, accessibility, and handset durability dominate mobile handset adoption for blue-collar trade workers; teenagers seek novelty through games, camera, and ringtones, and innovation through the latest trends in handset design; and white-collar workers seek multifunctionality, with the device acting as a mobile, an organizer, and a wireless internet access device.

Behavioural Criteria

Product-related methods of segmenting consumer goods and service markets include using behavioural methods (e.g. product usage, purchase, and ownership) as bases for segmentation. Observing consumers as they use products or consume services can be an important source of new ideas for new uses or product/service design and development. Furthermore, new markets for existing offerings can be signalled, as well as appropriate communication themes for promotion. Purchase, ownership, and usage are three very different behavioural constructs we can use to help profile and segment consumer markets.

> ### ▶ Research Insight 6.2
>
>
>
> ## To take your learning further, you might wish to read this influential paper.
>
> **Haley, R. I. (1968), 'Benefit segmentation: a decision-oriented research tool',** *Journal of Marketing*, 32, 30–5.
>
> In this article, Haley segmented the market for toothpaste purchasers based on the benefits users derived including: those who bought toothpaste to maintain white teeth (sociables), those who wished to prevent decay (worriers), those who liked the taste and refreshment properties (sensors), and those who bought on price (independents). Each group had particular demographic, behavioural, and psychographic characteristics. This approach to defining market segments based on benefits sought is still much in use today.
>
> @ Visit the **Online Resource Centre** to read the abstract and access the full paper.

Usage

A company may segment a market based on how often a customer uses its offerings, categorizing these into high, medium, and low users. This allows the development of service specifications or marketing mixes for each user group. For example, heavy users of public transport might be targeted differently to heavy users of private vehicles for car pooling activities. Consumer product use can be investigated from three perspectives:

1 Social interaction perspective—symbolic aspects of usage and the social meanings attached to the consumption of socially conspicuous products such as a car or house are considered (Belk, Bahn, and Mayer, 1982; Solomon, 1983). For example, Greenpeace launched a television campaign targeting owners of four-wheel drive cars highlighting the environmental social stigma of this car purchase.

Greenpeace campaigns against four-wheel drives
Source: Davison/Greenpeace.

2 Experiential consumption perspective—emotional and sensory experiences are considered as a result of usage, especially emotions such as satisfaction, 'fantasies, feelings and fun' (Holbrook and Hirschman, 1982). For example, Oxo gravy campaigns have emphasized how usage of Oxo can bring families together, and express family values such as love, sharing, and spending time together.

3 Functional utilization perspective—the functional usage of products and their attributes in different situations is considered (McAlister and Pessemier, 1982; Srivastava, Shocker, and Day, 1978). For example, how and when cameras are used, how often, and in what contexts.

Service providers often segment markets based on their customers' purchase behaviour. This might involve segmentation by loyalty to the service provider, or length of relationship, or some other mechanism.

Transaction and Purchase

The development of electronic technologies, such as electronic-point-of-sale (EPOS) computing systems, standardized product codes/article numbers in the USA and Europe and integrated purchasing systems (e.g. web, in-store, telephone) has facilitated a rapid growth in the collection of consumer purchase and transactional data. This provides an additional consumer characteristic upon which to base market segmentation. These systems allow retailers to track who buys what, when, for how much, in what quantities, and with what incentives (e.g. sales promotions). Companies now have the ability to monitor purchase patterns in a variety of geographical regions, at different times, or seasons of the year, for various product/service lines, and increasingly for differing market segments.

Transactional and purchase information is very useful for marketers to assess who are their most profitable customers. Analyzing the recency, frequency, and monetary value of purchases (RFM), marketers can identify the most profitable market segments. Customers who purchase most recently, frequently, and spend a high unit value per purchase (or over the life of the buyer–seller relationship) would be classified as profitable customers. However, transactional data are a record of behaviours, and might provide some insight into useful purchase trends. However, these will not provide deep insight into the reasons underlying purchase and consumption trends.

Market Insight 6.3 shows an example of the combined use of usage, transactional, and attitudinal data to profile and target banking segments.

▶ **Market Insight 6.3**

Banking On Segments

Barclays, a large UK-based bank, now adopts a hybrid segmentation model, incorporating attitudinal profiles and four types of segmentation as follows: 1) business type (personal, premier, private, small business); 2) operational segmentation by age and wealth; 3) attitudinal segmentation; and 4) executional segmentation, operationalized as 'triggers, events and propensity models' (see Figure 6.6).

▶ Market Insight 6.3 (continued)

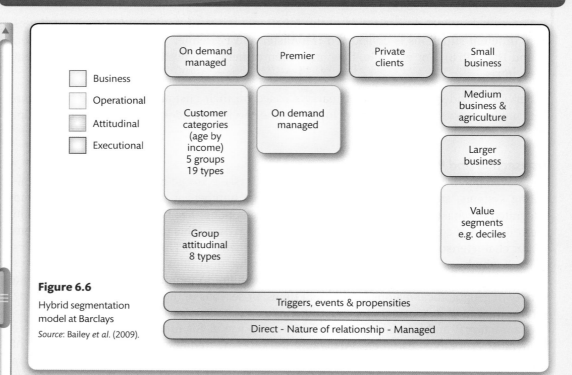

Figure 6.6

Hybrid segmentation model at Barclays

Source: Bailey *et al.* (2009).

The executional segmentation category focuses on how individual customers are treated. One approach is through 'triggers', for example, commercially significant occurrences on a customer's account. A late payment fee might indicate that a customer's needs have changed in some way. Or, a customer who has just taken out cash on their credit card might have a need for credit, and so be a possible target for a loan. The trigger information usually needs to be combined with an assessment of the customer's credit-status to determine whether a loan would be an appropriate offer for a customer who has just been charged a late payment fee, or an overdraft extension. Barclays also considers 'events' on customer accounts as well, e.g. when a customer's insurance requires renewal, or a mortgage comes to an end, or when moving house, getting married, and having children. Barclays focuses on executional segmentation by modelling customer responses to

Customer Action Prompts or 'CAPs'. This is referred to as 'propensity modelling'. The approach combines transactional data from current accounts and credit cards with external data sources, to provide a picture of customers' lifestyles, lifestages, and finances. They then merge propensity models to predict customers' likelihood of responding to particular promotional offers. (See Market Insight 15.3 for more information on how Barclays appeals to small businesses.)

Source: Bailey *et al.* (2009).

1 Why do you think Barclays use a hybrid approach in their segmentation?

2 Why do you think Premier customers are treated separately?

3 Think of your own bank and consider what characteristics the bank might use to segment people like you.

Media Usage

The logic of segmenting markets on the basis of frequency of readership, viewership, or patronage of **media vehicles** is well established. For example, Urban (1976) suggested that heavy and light magazine readership might respond differently to ads with different creative appeals. Potter *et al.* (1988) attempted to identify the profiles of five usage segments for video-cassette recorders (VCRs), a now defunct technology. Segmenting users on the basis of their media usage frequency can provide insights into whether a publisher attracts and retains consumers who are more or less responsive to an advertiser's communication. This information provides input when evaluating the efficiency and effectiveness of media. Furthermore, differences in frequency may lead to differences in response to repeated passive ad exposures, competing ads of other sponsors, and prior ad exposure.

Frequency of media usage has been the predominant measure of media usage experience. However, Olney, Holbrook, and Batra (1991) also identified viewing time as an important dependent variable in a model of advertising effects. Holbrook and Gardner (1993) have also argued that duration time is a critical outcome measure of consumption experiences and may be a useful behavioural indicator of experiential versus goal-directed orientations.

Segmentation in Business Markets

Business-to-business market segmentation is the identification of 'a group of present or potential customers with some common characteristic which is relevant in explaining (and predicting) their response to a supplier's marketing stimuli' (Wind and Cardozo, 1974). Unfortunately, B2B market segmentation has not been as well researched as consumer market segmentation (Bonoma and Shapiro, 1983). There are two main groups of interrelated variables used to segment business-to-business markets as presented in Table 6.4. The first involves organizational characteristics, such as **organizational size** and location, sometimes referred to as **firmographics**. Those seeking to segment markets where transactional marketing and the breakdown approach dominate should expect to start with these variables. The second group is based on the characteristics surrounding the decision-making process of buyer characteristics. Those organizations seeking to establish and develop particular relationships would normally expect to start with these variables, and build up their knowledge of their market and customer base.

▶ **Table 6.4** Segmentation bases used in business markets

Base type	Segmentation base	Explanation
Organizational characteristics	Organizational size	Grouping organizations by their relative size (multi-national corporations (MNCs) international, large, small to medium sized enterprizes (SMEs)) enables the identification of design, delivery, usage rates or order size, and other purchasing characteristics
	Geographical location	Often the needs of potential customers in one geographical area are different from those in another area
	Industry type (SIC codes)	Standard industrial classifications (SIC) are used to identify and categorize all types of industries and businesses

▶ **Table 6.4** continued

Base type	Segmentation base	Explanation
Buyer characteristics	Decision-making unit structure (DMU)	Attitudes, policies, and purchasing strategies used by organizations allow organizations to be clustered
	Choice criteria	The types of product/services bought and the specifications companies use when selecting and ordering products, services and equipment form the basis for clustering customers and segmenting business markets
	Purchase situation	Segmenting buyers on the way in which a buying company structures its purchasing procedures, the type of buying situation, and whether buyers are in an early or late stage in the purchase decision process

Organizational Characteristics

These factors concern the buying organizations that make up a business market. There are a number of criteria that can be used to cluster organizations, including size, geography, market served, value, location, **industry type**, usage rate, and **purchase situation**. Below we discuss the main three categories used. These are presented in Figure 6.7.

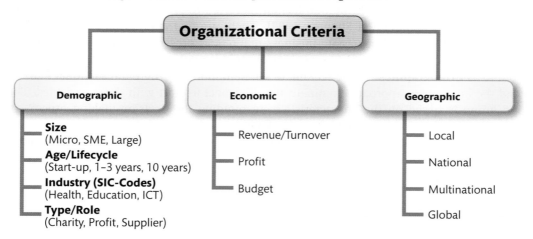

Figure 6.7

Segmentation by organisational characteristics. ICT, information communication technologies; SME, small and medium enterprises

Organizational Size

By segmenting organizations by size, we can identify particular buying requirements. Large organizations may have particular delivery or design needs based on volume demand, e.g. supermarkets such as France's Carrefour and Britain's Tesco pride themselves on purchasing goods in large quantities to enable them to offer cheaper-priced goods. The size of the organization may have an impact on the usage rates of a good or service, so organizational size is likely to be linked to whether an organization is a heavy, medium, or low buyer of a company's offerings.

Geographical Location

Targeting by geographical location is one of the more common methods used to segment business-to-business markets, and is often used by new or small organizations attempting to establish themselves. This approach is particularly useful as it allows sales territories to be drawn up around particular locations that salespersons can service easily. Such territories may be based on European regions, e.g. Scotland, England, and Wales, Scandinavia, Western Europe and Eastern Europe, and the Mediterranean. Alternatively, they may be based on specific regions within a country, e.g. in Eastern Europe sales territories may be based on individual nations (i.e. Poland, Czech Republic, Romania, and Hungary). However, this approach is increasingly less useful as the internet and associated websites increase the channels for distribution and communicating product and service offerings (see Chapter 17).

SIC Codes

Standard Industrial Classification (SIC) codes are often used to get an indication of the size of a particular market. They are easily accessible and standardized across most Western countries, e.g. the UK, Europe, and the USA. However, some marketers have argued that SIC codes contain categories that are too broad to be useful. Consequently, SIC codes have received limited application, although they do provide 'some preliminary indication of the industrial segments in [a] market' (Naudé and Cheng, 2003).

The SIC system was first introduced into the UK in 1948 to classify business establishments by the type of economic activity that they conducted. The classification has been revised many times since then because new products and the new industries that produce them have emerged. The need to take account of changes in industrial structures and industries is equally applicable to all international classifications and so they are revised from time to time to bring them up to date.

go online

Visit the **Online Resource Centre** and complete Internet Activity 6.2 to learn more about how we use SIC codes to segment business markets.

Market Insight 6.4 provides an example of how a SME used organizational characteristics and usage benefits to segment and cluster its business customers.

▶ Market Insight 6.4

B2B Safety Pilz!

In business-to-business markets, segmentation is often used to win a competitive advantage and is linked strongly with a strategy to achieve a sustainable differentiated position. The Pilz brand has stood for safety in automation for over 60 years. In 2009, Pilz was named as one of Germany's 100 most innovative small and medium enterprises (SMEs). As a leading, innovative automation technology company, Pilz are experts in the safety of human, machine, and the environment.

▶ Market Insight 6.4 (continued)

Characterized by their versatile range of applications, the organization provides worldwide, customer-oriented solutions in automation safety in all areas of mechanical engineering, be it the automotive, food and woodworking industries to airports, theatre, and rollercoasters.

Currently employing more than 1,300 staff worldwide, Pilz operates internationally as a technology leader in safe automation technology, with a head office in Germany, Pilz is represented by 24 subsidiaries and branch offices on all continents. Given its many and varied customer markets and bespoke customer solution offerings, Pilz segments its business customers by: industry type (e.g. packaging, airport), solution application (e.g. conveyor system), usage benefits (e.g. flexibility, price), and geography (e.g. Germany, Asia). Pilz business customers form small clusters based on similar needs in business application and usage benefits from Pilz customized offerings.

▶ Cluster 1: Conveyor System (e.g. Airport Schiphol)

▶ Cluster 2: Robotic Interpolation (e.g. FMCG – Chocolate Manufacturer)

▶ Cluster 3: Energy Supply (e.g. IBM Deutschland GmbH)

▶ Cluster 4: Manufacture (e.g. Dunlop Tyres)

To differentiate itself, Pilz positions itself to its customers on three core elements: as follows:

Total customer orientation: Pilz lives by and works alongside its customers, where real close customer proximity is evident at all levels and in all areas to instil confidence through individual consultation, flexibility, and reliable service. Technology leadership: Pilz is a world market leader through technology, oriented towards current market requirements and market leadership in key areas of safe automation, securing their leadership in research and technology.

Overall solutions: Pilz is a solution supplier for safe automation, providing both individual and overall solutions, from innovative products to comprehensive services.

Sources: Falson (2009); Anon. (2009b); www.pilz.com.

1 **What is the purpose of segmentation in B2B or industrial marketing?**

2 **What criteria or bases does Pilz use to segment its business markets?**

3 **What are the key elements Pilz uses to differentiate itself from its competitors?**

Customer Characteristics

These factors concern the characteristics of buyers within the organizations that make up a business market. There are a number of criteria that can be used to cluster organizations in this way including by decision-making unit, by purchasing strategies, by relationship type, attitude to risk, **choice criteria**, and purchase situation.

Decision-Making Unit

An organization's decision-making unit may have specific requirements that influence their purchase decisions in a particular market, e.g. policy factors, purchasing strategies, a level of importance attached to these types of purchases, or attitudes towards vendors and towards risk. These characteristics may help segregate groups of organizations for particular marketing programmes. Some organizations establish policies that govern purchasing decisions.

For example, a business may require specific delivery cycles to support manufacturing plans. Increasingly, organizations require that certain quality standards are met by their suppliers and that they are members of particular quality standards organizations (e.g. the ISO 9000 series).

Segmentation might be based on the closeness and level of interdependence already existing between organizations. Organizational attitude towards risk, and the degree to which an organization is willing to experiment through the acquisition of new industrial products can vary. This variance is partly a reflection of the prevailing culture and philosophy, leadership, and managerial style and can also be used as the basis for segmentation. The starting point of any business-to-business segmentation is a good database or customer relationship management system (see Chapter 15). It should contain customer addresses, contact details, and detailed purchase and transaction history. Ideally, it will also include the details of those buyers present in the customer company's **decision-making unit structure**.

Choice Criteria

Business markets can be segmented on the basis of the specifications of proposition that they choose. For example, an accountancy practice may segment its clients on the basis of those that seek 'compliance'-type accounting products such as audits and tax submission work, companies that require management accounting services, and companies that require a complex mix of both. A computer manufacturer may segment the business market for computers on the basis of those requiring computers with strong graphical capabilities (e.g. educational establishments, publishing houses) and computers with strong processing capabilities (e.g. scientific establishments). Companies do not necessarily need to target multiple segments, they might simply target a single segment, as Haagen-Dazs has done in the super-premium ice cream market.

Purchase Situation

There are three questions associated with segmentation by purchase situation that need to be considered. These are:

1 What is the structure of the buying organization's purchasing procedures? Centralized, decentralized, flexible, or inflexible?

2 What type of buying situation is present? New task (i.e. buying for the first time), modified rebuy (i.e. not buying for the first time, but buying something with different specifications from previously), or straight rebuy (i.e. buying the same thing again)?

3 What stage in the purchase decision process have target organizations reached? Are they buyers in early or late stages and are they experienced or new?

For example, a large services project management consultancy company like Serco in the UK might segment the market for service project management services into public and private services. The focus might be on fulfilling large government contracts that are put out to tender, that is where a group of selected buyers are offered the opportunity to bid for an exclusive franchise to deliver agreed services for a defined period of time. The service provider with the best bid is then selected accordingly by the tendering organization, using its own, sometimes secret and unpublished, choice criteria, and an exclusive contract is written for the winning supplier.

Typically in segmenting business markets, a service provider may use a mix of macro- and micro-industrial market segmentation approaches, by defining the customers a company wants to target using a macro-approach such as standard industrial classification or geographic region, and then further segmenting using the choice criteria for which they select a company. In other words, multi-stage market segmentation approaches can be adopted.

▶ **Research Insight 6.3**

To take your learning further, you might wish to read this influential paper.

Beane, T. P., and Ennis, D. M. (2001), 'Market segmentation: a review', *European Journal of Marketing*, 32, 5, 20–42.

Beane and Ennis' article provides a useful insight into the main bases for market segmentation and the strengths and weaknesses of the key statistical methods we use to analyze customer data to develop segmentation models. The article suggests there are many ways to segment a market and it is important to exercise creativity when doing so.

 Visit the **Online Resource Centre** to read the abstract and access the full paper.

Target Markets

The second important part of the STP process is to determine, which, if any, of the segments uncovered should be targeted and made the focus of a comprehensive marketing programme. Ultimately, managerial discretion and judgment determines which markets are selected and exploited and which are ignored. Kotler (1984) suggested that, for market segmentation to be effective, all segments must be:

▶ Distinct—is each segment clearly different from other segments? If so, different marketing mixes, will be necessary.

▶ Accessible—can buyers be reached through appropriate promotional programmes and distribution channels?

▶ Measurable—is the segment easy to identify and measure?

▶ Profitable—is the segment sufficiently large to provide a stream of constant future revenues and profits?

This approach to the evaluation of market segments is often referred to by the DAMP acronym, to make it easier to remember. Another approach to evaluating market segments uses a rating approach for different segment attractiveness factors, such as market growth, segment profitability, segment size, competitive intensity within the segment, and the cyclical nature of the industry (e.g. whether or not the business is seasonal, such as retailing, or dependent on government political cycles as are some large-scale defence contracts). Each of these segment attractiveness factors is rated on a scale of 0–10 and loosely categorized in the high, medium, or low columns, based on either set criteria, or subjective criteria, dependent on the availability of market and customer data and the approach adopted by the managers undertaking the segmentation programme (see Table 6.5).

Other examples of segment attractiveness factors might include segment stability (i.e. stability of the segment's needs over time), mission fit (i.e. the extent to which dealing with a particular segment fits the mission of your company, perhaps for political or historical reasons), and a whole host of other possibilities. Once the attractiveness factors have been determined, we can then weight the importance of each factor and rate each segment on each factor using the classifications in Table 6.5. This generates a segment attractiveness evaluation matrix, as shown in Table 6.6.

▶ **Table 6.5** Examples of segment attractiveness factors

Segment attractiveness factors	Rating		
	High (10–7)	Medium (6–4)	Low (3–0)
Growth	+2.5%	+2.5% to −2.0%	<2.0%
Profitability	>15%	10–15%	<10%
Size	<£5m	£1m–£5m	<£1m
Competitive intensity	Low	Medium	High
Cyclicality	Low	Medium	High

Source: McDonald and Dunbar (2004). Reproduced with permission. © Elsevier.

▶ **Table 6.6** Example of a segment attractiveness evaluation matrix

Segment attractiveness factors	Weight	Segment 1		Segment 2		Segment 3	
		Score	Total	Score	Total	Score	Total
Growth	25	6	1.5	5	1.25	10	2.5
Profitability	25	9	2.25	4	1.0	8	2.0
Size	15	6	0.9	5	0.9	7	1.05
Competitive intensity	15	5	0.75	6	0.9	6	0.9
Cyclicality	20	2.5	0.5	8	1.6	5	1
Total	100		5.9		5.65		7.45

Source: McDonald and Dunbar (2004). Reproduced with permission. © Elsevier.

Decisions need to be made about whether a single product is to be offered to a range of segments, whether a range of products should be offered to multiple segments or a single segment, or whether one product should be offered to a single segment. Whatever the decision, a marketing strategy should be developed to meet the needs of the segment and reflect an organization's capability with respect to its competitive strategy and available resources.

A segmentation exercise will have been undertaken previously as part of the development of the marketing strategy. The marketing communications strategist will not necessarily need to repeat the exercise. However, work is often necessary to provide current information about such factors as perception, attitudes, volumes, intentions and usage, among others. It is the accessibility question that is paramount: how can the defined group be reached with suitable communications? What is the media consumption pattern of the target audience? Where can they get access to our product and purchase it?

Targeting Approaches

Once identified, an organization should select its preferred approach to target marketing. Four differing approaches can be considered, see also Figure 6.8.

▶ The **undifferentiated approach**—there is no delineation between market segments, and instead the market is viewed as one mass market with one marketing strategy for the entire market. Although very expensive, this approach is selected in markets where there is limited segment differentiation, e.g. the Olympics marketed at a world market or certain government services.

▶ The **differentiated targeting approach**—there are several market segments to target, each being attractive to the marketing organization. To exploit market segments, a marketing strategy is developed for each segment, e.g. Hewlett Packard has developed its product

Figure 6.8

Target marketing approaches

range and marketing strategy to target the following user segments of computing equipment: home office users; small and medium businesses; large businesses; and health, education, and government departments. A disadvantage of this approach is the loss of economies of scale due to the resources required to meet the needs of many market segments.

▶ A **concentrated** or **niche marketing strategy**—where there are just a few market segments. This approach is often adopted by firms that either have limited resources to fund their marketing strategy, or adopt a very exclusive strategy in the market. Jordan's the cereal company originally used this approach to target just consumers interested in organic food products. This approach is also used by small to medium and micro-sized organizations, due mainly to their limited resources. For example, a local electrician may focus on the local residential market.

▶ A **customized targeting strategy**— where marketing strategy is developed for each customer as opposed to each

Jordan's used a niche strategy to market its organic food range

market segment. This approach predominates in B2B markets (e.g. marketing research or advertising services) or consumer markets with high-value, highly customized products (e.g. purchase of a custom-made car). For example, a manufacturer of industrial electronics for assembly lines might target and customize its product differently for Nissan, Unilever, and Levi's, given the differing requirements in assembly line processes for the manufacture of automobiles, foodstuffs, and clothing.

Segmentation Limitations

Market segmentation is a useful process for organizations to aggregate customer needs into distinct groups. However, it has been criticized for the following reasons:

▶ The process approximates offerings to the needs of customer groups, rather than individuals, therefore there is a chance that customers' needs are not fully met. **Customer relationship marketing** processes, and software, increasingly allow companies to develop customized approaches for individual customers.

▶ There is insufficient consideration of how market segmentation is linked to competitive advantage (see Hunt and Arnett, 2004). The product differentiation concept is linked to the need to develop competing offerings, but market segmentation does not stress the need to segment on the basis of differentiating the offering from competitors.

▶ It is unclear how valuable segmentation is to the manager. Suitable processes and models to measure the effectiveness of market segmentation processes are not yet available.

The processes involved in the target marketing process are not as precise as many authors imply. Dibb *et al.* (2001) suggest that segmentation plans in business-to-business markets often fail because businesses fail to overcome barriers encountered when implementing their plans. These include the following barriers:

▶ Infrastructure barriers—culture, structure, and the availability of resources prevent the segmentation process from ever starting, e.g. there may be a lack of financial resource or political will to collect the market data necessary for a segmentation programme, or an organizational culture might be rigidly product-oriented.

▶ Process issues—lack of experience, guidance, and expertise can hamper how segmentation is undertaken and managed. Typically, market research agencies and in-house market research teams use market data and statistical software packages to undertake this task. However, because the different statistical methods provide different results, care must be taken in determining which method to use and how to interpret these results when they are produced.

▶ Implementation barriers—once a new segmentation model is determined how do organizations move towards a new segmentation model? This may require a move away from a business model based on products (e.g. engine sizes for fleet buyers), to one based on customer needs. There is frequently insufficient information and practical guidance for managers to enable segmentation strategies successfully (Goller, Hogg, and Kalafatis, 2002).

Positioning

Having segmented the market, determined the size and potential of market segments, and selected specific target markets, the third part of the STP process is to position a brand within the target market(s). **Positioning** is the means by which goods and services can be differentiated from one another and so give consumers a reason to buy. It encompasses two fundamental elements. The first concerns the physical attributes, the functionality and capability that a brand offers, e.g. a car's engine specification, its design, and carbon emissions. The second positioning element concerns the way in which a brand is communicated and how consumers perceive the brand relative to other competing brands in the marketplace. This element of communication is vitally important as it is 'not what you do to a product, it is what you do to the mind of a prospect' (Ries and Trout, 1972) that determines how a brand is really positioned in a market.

Positioning concerns a product's attributes and design: how the product is communicated, and the way these elements are fused together in the minds of customers. It is not just the physical nature of the product that is important for positioning, and it is not just communication that leads to successful positioning. Claims (through communication) that a shampoo will remove dandruff will be rejected if the product itself fails to deliver. Positioning, therefore, is about how customers judge a product's value relative to competitors, its ability to deliver against the promises made and the potential customers have to derive value from the offering. To develop a sustainable position, we must understand the market in which the product is to compete and the way other brands are competing.

At a simple level, positioning takes place during the target market selection process. Strategic groups are the various clusters of brands that compete directly against each other. For example, in the car market, Tata, Toyota, and Mercedes each have brands that compete against each other in the high-end luxury car market. This strategic group consists of Jaguar, Lexus, and the Mercedes S-Class, respectively, among others. The specification and design of these cars are based on the attributes that customers in this segment deem to be important and are prepared to pay for. However, designing a car that includes key attributes alone is not sufficient. Successful positioning of each of these car brands is important in order that customers perceive how each brand is different and understand the value that each represents.

Key to this process is identifying those attributes considered to be important by consumers. These attributes may be tangible (e.g. the gearbox, transmission system, seating, and interior design) and intangible (e.g. the reputation, prestige, and allure that a brand generates). By understanding what customers consider to be the ideal standard or level that each attribute needs to attain and how they rate the attributes of each brand in relation to the ideal level, and each other, it becomes possible to see how a brand's attributes can be adapted and communicated to become more competitive.

Perceptual Mapping

Understanding the complexity associated with the different attributes and brands can be made easier by developing a visual representation of each market, known as perceptual maps. These 'maps' are used to determine how various brands are perceived according to the key attributes that customers value. **Perceptual mapping**, therefore, represents a geometric comparison of how competing products are perceived (Sinclair and Stalling, 1990). One thing to note is that the closer products/brands are clustered together on a perceptual map, the greater the competition. The further apart the positions, the greater the opportunity for new brands to enter the market, simply because the competition is less intense. For example, in the UK new car market there are numerous brands in the marketplace all competing with each other across differing core attributes, such as whether or not the car is needed for business purposes, for carrying more than three people, for carrying large items on a roof rack, whether or not it needs a large boot and so on. To show how the differing brands are positioned relative to each other using scores on the above attributes for each car brand, we can measure and map the brand positioning. Figure 6.9 shows the positioning of each of the main car brands in relation to the main product attributes but also indicates four clusters of car buyers in the UK new car buyers market.

The four clusters are Conservatives, Investors, Perfectionists, and Freshers. Conservatives buy based on perceptions of vehicle customization, interior comfort, and experience; Investors based on the value and appearance of the car; Perfectionists on perceptions of vehicle performance, reliability and the company's advertising; and Freshers buy on their perceptions of vehicle driving comfort and safety and purchase convenience. Figure 6.9 shows us many things. For example, it indicates that women prefer Mini, Suzuki, and Hyundai, whereas men

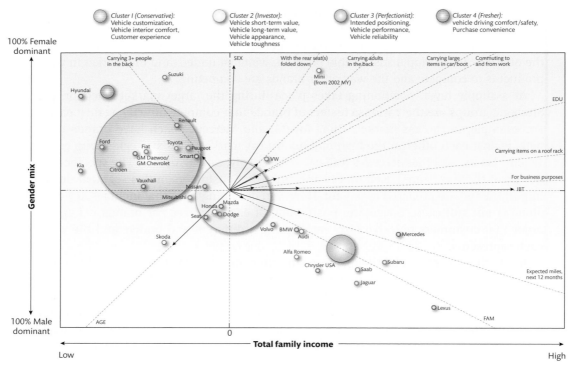

Figure 6.9

Perceptual map for UK new car buyers market

Sources: Leung, K.T. (2010), Road Vehicle State Estimation Using Low-Cost GPS/INS, Unpublished EngD Thesis, Cranfield: Cranfield University.

prefer Lexus, Jaguar, and Saab. Figure 6.9 also shows us that those on higher family incomes are more likely to prefer Lexus, Mercedes, and Subaru.

Perceptual mapping can provide significant insight into how a market operates. For example, it provides marketers with an insight into how their brands are perceived and it also provides a view about how their competitors' brands are perceived. In addition to this, substitute products can be uncovered based on their closeness to each other (Day *et al.*, 1979). All of the data reveal strengths and weaknesses that in turn can assist strategic decisions about how to differentiate on the attributes that matter to customers and how to compete more effectively in the target market. This is the principal value of perceptual mapping.

Positioning and Repositioning

Understanding how brands are positioned provides important inputs not only to the way a brand performs but also to the marketing communications used to support a brand. Through communications, and especially advertising, information can be conveyed about each attribute and in doing so adjust the perceptions customers have of the brand. Marketing communications can be used in one of two main ways to position brands, namely to position a brand either functionally or expressively (symbolically), see Table 6.7. Functionally positioned brands emphasize the features and benefits, whereas expressive brands emphasize the ego, social, and hedonic satisfactions that a brand can bring (see Chapter 18). Both approaches

▶ **Table 6.7** Product positioning strategies

Position	Strategy	Explanation
Functional	Product features	Brand positioned on the basis of the attributes, features, or benefits relative to the competition, e.g. Volvos are safe; Weetabix contains all the vitamins needed for the day; and Red Bull provides energy
	Price quality	Price can be a strong communicator of quality, typified by the lager Stella Artois, which is positioned in the UK as 'reassuringly expensive'. A high price can denote high quality; conversely, a low price can also denote low quality
	Use	By informing when or how a product can be used, we can create a position in the minds of the buyers, e.g. Kellogg's reposition their products to be consumed throughout the day, not just at breakfast. After Eight chocolate mints clearly indicate when they should be eaten
Expressive	User	By identifying the target user, messages can be communicated clearly to the right audience. So, Flora margarine was for men, and then it became 'for all the family'. Some hotels position themselves as places for weekend breaks, as leisure centres, or as conference centres
	Benefit	Positions can be established by proclaiming the benefits that usage confers on those that consume. The benefit of using Sensodyne toothpaste is that it enables users to drink hot and cold beverages without the pain associated with sensitive teeth and gums
	Heritage	Heritage and tradition are sometimes used to symbolize quality, experience, and knowledge. Kronenbourg 1664, 'Established since 1803', and the use of coats of arms by many universities to represent depth of experience are designed to convey trust, permanence, and longevity

make a promise: with regard to, for example, haircare, a promise to deliver cleaner, shinier, and healthier hair (functional) or hair that we are confident to wear because we want to be seen and admired, or because it is important that we feel more self-assured (expressive).

Technology, customer tastes, and competitors' new products are some of the reasons why markets change. If the position adopted by a brand is strong, if it was the first to claim the position and the position is being continually reinforced with clear, simple messages, then there may be little need to alter the position originally adopted. However, most marketers need to be alert and be prepared to reposition their brands as the relative positions occupied by brands, in the minds of customers, will be challenged and shifted around on a frequent basis. However, repositioning is difficult to accomplish, because of the entrenched perceptions and attitudes held by buyers towards brands and the vast (media) resources required to make the changes.

Repositioning is a task that revolves around a product and the way it is communicated. The following four ways outline how to approach repositioning a product, depending on the individual situation facing a brand. In some cases, a brand might need to be adapted before relaunch.

1 *Change the tangible attributes and then communicate the new proposition to the same market.* Regent Inns repositioned in 2007, ahead of the UK public place smoking restrictions, by moving the focus of bar and restaurant brands such as Walkabout, Jongleurs, and Old Orleans to food rather than drinks, changing lighting and seating to alter the atmosphere and ambience. The brands' logos were also refreshed (Godsell, 2007). In Britain, 118 118 the telephone helpline has repositioned itself to enable consumers to buy products and find out about retailers' deals via mobile phone and online in order to differentiate itself from Yell and BT (Ramsay, 2009).

2 *Change the way a product is communicated to the original market.* Vodafone have changed their global positioning in an attempt to throw off their 'stuffy' image. This has involved changing their strapline from 'Make the most of now' to 'Power to you' and communicating more inclusive values (Bussey, 2009).

3 *Change the target market and deliver the same product.* On some occasions repositioning can be achieved through marketing communications alone, but targeted at a new market. For example, Lucozade was repositioned from a drink for sickly children, a niche market with limited volume sales growth, to an energy drink for busy, active, and sports-oriented people, achieved through heavyweight advertising campaigns.

4 *Change both the product (attributes) and the target market.* For example, the Indian company Dabur needed to develop but had to reposition itself as an FMCG company, rather than retain its earlier position as an Ayurvedic medicine manufacturer. To do this it had to develop new product offerings and new packaging, it dropped the umbrella branding strategy, and adopted an individual branding approach. This was then communicated, using leading Bollywood actors and sports stars, to reach various new markets.

▶ Market Insight 6.5

I Don't Quite Get it!

The meaning that a piece of art conveys, its purpose and the artist's intended message, has for centuries fascinated people and been the source of discussion and debate. Many people when they visit an art gallery, very often, just don't understand what they are looking at, they don't quite get it. Some don't even visit at all. For Kiasma, the state-owned contemporary art museum in Helsinki, this was one thing they wanted to address.

Following several decades of debate, the museum was opened in 1998 and quickly became the most visited museum in Finland. However, the number of people enjoying the high culture offered at the museum began to fall steadily as competition for leisure time, media fragmentation, and work commitments reduced visitor numbers. To better understand peoples' behaviour and motivation and to find a new way of enabling them to interact with the art, a major research programme was undertaken. The research identified five distinct segments:

15% Passionates: Those people who are very interested in high culture. Often middle-aged, this group are open-minded, knowledgeable, and passionate about contemporary art.

20% Interested: Those people who are very interested in popular culture, with some interest in high culture.

▶ Market Insight 6.5

34% Moderates: Those with a moderate interest in both popular and high culture. This group would like to attend contemporary art shows.

20% Popularists: Those interested in popular culture but with no interest in high culture. Often young, this group perceived culture as difficult and had little intention to attend culture shows.

11% Negativists: Those not interested in any type of culture, not open to new ideas, and with no intention of visiting a contemporary art show.

The museum identified the Passionates, the Interested and the Moderates as the most attractive segments to target, and then developed a new positioning strategy. Targeted with individual campaigns, based on the members' media habits and attitudes towards culture, the core theme for the 10th anniversary, and a central message directed towards the Interested and Moderates segments, was 'I don't quite get it ...'. This focused on repositioning the art gallery as an enjoyable experience that was accessible to everyone. This repositioning strategy was designed to help audiences overcome the intimidation they felt when engaging with contemporary art and the academic issues they associated with this form of art. The core message was that it was alright not to understand high culture, but to just enjoy and be entertained through the feelings and the experience of art. Attendances are increasing as a result.

Sources: Jantti and Jarn (2009); www.kiasma.fi/.

1   Make a list of the type of media each of the segments might prefer.

Art: what do you see in this picture?

2   What might be some of the problems associated with positioning cultural attractions?

3   Rather than base the positioning of the Kiasma museum around freedom to be entertained and enjoyment, how else might cultural events be positioned?

▶ Research Insight 6.4

To take your learning further, you might wish to read this influential book.

Ries, A., and Trout, J. (2006), *Positioning: The Battle for your Mind*, London: McGraw-Hill Professional.

Al Ries and Jack Trout's book, originally published in 1981, remains the bible of advertising strategy. They define 'positioning' not as what you do to a product to make it acceptable to potential customers, but what you do to the mind of the prospect. Positioning requires an outside-in rather than an inside-out thinking approach.

 Visit the **Online Resource Centre** to read more about the book.

Skills for Employment

▶▶ We look for enthusiasm to succeed, plus a genuine desire to be part of a supportive culture where everyone is focused on one thing: our customers. ◀◀

Andrew Hicks, European Market Development Manager, 3M Display & Graphics

 Visit the **Online Resource Centre** to discover more tips and advice on skills for the workplace.

Chapter Summary

To consolidate your learning, the key points from this chapter are summarized below:

■ **Describe the principles of market segmentation and the STP process.**

Whole markets are sub-divided into different segments through the STP process. STP refers to the three activities that should be undertaken, sequentially, if segmentation is to be successful. These are segmentation, targeting, and positioning. Market segmentation is the division of a market into different groups of customers with distinctly similar needs and product/service requirements. The second part of the STP process determines which segments should be targeted with a comprehensive marketing programme. Having segmented the market and determined the size and potential of market segments and selected specific target markets, the third part of the STP process is to position a brand within the target market(s).

■ **Explain the characteristics and differences between market segmentation and product differentiation.**

Market segmentation is related to product differentiation. Given an increasing proliferation of tastes, marketers have sought to design product and service offerings around consumer demand (market segmentation) more than around their own production needs (product differentiation).

■ **Explain how market segmentation can be undertaken in both consumer and business-to-business markets.**

Data based on differing consumer, user, organizational, and market characteristics, is used to segment a market. These characteristics differ for consumer (B2C) and business (B2B) markets. To segment consumer goods and service markets, market information based on certain key customer-, product-, or situation-related criteria (variables) is used. These are classified as segmentation bases and include profile (e.g. who is my market and where are they?); behavioural (e.g. where, when, and how does my market behave?); and psychological criteria (e.g. why does my market behave that way?). To segment business markets two main groups of interrelated variables are used, organizational characteristics and buyer characteristics.

■ **Describe different targeting strategies.**

Once identified, the organization selects its target marketing approach. Four differing approaches exist: 1) undifferentiated (entire market with one strategy), 2) differentiated (target different segments with different strategies), 3) concentrated or niche (only target one segment from many segments), and 4) customized target marketing (target individual customers with individual strategies).

■ **Explain the concept of positioning.**

Positioning provides the means by which offerings can be differentiated from one another and give customers a reason to buy. It encompasses physical attributes—the functionality and capability that a brand offers, e.g. a car's engine specification, its design, and carbon emissions, and the way in which a brand is communicated and how customers perceive the brand relative to other competing brands in the marketplace. This perception element is vitally important as it is 'not what you do to a product, it is what you do to the mind of a prospect' (Ries and Trout, 1972) that determines how a brand is really positioned in a market.

■ **Illustrate how the use of perceptual maps can assist the positioning process.**

Perceptual maps are used in the positioning process to illustrate differing attributes of a selection of brands. They also illustrate the existing level of differentiation between brands; how our brand and competing brands are perceived in the marketplace; provide insight into how a market operates; and reveal strengths and weaknesses that can assist with making strategic decisions about how to differentiate the attributes that matter to customers and how to compete more effectively in the market.

 # Review Questions

1 Define market segmentation and explain the STP process.

2 What is the difference between market segmentation and product differentiation?

3 Identify four different ways in which markets can be segmented.

4 How do market segmentation bases differ in business-to-business and consumer markets?

5 How can market segmentation bases be evaluated when target marketing?

6 What are the different approaches to selecting target markets?

7 Describe the principle of positioning and why it should it be undertaken.

8 What are perceptual maps and what can they reveal?

9 Explain three ways in which brands can be positioned.

10 Make a list of four reasons why organizations need to reposition brands.

Worksheet Summary

Visit the **Online Resource Centre** and complete Worksheet 6.1. This will aid in learning about the STP process used to develop who to market to, in what way, and while differentiating from the competition.

Discussion Questions

1 Having read Case Insight 6.1, how would you advise Stagecoach to position its brand to the differing market segments?

2 In a group with other colleagues from your seminar/tutor group, discuss answers to the following questions.

    A Using the information in Table 6.8 on the champagne market, and a suitable calculator, determine what are the most potentially profitable segments in the marketplace.

    B What other data do we need to determine the size of the market (market potential)?

3 Discuss which market segmentation bases might be most applicable to:

    A A fashion retailer segmenting the market for womenswear.

    B A commercial radio station specializing in dance music and celebrity news/gossip.

    C A Belgian chocolate manufacturer supplying multiple retail grocers and confectionery shops across Europe, e.g. Godiva.

    D The Absolut Company headquartered in Sweden supplying high-quality vodka around the world.

    E The Burj al Arab luxury hotel in Dubai, United Arab Emirates, when segmenting the market for its exquisite (and very expensive!) hotel rooms.

▶ **Table 6.8** The champagne and sparkling wine market by segment

Social class	Indifferents (%) AP = £15, F = 1/ year	Sparkling wine advocates (%) AP = £10, F = 3/ year	Champagne charlies (%) AP = £25, F = 5/ year	Special occasion drinkers (%) AP = £30, F = 0.8/year	Non-drinkers (%) AP = £0, F= 0/ year
AB (n =8m)	22	12	13	32	21
C1 (n =14m)	23	12	9	30	26
C2 (n = 8m)	20	9	7	27	38
D (n =6m)	15	9	2	27	46
E (n =4m)	18	9	3	20	51

Notes: AP, average price, n, population size, F, no. of bottles purchased/year (all data hypothetical), % segment sizes per socio-economic group and segment descriptions only.

Source: Mintel, 2008.

4 Write a one-sentence description of the attributes and benefits that are attractive to target consumers for a product with which you are particularly familiar (e.g. Apple in the computer category or Samsung in the mobile phones category), using the statement provided below. Explain how these attributes and benefits are different from those of competitors. Your positioning statement might be as follows:

[Product A] provides [target consumers] with [one or two salient product attributes]. This distinguishes it from [one or two groups of competing product offerings] that offer [attributes/benefits of the competing products].

A Briefly describe the target market segment. This should summarize the defining characteristics of the segment (e.g. demographic, psychographic, geographic, or behavioural).

B Briefly explain your reasons for believing that the attributes/benefits of your positioning statement are important for your target segment. Draw a perceptual map that summarizes your understanding of the market and shows the relative positions of the most important competing products.

Visit the **Online Resource Centre** and complete the Multiple Choice Questions to assess your knowledge of Chapter 6.

go online

References

Anon. (2009a), 'Stella McCartney Falls Into the Gap', *Apparel Magazine*, July, 50, 11, 4.

—(2009b), 'What's new in automation?' Engineer, 7/27/2009, 294 (7777), 32.

Bailey, C., Baines, P., Wilson, H. and Clarke, M. (2009), 'Segmentation and customer insight in contemporary services marketing practice: why grouping customers is no longer enough', *Journal of Marketing Management* 25, 3/4, 227–52.

Bainbridge, J. (2010) 'Sector Insight: Childrenswear', *Marketing Magazine*, 10 March, retrieve from www.marketingmagazine.co.uk.

Beane, T. P., and Ennis, D. M. (1987), 'Market segmentation: a review', *European Journal of Marketing*, 32, 5, 20–42.

Belk, R. W., Bahn, K. D., and Mayer, R. N. (1982), 'Developmental recognition of consumption symbolism', *Journal of Consumer Research*, 9 (June), 4–17.

Berton, E., and Foreman, K. (2009), 'European Retailers Try To Stir Up Spending', *WWD: Women's Wear Daily*, 10 June, 197, 120, 4.

Bonoma, T. V., and Shapiro, B. P. (1983), *Segmenting the Industrial Market*, Lexington, Mass.: Lexington Books.

Bussey, N. (2009), 'Vodafone reveals thinking behind global repositioning', *Marketing*, 29 September, retrieve from www.brandrepublic.com/News/941741/Vodafone-reveals-thinking-behind-global-repositioning/?DCMP=ILC-SEARCH, accessed 3 February 2010.

Crittenden, V. L., Crittenden, W. F., and Muzyka, D. F. (2002), 'Segmenting the business-to-business marketplace by product attributes and the decision process', *Journal of Strategic Marketing*, 10, 3–20.

Day, G., Shocker, A. D., and Srivastava, R. K. (1979), 'Customer orientated approaches to identifying product markets', *Journal of Marketing*, 43, 4, 8–19.

Dibb, S., Simpkin, L., Pride, W. M., and Ferrell, D. C. (2001), *Marketing Concepts and Strategies*, Cambndye, Mass.: Houghton Mifflin.

Falson, S. (2009), *Safety Matters, Process & Control Engineering (PACE)*, 62, 10, 13–15.

Freytag, P. V., and Clarke, A. H. (2001), 'Business to business segmentation', *Industrial Marketing Management*, 30, 6 (August), 473–86.

Godsell, M. (2007), 'Branding: Regent Inns rethinks brands', *Marketing*, 25 April, retrieve from www.brandrepublic.com/News/652827/Branding-Regent-Inns-rethinks-brands/, accessed 3 February 2010.

Goller, S., Hogg, A., and Kalafatis, S. P. (2002), 'A new research agenda for business segmentation', *European Journal of Marketing*, 36, 1–2, 252–71.

Green, P. E. (1979), 'A new approach to market segmentation', *Business Horizons*, February, 61–73.

Griffith, R. L., and Pol, L. A. (1994), 'Segmenting industrial market', *Industrial Marketing Management*, 23, 39–46.

Haley, R. I. (1968), 'Benefit segmentation: a decision-oriented research tool', *Journal of Marketing*, 32, 30–5.

Holbrook, M. B., and Gardner, M. P. (1993), 'An approach to investigating the emotional determinants of consumption durations: why do people consume what they consume for as long as they consume it?', *Journal of Consumer Psychology*, 2, 2, 123–42.

—and Hirschman, E. C. (1982), 'The experiential aspects of consumer behaviour: consumer fantasies, feelings and fun', *Journal of Consumer Research*, 9 (September), 132–40.

Hooley, G. J., and Saunders, J. A. (1993), *Competitive Positioning: The Key to Market Success*, Englewood Cliffs, NJ: Prentice Hall.

Howaldt, K., and Mitchell, A. (2007), 'Can segmentation ever deliver the goods?', *Market Leader*, 36 (Spring), retrieve from www.warc.com, accessed 25 April.

Hunt, S. D., and Arnett, D. B. (2004), 'Market segmentation strategy, competitive advantage and public policy: grounding segmentation strategy in resource-advantage theory', *Australasian Marketing Journal*, 12, 1, 7–25.

Jantti, S-M., and Jarn, C. (2009), The insightful museum – how to create a customer centred marketing strategy, *ESOMAR, Consumer Insights*, retrieve from www.warc.com, accessed 26 March 2010.

Kotler, P. (1984), *Marketing Management*, international edn., Upper Saddle River, NJ: Prentice Hall.

Leung, K.T. (2010), *Road Vehicle State Estimation Using Low-Cost GPS/INS*, Unpublished EngD Thesis, Cranfield: Cranfield University.

McAlister, L., and Pessemier, E. (1982), 'Variety seeking behaviour: an interdisciplinary review', *Journal of Consumer Research*, 9 (December), 311–22.

McDonald, M., and Dunbar, I. (2004), *Market Segmentation: How to Do It, How to Profit from It*, Oxford: Elsevier.

Mintel (2008), *Champagne and Sparkling Wine – UK – March 2008*, retrieve from www.mintel.com, accessed 24 January 2010.

—(2010a), Childrenswear – UK – January 2010, *Mintel Report*, January. retrieve from: http://oxygen.mintel.com/sinatra/oxygen/display/id=479786, accessed 3 March 2010.

—(2010b), Supermarket sweeps up childrenswear sales, *Mintel Press Release*, retrieve from: www.mintel.com/press-centre/press-releases/488/supermarket-sweeps-up-childrenswear-sales, accessed 3 March 2010.

Naudé, P., and Cheng, L. (2003), 'Choosing between potential friends: market segmentation in a small company', paper presented at the *19th IMP Conference*, Lugano, Switzerland, retrieve from www.impgroup.org/conferences.php, accessed December 2007.

Olney, T. J., Holbrook, M. B., and Batra, R. (1991), 'Consumer response to advertising: the effects of ad content, emotions, and attitude toward the ad on viewing time', *Journal of Consumer Research*, 17 (March), 440–53.

Potter, S. J., Forrest, E., Sapolsky, B. S., and Ware, W. (1988), 'Segmenting VCR owners', *Journal of Advertising Research*, 28, 2, 29–39.

Ramey, J. and Hargitay, D. (2009), Price Is Paramount. *WWD: Women's Wear Daily*, 31 August, 198, 45, 20.

Ramsay, F. (2009), '118 118 to reposition itself as a transactional service', *Marketing*, 7 July 2009, retrieve from www.marketingmagazine.co.uk/news/918274/118-118-reposition-itself-transactional-service?DCMP=ILC-SEARCH, accessed 3 February 2010.

Ries, A., and Trout, J. (1972), 'The positioning era cometh', *Advertising Age*, 24 April, 35–8.

Sinclair, S. A., and Stalling, E. C. (1990), 'Perceptual mapping: a tool for industrial marketing: a case study', *Journal of Business and Industrial Marketing*, 5, 1, 55–65.

Smith, W. R. (1956), 'Product differentiation and market segmentation as alternative marketing strategies', *Journal of Marketing*, July, 3–8.

Solomon, M. R. (1983), 'The role of products as social stimuli: a symbolic interactionism perspective', *Journal of Consumer Research Conference*, 10 (December), 319–29.

Srivastava, R. K., Shocker, A. D., and Day, G. S. (1978), 'An exploratory study of the influences of usage situations on perceptions of product markets', paper presented at the *Advances in Consumer Research Conference*, Chicago.

Urban, C. (1976), 'Correlates of magazine readership', *Journal of Advertising Research*, 19, 3 (June), 7–12.

Wind, Y. (1978) 'Issues and advances in segmentation research', *Journal of Marketing Research*, 15 (August), 317–37.

—and Cardozo, R. N. (1974), 'Industrial market segmentation', *Industrial Marketing Management*, 3 (March), 155–66.

7 International Market Development

Learning Outcomes

After studying this chapter you should be able to:

► Define international market development as a key growth strategy

► Discuss the differences between multidomestic and global competitive strategies

► Discuss the key drivers for international market development

► Discuss the criteria used for international market selection

► Describe the factors in the foreign market environment that could influence an international marketing strategy

► Describe the various methods used for international market entry

▶ Case Insight 7.1

France Telecom, owner of Orange, one of the world's leading telecommunications operators, had consolidated sales of 53.5bn euros in 2008 and a customer base of more than 182m customers in 30 countries. Given such large numbers of customers what does Orange do to retain them? We talk to Sue Wilmot, Head of Customer Strategy in the customer marketing team, to find out more.

Sue Wilmot for Orange

Orange offers services including mobile and fixed line telephony, internet, and IPTV (internet TV) in 30 countries where the company operate for over 182m customers. By the end of 2008, the Group had 122m mobile customers worldwide and 13m broadband internet (ADSL) customers in Europe. It is the No. 3 mobile operator and the No. 1 provider of broadband internet services in Europe and, under the brand Orange Business Services, is a world leader in provision of telecommunication services to multinational companies. The group's strategy, characterized by a strong focus on innovation, convergence, and effective cost management, aims to establish Orange as an integrated operator and benchmark for new telecommunications services in Europe. Today, the group remains focused on its core activities as a network operator, while working to develop its position in new growth activities. To meet customer expectations, the group strives to provide products and services that are simple and user-friendly.

Customers are at the heart of everything we do at Orange group. As a result, it is essential we look after our existing customers and keep a loyal base for the future. To do this, we need to align both loyalty and retention activity to ensure we look after our customers, from the point at which they join Orange. However, there will always be instances where customers do want to leave as we work in a highly competitive industry and customers have alternatives and therefore we need a robust retention strategy to manage this.

Customer retention as a strategy is standardized across Europe but is localized at the implementation level given local market differences. What is highly important to some markets may not be as important to others due to the differences in customer behaviour, economic climate, maturity, and competitor situation. How we retain clients across multiple channels in different countries is based on the skills of the teams, the channel capabilities and the systems capabilities in different countries. The market conditions are also different across Europe, for example, although involuntary churn, i.e. non-payment of bills resulting in a customer leaving an operator, is an issue for most countries, it is certainly more of an issue in Romania and Spain than France.

These differences in retention practices and capabilities can be for different reasons. For involuntary churn, the culture and market conditions drive how much of an issue this is in local markets. France has not been as impacted by the recent recession as other countries such as Romania, Spain, and the UK. This recessionary factor, coupled with a culture in these countries of high borrowing, has led to consumers finding themselves in increasingly difficult personal economic circumstances where they cannot afford to pay their bills.

When looking at customer-initiated churn, how we address churn prevention through developing contact plans from day 1 of a customer's lifecycle is key. Traditionally, the customer lifecycle has been broken

▶ Case Insight 7.1

Orange, No.3 mobile operator and No.1 broadband provider in Europe

into three key periods; welcome, grow, and keep. But if we only consider 'keeping' a customer toward the end of their lifecycle, we are often reducing our chances of being able to 'save' that customer. This is particularly the case if a customer has experienced a problem throughout their lifetime with Orange, as if we don't manage the issues and subsequent satisfaction at this point we eventually worsen the problem. By not addressing this issue and the loyalty and retention of the customer until the end of a contract, we have fundamentally missed the opportunity to retain the customer as they are already dissatisfied with us . It is, therefore, little surprise the customer wants to leave when it comes to the end of the contract.

The problem for us, therefore, is how do we develop our customer contact plan to reduce customer churn given the different market conditions in European markets?

Introduction

Have you ever considered where the food you purchase and consume is produced or the clothes you are wearing right now have been manufactured? Have a look in your kitchen cupboard and your wardrobe—is it England, Europe, China, or perhaps South-East Asia? What about your mobile service provider, is their head office in the UK, USA, Sweden or maybe India? What about the last film you watched at the cinema—where was it filmed—America, India, or maybe Europe? In the twenty-first century we are consuming more products, reading more information, travelling overseas more than ever before. In 2008, the dollar value of world merchandise exports increased by 15% to US$15.8trn, whereas exports of commercial services rose 11% to US$3.7trn. However, in 2009, we saw a collapse in global demand brought on by the biggest economic downturn in decades. What effect has this had on how, where, and to whom we export products and market our product offerings?

In light of the increasing internationalization of world markets, increased foreign trade, changes in technology and the economic impact of foreign markets, **international marketing** is essential for the survival of many organizations. Even organizations that only compete in domestic markets are affected, as they compete increasingly with foreign organizations. An understanding of international business, marketing, and globalization is thus essential for marketing in the twenty-first century.

This chapter discusses the rise in international marketing and what marketers need to consider for effective international market development of their product offering. This includes how we approach international marketing, the criteria used to select attractive international markets, forces in international markets that shape our activities, and the differing methods for international market entry.

Market Development

Marketing strategy is about matching market opportunities to the organization's resources (what it can do) and objectives (what management wants to do). Successful strategies begin with identification of an attractive market opportunity. Early in the marketing strategy process, it is useful to develop or use an existing framework for exploring any opportunities. One framework was developed by Igor Ansoff, a Russian-born pioneer of strategic management and corporate planning (Ansoff, 1957). Often referred to as the **Ansoff matrix** (see Figure 7.1), the product–market matrix provides a useful framework for considering the relationship between strategic direction and market opportunities. This matrix provides four broad strategic options available to organizations, depending on whether the product and/or the market are considered new to the organization.

	Present Products	**New Products**
Present Markets	Market Penetration	Product Development
New Markets	Market Development	Diversification

Figure 7.1

Ansoff's matrix

Source: Adapted from Ansoff (1957).

The matrix illustrates that the element of risk increases the further the strategy moves away from known quantities—an existing product and/or existing market. Thus, product development (requiring a new product) and market development (a new market), typically involve a greater risk than penetration (existing product and existing market); with diversification (new product and new market) carrying the greatest risk of all. Although four types of opportunities are presented, some organizations can pursue more than one type of opportunity simultaneously. More detail about the Ansoff matrix can be found in Chapter 5. Here, we give specific attention to the strategy of 'market development'.

A **market development strategy** involves increasing sales by selling existing products in new markets, either by gaining new customers domestically or entering new markets internationally. So, we are trying to sell more of the same things to different people. We might target different geographical markets at home or abroad, or target different groups of people, perhaps a different demographic profile from our current customers. For example, Lucozade was first marketed for sick children and then rebranded to target athletes. Other examples include the use of military equipment for consumer purposes (e.g. miniature cameras in mobile phones originated from espionage), and, more controversially, the selling of cigarettes to women in the early 1930s/1940s. We currently see **franchise** chains like McDonald's expanding into new geographical locations domestically by targeting new audiences through differing distribution outlets like the McCafe and airport eateries. These are good examples of developing new markets domestically for an existing product.

A more risky strategy is entering a new international market with an existing product. To build brand awareness and minimize risk, organizations rely on the reputation of their brands in domestic markets. The entry of the Japanese, European, and American auto industry into China and India during the last decade is a good example of international market development. Here, we see players like Ford, Honda, Toyota, etc., trying to transfer their reputation in well-established Western markets to gain early footage in rapidly developing markets. Other examples include Cadbury Schweppes selling existing brands of chocolate bars in Africa, and McDonald's expanding their franchise and entering foreign markets such as China, Russia, and Brazil.

One of the main decisions is 'do we pursue new audiences in our domestic market or enter new international markets?'. Some of the main differences between domestic and international marketing include language, culture, complexity of research and decision-making, market knowledge, and marketing environment stability (see Table 7.1). For example, international markets are often seen as more unstable than domestic markets due to their sensitivity to fluctuations in currency rates, immigration patterns, and political and trade relations. Furthermore, development in international markets requires a higher degree of investment from the organization and a greater understanding of the changing nature of world markets.

▶ **Table 7.1** Key differences between domestic and international marketing

Domestic marketing	International marketing
Main language	Many languages
Dominant culture	Multicultural
Research relatively straightforward	Research is complex
Relatively stable environment	Frequently unstable environment
Single currency	Exchange rate problems
Business conventions understood	Conventions diverse and unclear

The Changing Nature of World Markets

Since the Second World War, international marketing has been driven by international trends in population migration, advances in technology, and the reduction in barriers to international trade. Importantly, barriers to international trade lowered considerably through the establishment of the World Trade Organization (WTO) and international agreements and trading blocs (e.g., European Union).

The World Trade Organization (WTO) developed from a system of trade negotiations founded in 1948, known as the General Agreement on Tariffs and Trade (GATT). GATT was initially meant to be a provisional agreement until its participant member states could devise the Charter for an International Trade Organization (ITO), an intended executive agency of the United Nations. However, the ITO never came to pass in its intended form, because of its ambitious agenda to provide rules for member state employment, investment practices, services, and commodity agreements. GATT was designed as a series of trade negotiations to reduce tariffs among negotiating countries in order to increase world trade by reducing the costs of doing international business. It proceeded through eight trade rounds incorporating around 123 countries by the final round, the Uruguay Round, which took place between September 1986 and April 1994. These negotiations transformed the GATT into the WTO.

Located in Geneva, Switzerland, the WTO was established on 1 January 1995. With 153 member countries, the WTO is a formidable and important operator in global trade agreements. Its mission is to:

▶ administer WTO trade agreements;

▶ provide a forum for trade negotiations;

▶ handle trade disputes between member countries;

▶ monitor national trade policies;

▶ provide technical assistance and training for developing countries; and

▶ cooperate with other international organizations.

go online

Visit the **Online Resource Centre** and complete Internet Activity 7.1 to learn more about the WTO and its activities to encourage global trade.

In the last 50 years, major regional trading blocs have also been developed in America (NAFTA), in Latin America (Mercosur), in Europe (European Union), and in South-East Asia (ASEAN) (see Table 7.2). Each trading bloc has its own unique character and customs, offering different opportunities and threats to international traders. For example, when the Single European Market was developed, a survey of senior marketing executives in Europe revealed the need to focus on the following issues:

▶ the growing importance of market segmentation;

▶ increasing industry concentration likely to occur;

▶ the emergence of worldwide competition;

▶ the implementation of prudent moves towards Eastern Europe; and

▶ a concern to develop European-style marketing including cross-border branding, advertising, and pricing (Lawrence, 1993).

▶ **Table 7.2** Origins and purposes of world trade blocs

Trade bloc name	Members	Formation date	Estimated combined GDP PPP	Purpose
Mercosur (derived from the Spanish Mercado Común del Sur)	Common Market of the 'Southern Cone' of the South Americas, a trading area incorporating Brazil, Argentina, Uruguay, Paraguay, and Venezuela	Formed in 1991 under the Treaty of Asunción and later amended based on the Protocol of Ouro Preto, negotiated in 1994	US$3.0trn (2009)	To promote free trade and free movement of goods, peoples, and currency
ASEAN (The Association of South-East Asian Nations)	Philippines, Indonesia, Thailand, Malaysia, and Singapore. Later between 1984 and 1999, Brunei Darussalam, Vietnam, Laos, Myanmar, and Cambodia	Formed in 1967 when the foreign ministers signed the ASEAN Declaration	US$2.8trn (2009)	To develop ties between Asian nations with a view to cooperation in international trade, security, and political affairs. To foster greater mutual respect for the independence, sovereignty, equality, territorial integrity, and national identity of all other member nations
EU (European Union)	27 countries by January 2007 including Austria, Belgium, Bulgaria, Cyprus, Czech Republic, Denmark, Estonia, Finland, France, Germany, Greece, Hungary, Ireland, Italy, Latvia, Lithuania, Luxembourg, Malta, the Netherlands, Poland, Portugal, Romania, Slovakia, Slovenia, Spain, Sweden, UK	Origins lie in the development of the European Steel and Coal Community in 1952, then the formation of the European Community in 1957. The Union was established in 1992 by the Treaty on European Union (the Maastricht Treaty)	US$14.4trn (2009)	To develop links between European nations to enhance security and rebuild Europe's post-war economies. To promote free trade and free movement of goods, people, and currency
NAFTA (The North American Free Trade Agreement)	USA, Canada, and Mexico	The agreement was an expansion of an earlier Canada–USA Free Trade Agreement signed in 1989. NAFTA came into effect in 1994	US$16.9trn (2009)	To eliminate barriers to trade and facilitate cross-border movement of goods and services. To promote fair competition. To increase investment in the territories of the parties. To provide protection and enforcement of intellectual property rights in each party's territory. To establish further trilateral, regional, and multilateral cooperation to expand and enhance the benefits of the NAFTA Agreement

Sources: Trade bloc websites; GDP PPP (gross domestic product, purchasing power parity) estimates, www.ciw.gov

More recently, country membership of the European Union has increased from 15 countries in 2004 to 27 countries in 2009 (with another three Croatia, Turkey, and the Former Yugoslav Republic of Macedonia currently being considered). According to the International Monetary Fund (IMF) in 2008, with over 500m citizens, the EU combined generated an estimated 30% share of the nominal gross world product and about 22% of the PPP gross world product, making it the world's largest trading group. By taking in new members from Eastern Europe as they develop, the EU offers even greater opportunities for export potential to firms inside and outside the EU as increased wealth fuels increased consumer demand for goods and services.

What is clear from an analysis of world trade is that, in reality, the leading multinational corporations in the world come from three major regions: the USA, Japan, and Europe (Rugman, 2000). Although there is increasing recognition of the importance of world trade, as organizations and countries increasingly trade their goods and services around the world, there are attempts by countries other than Japan, the USA, and the major European countries to develop their own trade regionally and internationally through trading blocs, often in collaboration with the three major trading regions.

go online

Visit the **Online Resource Centre** and follow the weblinks to learn more about each of these trading blocs and their respective governing bodies.

International Market Development

Entering international markets is a key market development strategy for organizational growth and has been a feature of civilizations for thousands of years. However, in the last century international trade has seen enormous growth in both scale and complexity. With this growth, different approaches have developed to international market development.

Approaches to International Market Development

International marketing means different things to different organizations. Some organizations take an ad hoc approach, only responding to customer export enquiries when they occur. Others proactively seek to develop an international marketing strategy in addition to their domestic strategy (e.g. H&M). However, for some, international market development is their only marketing strategy and their domestic operations are considered of minor importance. For example, the Australian beer, Foster's, focuses its efforts more on international markets than the domestic Australian market. The approach selected will depend on the resources available, the industry, and the type of product. For example, some products such as information technologies, electronics, and cars are international by nature. The high degree of investment in research and product development in these industries necessitates the move into international markets as domestic markets often do not provide enough sales. Irrespective of the motivation, we are seeing today a growing rise in international marketing activities with the main considerations for approach being the degree of risk and/or organization adaption required and the potential opportunities.

The EPRG classification (see Figure 7.2) by Perlmutter (1969) was one of the first to specify the various approaches for international market development. It highlights four approaches, the first two taking a more localized approach. An **ethnocentric approach** views the domestic market (home market) as the most important, with foreign markets not seen as representing a serious threat. With a **polycentric approach**, each overseas market is seen as a separate domestic market and the organization seeks to be seen as a local organization within that country. In some instances, each market has its own manufacturing and marketing operations, with only a limited overlap.

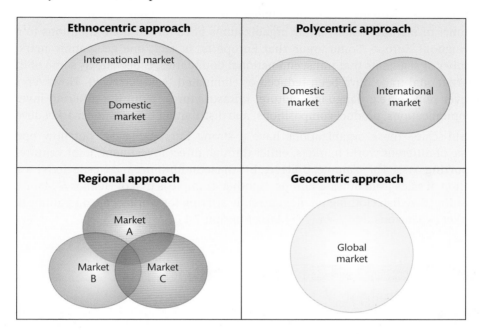

Figure 7.2
EPRG classification for international marketing

The last two take a more standardized approach. A **regional approach** groups countries together, usually on a geographical basis (e.g. Europe), and provides for the specific needs of consumers within those countries. In this instance, national boundaries are respected, but do not have the same importance as cultural differences. A **geocentric approach** sees the world as a single global market, with the organization looking for global segments (e.g. ageing market) and global opportunities to rationalize communications, production, and product development.

Another classification based on European organizations, was proposed by Lynch (1994) and includes five broad categories. These categories differ not only according to the organization's attitudes to international markets, but also the scale of the operations in markets being developed.

▶ Local-scale—these organizations operate within national and local boundaries and have little opportunity or desire to trade internationally. For example, the local convenience store or the car repair garage.

▶ National-scale—these organizations focus mainly on their domestic market, but might find a number of opportunities emerging from foreign markets in the form of ad hoc customer enquiries.

▶ Regional-scale—these organizations focus on specific regions within Europe as opposed to operating throughout Europe (e.g. Eastern or Western Europe, Scandinavian countries) and gain experience of operating abroad on a smaller scale. For example, Norwegian and Swedish organizations have a long tradition of trade relations with other Scandinavian countries as a first experience of cross-national trade.

▶ European-scale—with increasing changes to the European Union and the rise in the number of member states, many organizations have turned their attentions to marketing throughout Europe. Some argue that Europe is, in fact, one geographic market with a number of segments that transcend national boundaries, especially as some of the risks of international trade have been reduced or eliminated (e.g. currency). However, some will forever remain (e.g. language, culture, infrastructure), requiring differing investment in communications, product compositions, and distribution for effective market development.

▶ World-scale—these organizations have a strong European base, but now operate in a range of different world markets, either through direct investment, joint venture, or on an **exporting** basis. For example, Unilever, BP, GlaxoSmithKline, and Nestlé derive a significant portion of sales from outside Europe. Another example is that of Hennes & Mauritz (H&M), a leading Swedish clothing retailer currently striving for world-scale operations through its market expansions into Asia (see Market Insight 7.1).

▶ Market Insight 7.1

H&M Heads East

Hennes & Mauritz (H&M) was established in Sweden in 1947, but today H&M sells clothes and cosmetics in over 37 markets, employing more than 76,000 employees all working to the same philosophy: to bring customers fashion and quality at the best price. First quarter 2010 net profit for the international retailer was 3.74bn kronor ($514m), making H&M the number one fashion retailer across Europe, and the third-largest worldwide.

With great potential for international market development, H&M has expanded substantially in recent years and today operates more than 2,000 stores across 37 countries. Germany is the biggest market, followed by France, Sweden, and the UK. However, in recent years, the retailer has undertaken aggressive expansion throughout Asia. In April 2007, H&M landed in China with a splash, a particularly

H&M, the Swedish retailer, offers stylish womenswear
Source: H&M.

▶ Market Insight 7.1

bright, turquoise splash of images for the brand's new summery Kylie Minogue collection and the 'H&M loves Kylie' campaign promoted on thousands of billboards around Shanghai. Today, H&M has over 21 stores throughout China with sales in 2009 of SEK 1,614m.

About a year later (September 2008), H&M arrived in Japan, opening two stores in Tokyo, one in Ginza followed by one in Harajuku. These stores have already proved to be the most successful store launches in H&M's history. By 2010, H&M had a total of five stores across Japan with sales in 2009 of SEK 1,111m.

In February 2010, H&M opened its first store in Seoul, the fashion-conscious capital of Korea. Featuring international style inspiration with a full concept store of 2,600 metres on four floors, Karl-Johan Persson, CEO of H&M, commented that 'Korea is an exciting market and H&M looks forward to bringing style-

conscious shoppers in Seoul the inspiration to make their own personal fashion statement'.

Although H&M was relatively late to develop its international retail operations across Asia due to preoccupation with expansion in other foreign markets (e.g., Europe, USA), its business in Asia is built on the back of 30 years of manufacturing experience from across China.

Sources: Movius (2007); Kageyama (2008); Tapper-Hoel (2010); www.hm.com.

1 Using the EPRG classification, how would you classify H&M's approach to international marketing?

2 Using Lynch's (1994) study of European organizations, how would you classify the scale of H&M's operations?

3 Why was H&M 'late' to arrive in the Far East? Discuss.

▶ Research Insight 7.1

To take your learning further, you might wish to read this influential paper.

Lewis, K. S., Lim, F. A., and Rusetski, A. (2006), 'Development of archetypes of international marketing strategy', *Journal of International Business Studies*, 37, 4, 499–524.

This article provides a discussion of three separate characterizations of international marketing strategy: standardization–adaptation, concentration–dispersion, and integration–independence.

@ Visit the **Online Resource Centre** to read the abstract and access the full paper.

International Competitive Strategy

When entering international markets, the key competitive decision is do we standardize or adapt our marketing strategy and to what degree do we do this? In the analysis of the rise of global competition, Hout, Porter, and Rudden (1982) suggest that from a strategic point of

Figure 7.3
The spectrum of
competitive strategies

view, an organization can adopt either a local/global, a multi-domestic, or a global competitive approach to their international marketing strategy (see Figure 7.3).

Multi-domestic Competitive Strategy

In a **multi-domestic competitive strategy**, an organization pursues a separate marketing strategy in each of its foreign markets. It also views the competitive challenge independently from market to market. This is also referred to as a pure **adaptation orientation**, as an organization adapts its operations, buying or conducting market research into the particular country and developing a specific market strategy for that particular market. Through this, cultural, legal, language, communication, and geographical differences in each market are accommodated. For example, Marks and Spencer's formal businessmen's shirts suffered poor sales in the northern European market. Quality and design were identical to those sold in the UK market. However, research revealed that the M&S shirts lacked a key feature: breast pockets for items such as pens and cigarettes. Redesign resulted in an increase in sales. (See also Market Insight 7.2 about global versus local beer tastes.) A central headquarters might coordinate financial controls, research and development activities and marketing policies worldwide but strategy and operations are decentralized. Each subsidiary is viewed as a profit centre and expected to contribute earnings and growth consistent with market opportunity, with competition on a market-by-market basis (Hout, Porter, and Rudden, 1982).

▶ Market Insight 7.2

Global Beer: What's on Tap?

At some point globalization turns from a game of cross-border competition for market share among individual organizations into a contest about the key elements of the industry in which they compete—brands, relationships, and technology. For such industries as computers and soft drinks, this new form of globalization has already struck. It might be reasonable to think that the beer industry would tell a similar story. Reasonable, perhaps, but wrong.

Beer is surprisingly local. Until the middle of the last century, the short shelf life and difficulty of transporting beer meant that it could be sold only locally. Things have changed, but history has left its legacy. Research suggests that consumers may be getting somewhat more adventurous, but even where imports are readily available, most consumers in most countries continue to buy local brands produced by local brewers and sold through local stores, pubs, and restaurants at prices that vary widely in localities around the globe. As a result, the beer industry is a collection of tiny players. The top four command a 40% share of the world market, and the largest, the

▶ Market Insight 7.2

US brewer Anheuser-Busch InBev NV, makes more than 50% of its volume sales from its home market. Although no brewer comes close to dominating the world, in most countries, the top two or three brewers share more than 80% of the market. Two prominent exceptions, Germany and China, are themselves highly concentrated, but at the city or provincial rather than the national level.

Heineken now has the single best prospect of ranking among the global giants of the future. It has a global brand, a widespread presence, both in its own right and through alliances; and strong skills in such areas as marketing and production. Guinness is another international marketing success, with 10 million glasses of Guinness drunk in over 150 countries every day in 2007. Aside from Ireland, Guinness is brewed in 50 other markets, and whereas the UK, and Ireland seem to be falling out of love with stout, ale, the rest

of the world can't get enough of it. Anheuser-Busch In Bev NV is also in good shape, Belgium's Interbrew and South African Breweries are not far behind, and Carlsberg shows signs of regaining its position in the global running. Yet all of these organizations, Heineken included, are years away from replicating the global success of Coke or Nike.

Sources: Benson-Armer, Leibowitz, and Ramachandran (1999); Anon (2005); Word (2006); Euromonitor (2010).

1 **Why do you think some beer brands are so grounded in local appeal and struggle to find a 'global voice'?**

2 **What market factors contribute to such individual tastes when it comes to beer?**

3 **What could Heineken, Guinness, and Carlsberg learn from Coke or Nike in terms of pursuing an international marketing strategy?**

Heineken beer is marketed globally

Source: Heineken International.

Global Competitive Strategy

Globalization refers to the 'process by which the experience of everyday life is becoming standardized around the world' through the free flow of four major components: goods and services, people, capital, and information (Sirgy *et al.*, 2007). With this comes the increasing consolidation in many industries in world markets (e.g. pharmaceutical, financial services, and telecommunication industries) and acceleration by the new industrialized countries' (NICs) desire for modernity (e.g. East European countries like Poland and Slovenia and Asian countries like China and Taiwan). The importance of rising global trade, was indicated by Levitt (1983) in his statement that 'only global organizations will achieve long-term success by concentrating on what everyone wants rather than worrying about the details of what everyone thinks they might like'. However, there have also been detractors from this argument, those who argued that although it was appropriate to operate a global competitive approach to business, the key to success was to customize the offering (Quelch and Hoff, 1986) (i.e. adaptation).

A global competitive strategy follows a **standardization orientation**, wherein an organization operates as if the world were one large market (global market), ignoring regional and national differences, selling the same goods and services the same way throughout the world. The standardization approach operates on the belief that global culture is converging, or that the cultural differences are superficial (see Wind and Perlmutter, 1973; Levitt, 1983; Douglas and Douglas, 1987). The standardization approach has many immediate benefits including cost reductions, improved efficiency, enhanced customer preference, and increased competitive leverage (Herbig and Day, 1993). The problem with this approach is that cultural, legal, and national differences can inhibit trade—especially if an organization is incorrect in assuming the differences were superficial. Communication is one of the biggest barriers when marketing internationally and is heightened when using the standardization approach; the result of which is advertising messages being misrepresented or misunderstood, such as the famous communication blunders reported in Table 7.6.

To qualify as pursuing a global competitive strategy, an organization needs to be able to demonstrate two things: (1) selective contestability and (2) globally capability. **Selective contestability** means that the organization can contest any international market it chooses to compete in and is based on the core marketing principles of segmentation, targeting, and positioning. The ability to divide generic markets into meaningful sub-markets or segments, select those most attractive, and position the product offering appropriately is at the very heart of devising a competitive strategy, irrespective of whether the organization is competing in a regional, national, or global market. **Global capability** is the capability of an organization to bring its entire worldwide resources to bear on any competitive situation it finds itself in, regardless of where that might be. The idea of a global brand goes far beyond the organization's physical presence in a number of differing national markets and reflects the existence of a global image. It is this universal recognition that enables one to distinguish the organization pursuing a focused strategy in numerous national markets from a global player like Ford, McDonald's, Hilton, Google, and Levi's.

To distinguish if an organization is adopting a multi-domestic (adaption) or global (standardization) competitive strategy, Vijay (1997) recommends reviewing five key attributes (Table 7.3).

> **Table 7.3** Five key attributes of global strategy

Attribute	Description
Possessing a standard product (or core) that is marketed uniformly across the world	Both the product and service offering is marketed using the same marketing mix in differing national markets, representing what most regard as a global strategy
Sourcing all assets, not just production, on an optimal basis	If one were to pursue this to its ultimate level, one might find that nationalistic factors might well result in one finishing up with an essentially multi-domestic operation due to local requirements in capital ownership, employment, and so on
Achieving market access in line with the break-even volume of the needed infrastructure	Global competitor must be of sufficient size and generate sufficient volume/revenue in each of the markets in which it competes to justify the marketing investment needed to compete effectively
The ability to contest assets as much as products when circumstances require	This reflects the organization's ability to match its principal competitors in gaining access to and control over assets critical to its success, for example technology
Providing all functions (or competencies) with a global orientation, even they are primarily local in scope	This is the most difficult to achieve, and to measure, as it reflects the 'mental set' of those responsible for devising a strategy as well as those responsible for its execution

Source: Adapted from Vijay (1997).

go online

Visit the **Online Resource Centre** and complete Internet Activity 7.2 to learn more about how HSBC Plc positions itself as understanding local differences, with the aim of being the World's Local Bank.

Anti-Globalization Movement

In contrast to the perspectives mentioned above, there also exists an anti-globalization movement. **Anti-globalization** is a term most commonly used to refer to the political stance, social movement or as encompassing a number of separate social movements in which participants are united in opposition to the political power of large organizations, as exercised in trade agreements. These agreements are viewed as undermining democracy, the environment, labour rights, national sovereignty, the third world, and other concerns.

Protesters believe that global financial institutions (e.g. WTO) and trade agreements undermine local decision-making methods with many governments and free trade institutions seen as allegedly acting for the good of multinational organizations (e.g. Microsoft, McDonald's, Google). These organizations are also seen as having privileges that most people do not have: moving freely across borders, extracting desired natural resources, and utilizing a diversity of human resources. They are perceived to be able to move on after doing permanent damage to the natural capital and biodiversity of a nation, in a manner impossible for that nation's citizens. Activists also claim that large multinational organizations impose a kind of global monoculture. Some of the movement's common goals are, therefore, an end to the legal status of so-called corporate personhood and the dissolution or dramatic reform of the World Bank, IMF, and WTO. Two documentaries *The Corporation* (2003) and *Life and Debt* (2001) present very chilling and raw views of the socio-cultural impact of growing international trade relations and the multinational organization.

go online

Visit the **Online Resource Centre** and follow the weblinks to *The Corporation* to learn more about this documentary.

Promotional material for *The Corporation* film

▶ Research Insight 7.2

To take your learning further, you might wish to read this influential paper.

Levitt, T. (1983), 'Globalisation of markets', *Harvard Business Review*, May–June, 9–11.

This article provides a thought-provoking essay about the movement from an emphasis on customizing items to offering globally standardized products that are advanced, functional, reliable—and low priced.

Visit the **Online Resource Centre** to read the abstract and access the full paper.

Drivers of International Market Development

International marketing is driven by a number of key marketplace forces (see Figure 7.4). The most common drivers include:

▶ Excess stock—with excess stock and limited opportunity for sales in domestic markets, organizations seek international markets by which to offload some of this stock. This is an activity called **dumping** and is an international marketing version of 'clearance pricing', wherein excess stock is cleared onto another country's market at very low prices in order to liquidate capital. There is no long-term entry strategy, just a hit and run exercise.

▶ Historical accident—this was the reason behind the growth of Coca-Cola's international marketing operations. In 1928, Coca-Cola was the first ever sponsor of the Olympic Games,

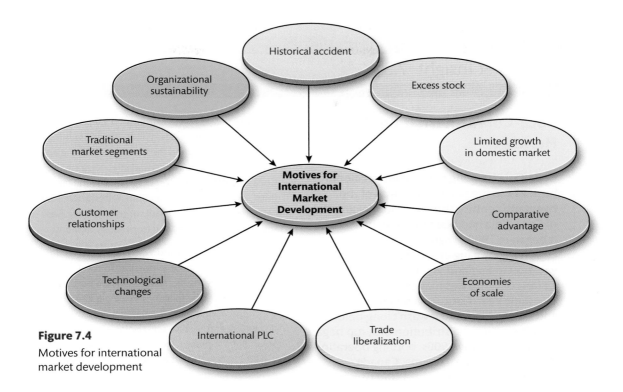

Figure 7.4

Motives for international market development

and, in the 1940s, US forces took the drink with them when they went into the Second World War. These historical events provided opportunities for Coca-Cola to build on with an aggressive distribution policy, resulting in the red and white livery being one of the most internationally recognizable brands (see Market Insight 7.3).

▶ Limited growth in domestic markets—if there is limited growth in the domestic market, an organization enters international markets to avoid the intensity of domestic competition. For example, given the intense competition in the home markets of the USA and Europe, and growth in the Chinese markets, the top four global brewers AB Inbev, SABMiller, Heineken, and Carlsberg have substantially increased volumes and global presence through acquisition activity in the last decade.

▶ Comparative advantage—certain regions and countries have developed core competencies in the production of certain products, the provision of raw resources, or skills in the workforce. This presents a comparative advantage for the manufacture and production of goods in these regions. For example, over 750m olive trees are cultivated worldwide, with about 95% in the Mediterranean region, and with most global olive oil production coming from Spain, Italy, and Greece. With respect to skills, certain countries offer differential labour costs and specialized skills, such as China and textile manufacturing, or India and the provision of business process outsourcing (BPOs) (e.g. customer call centres). This presents an advantage not only in labour and operating costs, but also, for some industries, savings in transport and import costs in manufacturing.

▶ Market Insight 7.3

Coca-Cola's International Heritage

Coca-Cola has long been an international business. In the first two decades of the twentieth century, the international growth of Coca-Cola had been rather haphazard. It began in 1900, when Charles Howard Candler, took a jug of syrup with him on vacation to England. A modest order for five gallons of syrup was mailed back to Atlanta. The same year, Coca-Cola travelled to Cuba and Puerto Rico, and it wasn't long before the international distribution of syrup began. Through the early 1900s, bottling operations were built in Cuba, Panama, Canada, Puerto Rico, the Philippines, and Guam (western Pacific island). In 1920, a bottling organization began operating in France as the first bottler of Coca-Cola on the European continent. Then came the 1928 Olympics and the Second World War.

In 1926, Robert W. Woodruff, chief executive officer and chairman of the board, committed the organization to international expansion by establishing a Foreign Department, which in 1930 became a subsidiary known as the Coca-Cola Export Corporation. By that time, the number of countries with bottling operations had almost quadrupled, and the organization had initiated a partnership with the Olympic Games that transcended cultural boundaries. Coca-Cola and the Olympic Games began their association in the summer of 1928, when an American freighter arrived in Amsterdam carrying the United States Olympic team and 1,000 cases of Coca-Cola. Forty thousand spectators filled the stadium to witness two firsts: the first lighting of the Olympic flame and the first sale of Coke at an Olympiad. Dressed in caps and coats bearing the Coca-Cola trademark, vendors satisfied the fans' thirst, while outside the stadium, refreshment stands, cafés, restaurants, and small shops called 'winkles' served Coke in bottles and from soda fountains.

During the Second World War, Coca-Cola set up bottling plants as close as possible to combat areas in Europe and the Pacific. More than 5bn bottles of Coke were consumed by military service personnel during the war, in addition to countless servings through dispensers and mobile, self-contained units in battle areas. But the presence of Coca-Cola did more than just lift the morale of the troops. In many areas, it gave local people their first taste of Coca-Cola. When peace returned, the Coca-Cola system was poised for unprecedented worldwide growth. From the mid-1940s until 1960, the number of countries with bottling operations nearly doubled. As the world emerged from a time of conflict, Coca-Cola emerged as a worldwide symbol of friendship and refreshment. The Coca-Cola organization is now operating in more than 200 countries and producing nearly 400 brands of Coca Cola.

Sources: Pendergrast (2000). www.thecoca-colacompany.com

1 **What key market forces were the drivers for internationalization of Coca-Cola?**

2 **What marketing elements were imperative for the successful international market strategy for Coca-Cola?**

3 **Was Coca-Cola in the right place at the right time or was this a planned international marketing strategy? Discuss.**

▶ Economies of scale—for some products the cost of development and production is high and thus requires mass production runs for effective return on investment, so to function effectively factories need to serve large world markets. Examples include consumer electronic goods and the automotive industry. A high degree of standardization is evident in the manufacture of certain car parts (e.g., the chassis) with superficial changes tailored for local markets (e.g. air conditioning). This enables car manufacturers to achieve economies of scale in certain parts (Pitcher, 1999).

▶ Trade liberalization—with the creation of trading blocs and the reduction of barriers to trade worldwide, we are seeing many organizations engaging in global competition with international firms in domestic markets and domestic organizations moving abroad to compete overseas as markets open up.

▶ International product lifecycle—this is when a product reaches a differing stage of the product lifecycle in differing countries. For example, the original Volkswagen Beetle ceased production in Germany in 1978, but soon after commenced production and sales in South America.

The original VW Beetle

▶ Technological changes—advances in electronic communications, such as the internet, have enabled increased ability to trade internationally. Online channels are increasingly being used to sell into new markets, taking advantage of low costs for international market entry online. This is a good way for SMEs to increase exports at a low cost, but this is greatly influenced by changes in the technological infrastructure internationally.

▶ Customer relationships—as organizations move abroad, so suppliers and intermediaries must consider the prospect as international marketing activities can be felt throughout the supply chain, from end consumer to the supplier and producer. For example, as Ford expands into foreign markets, its product components will also change and suppliers will need to match the requirements of Ford's new manufacturing and assembly production process. This is also true for service-based industries. However, the difference lies in that there will be an increasing need to locate an organization's services even closer to the customer, either through branch offices or subsidiaries strategically placed throughout a number of foreign markets. For example, A. C. Nielsen, one of the world's leading marketing research organizations, has research operations that span more than 100 countries. Headquartered in New York, the organization's major regional business centres are located in: Schaumburg, Illinois; Wavre, Belgium; Hong Kong; Sydney, Australia; Buenos Aires, Argentina; and Nicosia, Cyprus.

▶ Transnational market segments—the growth in groups of people with similar needs but who inhabit different countries, called transnational market segments, occurs because of migration (e.g. Malaysians working in Australia); similarities in demographics (e.g. baby boomers); or similarities in lifestyles (e.g. working women). From a conceptual perspective, a truly global organization should be dividing market segments up based on these similar characteristics across national borders. Country of residence or birth is becoming less and less relevant as migration increases and national borders diminish.

▶ Organizational sustainability—the broader the range of markets served, the less likely that failure in one market will result in overall organizational decline. Different markets are always at different stages of development and competitive intensity. Therefore, an international market portfolio will provide an organization with increased chance for organizational sustainability.

However, whatever the motivation for international market development, a planned approach considerably increases the chances for success. Once international market entry has been decided as an organizational growth strategy, certain decisions have to be made to increase the chances of success. These include determining:

▶ Which foreign markets to pursue?

▶ Which methods are the most suitable for entering new markets?

▶ Which strategy to adopt to appeal to the desired needs of foreign markets?

International Market Selection

Assessing market attractiveness is very important when considering international market development and involves a matching process between opportunities and threats in possible markets with the organization's own strengths and weaknesses. The quality of this assessment will have a big impact on the success or failure of the international marketing strategy (Anderson and Strandskov, 1998). A number of criteria are used to assess international market attractiveness, of which market size and growth are the two most important.

▶ Market size and growth rate—market size refers to the number of potential and current customers with a large market more likely to redeem increased sales volume than a small market. However, certain areas in the world grow in attractiveness whereas others decline. Ohmae (1985, 1992) was one of the first marketing writers to point to the domination of world markets by what he called the Triad—the three major world players of Europe, America, and Japan. However, this is susceptible to turbulent change. The rapidly developing countries of the Pacific Rim (i.e. China, Singapore, South Korea, and Taiwan), are going through a period of unparalleled economic growth. Income in their countries is still unevenly distributed in these populations; however, increasing prosperity has created markets hungry for Western luxury brands to reflect their rising personal wealth. Names like Burberry, Ralph Lauren, and new developing technologies appear prominently. As industrial sectors have grown in these areas, agriculture has decreased in importance, altering the mix of goods and services required for business markets and creating opportunities for information technologies, business services, and construction. For example, with rapid industrial development and a market of more than 1.3bn increasingly prosperous consumers, the attractiveness of China is widely viewed as outweighing the risk of investing capital. Furthermore, high growth rates are seen as considerably attractive due to lower perceived competition in these contexts than stable and declining markets. Whitelock and Jobber (1994) report that growth rate is a far more important consideration than market size.

▶ Market access—accessibility means that customers can be reached with marketing communications and distribution. Local industry structure, infrastructure, and local cultural norms can limit market access. For example, in Japan, the monolithic structure of the industry, in which the giant Sogo Sosha general trading organizations (GTC), such as Mitsubishi Corporation and Mitsui & Co., control everything, means that there are few openings for foreign entry, despite no legal problems with importing. Other countries have high tariffs on products in order to protect local industry, or media moguls or government bodies control the use of media channels, making access to certain market segments difficult (e.g. China).

▶ **Geographic proximity**—physical closeness of the market to the domestic market has a direct impact on resources. For example, trading between Australia and the UK requires larger resources than trade between the UK and other European countries such as France.

▶ **Psychological proximity**—this refers to the perceived cultural and societal similarities between countries. For example, some see greater cultural similarity between the USA and the UK than between the UK and France. Thus, organizations in the UK might perceive the USA as more attractive for possible trade relations. Psychological proximity is often based on language—the UK close to Canada, and even India given cultural, language, and historical similarities.

▶ Competition already in the market—intense market competition is unlikely to respond favourably to foreign market entrants, thus assessing competition is very important.

▶ Cost of entering the market—this can vary greatly between markets and strategies for market entry (exporting, direct distribution). For example, physical distribution costs can be extremely high in a country such as the USA or India where distances are large. In other countries distances might be comparably short, but distribution channels and supply chains are long and complex or lack the infrastructure to support them. For example, the telecommunications infrastructure in various African countries differs greatly from more established West European countries such as Germany and France.

▶ Profit potential—this is a factor of the number of potential customers and the profit margin in that market. Even though per unit profit margins would be small, a country with a large potential market might still be attractive for other reasons. For example, India and China might offer large future profit potential. Powerful buying groups, low per capita income, and strong competition are all factors that tend to reduce profit margins.

International market selection requires careful consideration. There is a need for sound market intelligence about the market environment and opportunities. In reality, market screening can be random, driven by customer enquiries or market demand for a product offering or knowledge gained through media or social networks. Visits to the potential markets will also be required for further insights and first-hand market knowledge and to aid the development of networks and relationships. Questions useful for international market screening are detailed in Table 7.4.

▶ **Research Insight 7.3**

To take your learning further, you might wish to read this influential paper.

Young, R. B., and Javalgi, R. G. (2007), 'International marketing research: A global project management perspective', *Business Horizons*, 50, 2, 113–22.

This article provides a useful insight into the importance and role of marketing research as the primary mechanism through which organizations understand their current, as well as potential, customers in international markets.

 Visit the **Online Resource Centre** to read the abstract and access the full paper.

▶ **Table 7.4** International market screening questions

Factor	Questions to consider
Market	▶ What stage is it in growth cycle?
	▶ Is there sufficient future demand or potential?
	▶ Are there established distribution channels?
	▶ How sophisticated is the infrastructure?
Product fit	▶ Is there opportunity in the market for this product?
	▶ Is there demand or interest in this type of product?
	▶ Would the product need to be adapted or changed in any way?
Competition	▶ Who are the existing competitors in this market—national and international?
	▶ How intense or aggressive is the competitive environment?
	▶ What degree of control or influence do existing competitors have in the marketplace?
	▶ What are some of the competitive barriers to entry?
	▶ What is likely to be the competitive response to our market entry?

Factor	Questions to consider
Market entry	▶ What entry methods are feasible for this market and the organization?
	▶ How much would market entry cost us?
	▶ Do we have any contacts in the market that could assist us?
	▶ How similar are the culture, values, attitudes to our domestic market?
	▶ How well do we understand the differences in this market?
Resources	▶ What do we need to invest to enter this market?
	▶ Are we going to have to employ staff locally or relocate staff to enter this market?
	▶ What training and/or education do we require to enter this market—culture, languages, exporting, etc.?
	▶ Do we need to invest in the establishment of new or differing distribution channels for market entry or can we rely on existing distribution channels?
Trade barriers	▶ What legal or regulatory factors will influence market entry or operations in the market?
	▶ Are the advertising and/or marketing research activities similar to our national market?
	▶ Will import tariffs or quotas apply to us?
	▶ Will we be able to take profits earned out of the country?
	▶ Are there any constraints on foreign organizations operating in this market?
	▶ Do we have to manufacture or produce our product to differing quality and/or health and safety standards?

International Marketing Environment

Understanding the international marketing environment of the countries or regions of interest provides the foundation for a market assessment and selection process. An analysis of environmental forces (as per Chapter 2) for foreign markets can help to identify which countries (e.g. Australia, France, Brazil) or regions (e.g. Western Europe, South America) should be given priority and which market entry strategy would be best suited to them. Young (2001) argues that, in contrast to domestic marketing strategies, international marketers pay too little attention to the potential impact that global socio-cultural, economic, legal/institutional, and political developments could have on their ability to enter and trade in a foreign market successfully.

Social Factors

Social factors are very important in international marketing activities. Differences in social structures, social values, gender roles, and family composition can affect what is and what is not acceptable in international marketing activities. The changing social structure is an important consideration. The role of women, the elderly, or the positioning of the family within society can have an impact on consumption patterns. In Western countries we are seeing changing family structures and household compositions as divorce and non-children families rise. We are also seeing more mothers returning to work, placing more reliance on grandparents for childcare responsibilities in regions like the UK, America, and Australia—changing the retirement age and lifestyle patterns of the greying consumer in these markets. This contrasts to the composition of other markets of more cross-generation households (e.g. China and Japan), where grandparents are considered a central part of the family unit and reside in the family household. Population movements are also influencing social factors through the migration of social values. Take Canada for example: immigration now accounts for 70% of Canada's population growth. An awareness of changes and differences in social structure and values is, therefore, imperative.

Cultural Factors

Culture is a set of learned behaviours that unites a group of people. Some of the areas comprising culture are language, education, religion, lifestyle, taboos, and norms. Culture affects how people define their wants and needs through consumption and how they interact. For example, DeBeers controls 80% of the £32.5bn world market in gem diamonds, but markets them differently to countries according to cultural norms. In the UK, a diamond ring is synonymous with getting engaged; in Spain, it is bought after the birth of a child; in Saudi Arabia, diamonds are an important wedding gift.

Giving diamonds: to a fiancé, a new child, or to the bride?

Culture also influences the way we interact. For example, following the movement of many call centre jobs to India, some have been transferred back to the UK. In 2005, Norwich Union (now Banco Santander) relocated customer calls for insurance claims back to the UK following a sequence of misunderstandings about flooding from immersion heaters. Local operators in India struggled to understand the claim as they didn't understand the heating systems. Clearly, for organizations serious about international marketing, cultural sensitivity is paramount. Table 7.5 outlines some behavioural factors that have been known to influence business conduct in international environments.

▶ **Table 7.5** Business conduct in international markets

Factor	Description
Time	▶ Attitudes towards punctuality
	▶ Sanctity of deadlines
	▶ Acquaintance time
	▶ Discussion time
Business cards	▶ When to offer them
	▶ Whether to translate them
	▶ Who gives them first
	▶ How to attend to them
Gifts	▶ Should they be given
	▶ Size/value
	▶ Should they be opened in front of the giver
Dress	▶ Dress codes
	▶ Formality
Entertainment	▶ Type/formality of social occasions
	▶ Table manners and etiquette
	▶ Cuisine
	▶ Cultural and religious taboos
	▶ Venues (e.g. restaurant, private home)
Space	▶ Office size and location
	▶ Selection, quality, and arrangement of furniture
Body language	▶ Greeting conventions (e.g. kiss, handshake, bow)
	▶ Facial and hand gestures and their meaning
	▶ Physical proximity
	▶ Touching and posture
Material possessions	▶ Is it appropriate to comment and admire?

Source: Mead (1990). © John Wiley & Sons Limited. Reproduced with permission.

Language is a critical cultural factor for entering foreign markets. In customer relationships it is becoming the norm to speak in a customer's own language; however, in many Western organizations, such as those from the UK, many executives assume that all foreigners can speak and negotiate in English (Kelly, 2002). Only about one-third of UK business executives have a foreign language, compared to executives from European organizations who often conduct business in a minimum of two languages. In countries such as Denmark, Finland, and Poland, over 80% of executives operate in at least one foreign language.

Language has further implications for marketing communications, be it brand names, organization slogans and advertising taglines, or product packaging. In French-speaking Quebec, Canada, KFC is known as PFK (Poulet Frit Kentucky); this is one of the few instances in which the KFC initialism is changed for the local language (even in France itself, it is called KFC). In several Spanish-speaking areas of the USA, KFC is known as PFK (Pollo Frito Kentucky). All forms of marketing communications have to be translated and back translated to ensure correct interpretation and meaning. This includes careful consideration of the variants. If communication is to be in Arabic then is it aimed at Tunisians or Iraqis, Egyptians or Yemenis? We must also analyse the style of the language and the target audience. If the audience is foreign business personnel, the vocabulary, grammar, and punctuation must reflect this. If the audience is informal or youth-oriented, then a more relaxed language should be used. Using the wrong language for the wrong audience can be devastating, and incorrect translations can result in customer frustration. See Table 7.6 for some examples.

▶ **Table 7.6** Language translations

Brand name	English translation	Language	Foreign translation
KFC	Finger-lickin good	Chinese	Bite your fingers off
Coors	Turn it loose	Spanish	Drink our beer and get diarrhoea
Pepsi	'Come alive: you're in the Pepsi generation'	Chinese	'Pepsi brings your ancestors back from the dead'
Microsoft	Vista	Latvia	'Vista' is a disparaging term for a frumpy old woman
Motorola	'Hellomoto' ring tone	India	Sounds like 'Hello, Fatty' in India
Ford	Pinto	Brazil	'Small male genitals'
Coca-Cola	The name Coca-Cola in China was first rendered as Ke-kou-ke-la	Chinese	'Bite the wax tadpole' or 'female horse stuffed with wax'
Schweppes	Schweppes Tonic Water	Italy	Schweppes Toilet Water
Salem cigarettes	'Salem—Feeling Free'	Japan	'When smoking Salem, you feel so refreshed that your mind seems to be free and empty'

Brand name	English translation	Language	Foreign translation
Parker Pen	'It won't leak in your pocket and embarrass you'	Mexico	'It won't leak in your pocket and make you pregnant'
Clairol	Introduced the 'Mist Stick', a curling iron	Germany	'Mist' is slang for manure. Not too many people had use for the 'manure stick'!
American Airlines	'Fly in Leather'	Latin American	Fly Naked
Electrolux	Nothing sucks like an Electrolux	USA	–

To adapt to cultural difference, organizations can use three internal processes (Mughan 1993): self-analysis—recognizing the situation from the customer's point of view and adapting behaviour accordingly; cultural training—particularly for personnel working or dealing direct with distributors or customers; and recruitment—the shortest route to widening the culture of an organization is through direct recruitment from the international labour market. One of the characteristics of most international organizations is the presence of a range of nationalities in senior management.

Consumption Attitudes

Attitudes can affect perceptions and customer reactions to a product, or the product's country of origin. For example, following the BSE crisis in the UK, the British beef industry had to invest in marketing to convince foreign markets that British beef was safe. A reliable strategy is to first enter international markets that have similar consumption attitudes to our domestic market, e.g. Irish organizations exporting to the UK, Swedish organizations to other Scandinavian markets, and New Zealand to Australia. Through these lower-risk strategies, organizations can develop knowledge and learning before entering markets regarded as very different in terms of consumption attitudes.

Monitoring trends and the context of the attitudes of the buying country are increasingly important in international market development. For example, mainland China had long been an unfriendly market for mid-range fashion, as consumer tastes tend to split into the extremes of mass and luxury. However, in recent years, a swelling demographic of young, white-collar, lower-middle-class women has created a demand for mid-price fashion, as evidenced by the successes of Zara, Gap, and H&M. The shift in consumer taste in China, however, is further reported as representative of a global trend. 'Fashion is not a matter of price. People tend to mix high- and low-priced items. It is a shift in customer attitude that is happening all over, including here' (Movius, 2007).

Some cultures have more negative attitudes than others towards foreign imports. Germans, for example, are more traditionalist, whereas the French and Italians are more open to foreign products (Paitra, 1993). Also, some organizations trade very effectively based on their country of origin, e.g. Foster's on the laid-back Australian attitude, Ikea on its Swedishness and clean Scandinavian design, McDonald's and Coca-Cola on the American dream, and, increasingly, Japan for precision and electronics.

Technological Factors

Technological development in the market can have many implications for marketing communications, new product development, and the overall success of market entry. In many international markets, new technology is increasingly changing the way that organizations go to market (Sclater, 2005). However, in developing markets, radio still remains the main channel for marketing communications, with limited TV diffusion. This highlights the importance of profiling the penetration of electronic technologies and the supporting infrastructure in potential new foreign markets.

Penetration rates of electronic technologies can reflect country population and/or region size, and can also be indicators of certain important market trends. In 2010, the world's population was estimated at 6.8bn and growing at over 80m annually. However, in terms of numbers of people who can, and do, access electronic technologies, only around 25% of the world's population has access to the internet, and only one-third of the world's population subscribes to mobile phones. Not all demographic groups have participated in the information revolution that has occurred since the 1980s: those who are poorer, less educated, and from rural areas have been slower to use both computers and the internet (Bikson and Panis, 1997; Tapscott, 1998). Thus, although certain electronic technologies are becoming everyday conveniences for some market segments, some clusters are being left out—at both the consumer and business levels.

Many customer needs and wants are further bound up with the technological infrastructure within which they reside. For example, the type of fuel used for cooking will depend on the country's use of natural resources and competitive infrastructure for utilities (gas, electric, etc.); the type of telephone used will depend on the telecommunications and economics infrastructure. Wireless telephony penetration frequently exceeds wireline (landline) penetration in developing countries. However, the needs and usage conditions of mobile phones differ considerably in developing markets from mature Western markets. Finnish mobile phone manufacturer Nokia Corp., looking for ways to make mobile handsets practical for people living in developing countries like India, learnt that features such as dustproof keypads were crucial in dry, hot countries with many unpaved roads. Its competitor, Motorola, has developed a slimmed-down mobile handset with only three essential functions to make it easier and more practical to use by customers with poor literacy. As such, customer needs and market conditions not only dictate access to marketing communications messages, but also product design in differing markets.

Economic Factors

The potential of any market is governed by the number of similar customers within that market, their purchasing power, and the health of the economic system. For example, with the collapse in global demand, the WTO forecasted that the global economic recession would drive exports down by roughly 9% in volume terms, the biggest such contraction since the Second World War. Basic information about per capita disposable income, consumption patterns, and unemployment trends can help to draw a picture of a market's economic health. Typical ways to assess the economic potential of a market include:

▶ measures of per capita income—these are often available but can conceal enormous disparities between the rich and poor in some countries. Evenly distributed incomes make for better marketing prospects, especially for middle-income purchases such as consumer durables;

▶ ownership rates of durables (e.g. cars);

▶ balance between urban and rural populations;

▶ prevailing rate of inflation;

▶ **gross national product** (GNP)—this is particularly relevant for the potential of industrial marketing;

▶ market size—this can be assessed from the existing levels of activity in the sector/industry in question and growth rate; and

▶ fluctuations in currency exchanges—these can have a dramatic impact on international marketing strategies, but can also provide attractive short-term opportunities, e.g. in tourism, changes in market exchange rates can have a knock-on effect on the attractiveness of a destination for overseas travellers. This is one key difference between international and domestic marketing.

In market attractiveness assessment, statistics of economic indicators per country are usually required from a number of sources, which, although they can pose comparison problems, can give some indication of a market's current or potential purchasing power.

Political—Legal Factors

Political and legal factors can also impose restrictions or provide opportunities in foreign marketing. For example, governments often intervene by assisting their country's industries to enter foreign markets or by placing obstacles in the way for prospective importers in order to protect domestic organizations. Measures invoked by governments in order to protect their domestic industries include the following:

▶ **quotas** to limit the amount of goods allowed in;

▶ duties, like a special tax on imports (which then makes them non-competitive on price);

▶ **non-tariff barriers** such as product legislation, which means that expensive adaptation needs to be made before the item is legally saleable in the **host country**.

Governments are also under pressure to assist in alleviating unemployment and stimulating economic activity. As such, many countries encourage foreign investment by providing tax concessions and support of various kinds to persuade international organizations to site their manufacturing units in depressed areas. This is true not only for production industries but also service industries.

Political conditions can also cause severe difficulties for international marketers, even to the point of having to withdraw from a market (e.g. Google from China, see Market Insight 7.4) or writing off an entire operation (e.g. Chrysler in post-revolutionary Iran). In some countries, a change in government may have little effect on commercial life, but in others the change can be dramatic (e.g. Iraq). Certain governments can restrict foreign investment and ownership by imputing conditions on market entry, such as through a joint venture with a local organization, with the local organization holding the larger percentage of ownership.

However, organizations need to look at more than just ownership restrictions: other examples of political and legal factors include employment law, health and safety regulations, financial law, patent protection, data protection, and electronic transactions legislation. For example, vending machines are an important delivery mechanism for Coca-Cola's distribution strategy; however, they are illegal in Russia. A mass of by-laws for food and drink retailing, real estate, and taxation—which require all sales to be conducted with a cash register—mean that vending machines can only be implemented with the assistance of 'security firms'.

▶ Market Insight 7.4

Censoring Google

The economy of the People's Republic of China is the fourth-largest in the world when measured by nominal GDP. With rapid industrial development and a market of more than 1.3bn increasingly prosperous consumers, the expected rewards of doing business in China are widely recognized. China is a very desirable market for internet companies, with nearly 384m Chinese consumers online in 2010, compared with just 10m only a decade before. Last year, the Chinese search engine market was worth an estimated $1bn and analysts expected Google to make about $600m from China in 2010. However, doing business in China requires foreign companies to abide by the country's political and legal systems, including its strict censorship laws.

Google launched google.cn in 2006, agreeing to censorship of its search results to obtain market access. For four years Google censored search results, in the hope of becoming the number one search engine in China; a goal it failed to achieve as, unlike most markets, Google comes second behind Baidu—a local search operator. As a foreign organization, Google was expected to operate under the laws of the country, much as eBay is banned from listing Nazi memorabilia in Germany. Self-censorship is the cost of doing business in China, and it is a price that Google decided was worth paying. Google's

decision to agree to China's requests on censorship in 2006 led to accusations it had betrayed its company motto—'Don't be evil'. Amnesty International has consistently called on Google (Yahoo and Microsoft) to stop collaborating with the Chinese authorities' censorship requirements, and to respect the right to freedom of expression for webusers in China. But at market entry in 2006, Google argued that it would be more damaging for civil liberties if it pulled out of China entirely.

In 2010 conditions changed. A spat of security breaches on Google email accounts, lower than forecasted ad-revenues, and acknowledgment that Google's corporate policies were incompatible with the self-censorship required to operate in China, had Google questioning its activities. On 22 March 2010, Google stopped censoring its internet search results in China and directed all traffic from its servers there to Hong Kong, This has been applauded by human rights and anti-censorship activists, as Google challenges China to end censorship.

Sources: Davies (2010); BBC News (2010); Carr (2010); www. amnesty.org; www.google.com.

1 Why is China seen as such an attractive market for a search engine?

2 What impact did Chinese censorship laws have on how Google entered the Chinese market in 2006?

3 Why, and how, has Google redesigned its market development strategy in China?

▶ Research Insight 7.4

To take your learning further, you might wish to read this influential paper.

Robertson, K. R., and Wood, V. R. (2001), 'The relative importance of types of information in the foreign market selection process', *International Business Review*, **10, 363–79.**

This article provides a useful study designed to investigate export decision-making. It specifically examines the relative importance of foreign market information used by international managers when choosing export markets.

@ Visit the **Online Resource Centre** to read the abstract and access the full paper.

Market Entry Method

An organization entering a foreign market must consider what method it will use to enter that market. This decision is complicated due to the differing objectives of management, the type of product offering, and the complexities of the market being entered. Six criteria should be taken into consideration when selecting the market entry method (Paliwoda 1993). These are displayed in Figure 7.5. The importance of each is dependent on the organization's international marketing objectives, e.g. how quickly they want to enter a market, how much they are prepared to invest, how much risk they are prepared to take, how flexible they want their marketing activities in the foreign market to be.

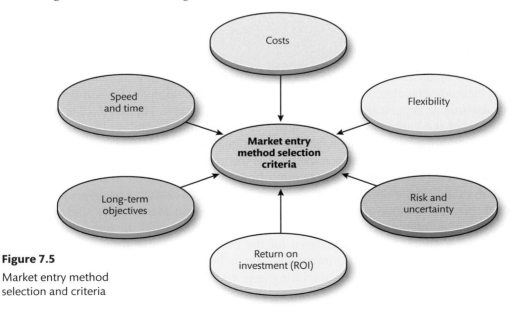

Figure 7.5

Market entry method selection and criteria

1 Speed and timing—some foreign market entry methods take months, whereas others can be put into action immediately. The organization needs to review how quickly it wishes to enter the market selected.

2 Costs—differing methods require differing levels of investment. Benefits and costs of each method need to be considered. How much is it going to cost to use a certain method and what are the direct and indirect benefits of each method considered?

3 Flexibility—some methods provide the organization with differing levels of flexibility over its activities in the new market, and future development opportunities. For example, some methods might require long-term contractual agreements or financial commitments.

4 Risk and uncertainty—there are numerous risk factors involved with entry into new and foreign markets. Some entry methods allow for reduction or management of risk and uncertainty, e.g. joint ventures or direct foreign investment in a foreign market can be seen as favourable politically in some markets, and thus can act to reduce **tariff barriers** and import quotas. However, these methods also require a larger degree of financial investment than indirect exporting or licensing.

5 Return on investment (ROI)—every organization has a different motivation for entering new foreign markets. This criterion coincides with the first and second criteria, speed and timing, and costs. Some organizations want a fast ROI through their market entry strategies, and thus the speed and timing of market entry is crucial to ensure quick return on foreign investment. For example, it may take years to build a factory in a foreign market, and thus it is more suitable to develop a partnership with an existing manufacturer in the local market who can provide this resource, increasing the speed of ROI.

6 Long-term objectives—the market entry strategy is just the first step in a long-term strategy for international marketing. An organization needs to review what it wants to achieve in the long term from its entry into the new foreign market as certain market entry methods will provide more flexibility for long-term opportunities than others.

Entry Method

Organizations might use one or a number of methods to enter international markets. The differing methods available vary according to the level of commitment, level of risks, and the level of rewards an organization can obtain. This is displayed in Figure 7.6. The higher the risk, the higher the likely rate of return; however, the options depend on the organization's ability to commit managerial, financial, and operational resources.

Some organizations move between methods as the importance of their international activities changes. However, other firms may jump from indirect exporting to direct investment, e.g. Nissan established a UK manufacturing base in the 1980s despite a relatively small share of the UK market, because of the impending Single European Market. The kind of product offering, whether operating in a consumer or industrial sector, and the level and nature of the competition are all factors considered for the best market entry strategy. For example, some products are more suited to international franchising (e.g. fast food restaurants, coffee houses), some to offshore manufacturing (e.g. textiles, car components), and others to exporting (e.g. regional products such as wine, cheese, chocolate, and luxury food items). The balance between support needs of the customer and the resources an organization has avail-

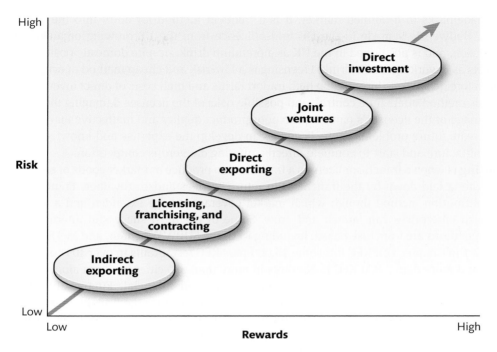

Figure 7.6
Market entry methods

able determines the international market entry method, especially for start-up organizations (Burgel and Murray, 2000).

Indirect Exporting

Indirect exporting takes place where production and manufacture of the product offering occurs in the domestic market and the services of another organization (an intermediary) are employed to sell the product in the foreign market. For example, Australian wineries are the fourth-largest exporters of wine, achieving rapid growth over the last 15 years through indirect exportation of Australian wines to foreign markets. The Australian Wine export market saw the sale of 764 ML of wine in 2009, worth A$2.3bn. An exporting manufacturer benefits from intermediaries' knowledge, their contact and business networks, and their experience in the foreign market the exporter wishes to enter. Given this reliance on the expertise of intermediaries, indirect exporting carries little risk and commitment as there is no direct investment in market development. This is a suitable strategy for market testing of product suitability, by a small organization with limited resources, and/or when dealing with small volumes of product offering for distribution.

Licensing, Franchising, and Contracting

Sometimes entering foreign markets involves the transfer of ideas, concepts, and processes, so that goods and services can be manufactured abroad—the market entry method of licensing, franchising, and/or contracting.

Licensing is an agreement under which an organization (the licensor) grants another organization (the licensee) the right to manufacturer goods, use patents, use particular processes, or exploit trademarks in a defined market. It is a frequent method for entry into the drinks market, e.g. Budweiser is made in the UK under licence from the US brewing organization Anheuser-Busch, and is positioned in the UK as a premium drink, despite domestic positioning in US markets as a working man's drink. Licensing is a low-risk and cheap method of accessing income from foreign markets by avoiding high import tariffs and high costs of direct investment. However, this method offers little control, and possible risks of the licensee damaging the reputation and image of the licensor's name due to poor product quality and ineffective marketing. It can also create future problems as the licensee can develop the expertise and knowledge for product manufacture and start to compete directly, offering dangerous competition.

Franchising is when a franchisor licenses a franchisee to produce or market goods or services to certain criteria laid down by the franchisor in return for fees and/or royalties. Franchising is both a distribution method though which market coverage can be extended and a system through which enterprises can launch and grow. Some of the most successful international marketing operations are franchise-based, including KFC, the SUBWAY® chain, and McDonald's (see Table 12.1 in Chapter 12). KFC has some 15,000-plus KFC restaurants in over 109 countries worldwide, and more than 2,870 KFC restaurants in more than 650 cities in China alone.

The two main benefits of franchising are managerial and financial. Financially, rapid growth in coverage of the market and penetration can be achieved for the franchisor with the franchisee bearing the risk through investment in capital assets (e.g. equipment, premises), working capital, and other operating costs. However, the effectiveness of this form of market entry method is reliant on the franchisor–franchisee relationship, the commitment of the franchisee, the resources and support provided by the franchisor, and market interest in the franchise. McDonald's is one of the largest and most lucrative franchises in the world and the leading franchise in Europe, established in 120 countries and serving 54m customers every day. However, as presented in Market Insight 7.5, it is Goody's, not McDonald's, that dominates the fast food market in Greece.

Subway, the successful international sandwich franchise
Source: Photo courtesy of the SUBWAY® chain.

Contracting is where a manufacturer contracts an organization in a foreign market to manufacture or assemble the product in the foreign market, thus avoiding the cost involved in physical distribution and logistics of the product offering abroad. Unlike licensing, the contractor has control over marketing. This method also provides a flexible approach to entering foreign markets, avoiding the problems of currency fluctuations, import barriers, and high costs, and knowledge required for international distribution.

▶ Market Insight 7.5

It's All Goody's in Greece

Greece is the one country where McDonald's does not dominate the fast food market. The Greek fast food restaurant Goody's enjoys overwhelming support from the Greek consumer. Goody's not only dominates the fast food market in Greece, but also this hamburger chain, originally from northern Greece, introduced franchising to the country in the late 1970s. The current Deputy Minister for Economy and Finance in Greece is one of the pioneer entrepreneurs who developed the Goody's 'concept' and launched the Thessaloniki restaurant as a franchise throughout Greece in 1975.

Greeks eat more Goody's burgers than McDonalds
Source: Goody's.

McDonald's opened its first restaurant in Greece in 1991. Today, there are 55 McDonald's restaurants employing 1,900 individuals throughout Greece. In contrast, there are over 200 Goody's restaurants in Greece, Cyprus, and Bulgaria, and, in 2010, Goody's was awarded Greek Retail Franchisor of the year. Goody's restaurants dominate the fast food market in Greece, leaving multinational giants such as McDonald's and KFC restaurants way behind.

Sources: Mortimer (2003); www.goodys.net; www.mcdonalds.gr.

1 Why do you think Goody's dominates the fast food market in Greece?

2 What do you recommend McDonald's do to build market share in Greece?

3 What do you think Goody's can do via marketing activities to protect and grow its market leadership in Greece?

Direct Exporting

Direct exporting involves the manufacturing organization itself distributing the product offering in foreign markets, direct to customers. Here, the organization treats its foreign customers like its domestic customers, taking responsibility for finding and selecting customers, agents, and distributors, and directly supporting their efforts. This approach is very time-consuming and expensive, and involves considerable investment, and can be a big step, particularly for smaller organizations. However, it gives the manufacturer more control and profits than does relying on intermediaries. Further advantages include direct access to market intelligence and also the building of a clear presence in the market.

Joint Ventures

A **joint venture** is when a foreign organization and a domestic organization join forces either by buying into each other, or by establishing a third jointly owned enterprise. The partners might feel that separately they do not have the resources to develop or enter into a foreign market. One might have cash, the other know-how and experience. The complementary strengths facilitate success, and sometimes a joint venture is the only way an organization can enter into or gain a foothold in a foreign market. Joint ventures tend to have a limited lifespan as each party's needs alter and develop over time. They work best in sectors where there is a high degree of local adaptation to the market. Figure 7.7 shows a list of factors that can contribute to a successful joint venture partnership.

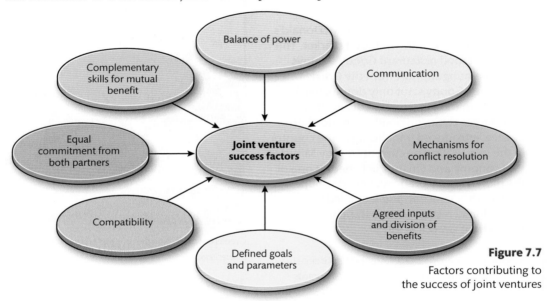

Figure 7.7

Factors contributing to the success of joint ventures

▶ Research Insight 7.5

To take your learning further, you might wish to read this influential paper.

Rundh, B. (2007), 'International marketing behaviour amongst exporting firms', *European Journal of Marketing*, 41, 1/2, 181–98.

This article provides a useful insight into factors affecting market entry through exporting to international markets for small and large organizations. Success factors relate to geographical proximity with the need for local representation and service and management commitment.

 Visit the **Online Resource Centre** to read the abstract and access the full paper.

Direct Investment

Direct investment or foreign manufacture involves some form of manufacture or production in the foreign or host country. Advantages include a commitment to the local market, speedy availability of parts and market detection of changes in local environment. The extent of direct investment can range from superficial assembly of product offering from parts to research and development-led innovation. Another means of market entry through direct investment is organization acquisition or takeover in the foreign market. For example, India's home textiles exporters are moving up the value chain and aiming at the lucrative US and Western markets.

Skills for Employment

▶▶ We look for people who are passionate about understanding our customers and putting them at the heart of our business, helping us to exceed their expectations in everything we do. You'll need to be creative, adaptable, enthusiastic and have the confidence to challenge current practice. Previous customer-focused work experience is essential. ◀◀

Kate Firth, Graduate Programme Manager, Sainsbury's

 Visit the **Online Resource Centre** to discover more tips and advice on skills for the workplace.

Chapter Summary

To consolidate your learning, the key points from this chapter are summarized below:

■ **Define international market development as a key growth strategy.**

A market development strategy involves increasing sales by selling existing products in new markets, either by targeting new audiences domestically or entering new markets internationally. International market development is growing in importance due to changes in the economic, social, and political landscape. International marketing activities are, therefore, receiving enormous growth in both scale and complexity. The main considerations are the degree of risk and adjustment an organization is willing to take and the identification of potential opportunities within foreign markets.

■ **Discuss the differences between a multi-domestic and global competitive strategy.**

In the last century international trade has seen enormous growth in both scale and complexity, resulting in emergence of different approaches to international market development. When entering international markets, the key competitive decision is do we standardize or adapt our marketing strategy and to what degree do we do this? In the analysis of the rise of global competition, Hout, Porter, and Rudden (1982) suggest that, from a strategic point of view, an organization can adopt a local/global, multi-domestic, or global competitive approach to its international marketing strategy. The decision is based on the type of product offering, the attitudes of the organization, and the resources available for market entry.

■ **Discuss the key drivers for international market development.**

In light of increasing internationalization of world markets, increased foreign trade, and international travel, international marketing is becoming a necessity for the survival of many organizations. Many factors motivate an organization to develop markets on foreign shores. These include: a historical accident (e.g. Coca-Cola), the need to move excess stock (e.g. dumping), limited growth in domestic markets, comparative advantages, economies of scale, trade liberalization, technological changes (e.g. internet), customer relationships, the development of transnational market segments through immigration, and organization sustainability.

■ **Discuss the criteria used for international market selection.**

Assessing market attractiveness is very important when considering international market development given that differing markets have very differing levels of attractiveness. Markets may be chosen according to the following criteria: market accessibility, market size, geographic proximity, psychological proximity, level and quality of competition already in the market, cost of entering the market, and a market's profit potential.

■ **Describe the factors in the foreign market environment that could influence an international marketing strategy.**

Understanding the marketing environment of the country of interest can form the foundation of a detailed market assessment and market selection process. The analysis of environmental forces can help to identify which countries or regions should be given priority and which market entry strategy would be best suited to that country/region. Factors to consider include: social, cultural, consumption attitudes, technological, economic, political, and legal factors.

■ **Consider the various methods for international market entry.**

The decision for market entry method is based on six main factors: speed and timing, costs and levels of investment required, flexibility, risk and uncertainty, expected return on investment (ROI), and long-term objectives. Once reviewed, the organization can select from a number of entry methods: indirect exporting, licensing, franchising, and contracting, direct exporting, joint ventures, and direct investment.

Review Questions

1   What factors influence the importance of an international market development strategy?

2   What are the key differences between multi-domestic and global competitive strategies?

3   What is the anti-globalization movement and why is it of increasing importance?

4   What criteria can an organization use to assess the attractiveness of a foreign market?

5   Outline the main environmental factors in the international marketing environment.

6   What are the differing methods for entering foreign markets?

7   What criteria should be considered when selecting an international market entry method?

8   What are the key differences between indirect and direct exporting?

9   What are the benefits of franchises in international marketing?

10   What are the key success factors for international joint ventures?

Worksheet Summary

Visit the **Online Resource Centre** and complete Worksheet 7.1. This will aid in learning about how market selection criteria can be used by a Chinese automobile manufacturer who wants to enter the European market, and how to identify which market entry method would be most suitable.

Discussion Questions

1 Having read Case Insight 7.1, how would you advise Orange to consider tailoring their customer contact plan to different market conditions across Europe?

2 What are the main criteria a SME should consider in its decision to enter a new international market?

3 Which of the following factors would have the greatest impact on a fashion retailers' assessment of the attractiveness of a foreign market: political–legal, social–cultural, or technological? Why?

4 What issues have Kentucky Fried Chicken (KFC) had to consider when expanding into new geographical markets across Asia?

5 Marketed heavily on their country-of-origin brand image, what impact do you think joint ventures with domestic vineyards or direct investment would have on the perception of wine brands in a foreign market?

6 Take note of the country of manufacture, assembly, and origin of your purchases. What countries and regions are represented? What impact do you think the political and legal environment has on their importation?

Visit the **Online Resource Centre** and complete the Multiple Choice Questions to assess your knowledge of Chapter 7.

go online

References

Anderson, P., and Strandskov, J. (1998), 'International market selection: a cognitive mapping perspective', *Journal of Global Marketing*, 11, 3, 65–84.

Anon. (2005), 'Guinness: the trials of the black stuff', *Brand Strategy*, 20 (7 February).

Ansoff, H. I. (1957), 'Strategies of diversification', *Harvard Business Review*, 25, 5, 113–25.

BBC News (2010), 'US worry at Chinese cyberattacks', BBC News, (14/01/2010), retrieve from: http://news.bbc.co.uk/go/pr/fr/-/1/hi/business/8458269.stm, accessed 13 January 2010.

Benson-Armer, R., Leibowitz, J., and Ramachandran, D. (1999), 'Global beer: what's on tap?', *McKinsey Quarterly*, 1, 110–22.

Bikson, T., and Panis, C. (1997), 'Computers and connectivity: current trends', in S. Kiesler (ed.), *Culture of the Internet*, Mahwah, NJ: Lawrence Erlbaum, 407–30.

Burgel, O., and Murray, G. (2000), 'The international market entry choices of start-up organizations in high-technology industries', *Journal of International Marketing*, 8, 2, 33–62.

Carr, P., (2010), 'Soul searching: Google's position on China might be many things, but moral it is not', *TechCrunch*, retrieve from www.techcrunch.com/2010/01/13/not-safe-for-wok/, accessed 13 January 2010.

Davies, C. (2010), 'Google China: Search engine's stand against censorship welcomes by campaigners', *The Guardian*, retrieve from www.guardian.co.uk/technology, accessed 13 January 2010.

Douglas, S., and Douglas, Y. W. (1987), 'The myth of globalisation', *Columbia Journal of World Business*, Winter, 19–29.

Euromonitor (2010), 'Alcoholic drinks and the great recession: The present and future of the global market',

Euromonitor Report, retrieve from www.euromonitor. com, accessed 10 April 2010.

Herbig, P. A. and Day, K. (1993), 'Managerial implications of the North American Free Trade Agreement', *International Marketing Review*, 10, 4, 15–35.

Hout, T., Porter, M. E., and Rudden, E. (1982), 'How global organizations win out!', *Harvard Business Review*, September–October.

Kageyama, Y. (2008), 'H&M opens shops in pricey Japan amid downturn', *USA Today,* 12 September 2008 retrieve from www.usatoday.com/money/economy/2008-09-12-213076897_x.htm, accessed 10 February 2010.

Kelly, J. (2002), 'Executives fail the business language test', *Financial Times*, 16 February, 4.

Lawrence, P. (1993), 'Developments in European business in the 1990s: the Single European Market in context', *Journal of Marketing Management*, 9, 3–9.

Levitt, T. (1983), 'The globalization of markets', *Harvard Business Review*, May–June, 2–11.

Lewis, K. S., Lim, F. A., and Rusetski, A. (2006), 'Development of archetypes of international marketing strategy', *Journal of International Business Studies*, 37, 4, 499–524.

Lynch, R. (1994), *European Business Strategies: The European and Global Strategies of Europe's Top Organizations*, London: Kogan Page.

Mead, R. (1990), *Cross-Cultural Management Communication*, New York: John Wiley & Sons.

Mortimer, R., (2003), 'How fast food and footie make an excellent match.' *Brand Strategy*, 170 (April), 10.

Movius, L. (2007), 'H&M heads east with first unit in Shanghai', *WWD: Women's Wear Daily*, 17 April, 193.

Mughan, T. (1993), 'Culture as an asset in international business', in J. Preston (ed.), *International Business: Texts & Cases*, London: Pitman, 78–86.

Ohmae, K. (1985), *Triad Power*, London: Macmillan.

—(1992), *The Borderless World: Power and Strategy in the Interlinked Economy*, London: Fontana.

Paitra, J. (1993), 'The euro-consumer: myth or reality?', in C. Halliburton and R. Hunerberg (eds), *European Marketing: Readings and Cases*, Boston: Addison-Wesley.

Paliwoda, S. (1993), *International Marketing*, 2nd edn, London: Butterworth-Heinemann.

Pendergrast, M. (2000), *For God, Country, and Coca-Cola: The Definitive History of the Great American Soft Drink*

and the Company That Makes It, 2nd edn, England: Basic Books.

Perlmutter, H. V. (1969), 'The tortuous evolution of the multinational corporation', *Columbia Journal of World Business*, January–February, 9–18.

Pitcher, G. (1999), 'Ford takes pole position in the battle for world wide domination', *Marketing Week*, 4 February, 25.

Quelch, J. A., and Hoff, E. J. (1986), 'Customising global marketing', *Harvard Business Review*, May–June, 59–68.

Robertson, K. R., and Wood, V. R. (2001), 'The relative importance of types of information in the foreign market selection process', *International Business Review*, 10, 363–79.

Rugman, A. (2000), *The End of Globalisation*, London: Random House Business Books.

Sclater, I. (2005), 'The digital dimension', *The Marketer*, May, 22–3.

Sirgy, M., Lee, D.-J., Miller, C., Littlefield, J., and Atay, E. (2007), 'The impact of imports and exports on a country's quality of life', *Social Indicators Research*, 83, 2, 245–81.

Tapper-Hoel, J. (2010), 'H&M opens its first store in South Korea', *H&M Press Release*, retrieve from www. hm.com/pl/investorrelations/pressreleases/__prfashion. nhtml?pressreleaseid=1002, accessed 11 April 2010.

Tapscott, D. (1998), *Growing Up Digital: The Rise of the Net Generation*, New York: McGraw-Hill.

Vijay, J. (1997), 'Global strategies in the 1990's', in *Mastering Management*, London: Financial Times, 572–7.

Ward, A. (2006), 'US brewers left to cry into their beers: competition from imports and local speciality brews are hitting home', *Financial Times*, 31 July, 23.

Whitelock, J., and Jobber, D. (1994), *'The impact of competitor environment on initial market entry in a new non-domestic market'*, paper presented at the Proceedings of the Marketing Education Group Conference, Coleraine.

Wind Y., and Perlmutter, H. V. (1973), 'Guidelines for developing international marketing strategies', *Journal of Marketing*, 37 (April), 14–23.

Young, S. (2001), 'What do researchers know about the global business environment?', *International Marketing Review*, 18, 2, 120–9.

The marketing mix principle

▶ Case Insight 8.1

3M is an innovative $23bn diversified technology company creating products to make the world healthier, safer, and more productive. Well-known brands include Scotch, Post-it, Scotchgard, Thinsulate, and Scotch-Brite. We speak to Andrew Hicks, European Market Development Manager, to find out how the company developed an innovative, new product, the Visual Attention Service.

Andrew Hicks for 3M

First set up in 1902, and now employing around 75,000 people worldwide, 3M has operations in more than 60 countries. It produces thousands of innovative products for customers and its 45 technology platforms touch nearly every aspect of modern life. The company has applied its expertise in RFID technology to deliver biometric passports; its healthcare knowledge to provide hospitals with infection prevention and detection solutions; and, in 2008, it launched the MPro range of pocket projectors.

3M's enduring success is built on constant innovation. To drive this, it invests heavily in R&D, spending over $1.40bn in 2008. It is fundamentally a science-based company, producing thousands of imaginative products, leading in scores of markets—from healthcare and highway safety to office products and optical films for LCD displays. The company's success begins with our ability to apply our technologies—often in combination—to an endless array of real-world customer needs.

We are organized into seven business divisions. Consumer and Office, Electro and Communications, Health Care, Industrial and Transportation Safety, Security and Protection Services, Optical Systems and Display and Graphics; the final division is a world leader in films that brighten the displays on electronic products, such as flat-panel computer monitors, cellular phones, personal digital assistants, and liquid crystal display (LCD) televisions.

The Digital-out-of-Home (DooH) department within Display and Graphics was set up in 2007. It encompasses electronic display technologies as well as software for content delivery and tools to optimize the performance of advertising messaging. DooH set up what became the 3M Visual Attention Service (3M VAS) to complement this portfolio. The service allows designers of creative messages to assess and optimize their visual impact before committing to production.

Researchers within the traffic safety business of 3M had identified that predictive attention modelling may have a commercial opportunity within the advertising industry. In the feasibility stage, the technical capability, projected costs, and potential market opportunity were assessed to determine whether to proceed with the investment required to bring the concept to market. At this stage, we undertook desk research to determine the distribution of our target market—creative agencies—by size, turnover, and specialization. Primary research with around 15 agencies helped to determine the value they would place on such a service and their likely throughput of images. These customers were given access to a beta version of the site to assess how they would use such a system. Combining the datasets allowed an estimate to be made of the potential usage levels for such a service. Through ethnographic research, 3M employees work-shadowed designers to understand the creative workflow and determine where in the process 3M VAS could offer greatest value. This research informed both the market opportunity assessment and the development of the appropriate marketing communications for this audience.

▶ Case Insight 8.1

3M's Visual Attention Service tests promotional material using visual heat maps

Once we determined that there was a likely market for the product, we looked at the service, the business plan, and the marketing communications plan. We knew we had to undertake a limited release of the service to allow feedback to be gained from lead users to validate the value and market opportunity. Finally, we undertook a full commercial global launch of the service, backed by advertising and promotional campaigns, and continued customer research to refine the offer.

However, as this was a new-to-the-world service and was also not a direct substitution for an existing service, there was no reference pricing in the marketplace. When potential customers were asked what they were prepared to pay, the value they perceived varied dramatically depending on the nature of the creative work the system was being used to assess. For example, the media space costs for a national billboard campaign for a major promotion would cost hundreds of thousands of pounds.

Anything that could validate the visual effectiveness of the creative design for adverts for this type of campaign, before committing the ads to print, would be extremely valuable to the advertiser. However, the number of campaigns of this type and the quantity of creative designs considered for these campaigns is relatively small. So this would be a high-cost, low-volume model.

On the other hand, thousands of designs are created every day for packaging, advertising and other marketing communications, where the level of investment and associated risk is much lower. In these cases, 3M VAS would still be of value, but the price that could be charged would be considerably lower—a low-cost, high-volume model.

The question for 3M was therefore: should it launch a low-volume, high-priced product or a high-volume, low-priced product?

Introduction

A Sony television, a train journey from Budapest to Berlin, a cappuccino at Costa Coffee, the *Guardian* newspaper, a copy of *Vogue* magazine, a haircut, and a manicure all have one thing in common. They are all **products**.

Now this might seem a bit strange, but the term product includes the tangible and intangible attributes related not just to physical goods but also to services, ideas, people, places, experiences, and even a mix of these various elements. Anything that can be offered for use and consumption, in exchange for money or some other form of value, is referred to as a product.

Tangibility refers to an item's ability to be touched and whether it is capable of being stored. For example, a bar of soap, a Rimmel lipstick, or a Vega factory conveyor belt are all tangible products and are capable of being touched and stored. A ferry trip from Sabah to Labuan in Malaysia, or a visit to Toni and Guy the hairdresser, cannot be touched and are not capable of being stored. These are intangible products and are referred to as services. Readers are directed to Chapter 13 for a detailed consideration of services and their characteristics.

Soap is a purely tangible good, whereas a financial services product, such as a pension or savings account, is a pure service. They lie at opposite ends of a spectrum, which is set out in Figure 8.1. In between the pure good and the pure service lie a host of goods/services combinations. Indeed, many organizations have developed the service aspect of their market offering in order to help differentiate themselves in the market.

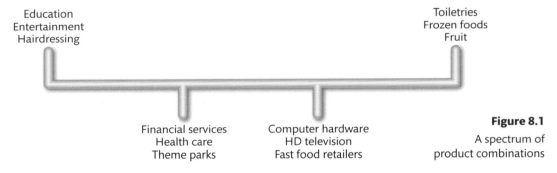

Figure 8.1

A spectrum of product combinations

This spectrum of product/service combinations incorporates strategies designed to increase the value offered to customers though improved services. However, developing the service element in order to provide a point of differentiation has not always been a successful strategy, as it can attract price competition. As prices fall, offerings can become commoditized and customers find it difficult to separate the value offered by competing firms. In an attempt to avoid this situation, some organizations have developed a third approach based around customer experiences.

The customer experiences strategy is neither based on brand tangible nor intangible attributes, but refers to the memories and fantasies that individuals retain or imagine, as a result of their interaction with an offering (Tynan and McKechnie, 2009). Memories of experiences related to product usage, events, visits, or activities are internalized, unlike products and services, which are generally external to each person. Indeed, the idea that people consume emotions is emerging as an important and influential aspect of the marketing discipline. The memories and fantasies concept is best illustrated through the activities of theme and leisure parks. Market Insight 8.1 considers customer experiences at Disney.

▶ Market Insight 8.1

Customer Experiences at Disney

Disney World is widely recognized as the master of managing customer experiences. At peak times the queues of people waiting for rides can be long, boring, and can distract from the overall experience at a theme park. One early solution was to reconstruct the physical queue into a 'snake' so that people felt they were moving forward, and it started at a point where visitors could see the ride or attraction. In addition to this Disney worked out the length of time people are prepared to wait before they need to be distracted. Now queues are entertained by videos, peripatetic characters, and mirrors, all carefully choreographed to commence at pre-determined intervals.

Destination Disney, the name for Disney's customer experience strategy, uses technology to help personalize the park experience. Through the use of global positioning satellites, wireless technology, smart sensors, and mobile devices, Disney tries to enhance the customer experience, influence visitor behaviour, and ease crowding throughout the parks.

One of the innovations was Pal Mickey, a 10.5-inch-tall stuffed doll. Visitors carried Pal Mickey into the park, and sensors received data wirelessly from one of the 500 infrared beacons. These were concealed in park lamp posts, rooftops, and bushes, and transmitted information from a Disney data centre. The doll giggled and vibrated when it received a new piece of information from a nearby beacon. Information about a parade, rides that have short queues, or just trivia about the area of the park the visitor was walking through was provided, keeping guests informed, up to date, and involved with the Disney experience.

1 In what other ways could digital technology be used to help improve the customer experience at a hotel, airline, or hospital?

2 What do you think guests expect to take away from their visit to a theme park?

3 Identify three other items that Disney could offer guests to make their visit more tangible.

The magical world of Disney
Source: © Disney.

Product Levels

When people buy products they are not just buying the simple functional aspect a product offers, there are other complexities involved in the purchase. For example, the taste of coffee granules is an important benefit arising from the purchase of a jar of instant coffee. However, in addition to this core benefit, people are also attracted to the **packaging**, the price, the strength of the coffee, and also some of the psychosocial associations that we have learnt about a brand. The Cafédirect brand, for instance, seeks to help people understand its ties with the Fairtrade movement and in doing so provide some customers a level of psychosocial satisfaction, through their contribution.

In order to understand these different elements and benefits, we refer to three different product forms: the core, the embodied, and the augmented product forms. These are depicted in Figure 8.2 and further outlined below.

▶ The core product—consists of the real core benefit or service. This may be a functional benefit in terms of what the product will enable you to do, or it may be an emotional benefit in terms of how the product or service will make you feel. Cars provide transportation and a means of self-expression. Cameras make memories by recording a scene, person, or object through the use of digital processes, or originally, film.

▶ The embodied product—consists of the physical good or delivered service that provides the expected benefit. It consists of many factors, for example the features and capabilities, the durability, design, packaging, and brand name. Cars are supplied with different styles, engines, seats, colours, boot space, whereas digital cameras are offered with a variety of picture qualities, screen sizes, pixels, zoom and telephoto features, editing, and relay facilities.

▶ The augmented product—consists of the embodied product plus all those other factors that are necessary to support the purchase and any post-purchase activities. For example, credit and finance, training, delivery, installation, guarantees, and the overall perception of customer service.

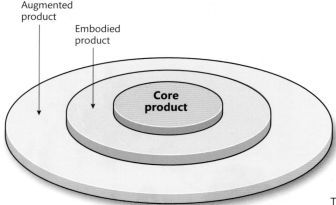

Figure 8.2
The three product forms

When these levels are brought together it is hoped that they will provide customers with a reason to buy and to keep buying. Each individual combination or bundle of benefits constitutes added value and serves to differentiate one sports car from another sports car, one disposable camera from another. Marketing strategies need to be designed around the actual and the augmented products as it is through these that competition occurs and people are able to understand how one disposable camera differs from another.

Understanding a brand and what it means to its core customers and their experience of a brand is vitally important. Pepsi's battle with Coca-Cola during the 1960s and 1970s saw it gradually reduce Coke's dominant market share. The battle culminated in 1985 when Coke abandoned its original recipe and introduced New Coke, a sweeter formulation designed to attract Pepsi's young market. Coke's customers boycotted New Coke, there was public outrage, and Pepsi became market leader, but only temporarily. New Coke was soon dropped and the original brought back and relaunched as Classic Cola, re-establishing its credentials with its customers and retrieving number one spot in a couple of months. The problem was that Coke had not appreciated the value that the product as a whole represented to its primary customers. The sum of the core, embodied, and augmented product, encapsulated as the brand Coca-Cola, drew passion from its customers and was overlooked by the market researchers when searching for a means to arrest Pepsi's progress.

The development of the internet and digital technologies has impacted on the nature of the product and the benefits accruing from product usage. This has opened opportunities for organizations to redefine their core and actual products, often by supplementing them with 'information' about the product or service, for example providing white papers or games designed to engage website visitors with the brand. Another approach has been to transform current products into digital products, for example Napster with music downloads. A further approach is to change the bundle of products offered, sometimes achieved by presenting an online catalogue that offers a wider array than the offline catalogue. See Chapter 17 for more information about these types of development.

Chaffey *et al.* (2009) refer to Ghosh (1998) and his early identification of the number of ways in which **digital value** can help augment products. For example, many companies provide evidence of the awards their products have won, whereas others parade testimonials, endorsements, and customer comments. These are designed to provide credibility, reduce risk, and enable people to engage with or purchase a brand. The key contribution of the internet, in this context, is that it offers digital value to customers, sometimes as a supplement and sometimes as a complete alternative to the conventional, established core product offering.

Classifying Products

Now that we understand that products may be tangible goods, intangible services, or even experiences, and that they consist of several layers, the next step is to classify or categorize products. This is important because only through understanding how customers think and feel about products, how they use products, and how their purchasing behaviours vary can marketing mixes and new products be developed that meet customer needs. Services are classified later in Chapter 13.

There are two main classifications, consumer products and business-to-business products. Consumer products are bought to satisfy personal and family needs and industrial and business products are bought either as a part of the business's operations or in order to make other products for resale. Although there are some products such as light bulbs and toilet tissue that are bought by both consumers and businesses, it is helpful to use this grouping simply because there are considerable differences in the way these two types of customers buy products and services. If you are unsure about buying behaviour issues we suggest you read Chapter 3.

Consumer Products

The first way of classifying consumer products is to consider them in terms of their durability. Durable goods such as bicycles, music players, and refrigerators can be used repeatedly and provide benefits each time they are used. Non-durable goods, such as yoghurt, newspapers, and plastic packaging, have a limited duration, often only capable of being used once. Services are intangible products and cannot be stored.

Durable goods often require a purchaser's high level of involvement in the purchase decision. There is **high perceived risk** in these decisions so consumers typically spend a great deal of time, care, and energy searching, formulating, and making the final decision. As a result, marketers need to understand these patterns of behaviour, provide, and make accessible sufficient amounts of appropriate information, and ensure there is the right type of service and support necessary to meet the needs of the target market.

Non-durable goods, typically food and grocery items, usually reflect low levels of involvement and buyers are not concerned which particular product they buy. Risk is perceived to be low and so there is little or no need (or time usually) to shop around for the best possible price. Buyers may buy on availability, price, habit, or brand experience.

One of the key characteristics of services is that they are intangible and another is that they are perishable. This means that they cannot be touched and because they are perishable they are not capable of being stored. Their use and consumption, therefore, has to be based on an 'on-demand' basis. Levels of involvement may be high or low and marketing mixes need to set up and deliver customer expectations. Due to their complexity, Chapter 13 is devoted to the marketing services.

A deeper and more meaningful way of classifying consumer products is to consider how and where consumers buy products. In Chapter 3, we considered different ways in which consumers make purchases. In particular, we looked at **extensive problem solving**, **limited problem solving**, and **routinized response behaviour**. Classifying products according to the behaviour consumers demonstrate when buying them enables marketing managers to develop more suitable and appropriate marketing strategies. Four main behavioural categories have been established; **convenience products**, **shopping products**, **speciality products**, and unsought products.

Convenience products are non-durable goods or services, and, as the name suggests, are bought because the consumer does not want to put very much effort, if any, into the buying decision. Routinized response behaviour corresponds most closely to convenience products as they are bought frequently and are inexpensive. Most decisions in this category are made through habit, and if a usual brand is not available an alternative brand will be selected or none at all as it would be too inconvenient to go and visit another store.

Convenience products may be sub-divided into three further categories. These are staples, impulse, and emergency products and are explained in Table 8.1.

▶ **Table 8.1** Categories of convenience products

Type of convenience product	Explanation
Staple products	Characteristically, staples are available almost everywhere. They include groceries such as bread, milk, soft drinks, and breakfast cereals but they also include petrol. They are bought frequently and form the basis of our daily pattern of behaviour. In France the daily purchase of a fresh French stick of bread or baguette constitutes an important part of social behaviour
Impulse products	These are products that consumers had not planned to buy but are persuaded at the very last minute to pick up and put in their trolley or basket. Typically, these items are located very near to the tills in supermarkets (the point of sale) so that while customers are waiting to pay for their planned or considered purchases they become attracted to these impulse items. Chewing gum, chocolate bars, and magazines are typical impulse purchases, unlike a bottle of milk or petrol, which are planned
Emergency products	Bought when a very special need arises; buyers are more intent on buying a solution than buying the right quality or image-related product. So, the purchase of a bandage when someone is cut or injured, a plumber when a pipe starts leaking in the middle of the night, or even umbrellas in the middle of summer when an unexpected downpour occurs, all constitute emergency products

All of these types of convenience products indicate that slightly different marketing strategies are required to make each of them work. However, one element common to all is distribution. If the product is not available when an emergency arises, or when a consumer is waiting to pay or walking towards the milk racks, then a sale will not be made. Pricing is important as customers know the expected price of convenience items and they may well switch brands if price exceeds that of the competition.

Shopping products are not bought as frequently as convenience products, and, as a result, consumers do not always have sufficient up-to-date information to make a buying decision. The purchase of shopping products such as furniture, electrical appliances, jewellery, and mobile phones requires some search for information, if only to find out about the latest features. Consumers give time and effort to planning these purchases, if only because the level of risk is more substantial than that associated with convenience products. They will visit several stores and use the internet and word-of-mouth communications for price comparisons, product information, and the experience of other customers. Not surprisingly, levels of brand loyalty are quite low as consumers are quite happy to switch brands in order to get the level of functionality and overall value they need.

The marketing strategies followed by manufacturers, and, to some extent, retailers, need to accommodate the characteristics of limited problem solving. Shopping products do not require the mass distribution strategies associated with convenience products. Here, a selective distribution strategy is required as consumers often want the specialist advice offered by knowledgeable, expert retailers. The volume of purchases is lower, so, although margins are higher, marketing communications have two important roles to play. The first is to establish a strong brand name so that when consumers are ready to start the purchase process they are able to associate a brand with the product category. The second is that manufacturers must use advertising, public relations, personal selling, and sales promotions to support retailers. This is necessary because between the manufacturer and the retailer they must provide customers with the information they need when and how they need it, the confidence to proceed, and an overall sense of value in the purchase.

Speciality products represent high risk, are very expensive, and are bought infrequently, often only once, and correspond to extended problem solving. People plan these purchases, search intensively for information about the object, and are often only concerned with a particular brand and in finding a way of gaining access to an outlet that can supply that brand. It is possible to find speciality products in many areas, e.g. limited edition sports equipment (Big Bertha golf clubs), rare paintings and artwork (Picasso's), custom cars, watches (Rolex), haute couture (Stella McCartney), and certain restaurants and holidays. All have unique characteristics, which to buyers means that there are no substitute products available or worth considering.

Rolex, a specialty product
Source: Courtesy of The Rolex Watch Company Limited.

Marketing strategies to support speciality products focus heavily on a very limited number of distribution outlets, and advertising that seeks to establish the brand name and values. The few retailers appointed to carry the item require detailed training and support so that the buyer experiences high levels of customer service and associated prestige throughout the entire purchase process.

Unsought products refer to a group of products that people do not normally anticipate buying, or indeed want to buy. Very often, consumers have little knowledge or awareness of the brands in the marketplace and are only motivated to find out about them when a specific need arises. So, a windscreen cracks or a water pipe bursts necessitating repairs and unsought products. In a similar way, life insurance was once sold through heavy pressurized selling as people did not see the need. That has changed through changes in legislation, but double glazing and timeshare holiday salespeople still have a reputation for getting people to buy their products and services who would not normally have bought them.

Business Products

Unlike some consumer products that are bought for personal and psychological rewards, business products are generally bought on a rational basis to meet organizational goals. These products are used to either enable the organization to function smoothly or they form an integral part of the products, processes, and services supplied by the organization for resale.

In the same way as consumer products are classified according to how customers use them, so business products are classified according to how organizational customers use them. Six main categories can be identified: equipment goods, raw materials, semi-finished goods, maintenance repair and operating goods, component parts, and business services.

Equipment goods cover two main areas and both concern the everyday operations of the organization: **capital equipment goods** and **accessory equipment goods**. Capital equipment goods are buildings, heavy plant, and factory equipment necessary to build or assemble products. They might also be major government schemes to build hospitals, motorways, and bridges. Whatever their nature, they all require substantial investment, are subject to long planning processes, are often one-off purchases designed to be used for a considerable amount of time, and require the involvement of a number of different people and groups in the purchase process. Accessory equipment goods should support the key operational processes and activities of the organization. Typically they are photocopiers, computers, stationery, and office furniture. These items cost less than capital equipment goods, are not expected to last as long as capital equipment goods, and are often portable rather than fixed. Whereas a poor capital equipment purchase may put the entire organization at risk, a poor accessory purchase will at worst be frustrating and slow down activities but is unlikely to threaten the existence of the organization.

Raw materials are the basic materials that are used in order to produce finished goods. Minerals, chemicals, timber, and food staples such as grain, vegetables, fruit, meat, and fish are extracted, grown, or farmed as necessary and transported to organizations that process the raw materials into finished or semi-finished products. Bought in large quantities, buyers often negotiate heavily on price as there is little to differentiate raw materials. However, these buying decisions can be influenced by non-product factors such as length of relationship, service quality, and credit facilities.

Semi-finished goods are raw materials that have been converted into a temporary state. Iron ore is converted into sheets that can be used by car and aircraft manufacturers, washing machines, and building contractors.

Maintenance, repair, and operating (MRO) goods are products, other than raw materials, that are necessary to ensure that the organization is able to continue functioning. Maintenance and repair goods such as nuts and bolts, light bulbs, and cleaning supplies are used to maintain the capital and accessory equipment goods. Operating supplies are not directly involved in the production of the finished goods nor are they a constituent part, but oil for lubricating machinery, paper, pens, and flash drives are all necessary to keep the overall organization functioning.

Component parts are finished, complete parts bought from other organizations. These components are then incorporated directly into the finished product. So, for example, Ford will buy in finished headlight assemblies and mount them directly into their Ford Fusion, Focus, or Transit models as appropriate.

Business services are intangible services used to enhance the operational aspects of organizations. Most commonly, these concern management consultancy, finance, and accounting, including auditing, legal, marketing research, IT, and marketing communications.

Product Range, Line, and Mix

In order to meet the needs of a number of different target markets, most organizations offer a variety of **products** and **services**. Although some offer an assortment based on an individual core product, it is rare that an organization offers just a single product. Consumer organizations, such as Gillette, offer a range of shaving products for men; industrial organizations, such as Oliver Valves, offer a range of valves for the offshore and onshore petrochemical, gas, and power generation industries. In order to make sense of, and understand, the relationships that one set of products have with another, a variety of terms have emerged. Table 8.2 sets out these different terms.

▶ **Table 8.2** Product range terminology

Product term	Explanation
Product mix	The total group of products offered by an organization: at Nokia this would mean all the phones and all the accessories they offer
Product line	A group of closely related products—related through technical, marketing, or user considerations, e.g. all the touchscreen phones offered by Nokia constitute a product line
Product item	A distinct product within a product line. Nokia's N8 is a product item
Product line length	The number of products available in a product line: the nine products available within the 'NSeries'
Product line depth	The number of variations available within a product line: the 12 types of touchscreen phone
Product mix width	The number of product lines within a product mix: 13 different forms of functionality offered by Nokia

Product Lifecycles

Underpinning the product lifecycle (PLC) concept is the belief that products move through a sequential, pre-determined pattern of development similar to the biological path that life-forms follow. This pathway, known as the **product lifecycle**, consists of five distinct stages, namely development, introduction, growth, maturity, and decline. Sales and profits rise and fall across the various lifestages of the product, as shown in Figure 8.3.

Products move through an overall cycle that consists of different stages. Speed of movement through the stages will vary, but each product has a limited lifespan. Although the life of a product can be extended in many ways, such as introducing new ways of using the product, finding new users, and developing new attributes, the majority of products have a finite

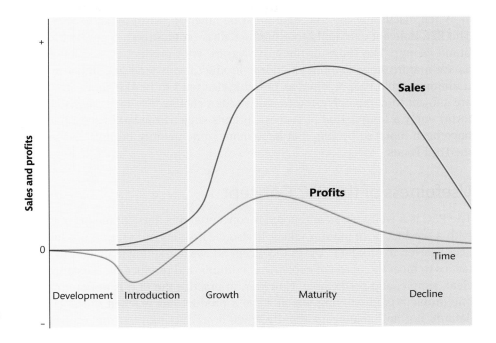

Figure 8.3

The product lifecycle

period during which management need to maximize their returns on the investment made in each of their products. In Sweden, mobile phones have an overall lifespan of 9–12 months so it is important to extend the sales period, especially through maturity. Apple and others do this through 'appstores'. The firm offers existing iPhone customers the possibility of purchasing additional applications and games (Leistén and Nilsson, 2009).

Just as the nature and expectations of customer groups differ at each stage so do the competitive conditions. This means that different marketing strategies, relating to the product and its distribution, pricing, and promotion, need to be deployed at particular times so as to maximize the financial return on a product's entire life.

The product lifecycle does not apply to all products in the same way. For example, some products reach the end of the introduction stage and then die as it becomes clear that there is no market to sustain the product. Some products follow the path into decline and then hang around sustained by heavy advertising and sales promotions, or they get recycled back into the growth stage by repositioning activities. Some products grow really quickly and then fade away rapidly. When Pot Noodle products were first introduced demand grew quickly, but then died off steeply at the end of the growth stage. The reason for this was that many people did not like the taste of these early products and so there was limited repeat buying.

The brands of many fast-moving consumer goods (FMCG) are sustained through a supermarket listing. Terminating a listed brand, and losing the shelf space to a competitor, is difficult to accept simply because getting the listing in the first place is so difficult and because of the substantial investment that has been put into the brand since its conception. In reality what happens is that the supermarket will delist an underperforming brand, unless the brand owner presents a suitable variant, capable of replacing the ailing brand (Clark, 2009).

When discussing the PLC care must be taken to clarify what exactly is being described. The PLC concept can apply to a product class (computers), a product form (a laptop), or a brand (Sony). The shape of the curve varies, with product classes having the longest cycle as the mature stage is often extended. Product forms tend to comply most closely with the traditional cycle shape, whereas brand cycles tend to be the shortest. This is because they are subject to competitive forces and sudden change. So, whereas hatchback cars (product form) enjoy a long period of success, brands such as the Ford Escort had shorter cycles and have been replaced by cars that have more contemporary designs and features, in this case, the Ford Focus.

Usefulness of the PLC Concept

The PLC is a well-known and popular concept and is a useful means of explaining the broad path a product or brand has taken. It also clearly sets out that no product, service, or brand lasts forever. In principle, the PLC concept allows marketing managers to adapt strategies and tactics to meet the needs of evolving conditions and product circumstances. In this sense it is clear, simple, and predictable. However, in practice the PLC is not of great use. For example, one problem is identifying which stage a product has reached in the cycle. Historical sales data do not help managers identify when a product moves from one stage to another. This means that it is difficult to forecast sales, and hence determine the future shape of the PLC curve.

The model worked reasonably well when the environment was relatively stable and not subject to dynamic swings or short-lived customer preferences. However, contemporary marketing managers are not concerned where their brand is within the product lifecycle: there are many other more meaningful ways and metrics to understand the competitive strength and development of a brand, e.g. benchmarking. Some brands do not follow the classical S-shaped curve, but rise steeply and then fall away immediately after sales reach a crest. These shapes reflect a consumer fad, a craze for a particular piece of merchandise, typified by fashion clothing, skateboards, and toys. So, great care is required when using the PLC, as its roles in commerce and when developing strategy are weak, but it is helpful generally as a way of explaining how brands develop (see Market Insight 8.2).

▶ Market Insight 8.2

LifeCycling Online Fashion

Firms such as Oli, ColorPlus, a premium Indian casualwear brand, YesStyle.com, who offer a range of Asian fashion online, and ASOS, the UK's market leader in online fashion retailing, each have thousands of product items on their websites and each can introduce hundreds of new items each week.

Understanding the principles underpinning the lifecycle can help these firms work out the length of each item's sales period, manage the stocking requirements, and plan for the introduction of new ranges. For example in the world of online fashion the following cycle might be evident:

▶ Market Insight 8.2

▶ Introduction—a new skirt is presented online, given lots of visibility, and is linked directly through newsletters and social media sites and also from the homepage. Some fashion leaders adopt the new skirt, while digital influencers who had been alerted previously to the launch, are given access to more detailed information, and, in some cases, samples.

▶ Growth—offline articles, online placements, and word-of-mouth help sales to grow Stock management becomes critical as it is essential not to disappoint customers.

▶ Maturity—competition becomes intense and it is necessary to remind audiences about the product online. More stock may be required to ensure continuity of supply. For example, a dress from the previous summer collection may still be selling well. At some point during this stage, the firm may cut the price to clear remaining stock. Sales provide an opportunity to make space in the warehouse for new products.

▶ Decline—the skirt becomes unfashionable and is replaced by a new design.

Each of these specific stages of development has different characteristics, requiring differing business and marketing approaches. This, in turn, has led to the development of software systems and applications that are geared to manage the individual characteristics of each stage. For example, Product Lifecycle Management (PLM) systems deal with online catalogues, design collaboration (enabling geographically dispersed employees to work on

Oli.co.uk, the online fashion house
Source: Courtesy of oli.co.uk.

designs together), style information (an item's sales history), and various facilities designed to integrate order tracking, invoicing, and operations activities.

Sources: www.worldfashionexchange.com/apparel-plm.aspx; www.straitstimes.com/BreakingNews/TechandScience/Story/STIStory_500942.html; www.asos.com; www.thetimes100.co.uk/studies/view.

1 How might the marketing activities change as an online fashion brand moves into the mature stage?

2 Use a major search engine to search and find the leading online fashion company in Australia, Canada, and another country of your choice. What do they all have in common?

3 Make brief notes about the needs customers have when buying fashion online. How might this change over the next five years?

▶ Research Insight 8.1

To take your learning further, you might wish to read this influential paper.

Wood, L. (1990), 'The end of the product life cycle? Education says goodbye to an old friend', *Journal of Marketing Management,* **6, 2, 145–55.**

This paper has been highlighted because it challenges the conventional wisdom about how useful the product lifecycle is. It identifies some of the problems associated with this popular concept and suggests that the concept is good for marketing education but not so good for marketing practitioners.

Visit the **Online Resource Centre** to read the abstract and access the full paper.

New Product Development

One of the key points that the product lifecycle concept tells us is that products do not last forever: their usefulness starts to diminish at some point and eventually nearly all come to an end, and die. There are many reasons for this cycle: technology is changing quickly so products are developed and adopted faster, lifecycles are becoming shorter, and so new products are required faster than before. In addition to this, global competition means that if an organization is to compete successfully and survive it will need to constantly offer superior value to its customers. One of management's tasks, therefore, is to be able to control the organization's range or portfolio of products and to anticipate when one product will become relatively tired and when new ones are necessary in order to sustain the organization and help it to grow.

The term 'new products' can be slightly misleading, as there can be a range of newness, both to the organization and to customers. Some new products might be totally new to both the organization and the market, for example the Dyson vacuum cleaner, with its cyclone technology, revolutionized the market, previously dominated by suction-based 'hoovers'. However, some products might only be minor product adaptations that have no real impact on a market other than offering an interesting new feature, e.g. features such as new colours, flavours, and pack sizes, and electronic facilities on CD players, digital cameras, and mobile personal players. Dyson offer their world-famous vacuum floor cleaners with a ball rather than four fixed wheels, improving manoeuvrability and providing a strong point of differentiation.

Unfortunately these 'new' products do not appear at the click of a pair of fingers. They have to be considered, planned, developed, and introduced carefully to the market. In order to ensure a stream of new products, organizations have three main options.

▶ Buy in finished products from other suppliers, perhaps from other parts of the world, or license the use of other products for specific periods of time.

▶ Develop products through collaboration with suppliers or even competitors.

▶ Develop new products internally, often through research and development departments (R&D) or through adapting current products through minor design and engineering changes.

Whatever the preferred route, they all necessitate a procedure or development pattern through which they are brought to the market. It would be wrong to suggest that there should be a uniform process (Ozer, 2003), as not only are there many approaches to new product development but also the procedures adopted by an organization reflect its attitude to risk, its culture, strategy, the product and market, and, above all else, its approach to customer relationships.

The success rate of new products is consistently poor. No more than one in ten new consumer products succeed and there are three main reasons for this, according to Drucker (1985):

1 There is no market for the product.

2 There is a market need but the product does not meet customer requirements.

3 The product's ability to meet the market need, although satisfactory, is not adequately communicated to the target market.

Successful new products are developed partly by understanding the market and partly by developing technology to meet the identified needs. Energizer batteries demonstrate this orientation with their 15-minute charger. The charger was designed to meet the needs of people who want batteries to cope with the demands of high-draining products such as digital cameras and who also want to reduce the recharge time. Advances in technology enabled Energizer to make their batteries last four times as long as alkaline batteries, and they reduced the recharge time from eight hours to just 15 minutes (Tiltman, 2006).

The development of new products is complex and high risk so organizations usually adopt a procedural approach. The procedure consists of several phases that enable progress to be monitored, test trials to be conducted, and the results analysed before there is any commitment to the market. The most common general new product development process (NPDP) is set out in Figure 8.4.

The NPDP presented here should be considered as a generalization, and it should be

Drained? Try Energiser's 15-minute battery charger
Source: Energizer Group Ltd.

understood that the various phases or episodes do not always occur in the linear sequence shown. Actions can overlap or even occur completely out of sequence, depending on the speed, complexity, and number of people or organizations involved in the NPDP. Apart from some minor issues, the process is essentially the same when developing new products for both consumer and business markets.

go online

Visit the **Online Resource Centre** and follow the weblink to the Product Development and Management Association (PDMA), to learn more about the professional development, information, collaboration, and promotion of new product development and management.

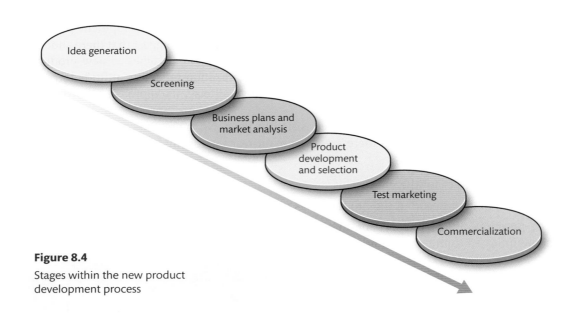

Figure 8.4

Stages within the new product development process

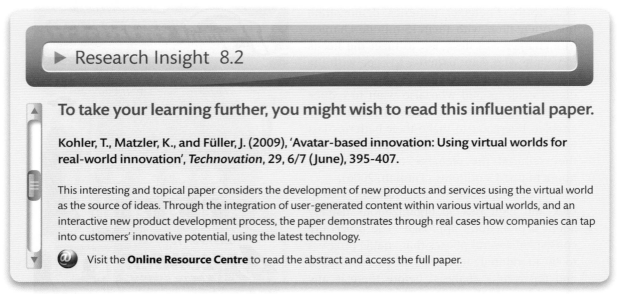

▶ Research Insight 8.2

To take your learning further, you might wish to read this influential paper.

Kohler, T., Matzler, K., and Füller, J. (2009), 'Avatar-based innovation: Using virtual worlds for real-world innovation', *Technovation*, 29, 6/7 (June), 395-407.

This interesting and topical paper considers the development of new products and services using the virtual world as the source of ideas. Through the integration of user-generated content within various virtual worlds, and an interactive new product development process, the paper demonstrates through real cases how companies can tap into customers' innovative potential, using the latest technology.

@ Visit the **Online Resource Centre** to read the abstract and access the full paper.

Idea Generation

Ideas can be generated through customers, competitors (through websites and sales literature analysis), market research data (such as reports), Research and Development departments, customer service employees, the sales force, project development teams, and secondary data sources such as sales records. What this means is that organizations should foster a corporate culture that encourages creativity and supports people when they bring forward new ideas for product enhancements and other improvements.

Screening

All ideas need to be assessed so that only those that meet pre-determined criteria are taken forward. Key criteria include the fit between the proposed new product idea and the overall corporate strategy and objectives. Another involves the views of customers, undertaken using concept testing. Other approaches consider how the market will react to the idea and what effort the organization will need to make if the product is to be brought to the market successfully. Whatever approaches are used, screening must be a separate activity to the idea generation stage. If it is not then creativity might be impaired.

Business Planning and Market Analysis

The development of a business plan is crucial, simply because it will indicate the potential and relative profitability of the product. In order to prepare the plan, important information about the size, shape, and dynamics of the market needs to be determined. The resultant profitability forecasts will be significant in determining how and when the product will be developed, if at all.

Product Development and Selection

In many organizations, several product ideas are considered simultaneously. It is management's task to select those that have commercial potential and are in the best interests of the organization and its longer term strategy, goals, and use of resources. There is a trade-off between the need to test and reduce risk and the need to go to market and drive income and get a return on the investment committed to the new product. This phase is expensive so only a limited number of projects are allowed to proceed into development. Those projects that are selected for further development have prototypes and test versions developed. These are then subjected to functional performance tests, design revisions, manufacturing requirements analysis, distribution analysis, and a multitude of other testing procedures.

Test Marketing

Before committing a new product to a market, most organizations decide to test market the finished product. By piloting and testing the product under controlled, real market conditions, many of the genuine issues as perceived by customers can be raised and resolved while minimizing any damage or risk to the organization and the brand. **Test marketing** can be undertaken using a particular geographical region or specific number of customer locations. The intention is to evaluate the product and the whole marketing programme under real working conditions. Test marketing, or field trials, enables the product and marketing plan to be refined or adapted in the light of market reaction, yet before release to the whole market. See Chapter 4 for more information about test marketing.

Commercialization

To commercialize a new product a launch plan is required. This considers the needs of **distributors**, end user customers, marketing communication agencies, and other relevant stakeholders. The objective is to schedule all those activities that are required to make the launch successful. These include communications (to inform audiences of the product's capabilities and to position and persuade potential customers), training, and product support for all customer-facing employees.

Any perceived rigidity in this formal process should disregarded. Many new products come to market via rather different routes, at different speeds and different levels of preparation. For example, LG's product development is closely aligned with its market research. They found that people wanted to get their washing done in one go at the weekend, they concerned about the environment, and had little or no experience or desire to do ironing. This led to the development of LG's steam washing machine. This has a large capacity drum, and uses steam rather than water (as in conventional washing machines), which is good for the environment. Steam also means fewer wrinkles, so less ironing (Barda, 2009).

▶ Market Insight 8.3

Developing Viagra: Determining Size

Pfizer was once a medium-sized pharmaceutical manufacturer. Now it is the world's leading player in a highly competitive sector. The reason for this considerable uplift in sales and profits was Viagra, the first drug to provide a cure for impotence. The development and launch of Viagra took 13 years, involved screening in excess of 1,500 compounds, and it is estimated that the research and development costs exceeded £600m.

Originally, Pfizer had invested in a research programme designed to find a treatment for angina. The angina trials proved unsuccessful, but some patients reported that they experienced penile erections as a side effect. Although this was noted by Pfizer, they were reluctant to develop further research using the 'angina' compounds, simply because formal research showed that only one in 20 men suffered from erectile dysfunction, that it was commonly accepted to be a psychological problem. Furthermore, who was going to allow themselves to be part of the testing procedure during the trials?

Despite these reservations and the associated business risk, Pfizer agreed to proceed. Plenty of people volunteered for the clinical trials between 1993 and 1996, which were an overwhelming success. This was followed by the issue of a full licence in 1998. In view of the 2.9m prescriptions made in the first three months alone (Pfizer.com), sales of $1.2bn in 2004, and the entry of two similar drugs into the market, it might be concluded that the original research failed to reflect the true size of the market.

Not only has Viagra helped millions of people, but also it has been a major new product success story. Despite the poor business case for the product during development, the inaccuracy of the market research was subsequently revealed by the demand for the drug.

Source: Adapted from Trott (2007).

1   **The Viagra case highlights the problems associated with developing a business case. What other problems might occur with the development of medicines?**

2   **To what extent is the business case and market analysis case stage useful?**

3   **Find examples of other recently launched new products. Where and how were they launched?**

---

go online

Visit the **Online Resource Centre** and complete Internet Activity 8.1 to learn more about how two leading FMCG companies approach the new product development process.

New Service Development

So far, the focus has been on the processes associated with developing new products, without reference to services. This is partly because researchers have given much more attention to the development issues with products and they perceive the development of new services as either problematic or very similar to that of products. This has changed in recent years as many Western economies have become increasingly service-orientated.

Of the few researchers in this area, Möller, Rajala, and Westerlund (2008) develop ideas based on the logic that value creation is key to the development of innovative service offerings and concepts. They distinguish three service innovation strategies. These are established services within competitive markets; incremental service innovation targeting value-added offerings; and radical service innovation, which aim to produce completely novel offerings.

Established services with a relatively stable value creation process are often generated under intense competitive behaviour in order to improve operational efficiency. Dell is cited as a business based on a simple concept, namely selling computer systems direct to customers. Dell's market leadership is the result of a constant focus on delivering positive product and service experiences to customers.

Incremental service innovation describes a value creation strategy in which services are developed to provide extra value. Working together, the service provider and client can produce more effective solutions. The prime example is Google, which, in addition to providing internet search services for individual consumers, provides search services for corporate clients, including advertisers, content publishers, and site managers. Google continually develops new service applications based on its back-end technology, and the use of linked PCs that respond immediately to each query. Google's innovation has resulted in faster response times, greater scalability, and lower costs.

Radical service innovation is concerned with value creation generated through novel or unusual service concepts. This requires new technologies, offerings, or business concepts, and involves radical systemwide changes in existing value systems. MySQL, the world's leading open-source database software producer uses this approach. By making the source code of the software freely available to everybody, the software is available to everyone to use and/or modify. However, all derivative works must be made available to the original developers. As a result, MySQL have been able to increase the number of users and developers, and subsequently offer their clients improved levels of service. This has led to increased financial performance.

Stages of Product/Service Innovation Development

It is helpful to view service innovation in the light of the product-service spectrum introduced at the start of this chapter. Services do not always need to be seen just as an extension or add-on to a product offering, they can be a way of creating value opportunities for clients. Shelton (2009) considers service innovation in the context of four stages of solution management maturity. The early stages of innovation maturity are characterized by a product-focus with a relatively small amount of services used only to augment and complement the products. The mature stages are characterized by much higher levels of service, some integrated with the products to provide solutions for customer problems.

▶ Stage 1—in this stage services are used as aftersales product support, e.g. parts and repair services. Service innovation is framed around maintaining the product, and ensuring that customers are satisfied with their product purchase. As a result, customers typically view the service and product business as distinct entities.

▶ Stage 2—this stage is characterized by aftersales services designed to complement the core product. Here, services should improve customer satisfaction with existing products, increase loyalty, and may generate additional purchases. Sheldon refers to Hewlett-Packard's 'PC Tune-Up', which, for a fee, provides a set of diagnostics to assess and manage customers.

▶ Stage 3—at this stage, the portfolio includes a full line of services and products designed to provide a clearly differentiated offering aimed at solving clients' lifecycle problems. Sheldon refers to Motorola's 'Total Network Care' (TNC), which provides end-to-end support services for wireless networks. Although the service organization is often consolidated into one identifiable business, products are still core to the company. End user customers see no major perceived boundaries between products and services.

▶ Stage 4—at this, the highest end of innovation maturity, firms seek to integrate the services dimension as part of their total offer. Known as 'servitization', this involves the provision of an integrated bundle of product/service solutions for the entire lifecycle of their customers, 'from cradle to grave'. These solutions are developed collaboratively with clients, and, therefore, require a deep understanding of the customer's overall business. These firms, often market leaders, generate innovative solutions through buyer/seller collaborative processes. Solutions are developed that are of mutual value. See Market Insight 8.4 for an example of servitization.

▶ Market Insight 8.4

Servitization Takes Off in Aerospace

Some organizations offer products and services as an integrated bundle, one where the services are an integral part of the core product. This is referred to as 'servitization' and enables customers to create the value they require rather than be dependent on suppliers.

Examples of servitization can be seen in many sectors, but manufacturers have been prominent in developing this form of strategy. Engine manufacturers, such as Rolls-Royce operating in the aerospace industry, do not just offer engines (a product) and neither do they offer engines plus training, delivery, and maintenance services. In order to compete through differentiation rather than price, Rolls-Royce offers commercial airline customers performance-based contracts. Baines *et al.* (2008) report that these contracts

▶ Market Insight 8.4

Rolls Royce engines: to buy or to lease, that is the question

link the manufacturer's compensation to product availability and the capability it delivers (e.g. hours flown). Rolls-Royce has registered trademarks for both 'Power by the Hour' and the more inclusive 'TotalCare' contracts. Such contracts provide airline operators with fixed engine maintenance costs, over an extended period of time (e.g. ten years). The TotalCare offering is an example of a product-centric servitization strategy.

In much the same way, GE offers a 'Complete Power Solutions' programme for its aircraft. In this, GE links its jet engine sales with a suite of financial and operational services, hence enabling a solution across the customer lifecycle.

Sources: Baines *et al.* (2008); Shelton (2009).

1 To what extent is servitization a glorified service contract? What is the real value of this approach?

2 Make brief notes about the issues customers have when buying high-value, high-technology products.

3 Which other industries might make good use of a servitization approach?

Servitization strategies have been used to create value in a number of different industries. Robinson, Clarke-Hill, and Clarkson (2002) report their use in the chemical industry, where price-led strategies tend to dominate in a commodity context. What is noticeable is that where commodity chemical firms have implemented servitization, one of the more prominent uses has been to help build relationships and reduce both the attitudinal and physical distance between partner organizations.

The Process of Adoption

The process by which individuals accept and use new products is referred to as adoption (Rogers, 1983). The different stages in the **adoption process** are sequential and are characterized by the different factors that are involved at each stage (e.g. the media used by each individual). The process starts with people gaining awareness of a product and moves through various stages of adoption before a purchase is eventually made. Figure 8.5 below sets out the various stages in the **process of adoption**.

In the knowledge stage, consumers become aware of the new product. They have little information and have yet to develop any particular attitudes towards the product. Indeed, at this stage consumers are not interested in finding out any more information.

The persuasion stage is characterized by consumers becoming aware that the innovation may be of use in solving a potential problem. Consumers become sufficiently motivated to find out more about the product's characteristics, including its features, price, and availability.

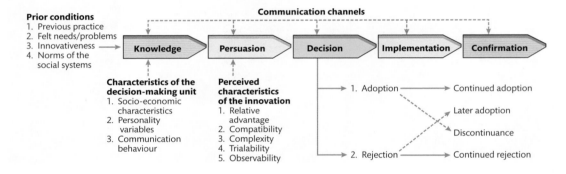

Figure 8.5

Stages in the innovation decision process of adoption

Source: Reprinted from Rogers (1983) with the permission of the Free Press. © 1962, 1971, 1983 by the Free Press.

In the decision stage, individuals develop an attitude toward the product or service and they reach a decision about whether the innovation will meet their needs. If this is positive they will go on to try the innovation.

During the implementation stage, the innovation is tried for the first time. Sales promotions are often used as samples to allow individuals to test the product without any undue risk. Individuals accept or reject an innovation on the basis of their experience of the trial. Note the way supermarkets use sampling to encourage people to try new food and drink products.

The final confirmation stage is signalled when an individual successfully adopts the product on a regular purchase basis without the help of the sales promotion or other incentives.

This model assumes that the adoption stages occur in a predictable sequence, but this cannot always be assumed to be the case. Rejection of the innovation can occur at any point, even during implementation and the very early phases of the confirmation stage. Generally, mass communications are going to be more effective in the earlier phases of the adoption process for products that buyers are actively interested in, and more interpersonal forms are more appropriate at the later stages, especially implementation and confirmation.

Diffusion Theory

Although we know that consumers may buy using both functional and emotional motives when purchasing, customers adopt new products at different speeds or timescales. Their different attitudes to risk, their level of education, experience, and needs, means that different groups of customers adopt new products at different and varying speeds. The rate at which a market adopts an innovation is referred to as the **process of diffusion** (Rogers, 1962). According to Rogers, there are five categories of adopters, as shown in Figure 8.6.

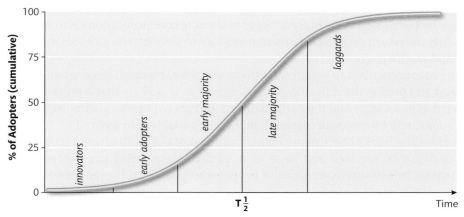

Figure 8.6

The process of diffusion

Source: Rogers (1962): fig. 5.1. © 1955, 2003 by Everett M. Rogers ©. 1962, 1971, 1983 by the Free Press.

▶ **Innovators**—this group, which constitutes 2.5% of the buying population, is important because they have to kick-start the adoption process. These people like new ideas, are often well educated, young, confident, and financially strong. This means that they are more likely to take risks associated with new products. Being an innovator in one product category, such as photography, does not mean a person will be an innovator in other categories. Innovative attitudes and behaviour can be specific to just one or two areas of interest.

▶ **Early adopters**—this group, 13.5% of the market, is characterized by a high percentage of opinion leaders. These people are very important for speeding up the adoption process. Consequently, marketing communications need to be targeted at these people, who, in turn, will stimulate word-of-mouth communications to spread information. Although early adopters prefer to let innovators take all the risks, they enjoy being at the leading edge of innovation, tend to be younger than any other group, and above average in education. Other than innovators, this group reads more publications and consults more salespeople than all others.

▶ **Early majority**—this group, which forms 34% of the market, is more risk-averse than the previous two groups. This group requires reassurance that the product works and has been proven in the market. They are above average in terms of age, education, social status, and income. Unlike the early adopters, they tend to wait for prices to fall and prefer more informal sources of information and are often prompted into purchase by other people who have already purchased.

▶ **Late majority**—a similar size to the previous group, the late majority are sceptical of new ideas and only adopt new products because of social or economic factors. They read few publications and are below average in education, social status, and income.

▶ **Laggards**—this group of people, 16% of the buying population, are suspicious of all new ideas and their opinions are very hard to change. Of all the groups, laggards have the lowest income, social status, and education, and take a long time to adopt an innovation, if at all.

The rate of diffusion, according to Gatignon and Robertson (1985), is a function of the speed at which sales occur, the pattern of diffusion as expressed in the shape of the curve, and the size of the market. This means that diffusion does not occur at a constant or predictable speed; it may be fast or slow. One of the tasks of marketing communications is to speed up the process so that the return on the investment necessary to develop the innovation is achieved as quickly and as efficiently as possible.

Marketing managers need to ensure that these variables are considered when attempting to understand and predict the diffusion process. However, it is likely that a promotional campaign targeted at innovators and the early majority, and geared to stimulating word-of-mouth communications, will be more successful than if these variables are ignored.

In his best-selling book, *The Tipping Point*, journalist Malcolm Gladwell (2002) compares the diffusion of goods, services, and ideas to an epidemic, spreading like a virus. He points out the important role of three categories of people who help the diffusion process:

▶ 'mavens' (see Feick and Price, 1987)—who have a voracious appetite for product and service information, passing this to others within a community;

▶ 'connectors'—whose social networks are extensive, bringing people within a community together; and

▶ 'salesmen'—who specialize in persuading people to adopt new goods, services, and ideas.

The difficulty in marketing is identifying these important groups of people. Increasingly, companies are using word-of-mouth marketing techniques to promote goods and services, particularly through blogs and websites where a selection of consumers are provided with free samples and asked to write their experiences on user websites.

Branding

Branding is a process by which manufacturers and retailers help customers to differentiate between various offerings in a market. It enables customers to make associations between certain attributes or feelings and a particular brand. If this differentiation can be achieved and sustained, then a brand is considered to have a competitive advantage. It is not necessary for people to buy brands in order to enjoy and understand them. Successful brands create strong, positive, and lasting impressions through their communications, and associated psychological feelings and emotions, not just their functionality through use.

Brand names provide information about content, taste, durability, quality, price, and performance, without requiring the buyer to undertake time-consuming comparison tests with similar offerings or other risk reduction approaches to purchase decisions. In some categories, brands can be developed through the use of messages that are entirely emotional or image-based. Many of the 'products' in FMCG sectors, where there is low customer involvement, use communications based largely on imagery. Other sectors, such as cars or pharmaceuticals, where involvement tends to be high, require rational information-based messages supported by image-based messages (Boehringer, 1996). In other words, a blend of messages may well be required to achieve the objectives and goals of the campaign.

What is a Brand?

Brands are products and services that have added value. This value has been deliberately designed and presented by marketing managers in an attempt to augment their offerings with values and associations that are recognized by, and are meaningful to, their customers. Although marketing managers have to create, sustain, protect, and develop the identity of the brands for which they are responsible, it is customer perception, the images they form of these brands, and the meaning and value that customers give to the brand that is important. Both managers and customers are involved in the branding process.

Chernatony and Dall'Olmo Riley (1998) identified 12 types of brand definition, but one of the more common interpretations is that a brand is represented by a name, symbol, words, or mark that identifies and distinguishes a product or company, from its competitors. However, brands consist of much more than these various elements. Brands have character, even personalities, and, in order to develop character, it is important to understand that brands are constructed of two main types of attributes: intrinsic and extrinsic.

Intrinsic attributes refer to the functional characteristics of a product, such as its shape, performance, and physical capacity. If any of these intrinsic attributes were changed, this would directly alter the product. Extrinsic attributes refer to those elements that are not intrinsic, and, if changed, do not alter the material functioning and performance of the product itself. These include devices such as the brand name, marketing communications, packaging, price, and mechanisms that enable consumers to form associations that give meaning to the brand. Buyers often use the extrinsic attributes to help them distinguish one brand from another, because in certain categories it is difficult for them to make decisions based on the intrinsic attributes alone.

▶ Research Insight 8.3

To take your learning further, you might wish to read this influential paper.

Doyle, P. (1993), 'Building successful brands; the strategic options', *Journal of Consumer Marketing,* 7, 2, 5–20.

This paper demonstrates that having a strong brand is not enough. Doyle shows that successful brands deliver against four criteria: a strong consumer proposition, integrated with other assets, being positioned within an attractive market, and being managed in order to realize the value of the brand's long-term cash flow.

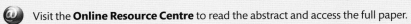 Visit the **Online Resource Centre** to read the abstract and access the full paper.

Why Brand?

Brands represent opportunities for both consumers and organizations (manufacturers and retailers) to buy and to sell products and services easily, more efficiently, and relatively quickly. The benefits are now considered from each perspective. Consumers like brands for the following reasons. They:

▶ Assist people to identify their preferred products.

▶ Reduce levels of perceived risk and in doing so improve the quality of the shopping experience.

▶ Help people to gauge the level of product quality.

▶ Reduce the amount of time spent making product-based decisions and, in turn, decrease the time spent shopping.

▶ Provide psychological reassurance or reward, especially for products bought on an occasional basis.

▶ Inform consumers about the source of a product (country or company).

Branding helps customers identify the products and services they prefer to use in order to satisfy their needs and wants. Equally, branding helps them to avoid the brands that they dislike as a result of previous use or because of other image, associations, or other psychological reasoning.

Consumers experience a range of perceived risks when buying different products. These might be financial risks (can I afford this?), social risks (what will other people think about me wearing this dress or going to this bar?), or functional risks (will this MP3 player work?). Branding helps to reduce these risks so that buyers can proceed with a purchase without fear or uncertainty. Strong brands encapsulate a range of values that communicate safety and purchase security.

In markets unknown to a buyer or where there is technical complexity (e.g. computing, financial services), consumers use branding to make judgements about the quality of a product. This, in turn, helps consumers save shopping time and again helps reduce the amount of risk they experience.

Perhaps above all other factors, branding helps consumers develop relationships based on **trust**. Strong brands are normally well trusted and annual surveys often announce that Nokia, Google, and Kellogg's are some of the most trusted brands. Similarly, these surveys declare those brands that are least trusted by consumers and very often these coincide with falling sales and reducing market share. Creating trust is important as it enables consumers to buy with confidence.

Many brands are deliberately imbued with human characteristics, to the point that they are identified as having particular personalities. These brand personalities might be based around being seen as friendly, approachable, distant, aloof, calculating, honest, fun, or even robust or caring. Marketing communications play an important role in communicating the essence of a brand's personality. By developing positive emotional links with a brand, consumers can find reassurance through their brand purchases.

Manufacturers and retailers enjoy brands for the following reasons. They:

▶ Enable premium pricing.

▶ Help differentiate the product from competitive offerings.

▶ Encourage cross-selling to other brands owned by the manufacturer.

▶ Develop customer loyalty/retention and repeat-purchase buyer behaviour.

▶ Assist the development and use of integrated marketing communications.

▶ Contribute to corporate identity programmes.

▶ Provide some legal protection.

Branding is an important way for manufacturers to differentiate their brands in crowded marketplaces. This, in turn, enables buyers to recognize the brand quickly and make fast, unhindered purchase decisions. One of the brand-owner's goals is to create strong brand loyalty to the extent that customers always seek out the brand, and become better prepared to accept cross-product promotions and brand extensions.

Perhaps one of the strongest motivations for branding is that it can allow manufacturers to set premium prices. Brands such as Andrex, Stella Artois, and L'Oréal charge a premium price, often around 20% higher than the average price in their respective product categories. Premium prices allow brand managers to reinvest in brand development, and in some markets this is important in order to remain competitive. However, it should not be assumed that the establishment of a brand will lead to automatic success. Many brands fail, sometimes because a firm fails to invest in a brand at the level required, or because management have not recognized or accepted the need to change, adapt, or reposition their brands as market preferences have moved on.

The greater the number of product-based brands, the greater the motivation for an organization to want to develop a corporate brand. Using this umbrella branding approach, organizations only need to invest heavily in one brand, rather than each and every product-based brand. This approach is not applicable to all sectors, although in business-to-business markets where there is product complexity, corporate branding is an effective way of communicating and focusing on a few core brand values.

Brands: Associations and Personalities

As suggested earlier, brands are capable of triggering **associations** in the minds of consumers, and these need not be based solely on a utilitarian or functional approach. These associations may sometimes enable consumers to construe a psychosocial meaning associated with a particular brand. The idea that consumers might search for brands with a personality that complements their self-concept is not new, as identified by McCraken (1986). Belk (1988) suggested that brands offer a means of self expression, whether this is in terms of who they want to be (desired self), who they strive to be (ideal self) or who they think they should be (ought self). Brands, therefore, provide a means for individuals to indicate to others their preferred personality, as they relate to these 'self' concepts.

This emotional and symbolic approach is intended to provide consumers with additional reasons to engage with a brand, beyond the normal functional characteristics a brand offers (Keller, 1998), which are so easily copied by competitors. Aaker (1997) refers to **brand personality** as the set of human characteristics that consumers associate with a brand. She developed the Brand Personality Scale, which consists of five main dimensions of psychosocial meaning, which subsumed 42 personality traits. The dimensions are sincerity (wholesome, honest, down-to-earth), excitement (exciting, imaginative, daring), competence (intelligent,

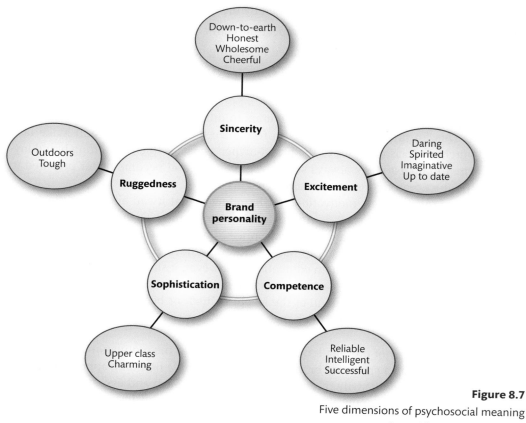

Figure 8.7

Five dimensions of psychosocial meaning

Source: Adapted from Aaker (1997).

confident), sophistication (charming, glamorous, smooth), and ruggedness (strong, masculine). These are depicted in Figure 8.7.

Aaker's initial research was conducted in the mid-1990s and revealed that in the USA, MTV was perceived to be best at excitement, CNN on competence, Levi's on ruggedness, Revlon on sophistication, and Campbells on sincerity.

These psychosocial dimensions have subsequently become enshrined as dimensions of brand personality. Aaker developed a five-point framework around these dimensions in order to provide a consistent means of measurement. The framework has been used frequently and cited many times by both academics and marketing practitioners. For example, Arora and Stoner (2009) report that various studies have found that consumers choose offerings which they feel possess personalities similar to their own personalities (Linville and Carlston, 1994; Phau and Lau, 2001). They prefer brands that project a personality that is consistent with their self-concepts. As Arora and Stoner (2009: 273) indicate, 'brand personality provides a form of identity for consumers that expresses symbolic meaning for themselves and for others'. Brand personality, therefore, can be construed as a means of creating and maintaining consumer loyalty, if only because this aspect is difficult for competitors to copy.

▶ Market Insight 8.5

A Finnish Association with Purity

Finlandia, a premium vodka brand, targeted at younger, upmarket drinkers, was built around functional associations with the clean, clear natural environment of Finland. In an attempt to raise awareness of the brand, a recent campaign called 'Pure Emotion' was launched. The strategy was to be achieved by shifting **brand associations** to one that engaged the target consumers emotionally. The campaign was made with the support of *the Independent* newspaper, itself a source of emotion, often depicted through travel, music, and sport.

The promotion launched with advertorial content in the newspaper's *Traveller* and *Independent* magazines. Teaser ads placed on the sports pages drove readers to the promotion, online at a co-branded microsite created at independent.co.uk. This was aimed at

encouraging readers/users to share videos, photos, and stories of their own 'Pure Emotion' experiences.

The microsite included three 'Pure Emotion' features, with people talking about their own emotional highs and lows in music, travel, and sport. There were also three 'user generated Pure Emotion' galleries, featuring stories, pictures, and video from independent.co.uk users, all about emotional moments from their lives. An online competition ran, based around the users' uploaded Pure Emotion content and attracted 1,213 competition entries. The microsite also featured a Finlandia advertorial and a gallery of 20 front pages of *the Independent* from the past year, underlining the emotional power of newspapers.

Text links to 'Pure Emotion' were included in *the Independent's* daily email newsletter to 80,000 subscribers and a marketing email to a 20,000-strong database. *the Independent's* campaign was tied in with the Finlandia Vodka Pure Emotion Exhibition at Camden's Proud Gallery, showing real people's pure

The winning photo, Finlandia's pure emotion competition
Source: Courtesy of Brown-Forman Beverages, Europe, Ltd.

Source: Courtesy of Brown-Forman Beverages, Europe, Ltd..

▶ Market Insight 8.5   (continued)

emotions in their own words through stories, images, and video clips. The brand also focused on its natural purity in an advertising takeover of Euston train station.

Source: Anon (2009).

1   Which other brands might you suggest focus on an emotional approach? Are they successful, and why?

2   If customers buy brands with a personality that reflects their own personalities, name three brands that you purchase regularly. How do these reflect your personality?

3   Visit www.interbrand.com and find brands where the use of emotion is prominent.

Customers assign a level of trust to the brands they encounter. Preferred brands signify a high level of trust and indicate that the brand promise is delivered. Marketing managers, therefore, need to ensure that they do not harm or reduce the perceived levels of trust in their brands. Indeed, actions should be taken to enhance trust. One way of achieving this is to use labels and logos to represent a brand's values, associations, and source. For example, all Apple products are signified, and identified by, the fruit with a bite removed; UK meat products carry a red tractor symbol. According to the National Farmers Union, the red tractor logo indicates that the meat was produced to exacting standards of food safety, kindness to animals, and environmental protection. This is intended to reassure customers about the origin and quality of the meat. A more recent symbol is that of a footprint. This refers to the carbon dioxide associated with the production and transportation of a brand. This emerged because some brands wanted a means of demonstrating the carbon savings they had made in their supply chains. Walkers Crisps and then Tesco were the first brands to use the symbol. However, as Charles (2009) points out, one of the issues arising from the use of the carbon footprint symbol is that consumers do not understand what the figures mean. This will take time, just as the Fairtrade brand was not established overnight.

Types of Brands

There are three main types of brands: manufacturer, distributor, and generic.

Manufacturer Brands

In many markets, and especially the FMCG sector, retailers are able to influence the way in which a product is displayed and presented to customers. As a result, manufacturers try to create brand recognition and name recall through their direct marketing communications activities with end users. The goal is to help customers identify the producer of a particular brand at the point of purchase. For example, Persil, Heinz, Cadbury, and Coca-Cola are strong manufacturers' brands, they are promoted heavily, and customers develop preferences based on performance, experience, communications, and availability. So, when customers are shopping they use the images they have of various manufacturers, combined with their own experiences, to seek out their preferred brands. Retailers who choose not to stock certain major **manufacturer brands** run the risk of losing customers.

Distributor (or Own-Label) Brands

The various organizations that make up the marketing channel often choose to create a distinct identity for themselves. The term distributor or own-label brand refers to the identities and images developed by the wholesalers, distributors, dealers, and retailers who make up the marketing channel. Wholesalers, such as Nurdin & Peacock, and retailers, such as Argos, Harvey Nichols, Sainsbury's, Next, and HMV, have all created strong brands.

This brand strategy offers many advantages to both the manufacturer, who can use excess capacity, and retailers, who can earn a higher margin than they can with manufacturers' branded goods and at the same time develop strong store images. Retailers have the additional cost of promotional initiatives, necessary in the absence of a manufacturer's support. Some manufacturers, such as Kellogg's, refuse to make products for distributors to brand, although others (Cereal Partners) are happy to supply a variety of competitors.

Occasionally, conflict emerges, especially when a **distributor brand** displays characteristics that are very similar to the manufacturer's market leader brand. Coca-Cola defended their brand when it was alleged that the packaging of Sainsbury's new cola drink was too similar to their own established design.

Generic Brands

Generic brands are sold without any promotional materials or any means of identifying the company, with the packaging displaying only information required by law. The only form of identification is the relevant product category, e.g. plain flour. Without having to pay for promotional support, these brands are sold at prices that are substantially below the price of normal brands. However, although briefly successful in the 1990s, their popularity has declined and manufacturers see no reason to produce these 'white carton' products. Only firms in the pharmaceutical sector use this type of brand.

Brand Strategies

Brands constitute a critical part of an organization's competitive strategy, so the development of strategies in order to manage and sustain them is really important. However, the original idea that brands provide a point of differentiation has been supplemented, not replaced, by an understanding of the relational dimension. Brands provide a way in which organizations can create and maintain relationships with customers. Therefore, brand strategies need to encompass relationship issues and to ensure that the way a customer relates to a brand is both appropriate and offers opportunities for cross-selling customers into other products and services in an organization's portfolio.

Brand Name

Choosing a name for a brand is a critical foundation stone because, ideally, it should enable all of the following to be accomplished:

▶ be easily recalled, spelled, and spoken;

▶ be strategically consistent with the organization's branding policies;

▶ be indicative of the product's major benefits and characteristics;

▶ be distinctive;

▶ be meaningful to the customer;

▶ be capable of registration and protection.

Brand names need to transfer easily across markets, and to do so successfully it helps if customers can not only pronounce the name but can also recall the name unaided. Sometimes problems can arise through interpretation. For example, Traficante is an Italian brand of mineral water, but in Spanish it means drug dealer. Clairol's curling iron, 'Mist Stick', had problems when launched in Germany because 'mist' is slang for manure (see Chapter 7).

One of the reasons that high-profile grocery brands are advertised so frequently is to create brand name awareness, so that when a UK customer thinks of pet food they think of Felix or Winalot, or a Swedish customer thinks of Mjau and Doggy. Names that are difficult to spell or are difficult to pronounce are unlikely to be accepted by customers. Short names such as Lego, Mars, Sony, Flash, or Shell have this strength.

Brand names should have some internal strategic consistency and be compatible with the organization's overall positioning. The Ford Transit, Virgin Atlantic, and Cadbury Dairy Milk are names that reflect their parent company's policies that the company name prefixes their product brand names. Some brand names incorporate a combination of words, numbers, or initials. The portable 'sat nav' brand Tom Tom GO 910 and Canon's Pixma MP600 photo printer use names that do not inform about the functionality, yet use a combination of words and numbers to reflect the parent company, product line to which they belong, and hint of their technological content.

A brand's functional benefit can also be incorporated within a name as this helps to convey its distinctive qualities. Deodorant brands such as Sure and Right Guard use this approach, although Lynx relies on imagery plus fragrance and dryness.

Most brands do not have sufficient financial resources to be advertised on TV or in any mainstream media. Therefore, it is not possible to convey brand values through imagery and brand advertising. For these brands it is important that the name of the brand reflects the functionality of the product itself. So, the super adhesive brand 'No More Nails', Cling Film, and 'Snap-on-Tools' all convey precisely what they do through their names. For these brands, packaging and merchandising is important in order to communicate with customers in-store.

Increasingly, brands are being developed through the use of social media. This is essentially about people talking, either spontaneously to one another, through blogs, or through formal or informal communities, about products and brands that they have experienced in some way. The role of brand managers is to listen to these conversations, and then adapt their brands accordingly. What this suggests is that the control and identity of a brand has moved from the brand-owner to the consumer. See Chapter 17 for a deeper insight into this issue.

Finally, brands can represent considerable value to their owners and so names need to be registered and protected for two main reasons. First, brand name protection helps organizations prevent others from copying and counterfeiting the brand. Although copying products is now commonplace, preventing the use of the brand name helps protect the brand-owners and enables them to maintain aspects of their brand positioning. The second reason for name registration is that the searches required when registering a name mean that the organization will not infringe the rights of others who already own the name. This can avoid costly legal arguments and delays in establishing a brand.

Branding Policies

Once a decision has been taken to brand an organization's products, an overall branding policy is required. There are three main strategies, individual, family, and corporate branding, and within these there are a number of brand combinations and variations in the way brands can be developed.

Individual Branding

Once referred to as a multibrand policy, individual branding requires that each product offered by an organization is branded independently of all the others. Grocery brands offered by Unilever (e.g. Knorr, Cif, and Dove) and Procter & Gamble (e.g. Fairy, Crest, and Head & Shoulders) typify this approach.

One of the advantages of this approach is that it is easy to target specific segments and to enter new markets with separate names. If a brand fails or becomes subject to negative media attention, the other brands are not likely to be damaged. However, there is a heavy financial cost as each brand needs to have its own promotional programme and associated support.

Family Branding

Once referred to as a multiproduct brand policy, family branding requires that all the products use the organization's name, either entirely or in part. Microsoft, Heinz, and Kellogg's all incorporate the company name as it is hoped that customer trust will develop across all brands. Therefore, promotional investment need not be as high. This is because there will always be a halo effect across all the brands when one is communicated and brand experience will stimulate word of mouth following usage. A prime example of this is Google, who have pursued a family brand strategy with Google Adwords, Google Maps, and Google Scholar to name a few. What is more impressive is that Google's shattering achievements have been accomplished in just ten years and without any spending on advertising or promotional materials.

Line family branding is a derivative policy whereby a family branding policy is followed for all products within a single line. Bosch is a technology company operating in the automotive, industry, and home markets. Many of its products are branded Bosch but they use line branding for their Blaupunkt and Qualcast brands in their car entertainment and garden products divisions.

Corporate Brands

Many retail brands adopt a single umbrella brand, based on the name of the organization. This name is then used at all locations and is a way of identifying the brand and providing a form of consistent differentiation, and form of recognition, whether on the high street or online. Major supermarkets such as Tesco in the UK, Carrefour in France, and ASDA Wal-Mart use this branding strategy to attract and help retain customers.

Corporate branding strategies are also used extensively in business markets, such as IBM,

ASDA, a corporate brand, synonymous with every day low pricing

Cisco, and Caterpillar, and in consumer markets where there is technical complexity, such as financial services. Companies such as HSBC, Prudential, and FirstDirect adopt a single name strategy. One of the advantages of this approach is that promotional investments are limited to one brand. However, the risk is similar to family branding where damage to one product or operational area can cause problems across the organization. For example, organizations such as Hitachi Corporation, Dell, Apple, Toshiba, Lenovo, and Fujitsu all recalled Sony batteries during the summer of 2006 on advice by Sony themselves. Sony announced that they were recalling certain batteries in laptops because they could fuse, as pieces of metal were left in their cells during the manufacturing process in Japan (Allison, 2006). The recall was said to cost up to $265m and involved approximately 6m batteries worldwide. The immediate impact on Sony's reputation was that they had to revise both income and profit forecasts.

Brand extensions are a way of capitalizing on the recognition, goodwill, and any positive associations of an established brand (Hem, Chernatony, and Iversen, 2003), and using the name to lever the brand into a new market. Mars successfully leveraged their confectionery bar into the ice cream market, and, in doing so, deseaonalized their sales by providing income in the summer when chocolate sales are normally at their lowest.

The attractiveness of brand extension is that time and money does not need to be spent building awareness or brand values. The key role for marketing communications is to position the new extended brand in the new market and give potential customers a reason to try it.

In the USA, Brandweek and TippingSprung run an annual survey of brand extensions. In 2007, PetSmart's PetHotel won best overall brand extension, joining Iams pet insurance, which won the same category in 2005. They found that not only are pet extensions very popular but those that are successful appear to be service-related (e.g. insurance, lodging) rather than product-driven.

go online

Visit the **Online Resource Centre** and follow the weblinks to Brandweek to learn more about current news in branding.

Successful brands are usually associated with a set of enduring brand values, often co-created by the brand and its loyal customers. These values provide the means through which brand extensions become possible, but understanding these values can be critical. For example, Harley-Davidson's (HD) values are essentially rugged and masculine, born out of the power and rumble associated with the motorbike. This had contributed to the development of the HD brand but was not understood or recognized when the chain of HD shops began selling wine coolers, baby clothes, and fragrances. This alienated its very loyal customers and the inappropriate products were withdrawn. Harley-Davidson had developed a strong brand by sticking consistently to making big, classic, US motorbikes and being proud about it. By moving away from this core activity and associating itself, through brand extensions, with categories that did not reflect the strong, masculine values, the brand alienated its customers and threatened the strength of the brand itself (Anon., 2006).

Licensing the trademark of an established brand and using it to develop another brand is proving to be another popular way of using brands. In return for a fee, one company permits another to use its trademark to promote other products over a defined period of time, in a defined area. Companies such as Disney use licensing because it provides revenue at virtually no cost and constitutes a form of marketing communications that takes the brand to new customers and markets. On the downside, brand licensing can proliferate the brand to the extent that the market is swamped with brand messages that fail to position the brand properly. In addition, problems with manufacturing or contractual compliance can lead to costly legal redress.

Licensing was for a long time a marketing activity that was the preserve of child-related toys, characters, and clothing. Now licensing is used increasingly with adult brands such as Gucci, Armani, Coca-Cola, and sports teams such as Manchester United, Formula One, and the Australian national cricket team.

Co-branding occurs when two established brands work together, on one product or service. The principle behind co-branding is that the combined power of the two brands generates increased consumer appeal and attraction. It also enables brands to move into markets and segments where they would normally have great difficulty in establishing themselves. Another reason for co-branding is that it enables organizations to share resources based on their different strengths. The co-branding arrangement between Microsoft and the UK charity NSPCC (National Society for the Prevention of Cruelty to Children) gives the charity access to the financial resources of Microsoft for marketing communications to reach new donors and raise awareness of their cause. Microsoft benefits from its association with a softer brand, one that helps reposition Microsoft as a brand that cares.

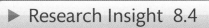

▶ Research Insight 8.4

To take your learning further, you might wish to read this influential paper.

Chernatony, L. de, Harris, F., and Dall'Olmo Riley, F. (2000), 'Added value: its nature, roles and sustainability', *European Journal of Marketing*, 34, 1–2, 39–56.

This paper explores the meaning of added value, a key concept in branding. Based on research involving 'brand experts', the paper examines what the term means and how it is interpreted by both academics and those who practice branding for a living.

 Visit the **Online Resource Centre** to read the abstract and access the full paper.

Brand Equity

Brand equity is a measure of the value of a brand. It is an assessment of a brand's wealth, sometimes referred to as goodwill. Financially, brands consist of their physical assets plus a sum that represents their reputation or goodwill, with the latter far exceeding the former. So, when Premier Foods, who own Branston sauces and Ambrosia Creamed Rice, paid £1.2bn to buy Rank Hovis McDougall (RHM), who own Oxo, Hovis, and Mr Kipling cakes, in 2006, they bought the physical assets and the reputation of RHM brands, the sales of which amount to £1.6bn annually (OFT, 2007).

Brand equity is considered important because of the increasing interest in trying to measure the return on promotional investments and pressure by various stakeholders to value brands for balance sheet purposes. A brand with a strong equity is more likely to be able to preserve its customer loyalty and so fend off competitor attacks.

There are two main views about how brand equity should be valued; from a financial and from a marketing perspective (Lasser, Mittal, and Sharma, 1995). The financial view is founded on a consideration of a brand's asset value that is based on the net value of all the cash the brand is expected to generate over its lifetime. The marketing perspective is grounded in the images, beliefs, and core associations consumers have about particular brands, and the degree of loyalty or retention a brand is able to sustain. Measures of market awareness, penetration, involvement, attitudes, and purchase intervals (frequency) are typical. In an attempt to overcome these two approaches, Feldwick (1996) suggests that there are three parts associated with brand equity:

▶ brand value, based on a financial and accounting base;

▶ brand strength, measuring the strength of a consumer's attachment to a brand; and

▶ brand description, represented by the specific attitudes customers have towards a brand.

Brand equity is strongly related to marketing and brand strategy because this type of measurement can help focus management on brand development. However, there is little agreement about what is to be measured and how and when it is measured. Ambler and Vakratsas (1998) argue that organizations should not seek a single set of measures simply because of the varying circumstances and contextual factors that impinge on brand performance. In reality, the measures used by most firms share many common elements.

go online

Visit the **Online Resource Centre** and complete Internet Activity 8.2 to learn more about luxury designer fashion brands and their differing marketing strategies.

Skills for Employment

> ▶▶ To work at 3M you need to be a free thinker and have plenty of drive and ambition. It's creativity and innovation that sets us apart as a company and so that's what we look for in our new graduate recruits. ◀◀
>
> Andrew Hicks, European Market Development Manager, 3M Display & Graphics
>
> Visit the **Online Resource Centre** to discover more tips and advice on skills for the workplace.

Chapter Summary

To consolidate your learning, the key points from this chapter are summarized below:

■ **Explain the nature and characteristics of products and describe the product/service spectrum.**

A product encompasses all the tangible and intangible attributes related not just to physical goods but also to services, ideas, people, places, experiences, and even a mix of these various elements. Anything that can be offered for use and consumption, in exchange for money or some other form of value, is referred to as a product. The product/service spectrum recognizes that many products combine physical goods with a service element.

- **Identify and describe the various types of products and explain particular concepts relating to the management of products, including the product lifecycle.**

  Consumer and business products are classified in different ways but both classifications are related to the way customers use them. Consumer products are bought to satisfy personal and family needs, and industrial and business products are bought either as a part of the business's operations or in order to make other products for resale. In order to meet the needs of different target markets, most organizations offer a range of products and services, which are grouped together in terms of product lines and product mix. Products are thought to move through a sequential pattern of development, referred to as the product lifecycle. It consists of five distinct stages, namely development, birth, growth, maturity, and decline. Each stage of the cycle represents a different set of market circumstances and customer expectations that need to be met with different strategies.

- **Explain the processes and issues associated with the development of new products and services and how they are adopted by markets.**

  The development of new products is complex and high risk, so organizations usually adopt a procedural approach. The procedure consists of several phases that enable progress to be monitored, test trials to be conducted, and the results analysed before there is any commitment to the market. The development of new services follows a similar staged process, whereby additional services are added to a core product until a point is reached where the service and the core product are integrated into a bundled offering. This is known as servitization. The processes of adoption and diffusion explain the way in which individuals adopt new products and the rate at which a market adopts an innovation.

- **Describe the principles of branding and explain the different types of brand.**

  Brands are products and services that have added value. Brands help customers to differentiate between the various offerings and to make associations with certain attributes or feelings with a particular brand. There are three main types of brands: manufacturer, distributor, and generic.

- **Understand ideas concerning brand associations and brand personalities**

  Brands are capable of triggering associations in the minds of consumers. These associations may sometimes enable consumers to construe a psychosocial meaning associated with a particular brand. This psychosocial element can be measured in terms of the associations consumers make in terms of five key dimensions: sincerity, excitement, competence, sophistication, and ruggedness. Brand personality provides a form of identity for consumers that expresses symbolic meaning for themselves and for others.

- **Explain the benefits that branding offers both customers and organizations.**

  Brands reduce risk and uncertainty in the buying process. They provide a snapshot of quality and positioning helping customers understand how one brand relates to another. As a result, branding helps consumers and organizations to buy and sell products easily, more efficiently, and relatively quickly.

- **Understand why the value of a brand is important and explain some of the issues associated with brand equity.**

  Brand equity is a measure of the value of a brand. It is an assessment of a brand's wealth, sometimes referred to as goodwill. Financially, brands consist of their physical assets plus a sum that represents their reputation or goodwill, with the latter far exceeding the former. There are two main views about how brand equity should be valued, namely financial and marketing perspectives.

Review Questions

1   Draw the spectrum of product/service combinations and briefly explain its main characteristics.

2   Identify the three levels that make up a product.

3   Describe the three types of convenience good and find examples to illustrate each of them.

4   Explain the difference between durable and non-durable consumer goods.

5   Write brief notes that explain each of the six types of business products.

6   Explain the product lifecycle and identify the key characteristics that make up each of the stages.

7   What are the main stages associated with the new product development process?

8   Why should marketers know about the process of adoption?

9   Why is branding important to consumers and to organizations?

10   Write brief notes explaining the two main views about brand equity.

Worksheet Summary

Visit the **Online Resource Centre** and complete Worksheet 8.1. This will help you learn about the process of developing a new product offering and devising a suitable new brand name.

Discussion Questions

1   Having read Case Insight 8.1, how would you advise 3M about whether it should launch a low-volume, high-priced product or a high-volume, low-priced product?

2   Consider the different types of consumer product and discuss how this knowledge can assist those responsible for marketing these products.

3   As a marketing assistant assigned to a major grocery brand (of your choice), you have noticed that your main brand competitors are pursuing marketing strategies that are significantly different from those of your brand. You have mentioned this to your manager who has asked you to prepare a briefing note explaining why this might be. As part of your note you have decided to refer to the role and impact of the product lifecycle on the strategies assigned to grocery brands. Your task, therefore, is to prepare a brief report in which you explain the nature of the product lifecycle and discuss how it might be used to improve your brand's marketing activities.

4   Discuss the view that it is not worth the huge investment necessary to develop new products, when it is just as easy to copy the market leader's products.

5   The celebrity chef Gordon Ramsay owns and runs a series of high-profile restaurants. He is opening restaurants worldwide, stars in his own ground-breaking chef/food-based TV programmes, and has a number of books and other business interests. Discuss the view that celebrities cannot be brands as they do not meet the common brand criteria.

Visit the **Online Resource Centre** and complete the Multiple Choice Questions to assess your knowledge of Chapter 8.

go online

References

Aaker, J. (1997), 'Dimensions of Brand Personality', *Journal of Marketing Research*, 34 (August), 347–56.

Allison, K. (2006), 'Apple recall deepens Sony battery crisis', *Financial Times*, 24 August, retrieve from www.ft.com/cms/s/c2eab782-3394-11db-981f-0000779e2340,_i_rssPage=6700d4e4-6714-11da-a650-0000779e2340.html, accessed December 2007.

Ambler, T., and Vakratsas, D. (1998), 'Why not let the agency decide the advertising', *Market Leader*, 1 (Spring), 32–7

Anon. (2006), http://brandfailures.blogspot.com/2006/11/extension-brand-failures-harley.html, accessed December 2007.

—(2009), 'Creative solution Finlandia', *Campaign*, 4 September, 24.

Arora, R., and Stoner, C. (2009), 'A mixed method approach to understanding brand personality', *Journal of Product & Brand Management*, 18, 4, 272–83.

Baines, T., Lightfoot, H., Peppard, J., Johnson, M., Tiwari, A. Shehab, E., and Swink, M. (2009), 'Towards an operations strategy for product-centric servitization', *International Journal of Operations & Production Management*, 29, 5, 494–519.

Barda, T. (2009), 'The science of appliances', *The Marketer* (May), 25–7.

Belk, R. (1988), 'Possessions and the Extended Self', *Journal of Consumer Research*, 15, 2, (September), 139–68.

Boehringer, C. (1996), 'How can you build a better brand?', *Pharmaceutical Marketing*, July, 35–6.

Chaffey, D., Mayer, R., Johnston, K., and Ellis-Chadwick, F. (2009), *Internet Marketing*, 4th edn, Harlow: FT/Prentice Hall.

Charles, G. (2009), 'Get to grips with the carbon agenda', *Marketing*, 30 September, 26–7.

Chernatony, L. de, and Dall'Olmo Riley, F. (1998), 'Defining a brand: beyond the literature with experts' interpretations', *Journal of Marketing Management*, 14, 417–43.

—Harris, F., and Dall'Olmo Riley, F. (2000), 'Added value: its nature, roles and sustainability', *European Journal of Marketing*, 34, 1/2, 39–56.

Clark, N. (2009), 'Knowing when to swing the axe', *Marketing*, 18 February, 30–1.

Doyle, P. (1993), 'Building successful brands: the strategic options', *Journal of Consumer Marketing*, 7, 2, 5–20.

Drucker, P. F. (1985), 'The discipline of innovation', *Harvard Business Review*, 63, May–June, 67–72.

Feick, L. F. and Price, L.L. (1987), 'The market maven: a diffuser of marketplace information', *Journal of Marketing*, 51 (January), 83–97.

Feldwick, P. (1996), 'What is brand equity anyway, and how do you measure it?', *Journal of Marketing Research*, 38, 2, 85–104.

Gatignon, H., and Robertson, T. S. (1985), 'A Propositional Inventory for New Diffusion Research', *Journal of Consumer Research*, 11 (March), 849–67.

Ghosh, S. (1998), 'Making business sense of the internet', *Harvard Business Review*, March–April, 127–35.

Gladwell, M. (2002), *The Tipping Point: How Little Things Can Make a Big Difference*. Boston: Back Bay Books.

Hem, L., Chernatony, L. de, and Iversen, M. (2003), 'Factors influencing successful brand extensions', *Journal of Marketing Management*, 19, 7–8, 781–806.

Keller, K.L. (1998), *Strategic Brand Management: Building, Measuring, and Managing Brand Equity*, Upper Saddle River, NJ: Prentice-Hall.

Lasser, W., Mittal, B., and Sharma, A. (1995), 'Measuring customer based brand equity', *Journal of Consumer Marketing*, 12, 4, 11–19.

Leistén, J., and Nilsson, M. (2009), *Crossing the chasm: Launching and re-launching in the Swedish mobile phone industry*, Dissertation, Jönköping International Business School retrieve from http://hj.diva-portal.org/smash/record.jsf?pid=diva2:158025, accessed 19 March 2009.

Linville, P., and Carlston, D. E. (1994). 'Social cognition of the self.' In P. G. Devine, D. L. Hamilton, and T. M. Ostrom (Eds), *Social Cognition: Impact on Social Psychology* (143–93). San Diego: Academic Press.

McCraken, G. (1986), 'Culture and consumption: a theoretical account of the structure and movement of the cultural meaning of consumer goods', *Journal of Consumer Research*, 13 (June), 71–84.

Möller, K., Rajala, R. and Westerlund, M,. (2008), Service innovation myopia? a new recipe for client/provider value creation, *California Management Review*, 50, 3 (Spring), 31–48.

OFT (2007), www.oft.gov.uk/shared_oft/mergers_eaoz/361227/premier.pdf, accessed 2 December 2007.

Ozer, M. (2003), 'Process implications of the use of the internet in new product development: a conceptual analysis', *Industrial Marketing Management*, 32, 6 (August), 517–30.

Phau, I., and Lau, K.C. (2001), 'Brand Personality and consumer self-expression: Single or dual carriageway?', *Journal of Brand Management*, 8, 6, 428–44.

Robinson, T., Clarke-Hill, C. M. and Clarkson, R. (2002), 'Differentiation through service: a perspective from the commodity chemicals sector', *The Service Industries Journal*, 22, 3, (July), 149–66.

Rogers, E.M. (1962), *Diffusion of Innovations*, 1st edn, New York: Free Press.

—(1983), *Diffusion of Innovations*, 3rd edn, New York: Free Press.

Shelton, R. (2009), 'Integrating product and service innovation', *Research Technology Management*, 52, 3 (May/June), 38–44.

Tiltman, D. (2006), 'In with the new', *Marketing*, 1 February, 37–8.

Trott, P. (2007), 'The long and difficult 13 year journey to the marketplace: a case study of Pfizer's Viagra', unpublished, Internal Working Case Study, University of Portsmouth, January.

Tynan, C., and McKechnie, S (2009), 'Experience Marketing: a review and reassessment', *Journal of Marketing Management*, 25, 5–6, 501–17.

Wood, L. (1990), 'The end of the product life cycle? Education says goodbye to an old friend', *Journal of Marketing Management*, 6, 2, 145–55.

9 | Price Decisions

Learning Outcomes

After reading this chapter, you will be able to:

▶ Define price, and understand its relationship with costs, quality, and value

▶ Explain the concept of price elasticity of demand

▶ Describe how consumers and customers perceive price

▶ Explain cost-, competitor-, demand-, and value-oriented approaches to pricing

▶ Understand how to price new offerings

▶ Understand the conditions under which a price war is more or less likely to ignite

▶ Explain how pricing operates in the business-to-business setting

▶ Case Insight 9.1

P&O Ferries now operates in competition with low-cost airlines as well as low-cost ferry operators. How does it make its pricing decisions? We speak to Simon Johnson to find out more.

Simon Johnson for P&O Ferries

P&O Ferries was part of the Peninsular and Oriental Steam Navigation Company. The company was taken over after 169 years of independence by Dubai Ports World (DPW), a large Middle Eastern ports operator, in 2006 for £3.92bn, at a 15% premium above the offer from Singapore's ports operator, PSA. P&O is probably best known in the UK for its operation of ferries between the UK, Belgium, France, the Netherlands, and Spain, but it also operates container terminals and logistics operations in over 100 ports, offering its new owner the opportunity to expand its global reach.

However, the ferry division's outlook had not been so rosy a couple of years earlier. By the end of 2004, the challenge facing our marketing team was substantial. Ferry travel was in long-term decline as a result of the competition from low-cost airlines and the reduction of duty-free incentives, which had driven the 'booze

P&O *Pride of Canterbury* ship
Source: P&O Ferries.

▶ Case Insight 9.1

cruise' day-tripper market—people who travelled from Dover in the UK to Calais in France for cheaper wine, beers, and spirits. In addition, the popularity of France as a holiday destination for the British was in decline. Ferry travel was starting to look outmoded. Annual passenger volumes for P&O on the Dover–Calais route dropped from around 10m in 2003 to just over 7m by 2005.

But this wasn't all. Within the ferry market itself, we faced stiff competition on key routes from a new breed of low-cost ferry operators such as Speedferries and Norfolk Line, which had resulted in significant over-capacity in the market. Rising crude oil prices, a declining advertising share of voice (as low-cost airlines spent more and more on advertising), and an ageing ferry fleet added to our woes.

The company research we carried out among existing and lapsed passengers indicated that the low-cost

airline model—of flexible, demand-based pricing and online ticket buying—had become widely understood by, and acceptable to, customers. To survive, we felt that P&O needed to do something similar with its own pricing approach. Research identified two key customer groups: the ferry *loyalists* who had stuck with the company despite intense competition and the *convertibles*, who could be persuaded to shift back to ferry travel having lapsed. We made the decision to develop a campaign with the key objective of delivering more customers, more cost-effectively, online. Advertising messages that seemed to resonate were that travelling by ferry was more relaxing and less hassle than travelling by air, and customers wanted a simplified pricing structure, demonstrating greater value for money.

If you were developing the ticket pricing policy, how would you design it to clearly demonstrate value for money?

Introduction

When did you last buy something you thought was really expensive? Did you wonder if others would think it was expensive too? Just when is a price expensive and when is it not? How do companies actually set prices? What procedures do they use? Clearly, price wars are self-defeating, so why do companies get involved in them in the first place? These are just some of the questions we set out to consider in this chapter.

Our understanding of pricing, and costing has been developed mainly through accounting practice. Economics has also contributed to our understanding of pricing through models of supply and demand, operating at an aggregate level (i.e. across all customers in an industry). Psychology has also contributed greatly to our understanding of customers' perceptions of prices. Marketing as a field integrates all these components to provide a better understanding of how the firm manipulates price to achieve higher profits and maintain satisfied customers.

In this chapter, we provide an insight into how customers respond to price changes, what economists call **price elasticity** of demand. We consider pricing decisions in relation to developing differentiated or low-cost approaches and the pricing of services. As a topic, pricing is perhaps the most difficult component of the marketing mix to understand because the price of a good is linked to the cost of all the many and various elements that come together to make a particular product or service. The marketing manager seldom controls costs and prices of a particular product, and usually refers to the accounting department, or marketing controller, to set prices for particular goods and services.

We also provide an indication of how to set prices for new products and services, and how to change prices to existing products and services. As making price changes for products and services often invokes a response from competitors, who may also drop their prices, we include a section on how to avoid competitive price wars. In some markets, a company does not control its own price setting, and so we also consider in this chapter some of the markets where prices are regulated by government. Finally, we consider briefly how the internet is affecting pricing, particularly in the newly formed consumer-to-consumer market.

The Concept of Pricing and Cost

Pricing

Pricing is a very complex component of the marketing mix. The term **price** has come to encompass any and all of the following meanings: 'the amount of money expected, required, or given in payment for something; something expended or endured in order to achieve an objective; the odds in betting and also archaic value; worth' (Concise Oxford English Dictionary, 2010). In marketing terms, we consider price as the amount the customer has to pay or exchange to receive a good or service. For example, when purchasing a McDonald's happy meal for children (incorporating a burger, small fries, drinks and a toy), the price exchanged for the meal might be say $1.29, £1.99, 135 rupees, or 20 yuan depending on where you live. The £1.99 element is the price, the assigned numerical monetary worth of the hamburger. However, this notion of pricing a good or service is often confused with a number of other key concepts used in marketing when discussing how and why we set pricing levels, particularly cost and value.

go online

Visit the **Online Resource Centre** and follow the weblink to the Professional Pricing Society (PPS) to learn more about pricing and the pricing profession.

Proposition Costs

To price an offering properly, we need some idea of what the offering costs us to make, produce, or buy. Cost represents the total money, time, and resources sacrificed to produce or acquire a good or service. For example, the costs incurred to produce the McDonald's hamburger meal discussed above will include the cost of heat and light in the restaurant, advertising and sales promotion costs, costs of rent or of the mortgage interest accrued from owning the restaurant, management and staffing costs, and the franchise fees paid to McDonald's central headquarters to cover training, management, and marketing. Furthermore, there are costs associated with the distribution of the product components to, and from, farms and other catering suppliers to the restaurants. There are the costs of computer systems and purchasing systems. There are the costs of the packaging, bags, and extras like gifts and toys.

▶ **Table 9.1** Examples of fixed and variable costs

Fixed costs	Variable costs
Manufacturing plant and equipment (in a business selling product)	Equipment servicing costs
Office buildings	Energy costs
Cars and other vehicles	Mileage allowances
Salaries	Overtime and bonus payments
Professional service fees (e.g. legal)	Professional services fees (e.g. legal) in a business with a strong regulatory regime (e.g. pharmaceuticals)

Typically, a firm will determine what their **fixed costs** are, and what their **variable costs** are for each proposition. These items vary for individual industries but Table 9.1 provides some indication of what these are in general. Fixed costs are costs that do not vary according to the number of units of goods made or services sold, so are independent of sales volume. In a McDonald's restaurant this could include the cost of heating and lighting, rent, and staffing costs. In contrast, variable costs vary according to the number of units of goods made or services sold. For example, with the production of McDonald's hamburger meals, when sales and demand decrease, fewer raw goods such as hamburger ingredients, product packaging, and novelty items such as toys are required, so less spending on raw materials occurs. However, when sales increase, more raw materials are used and spending rises.

The Relationship between Pricing and Proposition Costs

The relationship between price and costs is important because costs should be substantially less than the price assigned to a proposition, otherwise the firm will not sell sufficient units to obtain sufficient revenues to cover costs and make long-term profits (see equations below).

$$\text{Total Revenue} = \text{Volume Sold} \times \text{Unit Price.}$$
$$\text{Profit} = \text{Total Revenue} - \text{Total Costs.}$$

The price at which a proposition is set is strategically important because increases in price have a disproportionately positive effect on profits and decreases in price have a disproportionately negative effect on profits. For example, in one study (Marn and Rosiello, 1992) it was identified that a:

▶ 1% improvement in price brings an 11.1% improvement in operating profit;

▶ 1% improvement in variable costs only brings a 7.8% improvement in operating profit;

▶ 1% improvement in volume sales brings a 3.3% improvement in operating profit; and

▶ 1% improvement in fixed costs brings only a 2.3% improvement in operating profits.

Put another way, a 1% profit increase, where the normal profit on sales is 10%, is equivalent to a 10% gain on return on investment, and a 1% profit increase where the normal profit on sales is 5% represents a 20% improvement on return on investment (Walker, 1967). Therefore, where we can, we should be looking to increase prices every time.

However, deciding how to price a proposition is not simple. Take the example presented earlier for McDonald's. A firm like McDonald's might well have 100 products on any one restaurant menu (including meals, individual burgers, ice creams, drinks, salads, etc.) in any one country. If we bear in mind that different countries have slightly different menus to incorporate food products for local tastes (for example, the Chicken Maharaja Mac™ in India where beef and pork are not eaten, and the McArabia™ Grilled Kofta available in Jordan), then we can imagine that, worldwide, McDonald's must have an enormous menu of products, despite the appearance of standardization. But how do we cost and price each individual product? The first step is to determine costs but, in any one restaurant, how do we allocate fixed costs such as heat and light, rent and tax, to each of the individual products sold? And once we've allocated the fixed costs, how do we determine the variable costs for each product? Once we've allocated fixed costs and determined the variable costs associated with a product, we set the initial price of a product. But costs of components, such as heat and light, and other costs change constantly. How do we determine whether or not we need to change our prices on any one item after we've set them because of the changes in component costs? After all, we can't keep changing prices every single time a component cost changes. So, at what point do we decide to change a product price?

From this short example, we can see that determining a product's cost is a complex task. Because of the cost of information, to increase the accuracy of the cost data, we need to spend more time collecting and analysing the data. Determining costs is an exercise where we trade-off accuracy with the benefits and costs of data collection, storage, and processing (Babad and Balachandran, 1993). Determining costs and prices is made more difficult when organizations are divided into separate profit centres, selling on to other divisions within the same company, especially when these adopt inefficient **transfer pricing** mechanisms (Ward, 1993). For example, Airbus, the airline company owned by parent EADS (European Aeronautic Defence and Space Company), assembles its planes using parts made in several European countries. When these parts are made by the respective divisions, they are sold on using a process known as transfer pricing to the main holding company, which assembles the plane from its component parts. But it's not just costs that matter; we might observe changes in demand for our products, as customers' desires change. In setting pricing levels, we must also consider our customers' perceptions of prices.

Customer Perceptions of Price, Quality, and Value

Researchers are concerned with how individuals react to the way products are priced, questioning how consumers perceive prices and why they perceive them as they do. Here, we take into account individual perceptions of proposition quality and value and their relationship to customer response to the pricing levels assigned to a product offering.

Proposition Quality

Quality is a very important concept when considering proposition pricing levels. Quality is defined as 'the standard of something as measured against other things of a similar kind; general excellence; archaic high social standing' (Concise Oxford English Dictionary, 2010). The International Organization for Standardization has defined quality as the 'degree to which a set of inherent characteristic fulfils requirements' (ISO 9000). In this context, quality of both goods and services relates to standards to which that product or service performs as a need-satisfier. For example, a very high-quality car will more than satisfy both our aesthetic needs for aerodynamic beauty and our ego and functional needs for high-performance road handling, speed, and power. But quality is not a single standard in a product or service. It encompasses many standards as there are many levels at which our needs might or might not be satisfied.

Quality is multifaceted (i.e. different functional and non-functional needs) and multilayered (i.e. differing levels or intensities of satisfaction). The American Society for Quality defines quality as a subjective term, suggesting that each person has his or her own definition of quality. So, we prefer to talk of 'perceived quality'. We find consumers have differing views of the quality of the product offering they have purchased, e.g. some might be very dissatisfied, and some highly satisfied, with exactly the same product offering.

The Relationship between Quality and Pricing Levels

The relationship between price and perceived quality is complex. There is an assumption that as price increases so does quality, and that, in general, price reflects quality. But this is not always the case. For example, 'snob' consumers in the fashion clothing and perfume sectors (see Amaldoss and Jain, 2005; Yeoman and McMahon-Beattie, 2006) assume that higher prices reflect higher quality garments and fragrances. The general idea that price indicates quality (**perceived quality**) assumes that the prices are objectively determined by the interaction of supply and demand in competitive markets (Sjolander, 1992). In truth, people within firms set prices, often dispassionately, so as to try to obtain the maximum profit possible. Various studies conducted to determine whether or not price bears a relation to quality have found that a general price–perceived quality relationship does not, in fact, exist (Zeithaml, 1988; Sjolander, 1992), except perhaps for wine and perfume (Zeithaml, 1988). However, a study specifically designed to understand the relationship between price and quality in a world where price information is increasingly available online (Boyle and Lathrop, 2009) has found that US consumers believe that higher prices correspond with higher quality for **consumer durables** (e.g. cars, televisions), but are less likely to perceive this with non-durables (e.g. foodstuffs).

The Relationship between Perceived Value, Product Quality, and Pricing Levels

Value is defined as 'the regard that something is held to deserve; importance or worth; material or monetary worth; the worth of something compared to its price; at £12.50 the book is good value' (Concise Oxford English Dictionary, 2010). In marketing terms, value refers to what we get for what we pay. It is often expressed as the equation:

$$\text{Value} = \frac{\text{quality}}{\text{price}}$$

This approach to value indicates that to increase a customer's perception of the value of a product offering, we must either lower the price, or increase the quality. In some ways, this is a simplistic concept of value. There are other intervening effects on the value we perceive a proposition to hold. Sometimes our initial assessment is faulty, or needs to be reconsidered. Sometimes as customers we are not skilled to recognize or evaluate quality, e.g. the average wine drinker would not regard themselves as knowledgeable about wine and so might find it hard to work out the product quality.

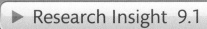

▶ Research Insight 9.1

To take your learning further, you might wish to read this influential paper.

Zeithaml, V. A. (1988), 'Consumer perceptions of price, quality and value: a means–end model and synthesis of evidence', *Journal of Marketing*, 52 (July), 2–22.

This article was the first to provide evidence into how pricing relates to costs, quality, and value from a customer perspective. The authors suggest marketers research customer understanding of quality and how they measure it, over time in both monetary and non-monetary terms in order to develop propositions of increasing customer value.

 Visit the **Online Resource Centre** to read the abstract and access the full paper.

Measuring Customer Price Perceptions

One way of determining how customers perceive prices is to ask them. In an online consumer survey conducted at Bentley College and Emory University in the USA (Sheth, Sisodia, and Barbulescu, 2006), when American consumers were asked to provide their perceptions of price (i.e. positive, negative, or neutral) across a range of product and service categories, they had strongly negative perceptions of the price of replacement razor cartridges and prescription drugs with 53% having negative perceptions of price. By contrast, only around 8% had negative perceptions about the price of computers. Airline ticket pricing was fairly poorly regarded, with 27% of the sample having negative perceptions. Most consumers seemed to have neutral opinions on household appliances, possibly indicating either that they have relatively little experience of shopping in this field and/or that they are not conscious of the prices charged for these items. The point is that we hold certain prices in our minds for certain items and when companies deviate from those prices we can perceive them to be unfair. For marketers the key question is what influences how customers perceive prices. We turn to this important topic next.

External Influences on Customer Price Perceptions

Reference Prices

Why do consumers see some prices as fairer than others and some products as of higher value than others? If we are to be able to price a good or service according to customer needs, we must have some idea of what customers think is a fair price to pay for that good or service, or what they expect to pay, or what they think others might pay.

Marketers call these prices **reference prices**. There is usually a price band that customers judge the purchase price of goods and services against in their own minds. Reference prices can be viewed as predictive price expectations in the consumers' own minds, brought about through prior experience with those products and services or through word-of-mouth discussions with others. They depend on brand choice, purchase quantity, purchase timing (e.g. products bought at Christmas time in West European markets tend to be more expensive than at other times), price history, promotion history, the shop visit history, whether or not the visit was planned, the store choice, whether or not the price was well advertised, whether or not the product is frequently purchased, whether there are different components of the product or service that make it easy to understand the pricing structure, and customer characteristics such as price sensitivity, brand loyalty, and so on. Reference prices do vary across consumers and so there is a clear opportunity to segment and target consumers on the basis of reference price (Mazumdar, Raj, and Sinha, 2005). Think about it yourself. How much would you be prepared to pay for a haircut? A woman's cut-and-blow-dry haircut might cost between £40 and £100. So a salon charging £4 for a woman's haircut and another charging £400 would catch her eye. She probably would not trust the first place with a price of £4. She might well think that they would damage her hair or make a poor job of it. Equally, the £400 haircut, a haircut at a celebrity price, would have to be pretty special. So, the woman's reference price band for a haircut in the UK is around £40–100 or so and a man's is around £10–50.

But, in addition to deciding whether or not a price is fair (how products and services ought to be priced), or what they expect to pay (expectation-based pricing) or what significant others would pay (so-called aspirational pricing), we also need to know whether or not customers are actually conscious of prices in a particular category or not. Most people do not have as good a knowledge of prices as they think. Think of your mum and dad or a friend or a relative significantly older than you. Do they know the ticket price for a gig? Do you know the price of a good-quality dining table? As an industrial buyer, how much should you pay for the installation and servicing of a new HR computer system, say Peoplesoft, designed to keep records for about 5,000 staff? We use these examples to indicate that our experience of prices contributes to what we know about reference prices, but also to explain that our experience, by its very nature, is limited to what we have done in the past. This is nicely illustrated by the American TV gameshow, *The Price is Right*, where contestants very often do not know the prices of many common household items (Anderson and Simester, 2003). In fact, there are certain groups of grocery items that supermarket shoppers are more likely to know, and it is these items that supermarkets frequently discount, and advertise, to attract shoppers, not the other lesser known items, where prices may even be raised. Examples include everyday items such as bread, milk, and tins of baked beans. Shoppers assume that because these items are discounted, all other items must be similarly discounted. So, if people do not know the prices of goods and services, how can they possibly determine whether or not those prices are fair or reasonable?

To be fair to grocery shoppers, estimating reference prices is subject to seasonality for items such as flowers, fruit, and vegetables (particularly the more exotic varieties from around the world), quality and sizes of items are not universal across companies' offerings, product designs vary over time, and customers may not purchase some goods frequently (Anderson and Simester, 2003). Instead, when customers assess prices, they estimate value using **pricing cues**, because they do not always know the true cost and price of the item that they are purchasing. These pricing cues include sale signs, odd-number pricing, the purchase context, and price bundling and rebates.

Sale Signs

Sale signs act as cues by indicating to a potential customer that there is a bargain to be had. This entices the customer to purchase because it also suggests to the buyer that the item is desirable and so may be bought by another customer if you are not quick enough to buy it. The sale sign uses one of the most persuasive devices known in marketing, the notion of scarcity. The more scarce we perceive a product or service to be, the more we are likely to want it (Cialdini, 1993), often regardless of whether we even need it.

Odd-Number Pricing

Another pricing cue is the use of odd-number endings, prices that end in nine. Have you ever wondered why the Sony PlayStation you bought was say $199, or £149, or 749 (Polish) zloty? Why not simply round it up to $200, £150, or 750 zloty? According to Anderson and Simester (2003), raising the price of a woman's dress in a national mail order catalogue from $34 to $39 increased demand by 33% but demand remained unchanged when the price was raised to $44! The question is why did the increase in demand take place when there was an increase in price? It is unlikely that there would have been such an increase if the item had been priced at $38. The reason for this is that we perceive the first price as relative to a reference price of £30 (which is £33 rounded down to the nearest unit of ten) and more expensive, whereas the second price of $39 we perceive as cheaper than a reference price of $40 (which we rounded up to the nearest ten). (See Market Insight 9.1.)

▶ Market Insight 9.1

Pricing Illusions

Consider the situation where you are looking for a pair of sunglasses while shopping in the airport lounge. Let's say you are flying to Thailand for your holidays and you are shopping at Frankfurt or Heathrow airport. You see two particular pairs of sunglasses at, say, Sunglass Hut, that you consider buying, Pair A and B. Both are on sale and both show the original and new discounted prices on their price tickets as shown in Table 9.2. Which pair of sunglasses would you consider is the better bargain at the new discounted price, Pair A or Pair B? Don't think about it for too long, just decide which you think offers the best discounted price.

Seeing is deceiving, for pricing at least

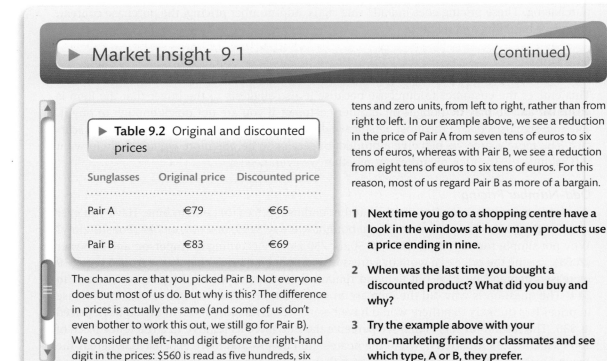

▶ Market Insight 9.1   (continued)

▶ **Table 9.2** Original and discounted prices

Sunglasses	Original price	Discounted price
Pair A	€79	€65
Pair B	€83	€69

The chances are that you picked Pair B. Not everyone does but most of us do. But why is this? The difference in prices is actually the same (and some of us don't even bother to work this out, we still go for Pair B). We consider the left-hand digit before the right-hand digit in the prices: $560 is read as five hundreds, six

tens and zero units, from left to right, rather than from right to left. In our example above, we see a reduction in the price of Pair A from seven tens of euros to six tens of euros, whereas with Pair B, we see a reduction from eight tens of euros to six tens of euros. For this reason, most of us regard Pair B as more of a bargain.

1 Next time you go to a shopping centre have a look in the windows at how many products use a price ending in nine.

2 When was the last time you bought a discounted product? What did you buy and why?

3 Try the example above with your non-marketing friends or classmates and see which type, A or B, they prefer.

Purchase Context in Pricing

Another important element in pricing is the purchase context. In some cases, the purchase context can be used as a frame of reference by the customer in determining prices. Confused. com, an insurance comparison website, used this technique when advertising the message, 'save a pair of jeans on your car insurance', indicating customers could get a cheaper deal by using their website and still buy a pair of jeans with the difference saved. Our perception of risk is greater if we are continually reminded of it than if we consider it only at the point of purchase. For example, gyms use the technique of charging a monthly fee, even though they often demand a one-year membership agreement, for precisely this reason. In fact, a monthly price (instead of an annual, semi-annual, or quarterly charge) drives a higher level of gym attendance as customers are more regularly reminded of their purchase. So, the way you set your price does not just influence demand but it also drives how buyers use your product and service (Gourville and Soman, 2002).

Research shows that if we are exposed to higher priced items first, our reference prices are anchored at the higher level, whereas if we are exposed to lower prices, they are anchored at the lower level (Smith and Nagle, 1995). Consequently, salespeople should show customers around product ranges by starting with products in descending price order rather than ascending price order. For example, in a car showroom we should show the BMW 7 series first then take the customer to the 3 series rather than vice versa. It makes sense also to redesign catalogues to include more expensive items in the earlier pages (Nunes and Boatwright, 2001) because of this effect.

Interestingly enough, location also has an impact on price perceptions. For example, we are prepared to pay more for a drink of, say, Absolut vodka from the hotel mini-bar than we are from the hotel bar or for an equivalent measure from a bottle from the supermarket. This indicates the context-specific nature of price perceptions.

go online

Visit the **Online Resource Centre** and complete Internet Activity 9.1 to learn more about the impact the purchase context (e.g., time of day, week, online versus telephone booking etc.) has on the pricing of budget airline services.

Price Bundling and Rebates

Marketers highlight their prices to customers through bundling other products, services, and gains into an offering to make the price look more reasonable. For example, magazines frequently bundle CDs/DVDs and other gifts in with the magazine to make it appear more attractive, which is called **pure price bundling**. Sunday newspapers (in Britain, France, Thailand, Sweden) often contain numerous supplements (e.g. fashion, entertainment, property) to make the newspaper appear greater value for money. New cars are often sold with three years' warranty on parts to provide the customer with the peace of mind of knowing that they should not have to pay for any car parts to be repaired within the period of the warranty. Mobile phone manufacturers offer monthly price packages with international call packages, and text message packages bundled in with different types of account, and these bundles are also available independently (so-called **mixed price bundling**).

But price bundles do not always mean the company giving the customer other products or services. We might simply be offered a rebate, i.e. given money back. Car manufacturers like Ford have often used rebates to encourage customers to move from considering less expensive base models to upgrade to higher priced models. The lost revenues from purchases of the lower priced models are often offset by the purchases of the higher priced models even after the rebate (Cross and Dixit, 2005). Credit card companies often offer cashback schemes on money spent on their credit cards, as a proportion of the total amount spent.

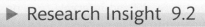

▶ Research Insight 9.2

To take your learning further, you might wish to read this influential paper.

Smith, G. E., and Nagle, T. T. (1995), 'Frames of reference and buyers' perceptions of price and value', *California Management Review*, 38, 1, 98–116.

A useful article summarizing in a practical way the psychological basis of how customers form frames of reference for prices, how they perceive risk, how current and past prices affect perceptions, the importance of context on price perception, and of odd price endings, and the implications that they have for marketing practice.

 Visit the **Online Resource Centre** to read the abstract and access the full paper.

Pricing Objectives

How a company prices its products depends on what its pricing objectives are. Typically, these can be financial with offerings priced to maximize profit or sales or to achieve a satisfactory level of profits or sales, or a particular return on investment. Companies may price by offering discounts for quick payment. A firm's pricing objectives could be marketing-based, e.g. pricing to achieve a particular market share (so-called market penetration pricing), or to position the brand so that it is perceived to be of a certain quality. Sometimes companies price their products and services just to survive, e.g. pricing to discourage new competitors from entering the market by pricing products and services at a lower rate or lowering prices to maintain sales volumes when competitors lower their prices. Alternatively, a company might price to avoid price wars, maintaining prices at levels similar to its competitors, so-called competitor-oriented pricing. Finally, a company may price to achieve certain social goals. There are many ways in which a company can price its products and services. The important consideration is whether or not the pricing objective is reasonable and measurable. Often companies pursue more than one pricing objective simultaneously and some pricing objectives may be incompatible with each other. For example, pricing to increase cash flow by offering quick payment discounts is not compatible with maximizing profitability. It is, however, compatible with obtaining a satisfactory profitability, so long as the discounts offered are not greater than the cost of goods sold.

Pricing Approaches

Price-setting depends on various factors, including how price affects demand, how sales revenue is linked to price, how cost is linked to price, and how investment costs are linked to price (Doyle, 2000). Price setting also depends on how sales revenue relates to price. Raising prices tends to increase revenue up to a point, but then further increases in unit price produce declining increases in revenue. The relationship between price and sales revenue corresponds to the bell curve shape (see Figure 9.1).

Costs also tend to vary with price in a linear fashion as higher prices reduce volume sales producing lower total costs (see Figure 9.2). Third, investment costs, including both **working capital** and **fixed capital** (cost of plant and machinery etc.), also affect prices, with lower prices tending to require higher sales volume targets to be set, with correspondingly higher levels of investment. Investments tend to be made at fixed intervals (e.g. on a six-monthly cycle), with investment costs dropping compared to price increases (and sales volumes decreases) and so the relationship between investment and price looks something like a downward staircase (see Figure 9.3).

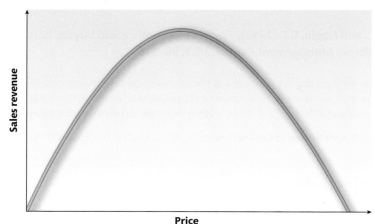

Figure 9.1

How price relates to sales revenue

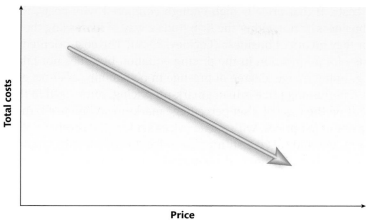

Figure 9.2
How price relates to total costs

Figure 9.3
How price relates to investment costs

Broadly, there are four types of pricing approaches, each of which is described in the following sections:

1 the cost-oriented approach (with prices set based on costs);

2 the demand-oriented approach (with prices set based on price sensitivity and levels of demand);

3 the competitor-oriented approach (with prices set based on competitors' prices); and

4 the value-oriented approach (with prices set based on what customers believe to offer value).

The Cost-Oriented Approach

Considered to be the original theory of pricing, this approach advances the idea that the most important element of pricing is the cost of the component resources that combine to make up the product. So, the marketer sells output at the highest price possible, regardless of the firm's own preference or costs. If that price is high enough compared with costs, the firm earns a profit and stays in business. If not, either the firm finds a way of increasing the price or lowering costs or both, or they go out of business (Lockley, 1949). The cost-oriented approach considers the total costs of a proposition in the pricing equation but does not take into account non-cost factors, e.g. brand image, degree of prestige in ownership, or effort expended.

One approach to determining price is using mark-up pricing, often used in the retail sector. This method operates on the base of a set percentage mark-up. When used, the cost-oriented method leads to the use of list prices, with single prices set for all customers. We simply add a mark-up to the cost of X% and this constitutes the price. In British supermarket retailing the mark-up is around 6–8%, but in American supermarket retailing is often even less at around 4% or less. Mark-ups on wine served in restaurants are typically between 200% and 300%. The cost-oriented approach requires us first to determine the price we set that just covers our costs. This is known as break-even pricing. It represents the point at which our total costs and our total revenues are exactly equal.

To exemplify the concept of mark-up pricing further, we can use the example of a computer company selling high-quality laptop computers, at a cost of £1,000 per unit to make. Suppose the computer company uses the mark-up pricing method and adds 40% (or 0.4 when expressed as a decimal figure between 0 and 1). The final price set would be given by the equation below:

$$\text{Price} = \frac{\text{unit item cost}}{1 - \text{mark-up}} = \frac{£1,000}{(1 - 0.4)} = £1,667$$

If we consider that in a supply chain there is typically more than one customer interaction, as we move along the supply chain, each partner takes their share, adding to the costs and the final selling price. So a toy, say a teddy bear, bought by a UK importer from a Chinese toy manufacturer based in Hong Kong, typically free on board (which means all costs after placing onto the ship are borne by the importer), brought to Britain, warehoused, stored, financed, and eventually sold at £5.90 (in cases of 12), may well have cost around £4.50 to that importer. The eventual retail price would probably be around the £10 retail price point, i.e. £9.99. The mark-up here for the retailer is 69% = (£9.99 – £5.90)/£5.90. The mark-up for the importer is much lower at 31% = (£5.90 – £4.50)/(£4.50). However, the importer may well buy a container of the teddy bears, comprising say 4,800 individual teddy bears (400 boxes, each containing 12 units), and sell these over three months between August until October for the Christmas retail season. The retailer, by contrast, may sell only six boxes of 12 during the period October until December, so the retailer has to make a higher profit on a smaller volume with a wider range of items to give the customer some choice.

The cost-oriented approach does not always mean that we use a mark-up pricing approach. In some industries, prices are set based on fixed formulae, which are set with a supplier's costs in mind. For example, in the ethical prescription pharmaceutical industry, in France, Italy, and Spain, government-fixed formulae dictate prices with limited scope for pharmaceutical manufacturers to negotiate, whereas in the UK and Germany, the tradition has been for the country's national health authorities not to fix individual product prices but to set an overall level of profitability with which the pharmaceutical manufacturer must agree, based on a submission of their costs (Attridge, 2003).

The Demand-Oriented Approach

With the demand approach to pricing, the firm sets prices according to how much customers are prepared to pay. One of the best-known types of companies to operate this approach to pricing is the airline industry, where different groups of customers pay different amounts for airline seats with varying levels of service attached. Most airline companies operate three types of cabin service. Emirates, for instance, offers First Class, Business Class, and Economy with the following core benefits:

▶ First Class—offers wide aisles and individualized comfortable sleeper seats (and separate cabins with their own mini-bar and vanity desk on selected long-haul flights), seven-course meals on long-haul flights, a selection of fine wines, an award winning in-flight entertainment service, complimentary limousine transfer service, and free entry into the Emirates Lounge executive club at selected airports.

▶ Business Class—offers complimentary limousine transfer service, enhanced legroom between seats (but less than First Class), double seating arrangements, luxury seating transforming into a lie flat bed, an award-winning in-flight entertainment service (but with fewer options than First Class), five-course meals on long-haul flights, and free entry into the Emirates Lounge executive club at selected airports.

▶ Economy Class—comfortable seating with seating arrangements in banks of three to five seats, reclining seating, and an award-winning in-flight individual entertainment service.

Other benefits, including premier access through immigration lanes, instant seat upgrades and priority seats, are available through the Emirates membership and loyalty scheme, which has three tiers of membership, blue, silver and gold, dependent on the number of miles a passenger has flown with the carrier. By contrast, the low-cost carriers in Europe, such as Ryanair and easyJet, operate fairly sophisticated yield management systems, which set prices to ensure planes operate at full capacity but usually price tickets at substantially less than the national airline carriers such as British Airways, Lufthansa, Air France, and so on, at least in the period when tickets first become available. The result is a low-margin, yield-based pricing policy.

Companies operating a demand pricing policy should be wary of overcharging their customers, particularly where customers' requests are urgent. Examples include emergency purchases such as funeral services, or prescription pharmaceutical products for life-threatening diseases. When companies do set charges that are perceived to be unfair, they are liable to claims of **price gouging**. In the pharmaceutical industry, allegations of so-called price gouging are frequent (Hartley, 1993; Spinello, 1992), because, unlike most industries, there are few or no alternative brands available. It is for this reason that governments regulate prices of pharmaceutical products, to ensure that those products reach all patients, not only those who can personally afford to pay for them privately.

The Competitor-Oriented Approach

With this approach, companies set prices based on competitors' prices, the so-called going rate. This is also called 'me-too' pricing. The advantage of this approach is that when your prices are lower than your competitors, customers are more likely to purchase from you, providing that they know that your prices are lower, which is not always the case. (See Market Insight 9.2.)

▶ Market Insight 9.2

Tesco's Price Check Service

The leading British supermarket Tesco now retails grocery products around the world (e.g. in Japan, in Hungary, in Thailand with a local partner, as Tesco Lotus, and in the USA as Fresh and Easy). In Britain, it has by far the largest market share of the retail grocery market with around 25.7% of the food retail market by value in 2008, against its nearest competitors' shares of 13.7% (ASDA Wal-Mart), 12.9% (Sainsbury's), and 9.6% (Morrisons). In order to remain competitive,

Tesco conducts online mystery shopping exercises, where market researchers obtain competitors' product pricing information, to compare the prices of baskets of items against the prices charged by its key competitors (i.e. ASDA Wal-Mart and Sainsbury's) for equivalent baskets. Tesco call the scheme Tesco Price Check and make the results of the exercise available to its customers online, with a facility allowing customers to search the website for the cheapest store on any one particular item.

Tesco's Price Check comparison service, available online

Source: Courtesy of Tesco Stores Limited.

▶ Market Insight 9.2

In order to defend its low-price image and reputation, Tesco has resorted in the past to taking ASDA Wal-Mart, its main supermarket rival, to the Advertising Standards Authority (ASA), over ASDA's claim to be 'officially Britain's lowest priced supermarket'. The marketspace to be perceived by supermarket customers as offering the best value is, therefore, hotly contested. The point, however, is do you have to be the lowest priced supermarket to offer the best value?

Sources: Barnes (2004); Mintel (2009); www.tesco.com/price_check_search.

1 Do you think the cost of collecting all this competitor data on prices is justified commercially? Why?

2 How might Tesco use this price data in determining their own prices? What is the difference between promotional pricing and everyday low pricing and when might you use each one?

3 What other data do Tesco need to determine how customers perceive competing prices from different supermarkets?

Esso, the global oil company and petrol retailer, for many years offered a scheme that it called Price Watch where it would give customers refunds of the petrol price difference within a specified distance if they could buy cheaper petrol at a competing garage. The scheme was designed to cement the value proposition firmly in customers' minds. The problem has been that Esso can no longer match supermarkets on petrol prices because the supermarkets have lower storage and distribution costs (Lewis, 2001).

Price guarantee schemes like the one outlined above are aimed at providing customers with the peace of mind of knowing that the company they are purchasing from is competitive in price. In reality, such schemes are often expensive to operate as they require continuous monitoring of the full range of competitors' prices, and a strong focus on cost control to maintain those competitive prices in the first place. Adopting a competitor-oriented pricing strategy can, and often does, lead to price wars. But supermarket retailing is highly competitive in most major markets around the world, as there are frequently relatively few players in the market. In Australia, supermarket retailing is dominated by Coles and Woolworths/Safeway. When Coles introduced everyday low pricing, Woolworths introduced its 'price roll back' scheme, particularly in relation to milk and petrol prices (Sankey, 2003).

Price wars occur when competitors' pricing policies are almost exclusively focused on competitors rather than customers, when price is pushed downwards, and when pricing results in interactions between competitors that lead to unsustainable prices. In a review of more than 1,000 price wars, researchers found that price wars could usually be averted if companies responded to market-based, firm-based, product-based, and consumer-based early warning signals. In other words, some firms under certain circumstances within certain industries were more susceptible to price wars than others (see Market Insight 9.3; Table 9.3).

▶ Research Insight 9.3

To take your learning further, you might wish to read this influential paper.

Heil, O. P., and Helsen, K. (2001), 'Toward an understanding of price wars: their nature and how they erupt', *International Journal of Research in Marketing*, 18, 83–98.

The above article uniquely covers a very important topic of considerable interest to practitioners; a topic that has received surprisingly little attention in the academic marketing literature. Price wars are defined by how they can be characterized when they do happen, and what to look out for before they are about to happen in order for marketers to avoid cut-throat price competition.

@ Visit the **Online Resource Centre** to read the abstract and access the full paper.

▶ Market Insight 9.3

Harry Potter Price Magic!

The Harry Potter series has been a global phenomenon, making its author, J. K. Rowling, a worldwide celebrity and the inspiration behind what by 2009 has become a $4bn brand. Over 450 million copies of the seven books in the series have been sold around the world, sparking successful Blockbuster film tie-in movies for all seven instalments. *The Sunday Times* rich list placed Rowling as the 101st richest person in Britain in 2009 with a personal fortune of £499m from books and film rights—not bad for a single parent from Edinburgh! When the seventh and final book in the Harry Potter series, *Harry Potter and the Deathly Hallows* was released in 2007, everyone expected it to sell a lot of copies. But no one expected it to sell 11m copies in the UK and the USA alone in the first 24 hours! The need to own a copy among young and old readers alike meant huge crowds of people queuing at supermarkets and bookshops around the world.

The prospect of so many customers queuing up was too much for many supermarkets. They either worried

▶ Market Insight 9.3

that other supermarkets might steal their customers or were keen themselves to steal a march on their competitors by selling the book at a discount price to lure customers to buy their weekly shop. Despite the £17.99 recommended retailer price suggested by the publisher Bloomsbury, ASDA discounted the book to £5.00 in Britain after initially offering a pre-order price of £8.87. Morrisons swiftly followed suit, selling its copies at £4.99 and Tesco sold a copy for £5 if shoppers spent £50 in-store. Sainsbury's stayed above the fray, keeping its price at £8.87. Booksellers, who could not compete with the supermarket's deep discounting, kept their prices around the £10 price band. What was particularly interesting about this episode, however, was that the publisher made a statement saying that the supermarkets were selling the book at cheaper prices than they had actually paid for them.

But such supermarket madness wasn't just in evidence in Britain. It was happening around the world. In Malaysia, discounting of the book to 69.90 Ringgit by supermarket groups, Carrefour and Tesco, compared to the price of 109.90 Ringgit offered by booksellers, caused such an uproar that the independent members of the Malaysian Booksellers Association threatened to return copies to the publishers. Selling the books at below-cost seems like an odd way of doing business, but consider that the sales obtained from all the extra demand from customers coming in to buy their final copy of Harry would have more than compensated—now there's a spot of (marketing) wizardry!

Sources: Cobb (2007); Brown and Patterson (2009); Haycock (2007); Kaur (2007); www.jkrowling.com; http://business.timesonline.co.uk/tol/business/specials/rich_list/rich_list_search.

1 Why did the supermarkets set the price of their new release Harry Potter books so low?

2 Can supermarkets price all their books at such low prices or not? Why do you say this?

3 What other price wars do you know of, or can you remember? What sector were they in?

▶ **Table 9.3** Circumstances under which price wars are more or less likely to occur

Circumstances under which price wars are more likely to occur:

1 As market entry occurs and an entrant gains or is expected to gain a sizeable market position

2 When an industry possesses excess production capacity; this will also stimulate the intensity of the price war

3 When markets have marginal or negative growth prospects

4 Where market power within an industry is highly concentrated

5 Where barriers to exit are greater (meaning it is more difficult to leave an industry, e.g. because of high investment costs)

6 Where financial conditions of at least one firm in the industry worsen or as a firm approaches bankruptcy

7 Where the product concerned is of strategic importance to the company

8 When a product is more like a commodity and so does not command a price premium

9 When firms introduce very similar products to one another

10 When there is little brand loyalty in evidence from customers, and

11 When customers are more highly price-sensitive; this also increases the intensity of the price war

> Circumstances under which price wars are less likely to occur:
>
> 1   One or more firms have established a reputation for strong and tough responses to past price wars
>
> 2   Where markets have intermediate levels of market power concentration (in other words, neither suppliers nor buyers are dominant in a market)

Calculating and anticipating competitors' responses is important when setting prices and responding to competitors' price cuts. We should analyse consumer responses when a competitor starts to cut prices but if purchase behaviour changes only modestly or temporarily, other marketing mix elements (such as promotion, distribution or product differentiation) may be more likely to win back customers (van Heerde, Gijsbrechts, and Pauwels, 2008).

But we do not always have to respond with a price cut in this situation. Instead, we might respond with improvements in service quality, to offer the customer greater value for money as a defensive strategy to offset the competitor's price reductions (Rust, Danaher, and Varki, 2000). In the UK, the household energy market in 2010 was on the brink of entering into a price war, when British Gas cut its prices by 7%, sparking similar cuts from E.ON and RWE and other energy companies. The problem has arisen partly because wholesale gas prices are so low due to a 10% decline in industrial demand as a result of the recession and increased supply through newly developed liquefied natural gas terminals (Pagnamenta, 2010).

The Value-Oriented Approach

Even in the consumer durables category (e.g. furniture, white goods—washing machines and refrigerators—carpets), where we might expect customers to be less price-sensitive, firms have long since practised pricing approaches with their customers' considerations in mind (Foxall, 1972). We term this the value-oriented approach to pricing, because prices are set based on buyers' perceptions of specific product/service attribute values rather than on costs or competitors' prices. It operates in direct contrast to the cost-oriented approach.

The idea is that we no longer live in an era where goods and services are priced at what people can afford to pay, because resources used to make products and services are no longer scarce. We live in an era where resources are more plentiful, where consumers have much of what they need, and so are more interested in obtaining even more value from the goods and services that they buy. We have shifted from the neoclassical economics perspective of the economics of scarcity to the modern perspective of the economics of plenty as we accelerate into the twenty-first century.

With value-based pricing, the pricing process begins with the customer, determining what value they derive from the product or service, then determining price, rather than the opposite approach used in cost-oriented pricing, where costs are determined first, then price is set.

In value-based pricing, the determination of value is undertaken using customer research first. The result may be that the company does not necessarily offer a cheaper price. In fact, it could mean a higher priced offering. If that offering was to represent true value to the customer, they must feel that it has more benefits than equivalent offerings. A good example of a brand using this approach is L'Oréal Paris, which has for a long time advertised its products using spokesmodels, e.g. Bollywood actress and former Miss World, Aishwarya Rai, and British pop sensation and television personality, Cheryl Cole, on the basis that we should use their products 'because we're worth it'. Research has indicated that when a brand can generate revenues over and above those that are obtained by an own-label or generic version of the offering, so-called revenue premiums, this acts as a useful measure for brand equity (Ailawadi, Lehmann, and Neslin, 2003). And brand equity is important, because it contributes to company valuations when they are sold, acquired, or merged. Companies, therefore, are increasingly focusing on trying to generate price premiums for their propositions. However, a price premium is no good if it's not considered fair. Consequently, when setting value-based prices we should consider the following six questions:

1 What is the market strategy for the segment? What does the supplier want to accomplish?

2 What is the differential value that is transparent to customers? (In other words the value between this proposition and the next best alternative, and this assumes that the differential value can be verified with the customer's own data.)

3 What is the price of the next best alternative?

4 What is the cost of the supplier's proposition?

5 What pricing tactics will be used initially (e.g. price discounting)?

6 What is the customer's expectation of a 'fair' price? (Anderson, Wouters, and Van Rossum, 2010). (See Market Insight 9.4.)

▶ Market Insight 9.4

The Birkin Bag—Worth Its Wait in Gold?

A more extreme example of the value-oriented approach to pricing is that adopted by Hermès in the development of its über-stylish, hard to get hold of, Birkin bag, a bag so revered that it, and references to it, keep appearing in American television shows like *Sex and the City* and *Will and Grace*. The bag was named after, and first made for, British actress, Jane Birkin, reportedly after she met Hermès CEO, John-Louis Dumas on a flight to Paris from London in 1984 when she complained that she could not find a leather weekend bag.

In luxury markets, where prices can often seem extreme to the average person in the street, the key is to extend the price range and positioning of the brand so much that it drives the aspirations and fantasies of the wealthiest people in the world. Pricing in these situations may be decided based on a form of

Victoria Beckham, the fashion icon, with her Birkin bag © Corbis

▶ Market Insight 9.4 (continued)

reverse-demand curve, especially as some groups of people (i.e. the risk-averse and the prestige-conscious) view price as an indicator of quality. In other words, people are prepared to pay more for them the more expensive they are, simply for 'snob' value, for the sake of their own expensiveness, or because of their uniqueness (Amaldoss and Jain, 2005; Yeoman and McMahon-Beattie, 2006; Zeithaml, 1988). The Birkin bag is a case in point, with the price ranging from a cool $6,500 to a sky-high $200,000 depending on size, skin (some are made from saltwater crocodile skin), colour, whether or not it's bejewelled, and celebrity appeal (Kingston, 2008). But, finally, all has been revealed. In a novel by Michael Tonello, entitled *Bringing Home the Birkin: My Life in Hot Pursuit of the World's Most Coveted Handbag,* the author reveals that the custom-made bag is often made available only to select customers in select stores who develop relationships with particular sales assistants and only after spending considerable amounts of money in-store. The bag is, therefore, sometimes given to high-value customers as a prize, whereas other customers wait years to receive one (Kingston, 2008).

What this highlights is that the challenge with the value-oriented approach to pricing is the need to ensure that you do not price a product or service so high that customers feel cheated rather than recognizing the true value of the product—enhanced by the scarcity of the product in this case.

1 When a product is very valuable, do you think it is harder or easier to set its price? Why?

2 What approach to pricing is Hermès using here? What about when they give the Birkin bag away to high-value customers who've spent a small fortune on other expensive items?

3 What other examples of luxurious products can you think of which are priced at very high levels? Why do some people continue to buy them, do you think?

Pricing and Transactional Management

Over the past few decades, electronic technologies such as marketing information systems (MkIS), database technologies, and more recently internet-enabled technologies, have been changing the rules of strategic pricing and pricing decisions. Pricing strategies such as 'real-time' or 'dynamic' pricing have increasingly developed in both B2C and B2B markets through online price comparison decision aids and online auctions.

go online

Visit the **Online Resource Centre** and follow the weblink to Kelkoo, an example of an online price comparison decision aid.

We are also seeing electronic technologies influence how retailers manage stock pricing and how we actually buy or conduct a financial transaction—bringing into reality the idea of the cashless society.

With the ease with which information can be exchanged, we are also seeing the proliferation of web-based information brokers with information offerings of product and price comparisons. In the internet age, price comparison websites are an increasingly common feature of the electronic landscape. Examples in the UK include www.comparethemarket.com and www.gocompare.com. Like their counterparts in the USA (e.g. www.pricescan.com) and France (e.g. www.monsieurprix.com), these companies are rapidly developing large customer databases. Examples of compared services include complex services such as gas and electricity supply, insurance, mobile phone packages, and travel, as well as standard products like cars and car breakdown cover. The implication for large companies is clear. Marketers now work in a much more price-transparent environment, where both on- and

Comparison websites such as GoCompare are making the market much more price-transparent

Source: Courtesy of GoCompare. Go-compare.com, the comparison website.

offline customers want to know what the prices are, presented as simply as possible. Price comparison websites are having a dramatic impact on business for some of the organizations whose prices they are comparing against, as they are coming to be seen as overpriced compared to their competitors.

go online

Visit the **Online Resource Centre** and complete Internet Activity 9.2 to learn more about the role and importance of online auctions to price setting and consumer decision-making.

Pricing Policies

In reality, when setting prices the company has to trade-off the factors associated with competition, e.g. how much competitors are charging for similar products/services, factors associated with cost; how much the individual components that make up our product/service cost, factors associated with demand; how much of this product or service will we sell at what price, and factors associated with value; and what components of the product/service does the customer value and how much are they prepared to pay for them. Most pricing decisions are trade-offs between these and other factors. So, although there are four main pricing approaches outlined in this chapter, there are in fact many different possible pricing policies that could be used including the following:

▶ List pricing—an unsophisticated approach to pricing where a single price is set for a product or service. Hotels frequently try to charge what they call 'rack rates' for hotel conferencing facilities, which combine residential accommodation for a set number of delegates with daytime accommodation for a seminar/workshop/conference, refreshments, and lunch.

▶ Loss-leader pricing—occurs where the price is set at a level lower than the actual cost incurred to produce it. This pricing tactic is often used in supermarkets on popular, price-sensitive items (e.g. baked beans, milk) to entice customers into the store. The loss incurred on these items is made up by increasing the prices of other less price-sensitive items or absorbed as a short-term promotional cost on the basis that it brings in more customers.

▶ Promotional pricing—occurs when companies temporarily reduce their prices below the standard price for a period of time to raise awareness of the product or service to encourage trial, and raise brand awareness in the short term. Such pricing approaches incorporate the use of loss-leaders, sales discounts, cash rebates, low-interest financing (e.g. some car manufacturers, e.g. Peugeot UK, have offered low or 0% interest-free financing deals), and other price-based promotional incentives.

▶ Segmentation pricing—where varying prices are set for different groups of customers, e.g. Unilever's ice cream is offered as various different ice cream products at differing levels of quality and price ranging from their superpremium (e.g. Ben & Jerry's ice cream available in video shops, cinemas, and elsewhere) to economy offerings (e.g. standard low-priced vanilla ice cream available in supermarkets). Economists refer to this approach as **price discrimination**.

▶ Customer-centric pricing—Cross and Dixit (2005) suggest that companies can take advantage of customer segments by measuring their value perceptions, measuring the value created, and designing a unique bundle of products and services to cater to the value requirements of each segment, and continually assess the impact this has on company profitability, taking advantage of up-selling, e.g. offering a customer a more expensive product or service in the same category and cross-selling, e.g. selling other, different products and services to the same customer.

▶ Market Insight 9.5

At What Price, An English Degree?

After the British government passed the Higher Education Act in 2004, universities in England were able to offer variable tuition fees for undergraduate degrees for home students (from the UK and EU) from autumn 2006. From September 2010, fees are capped at £3,290 per annum (about €3,700). In reality, only a handful of university courses will charge less than this fee, not least because many believe the true cost of educating a student to be far higher.

What was different about this pricing approach, however, was that from 2006, students paid nothing upfront as they had in the past. Or rather, their parents paid nothing upfront as they were usually the ones paying the fees. Instead, the government pays the tuition fee to the university, and the student pays it back once they graduate, and as long as they earn over £15,000. For international students (from outside the EU), fees remain uncapped, which means that they can be up to two or three times higher than the rate for home students.

The cap on the rate, however, could be removed for the home student tuition rate dependent on advice received from a review of higher education funding by Lord Browne, and some courses, for example medical degrees, may be able to charge up to £20,000 per year because they lead to well-paid jobs. Oxford University, has long argued that the fee is not high enough and does not reflect the true cost of teaching an undergraduate course (Halpin, 2005). There is also an argument that it costs a lot more to run a course in physics or chemistry (with the need for sophisticated equipment and laboratories) than it does to run a course in the humanities.

However, in a more austere financial environment with the British government cutting funding by £900m by 2013, particularly for teaching as opposed

Oxford University believes its degrees should be priced higher

to research, it seems inevitable that degree prices will be set by the market, particularly as competition for places is still very buoyant, with international demand for places increasing. Universities will also still be expected to provide bursaries to support home students from poorer backgrounds. Given this situation, what financial incentive is there for English universities to target home students if the price cap is not removed?

Sources: Anon (2010); Baker (2007).

1 **What pricing policy has been adopted by most universities in England after the introduction of so-called top-up fees?**

2 **Do you think it is fair that universities charge home (UK and EU) students a different price for undergraduate degrees compared with international students? Why do you say this?**

3 **If there was no government regulation on how universities might charge for undergraduate degrees, what are the main approaches that you could use to work out the price of a degree?**

Pricing for New Propositions

When launching new products and services, we adopt one of two particular pricing strategies. With the first approach, we charge a higher price initially and then reduce the price, recouping the cost of the research and development investment over time from sales to the group of customers that is prepared to pay the higher price (hence 'skimming' the market). In the second approach, we charge a lower price in the hopes of generating a large volume of sales and recoup our research and development investment that way (hence market penetration).

Figure 9.4 shows both market penetration and market skimming price strategies and their hypothetical impact on quantity demanded, Q1 and Q2 respectively. For any given demand curve, the market skimming price offers a higher unit price than the market penetration price. The actual amount sold at each of these unit prices depends on the price elasticity of demand, and a more inelastic product demand curve would give greater revenue from a market skimming price than a market penetration price as the quantity sold would not be so different between the two prices. On average the market skimming price is likely to yield a lower quantity of goods/services sold than the market penetration price.

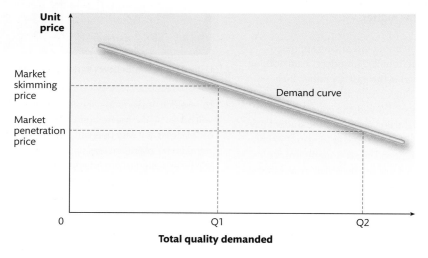

Figure 9.4

New product/service pricing strategies

Source: Adapted from Burnett (2002). Reproduced with the kind permission of the author, John Burnett.

The skim pricing approach is a fairly standard approach for high-technology goods and services or those products and services that require substantial research and development cost input initially e.g. prescription pharmaceuticals. In 1981, the then-UK pharmaceutical giant Glaxo priced its new anti-ulcer drug Zantac at a significant premium price compared to the market leader in major markets (UK, Italy, France, Germany, USA, and Japan), SmithKlineBeecham's billion-dollar blockbuster drug Tagamet. It did this despite the fact that there was little obvious improvement in performance of the drug, although it arguably had fewer side effects. The decision to price higher than the market leader ran counter to what the market research advice was recommending, which was to price at 10% below the market leader to penetrate the market, and was taken by the then-Glaxo CEO, Sir Paul Girolami. Sir Paul felt that Glaxo's previous major blockbuster drug, Ventolin, had been launched at a

> ▶ **Table 9.4** Conditions for effective skim pricing

1	When companies need to recover their research and development investment quickly
2	When demand is likely to be price-inelastic
3	Where there is an unknown elasticity of demand as it is safer to offer a higher price and then lower it, than offer a lower price and try to increase it
4	Where there are high barriers to entry within the market
5	Where there are few economies of scale or experience
6	Where product lifecycles are expected to be short

competitive price despite being better (in terms of performance) than existing competitors but had failed to reach its true market potential as a result. He decided to price Zantac differently, at what he felt the customer would be prepared to pay for a drug that Glaxo marketed as safer and had no side effects, particularly on patients' sex lives (Angelmar and Pinson, 1992). The skim pricing approach is particularly appropriate under certain conditions (Dean, 1950; Doyle, 2000). These conditions are shown in Table 9.4.

The market penetration pricing approach is often used for fast-moving consumer goods and consumer durables items, where the new product introduced is not demonstrably different from existing formulations available. So, if a car manufacturer introduced a new coupé, which was relatively similar to its previous model, and had no new features, and was not significantly better than competing models, it would probably be priced using the market penetration pricing approach. Similarly, items aimed at capturing price-sensitive customers might well adopt this approach. In the multiple retail grocery market during the recession in the late 2000s, for example, the discount grocery stores Aldi, Netto, and Lidl, and the mainstream supermarkets, Tesco, Sainsbury's, and Morrisons all achieved some success at the till as consumers shifted from eating out to eating in to save money. In a recessionary environment, customers are particularly sensitive to the value they receive when purchasing consumer offerings or procuring business goods and services. The approach should be used under certain conditions when it is more likely to be most effective (Dean, 1950; Doyle, 2000), as outlined in Table 9.5.

> ▶ **Table 9.5** Conditions for effective market penetration pricing

1	Where there is a strong threat of competition
2	When our product/service is likely to exhibit a high price elasticity of demand in the short term
3	Where there are substantial savings to be made from volume production
4	Where there are low barriers to entry
5	Where product lifecycles are expected to be long
6	Where there are economies of scale and experience to take advantage of

Aldi, the discount supermarket group, courtesy of Aldi
Source: Aldi.

▶ Research Insight 9.4

To take your learning further, you might wish to read this influential paper.

Dean, J. (1950), 'Pricing policies for new products', *Harvard Business Review*, November, 45–53 (reprinted with retrospective commentary in *HBR*, November–December, 1978).

This is a seminal paper introducing the reader to the concepts of price skimming and penetration pricing as pricing policies for pioneer product marketers. The author indicates that the new product should be priced through the customers' eyes, by consideration of the rate of return of a customer's investment. Reprinted twice since its original publication in *Harvard Business Review*, this article remains a classic, as true today as it was when it was first written.

 Visit the **Online Resource Centre** to read the abstract and access the full paper.

Pricing in the Business-to-Business Setting

Business-to-business markets exist on the basis that firms sell products and services to one another rather than to end users. The demand for their products and services comes from the demand for the finished goods and services required by the end user (see Chapter

14). Business markets are also different in the sense that buyers are usually professionally trained purchasing executives, often professionally accredited (e.g. the Chartered Institute of Purchasing and Supply in the UK), and have frequently attended training programmes to familiarize themselves with the products and services bought within their own organizations. Their function within the company as organizational buyers is a highly technical one, even for an apparently simple product. For example, German buyers of stationery based in Frankfurt would typically need to know for a simple pen set in blister packaging what the market prices are for various types of stationery products and the components that make them up. For instance, the pens themselves may be bought in Italy, packaging and printing from China, refills from Germany, and the final product assembled in Bulgaria. They would typically make their purchases either at a trade fair, at their own premises having been visited by various sales representatives, at the showrooms and offices of the various companies from which they buy, or online using an extranet website or an e-procurement portal. Because the buying function is technical, the relationship between the buyer and the supplier is even more important.

The buyer–seller relationship is the fundamental component of the business-to-business marketing interaction. Pricing has an important function in this relationship. If a buyer thinks he or she is being overcharged, he or she will quickly look elsewhere. Equally, if a seller is forced to make a sale too cheaply and is reprimanded for this by her superiors, she will not wish to sell at that lower price in future, and the relationship may be equally damaged. Under such circumstances, the seller may then seek to sell elsewhere.

In the business-to-business context, the discussion of price takes place between the buyer and the seller in an atmosphere where both are trying to make the best commercial decision for their organizations. The seller wants to sell at a high price to make the maximum profit, and the buyer wants to buy at a low price to lower his or her own costs and maximize profits. Their task is to resolve their mutual needs in a win–win situation (otherwise if one side is taken advantage of, the relationship is less likely to last in the longer term).

From the business-to-business seller's perspective, there are numerous approaches to pricing products and services including the following:

▶ Geographical pricing—prices are determined on the basis of customer location (e.g. pharmaceutical companies often sell their prescription drugs at varying prices in different countries at levels set by the governments themselves rather than the pharmaceutical companies). This might include FOB (free on board) factory prices where the price represents the cost of the goods and the buyer must pay for all transport costs incurred. FOB destination pricing is where the manufacturer agrees to cover the cost of shipping to the destination but not transport costs incurred on arrival at the port (air or sea).

▶ Negotiated pricing—prices are set according to specific agreements between a company and its clients or customers (e.g. professional services such as architectural or structural engineering practices or IT installation and servicing). This approach typically occurs where a sale is complex and consultative, but sales and marketing representatives should beware of conceding on price too quickly before properly understanding a client's needs for the product or service (Rackham, 2001).

▶ Discount pricing—companies reduce the price of a good or service on the basis that a customer is prepared to commit either to buying a large volume of that good or service now, or in the future, or paying for it within a specified time period. Large retailers work on the discount principle when buying goods for their stores. Their mighty procurement budgets and long experience ensure that they buy at cheaper prices from their manufacturer suppliers and so lower their costs. Consequently, they can set their own cheaper prices to their retail customers. Sometimes, discount pricing works on the basis of payment terms. For example in the British toy and gift market, where retail buyers are used to buying their goods on credit, suppliers frequently offer their retail buyers discounts for quicker payment (e.g. 5% discount for payment within seven days, 2.5% for 14 days). However, each time a product or service price is reduced, we disproportionately reduce the operating profit (Marn and Rosiello, 1992).

▶ Value-in-use pricing—this approach focuses our attention on customer perceptions of product attributes and away from cost-oriented approaches. It uses an approach that prices products and services according to what the customer is prepared to pay for individual benefits received from that proposition so the company must first ascertain what benefit components the customer perceives to be important, then quantify those benefit values, then determine the price equivalence of value, then rate competitive and alternative products to provide a benchmark for price determination, then quantify the value in use (i.e. the value in using our product vis-à-vis our competitors), and only then is the price actually fixed (see Christopher, 1982, for a more detailed discussion). The approach is a particularly useful one for industrial products and services, although the actual process of price determination is complex.

▶ Relationship pricing—this approach to pricing is based on understanding a customer's needs and pricing the product or service according to these needs to generate a long-term relationship. This could mean offering good financial terms, perhaps credit or more lenient time periods for payment, or discounts based on future sales revenue. The difficulty with this approach is that it relies on a greater degree of trust and commitment between the two companies particularly on the part of the seller in relation to the buyer. Where this trust is misplaced, the seller incurs an **opportunity cost**.

▶ Transfer pricing—this occurs in very large organizations where there is considerable internal dealing between different divisions of the company and across national boundaries. Prices may be set at commercial rates, on the basis of negotiated prices between divisions, or using a cost-based approach. It entirely depends on whether each division is a cost- or profit-centre. The danger is that such internal dealings can sometimes mean that the final product or service is priced at too high a level for the customer. A good example of a company that adopts this approach is Airbus Industries, the European aircraft manufacturer, owned by parent company EADS (European Aeronautic Defence and Space Company), which constructs its planes built from components made in several different countries.

▶ Economic value to the customer (EVC) pricing—this approach works on the basis that a company prices an industrial good or service according to its value to the purchasing organization typically through a comparison with a reference or market-leading product or service, taking into consideration not only the actual purchase price of the product or service, but also the start-up and post-purchase costs to give an overall indication of how much better your pricing structure is, compared with that of a competitor. A worked example of economic value to the customer (EVC) pricing is outlined below.

EVC pricing works by calculating total lifetime costs for a business-to-business product or service in comparison to a reference product or service and the adjustment of the purchase price to reflect the value the customer requires or the seller is prepared to offer. In this case, we use the example of a company developing CRM (customer relationship management) systems for the financial services sector. In the case of the Reference System—typically we use the market-leading product or service as this acts as a well-known benchmark—the system actually costs £50,000 initially, but requires expenditure of a further £20,000 on start-up costs, including say staff training on the system, and staff time in loading and testing the software's compatibility with the firm's other software systems. Maintenance costs of the database developed from using the software system over a three-year period come to a further £30,000, mainly consisting of data input, cleaning and processing time particularly in relation to system interoperability and database translation issues between software packages. Overall, the total lifetime profit from purchasing the market-leading CRM system is £100,000 because, although it costs £100,000 over three years, it also generates £200,000 in extra income.

However, our company developing CRM software systems has two alternative products, System A and System B. Let's consider System A first. In comparison with the market-leading product, it offers slightly cheaper start-up costs at £15,000 because it is easier to use and requires less staff training. It also has substantially lower maintenance costs because data input is made substantially easier as the software uses the majority of the company's existing database systems and so reduces software interoperability problems. In total, the system costs £20,000 less than the reference product, but is estimated to bring the same extra revenue of £100,000. In total, the system will cost £80,000. Therefore, the economic value to the customer of purchasing System A is the total lifetime cost/profit associated with System A less the cost of the purchase of the system = £70,000. When we come to sell System A to our CRM system buyer, we can offer the buyer any price between £50,000 and £70,000 to remain competitive and still offer a differential price advantage over the market leader.

We can also offer our CRM buyer another system. System B, by contrast, has the same start-up costs and maintenance costs as the market leader. However, it also has sophisticated predictive up-selling and cross-selling functions, which allow the financial services company to generate higher revenue from the database developed of £350,000 compared with the £200,000 generated from the Reference System or System A. In this case, the total lifetime profit of the system is £250,000. Therefore, the economic value to the customer of purchasing

▶ **Table 9.6** Economic value to the customer (EVC) analysis

Cost item	Reference system	System A	System B
EVC	n/a	£70,000	£190,000
Extra revenue generated (three years)	£200,000	£200,000	£350,000
Purchase price	£50,000	£50,000	£50,000
Start-up costs (year 1 only)	£20,000	£15,000	£20,000
Maintenance costs (three years)	£30,000	£15,000	£30,000
Total lifetime cost (-)/profit (+)	+£100,000	+£120,000	+£250,000

System B is the total lifetime cost/profit associated with System B less the cost of the purchase of the system = £190,000. The CRM company can offer the financial service company System B for any price between £50,000 and £190,000. In reality, however, it would probably be difficult to justify a price towards the higher figure, because the extra revenue generated is estimated and uncertain.

Tendering and Bidding

In business-to-business markets, companies bid for the right to provide products and services for a fixed period of time to a successful bidder through a competitive bidding process. In other words, a company sets up a form of competition (the tender process) where they either ask a number of selected companies (their 'preferred suppliers'), or they set an open competition where they ask any number of companies to put together a proposal for a set of services or the supply of products and services (known as a bid), which has to be submitted by a set deadline. Where a company does not have a pool of preferred suppliers, or wants to widen its pool of potential suppliers, this phase is sometimes preceded by an initial phase where the company invites 'expressions of interest' from interested potential suppliers. The submissions are then screened by the company, which removes those companies that it does not want to deal with, and the rest are advanced to the next phase of the competition. The company goes on to consider the individual full bids in some form of ranking process, often requiring the bid submitters to make a presentation and discuss the detail of their bids individually. On the basis of those bids and the presentation, either the company will make a choice of who they want to supply their company, or they will take the process to a second round or third round of bidding, and so on. Eventually, they will decide to which company they want to award the temporary contract. The tendering process is a set requirement for the provision of public services and goods in the European Union above certain financial values of contract with strict rules on how the contracts must be promoted and awarded.

Private companies dealing with private companies tend to adopt the same forms of bidding and tendering, but without the same level of strict regulation. Generally, the formal tendering and bidding process takes a considerable period of time, effort, and expense. Bidding processes like that described are common in industrial markets, and are used around the world as a means to introduce competition, particularly to the provision of public sector services, such as in telecommunications, public utilities (such as gas, electricity, and water), transport (e.g. train, underground, monorail, maglev), oil and gas exploration, defence contracting, and so on. The difficulty in designing, writing, and submitting a suitable contract is that the details of competitors' bids usually remain highly confidential. When trying to second-guess competitors' bid prices, it is important to use the sales force as a source of intelligence (as they often pick up information from talks with friendly companies that they supply and even colleagues in other companies at industry events). The manager should know his or her own profitability when determining the price and aim to discover the winning bidder's name and price on lost jobs, although this is not always possible (Walker, 1967). Ross (1984) argues that it is often better not to ask 'what price will it take to win this order?' but 'Do we want this order, given the price our competitors are likely to quote?'. There is the notion of the **winner's curse**, where the winning bidder obtains an unprofitable contract that she or he is duty-bound to deliver because their bid price was set so low so that they won the contract.

Skills for Employment

▶▶ One of the most important attributes candidates can demonstrate is marketing theory's application in real life. It is important to demonstrate knowledge of how things work, how things affect each other (e.g. cost/benefit analysis) to be able to take a holistic approach to marketing from long-term strategy writing to tactical decision-making. In the dynamic marketing environment it is all about adaptability. The use of theoretical modelling to help quickly assess situations and make commercial decisions is a critical tool and ensures reduced risk, while maximizing chances of success. ◀◀

Gwyn Davis, Marketing Manager, ZSL London Zoo

 Visit the **Online Resource Centre** to discover more tips and advice on skills for the workplace.

Chapter Summary

To consolidate your learning, the key points from this chapter are summarized below.

■ **Define price, and understand its relationship with costs, quality, and value.**

Price, costs, quality, and value are all interrelated. Price is what a product or service is sold for and cost is what it is bought for. When value is added to a proposition the price that can be obtained exceeds the cost. Price and cost are often confused and assumed even by major international dictionaries to be the same thing. They are not. Quality is a measure of how well a product or service satisfies the need it is designed to cater for. Value is a function of the quality of a good or service as a proportion of the price paid.

■ **Explain the concept of price elasticity of demand.**

Price elasticity of demand allows us to determine how the quantity of a good or service relates to the price at which it is offered. Inelastic goods and services are defined as such because increases (decreases) in price produce relatively smaller decreases (increases) in sales volumes, where elastic goods have larger similar effects. Understanding price elasticity helps us devise demand-oriented pricing mechanisms.

■ **Describe how customers and consumers perceive price.**

Understanding how customers and consumers perceive pricing helps in setting prices. Customers have an idea of reference prices based on either what they ought to pay for a good or service, what others would pay, or what they would like to pay. Their knowledge of actual prices is limited to well-known and frequently bought and advertised goods and services. Consequently, customers tend to rely on price cues such as odd-number pricing, sale signs, the purchase context, and price bundles when deciding whether or not value exists in a particular proposition.

■ **Explain cost-, competitor-, demand-, and value-oriented approaches to pricing.**

There are a variety of different pricing policies that can be used dependent on whether we are pricing for a consumer or industrial proposition. They tend to be either cost-oriented (based on what we paid for it and what mark-up we intend to add), competitor-oriented (the so-called going rate or based on what price competitors sell a product or service at), demand-oriented (based on how much of a good or service can be sold at what price), or value-oriented (what attributes of the product or service are of benefit to our customer and what will they pay for them?).

- **Understand how to price new offerings.**

  The two dominant approaches to pricing new propositions are the market skimming pricing method and the market penetration pricing method. The former is favoured when a company needs to recover its R&D investment quickly, when customers are price-insensitive or of unknown price-sensitivity, when product lifecycles are short, and barriers to entry to competitors are high. The latter is favoured when these conditions are not in existence.

- **Understand the conditions under which a price war is more or less likely to ignite.**

  Price wars can devastate companies. Research indicates that it is better to avoid price wars by recognizing early warning signals. Eleven signals are outlined, which indicate when price wars are more likely, including factors related to the industry (e.g. low growth rates), the firm itself (e.g. where the product is of strategic importance to the company), the product category (e.g. where it is a commodity), and the nature of the customers (e.g. where they are price-sensitive), and that reduce the incidence of price wars, e.g. when competitors have a reputation for swift retaliatory pricing actions and when there are intermediate levels of market power.

- **Explain how pricing operates in the business-to-business setting.**

  There are a variety of pricing approaches used in the business-to-business setting, including the following: geographical, negotiated, discount, value-in-use, relationship, transfer, and economic value to the customer. Business-to-business pricing differs in the sense that buyers are frequently expert in purchasing goods and services for their organizations. They are likely to pay particular attention to the value that they derive from the offering. Companies and organizations, particularly government organizations, frequently purchase goods and services from suppliers through tenders inviting companies to submit bids, containing their proposals, terms and conditions and prices.

 Review Questions

1 Define price, cost, quality, and value in your own words.
2 Explain the concept of price elasticity of demand, naming examples of products that are both price elastic and price inelastic.
3 What are pricing cues?
4 What pricing policies are most appropriate for which situations?
5 What are the main business-to-business pricing policies?
6 What are the main two approaches to pricing for new products and services?
7 When should you use price skimming as a pricing approach?
8 When should you use market penetration as a pricing approach?
9 How is business-to-business pricing different?
10 Describe in your own words the economic value to the customer pricing approach.

Worksheet Summary

Visit the **Online Resource Centre** and complete Worksheet 9.1. This aid in learning about how external influences can affect our perceptions of the price for pizza and how we can use different approaches to set pizza pricing.

Discussion Questions

1 Having read Case Insight 9.1, what approach to ticket pricing would you advise P&O Ferries to adopt? Why do you think this approach would be more effective than the alternative possibilities?

2 A range of scenarios are presented below in which you are given some information on the price context. What pricing policy would you use when setting the price in the following situation (state the assumptions under which you are working when you decide on which one)?

   A The owner of a newly refurbished themed Irish pub in a central city location (e.g. Paris or Gothenburg) wants to set the prices for his range of beers with the objective of attracting a new customer base.

   B The product manager at Italian car maker Alfa Romeo wants to set the price range for the Alfa Romeo Giulietta in the UK launched in Summer 2010. (www.alfaromeogiulietta.co.uk).

   C You are the manager at a large well-known consulting services organization (e.g. Boston Consulting Group) in Sweden, and your client, from a €20m turnover medium-sized import/export company, commissions a study from you on how they can improve their marketing operations. What further information would you require in order to price such a study and what pricing approach would you adopt and why?

3 How would you go about determining the price-sensitivity of your customers if you were an airline marketing manager and you wanted your aeroplanes to operate at full capacity throughout the week, including very early and very late flight slots not just at weekends and in the mornings?

4 Identify an entrepreneur or shop owner that you know. Ask them how they set their prices for the propositions that they sell? What pricing policies do you think they use?

5 Research and examine the prices of five different items in two different jewellery shops (selling similar or identical products and pack sizes in each where possible to allow comparison). What are the average prices for each of the items and how does each shop compare with the other?

Visit the **Online Resource Centre** and complete the Multiple Choice Questions to assess your knowledge of Chapter 9.

go online

References

Ailawadi, K., Lehmann, D. R., and Neslin, S. A. (2003), 'Revenue premium as a outcome measure of brand equity', *Journal of Marketing*, 67 (October) 1–17.

Amaldoss, W., and Jain, S. (2005), 'Pricing of conspicuous goods: a competitive analysis of social effects', *Journal of Marketing Research*, 42 (February), 30–42.

Anderson, E., and Simester, D. (2003), 'Mind your pricing cues', *Harvard Business Review*, September, 96–103.

Anderson, J.C.; Wouters, M., and Van Rossum, W. (2010), 'Why the highest price isn't the best price', *Sloan Management Review*, 51, 2, 69–76.

Angelmar, R., and Pinson, C. (1992), 'Zantac A', *Case Study* 592-045-1, Fontainbleau, France: INSEAD.

Anon. (2010), 'Frustrated ambitions', *The Economist*, 6–12 February, 35.

Attridge, J. (2003), 'A single European market for pharmaceuticals: could less regulation and more negotiation be the answer?', *European Business Journal*, 15, 3, 122–43.

Babad, Y. M., and Balachandran, B. V. (1993), 'Cost driver optimisation in activity-based costing', *Accounting Review*, 68, 3, 563–75.

Baker, M. (2007), 'What price a university degree?', BBC News 24, 17 February, retrieve from http://news.bbc.co.uk/1/hi/education/4749575.stm, accessed 15 June 2007.

Barnes, R. (2004), 'Tesco complains to ASA over Asda low-price ads', *Marketing*, 8 November.

Boyle, P.J. and Lathrop, E.S. (2009), 'Are consumers perceptions of price-quality relationships well-calibrated?', *International Journal of Consumer Studies*, 33, 58–63.

Brown, S., and Patterson, A. (2009), 'Harry Potter and the service-dominant logic of marketing: a cautionary tale', *Journal of Marketing Management*, 25, 5/6, 519–33.

Burnett, J. (2002), *Core Concepts in Marketing*, London: John Wiley and Sons.

Christopher, M. (1982), 'Value-in-use pricing', *European Journal of Marketing*, 16, 5, 35–46.

Cialdini, R. B. (1993), *Influence: The Psychology of Persuasion*, New York: Quill William Morrow.

Cobb, C. (2007), 'Harry Potter's PR magic', *Public Relations Tactics*, August, 9–10.

Concise Oxford English Dictionary (2010), 'Price', 'Value', 'Quality', retrieve from www.oxfordreference.com, accessed 4 February 2010.

Cross, R. G., and Dixit, A. (2005), 'Customer-centric pricing: the surprising secret for profitability', *Business Horizons*, 48, 483–91.

Dean, J. (1950), 'Pricing policies for new products', *Harvard Business Review*, November, 45–53.

Doyle, P. (2000), *Value-Based Marketing: Marketing Strategies for Corporate Growth and Shareholder Value*, Chichester: John Wiley and Sons.

Foxall, G. (1972), 'A descriptive theory of pricing for marketing', *European Journal of Marketing*, 6, 3, 190–4.

Gourville, J., and Soman, D. (2002), 'Pricing and the psychology of consumption', *Harvard Business Review*, September, 90–6.

Halpin, T. (2005), 'Oxford may cut undergraduates to save £200m', *The Times*, 21 September, 2.

Hartley, R. F. (1993), *Business Ethics: Violations of the Public Trust*, New York: John Wiley and Sons.

Haycock, G. (2007), 'UK supermarkets extend price war on Potter books', retrieve from www.reuters.com/article/idUSL2083170420070720, accessed 10 April 2010.

Heil, O. P., and Helsen, K. (2001), 'Toward an understanding of price wars: their nature and how they erupt', *International Journal of Research in Marketing*, 18, 83–98.

Kaur, M. (2007), 'Potter price war: booksellers to meet next week to decide next move', *The Star*, 22 July, retrieve from http://thestar.com.my/news/story.asp?file=/2007/7/22/nation/20070722114014&sec=nation, accessed 10 April 2010.

Kingston, A. (2008), 'How to get the un-gettable bag', *Maclean's*, 3 March, 74.

Lewis, L. (2001), 'Esso and Price Watch to go', *The Independent on Sunday*, 18 November, retrieve from www.independent.co.uk/news/business/news/esso-and-price-watch-to-go-617288.html, accessed 7 February 2010.

Lockley, L. C. (1949), 'Theories of pricing in marketing', *Journal of Marketing*, 13, 3, 364–7.

Marn, M. V., and Rosiello, R. L. (1992), 'Managing price, gaining profit', *Harvard Business Review*, September–October, 84–94.

Mazumdar, T., Raj, S. P., and Sinha, I. (2005), 'Reference price research: review and propositions', *Journal of Marketing*, 69 (October), 84–102.

Mintel (2009), *Food Retailing—UK: November 2009*, London: Mintel, retrieve from www.mintel.com, accessed 4 February 2010.

Nunes, J. C., and Boatwright, P. (2001), 'Pricey encounters', *Harvard Business Review*, July–August, 18–19.

Pagnamenta, R. (2010), 'British Gas sparks a price war as bills fall for 8m households', *The Times*, 5 February.

Rackham, N. (2001), 'Winning the price war', *Sales and Marketing Management*, 253, 11 (November), 26.

Ross, E. B. (1984), 'Making money with proactive pricing', *Harvard Business Review*, November–December, 145–55.

Rust, R. T., Danaher, P. J., and Varki, S. (2000), 'Using service quality data for competitive marketing decisions', *International Journal of Service Industry Management*, 11, 5, 438–69.

Sankey, J. (2003), 'Retail wars just boomerang back', *Precision Marketing*, 29 August, 3.

Sheth, J. N., Sisodia, R. S., and Barbulescu, A. (2006), 'The image of marketing', in J. N. Sheth and R. S. Sisodia (eds), *Does Marketing Need Reform*, New York: M. E. Sharpe, Inc., 26–36.

Sjolander, R. (1992), 'Cross-cultural effects of price on perceived product quality', *European Journal of Marketing*, 26, 7, 34–44.

Smith, G. E., and Nagle, T. T. (1995), 'Frames of reference and buyer's perceptions of value', *California Management Review*, 38, 1, 98–116.

Spinello, R. A. (1992), 'Ethics, pricing and the pharmaceutical industry', *Journal of Business Ethics*, 11, 617–26.

van Heerde, H.J.,; Gijsbrechts, E., and Pauwels, K. (2008), 'Winners and losers in a major price war', *Journal of Marketing Research*, 45, 5, 499–518.

Walker, A. W. (1967), 'How to price industrial products', *Harvard Business Review*, September–October, 125–32.

Ward, K. (1993), 'Gaining a marketing advantage through the strategic use of transfer pricing', *Journal of Marketing Management*, 9, 245–53.

Yeoman, I., and McMahon-Beattie, U. (2006), 'Luxury markets and premium pricing', *Journal of Revenue and Pricing Management*, 4, 4, 319–28.

Zeithaml, V. A. (1988), 'Consumer perceptions of price, quality and value: a means–end model and synthesis of evidence', *Journal of Marketing*, 52 (July), 2–22.

10 An Introduction to Marketing Communications

Learning Outcomes

After studying this chapter you should be able to:

▶ Explain three models of communication and describe how personal influences can enhance the effectiveness of marketing communication activities

▶ Describe the nature, purpose, and scope of marketing communications

▶ Understand the role and various tasks of marketing communications

▶ Explain the key characteristics associated with developing promotional messages

▶ Understand the models used to explain how marketing communications and advertising are considered to work

▶ Describe what culture is and explain how it can impact on the use of marketing communications

▶ Case Insight 10.1

The British Airways London Eye uses marketing communications in a number of interesting ways and has become the UK's most popular visitor attraction. We speak to Helen Bull to find out more.

Helen Bull for the London Eye

The British Airways London Eye is the world's tallest observation wheel at 135 metres high, and, since opening at the turn of the century, has become an iconic landmark, with a status that can be compared with Tower Bridge, Big Ben, Eros, and the Tower of London. The London Eye has become the most popular paid-for UK visitor attraction, visited by over 3.5m people a year; that is an average of 10,000 a day.

At the London Eye we use marketing communications in a number of interesting ways. During the construction phase, for example, public relations was used to build high pre-opening interest and awareness and to challenge any negative perceptions associated with ferris wheels or thrill rides. We gave the media access to key individuals and organizations throughout this period in order to win public favour by involving them in the entire process and giving them ownership of what would become a global icon. For the same reason, the media was given access to the construction site at regular key stages of the build, the biggest day being the raising of the wheel from barges on the River Thames. The London Eye project was watched by millions of people on a daily basis and we used regular, consistent media exposure to keep the public interested and instil a sense of pride in Londoners. By the time the London Eye was due to open, hundreds of thousands of people had already pre-booked their tickets.

Advertising is used as part of our marketing communications to drive both awareness and footfall. Building awareness with target audiences ensures that the London Eye as a global icon is at the forefront of everyone's mind. Through advertising, the London Eye targets audiences in London and the South-East as well as visitors to London once they arrive in the capital.

Other marketing activity includes seasonal campaigns, sales promotions, and the tactical distribution of leaflets. Seasonal campaigns centre around key periods such as Easter, Christmas, and Halloween where we target Londoners and the South-East market. The latter makes it ideal to focus on local London media, such as the *Evening Standard*, all the free London papers, and marketing emails.

Sales promotions are used to drive incremental off-peak revenue and visitors. These kinds of campaigns are normally used tactically to encourage guests to trial additional products and also to extend brand communication. Leaflets are distributed via British Tourist Authority offices worldwide, trade clients, and Tourist Information Centres throughout the UK. In addition, 'word-of-mouth' plays a key role to encourage visits to the London Eye. More than 30% of London Eye guests visit as the result of a recommendation from family or friends. There is a definite consumer trend towards trusting word-of-mouth and personal recommendations above any form of advertising.

It is extremely important for us to build relationships with industry representative organizations such as

▶ Case Insight 10.1   (continued)

The BA London Eye: the world's tallest observation wheel

Visit London and Visit Britain who actively go out to other territories around the world to promote London and Britain as a destination. Through working with these organizations, the London Eye is able to target audiences in desired countries and areas as well as specific demographics. At the London Eye we also undertake a number of sales missions to different countries where key salespeople will meet with travel agents and organizers in a small group or on an individual basis in order to communicate and educate buyers on the London Eye portfolio of products. In the world of corporate events as well as journalist familiarization trips, personal communications make a much bigger impact.

In March 2007, we knew our 25 millionth visitor would be arriving and two important questions emerged. How should we celebrate the occasion and how should we use marketing communications to mark it?

Introduction

Have you ever wondered how organizations manage to communicate with so many different people and organizations? Well, this is the first of two chapters that explain how this can be accomplished through the use of marketing communications. This one introduces and explains what marketing communications is. The following chapter considers each of the communication tools and media, and explains how marketing communications can be planned.

The overall purpose of this chapter is to introduce some of the fundamental ideas and concepts associated with marketing communications. In order to achieve this, the chapter commences with a consideration of communication theory. This is important because it provides a basis on which it is easier to appreciate the different ways in which marketing communications is used.

Following a definition, we explain the role and tasks of marketing communications. Again, this is important as it specifies the scope of the subject and provides a framework within which to appreciate the various communication activities undertaken by organizations. The tools and media used by marketing communications are an important aspect of this topic. Although the next chapter is devoted to a fuller examination of each of them, a brief overview is presented here.

Marketing communications is about shared meaning and that means developing messages that can be understood and acted on by target audiences. We present some principles by which marketing messages are communicated and then consider how marketing communications might work. This chapter concludes with an overview of what culture is and how it can impact on marketing communications.

Introducing Marketing Communications

Marketing communications, or **promotion** as it was originally called, is one element of the marketing mix. It is used to communicate elements of an organization's offering to a target audience. This offer might refer to a product, a service, or the organization itself as it tries to build its reputation. However, this is a broad view of marketing communications and we need to understand the various issues, dimensions, and elements that make up this important communication activity. For example, there are the communications experienced by audiences relating to both their use of products (how good is this hairdryer?) and the consumption of associated services (just how good was the service when I was in IKEA?).

There are communications arising from unplanned or unintended experiences (empty stock shelves or accidents) and there are planned marketing communications (Duncan and Moriarty, 1997), which is the main focus of this and the following chapter. These are all represented in Figure 10.1 (Hughes and Fill, 2007), which is the point at which we start our exploration of marketing communications.

Figure 10.1 depicts not just the breadth but also the complexity of managing marketing communications. However, this framework fails to provide any detailed understanding, particularly of the planned marketing communications element. This component is really important because it has the potential not only to present products and services in the best possible way but also to influence people's expectations about both product and service experiences.

Organizations plan, design, implement, and evaluate their marketing communication activities. Often referred to as campaigns, these activities involve the delivery of messages either to or with target audiences, through various communication tools and media.

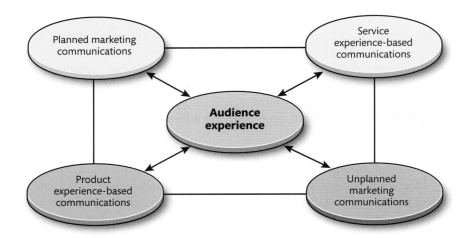

Figure 10.1

A macro perspective of the marketing communications mix

Source: Hughes and Fill (2007). Adapted with the kind permission of Emerald Group Publishing Limited and Westburn Publishers.

This chapter is intended to help understand some of the fundamental ideas associated with planned marketing communications. It sets out the broad scope of the subject and enables readers to appreciate the complexity and diversity of this fascinating subject.

Visit the **Online Resource Centre** and follow the weblink to the European Association of Communication Agencies (EACA) to learn more about advertising, media and sales promotion activities across Europe.

go online

See Market Insight 10.1 for an example of marketing communications drawing on a well-known brand.

▶ Market Insight 10.1

'No Worries' claim Foster's

Foster's is an established brand in the standard lager sector, targeted at 18–34-year-old men. Research gathered during the 2008/9 recession, indicated that people wanted to be involved with a more stress-free world. Foster's response was to develop a multimillion-pound TV campaign aimed at rejuvenating and repositioning their brand. Foster's have used humour extensively in previous advertising, for example the

Crocodile Dundee campaigns featuring the actor Paul Hogan. The new campaign extended the humour proposition and was designed to tap into the Aussie 'no worries' attitude, arguing that all UK drinkers need is to 'get some Australian in you'.

The campaign, which uses TV, cinema and radio, digital activity and CRM work, broke during ITV1's live coverage of England's World Cup 2010 qualifier against Andorra. It consists of two TV commercials, one called 'Backpacker' and the other, 'Deep Sea'.

▶ Market Insight 10.1

Foster's, the laid back Australian beer
Source: Courtesy of Heineken UK Limited.

The previous campaign used a functional approach, one which featured lads going to extreme lengths to keep their beer cold. That campaign used the strapline: 'Foster's. You wouldn't want a warm beer, would you?'. Now the goal was to refresh the brand and this was to be achieved using a more emotional approach. The ads feature a character in a stressful situation but behaving in an unexpectedly laidback manner. This is because they have 'a bit of Australian' in them. Their part Australian nature enables them to respond to in a typical 'No Worries' manner, leading to the new end-line 'Foster's—get some Australian in you'.

Source: Sweney (2009); Utalk (2009a).

1　**What do functional and emotional approaches mean? Find three examples of each, in any sector of your choice.**

2　**How are other standard lager brands in your country positioned?**

3　**Think of two other functional and two other emotional approaches that Foster's might use to communicate with their target audiences?**

Communication Theory

We start with a consideration of communication theory. This is important as it helps explain how and why certain marketing communication activities take place. Communication is the process by which individuals share meaning. It is necessary, therefore, that participants are able to interpret the meanings embedded in the messages they receive, and then, as far as the sender is concerned, able to respond coherently. The act of responding is important as it completes an episode in the communication process. Communication that travels only from the sender to the receiver is essentially a one-way process and the full communication process remains incomplete. This form of communication is shown in Figure 10.2.

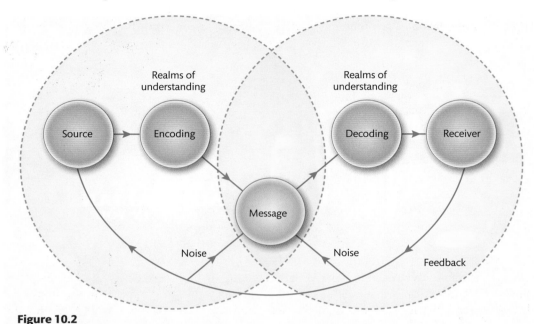

Figure 10.2

A linear model of communications

Source: Based on Schramm (1955) and Shannon and Weaver (1962).

When Cadbury present their Dairy Milk chocolate bar on a poster in the London underground, the person standing on the platform can read it, understand it, and may even enjoy being entertained by it. They do not, however, have any immediate opportunity to respond to the ad in such a way that Cadbury can hear, understand, and act on the person's comments and feelings. When that same ad is presented on a website or a sales promotion representative offers that same person a chunk of Cadbury Dairy Milk when they are shopping in a supermarket, there are opportunities to hear, record, and even respond to the comments that person makes. This form of communication travels from a sender (Cadbury) to a receiver (the person in the supermarket) and back again to Cadbury, and is referred to as a two-way communication and represents a complete communication episode. This type of communication is depicted in Figure 10.3.

These basic models form the basis of this introduction to communication theory. For those involved in managing and delivering marketing communications it is important that these processes and associated complexities are understood. Through knowledge and understanding of the communications process, they are more likely to achieve their objective of sharing meaning with each member of their target audiences. This not only helps create opportunities to interact with their audiences but also encourages some people to develop a dialogue, the richest and most meaningful form of communication.

Understanding the way communication works, therefore, provides a foundation on which we can better understand the way marketing communications not only works, but also how it can be used effectively by organizations.

go online

Visit the **Online Resource Centre** and follow the weblink to the International Association of Business Communicators (IABC), a business network with the aim of improving marketing communications effectiveness among communication professionals.

Three main models or interpretations of how communication works are considered here. These are the linear model, the two-way model, and the interactive model of communication.

The Linear Model of Communication

The linear model of communication is regarded as the basic model of mass communications. First developed by Wilbur Schramm (1955), the key components of the linear model of communication are set out in Figure 10.2.

The model can be broken down into a number of phases, each of which has distinct characteristics. The linear model emphasizes that each phase occurs in a particular sequence, a linear progression, which, according to Theodorson and Theodorson (1969), enables the 'transmission of information, ideas, attitudes, or emotion from one person or group to another (or others), primarily through symbols'. The model and its components are straightforward, but it is the quality of the linkages between the various elements in the process that determines whether the communication will be successful.

The source is an individual or organization that identifies a problem requiring transmission of a message. The source of a message is an important factor in the communication process. First, the source must identify the right problem, and second, a **receiver** who perceives a source to lack conviction, authority, trust, or expertise is not likely to believe the messages sent by that source.

Encoding is the process whereby the source selects a combination of appropriate words, pictures, symbols, and music to represent the message to be transmitted. The various bits are 'packed' in such a way that they can be unpacked and understood. The goal is to create a message that is capable of being comprehended easily by the receiver.

Once encoded, the message must be put into a form that is capable of transmission. It may be oral or written, verbal or non-verbal, in a symbolic form or in a sign. The channel is the means by which the message is transmitted from the source to the receiver. These channels may be personal or non-personal. The former involves face-to-face contact and **word-of-mouth** communications, which can be extremely influential. Non-personal channels are characterized by mass media advertising, which can reach large audiences. Whatever the format chosen, the source must be sure that what is being put into the message is what they want to be decoded by the receiver.

Once the receiver, an individual or organization, has seen, heard, smelt, or read the message they decode it. In effect they are 'unpacking' the various components of the message, starting to make sense of it and give it meaning. The more clearly the message is encoded the easier it is to 'unpack' and comprehend what the source intended to convey when they constructed the message. **Decoding**, therefore, is that part of the communication process where receivers give meaning to a message.

Once understood receivers provide a set of reactions referred to as a response. These reactions may vary from an emotional response based on a set of feelings and thoughts about the message to a behavioural or action response.

Feedback is another part of the response process. It is important to know not just that the message has been received but also that it has been correctly decoded and the right meaning attributed. However, although feedback is an essential aspect of a successful communication event, feedback through mass media channels is generally difficult to obtain, mainly because of the inherent time delay involved in the feedback process. Feedback through **personal selling**, however, can be instantaneous, through explicit means such as questioning, raising objections, or signing an order form. For the mass media advertiser, the process can be vague and prone to misinterpretation. If a suitable feedback system is not in place then the source will be unaware that the communication has been unsuccessful and is liable to continue wasting resources. This represents inefficient and ineffective marketing communications.

Noise is concerned with influences that distort information and, which, in turn, make it difficult for the receiver to correctly decode and interpret the message as intended by the source. So, if a telephone rings, or someone rustles sweet papers during a sensitive part of a film screened in a cinema, the receiver is distracted from the message.

The final component in the linear model concerns the 'realm of understanding'. This is an important element in the communication process because it recognizes that successful communications are more likely to be achieved if the source and the receiver understand each other. This understanding concerns attitudes, perceptions, behaviour, and experience: the values of both parties to the communication process. Effective communication is more likely when there is some common ground, a realm of understanding between the source and receiver.

One of the problems associated with the linear model of communication is that it ignores the impact that other people can have on the communication process. People are not passive, they actively use information and the views and actions of other people can impact on the way information is sent, received, processed, and given meaning. One of the other difficulties with the linear model is that it is based on communication through mass media.

Developed at a time when first radio and then TV, with a just a few channels, were the only media available, it can be seen why the model was developed. Today there are hundreds of TV channels, audiences now use the internet, mobile phones, and an increasing array of digital equipment to manage their work, leisure, and entertainment. Increasing numbers of people now engage with interactive-based communications, and in some circumstances organizations and individuals can be involved in real dialogue, such as online gaming. The linear model, therefore, is no longer entirely appropriate.

The Two-Step Model of Communication

One interpretation of the linear model is that it is a one-step explanation. Information is directed and shot at prospective audiences, rather like a bullet is propelled from a gun. However, we know that people can have a significant impact on the communication process and the **two-step model** goes some way to reflecting their influence.

The two-step model compensates for the linear or one-step model because it recognizes the importance of personal influences when informing and persuading audiences to think or behave in particular ways. This model depicts information flowing via various media channels, to particular types of people to whom other members of the audience refer for information and guidance. There are two main types of influencer. The first is referred to as an **opinion leader** and the other is an **opinion former**. The first is just an ordinary person who has a heightened interest in a particular topic. The second is involved professionally in the

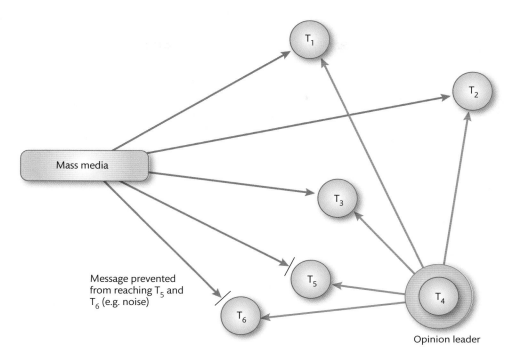

Figure 10.3

The two-step model of communications

Source: *Marketing Commmunications*, 4th edn, Fill, C., Pearson Education Limited (2006).
Reproduced with the kind permission of Pearson Education Limited.

topic of interest. These are discussed in more detail later in this chapter, but they both have enormous potential to influence audiences. This may be because messages from personal influencers provide reinforcement and message credibility or it might be because this is the only way of reaching the end user audience.

The Interaction Model of Communications

This model is similar to the two-step model but it contains one important difference. In this interpretation the parties are seen to interact among themselves and communication flows among all the members in what is regarded as a communication network (Figure 10.4). Mass media is not the only source of the communication.

Unlike the linear model, in which messages flow from the source to the receiver, through a channel, the **interaction model** recognizes that messages can flow through various channels and that people can influence the direction and impact of a message. It is not necessarily one-way but interactive communication that typifies much of contemporary communications.

Interaction is an integral part of the communication process. Think of a conversation with a friend: the face-to-face oral-, and visual-based communication enables both of you to consider what the other is saying, and to react in whatever way is appropriate. Mass communication does not facilitate this interactional element and so the linear model might, therefore, be regarded as an incomplete form of the pure communication process.

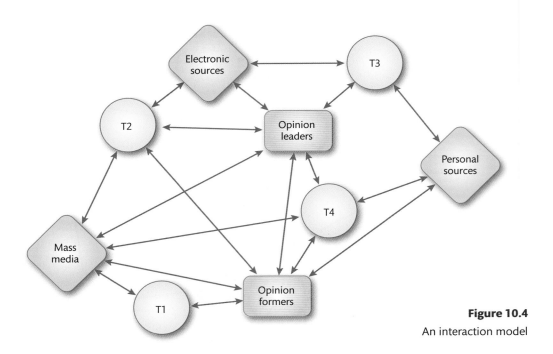

Figure 10.4

An interaction model

Interaction is about actions that lead to a response and much attention is now given to the interaction that occurs between people. However, care needs to be taken because the content associated with an interactional event might be based on an argument, a statement of opinion, or a mere casual social encounter. What is important here is interaction that leads to mutual understanding. This type of interaction concerns 'relationship specific knowledge' (Ballantyne, 2004). That is, the interaction is about information that is relevant to both parties. Once this is established, increased levels of trust develop between the participants so that eventually a dialogue emerges between communication partners. Interactivity, therefore, is a prelude to dialogue, the highest or purest form of communication.

Dialogue occurs through reasoning, which requires both listening and adaptation skills. Dialogue is concerned with the development of knowledge that is specific to the parties involved and is referred to as 'learning together' (Ballantyne, 2004: 119). The development of digital technologies has been instrumental in enabling organizations to provide increased interaction opportunities with their customers and other audiences. Think of the number of times when watching TV that you are prompted to press the red button to get more information. For example, many news programmes now encourage viewers to phone or send in their emails and pictures about particular issues. This is an attempt to get audiences to express their views about a subject and in doing so promote access to and interaction with the programme. Whereas interaction at one time only really occurred through personal selling, it is now possible to interact, and so build mutual understanding with consumers, through the internet and other digital technologies. Indeed, Hoffman and Novak (1996) claim that interactivity between people is now supplemented by interactivity between machines. This means that the interaction, or indeed dialogue, that previously occurred through machines can now occur with the equipment facilitating the communication.

Visit the **Online Resource Centre** and complete Internet Activity 10.3 to learn more about internet advertising, a form of machine interactivity with the internet.

go online

Personal Influencers

As mentioned earlier two main types of personal influencer can be recognized: opinion leaders and opinion formers. These are now discussed in turn.

Opinion Leaders

Studies by Katz and Lazarsfeld (1955) into American voting and purchase behaviour led them to conclude that some individuals were more predisposed to receiving information and then reprocessing it to influence others. They found that these individuals had the capacity to be more persuasive than information received directly from the mass media. They called these people opinion leaders and one of their defining characteristics is that they belong to the same peer group as the people they influence, they are not distant or removed.

It has been reported in subsequent research that opinion leaders have a greater exposure to relevant media and as a result have more knowledge/familiarity and involvement with a product category than others. Non-leaders, or **opinion followers**, turn to opinion leaders for advice and information about products and services they are interested in. **Opinion leaders** are also more gregarious and more self-confident than non-leaders and are more confident of their role as an influencer (Chan and Misra, 1990). It is not surprising, therefore, that many marketing communication strategies are targeted at influencing opinion leaders as they will, in turn, influence others. This approach has been used to convey particular information and help educate large target audiences through TV and radio programmes. For example, TV programmes such as *Coronation Street*, *Eastenders*, and *Emmerdale* and radio programmes such as *The Archers* (soaps), have been used as opinion leadership vehicles to bring to attention and open up debates about many controversial social issues, such as contraception, abortion, drug use and abuse, and serious illness and mental health concerns.

▶ Market Insight 10.2

It was Shouted not Wispa'd

One common approach when launching new brands such as cigarettes, and both alcoholic and soft drinks, is to encourage staff at nightclubs and other venues appropriate to the target market to be seen drinking/using the product. The use of these people is deliberate because they are of the same age and peer group as the club guests. They are, therefore, perceived as opinion leaders, and, when seen consuming the brand in the right context, can provide the necessary credibility for a new brand. This not only helps to inform clubbers of the availability of the brand and that it is cool to be seen drinking it, but it can also motivate subsequent purchase. It is quite common for free samples to be available as this encourages people to experience the brand at little or no risk.

The power of word-of-mouth should not be underestimated. The Cadbury Wispa chocolate bar was introduced in 1981 and then dropped in 2003. This caused public outrage and Wispa fans joined as a concerted effort to get the brand re-established, resulting in 93 Bring Back Wispa groups on Facebook including 800,000 Wispa fans plus increasing levels

▶ Market Insight 10.2

(Previous page)
Bringing back the much-loved Wispa
Source: © 2010 Cadbury.

of activity on rival networks. Clips of Wispa TV advertisements from the bar's heyday in the 1980s were posted on YouTube and similar sites, with fans appealing for missing examples. There was even an invasion of Wispa supporters at the stage of the Glastonbury festival. All of this plus blogs and internet discussion threads persuaded Cadbury that there was a strong and vibrant market for Wispa. In 2007, Cadbury re-launched a limited edition of Wispa and sold 20m bars in seven weeks. Following this success, Cadbury then announced that Wispa would return permanently and it was the no. 1 selling chocolate bar in 2009.
Sources: Wainwright (2007); Tualk (2009b).

1 Using a product or brand with which you are familiar, think about three ways in which planned opinion leadership might be used to develop the brand.

2 Think of a hobby or pastime that you might enjoy. Now, out of all your friends and social networks and contacts, who would you ask for advice about taking up the pastime? Why did you choose them?

3 Do you believe that paying or rewarding opinion leaders is an authentic way to develop word-of-mouth communication?

Opinion Formers

The other main form of independent personal influencer is **opinion formers**. They are not part of the same peer group as the people they influence. Their defining characteristic is that they exert personal influence because of their profession, authority, education, or status associated with the object of the communication process. They provide information and advice as part of the formal expertise they are perceived to hold. For example, shop assistants in music equipment shops are often experienced musicians in their own right. Aspiring musicians seeking to buy their first proper guitar will often consult these perceived 'experts' about guitar brands, styles, models, and associated equipment such as amplifiers. In the same way, doctors carry such conviction that they can influence the rate at which medicines are consumed. Drug manufacturers such as GlaxoSmithKline and Pfizer often launch new drugs by enlisting the support of eminent professors, consultants, or doctors who are recognized by others in the profession as experts. These opinion formers are invited to lead symposia and associated events and in doing so build credibility and activity around the new product.

Organizations target their marketing communications at opinion leaders and formers in order to penetrate the market more quickly than relying on communicating directly with the target audience. However, in addition to these forms of influence, reference needs to be made to spokespersons. There are some potential problems that advertisers need to be aware of when considering the use of celebrities. First, does the celebrity fit the image of the brand and will the celebrity be acceptable to the target audience, now and in the long run? So, should the lifestyle of the celebrity change, what impact will the change have on the target audience and their attitude towards the brand? For example, the well-publicized allegations about the behaviour of the supermodel Kate Moss led to several sponsorship and brand endorsement contracts being lost (e.g. H&M and Burberry), although it is alleged that her overall income actually increased as a result of the publicity, and sales through her new Topshop brand have soared.

The second problem concerns the impact that the celebrity makes relative to the brand. There is a danger that the receiver remembers the celebrity but not the message or the brand. The celebrity becomes the hero, rather than the product being advertised.

All of the models of communication discussed have a role to play in marketing communications. Mass media communication in the form of broadcast TV and radio is still used by organizations to reach large audiences. Two-way and interaction forms of communication are used to reach smaller, specific target audiences and to enable a range of people to contribute to the process. Interaction and dialogue are higher levels of communication and are used increasingly to generate personal communication with individual customers. The skill for marketing practitioners is to know when to move from one-way, to two-way, to interactive, and then dialogue-based marketing communications.

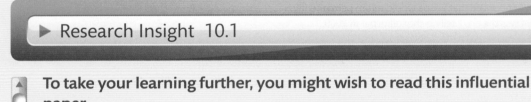

▶ Research Insight 10.1

To take your learning further, you might wish to read this influential paper.

Kitchen, P. (1993), 'Marketing communications renaissance', *International Journal of Advertising*, 12, 4, 367–86.

This paper provides a helpful review of the literature in relation to developments in marketing communications in the early 1990s, at a time when initial ideas about integrated marketing communications were emerging. It signals changes in public relations and shows how advertising, sales promotion, and personal selling were adapting to a changing environment.

 Visit the **Online Resource Centre** to read the abstract and access the full paper.

The Role of Marketing Communications

Now that ideas about how communication works have been established, it is time to examine what marketing communications is and the tasks it undertakes. Marketing communications is a relatively new term for what was previously referred to as promotion. As was discussed in Chapter 1, promotion is one of the Ps of the marketing mix, and is responsible for the communication of the marketing offer to the target market. Although recognizing that there is implicit and important communication through the other elements of the marketing mix (for example, a high price is symbolic of high quality), it is the task of a planned and integrated set of activities to communicate effectively with each of an organization's stakeholder groups.

Fundamentally, marketing communications comprises three elements: a set of tools, the media, and messages. The five common tools are advertising, sales promotion, personal selling, direct marketing, and public relations. In addition there are a range of media, such as TV, radio, press, and the internet, which are used to convey messages to target audiences.

These various tools have been developed in response to changing market and environmental conditions. For example, public relations is now seen by some to have both a product and a corporate dimension. Direct marketing is now recognized as an important way of developing closer relationships with buyers, both consumer and organizational, whereas new and innovative forms of communication through sponsorship, floor advertising, video screens on supermarket trolleys and checkout coupon dispensers, and the internet and associated technologies, mean that effective communication requires the selection and integration of an increasing variety of communication tools and media. Communication is no longer restricted to promoting and persuading audiences as the tasks are now much broader and strategic.

Today, the term marketing communications is a more appropriate and established term used to reflect an organization's communication activities.

Marketing communications are used to achieve one of two principal goals. The first concerns the development of brand values. Advertising, and to some extent public relations, have for a long time concentrated on establishing a set of feelings, emotions, and beliefs about a brand or organization. Brand communication seeks to make us think positively about a brand, helps us to remember and develop positive brand attitudes in the hope that when we are ready to buy that type of product again, we will buy brand X because we feel positively about it.

The alternative and more contemporary goal is to use communications to make us behave in particular ways. Rather than spend lots of money developing worthy and positive attitudes towards brands, the view of many today is that we should use this money to encourage people to behave differently. This might be through buying the product, or driving people to a website, requesting a brochure, or making a telephone call. This is called behaviour change and is driven by using messages that provide audiences with a reason to act or what is referred to as a **call-to-action**.

So, on the one hand, communications can be used to develop brand feelings, and, on the other, to change or manage the behaviour of the target audience. These are not mutually exclusive, for example, many TV advertisements are referred to as direct-response ads because not only do they attempt to create brand values but they also carry a website address, telephone number, or details of a special offer (sales promotion). In other words, the two goals are mixed into a hybrid approach.

The success of marketing communication depends on the extent to which messages engage their audiences (see Market Insight 10.3). These audiences can be seen to fall into three main groups.

▶ Customers—these may be consumers or they may be end user organizations.

▶ Channel members—each organization is part of a network of other organizations such as suppliers, retailers, wholesalers, value added **resellers**, distributors, and other retailers, who join together, often freely, to make the product or service available to end users.

▶ General stakeholders—organizations and people who either influence or are influenced by the organization. These may be shareholders, the financial community, trade unions, employees, local community, and others.

▶ Market Insight 10.3

Marketing the British Army: Start Thinking Soldier

For a long time the recruitment strategy used by the British Army involved TV and print campaigns. These were then used to drive people to their website where more information could be obtained. Now the strategy being deployed by the British Army seeks to provide potential recruits an experience of what life is like in the army. The experience is developed at the website and for some, at purpose-built 'Show Rooms'. Therefore, the overall campaign, called 'Start Thinking Soldier', combines interactive and experiential approaches.

The campaign is driven by the use of TV ads, which are used to provide awareness and stimulate interest in the opportunities available. The ads also drive people to the 'Start Thinking Soldier' website. At the site, in addition to links to a variety of jobs and roles plus a forum to chat with real soldiers, there are opportunities for people to experience life in the army. Visitors are presented with a variety of interactive situations, where skills such as observation and target practice are tested. Each of the situations are based on reality and each is designed to provide an insight into what life is like in the army.

The army has also built a small number of Show Rooms in the London area. These enable people to experience simulations such as firing a rifle and riding in a tank, plus obtaining information about a range

The Start Thinking Soldier campaign markets the army as an exciting career option

▶ Market Insight 10.3

of back-office positions. All of these are designed to provide a taste of life as a soldier.

Sources: Thomas (2009); Charles (2009); www.armyjobs.mod.uk/startthinkingsoldier.

1 Putting aside any opinions you may have about the army generally, what do you think about this approach used by the army to reach their target market?

2 Identify two other products or services that try to use an experiential strategy.

3 Visit the websites of armies in two different countries. What are the core messages they convey?

Marketing communications, therefore, involves not just customers but also a range of other stakeholders. Marketing communications can be used to reach consumers as well as business audiences.

As explained earlier in Chapter 1, the concept of exchange is central to our understanding of marketing. For an exchange to take place there must be two or more parties, each of whom can offer something of value to the other and who are prepared to enter freely into the exchange process, a transaction. There are of course many types of exchange but two are of particular importance: transactional exchanges and collaborative exchanges.

▶ **Transactional exchanges** (Bagozzi, 1978; Houston and Gassenheimer, 1987) are transactions that occur independently of any previous or subsequent exchanges. They have a short-term orientation and are primarily motivated by self-interest. So, when a consumer buys an MP3 player, a brand that they have not bought before, then a transactional exchange can be identified.

▶ **Collaborative exchanges** (Dwyer, Schurr, and Oh, 1987) have a longer term orientation and develop between parties who wish to build long-term supportive relationships. So, when a consumer buys their third product from the same brand as the MP3 player, perhaps from the same dealer, collaborative exchanges are considered to be taking place.

These two types of exchange transactions represent the extremes of a spectrum. In mature industrial societies transactional exchanges have tended to dominate commercial transactions, although recently there has been a substantial movement towards collaborative exchanges. Each organization has a mix of audiences so it should not be surprising that they use a range of communication tools and media to suit different exchange preferences of customers, suppliers, and other stakeholder audiences.

The impact on marketing communications is essentially about the choice of tools, media, and messages. Audiences who prefer transactional exchanges might be better engaged with advertising and mass media-based communications, with messages that are impersonal and largely rational and product-focused. Audiences that prefer more collaborative exchanges should be engaged through personal, informal, and interactive communications, with messages that are generally emotional and relationship-oriented.

Shoes can be purchased from a range of different retail outlets and the store they are purchased from is often insignificant, especially as price can be an important purchasing factor. The approach adopted by Clarks, the shoe company, recognizes the importance of building a long-term relationship with their customers. The First Shoes campaign run by Clarks demonstrates good marketing communications and is based on the significance of a child's first pair of shoes and what they can mean to the parents. These tiny shoes are often kept for years and years as a memento. Clarks now provide a souvenir of the occasion in the form of a free, framed Polaroid photograph of a child's very first shop visit and fitting. A simple campaign that engages audiences with an important event, but it also enables both the parents and Clarks to remember the event through longer term memories. What might have been a transactional exchange is transformed into one that is more collaborative and relationship-oriented.

What is Marketing Communications?

Quite naturally, definitions of marketing communication have evolved as the topic and our understanding have developed. Original views assumed that these types of communication were used to persuade people to buy products and services. The focus was on products, one-way communications, persuasion, and there was a short-term perspective. In short, an organization's products and services were *promoted* to audiences.

However, this perspective has given way to the term marketing communications. This was partly a result of an increase in the tasks that the communications departments were expected to undertake and a widening of the tools and media that could be used. At the same time there has been a shift from mass to personal communications and a greater focus on integration activities. The following represents a contemporary definition of marketing communications.

> Marketing communications is a management process through which an organisation attempts to engage with its various audiences. By understanding an audience's communications environment, organisations seek to develop and present messages for its identified stakeholder groups, before evaluating and acting upon the responses. By conveying messages that are of significant value, audiences are encouraged to offer attitudinal and behavioural responses (Fill, 2009).

There are three main aspects associated with this definition: engagement, audiences, and responses.

▶ **Engagement**—what are the audiences' communications needs and is it possible to engage with them on their terms using one-way, two-way, or dialogic communications?

▶ Audiences—which specific audience(s) do we need to communicate with and what are their various behaviour and information-processing needs?

▶ Responses—what are the desired outcomes of the communication process? Are they based on changes in perception, values, and beliefs or are changes in behaviour required?

Marketing communications can, therefore, be considered from a number of perspectives. Although it is a complex activity and used by organizations with varying degrees of sophistication, it is undoubtedly concerned with the way in which audiences are encouraged to perceive an organization and/or its offerings. It should, therefore, be regarded as an audience-centred activity.

▶ Market Insight 10.4

Stunts, Media, and T-Mobile

T-Mobile launched a campaign in 2009 that typifies the way in which marketing communications can now work. The campaign was audience-orientated, driven by digital media yet incorporated traditional advertising through broadcast and outdoor media. The campaign also harnessed the power of public relations.

The goal was to help people see how they could create and share magical moments using T-Mobile. This was achieved through two key events and YouTube, among other facilities. In January a mass-choreographed dance, involving unsuspecting commuters, was staged at Liverpool Street Station in London. A 2.5-minute ad, featuring footage from the dance, was delivered through broadcast media during Channel 4's *Big Brother*.

In April, a mass-singalong was held in Trafalgar Square with people invited to attend through Facebook, Twitter, and SMS. Over 13,000 people turned up for the event, which was filmed and again turned into an ad.

Videos from both events were hosted on T-Mobile's branded YouTube and received 23m hits. The events were taken on a roadshow tour and one Facebook group re-enacted the dance with 2,000 people at Liverpool Street Station. As if that was not enough, outdoor advertising was used in the form of bus advertising and media relations ensured the unusual events were mentioned in the news, entertainment, and business media. The results? Handset sales up 22%, and T-Mobile stores experience the highest ever recorded number of visitors.

Sources: Benady (2009); Byrne (2010).

1 **Apply the three elements from the definition of marketing communications to the T-Mobile campaign. How well do they fit?**

2 **How does your mobile phone service provider use marketing communications?**

3 **Go to www.campaignlive.co.uk/news/873966/ Campaign-video—behind-scenes-TMobiles-new-shoot/?DCMP=ILC-SEARCH and watch the video. Why was YouTube a central element in the campaign?**

T-Mobile stages a mass choreographed dance with unsuspecting train commuters

Source: © 2010 T-Mobile (UK) Ltd.

The Tasks of Marketing Communications

However, promotion (essentially persuasion) alone is insufficient as marketing communications undertakes other tasks in the name of engaging audiences. So, what is it that marketing communications does and why do organizations use it in varying ways? Well, fundamentally, marketing communications can be used to engage audiences by undertaking one of four main tasks, referred to by Fill as the **DRIP** model (Fill, 2002). In no particular order, communications can be used to differentiate brands and organizations, to reinforce brand memories and expectations, to inform, that is make aware and educate audiences, and finally to persuade them to do things or to behave in particular ways. See Table 10.1 for an explanation of each of these tasks.

These tasks are not mutually exclusive, indeed campaigns might be designed to target two or three of them. For example, the launch of a new brand will require that audiences be informed, made aware of its existence, and enabled to understand how it is different from competitor brands. A brand that is well established might try to reach lapsed customers by reminding them of the key features and benefits and offering them an incentive (persuasion) to buy again. For example, Your M&S is a bi-monthly magazine designed to showcase what is new in Marks and Spencer's stores and give fashion and style advice. However, it only features products available at M&S. The magazine is an integral part of the company's communication mix and is used, among many things, to engage customers with the brand and drive readers into the store to shop. To that extent, an in-house survey found that 57%

▶ **Table 10.1** The key DRIP tasks for marketing communications

Marketing communications tasks	Explanation
To differentiate	In many markets there is little to separate brands (e.g. mineral water, coffee, printers). In these cases it is the images created by marketing communications that help differentiate one brand from another and position them so that consumers develop positive attitudes and make purchasing decisions
To reinforce	Communications may be used to *remind* people of a need they might have or of the benefits of past transactions with a view to convincing them that they should enter into a similar exchange. In addition, it is possible to provide *reassurance* or comfort either immediately prior to an exchange or, more commonly, post purchase. This is important as it helps to retain current customers and improve profitability. This approach to business is much more cost-effective than constantly striving to lure new customers
To inform	One of the most common uses of marketing communications is to *inform* and make potential customers aware of the features and benefits of an organization's offering. In addition, marketing communications can be used to educate audiences, to show them how to use a product or what to do in particular situations
To persuade	Communication may attempt to *persuade* current and potential customers of the desirability of entering into an exchange relationship

of readers, that is nearly 2.53 million people, visited an M&S store as a result of reading the magazine. It also found that 30% of readers had bought a product featured in its magazine (Alarcon, 2008).

Marketing Communication Messages

The importance of sending the right message was established earlier when considering communication theory. From a receiver's perspective, the process of decoding and giving meaning to messages is affected by the volume and quality of information received and the judgment they make about the methods and how well the message was communicated. We also know that, in order for a message to be processed successfully, messages should reflect a balance between the need for information and the need for pleasure or enjoyment in consuming the message. Messages can be categorized as either product-oriented and rational or customer-oriented and based on feelings and emotions.

As a general guideline, when audiences experience high involvement, the emphasis of the message should be on the information content, with the key attributes and the associated benefits emphasized. This style is often factual and product-oriented. If audiences experience low involvement then messages should attempt to gain an emotional response. There are, of course, many situations where both rational and emotional messages are needed by buyers in order to make purchasing decisions. Nokia, the Finnish mobile phone manufacturer, announced early in 2007 that it was reviewing its global advertising and that it was intending to put emotional engagement at the centre of its brand strategy and communications (Kemp, 2007).

The presentation of messages should reflect the degree to which factual information or emotional content is required for the message to command attention and then be processed. There are numerous presentational or executional techniques, but Table 10.2 outlines some of the more commonly used appeals.

▶ **Table 10.2** Information and emotional appeals

Information-based messages

Factual	Messages provide rational, logical information, and are presented in a straightforward, no-frills manner
Slice of life	Uses people who are similar to the target audience and presented in scenes to which the target audience can readily associate and understand. For example, washing powder brands are often presented by stereotypical 'housewives', who are seen discussing the brand in a kitchen
Demonstration	Brands are presented in a problem-solving context. So, people with headaches are seen to be in pain, but then take brand x, which resolves the problem
Comparative	In this approach, brand x is compared favourably, on two or three main attributes, with a leading competitor

Emotion-based messages	
Fear	Products are shown either to relieve danger or ill health through usage (e.g. toothpaste) or they can dispel the fear of social rejection (anti-dandruff shampoos)
Humour	The use of humour can draw attention, stimulate interest, and place audiences in a positive mood
Animation	Used to reach children and as a way of communicating potentially boring and uninteresting products (gas, insurance) to adults
Sex	Excellent for getting the attention of the target audience, but unless the product is related (e.g. perfume, clothing) these ads generally do not work
Music	Good for getting attention and differentiating between brands
Fantasy and surrealism	Used increasingly to provide a point of differentiation and brand intrigue (e.g. mobile phone networks)

go online

Visit the **Online Resource Centre** and complete Internet Activity 10.1 to learn more about how Bacardi uses product demonstration and a digital media format (.mp3) to inform target audiences how to make a Bacardi Mojito.

The Marketing Communications Mix

We learnt earlier that marketing communications activities concern the use of three main elements; 1) tools, 2) media, and 3) messages. These are considered here briefly, although a fuller exposition of the tools and media can be found in Chapter 12.

The traditional **marketing communications mix** consists of a set of five primary tools. These are advertising, sales promotion, direct marketing, public relations, and personal selling. Additionally, these tools, and, in particular, advertising, use media in order to reach their audiences. Tools and media are not the same as they have different characteristics and are used for different purposes.

The five primary tools of marketing communications are used in various combinations and with different degrees of intensity in order to achieve different communication goals with target audiences.

Media enable messages to be delivered to target audiences. Some media are owned by organizations (a building or delivery van can constitute media), but in most cases media to reach large audiences are owned by third-party organizations. As a result, clients have to pay media owners for the right to send their messages through their media vehicles.

For a long time the range of available media was fairly limited, but since the early 1990s the array of media has been growing rapidly and changing the media landscape. Now there is a huge choice of media so that media selection has become crucial when trying to reach increasingly smaller audiences. The cost of some media can be immense, although in many cases fees are related to the number of people reached through a media vehicle. Space (or time) within traditional media is limited and costs rise as demand for the limited space/time and audience size increases. As a generalization, space within digital media is unlimited and so contact costs fall as audience size increases.

For a consideration of each of the tools and key media readers are advised to read Chapter 11.

Word-of-Mouth

Planned marketing communications have traditionally used paid-for media to convey messages to target audiences. However, as mentioned previously in respect of opinion formers and leaders, some messages are best relayed through personal communications. This type of communication does not involve any payment for media because communication is freely given through word-of-mouth conversation.

Word-of-mouth communication is 'interpersonal communication regarding products or services where the receiver regards the communicator as impartial' (Stokes and Lomax, 2002).

Personal influence within the communication process is important. This is because customers perceive word-of-mouth recommendations as objective and unbiased. In comparison to advertising messages, word-of-mouth communications are more robust (Berkman and Gilson, 1986). Word-of-mouth messages are used either as information inputs prior to purchase or as a support and reinforcement of their own purchasing decisions.

People like to talk about their product (service) experiences. The main stimulus for behaviour is that the product or service in question either gave them particular pleasure or displeasure. These motivations to discuss products and their associative experiences vary between individuals and with the intensity of the motivation at any one particular moment. One hotel gave away teddy bears to guests on the basis that the guests would be happy to talk about their stay at the hotel, with the teddy bear acting as a prompt to provoke or induce conversation.

For every single positive comment there are ten negative comments. For this reason, word-of-mouth communication was once seen as negative, unplanned, and as having a corrosive effect on a brand's overall communications. Today, organizations actively manage word-of-mouth communications in order to generate positive comments and as a way of differentiating themselves in the market. e-viral marketing or 'word-of-mouse' communication is an electronic version of the spoken endorsement of a product or service. Often using humorous messages, games, video clips, and screen savers, information can be targeted at key individuals who then voluntarily pass the message to friends and colleagues and in doing so bestow, endorse, and provide the message with much-valued credibility.

For organizations it is important to target messages at those individuals who are predisposed to such discussion, as it is likely that they will propel word-of-mouth recommendations. The target, therefore, is not necessarily the target market, but opinion leaders within target markets, individuals who are most likely to volunteer their positive opinions about the offering, and who, potentially, have some influence over people in their peer group.

▶ Research Insight 10.2

To take your learning further, you might wish to read this influential paper.

Duncan, T., and Moriarty, S. (1998) 'A communication-based marketing model for managing relationships', *Journal of Marketing,* **62 (April), 1–13.**

This is one of the most important academic papers in the field of marketing communications. It is important because it led the transition from a functional perspective of integrated marketing communications to one that emphasized its role within relationship marketing.

 Visit the **Online Resource Centre** to read the abstract and access the full paper.

How Marketing Communications Works

Ideas about how advertising, and then promotion, works have been a constant source of investigation, endeavour, and conceptual speculation. To suggest that a firm conclusion has been reached would be misleading and untrue. However, particular ideas have stood out and have played a more influential role in shaping our ideas about this fascinating topic. Some of these are presented here.

The first important idea about how advertising works was based on how the personal selling process works. Developed by Strong (1925), the **AIDA** model has become extremely well known and used by many practitioners. AIDA refers to the need to first create awareness, secondly generate interest, then drive desire, from which action (a sale) emerges. As a broad interpretation of the sales process this is generally correct but it fails to provide insight into the depths of how advertising works. Thirty-six years later, Lavidge and Steiner (1961) presented a model based on what is referred to as the **hierarchy of effects** approach. Similar in nature to AIDA, it assumes that there are a series of steps a prospect must pass through in order for a purchase to be made. It is assumed, correctly, that advertising cannot generate an immediate sale because there are a series of thought processes that need to be fulfilled prior to action. These steps are represented in Figure 10.5.

These models have become known as hierarchy of effects (HoE) models, simply because the effects (on audiences) are thought to occur in a top-down sequence. Some of the attractions of these HoE models and frameworks are that they are straightforward, simple, easy to understand, and, if creating advertising materials, provide a helpful broad template on which to develop and evaluate campaigns.

However, although attractive, this sequential approach has several drawbacks. People do not always process information nor do they always purchase products following a series of sequential steps. This logical progression is not reflected in reality when, for example, an impulse purchase is followed by an emotional feeling toward a brand. There are also questions about what actually constitutes adequate levels of awareness, comprehension, and

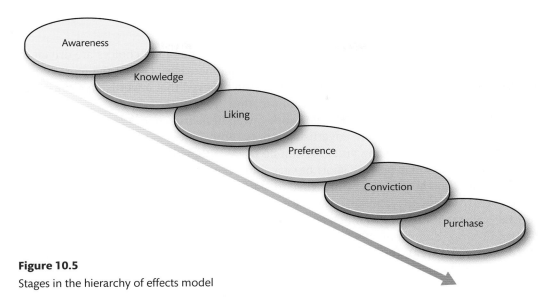

Figure 10.5
Stages in the hierarchy of effects model

conviction, how can it be known which stage the majority of the target audience has reached at any one point in time, and is this purchase sequence applicable to all consumers for all purchases?

The Strong and the Weak Theories of Advertising

So, if advertising cannot be assumed to work in just one particular way what other explanations are there? Of the various models put forward, two in particular stand out. These are the strong (Jones, 1991) and the weak (Ehrenberg, 1974) theories of advertising.

The Strong Theory of Advertising

According to Jones (1991), advertising is capable of persuading people to buy a product that they have not previously purchased. Advertising can also generate long-run purchase behaviour. Under the **strong theory**, advertising is believed to be capable of increasing sales for a brand and for the **product class**. These upward shifts are achieved through the use of manipulative and psychological techniques, which are deployed against largely passive consumers, who, possibly due to apathy, are either generally incapable of processing information intelligently or have little or no motivation to become involved.

This interpretation is a persuasion view and corresponds very well to the HoE models referred to earlier. Persuasion occurs by moving buyers towards a purchase by easing them through a series of steps, prompted by timely and suitable promotional messages. It seems that this approach correlates closely with new products where new buying behaviours are required.

The strong theory has close affiliation with an advertising style that is product-oriented, where features and benefits are outlined clearly for audiences, and where pack shots are considered important.

The Weak Theory of Advertising

Contrary to the strong perspective is the view that a consumer's brand choices are driven by purchasing habit rather than by exposure to promotional messages. One of the more prominent researchers in this area is Ehrenberg (1997), who believed that advertising represented a weak force and that consumers are active information processors.

Ehrenberg proposed that the **ATR** framework (awareness–trial–reinforcement) is a more appropriate interpretation of how advertising works. Both Jones and Ehrenberg agree that awareness is required before any purchase can be made, although the elapsed time between awareness and action may be very short or very long. Out of the mass of people exposed to a message, a few will be sufficiently intrigued to want to try a product (trial), the next phase. Reinforcement follows to maintain awareness and provide reassurance to help customers repeat the pattern of thinking and behaviour. Advertising's role is to breed brand familiarity and identification (Ehrenberg, 1997).

According to the **weak theory**, advertising is employed as a defence, to retain customers, and to increase product or brand usage. Advertising is used to reinforce existing attitudes, not necessarily to drastically change them. This means that when people say that they 'are not influenced by advertising' they are in the main correct.

Both the strong and the weak theories of advertising are important because they are equally right and they are equally wrong. The answer to the question 'how does advertising work?' lies somewhere between the two and is dependent on the context. For advertising to work, involvement is likely to be high and so here the strong theory is the most applicable. However, the vast majority of product purchase decisions generate low involvement, and so decision-making is likely to be driven by habit. Here, advertising's role is to maintain a brand's awareness with the purchase cycle.

A Composite Approach

Most of the frameworks presented so far have their roots in advertising. If we are to establish a model that explains how marketing communications works, a different perspective is required, one that draws on the key parts of all the models. This is possible as the three key components of the attitude construct lie within these different models. Attitudes have been regarded as an important aspect of promotional activity, and advertising is thought to be capable of influencing the development of positive attitudes towards brands.

The three stages of attitude formation are that we learn something (cognitive or learning component), feel something (an affective or emotional component), and then we act on our attitudes (behavioural or the conative component). So, in many situations we learn something, feel something towards a brand, and then proceed to buy or not buy. These stages are set out in Figure 10.6.

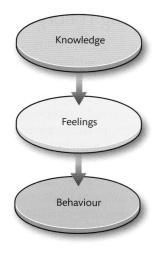

Figure 10.6

Attitude construct—linear

The HoE models and the strong theory contain this sequential approach of learn, feel, do. However, we do not always pass through this particular sequence and the weak theory puts greater emphasis on familiarity and reminding (awareness) than the other components.

So, if we look at Figure 10.7, we can see that these components have been worked into a circular format. This means that when using marketing communications it is not necessary to slavishly follow each component in turn. The focus can be on what the audience requires and this might be on the learning, feeling, or doing components, as determined by the audience. In other words, for marketing communications to be audience-centred, we should develop campaigns based on the overriding need of the audience at any one point in time, based on the need to learn, to feel, or to behave in particular ways.

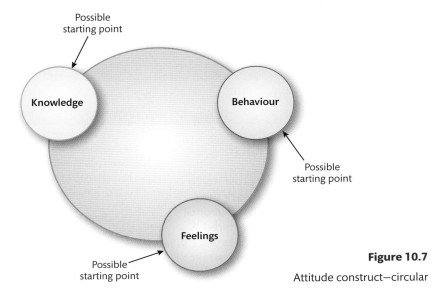

Figure 10.7

Attitude construct—circular

▶ **Learn**

Where learning is the priority, the overall goal should be to inform or educate the target audience. If the product is new it will be important to make the target audience aware of the product's existence and to inform them of the brand's key attributes and benefits. This is a common use for advertising as it has the capacity to reach both large and targeted audiences. Other than making them aware of the product's existence, other tasks include showing the target audience how a brand is superior to competitive offerings, perhaps demonstrating how a product works and educating the audience about when and in what circumstances the brand should be used.

▶ **Feel**

Once the audience is aware of a brand and knows something about how it might be useful to them, it is important that they develop a positive attitude towards the brand. This can be achieved by presenting the brand with a set of emotional values that it is thought will appeal and be of interest to the audience. These values need to be repeated in subsequent communications in order to reinforce the brand attitudes.

Marketing communications should be used to involve and immerse people in a brand. So, for example, advertising or product placement within films and music videos will help show how a brand fits in with a desirable set of values and lifestyles. Use of suitable music, characters that reflect the values of either the current target audience or an aspirational group, a tone of voice, colours, and images all help to create a particular emotional disposition and understanding about what the brand represents or stands for. For some people, advertising only works at an emotional level and the cognitive approach is irrelevant.

▶ **Do**

Most organizations find that to be successful they need to use a much broader set of tools, and that the goal is to change the behaviour of the target audience. This behavioural change may be about getting people to buy the brand, but it may often be about motivating them to visit a website, call for a brochure, fill in an application form, or just encouraging them to visit a shop and sample the brand free of money and any other risk. This behavioural change is also referred to as a 'call-to-action'.

▶ Market Insight 10.5

Why Compare Meerkats?

Price comparison sites have proliferated in recent years, mainly because of their functionality. The key benefit is that once a person's enquiry details are entered, a search of hundreds of prices takes place in a few seconds. Previously, it used to take all morning to contact three or four insurers by phone.

Competition is intense and size is important as the larger operators have the advertising spend necessary to gain name recognition, recall and search to achieve market share. When comparethe market.com considered their options the outlook was not good. Fourth in the market where name familiarity is key (and their name was unmemorable), their identity and name were very similar to their nearest competitor (gocompare), they had no single point of differentiation, and they were last to the market. They needed a distinct place in the market.

Most sites were the same and the messages were very similar, based around price-saving claims. It is easy to get people to remember 'compare' led brand names, but getting them to differentiate them accurately and to attribute the right benefit claims to the right brand, was not. The single key element that distinguished this brand from the competition was the word 'market'

in their name. So, rather than a rational attribute-based positioning like their competitors, who were perceived to be irritating and disliked, another option was to differentiate through entertainment.

The **client brief** requested that the agency find a way of side stepping the high cost per click on the word market (which is over £5). The task was to find a way of introducing a cheaper term or phrase into the advertising that could exist alongside 'market'. To keep costs down, comparison sites need to stimulate people to type in their brand name. This is because Google charge more if they search for something generic (i.e. car insurance), less if the search is by brand name.

The result was Aleksandr Orlov, a Russian meerkat and founder of www.comparethemeerkat.com, a site for comparing meerkats. Orlov is constantly frustrated by the confusion between comparethemarket.com and comparethemeerkat.com. This idea caught the imagination of the audience and the comparethemeerkat.com campaign site was used to develop the joke by encouraging users to actually compare meerkats, and select your particular meerkat. As a bonus, the cost per click on meerkats was approximately 5p, not the £5 required on the word 'market'.

The TV campaign proved to be a tremendous success and captured the imagination of thousands of people.

▶ Market Insight 10.5

comparethemarket.com's successful advert used the meerkat character, Alexsandr Orlov

Source: Courtesy of comparethemarket.com.

The campaign included a website, a community on Facebook, and direct access to the brand hero through Twitter.

Facebook was used for people to upload meerkat suggestions, meerkat photos, and ideas for new marketing launches (toys, ringtones, etc.). A blog was created uploading content, pictures, videos, and notes on a weekly basis. Aleksandr was claimed to be the first UK advertising character to have his own Twitter account. He shares links, photos, his daily thoughts, and answers specific questions that his fans tweet him. Twitter is used to find real people to appear as part of his new Testimonials page on his website. At the time of writing it was claimed that Aleksandr had over 700,000 Facebook fans and over 37,000 followers on Twitter.

The campaign achieved all of its 12-month objectives in just nine weeks. It also propelled the brand to the no. 1 position in terms of spontaneous awareness and consideration, slashed the cost per visit by 73% and increased quote volumes by over 83%. (See Market Insight 12.4 for more on Comparison Shopping Engines.)

Sources: Jukes (2009); VCCP (2009); Ramsay (2009).

1 **Which part of the attitude construct was the www.comparethemeerkat.com idea trying to influence?**

2 **How have www.comparethemeerkat.com tried to use word-of-mouth communications?**

3 **What is your opinion of the strategy used by www.comparethemeerkat.com? Justify your response.**

When the accent is on using marketing communications to drive behaviour and action, **direct-response advertising** can be effective. It is said that 40% of TV ads have a telephone number or website address. However, sales promotion, direct marketing, and personal selling are particularly effective at influencing behaviour and calling the audience to act.

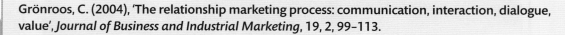

▶ Research Insight 10.3

To take your learning further, you might wish to read this influential paper.

Grönroos, C. (2004), 'The relationship marketing process: communication, interaction, dialogue, value', *Journal of Business and Industrial Marketing*, 19, 2, 99–113.

Professor Grönroos is a leading researcher within the services marketing sector. In this paper he suggests that if the interaction and marketing communications processes are geared towards customers' value processes, then a relationship dialogue may develop.

@ Visit the **Online Resource Centre** to read the abstract and access the full paper.

Cultural Aspects of Marketing Communications

Marketing communications has the potential to influence more than just customers. Indeed it can be used by a wide range of other stakeholders, such as suppliers, employees, religious and faith groups, trade unions, and local communities.

The tools, media, and messages used by organizations influence and are influenced by the culture and environment in which they operate. Culture and related belief systems are significant factors in the way organizations choose to communicate in the different areas and regions in which they operate. At a broad level, for example, cases of the strong theory of advertising are observed more frequently in North America, whereas examples of the weak theory are quite prevalent in Europe.

In this final part of the chapter, consideration is given to some of the cultural issues associated with marketing communications.

Culture

Culture refers to the values, beliefs, ideas, customs, actions, and symbols that are learnt by members of particular societies. Marketing communications should be an audience-centred activity, whether those audiences are located domestically or anywhere around the globe. Therefore, as there are so many international, regional, and local communities, each with cultural variances, so the development of marketing communications for these audiences must be based on a sound understanding of their culture.

Culture is important because it provides individuals within a society with a sense of identity and an understanding of what is deemed to be acceptable behaviour. According to Hollensen (2005), it is commonly agreed that culture has three key characteristics: that culture is learned, interrelated, and shared. See Table 10.3 for a fuller account of these variables.

These boundaries between cultures are not fixed or rigid, as this would suggest that cultures are static. Instead they evolve and change as members of a society adjust to new technologies, government policies, changing values, and demographic changes, to mention but a few dynamic variables. Unsurprisingly, therefore, brands and symbols used to represent brands have different meanings as they are interpreted in the light of the prevailing culture.

Culture consists of various layers. Hollensen (2005) refers to a nest of cultures, with one inside another, a structure that is similar to a 'Russian doll' (Figure 10.8).

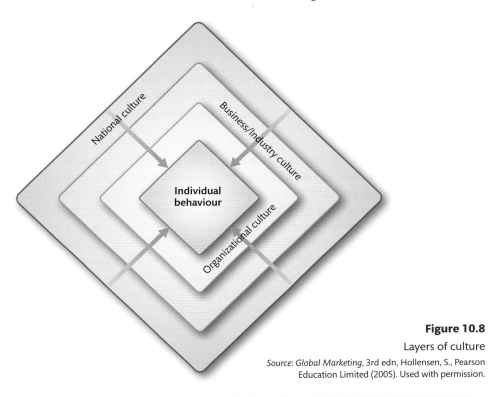

Figure 10.8

Layers of culture

Source: *Global Marketing*, 3rd edn, Hollensen, S., Pearson Education Limited (2005). Used with permission.

▶ **Table 10.3** Characteristics of culture

Cultural characteristic	Explanation
Learned	Culture is not innate or instinctual otherwise everyone would behave in the same way. Human beings across the world do not behave uniformly or predictably and they learn values and behaviours that are shared with common groups. Therefore, different cultures exist and there are boundaries within cultures, framing behaviours, and lifestyles
Interrelated	There are deep connections between different elements within a culture. Therefore, family, religion, business/work, and social status are interlinked
Shared	Cultural values are passed through family, religion, education, and the media. This progression of values enables culture to be passed from generation to generation. This is important as it provides consistency, stability, and direction for social behaviour and beliefs

Source: Adapted from Hollensen (2005).

Here, it can be imagined that the buyer in one country and a seller in another are faced with several layers of culture, all interrelated and all influencing an individual's behaviour.

▶ National culture—sets out the cultural concepts and the legislative framework governing the way business is undertaken.

▶ Industry/business culture—particular business sectors adopt a way of doing business within a competitive framework. The shipping business, for example, will have its own way of conducting itself based on its own heritage. As a result all participants know what is expected and understand the rules of the game.

▶ Organizational culture—not only does an organization have an overall culture but the various sub-cultures also have a system of shared values, beliefs, meanings, and behaviours.

▶ Individual behaviour—each individual is affected by and learns from the various cultural levels.

Marketing communications, at both a formal and informal level, needs to assimilate these different levels to ensure that an individual's behaviour is understood and the decision-making processes and procedures within which they operate are appreciated. In many markets there is little to separate brands (e.g. mineral water, coffee, printers). In these cases it is the images created by marketing communications that help differentiate one brand from another and position them so that consumers develop positive attitudes and make purchasing decisions. The way in which different societies perceive these same brands is a reflection of the cultural drivers that frame people's perceptions.

 ## Skills for Employment

> ▶▶ The best marketing practitioners are often great lateral thinkers. They can address questions such as: 'How do I get our message to our relevant audience? What message will appeal to them most? Where is there a gap in the market and how can I fill it?' ◀◀
>
> Simon Harrop, CEO, BRAND sense agency
>
> Visit the **Online Resource Centre** to discover more tips and advice on skills for the workplace.

 ## Chapter Summary

To consolidate your learning, the key points from this chapter are summarized below:

■ **Explain three models of communication and describe how personal influences can enhance the effectiveness of marketing communication activities.**

The linear or one-way model of communication is the traditional mass media interpretation of how communication works. The two-way model incorporates the influence of other people in the communication process, whereas the interactional model explains how communication flows not just between sender and receiver but throughout a network of people. Interaction is about actions that lead to a response and, most importantly in an age of interactive communication, interactivity is a prelude to dialogue, the highest or purest form of communication.

- **Describe the nature, purpose, and scope of marketing communications.**

  Marketing communications, or promotion as it was originally called, is one of the Ps of the marketing mix. It is used to communicate an organization's offer relating to products, services, or the overall organization. In broad terms the management activity consists of several components. There are the communications experienced by audiences relating to both their use of products and the consumption of associated services. There are communications arising from unplanned or unintended experiences and there are planned marketing communications.

- **Understand the role and various tasks of marketing communications.**

  The role of marketing communications is to engage audiences and there are four main tasks that it can be used to complete. These tasks are summarized as DRIP, that is, to differentiate, reinforce, inform, or persuade audiences to behave in particular ways. Several of these tasks can be undertaken simultaneously within a campaign.

- **Explain the key characteristics associated with developing promotional messages.**

  The main issues associated with message development concern the balance between providing sufficient product/service-related information and emotional content. When the customer experiences high involvement, the informational content should dominate. When audiences experience low involvement, the emotional aspects should be emphasized.

- **Understand the models used to explain how marketing communication is considered to work.**

  These models have evolved from sequential approaches such as AIDA and the HoE models. A circular model of the attitude construct helps understanding of the tasks of marketing communication, namely to inform audiences, to create feelings and a value associated with products and services, and to drive behaviour.

- **Describe what culture is and explain how it can impact on the use of marketing communications.**

  Culture refers to the values, beliefs, ideas, customs, actions, and symbols that are learned by members of particular societies. Culture is important because it provides individuals, within a society, with a sense of identity and an understanding of what is deemed to be acceptable behaviour. Culture is learnt, the elements are interrelated, and culture is shared among members of a society or group.

  Organizations that practice marketing communications in international environments have to be fully aware of the cultural dimensions associated with each of their markets. In addition they need to consider whether it is better to use a standardized approach and use the same unmodified campaigns across all markets, or adapt campaigns to meet the needs of local markets.

 Review Questions

1 Draw the linear model of communication and briefly explain each of the main elements.
2 Make brief notes outlining the meaning of interaction and how dialogue can develop.
3 Describe the main differences between opinion leaders and opinion formers.
4 Explain the key role of marketing communications and find examples to illustrate the meaning of each element in the DRIP framework.
5 What constitutes the marketing communications mix?
6 What is a hierarchy of effects model?

7 Write brief notes explaining the strong and the weak theories of advertising.

8 Using examples, explain the difference between informational and emotional messages.

9 Why is the circular interpretation of the attitude construct better than the linear form?

10 Hollensen (2005) argues that culture is made up of three elements and four layers. Name them.

Worksheet Summary

Visit the **Online Resource Centre** and complete Worksheet 10.1. This will aid in learning about the role marketing communications played in your decision as to which university to attend and who influenced your decision?

Discussion Questions

1 Having read Case Insight 10.1, how would you advise the marketing team at the London Eye to celebrate the 25 millionth visitor and how would you recommend they use marketing communications to mark the occasion?

2 Consider the key market exchange characteristics that will favour the use of linear or one-way communication and then repeat the exercise with respect to interactional communication. Discuss the differences and find examples to illustrate these conditions.

3 Day Birger et Mikkelsen is a leading Danish fashion retailer, providing a range of fashion clothing for young people aged 18–35. As a marketing assistant you have just returned from a conference at which the role of personal influencers was highlighted. You now wish to convey your new knowledge to your manager. Prepare a brief report in which you explain the nature of opinion leaders and formers, and discuss how they might be used by Day Birger et Mikkelsen to improve their marketing communications. Using at least three examples, make it clear who you think would make good opinion formers for Day Birger et Mikkelsen.

4 Discuss the extent to which marketing communications should be used by organizations just to persuade audiences to buy products and services.

5 To what extent should organizations operating a standardization policy consider the culture of the countries they are operating in?

Visit the **Online Resource Centre** and complete the Multiple Choice Questions to assess your knowledge of Chapter 10.

go online

References

Alarcon, C. (2008), 'Customer titles extend reach', *Marketing Week*, 30 October, retrieve from www.marketingweek.co.uk/in-depth-analysis/customer-titles-extend-reach/2063120.article, accessed 12 September 2009.

Bagozzi, R. (1978), 'Marketing as exchange: a theory of transactions in the market place', *American Behavioural Science*, 21, 4, 257–61.

Ballantyne, D. (2004), 'Dialogue and its role in the development of relationship specific knowledge', *Journal of Business & Industrial Marketing*, 19, 2, 114–23.

Benady, D. (2009), 'Advertising to the YouTube generation', *Marketing*, 25 November, 34–5.

Berkman, H., and Gilson, C. (1986), *Consumer Behavior: Concepts and Strategies*, Boston: Kent Publishing Co.

Byrne, C. (2010), 'Ad agency reputation survey reveals 'disconnect' between advertisers and their clients', *The Guardian*, 22 March 2010, retrieve from http://browse.guardian.co.uk/search?search=T-Mobile+Dance&No=10&sitesearch-radio=guardian, accessed 22 March 2010.

Chan, K. K., and Misra, S. (1990), 'Characteristics of the opinion leader: a new dimension', *Journal of Advertising*, 19, 3, 53–60.

Charles, G. (2009), 'Army tests show room recruitment initiatives', *Marketing*, 8 April, 1.

Duncan, T., and Moriarty, S. (1998), 'A communication-based marketing model for managing relationships', *Journal of Marketing*, 62 (April) 1–13.

Dwyer, R., Schurr, P., and Oh, S. (1987), 'Developing buyer–seller relationships', *Journal of Marketing*, 51 (April), 11–27.

Ehrenberg, A.S.C. (1974), 'Repetitive advertising and the consumer', *Journal of Advertising Research*, 14 (April), 25–34

—(1997), 'How do consumers come to buy a new brand?' *Admap*, March, 20–4.

Fill, C. (2002), *Marketing Communications: Contexts, Strategies and Applications*, 3rd edn, Harlow: FT/Prentice Hall.

—(2009), *Marketing Communications: Interactivity, Communities and Content*, 5th edn, Harlow: FT/Prentice Hall.

Hoffman, D. L., and Novak, P. T. (1996), 'Marketing in hyper computer-mediated environments: conceptual foundations', *Journal of Marketing*, 60 (July), 50–68.

Hollensen, S. (2005), *Global Marketing*, 3rd edn, Harlow: FT/Prentice Hall.

Houston, F., and Gassenheimer, J. (1987), 'Marketing and exchange', *Journal of Marketing*, 51 (October), 3–18.

Hughes, G., and Fill, C. (2007), 'Redefining the nature and format of the marketing communications mix', *The Marketing Review*, 7, 1 (March), 45–57.

Jones, J. P. (1991), 'Over-promise and under-delivery', *Marketing and Research Today*, November, 195–203.

Jukes, M (2009), 'Creative review: Comparethemarket.com', 26 February, retrieve from www.brandrepublic.com/InDepth/Features/930643/APG-Creative-Strategy-Awards—Comparethemarketcom-meerkat-campaign-VCCP, accessed 20 September 2009.

Katz, E., and Lazarsfeld, P. F. (1955), *Personal Influence: The Part Played by People in the Flow of Mass Communication*, Glencoe, Ill.: Free Press.

Kemp, E. (2007), 'Nokia strategy rethink spurs global as review', *Marketing*, 24 January, 2.

Lavidge, R. J., and Steiner, G. A. (1961), 'A model for predictive measurements of advertising effectiveness', *Journal of Marketing*, 25, 6 (October), 59–62.

Ramsay, F. (2009), 'Building on Animal Magic', *Marketing*, 19 August, 20–1.

Schramm, W. (1955), 'How communication works', in W. Schramm (ed.) *The Process and Effects of Mass Communications*, Urbana, Ill.: University of Illinois Press, 3–26.

Shannon, C., and Weaver, W. (1962), *The Mathematical Theory of Communication*, Urbana, Ill.: University of Illinois Press.

Stokes, D., and Lomax, W. (2002), 'Taking control of word of mouth marketing: the case of an entrepreneurial hotelier', *Journal of Small Business and Enterprise Development*, 9, 4, 349–57.

Strong, E. K. (1925), *The Psychology of Selling*, New York: McGraw-Hill.

Sweney, M. (2009), 'Foster's ads return to lager's "no worries" Australian roots', *The Guardian*, 10 June, retrieve from www.guardian.co.uk/media/2009/jun/10/fosters-ad, accessed 17 September 2009.

Theodorson, S. A., and Theodorson, G. R. (1969), *A Modern Dictionary of Sociology*, New York: Cromwell.

Thomas, J. (2009), 'The value of experience', *Marketing*, 15 April, 14.

Utalk (2009a), www.utalkmarketing.com/Pages/CreativeShowcase.aspx?ArticleID=14313.

—(2009b), How Cadbury re-launched the Wispa bar, retrieved 16 September 2009 from www.utalkmarketing.com/Pages/Article.aspx?ArticleID=14896, accessed 16 September 2009.

VCCP (2009), Comparethemarket.com 'meerkat campaign', campaignlive.co.uk retrieve from www.brandrepublic.com/InDepth/Features/930643/APG-Creative-Strategy-Awards---Comparethemarketcom-meerkat-campaign-VCCP, accessed 17 September 2009.

Wainwright, M. (2007), 'Whisper it softly … 80s favourite revived', *The Guardian*, 18 August retrieve from www.guardian.co.uk/uk/2007/aug/18/lifeandhealth.foodanddrink, accessed 16 September 2009.

11

Marketing Communications: Tools Media, and Planning

Learning Outcomes

After studying this chapter you should be able to:

▶ Describe the role and configuration of the marketing communications mix

▶ Explain the role and characteristics of each of the primary tools of the communication mix

▶ Understand and set out the criteria that should be used to select the right communication mix

▶ Outline the characteristics of the different media and how they are categorized

▶ Explain how marketing communication activities are planned and implemented

▶ Describe the different activities associated with managing marketing communications

▶ Consider the principles and issues associated with integrated marketing communications

▶ Case Insight 11.1

London Zoo, located in Regent's Park in the centre of London, has changed its name to ZSL London Zoo. Why? We speak to James Bailey to find out more.

James Bailey for ZSL London Zoo

Following a segmentation exercise, it was revealed that 18% of the UK population are what we call 'open conservationists'. These people would be more likely to visit zoos if they were aware of the conservation work that zoos did. This presented us with an opportunity, an opportunity to increase the potential audience within 90 minutes' drive time by 1.4m people. We believe that if we could make London Zoo more synonymous with conservation it would give these people permission to visit the Zoo.

So, we changed the name to ZSL to reflect the conservation work of the Zoological Society of London, a charity that operates London Zoo and the sister Zoo, Whipsnade. ZSL carries out conservation work in 30 countries around the world, but there is very little awareness about ZSL. By using ZSL as a master brand, we hope to accelerate the awareness of ZSL and prompt people to ask the questions: who is ZSL and what do they do? Once people become more aware of ZSL and its work they will associate the two zoos with conservation.

To attract visitors, ZSL use a range of marketing communications tools and media. Public relations is very important as it allows us to convey the wider message of ZSL's conservation work, and personal selling has become more important recently as we strive to develop relationships with key customers in the travel trade industry so that they sell more tickets to their own clients through various distribution outlets.

Direct marketing is used to target specific consumer and trade groups, using a mixture of direct mail and email communications. Advertising is a key tool and is used to sell tickets. Sales promotion is not a key tool as ZSL need to maintain high levels of per capita income, although we did discount heavily to get people back to the zoo following the bombs in London in 2005.

The main visitor season commences during the spring each year and runs through to the end of September. In order to maximize the number of visitors in this period, the use of the various tools and media is very important. The objectives that we set ourselves also determine the mix. Budget constraints play a key part in determining the media used. We use a media agency to help and advise on the mix and to do this we provide the agency with information such as the demographics of the target market, which they then run against TGI data. This analysis produces a whole range of different tactics that are appropriate for our target market. We then use our knowledge of the market to make the final decision.

When we launched 'Gorilla Kingdom' we needed to promote the exhibit as a key attraction. Once the product was named, the brand developed, and the creative direction established, the crucial question was which tools and which media we should use?

Which tools and media would you use to attract visitors to see Gorilla Kingdom?

(Previous page)

An advert for the rebranded ZSL London Zoo

Source: ZSL London Zoo.

Introduction

What are the 'touchpoints' that you have with your mobile phone provider? Email, telephone, direct mail items, and snail mail for personal communications? What about TV ads, web-pages, articles and ads in magazines, posters, and perhaps news items that generate general brand awareness? Organizations use a variety of tools and media to engage their audiences. Collectively, these are referred to as the **marketing communications mix**, a set of five tools and a variety of **media** that can be used in various combinations, and different degrees of intensity, in order to communicate with target audiences. The five principal marketing communications tools are: **advertising**, **sales promotion**, **public relations**, **direct marketing**, and **personal selling**.

In addition to this mix of tools there is the media, used primarily, but not exclusively, to deliver advertising messages to target audiences. Although the term media refers to any mechanism or device that can carry a message, we refer to paid-for media, processes, and systems that are owned by third parties, such as the News Corporation (they own *The Sun* and *The Sunday Times* newspapers plus the BSkyB TV platform), Condé Nast (who own *Tatler*, *Vanity Fair*, and *Vogue* magazines, among others), Singapore Press Holdings (who own the *Business Time*s in Singapore), and Time Warner Inc., a 'leading media and entertainment company, whose businesses include interactive services, cable systems, filmed entertainment, TV networks and publishing'. These organizations rent out time and space to client organizations so that they can send their messages and make content available to various audiences. The list of available paid-for media is expanding all the time but it is possible to identify six key classes of media. These are broadcast, print, outdoor, in-store, digital, and other (which includes both cinema and ambient media). All of these are explored in this chapter.

On completing this chapter readers should understand the main characteristics associated with the principal tools and media. This means that it is possible to configure different mixes of tools and media and that these can be shaped to achieve different goals. This chapter also considers the marketing communications planning process and some of the issues associated with this important management activity, including **integrated marketing communications**.

The Role and Purpose of the Marketing Communications Mix

Up until the mid-1980s organizations were able to use a fairly predictable and stable range of tools and media. Advertising was used to build awareness and brand values, sales promotions were used to stimulate demand, public relations conveyed goodwill messages about organizations, and personal selling was seen as a means of getting orders, particularly in the business-to-business market. However, there have been some major changes in the environment and in the way organizations communicate with their target audiences. New technology has given rise to a raft of different media and opportunities for advertisers to reach their audiences. We now have access to hundreds of commercial TV and radio channels, not just a few. Cinemas show multiple films at multiplex sites, and the internet has transformed the way in which we communicate, educate, inform, and entertain ourselves.

This expansion of the media is referred to as **media fragmentation**. At the same time people have developed a whole host of new ways to spend their leisure time; they are no longer locked in and restricted to a few media. This expansion of media choice is referred to as **audience fragmentation**. So, although the range and type of media has expanded, the size of audiences that each medium commands has generally shrunk.

For organizations, one of the key challenges is to find the right mix of tools and media that allow them to reach their target audiences economically. To do this they have had to revise and develop their marketing communication mixes in order to reach their audiences. For example, in the 1990s there was a dramatic rise in the use of direct-response media as direct marketing emerged as a new tool to be added to the mix. Now, the internet and digital technologies have enabled new interactive forms of communication, where the receiver has greater responsibility for their part in the communication process and is encouraged to interact with the sender. As a result of these changes, many organizations are reducing their investment in traditional media and putting it into digital media (see Chapter 17).

go online

Visit the **Online Resource Centre** and complete Internet Activity 11.1 to learn more about how Toyota uses an interactive website to inform its target audience about a complex product offering, its Hybrid Synergy Drive.

The role of the mix has changed from one based on persuading customers in the short term to buy products and services, to a longer term perspective, whereby the mix is intended to facilitate communication with a wide range of stakeholders, and on a broader range of issues. New goals such as developing understanding and preference, reminding and reassuring customers, have now become accepted as important aspects of marketing communications.

The pursuit of integrated marketing communications has become a popular activity and some organizations are trying to use the mix to help develop relationships not just with key customers, but also with key suppliers and other important stakeholders. Today, therefore, an increasing number of organizations are reformulating the mix to encourage customer retention, not acquisition.

▶ Market Insight 11.1

Sainsbury's Campaign Works up a Treat

The UK supermarket Sainsbury's has been running the 'Try something new today' campaign, with great success since 2005. 'Try' works by giving people recipe and food ideas, which they use and top up the shopping baskets each time they shop. However, 'Try' works when the economy is strong, so, when the credit crunch started to bite, Sainsbury's realized they needed to adapt their campaign if their growth rates were to be extended.

Following research into peoples' perceptions of food and meal prices, Sainsbury's developed a set

▶ Market Insight 11.1

of communication objectives designed to show that Sainsbury's food is not only great quality but also great value and to inspire people to 'Try something new' to help reduce their shopping bill. They wanted to challenge people with the fact that you can feed your family for under £5 at Sainsbury's, hence the idea 'feed your family for a fiver'.

In order to deliver this promise, Sainsbury's created a range of 30 family meals with Sainsbury's products. Each meal had to cost under £5, all ingredients had to be at their standard everyday low prices (and not on promotion), all would need to be substantial enough for a hungry family of four, meals would need to centre around a good portion of protein, include a range of items from 'basics' to 'Taste the difference' to show that Sainsbury's offers value across the store and maintain the inspiration expected of 'Try''s food ideas.

From this point, the campaign needed to be communicated and an integrated tools and media campaign was run for the five months ending in August 2008. The campaign used TV and print advertising. The former was anchored around four 30″ TV executions, each featuring a shopper being challenged by Jamie Oliver with the idea that he could help them feed their family for a fiver at Sainsbury's ('Meatballs', 'Bacon Pasta', 'Salmon Fishcakes', 'Lamb Burgers'). The magazine and press advertising featured the meal ideas, with some executions featuring five meal ideas to help shoppers plan a week's meals.

Instore 'Tip cards' were provided free of charge, each showing products and cooking instructions. Point of Purchase materials were used to assist shoppers locate ingredients they needed. Digitally the Sainsbury's website provided full information on all the ingredients and recipes necessary to make each meal.

The impact was immediate as tracking and qualitative research showed buzz around the campaign, with the idea being spontaneously and accurately played back by respondents. Recognition built to 80% over the campaign period, the highest ever score for a Jamie

Sainsbury's 'try something new today' campaign aims at changing people's shopping habits

Oliver TV campaign. Tracking showed perceptions of Sainsbury's value shifting from the outset. All ingredients featured in the meal ideas saw strong sales uplifts. The campaign cost £6.9m in total and it was calculated that the campaign delivered £203m in sales and a profit of £31.6m.

Perhaps the most telling testimony was that their four main competitors developed campaigns on the same principle. M&S's 'Dine in for £10' promotion was launched a month after the Sainsbury's campaign. ASDA launched its 'Feed the family for less' campaign in press and TV in May, and Tesco and Morrisons offered similar deals in July. (See also Market Insight 3.3 for more on Jamie Oliver's endorsement of Sainsbury's.)

Source: Buck and Roach (2009); King (2009); www2.sainsburys. co.uk/YourIdeas/forums/showthread.aspx?PostID=12765.

▶ Market Insight 11.1   (continued)

1   Why did Sainsbury's use TV and print advertising when their customers were captive in their supermarkets?

2   In addition to creating awareness, what else might the TV campaign have set out to achieve?

3   Is Jamie Oliver an opinion leader or opinion former?

Each of the tools of the marketing communications mix has developed in an offline environment. However, the development of the internet has presented new opportunities for each of the tools to be delivered through online media. Many organizations have found that the principles through which particular tools work offline do not apply in an online environment. New approaches and ideas have been sought and there is no established way of operating in an online context.

The marketing communications mix is a vital part of the process that conveys added value to stakeholders. It is expected that marketing communications, and the mix of tools and media it uses, needs to embrace a wider remit, to move beyond the product information model and become an integral part of an organization's overall communications and relationship management strategy. Above all else, the marketing communications mix should be utilized as an audience-centred activity. (See Market Insight 11.1 for the marketing communications mix used by Sainsbury's.)

▶ Research Insight 11.1

To take your learning further, you might wish to read this influential paper.

Vakratsas, D., and Ambler, T. (1999), 'How advertising works: what do we really know?', *Journal of Marketing*, 63 (January), 26–43.

In an attempt to understand the interaction between consumers and advertising the authors review more than 250 journal articles and books. They conclude that there is no support for any particular hierarchical model that explains how advertising works. They propose that advertising should be considered in terms of affect, **cognition**, and experience (see the general model proposed in Chapter 11) and that understanding the context is absolutely imperative (e.g. goals, product category, competition, other aspects of mix, stage of product lifecycle, and target market).

   Visit the **Online Resource Centre** to read the abstract and access the full paper.

Selecting the Right Mix of Tools

Table 11.1 sets out the principal characteristics of the five main tools of the marketing communications mix.

The principal tools presented in Table 11.1 subsume other tools such as product placement, sponsorship, and exhibitions. Although the table suggests that the tools are independent entities, each with their own skills and attributes, a truly effective mix works when the tools are used to complement each other and are designed to work as an interacting unit. One of the challenges facing marketing communication managers is to extract the full potential from the tools selected. Only by appreciating their characteristics is it really possible to get an insight into how to select the right mix of tools for each communication task.

▶ **Table 11.1** The principal characteristics of the five main tools of the marketing communications mix

Marketing communications tools	Overview
Advertising	Advertising is a non-personal form of communication, where a clearly identifiable sponsor pays for a message to be transmitted through media. One of the distinctive qualities that advertising brings to the mix is that it reaches large, often mass audiences in an impersonal way. The role of advertising is to engage audiences and this engagement is dependent on the context in which the communication occurs
Sales promotion	Sales promotions offer a direct inducement or an incentive to encourage customers to buy a product/service. These inducements can be targeted at consumers, distributors, agents, and members of the salesforce. Sales promotions are concerned with offering customers additional value, in order to induce an immediate sale. These sales might well have taken place without the presence of an incentive, it is simply that the inducement brings the time of the sale forward. The key forms of sales promotion are sampling, coupons, deals, premiums, contests and sweepstakes and in the trade, various forms of allowance
Public relations	Public relations is used to influence the way an organization is perceived by various groups of stakeholders. One of the key characteristics that differentiates public relations from the other tools is that it does not require the purchase of airtime or space in media vehicles, such as TV magazines or online. This means that these types of message are low-cost and are perceived to be extremely credible. It is a management activity that attempts to shape the attitudes and opinions held by an organization's stakeholders. It attempts to identify its own policies with the interests of its stakeholders and formulates and executes a programme of action to develop mutual goodwill and understanding. Through this process relationships are developed, which are in the long-term interests of all parties. The key forms of public relations are sponsorship, publicity, lobbying, public affairs, issues management, crisis communications, and investor relations

> ▶ **Table 11.1** (continued)

Marketing communications tools	Overview
Direct marketing	The primary role of direct marketing is to drive a response and shape the behaviour of the target audience with regard to a brand. This is achieved by sending personalized and customized messages, often requesting a 'call-to-action', designed to provoke a change in the audience's behaviour. Direct marketing is used to create and sustain a personal and intermediary-free communication with customers, potential customers, and other significant stakeholders. In most cases this is a media-based activity and offers great scope for the collection and utilization of pertinent and measurable data. One of the key benefits of direct marketing is that there is limited communication wastage. The precision associated with target marketing means that messages are sent to, received, processed, and responded to by members of the target audience, and no others. This is unlike advertising, where messages often reach some people who are not targets and are unlikely to be involved with the brand. Some of the principal techniques are direct mail, telemarketing, email, and internet-based communications
Personal selling	Personal selling involves interpersonal communication through which information is provided, positive feelings developed, and behaviour stimulated. Personal selling is an activity undertaken by an individual representing an organization, or collectively in the form of a salesforce. It is a highly potent form of communication simply because messages can be adapted to meet the requirements of both parties. Objections can be overcome, information provided in the context of the buyer's environment, and the conviction and power of demonstration can be brought to the buyer when requested. The role of personal selling is largely one of representation, but it is the most expensive tool in the mix and the reach of personal selling is the most limited

An overview of each of the tools should highlight a number of characteristics that are shared among all of the tools. These are the degree to which a tool and the message conveyed is controllable, the credibility of the message conveyed, the costs of using a tool, the degree to which a target audience is dispersed, and the DRIP task that marketing communications is required to accomplish. These five elements can serve as a starting point when selecting the right marketing communications mix and each is considered in turn.

Table 11.2 provides a summary of the relative strengths of each of the tools of the communications mix against these criteria. However, although depicted individually, the elements of the mix should be regarded as a set of complementary instruments, each potentially stronger when it draws on the potential of the others. The tools are, to a limited extent, partially interchangeable, and in different circumstances different tools should be used to meet different objectives. For example, in a business context, personal selling will be the predominant tool, whereas in a consumer market context, advertising has traditionally reigned supreme.

What is clear is that the nature, configuration, and use of what was once called the promotional mix has changed. No longer can the traditional groupings of tools be assumed to be the most effective forms of communication. The role of the media in the communication process

▶ **Table 11.2** The relative strength of the tools of the marketing communication mix

	Advertising	Sales promotion	Public relations	Direct marketing	Personal selling
Level of control	Medium	High	Low	High	Medium
Level of cost	High	Medium	Low	Medium	High
Level of credibility	Low	Medium	High	Medium	Medium
Level of dispersion					
High	Low	Medium	High	High	Medium
Low	Medium	High	High	Medium	High
Primary tasks	Differentiating informing	Persuading	Differentiating informing	Persuading reinforcing	Persuading

is now much more significant than it has ever been. The arrival and development of digital media expands opportunities for people and organizations to converse globally, personally, more speedily, and factually.

Word-of-mouth communication now plays a more significant part in contemporary communications, especially as communications-literate consumers are increasingly sceptical of the message conveyed by many organizations.

go online

Visit the **Online Resource Centre** and follow the weblinks to the Federation of European Direct and Interactive Marketing Association (FEDMA) and the Institute of Promotional Marketing (IPM) to learn more about the communication tools of direct marketing and sales promotions.

The Media

Once a client has decided on the message to be conveyed to a target audience, decisions need to be made about how and when a message is to be conveyed. Technically, all messages need to be conveyed through media. Some media are owned by the organization, for example the salesforce or the signage outside a building. However, these media do not enable messages to reach a very large or targeted audience and neither do they allow for specific product- or service-oriented messages to be conveyed to particular target audiences. In most circumstances, therefore, client organizations need to use the media owned by others, and pay a fee for renting the space and time to convey their messages. The next section considers the role of the media, and then examines digital media before considering the principles of direct response media.

Media Characteristics

In order to make sense of the vast array of available media, it is helpful to use a categorization system. Here, we will consider three media categories; classes, types, and vehicles. At the broadest level, six main classes of media can be identified. These are broadcast, print, outdoor (now referred to as out-of-home by some), digital, in-store, and other media.

Within each of these classes there are particular types of media. For example, within broadcast there are TV and radio, and within the print class there are newspapers and magazines. Within each type of medium there are a huge number of different media vehicles that can be selected to carry a client's message. For example, within UK TV there are terrestrial networks (Independent TV Network, Channel 4, and Channel 5) and the satellite (BSkyB) and cable (Virgin Media) networks. In print, there are consumer magazines such as Elle and *HELLO!* and business-oriented magazines such as *The Grocer* and *The Economist*.

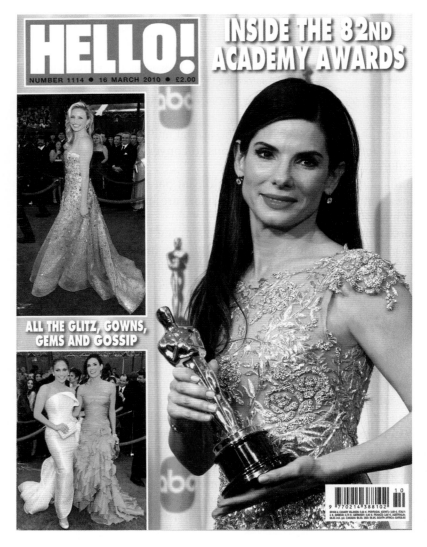

HELLO! The Celebrity news bible offers opportunities to advertisers
Source: HELLO! Ltd.

Table 11.3 provides a summary of the main classes, types, and media vehicles.

▶ **Table 11.3** A summary of the main media

Class	Type	Vehicles
Broadcast	TV	*Coronation Street, X Factor*
	Radio	*Heart FM, Classic FM*
Print	Newspapers	*The Sunday Times, The Mirror, Daily Telegraph*
	Magazines: consumer	*Cosmopolitan, FHM, Woman*
	business	*The Grocer, Plumbing News*
Outdoor	Billboards	96 and 48 sheet
	Street furniture	Adshel
	Transit	London Underground, taxis, hot-air balloons
Digital media	Internet	Websites, email, intranet
	Digital TV	Teletext, SkyText
	CD-ROM: DVD	Various: music, educational, entertainment
In-store	Point of purchase	Bins, signs, and displays
	Packaging	The *Coca-Cola* contour bottle
Other	Cinema	*Pearl and Dean*
	Exhibitions	Ideal Home, The Motor Show
	Product placement	Films, TV, books
	Ambient	Litter bins, golf tees, petrol pumps
	Guerrilla	Flyposting

Source: Fill (2009). Used with permission.

The development of digital media has had a profound impact on the way client organizations communicate with their audiences. Generally, there has been a trend to reduce the amount of traditional media used and an increase in the amount of digital and online media used. For example, in August 2009, Gap announced it was dropping TV advertising completely for the launch of a range of jeans and just using social media (see Market Insight 11.3). Reports that TV and print advertising is dead have been proven to be premature, but it is clear that the balance within the mix of media used by organizations is changing and new ways of delivering messages are evolving.

go online

Visit the **Online Resource Centre** and complete Internet Activity 11.2 to learn more about the differing media that was used for the Ray-Ban 'Neverhide' campaign.

▶ **Table 11.4** An overview of each class of media

Class of media	Overview
Print	Newspapers and magazines are the two main media in the print media class; others include custom magazines and directories. Print is very effective at delivering messages to target audiences as it allows for explanation in a way that most other media cannot. This may be in the form of either a picture or a photograph demonstrating how a product should be used. Alternatively, the written word can be used to argue why a product should be chosen and detail the advantages and benefits that consumption will provide for the user
Broadcast	Advertisers use broadcast media (TV and radio) because they can reach mass audiences with their messages at a relatively low cost per target reached. Broadcast media allow advertisers to add visual and/or sound dimensions to their messages. This helps them to demonstrate the benefits of using a particular product and can bring life and energy to an advertiser's message. TV uses sight, sound, and movement, whereas radio can only use its audio capacity to convey meaning. Both media have the potential to tell stories and to appeal to people's emotions when transmitting a message. These are dimensions that the printed media find difficult in achieving effectively within an advertiser's time and cost parameters
Digital	Digital media embrace more than just the internet and online marketing. Although significant and extremely important, the digital media spectrum involves three key additional areas; wireless, mobile, and interactive TV. Within each of these areas there are many sub-sections, each of which provides a variety of media opportunities. These present clients with opportunities to communicate with their audiences in radically different ways from those previously available. Generally, most traditional media provide one-way communications, where information passes from a source to a receiver but there is little opportunity for feedback, let alone interaction. Digital media enables two-way, interactive communication, with information flowing back to the source and again to the receiver, as each participant adapts their message to meet the requirements of their audience. For example, banner ads can provoke a click, this takes the receiver to a new website where the source presents new information and the receiver makes choices, responds to questions (e.g. registers at the site), and the source again provides fresh information. Indeed, the identity of the source and receiver in this type of communication becomes less clear. These interactions are conducted at high speed, low cost, and usually with great clarity. People drive these interactions at a speed that is convenient to them; they are not driven by others. Space (or time) within traditional media is limited so costs rise as demand for the limited space/time increases. To generalize, as space is unlimited on the internet, so costs per contact fall as more visitors are received
In-store	There are two main forms of in-store media, point-of-purchase (POP) displays and packaging. Retailers control the former and manufacturers the latter. The primary objective of using in-store media is to get the attention of shoppers and to stimulate them to make purchases. The content of messages can be controlled easily by both retailers or manufacturers. In addition, the timing and the exact placement of in-store messages can be equally well controlled. There are a number of POP techniques, but the most used are window displays, floor and wall racks to display merchandise, posters and information cards, plus counter and checkout displays. Packaging has to protect and preserve products, but it also has a significant communication role and is a means of influencing brand choice decisions

> ▶ **Table 11.4** (continued)

Outdoor	Outdoor media consist of three main formats: street furniture (such as bus shelters), billboards (which consist primarily of 96-, 48-, and 6-sheet poster sites), and transit (which includes buses, taxis, and the underground). The key characteristic associated with outdoor media is that they are observed by their target audiences at locations away from home, and they are normally used to support messages that are transmitted through the primary media, namely broadcast and print. Outdoor media can, therefore, be seen to be a secondary, but important support media for a complementary and effective media mix
Other	Two main media can be identified, cinema and ambient. Cinema advertising has all the advantages of TV-based messages such as the high-quality audio and visual dimensions, which combine to provide high impact. However, the vast majority of cinema visitors are people aged 18–35 so if an advertiser wishes to reach different age group segments, or perhaps a national audience, not only will cinema be inappropriate but also the costs will be much higher than those for TV. Ambient media are regarded as out-of-home media that fail to fit any of the established outdoor categories. Ambient media can be classified according to a variety of factors. These include posters (typically found in washrooms), distribution (e.g., ads on tickets and carrier bags), digital media (in the form of video and LCD screens), sponsorships (as in golf holes and petrol pump nozzles), and aerials (in the form of balloons, blimps, towed banners)

The Changing Role of the Media

For a long time commercial media have been used to convey messages designed to develop consumers' attitudes and feelings towards brands. Today, many of the messages are designed to provoke audiences into responding, either physically, cognitively, or emotionally. The former is referred to as an attitudinal response, the latter a behavioural response. It follows that attitude- and behavioural-oriented communications require different media.

Direct-response media are characterized by the provision of a telephone number or web address. This is the mechanism through which receivers can respond to a message. Direct mail, telemarketing, and door-to-door activities are the main direct-response media, as they allow more personal, direct, and evaluative means of reaching precisely targeted customers. However, in reality, any type of media can be used, simply by attaching a telephone number, website address, mailing address, or response card. Table 11.5 sets out the main media used within direct-response marketing.

Direct-response media also allow clients the opportunity to measure the volume, frequency, and value of audience responses. This enables them to determine which direct-response media work best and so helps them become more efficient as well as effective. Estimates vary, but somewhere between 30% and 40% of all TV advertisements are now direct response. Direct-response TV (DRTV) is attractive to service providers such as those in financial services, charities, and tourism, but, increasingly, grocery brands such as Tango and Peperami have used this format. The growth in video advertising reflects the involvement of people in their online activities.

The complementary nature of TV and online media was revealed by a Deloitte/YouGov report published in 2009. This found that 44% of consumers research a service online only after watching a TV ad. Over half of the respondents claimed to watch TV and use the internet

▶ **Table 11.5** Direct-response (DR) media

Types of DR media	Explanation
Direct mail	Direct mail refers to personally addressed advertising that is delivered through the postal system. It can be personalized and targeted with great accuracy, and its results are capable of precise measurement. Direct mail can be expensive, at anything between £250 and £500 per 1,000 items dispatched. It should, therefore, be used selectively and for purposes other than creating awareness
Telemarketing	The telephone provides interaction, flexibility, immediate feedback, and the opportunity to overcome objections, all within the same communication event. Telemarketing also allows organizations to undertake separate marketing research, which is both highly measurable and accountable in that the effectiveness can be verified continuously and call rates, contacts reached, and the number and quality of positive and negative responses are easily recorded and monitored
Carelines	Carelines and contact centres enable customers to complain about a product performance, and related experiences, seek product-related advice, make suggestions regarding product or packaging development, and comment about an action or development concerning the brand as a whole
Inserts	Inserts are media materials that are placed inside magazines or direct mail letters. These provide factual information about the product or service and enable the recipient to respond to the request of the direct marketer. This request might be to place an order, visit a website, or post back a card for more information, such as a brochure. Inserts are popular because they are good at generating leads, even though their cost is substantially higher than a four-colour advertisement in the magazine in which the insert is carried
Print	There are two main forms of direct-response advertising through printed media: first, catalogues, and second, magazines and newspapers. Consumer direct print ads sometimes offer an incentive, and are designed explicitly to drive customers to a website, where transactions can be completed without reference to retailers, dealers, or other intermediaries
Door-to-door	Although the content and quality can be controlled in the same way, door-to-door response rates are lower than direct mail because of the lack of a personal address mechanism. Door-to-door can be much cheaper than direct mail as there are no postage charges to be accounted for
Radio and TV	TV has much greater potential than radio as a direct-response mechanism because it can provide a visual dimension. Originally, pricing restrictions limited the use of TV in this context, but now following deregulation, nearly half of all TV ads carry a response mechanism
Digital media	The recent development of digital technologies, and the impact on digital TV, internet, email, viral marketing, blogging, and social networking sites, now represents major new forms of interactive and direct marketing opportunities. Driven initially by developments in home shopping and banking facilities that were attractive to particular target groups, these facilities have now become fully interactive. As a result, these services are now accessible by a much wider audience and encompass leisure and entertainment opportunities

at the same time. The report revealed that TV was seen by consumers as the most impactful form of advertising (64%), whereas search and online display were the least impactful, 12% and 8% respectively. What this reinforces is the notion that TV can drive people online because TV is good at display ads and brand building, whereas online advertising is best at search (Berne, 2009).

go online

Visit the **Online Resource Centre** and follow the weblink to the Radio Advertising Bureau (RAB) to learn more about how the role and importance of radio in today's fragmented media landscape.

▶ Market Insight 11.2

Cash4Gold goes Direct

Cash4Gold launched in the USA in April 2007, and over 900,000 people have since used the pioneering gold-buying service. The service was introduced to the UK in 2009 and quickly became one of the country's top direct-response advertisers. The campaign was structured into two main phases. The first was built around TV and print advertising. The TV work was based on using daytime TV ad spots to reach a highly targeted audience, people who are attracted to the idea of turning their unwanted bits of gold, such as gaudy bracelets, dental crowns, or half of a pair of earrings, into cash. Cash4Gold's brash branding spelt its message out loud and clear, that there is money available for unwanted gold. Brand response advertising for this type of product is capable of building awareness quickly.

Cash4Gold is endorsed by Goldie and MC Hammer, two celebrities who quite like gold!

Source: Courtesy of Cash4Gold.

> ▶ **Research Insight 11.2**
>
> **To take your learning further, you might wish to read this influential paper.**
>
> Kent, M. L., Taylor, M., and White, W. J. (2003), 'The relationship between web site design and organisational responsiveness to stakeholders', *Public Relations Review*, 29, 1 (March), 63–77.
>
> As the title indicates, this paper examines the relationship between website design and organizational responsiveness to stakeholder information needs. Written at a time when there was little or no empirical evidence about the extent to which new technologies can assist organizations to develop relationships, this paper provides an interesting and readable first insight.
>
> @ Visit the **Online Resource Centre** to read the abstract and access the full paper.

Other Promotional Methods and Approaches

The media and audience fragmentation referred to previously in this chapter has forced organizations to adapt to changing market conditions. The switch in emphasis from mass media to digital media has also been complemented by an increase in the use of what might be regarded as support tools and media. So far in this chapter, the marketing communications mix has been presented as a set of five tools and various media. However, in addition to these five primary tools are numerous other tools and communication instruments that are used by organizations to reach their audiences. In many cases they can be regarded as tools or media that support the primary mix, although they can be used in their own right, as stand-alone methods of communications. Some of these other tools are briefly considered here.

Sponsorship, normally associated with public relations but with strong associations with advertising, has become an important communication activity for many organizations. Sponsorship is a commercial activity, whereby one party permits another an opportunity to exploit an association with a target audience in return for funds, services, or resources (Fill, 2009). Organizations are using different forms of sponsorship activities to generate awareness, brand associations, and to cut through the clutter of commercial messages.

> ▶ **Market Insight 11.4**
>
> **O2 Sponsors Experiences**
>
> O2 use sponsorship in a number of different ways, but the overriding goal is to create new experiences for customers, potential customers, and partners. Their sponsorship strategy is an integral part of their commitment to music, sport, and entertainment, and the interactive partnerships developed with customers and

▶ Market Insight 11.4

partners. The sponsorships undertaken range from the substantial, planned, and organized events to those that are more individual, and seemingly spontaneous activities.

By far the largest organized sponsorship activity incorporates the O2 Arena. Apart from enabling visitors to experience the brand through the events held at the Arena, it generates enormous coverage and exposure for the brand. In its first year the O2 Arena staged 149 performances by 60 acts, including some of the world's top music artists; 1,719,309 tickets had been sold as at 31 March, there had been in excess of 7.5m visitors, of which over 1m visited The Tutankhamen exhibition. O2 customers benefit from exclusive content from leading artists and are given priority access to tickets for shows, major sports events, and exhibitions. More than 12m voice calls have been made from the venue and approximately 300 texts per minute have been sent from the venue during major events.

Other sponsorships include the England rugby team, and, in 2008, O2 introduced its 'Scrum in the Park'

event. This allowed rugby fans the opportunity to meet the team and even test their skills. At a more spontaneous level, O2 'angels' deliver random acts of kindness such as distributing ice creams and cold water on hot days or free phone-charging facilities at music festivals. O2-branded London taxis gave O2 customers free rides during the period 6–7 p.m. as a happy-hour contribution. Many O2-branded taxis in London and Birmingham are fitted with hands-free phones and charging units offering free facilities to existing and potential customers.

Sources: www.o2.com/about/why_sponsor.asp; Kemp, E. (2008).

1 **Apart from generating experiences, what other major benefit do O2 get from using sponsorship?**

2 **To what extent do you believe the O2 Arena will be a useful long-term sponsorship for O2?**

3 **Select another mobile operator in a country of your choice, and find out if they use sponsorship and if they do, what do they sponsor?**

Product placement is also a form of sponsorship and represents a relationship between film/TV producers and managers of brands. Through this arrangement, brand managers are able, for a fee, to present their brands 'naturally' within a film or entertainment event. Such placement is designed to increase brand awareness, develop positive brand attitudes, and possibly lead to purchase activity.

Field marketing is about providing support for the salesforce and merchandising personnel. One of the tasks is concerned with getting free samples of a product into the hands of potential customers. Another task is to create an interaction between the brand and a new customer, and another is to create a personal and memorable brand experience for potential customers.

Exhibitions are held for both consumer and business markets. Organizations benefit from meeting their current and potential customers, developing relationships, demonstrating products, building industrywide credibility, placing and taking orders, generating leads, and gathering market information. For customers, exhibitions enable them to meet new or potential suppliers, find out about new products and leading-edge brands, and get up to date with market developments.

In business markets, exhibitions and trade shows can be an integral element of the marketing communications mix. Meeting friends, customers, suppliers, competitors, and prospective customers is an important sociological and ritualistic event in the communications calendar for many companies.

Viral marketing is a fairly recent development based on the credibility and reach associated with word-of-mouth communications. Numerous definitions have been proposed, many of which can be found in Vilpponen, Winter, and Sundqvist (2006). According to Simmons (2006: 1), the term viral marketing refers to 'how the content—be it a joke, picture, game or video—gets around'. Developing this idea, Porter and Golan (2006: 33) refer to viral marketing in terms of how these materials are communicated and suggest that it commonly involves the 'unpaid peer-to-peer communication of provocative content originating from an identified sponsor using the internet to persuade or influence an audience to pass along the content to others'.

There are many other, largely digital, methods of communicating with target audiences: mobile communications, SMS, blogging, and podcasting to name a few. These are considered in greater depth in Chapter 17.

Marketing Communications Planning

This part of the chapter examines the issues associated with managing marketing communications activities. Management's task is to formulate and implement a communication strategy that blends the right mix of tools and media in order to deliver the right messages in the right place, at the right time, for the right audience. To accomplish this, there are inevitably a series of issues that need to be addressed before decisions can be made. These 'issues' embrace a range of activities, such as developing strategy in the light of both audience and brand characteristics, agreeing communication objectives, and then formulating, implementing, and evaluating marketing communication strategies and plans, many of which need to be integrated, an important topic itself in contemporary marketing communications.

Further issues concern the creation of the right message, the configuration of the right mix of tools and media, the allocation of financial and human resources, the coordination and control of related activities, and the management of various relationships. These relationships are not just those with internal colleagues, critical as these are, but they also encompass those external stakeholders who work with the organization in order to deliver particular elements of a marketing communications plan. For example, they might provide research information, they might be agencies that design the message (or creative as it is referred to in the trade), or those who plan and buy media in order for the message to be conveyed to the target audience.

Marketing communications planning is a systematic process involving a series of procedures and activities that lead to the setting of marketing communications objectives and the formulation of plans for achieving them. The aim of the planning process is to formulate and convey messages to particular target audiences that encourage them to think, emote, behave, or respond in particular ways. It is the skill and responsibility of those in charge of marketing communications planning to ensure that there is the right blend of communication tools, that they create memorable messages, and convey them through a suitable media mix.

In order to better understand what a marketing communications plan should achieve, it is helpful to appreciate the principal tasks facing marketing communications managers. These are to decide:

- ▶ Who should receive the messages?
- ▶ What should the messages say?
- ▶ What image of the organization/brand are receivers expected to retain?
- ▶ How much is to be spent establishing this new image?
- ▶ How are the messages to be delivered?
- ▶ What actions should the receivers take?
- ▶ How do we control the whole process once implemented?
- ▶ What was achieved?

For many reasons, planning is an essential management activity, and, if planned marketing communications are to be developed in an orderly and efficient way, the use of a suitable framework is necessary. A framework for integrated marketing communications plans is presented in Figure 11.1.

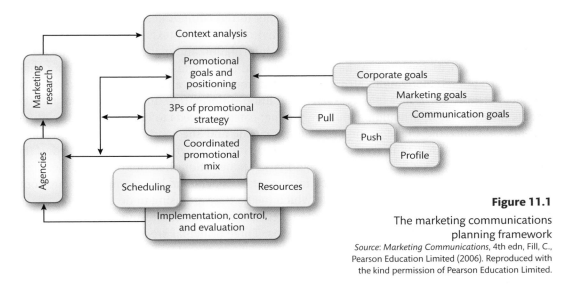

Figure 11.1

The marketing communications planning framework

Source: Marketing Communications, 4th edn, Fill, C., Pearson Education Limited (2006). Reproduced with the kind permission of Pearson Education Limited.

The **marketing communications planning framework** (MCPF) provides a visual guide to what needs to be achieved and brings together the various elements into a logical sequence of activities. As with all hierarchical planning models, each level of decision-making is built on information generated at a previous level in the model. Another advantage of using the MCPF is that it provides a suitable checklist of activities that need to be considered. The MCPF represents a sequence of decisions that marketing managers undertake when preparing, implementing, and evaluating communication strategies and plans. This framework reflects a deliberate or planned approach to strategic marketing communications.

However, marketing communications planning is not always developed as a linear process in practice, as depicted in this framework. Indeed, many marketing communications decisions are made outside any recognizable framework as some organizations approach the process as an integrative and sometimes spontaneous activity. However, the MCPF approach presented here is intended to highlight the tasks to be achieved, the way in which they relate to one another, and the order in which they should be accomplished.

Elements of the MCPF

A marketing communications plan should be developed for each level of communications activity, from strategy to individual tactical aspects of a campaign. The difference between them is the level of detail that is included.

Context Analysis

The marketing plan is the bedrock of the **context analysis** (CA). This will already have been prepared and contains important information about the target segment, the business and marketing goals, competitors, and the timescales in which the goals are to be achieved. The CA needs to elaborate and build on this information in order to provide the detail so that the plan can be developed and justified.

The first and vital step in the planning process is to analyse the context in which marketing communications activities are to occur. Unlike a situation analysis used in general planning models, the context analysis should be communications-oriented and use the marketing plan as a foundation. There are four main components to the communications context analysis: the customer, business, internal, and external environmental contexts.

Understanding the customer context requires information and market research data about the target audiences specified in the marketing plan. Here, detailed information about their needs, perceptions, motivation, attitudes, and decision-making characteristics relative to the product category (or issue) is necessary. In addition, information about the media and the people they use for information about the product category needs to be determined.

Understanding the business or marketing context, and the marketing communications environment in particular, is also important as these influence what has to be achieved. If the marketing strategy specifies growth through market penetration then not only will messages need to reflect this goal but also it will be important to understand how competitors are communicating with the target audience and which media they are using to do this.

Analysis of the internal context is undertaken to determine the resource capability with respect to supporting marketing communications. Three principal areas need to be reviewed:

▶ people resources (are people, including agencies, with suitable marketing communications skills available?);

▶ financial resources (how much is available to invest in marketing communications?); and

▶ technological resources (are the right systems and processes available to support marketing communications?).

The final area to be reviewed is the wider external context. Similar to the areas considered during the strategic analysis, emphasis is given to the political, economic, societal, ecological, and technological conditions. However, stress needs to be given to the impact on marketing communications. For example, if economic conditions get tough then people have lower levels of disposable income. Sales promotions, promotional offers, and extended credit terms become more attractive in this context.

The context analysis provides the rationale for the rest of the plan. It is from the CA that the marketing objectives (from the marketing plan) and the marketing communications objectives are derived. The type, form, and style of the message are rooted in the characteristics of the target audience, and the media selected to convey messages should be based on the nature of the tasks, the media preferences and habits of the audience, and the resources available.

Marketing Communications Objectives

Many organizations assume that their marketing communications goals are the same as their sales targets. This is incorrect because there are so many elements that contribute to sales, such as competitor pricing, product attributes, and distributor policies, that making marketing communications solely responsible for sales is naive and unrealistic. Ideally, marketing communications objectives should consist of three main elements, corporate, marketing, and communications objectives.

▶ **Corporate objectives** are derived from the business or marketing plan. They refer to the mission and the business area that the organization believes it should be in.

▶ **Marketing objectives** are derived from the marketing plan and are sales-oriented. These might be market share, sales revenues, volumes, ROI (return on investment), and other profitability indicators.

▶ **Communications objectives** are derived from the context analysis and refer to levels of awareness, perception, comprehension/knowledge, attitudes, and overall degree of preference for a brand. The choice of communications goal depends on the tasks that need to be accomplished.

These three elements constitute the overall set of marketing communications objectives. They should be set out in **SMART** terminology, that is, each should be specific, measurable, achievable, realistic, and timed. However, many brands need to refine the way they are perceived by customers, commonly referred to as a brand's position. Positioning is not applicable to all communications plans, e.g. government-sponsored information campaigns do not have a positioning goal.

However, most commercial and brand-oriented communication programmes need to be seen to occupy a clear position in the market. So, at this point in the planning process, the brand's positioning intentions are developed and these should be related to the market, the customers, or a product dimension. The justification for this will have been identified in the context analysis.

Marketing Communications Strategy

The marketing communications strategy is derived from the objectives and context analysis. There are three types of strategy: pull for the end user markets, push for the trade and channel intermediaries, and profile designed to reach all significant stakeholders. The DRIP roles of marketing communications, established in Chapter 10, can be used to elaborate the relevant strategy to be pursued. For example, if a new brand is being launched, the first task will be to inform and differentiate the brand for members of the trade before using a **pull strategy** to inform and differentiate the brand for the target end user customers. For example, when Diageo launched its Johnny Walker Whisky brand into the Greek market, it first informed and then educated its key distributors and business partners about how each brand should be presented and served. This was achieved by the slightly unusual approach of acting out the style and image of each brand through a theatrical performance. Naturally, this was followed by a tasting session to familiarize the distributors with each brand's attributes (Anon., 2006).

An organization wishing to signal a change of strategy and/or a change of name following a merger or acquisition may choose to use a profile strategy and the primary task will be to inform about the name change. An organization experiencing declining sales may choose to remind customers of a need or it may choose to improve sales through persuasion.

A traditional pull strategy in the grocery sector used to be based on delivering mass media advertising supported by below-the-line communications, most notably sales promotions delivered in-store and through direct mail and email to registered customers (e.g. Tesco Clubcard customers). The decision to use a pull strategy should be supported by a core message that will try to differentiate (position), remind or reassure, inform, or persuade the audience to think, feel, or behave in a particular way. This approach can be interpreted as a pull/remind or pull/position communication strategy, as this describes the audience and direction of the strategy and also clarifies what the strategy seeks to achieve.

go online

Visit the **Online Resource Centre** and complete Internet Activity 11.3 to learn more about how Honda used a pull strategy to target purchasers of its Honda Civic.

A push strategy should be treated in a similar way. The need to consider the core message is paramount as it conveys information about the essence of the strategy. Push/inform, push/position, or push/key accounts/discount might be examples of possible terminology.

Although these three strategies are represented here as individual entities, they are often used as a 'cluster'. For example, the launch of a new toothpaste brand will involve a push strategy to get the product on the shelves of the key supermarkets and independent retailers. The strategy would be to gain retailer acceptance of the new brand and to position it for them as a profitable new brand. The goal is to get the toothpaste on the retailers' shelves. To achieve this, personal selling supported by trade sales promotions will be the main marketing communications tools. A push strategy alone would be insufficient to persuade a retailer to stock a new brand. The promise of a pull strategy aimed at creating brand awareness and customer excitement needs to be created, accompanied by appropriate public relations activities, and any initial sales promotions necessary to motivate consumers to change their brand of toothpaste. The next step is to create particular brand associations and thereby position the brand in the minds of the target consumer audience. Messages may be primarily informational or emotional, but will endeavour to convey a brand promise. This may be accompanied or followed by the use of incentives to encourage consumers to trial the product. To support the brand, carelines and a website will need to be put in place to provide credibility, as well as a buyer reference point.

Communications Methods

This part of the plan is relatively complex as a number of activities need to be accomplished. For each specified target audience in the strategy, a creative or message needs to be developed. This should be based on the positioning requirements and will often be developed by an outside communications agency.

Simultaneously, it is necessary to formulate the right mix of communication tools to reach each particular audience. In addition, the right media mix needs to be determined, both on- and offline. Again, this task will most probably be undertaken by media experts. Here, integration is regarded as an important feature of the communication mix. For example, when LG Electronics launched

A demonstrator shows off the premium HDTV

Source: Courtesy of LG Electronics. © You SUNG-HO/Reuters/Corbis

its global campaign in May 2007 for its premium 'Full HD' 1080p flat-panel high-definition TVs (HDTVs) they used both offline and online advertising formats. These featured broadcast, print, outdoor, and online in three creative concepts that all feature an LG Red Couch, their symbol of the consumers' all-encompassing high-definition viewing experience. The LG campaign also incorporated LG's corporate sponsorship of the Cannes Film Festival and targeted public relations activities highlighting the Full HD technology and flat-panel designs. The selected media reflected the product's key purpose.

The Schedule

The next step is to schedule the way in which the campaign is to be delivered. Events and activities should be scheduled according to the goals and the strategic thrust. So, if it is necessary to communicate with the trade prior to a public launch, those activities tied into the push strategy should be scheduled prior to those calculated to support the pull strategy.

Similarly, if awareness is a goal then, funds permitting, it may be best to first use TV and poster ads offline plus banners and search engine ads online, before using sales promotions (unless sampling is used), direct marketing, point of purchase, and personal selling.

Resources

The resources necessary to support the plan need to be determined. These refer not only to the financial issues but also to the quality of available marketing expertise. This means that internally the right sort of marketing knowledge may not be present and may have to be recruited. For example, if launching a customer relationship management system (CRM) initiative, then it will be important to have people with knowledge and skills related to running CRM programmes. With regard to external skills, it is necessary that the current communications agencies are capable of delivering the creative and media plan.

This is an important part of the plan, one that is often avoided or forgotten about. Software project planning tools, simple spreadsheets, or Gantt charts can be used not only to schedule the campaign but also to chart the resources relating to the actual and budgeted costs of using the selected tools and media.

Control and Evaluation

Campaigns, once launched, should be monitored. This is to ensure that should there be any major deviance from the plan, opportunities exist to get back on track as soon as possible. In addition, all marketing communications plans should be evaluated. There are numerous methods to evaluate the individual performance of the tools and the media used, but perhaps the most important measures concern the achievement of the communication objectives.

Feedback

The marketing communications planning process is completed when feedback is provided. Not only should information regarding the overall outcome of a campaign be considered but also individual aspects of the activity. For example, the performance of the individual tools used within the campaign, whether sufficient resources were invested, the appropriateness of the strategy in the first place, whether any problems had been encountered during implementation, and the relative ease with which the objectives were accomplished, are aspects that need to be fed back to all internal and external parties associated with the planning process.

This feedback is vitally important because it provides information for the context analysis that anchors the next campaign. Information fed back in a formal and systematic manner constitutes an opportunity for organizations to learn from their previous campaign activities, a point often overlooked and neglected.

Managing Communications Activities

Over the past five years there have been some sizeable changes to the way the marketing communications industry is structured, not just in the UK but across the globe. One of the most important of these has been the emergence of a number of powerful and dominant industry groups, such as WPP and the News Corporation, the business interests of which span cross-media ownership, content development, and delivery. The battle in 2007 between Virgin Media and BSkyB over fees to deliver Sky content through Virgin Media reflects the criticality of some of these issues. The changing industry structure is partly a response to several variables, namely developments in technology, the configuration of the communications mix and media used by organizations, and the way in which client-side managers are expected to operate.

There can be no doubt that technology has had a dramatic impact on the communications industry. As a result, the way organizations use the communications mix has changed considerably. Traditionally, clients working in consumer markets preferred to place the majority of their media advertising into offline, mass media vehicles. Similarly, the salesforce was the dominant tool of the mix used by organizations operating in business markets. Today, the use of sponsorship, direct and event marketing, and online, digitally driven interactive communications is growing at the expense of offline mass media advertising and sales promotions in consumer markets. Many organizations in the business-to-business market have slashed the size of their salesforces, partly to cut costs but also to use technology more efficiently.

The reasons for these shifts in behaviour are indicative of the increasing attention and accountability that management is attaching to the communication spend. Increasingly, marketing managers are being asked to justify the amounts they spend on their budgets, including advertising and sales promotion. Senior managers now want to know the return they are getting on their marketing communication investments. This is because there is pressure to use their scarce resources more effectively and efficiently so that they can meet their corporate and business-level objectives.

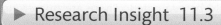

▶ Research Insight 11.3

To take your learning further, you might wish to read this influential paper.

Jones, J. P. (1990), 'Ad spending: maintaining market share', *Harvard Business Review*, January–February, 38–42.

This paper provided a first and important link between advertising strategy and budgeting. The paper is built on the research findings emanating from a very large sample of brands. It draws some interesting conclusions about the level of advertising investment relative to market share.

 Visit the **Online Resource Centre** to read the abstract and access the full paper.

It might be safely assumed that the final aspect of a manager's responsibilities concerns the measurement of their marketing communications activities. This is partly correct but measurement and evaluation should be an ongoing activity, used throughout the development and implementation of a campaign. The importance of evaluating marketing communications activities should not be underestimated. The process can provide a potentially rich source of material for the next campaign and the ongoing communications that all organizations operate. Unfortunately, many organizations choose to either ignore or not to devote too many resources or significance to this aspect of their work. However, in an age of increasing accountability, measuring and determining just how well a campaign ran and what was accomplished is an essential part of marketing communications. Table 11.6 sets out some of the more common techniques used to measure marketing communications.

▶ **Table 11.6** Evaluation methods: marketing communications tools

Marketing communication tool	Method of testing
Advertising	Pretesting—*unfinished* ads—concept testing, focus groups, consumer juries
	Pretesting—*finished* ads—dummy vehicles, readability test, theatre tests
	Physiological—pupil dilation, eye tracking, galvanic skin response, tachistoscopes, electrocephalographs
	Post-testing—enquiry tests, recall tests, recognition tests, sales-tracking studies, financial analysis, likeability
Sales promotion	Trial, sales, stock turn, redemption levels
Public relations	Press cuttings, content analysis, media evaluation, tracking studies, recruitment levels
Direct marketing	Response rates, sales, opening/reading ratios, trial
Personal selling	Activities, costs, knowledge and skills, sales, performance ratios, territory analysis, team outputs, customer satisfaction

Integrated Marketing Communications

So far in this chapter we have looked briefly at the five main tools, the media, and ideas about how messages should be developed. However, in order for these to work most effectively and most efficiently, it makes sense to bring them together so that they work together as a unit. In doing so, they will have a greater overall impact and bring benefits to organizations, as well as audiences. This bringing together is referred to as **integrated marketing communications**, or IMC.

Integrated marketing communications has become a popular approach with both clients and communications agencies. Ideas about IMC originated in the early 1990s and IMC was regarded as a means of orchestrating the tools of the marketing communications mix, so that audiences perceive a single, consistent, unified message whenever they have contact with a brand. Duncan and Everett (1993) referred to this new, largely media-oriented approach as *orchestration*, *whole egg*, and *seamless* communication. Since this time, many authors have explored ideas concerning IMC, and, more recently, Duncan (2002), Grönroos (2004), and Kitchen *et al.* (2004) have provided various definitions and valuable insights into IMC. For our purposes the following definition is used:

> IMC is a strategic approach to the planned management of an organisation's communications. IMC requires that organisations coordinate their various strategies, resources and messages in order that it engage coherently and meaningfully with target audiences. The main purpose is to develop relationships with audiences that are of mutual value (Fill, 2006).

Embedded within this definition are links with both business-level and marketing strategies plus confirmation of the importance of the coherent use of resources and messages. What should also be evident is that IMC can be used to support the development and maintenance of effective relationships, a point made first by Duncan and Moriarty (1998) and then by Grönroos (2004) and Ballantyne (2004). Some, such as Peltier, Schibrowsky, and Schultz (2003) advocate interactive integrated marketing communications (IIMC) based on the premise that all marketing communication should be based on customer databases. However, this is not a widely held view as IMC can work without having to be database-fed, or interactive in that sense.

One quite common use of an integrated approach can be seen in the use of the tools. For example, rather than use advertising, public relations, sales promotions, personal selling, and direct marketing separately, better to use them in a coordinated manner. So, organizations often use advertising or sales promotion to create awareness, and then involve public relations to provoke media comment, and then reinforce these messages through direct marketing or personal selling. The internet can also be incorporated to encourage comment, interest, and involvement in a brand yet still convey the same message in a consistent way. Mobile communications are used to reach audiences to reinforce messages and persuade audiences to behave in particular ways, wherever they are. However, the rise of digital media poses problems for IMC and for planning marketing communications activities. Some of these issues concern metrics and measurement, budgeting, brand control, and content development (Winer, 2009).

Another important aspect of integration concerns the question 'what else should be integrated?'. Well, one element might be the planning and campaign development process. Using an integrated approach during the planning phase can serve to integrate clients, agencies, suppliers, and employees, as well as other resources.

IMC has emerged for many reasons, but two main ones concern customers and costs. First, organizations began to realize that their customers are more likely to understand a single message, delivered through various sources, rather than try to understand a series of different messages transmitted through different tools and a variety of media. IMC, therefore, is concerned with harmonizing the messages conveyed through each of the promotional tools, so that audiences perceive a consistent set of meanings within the messages they receive. The second reason concerns costs. As organizations seek to lower their costs, it is becoming clear that it is far more cost-effective to send a single message, using a limited number of agencies and other resources, rather than develop several messages through a number of agencies.

At first glance IMC might appear to be a practical and logical development that should benefit all concerned with an organization's marketing communications. However, there are issues concerning the concept, including what should be integrated, over and above the tools, media, and messages. For example, what about the impact of employees on a brand, and the other elements of the marketing mix, as well as the structure, systems, processes, and procedures necessary to deliver IMC consistently through time? There is some debate about the nature and contribution IMC can make to an organization, if only because there is a no main theory to underpin the topic (Cornelissen, 2003).

Although IMC has yet to become an established marketing theory, the original ideas inherent in the overall approach are intuitively appealing and appear to be of value. However, what is integration to one person may be coordination and good practice to another, and, until there is a theoretical base on which to build IMC the phrase will continue to be misused, misunderstood, and used in a haphazard and inconsistent way.

▶ Market Insight 11.5

Integrated or Coordinated Marketing Communications?

Many campaigns claim to be integrated, yet the only evidence appears to be that it is the tools and media which are combined so that the same message is conveyed through all media channels. For example, in July 2009, Samsung launched 'Jet', a super-fast smart phone and used a £5m integrated campaign, based on a marketing strategy designed to drive brand preference and loyalty. The

The Nivea Sun bus, part of their integrated 'sunwise' campaign

▶ Market Insight 11.5

campaign was called 'Impatience is a Virtue', and illustrated different cases of people waiting, such as a person waiting to be served in a café and someone waiting for a bus. The voiceover informs us that we hate waiting, but that it can be a virtue as it has driven civilization to build and create things to rid us of waiting. Examples given include the jet plane, suggesting that the name of the new model further points to the function of the handset itself. The integrated campaign was based around TV as the lead medium, and included cinema, press, poster, digital, retail, PR, and below-the-line activity.

A quick scan of the marketing press shows that the word integrated is used frequently to describe campaigns. For example, Nivea Sun ran a nationwide 'Sunwise' roadshow to promote sun safety and the brand's Children's Sun Spray range. The integrated programme was based on the Nivea Sun bus, which features areas for kids to explore. This was supported by TV and press activity.

Hotel company Ibis used an integrated campaign to drive leisure bookings and included online promotions on several travel websites, as well as national press and outdoor ads.

Volkswagen used an integrated campaign to illustrate how Volkswagen vans are a good investment in the recession. They used TV, radio, digital, experiential, retail, press, and PR elements.

Sources: Alarcon (2009); Wood (2009); Golding (2009); Anon. (2009); Charles-Kay (2009).

1   Just because a client wants an integrated programme does not mean that all agencies can deliver it. Go to the article in *Campaign* and see how one agency has approached the issue of integration. www.campaignlive.co.uk/news/features/941045/Close-up-Inside-MBA/?DCMP=ILC-SEARCH.

2   Go to the article by Williams (2009b) in *Campaign* and write notes for and against the IMC concept. www.campaignlive.co.uk/news/features/912812/Close-Up-Does-UK-deliver-integration/.

3   How would you respond if requested to describe what an integrated campaign means?

▶ Research Insight 11.4

To take your learning further, you might wish to read this influential paper.

Cornelissen, J. P. (2001), 'Integrated marketing communications and the language of marketing development', *International Journal of Advertising*, 20, 4, 483–98.

Cornelissen has written many papers about IMC and associated communication management and planning issues. His view of the subject provides a useful counterbalance to the whole-hearted support expressed by most other IMC authors and that alone is good reason to read this paper.

@ Visit the **Online Resource Centre** to read the abstract and access the full paper.

Skills for Employment

▶▶ Learn everything about the company before you go for the interview. Find out everything they do, who their competitors are, what products they have, what markets they operate in, advertising campaigns they have done, etc. A passion for your work, hunger to learn, and willingness to roll your sleeves up and get stuck in are key things I look for in entry-level candidates. There is nothing worse than a candidate coming to an interview for a job in my marketing team and not finding out these things first. ◀◀

Gwyn Davis, Marketing Manager, ZSL London Zoo

 Visit the **Online Resource Centre** to discover more tips and advice on skills for the workplace.

 Chapter Summary

To consolidate your learning, the key points from this chapter are summarized below:

■ **Describe the configuration and role of the marketing communications mix.**

Organizations use the marketing communication mix to engage their various audiences. The mix consists of five tools and six classes of media. The tools include advertising, sales promotion, public relations, direct marketing, and personal selling. Advertising uses paid-for media to convey messages to the target audiences. Tools and media are not the same, as the former are methods or techniques, whereas the media are the means by which messages are conveyed to the target audience.

■ **Explain the role and characteristics of each of the primary tools of the communication mix.**

Each of the tools communicates messages in different ways and achieves different outcomes. Advertising can differentiate, reinforce, and build awareness but is not very good at getting responses or driving behaviour. Sales promotions are persuasive, public relations can inform audiences and differentiate organizations and brands, whereas direct marketing is strong at generating responses from target audiences: that is, persuading them to behave in particular ways. The final tool, personal selling, is competent at all the DRIP tasks but excels at persuasion.

■ **Understand and set out the criteria that should be used to select the right communication mix.**

Using a set of criteria can help simplify the complex and difficult process of selecting the right marketing communications mix. There are five key criteria, namely: the degree of control over a message, the credibility of the message conveyed, the costs of using a tool, the degree to which a target audience is dispersed, and the task that marketing communications is required to accomplish.

■ **Outline the characteristics of the different media and how they are categorized.**

Each medium has a set of characteristics that enable it to convey messages in particular ways to a target audience. For example, TV uses sight and sound, radio just sound, outdoor usually just sight, and digital media can use sound, touch, and sight. Three media categories can be identified: classes, types, and vehicles. There are six main classes of media, broadcast, print, outdoor, digital, in-store, and other media. There are many types of media, such as TV and radio, newspapers and magazines. Within each type of medium there are a huge number of different media vehicles that can be selected to carry a client's message.

■ **Explain how marketing communication activities are planned and implemented.**

Marketing communication planning is a systematic process that leads to the setting of marketing communication objectives and the formulation of plans for achieving them. The marketing communications planning framework (MCPF) provides a structure and checklist though which the sequence of decisions that marketing managers undertake when preparing, implementing, and evaluating communication strategies and plans can be designed. The framework reflects a deliberate or planned approach to strategic marketing communications, one that may not always occur in practice.

■ **Describe the different activities associated with managing marketing communications.**

There is a large range of tasks associated with managing marketing communications. At one level, there are decisions to be made about the overall strategy and direction of the marketing communications, and issues associated with the process and, of course, the content of marketing communications plans. At another level, decisions need to be made about the right mix of tools and media necessary to engage with target audiences, and to decide about what is to be said in the message and how it is to be presented. Behind all of these activities are issues associated with the management of resources, both human and financial, and the agency relationships necessary to generate the communication materials. Once implemented, management is still involved through the control, monitoring, evaluation, and feedback processes.

■ **Consider the principles and issues associated with integrated marketing communications.**

Rather than use advertising, public relations, sales promotions, personal selling, and direct marketing separately, integrated marketing communications is concerned with working with these tools (and media) as a coordinated whole. So, organizations often use advertising to create awareness, then involve public relations to provoke media comment, sales promotion to create trial and then reinforce these messages through, direct marketing or personal selling in order to persuade audiences. The internet can also be incorporated to encourage comment, interest, and involvement in a brand, yet still convey the same message in a consistent way. Mobile communications are used to reach audiences to reinforce messages and persuade audiences to behave in particular ways, wherever they are.

 Review Questions

1 Make brief notes about the nature and role of the marketing communications mix and explain how the role has changed.

2 Write a definition for advertising, public relations, and one other tool from the mix. Identify the key differences.

3 Explain the main reason why organizations like to use direct-response media.

4 Explain how technology has influenced the use of personal selling.

5 Identify and explain the five criteria that can be used to select the right mix of communication tools.

6 Write a list that categorizes the media. Find a media vehicle to represent each type of media.

7 To what extent are online and digital media likely to replace the use of traditional media?

8 Discuss the view that if marketing communications strategy is about being audience-centred then there is little need to prepare a context analysis.

9 Draw the marketing communications planning framework. Try this first without referring to the diagram. If stuck refer to the diagram.

10 Explain the principles of integrated marketing communications.

 ## Worksheet Summary

Visit the **Online Resource Centre** and complete Worksheet 11.1. This will aid in learning about how we can use the different marketing communication tools and differing media channels to communicate information about a FMCG to our target audiences.

 ## Discussion Questions

1 Having read Case Insight 11.1, how would you advise ZSL London Zoo about which tools and media they should use to attract visitors to see Gorilla Kingdom?

2 Discuss the view that the role of the marketing communications mix should change as it was developed in an age when communications were based essentially on mass media communications.

3 Select an organization you are either familiar with or would like to work for. Visit their website and try to determine their use of the marketing communications tools and media. How could their mix of tools and media be improved?

4 Select an organization in the consumer technology industry or one which you would like to work for. Visit their website and see their ad archive and then read the press releases. Try to determine their approach to marketing communications. Now visit the website for their main competitor and again, determine their marketing communications. Discuss the similarities and differences.

5 Zylog is based in Sweden and manufactures and distributes a range of consumer electronic equipment. Annike Karlsson, Zylog's new marketing manager, has indicated that she wants to introduce an integrated approach to the firm's marketing communications. However, Zylog does not have any experience of IMC and their current communications agency, Red Spider, has started to become concerned that it may lose the Zylog account. Discuss the situation facing Zylog and suggest ways in which they might acquire the expertise they need. Then discuss ways in which Red Spider might acquire an IMC capability.

 Visit the **Online Resource Centre** and complete the Multiple Choice Questions to assess your knowledge of Chapter 11.

  go online

References

Alarcon, C. (2009), 'Samsung launches Jet with integrated campaign,' *Marketing Week*, 7 July, retrieve from www.marketingweek.co.uk/samsung-launches-jet-with-integrated-campaign/3002056.article, accessed 25 September 2009.

Anon. (2006), *Diageo (Greece) Theatrical Staff Seminar*, retrieve from www.warc.com, accessed 28 March 2007.

—(2008), Case Study O2, *Design Case Studies, Marketing*, p. 15.

—(2009), 'Ibis in autumn break activity', *Marketing*, 2 September 2009 retrieve from www.marketingmagazine.co.uk/news/931304/Ibis-autumn-break-activity?, accessed 27 September 2009.

Ballantyne, D. (2004), 'Dialogue and its role in the development of relationship specific knowledge', *Journal of Business & Industrial Marketing*, 19, 2, 114–23.

Berne, S. (2009), 'Four in ten viewers driven online by TV ads', *NewMediaAge*, 19 August, retrieve from www.nma.co.uk/four-in-ten-viewers-driven-online-by-tv-ads/, accessed 25 September 2009.

Buck, H. and Roach, T. (2009), 'How to Feed your Family for a Fiver', Marketing Society Awards for Excellence, retrieve from www.marketing-society.org.uk/Assets/documents/pdfs/marketing-communications-sainsbury.pdf, accessed 22 September 2009.

Charles-Kay, L. (2009), 'Volkswagen promotes commercial vehicles integrated campaign', *Marketing*, 1 July, retrieve from www.marketingmagazine.co.uk/news/917262/Volkswagen-promotes-commercial-vehicles-integrated-campaign?, accessed 27 September 2009.

Cornelissen, J. P. (2003), 'Change, continuity and progress: the concept of integrated marketing communications and marketing communications practice', *Journal of Strategic Marketing*, 11 (December), 217–34.

Duncan, T. (2002), *IMC: Using Advertising and Promotion to Build Brand*, international edn, New York: McGraw Hill.

—and Everett, S. (1993), 'Client perceptions of integrated marketing communications', *Journal of Advertising Research*, 3, 3, 30–9.

—and Moriarty, S. (1998), 'A communication-based marketing model for managing relationships', *Journal of Marketing*, 62 (April), 1–13.

Farber, A.(2009), 'Gap to follow web campaign with UK ecommerce site', *Marketing Week*, 9 September, retrieve from www.marketingweek.co.uk/news/gap-to-follow-web-campaign-with-uk-ecommerce-site/3004248.article, accessed 27 April 2010.

Fill, C. (2002), *Marketing Communications*, 3rd edn, Harlow: FT/Prentice Hall.

—(2006), *Simply Marketing Communications*, Harlow: FT/Prentice Hall.

—(2009), *Marketing Communications: Interactivity, Communities and Content*, 5th edn, Harlow: FT/Prentice Hall.

Golding, A. (2009), 'Nivea uses experiential events to promote children's sunscreen brand', *Marketing*, 7 May 2009, retrieve from www.marketingmagazine.co.uk/news/904057/Nivea-uses-experiential-events-promote-childrens-sunscreen-brand?, accessed 27 September 2009.

Grönroos, C. (2004), 'The relationship marketing process: communication, interaction, dialogue, value', *Journal of Business and Industrial Marketing*, 19, 2, 99–113.

Hosea, M. (2009), 'Worth its weight in gold', *Marketing Week*, 17 September, retrieve from www.marketingweek.co.uk/worth-its-weight-in-gold/3004489.article, accessed 25 September 2009.

Howard, J. (2009), 'Adwatch Review: Cash4Gold.com', *Marketing*, 25 August, retrieve from www.marketingmagazine.co.uk/news/928887/Adwatch-Review-Cash4Goldcom?, accessed 25 September 2009.

Kemp, E. (2008), 'O2 unveils major repositioning and fresh strapline', *Marketing*, 4 April, retrieven from www.brandrepublic.com/News/800044/o2-unveils-major-repositioning-and-fresh-strapline, accessed 17 July 2010.

King, I. (2009), 'Beneath the basic story', *The Times*, 13 May, retrieve from http://business.timesonline.co.uk/tol/business/columnists/article6276638.ece, accessed 26 April 2010.

Kitchen, P., Brignell, J., Li, T., and Spickett Jones, G. (2004), 'The emergence of IMC: a theoretical perspective', *Journal of Advertising Research*, 44 (March), 19–30.

McEleny, C (2009), 'Gap ditches TV ads in favour of social media', *New Media Age*, 17 August. retrieve from www.nma.co.uk/gap-ditches-tv-ads-in-favour-of-social-media/3003521.article?nl=DN, accessed 24 September 2009.

Peltier, J.W., Schibrowsky, J.A. and Schultz, D. E. (2003), 'Interactive integrated marketing communication: combining the power of MC, the new media and database marketing', *International Journal of Advertising*, 22, 93–115.

Porter, L., and Golan, G. J. (2006), 'From subservient chickens to brawny men: a comparison of viral advertising to TV advertising', *Journal of Interactive Advertising*, 6, 2, 30–8.

Quenqua, D. (2009), 'The Gap Steps Up to Social Media in New Denim Campaign', ClickZ, 17 Aug, retrieve from www.clickz.com/3634707, accessed 27 April 2010.

Silverman, G. (2006), 'How can I help you?', FT Magazine, 4–5 February, 16–21.

Simmons, D. (2006), 'Marketing's viral goldmine'. *BBC News website*, retrieve from http://news.bbc.co.uk/1/hi/programmes/click_online/5179166.stm

Simms, J. (2007), 'User-generated ads kick off at Super Bowl', *Marketing*, 30 January retrieve from www.marketingmagazine.co.uk/news/629145/User-generated-ads-kick-off-Super-Bowl?, accessed 25 September 2009.

Vilpponen, A., Winter, S., and Sundqvist, S. (2006), 'Electronic word-of-mouth in online environments: exploring referral network structure and adoption behavior', *Journal of Interactive Advertising*, 6, 2 (Spring), 71–86.

Williams, M. (2009a), 'Cash4Gold asks public to choose UK brand spokesman', Campaignlive, 14 September, retrieve from www.brandrepublic.com/News/938083/Cash4Gold-asks-public-choose-UK-brand-spokesman/?, accessed 25 September 2009.

—(2009b), 'Close-Up: Does the UK deliver on integration?' *Campaign*, 5 June, retrieve from www.brandrepublic.com/Campaign/Features/Analysis/912812/Close-Up-Does-UK-deliver-integration/?, accessed 27 September 2009.

Winer, R.S. (2009), 'New communications approaches in Marketing: Issues and Research Directions', *Journal of Interactive Marketing*, 23, 108–117.

Wood, R. (2009), 'Samsung rockets with new Jet', *Media Week*, 12 August, retrieve from www.mediaweek.co.uk/news/926809/Samsung-rockets-new-Jet/, accessed 25 September 2009.

12 Retailing and Channel Management

● Learning Outcomes

After studying this chapter you should be able to:

▶ Define what a channel of distribution is and key considerations in managing a channel strategy

▶ Discuss the differing types of intermediaries and their roles in the distribution channel

▶ Differentiate between different distribution channel structures and selection criteria

▶ Discuss the factors influencing channel design, structure, and strategy

▶ Distinguish between the logistical functions for effective management

▶ Discuss the role, function, and importance of retailers in the distribution channel

▶ Compare and contrast the differing types of retailers

▶ Case Insight 12.1

Founded in 1921, HMV opened its first store in Oxford Street, London. Long regarded as one of Europe's leading music retailers, today HMV is more a multiple entertainment hub than a pure music retailer. We speak to Gennaro Castaldo to find out how HMV is adapting to changing customer and market expectations.

Gennaro Castaldo for HMV

With its origins in retailing, HMV has grown to comprise over 270 stores with sales of £1.15bn in the UK and Ireland (HMV UK), with a further 130 stores throughout Canada, Hong Kong and Singapore, with sales of £253.8m (HMV International). However, HMV is far more than a music retailer. With rapid innovations in the development of technology coupled with changing customer preferences in entertainment consumption, HMV today is more a hub for entertainment. HMV's aim has always been to give customers access to the music and entertainment that they love, the way they want to enjoy it.

Over the last century we have seen the way music and entertainment content is made available to customers continually change. However, today's digital technology has gone one step further and changed not only consumption patterns but also the business model of music retailing forever. Digital technology has made downloads not just possible but a customer preference, with increased access via a variety of internet-based PC and mobile platforms. CD albums still represent about 85% of all legal sales in the UK, but there is a definite long-term downward trend to this market. In contrast, sales of singles have seen nine out of ten purchases made in digital form. Record labels and retailers alike are struggling to adapt their business models in light of this new digital landscape. Multicategory supermarket retailers also sell music and entertainment products rendering increased competition across the sector. Questions continue to remain about the long-term viability of selling recorded music and entertainment products.

To adapt, HMV is diversifying its product and channel offering, and further investing in adjacent businesses to provide a multichannel entertainment experience for its customers. HMV's aim is to be seen LESS as a one-dimensional music retailer, and MORE as a multichannel entertainment hub where consumers can 'get closer' to the music, film, and games they love, however they wish to enjoy them.

With over tens of millions of customers visiting our multiple channels, and our HMV website generating over 55m customer visits alone in 2009, we operate a multichannel strategy. The *HMV product portfolio* includes not just music albums and singles, but also DVD and Blu-ray, games and technology, and related entertainment products such as licensed artist and film franchise merchandising. In the UK in 2009, 45% of HMV sales came from visual (DVD and Blu-ray), 28% from music, 24% from games and technology, and 3% from related entertainment products. *Live in-store events* include hundreds of artist personal appearances each year, ranging from album signings to live in-store performances. For *online engagement* we use a website, email marketing, and social media strategy (i.e. Twitter, YouTube, Facebook), and a customer rewards programme across channels (*purehmv*) to engage with customers' entertainment experiences. Critical to this is our employee strategy, spanning 8,000 employees in five countries, focused on providing *specialist entertainment knowledge* with a staff ethos *'to be original, be fanatic and work hard together to get customers closer to the music, film, and games they love'*.

▶ Case Insight 12.1

At HMV, retail is just one part of a multi-channel strategy

HMV is also diversifying further the channels through which we offer our customers live entertainment experiences. We continue to invest in entertainment venues, with 11 concert venues in total, co-owning (with MAMA Group) the legendary HMV Hammersmith Apollo and the HMV Forum (London), the HMV Picture House (Edinburgh) and investing in summer festivals such as Lovebox, Godskitchen, Global Gathering, and the Great Escape. We are also experimenting with cinema (in Wimbledon, S.W. London) through a partnership with Curzon Artificial Eye and rolling out an online gaming facility called Gamerbase across stores.

HMV is no longer a one-dimensional music retailer, but rather an entertainment hub using multiple channels to foster customer entertainment experiences—be it at home, in-store, online, or at live entertainment venues.

If you were HMV, what would you do to manage its multiple-channel entertainment hub to foster continued positive customer experiences?

Introduction

Where do you do your banking or buy your groceries? How do you purchase tickets for a concert, a football match, or an airline flight? At what time of the day do you pay your electricity or phone bills? For many people, the time and place at which they deal with these things have changed. We can get cash 24 hours a day, 365 days per year, from automatic teller machines (ATMs). Bills can be paid and banking completed any time at home or at work, on the phone or through the internet, and drink and snack dispensing machines now appear on railway station platforms, airline terminals, in shopping malls, and hospital waiting rooms. These examples demonstrate that in the last two decades **place (or distribution)** has undergone substantial change.

Many organizations believe that they play a relatively small part in their marketing activities, seeing distribution as only the activities involved in transporting goods physically from where they are manufactured to the customer. However, as competition increases, and margins are reduced, the focus on distribution efficiency and effectiveness continues to dramatically increase. If goods do not arrive in the proper place, or in the proper condition, no sale can be made (Douglas, James, and Ellram, 1998).

This chapter demonstrates that distribution embraces a broader concept than just the delivery of goods. It includes understanding the strategic importance of distribution channels, member roles in the channel, and the rising importance of customer service. This chapter introduces you to the fundamental principle of 'place' in the marketing mix and to management decisions concerning distribution channels, channel members, and logistics management. For consumer markets, retailing is a very important part of the distribution channel, so we also provide a detailed discussion of retailing and wholesaling.

Place

'Place' or distribution concerns how to place the optimum amount of goods and/or services before the maximum number of a target market at the times and locations they want. The way distribution occurs can be physical, like supplying a music album or DVD through one of HMV's stores; a service, such as a training on how to use editing software to create our own music; or electronic, such as downloading the latest singles from iTunes. Irrespective of the mode used, distribution activities have a direct effect on other marketing elements. For example, Europe's largest clothing maker and retailer, Inditex has seen its clothing sales rise by over 25% in recent years because it adds new stock in its Zara stores twice a week, keeping its stock up to date with the latest fashion trends. It achieves this by manufacturing over 40% of its stock in Spain or Portugal; although more costly in production, Inditex can get new trends into European and American stores twice as fast than if they have to wait for delivery for stock manufactured in Asia. This shows that distribution activities have a direct effect on Inditex and Zara's brand and retailing strategy.

Distribution activities are a vital element in creating customer value. A product will provide customer value and satisfaction only if it is available to the customer when and where it is needed, and in the appropriate quantity (Douglas, James, and Ellram, 1998). Sometimes this requires organizations to think outside the box of traditional delivery channels. For example, in order to reach the 600,000 rural villages in India, Samsung, partnered with the Indian Farmers Fertiliser Cooperative Ltd to sell its handsets. With this distribution channel it can now reach over 90% of the villages in India. Factors that influence customer perceptions of distribution quality include:

▶ dependability—consistency of service;

▶ time in transit;

▶ market coverage;

▶ the ability to provide door-to-door service;

▶ flexibility—handling and meeting the special needs of shippers;

▶ loss and damage performance; and

▶ the ability to provide more than a basic product delivery service.

As product delivery has a direct effect on customer evaluations of service quality and satisfaction, we need to understand what it is customers want from our distribution activities. Do they want speedy delivery, a reliable supply of products, a good range of choice or product assortment, increased availability, convenience, service and support, a good price, or aftersales service? Insight to these questions helps inform effective distribution and channel management strategies, but these too are dependent on the buyer type and type of product being delivered. For more information on how Nokia reaches customers in China, see Market Insight 12.1.

▶ Market Insight 12.1

Nokia Reaches out in China

The People's Republic of China is a highly attractive marketplace for Western companies looking to expand their global sales. After the USA and Japan, its economy is regarded as the third-largest in the world, with a nominal GDP of US$4.91trn (2009). It is not only the fastest growing major economy in the world, but has been the fastest growing major economy for the past 30 years, with an average annual GDP growth rate over 10%. This has made it especially attractive to the Finnish mobile manufacturer Nokia.

Nokia is the largest mobile phone manufacturer in the world and China is its largest market contributing over 16% of its global sales. But delivering to Chinese consumers has not been without its challenges. The organization entered China in the early 1990s, and initially supplied network equipment to Chinese manufacturers, through joint ventures with local companies. With a better understanding of the local market, by the end of the 1990s, China emerged as Nokia's second-largest market after the USA; however, Motorola was still the market leader. By early 2000, Nokia began losing sales significantly to local Chinese companies due to the limited range of Nokia handsets

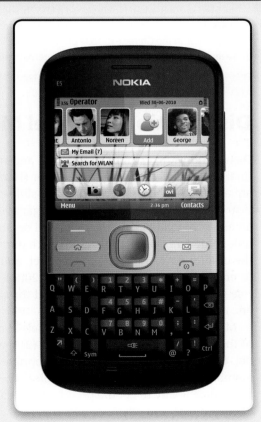

Nokia, the world's largest mobile handset manufacturer

Source: Copyright © Nokia 2010.

▶ Market Insight 12.1   (continued)

in the country and limited distribution to rural China where demand was rapidly growing.

To address these challenges, Nokia revamped its product strategies and invested heavily in its distribution system. This included decentralizing Nokia's distribution operations, increasing the number of regional distributors, hiring third-party representatives, opening sales offices all across the country, and engaging in direct distribution to end consumers through retail outlets across the country. These changes had a positive impact on sales—by 2005, Nokia emerged as the leading handset manufacturer in the country and China was Nokia's largest market. Nokia's position was further secured in 2008, when Nokia signed a US$2bn deal with China P&T Appliances' China Postel, the leading distributor in the Chinese mobile phone market. With revenues from China in 2009 of $8.6bn, remaining

flat year-over-year, despite a 5% decrease in market share to 35% in 2009, Nokia's position in the country still remains strong. With China constituting the largest market in the world, with around 750m mobile subscribers, an effective distribution strategy to reach the Chinese consumer when, where, and how they want it, is of critical importance for Nokia to defend its market leader position.

Sources: Datamonitor (2009); Wai-yin Kwok (2008); www.nokia.com

1   **What were the reasons Nokia lost sales to local Chinese organizations?**

2   **What did Nokia do to overcome these challenges?**

3   **What impact could the US$2bn deal have on Nokia's position in China?**

Distribution Channel Management

Distribution ranges from production and manufacturing to logistics, warehousing, and the final delivery of goods to the customer (Handfield and Nichols, 1999). Very few organizations are able to deliver products to all possible customers, and thus rely on other parties, such as distributors, for assistance. These organizations form what we call a **distribution channel**, an organized network of agencies and organizations that perform all the activities required to link producers and manufacturers with purchasers and consumers (Bennet, 1988). The aim is the orderly flow of material, personnel, and information throughout the distribution channel to ensure product delivery (Russell, 2000). Distributors perform an important intermediary role in matching supply with demand through their interactions with suppliers, manufacturers, and end customers.

Management of distribution channels concerns two key elements: (1) managing the design of the channel and its activities, and (2) managing the relationship of members in the channel. First, we need to design an appropriate channel structure, channel length, and select the members of the channel and their roles. This helps us to determine what is the most effective and efficient way to get the product to the customer. How can we reach the optimum number of customers? And what organizations do we need to help us achieve this? Next, we turn our attention to managing the social, political, and economic relationships of channel members (Gandhi, 1979). A good understanding of the relationships in the channel will help to improve the effectiveness and efficiency of product delivery.

Channel decisions are some of the most important decisions that a manager faces. An organization's pricing strategies will depend on whether the product is distributed through mass retailers or high-quality speciality stores. Likewise, salesforce and advertising decisions will depend on how much persuasion, training, motivation, and support dealers in the channel need. If an organization does not pay sufficient attention to the distribution channel, it will be detrimental to its marketing efforts. Some organizations have actually created an industry in improved distribution. Serving Europe for more than 20 years, the FedEx EuroOne Network offers next-day service with late collections and early deliveries, linking hundreds of European cities, and covering more than 40,000 postcodes.

Key Considerations

When managing distribution channels, we need to consider a number of factors to make sure the channel best suits the organization's objectives. This includes balancing the three elements of economics, coverage, and control.

▶ **Economics** requires us to recognize where costs are being incurred and profits being made in a channel to maximize our return on investment.

▶ **Coverage** is about maximizing the product's availability in the market for the customer, satisfying the desire to have the product available to the largest number of customers, in as many locations as possible, at the widest range of times.

▶ **Control** refers to achieving the optimum distribution costs without losing decision-making authority over the product, how it is priced, promoted, and delivered in the distribution channel.

Sometimes, by covering a wide range of delivery times and locations through the use of intermediaries, the organization sacrifices some control in decision-making. Intermediaries start changing the price, image, display, and so on as they seek to maximize sales of a whole range of products, including the products of competitors. Think about the positions of Nokia, Samsung, and Sony Ericsson. In order to get the maximum number of customers using their mobile phone handsets, they need to have the maximum number of retailers and mobile phone networks promoting and selling their phones. But the same networks and retailers also sell the handsets of their competitors. As the retailers and networks compete to sign up customers, they push for lower prices, or they demand advertising subsidies to help them sell the phones. So Nokia, Samsung, and Sony Ericsson may discover that their phones are being sold at very low prices, and their brand image being compromised, by retailers and networks who are desperately seeking to maximize their own sales. What happens if Motorola reduce the number of retailers or networks they deal with in order to increase control over their marketing mix? The danger, of course, is that their competitors will gain market share by continuing to deal with these retailers and networks. In contrast, Apple has specific policies on what distributors can and cannot discount on its products like the iPhone, whereas Google challenged the accepted mobile delivery model altogether in 2009, by launching its own online storefront for the Google Nexus One handset. All face a trade-off between economics, coverage, and control.

go online

Visit the **Online Resource Centre** and follow the weblink to the Institute of Supply Chain Management (ISM), to learn more about the profession and activities of managing the distribution and supply chain.

Intermediaries

Organizations often rely on **intermediaries**, independent organizations that provide a link between producers and end consumers, assisting the physical movement of the product and the transfer of legal title to the end consumer. They perform various functions such as managing inventory, physical delivery, and financial services, enabling organizations to offer just about everything a buyer wants, from availability, speed of delivery, reliable supply, range of choice in product assortment, and so on. Figure 12.1 displays a number of the benefits offered by intermediaries.

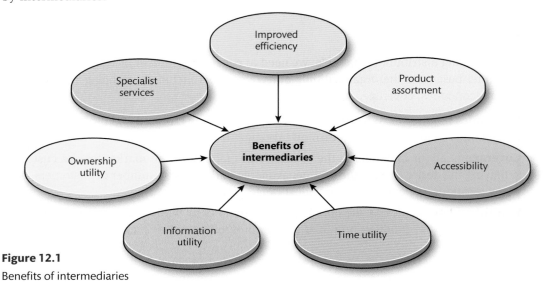

Figure 12.1

Benefits of intermediaries

The benefits of intermediaries include some or all of the following:

▶ Improved efficiency—producers usually manufacture a small range of products in large quantities, whereas consumers consume a wide range of products in small quantities. An intermediary such as a wholesaler improves efficiency in the delivery channel by breaking large deliveries from producers into single units and assorting them into a range of goods available for retailers (i.e. product assortment efficiency).

▶ Accessibility—usually the location where production occurs is miles from the point of usage or consumption. Think about clothes purchased on the high street; these can be manufactured as far afield as China or India. Intermediaries assist by bringing the product to a more convenient location for purchase, providing place utility.

▶ **Time utility**—manufacturing, purchase, and consumption can also occur at differing points in time. The product might be manufactured during the day but purchased and consumed at the weekend. Intermediaries such as retailers provide time utility.

▶ **Ownership utility**—through intermediaries like retailers, products are available immediately from the intermediaries' stocks, enabling ownership to pass to the consumer within a limited amount of time.

▶ Specialist services—intermediaries might also provide specialist services such as aftersales, maintenance, installation, or training services to increase the effective use of the product.

These services are best offered and performed by those closest to the purchaser or user of the product.

▶ **Information utility**—sometimes intermediaries also provide information about the product to aid sales and product usage. The internet has further led to the development of a new type of intermediary, an information intermediary (e.g. Expedia, Google), the key role of which is to manage information to improve the efficiency and effectiveness of the distribution channel.

These benefits are offset by certain disadvantages. With an increasing number of inter-mediaries, and certain types in a distribution channel, a lack of control over the product can result. Manufacturers are often at the mercy of intermediaries in terms of where their product is placed in-store and how much it is finally priced for. Furthermore, intermediaries might be susceptible to competitor inducement such as trade promotions. For many manufacturers and producers, intermediaries often become a market in their own right, requiring considerable time, money, and personnel to support and develop a relationship with them. Sony provides a good example of the effect a supplier's brand can have on the activities and behaviour of intermediaries such as retailers in the electronics sector. Despite product similarity, Sony remains a premium electronics brand, and any electrical retailer without the Sony brand in stock will suffer in terms of store traffic as shoppers will expect to see it. Thus, Sony has sup-plier power in this way and can negotiate high margins and better shelf positioning for its products than its rivals (combining both **pull** and **push strategies**).

go online

Visit the **Online Resource Centre** and complete Internet Activity 12.1 to learn more about the role of intermediaries in the supply chain within the film and TV industry.

Member Channel Functions

Channel members perform a number of functions within the distribution channel. As shown in Figure 12.2, these functions have evolved since the 1980s from as few as five key functions to as many as 11 (Michman, 1990). Managing the distribution functions involves managing the sourcing of organizational resources upstream from manufacturers and suppliers and dis-tributing resources downstream to customers. The aim is to provide a reliable and responsive service to meet customer orders with a guaranteed delivery date, of the right amount, with

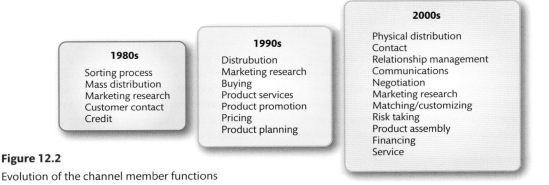

1980s
Sorting process
Mass distribution
Marketing research
Customer contact
Credit

1990s
Distrubution
Marketing research
Buying
Product services
Product promotion
Pricing
Product planning

2000s
Physical distribution
Contact
Relationship management
Communications
Negotiation
Marketing research
Matching/customizing
Risk taking
Product assembly
Financing
Service

Figure 12.2
Evolution of the channel member functions

the expected level of quality. To achieve this, there is often a trade-off between the customer objectives of time, quality, and accessibility, and the cost to the supplier or distributor. The main strategy is to offer maximum flexibility in meeting customer requirements for a range of products, in any quantity, without incurring significant costs. See Market Insight 12.2 for an example of how Red Bull used a unique distribution strategy to penetrate the market and create a new drinks category, energy drinks.

▶ Market Insight 12.2

Red Bull Grows Wings

If the mantra for retailers is 'location, location, location', the rallying cry for small beverage companies is 'distribution, distribution, distribution'. However, with Coca-Cola and Pepsi owning the widest and most powerful distributor networks, especially in the USA, penetrating these networks can prove very difficult, especially for a small beverage manufacturer like Red Bull GmbH.

Red Bull GmbH, founded in 1984, is the most powerful Austrian brand in the world and is credited with creating the energy drinks category. The organization built its market share by securing unusual distribution outlets and piggybacking on established distributors. As the drink caught on, the organization began taking a narrow approach to distribution. The organization built a network of student sales representatives each with contacts with small distributors, insisting that they sell only Red Bull, then set up warehouses and hired students to load up delivery vans and deliver the product. These start-up distributors focused their entire energies on getting Red Bull fully stocked in stores with prominent shelf placement.

Red Bull, the world's most powerful Austrian brand

The sales team visited key on-premise accounts such as new or hot clubs and trendy bars. When owners began buying a few cases, they would receive a Red Bull branded cooler and other POP items. The organization adopted on-premise accounts (vs. retailers) first, giving the product lots of visibility and providing fertile ground for new drink trends. These young emerging distributors also found it faster to deal with individual accounts, not big chains and their authorization process. These tactics soon developed into more than a guerrilla strategy building buzz at clubs. Sales teams started to open off-premise accounts at convenience stores near colleges, gyms,

▶ Market Insight 12.2

health-food stores, and supermarkets. The mission was to find out where the target market (men and women aged 16–29) hung out and what interested them, and then to get the message out to the right clubs and at the right events.

The success of this early distribution strategy is evident today with more than 3.906bn cans of Red Bull sold in over 160 countries, generating 3.323bn euros in turnover in 2009. However, soon Red Bull outgrew these tactics. Today, Red Bull's distribution strategy is very different, with its logistics and distribution plan fitting its enormous expansion strategy. The organization has created a supply chain strategy that blends logistics and transportation with the need for flexibility and expansion. The effort

included new approaches toward transportation and to warehousing, and to how those two wings of logistics fit in together.

Sources: Hein (2001), 2004; Page (2005); Anon. (2010); www.redbull.com

1 How did Red Bull balance economics, coverage, and control in its early distribution strategy?

2 What specific benefits did this 'student sales rep' approach offer Red Bull?

3 Why do you think the early on-premise distribution strategy was attractive to Red Bull?

Distribution Channel Strategy

When devising a distribution channel strategy, several key decisions need to be made in order to serve customers and establish and maintain buyer–seller relationships. These are summarized in Figure 12.3. The first decision is selecting how the channel will be structured. If the channel requires intermediaries, we need to consider the type of market coverage we want, the number and type of intermediaries to use, and how we should manage the relationships between members in the channel. These choices are important as they can affect the benefits provided to customers.

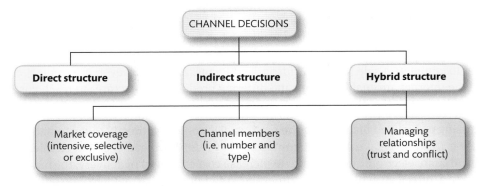

Figure 12.3

Distribution channel strategy decisions

Channel Structure

Distribution channels can be structured in a number of ways. Three examples of how relationships between producers, intermediaries, and customers can be structured include 'direct', 'indirect', or 'hybrid' channel structures. A direct structure involves selling directly to customers with minimal involvement from other organizations; an indirect structure uses intermediaries; and a hybrid structure combines both. These are displayed in Figure 12.4. The degree of efficiency that an intermediary can introduce to the performance of a distribution channel is what ultimately determines what form a channel structure will take. We will now consider the advantages and disadvantages of each of type of channel structure.

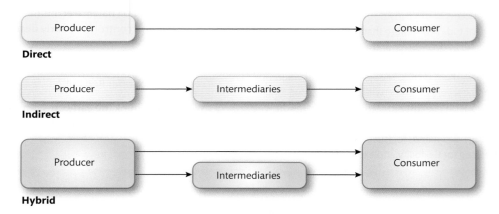

Figure 12.4
Distribution channel structure

Direct Distribution Channel Structure

In direct channels, the producer uses strategies to reach end customers directly rather than dealing via an intermediary like an agent, broker, retailer, or wholesaler (see Figure 12.4). Have you ever been to a farmers' market and purchased produce directly from a farmer, or downloaded music from the MySpace site of a local band? These are examples of direct distribution. The advantages of this structure include the producer or manufacturer maintaining control over their product and profitability, and building strong customer relationships. However, this structure is not suitable for all products. It is ideally suited to those products that require significant customization, technical expertise, or commitment on behalf of the producer to complete a sale (Parker, Bridson, and Evans, 2006). However, electronic technologies like the internet are enabling more and differing product manufactures to reach customers directly. Efficiency of the **direct channel structure** is being improved in the following ways:

▶ Processing orders and distributing the product electronically directly to customers—Adobe Reader is free universal software manufactured by Adobe Systems Inc. that enables users to read and share electronic documents. To increase cost efficiency of delivery, the organization employs a direct structure via the internet, providing digital delivery, installation, and customer support.

▶ Supporting the physical distribution of the product offering directly to customers—one of the most well-known examples of this is Dell Computer Corp.'s system. Dell sells computer equipment through the organization website, using telesales for product ordering, database technology for order processing, tracking, and inventory and delivery management. The organization further physically distributes its product offering though organization-employed delivery and installation staff.

The disadvantages of a direct channel structure typically include the amount of capital and resources required to reach customers directly, resulting in the potential loss of economies of scale. Manufacturers might also suffer from offering a low variety of products, which are not consistent with the needs of the buyer. This is especially apparent in B2C markets, such as fast-moving consumer goods (FMCGs). Imagine having to shop for bread, milk, and a soft drink at three differing retail outlets owned by each product manufacturer. Few consumers today would purchase their products from individual manufacturers due to the inconvenience and time costs involved. Thus, retailers fulfil the needs of end consumers for product variety, something a direct channel of distribution would not necessarily fulfil.

Indirect Distribution Channel Structure

In an **indirect channel structure**, the producer concentrates on the skills and processes involved in producing the product and relies on one or more intermediaries for distribution. An example here is Procter & Gamble, who focus their resources and expertise on developing new types of FMCGs, and Sainsbury's who alternatively focus on making these new products available to end consumers. An intermediary must add some value that the producing organization cannot offer. Equally, the producing organization must add some value for the intermediary.

Using intermediaries often involves a trade-off between the benefits gained and the costs incurred, both financial and strategic. The benefits include reaching more of the target market by exploiting the networks and relationships of intermediaries. This further allows the producer to concentrate resources and skills on the areas where it is most competent, and where it can achieve maximum return. The main disadvantages can involve the sharing of profits, one of the major sources of channel conflict. Why should an intermediary spend further resources on managing the product the way the producer would prefer if the return on investment is not profitable?

Another source of channel conflict comes from the sharing of control between the producer and the intermediary. Sometimes the producer has no direct relationship with the customer and is, therefore, dependent on the intermediary for sales information and customer feedback. Electronic technologies such as scanning technologies, databases, and the development of RFID (radio frequency identification) have improved the efficiencies of data and information sharing throughout distribution channels. The Tesco Clubcard scheme is an excellent example in which producers such as Unilever and Procter & Gamble, as well as intermediaries such as transport carriers, receive a large stream of data and information about the sale and delivery of products. (See Chapter 15 for more on loyalty and retention programmes.)

Hybrid Distribution Channel Structure

An increasing number of organizations are adopting a multiple or **hybrid channel structure** to distribute goods and services (Park and Keh, 2003). Here, the producer controls some distribution channels and intermediaries control others. For example, many airlines sell their tickets directly to consumers through the internet, but also rely on travel agents. Music labels also sell their CDs directly, using catalogues and the internet, as well as via music retailers such as

Record labels sell their music directly and through intermediaries like HMV

HMV. Consider the options for purchase of a mobile handset. This could occur directly from the Nokia website, from a service provider such as Orange, or perhaps at Tesco while picking up some bread and milk? What we are seeing is growth in the use of hybrid channels in the mobile telecommunications industry. Samsung, Sony Ericsson, and Nokia are using service providers, electronic retailers, and wholesale discount clubs alongside their own direct internet and telesales channels to market and deliver their mobile phone handsets.

The benefits of the hybrid channel structure include:

▶ increased reach to a target audience by exploiting existing direct networks, marketing efforts, and relationships of intermediaries;

▶ the producer has greater control over prices, communication, and promoting directly to customers;

▶ greater compliance from intermediaries as the producer also acts like a competitor, although this could reduce the loyalty the intermediary feels towards the producer;

▶ optimized margins to the producer (from the direct distribution channel), and increasing the bargaining power of the producer as dependence on the intermediary is reduced; and

▶ developing direct relationships with customers, a source of useful information.

The sharing of the profits, however, among channel members can create a source of distribution channel conflict, especially as intermediaries perceive the producer now as a competitor as well as a supplier. This structure may also confuse customers who don't understand which distribution channel they should use. Hybrid channel strategies are being used more following the growth in use of the internet, increasing the ability and efficiency with which consumers and manufacturers can interact (Park and Keh, 2003). At the same time, technologies are increasing the efficiency of information exchange between producers and intermediaries (e.g. through EDI (electronic data interchange) and extranets). See Market Insight 12.3 for an example of how a fashion house manages its distribution channels.

▶ Market Insight 12.3

Fast Fashion

According to Amancio Ortega, the founder of Zara, to be successful 'you need to have five fingers touching the factory and five touching the customer'. Translation: control what happens to a product until the customer buys it. In adhering to this philosophy, Zara has developed a super-responsive supply chain. The organization can design, produce, and deliver a new garment to its 1,395 stores across 74 countries in just 24 hours in Europe and 40 hours in America and Asia. Such a pace is unheard of in the fashion business, where designers typically spend months planning for the next season.

This success stems from a holistic approach to supply chain management that optimizes the entire chain instead of focusing on individual parts. In the process, Zara defies most of the current conventional wisdom about how supply chains should be run. Unlike so many of its peers, which rush to outsource, Zara keeps almost half of its production in-house. Zara carries out all operations under the same roof at its La Coruña headquarters. Informality rules the roost, and functions such as design, production, and marketing all rub shoulders with each other. This set-up removes the need for information to travel through widely dispersed channels. It shortens delays, minimizes bureaucracy, provides the opportunity for more immediate comment and feedback, allows speedier decision-making, and lessens the potential impact

Merchandising is important at Zara, the fast fashion retailer

Source: Zara/Intidex.

> ▶ Market Insight 12.3   (continued)

of changes in circumstances such as an amendment to retail orders. This reduces the risk of loss through overproduction.

Zara's self-reinforcing system is built on three principles:

▶ Close the communication loop. Zara's supply chain is organized to transfer both hard data and anecdotal information quickly and easily from shoppers to designers and production staff. It's also set up to track materials and products in real time every step of the way, including inventory on display in the stores. The goal is to close the information loop between the end users and the upstream operations of design, procurement, production, and distribution as quickly and directly as possible.

▶ Stick to a rhythm across the entire chain. At Zara, rapid timing and synchronicity are paramount. To this end, the organization indulges in an approach that can best be characterized as

'penny foolish, pound wise'. It spends money on anything that helps to increase and enforce the speed and responsiveness of the chain as a whole.

▶ Leverage capital assets to increase supply chain flexibility. Zara has made major capital investments in production and distribution facilities, and uses them to increase the supply chain's responsiveness to new and fluctuating demands. It produces complicated products in-house and outsources the simple ones.

Sources: Vitzthum (2001); Ferdows, Lewis, and Machuca (2004); Anon. (2005); Hamilton (2007); www.zara.com

1 **Describe the distribution channel structure adopted by Zara.**

2 **Outline the advantages of this channel structure for Zara.**

3 **Outline the disadvantages of this channel structure for Zara.**

Members of Channel Intermediaries

Once we have decided to use a channel structure requiring intermediaries, we must then decide which type of intermediary to use. There are several different types of intermediaries, including the following:

▶ **Agents** or brokers—these act as a principal intermediary between the seller of a product and buyers, bringing them together, without taking ownership of the product offering. These intermediaries have the legal authority to act on behalf of the manufacturer. For example, universities often use agents to recruit students in overseas markets (e.g. China, India).

▶ **Merchant**—a merchant performs in the same way as an agent, but takes ownership of the product.

▶ **Distributors** or dealers—these distribute the product. They offer value through services associated with selling inventory, credit, and aftersales service. Often used in B2B markets, they can also be found dealing directly with consumers, e.g. automobile distributors.

▶ **Franchise**—a franchisee holds a contract to supply and market a product to the requirements or blueprint of the franchisor, the owner of the original product. The contract might cover many aspects of the design of the product such as marketing, product assortment, or service delivery. The uniformity of differing branches of McDonald's and KFC is an indication of franchisee contracts; however, franchise agreements are not just used in the fast food sector. Table 12.1 provides a list of the top ten franchises in Europe in 2009, spanning various product categories.

go online

Visit the **Online Resource Centre** and follow the weblink to the European Franchise Association (EFA) to learn more about business franchise collaboration activities across Europe.

▶ **Wholesalers**—a wholesaler stocks goods before the next level of distribution and takes both legal title and physical possession of the goods. In B2C markets, wholesalers do not usually deal with the end consumer but with other intermediaries (e.g. retailers). In B2B markets, sales are made direct to end customers. Examples include Costco Wholesalers in the USA, and Makro in Europe.

▶ **Retailers**—these intermediaries sell directly to end consumers and may purchase direct from manufacturers or deal with wholesalers. This is dependent on their purchasing power and the volume purchased. Leading retailers include Wal-Mart, Marks and Spencer, Carrefour, and electronics retailers such as Media-Saturn.

▶ **Table 12.1** Top European franchises by rank

Franchise	Origin country	Industry	Rank
7-Eleven	Japan	Food: convenience	1
McDonald's	USA	Food: restaurants	2
Subway	USA	Food: sandwich and coffee shop	3
Kumon Inst. of Education Co. Ltd.	Japan	Education: children	4
Spar	Netherlands	Food: convenience stores	5
Vival	France	Food: convenience stores	6
Pizza Hut	USA	Food: restaurants	7
Janl-King	USA	Commercial hygiene	8
Burger King	USA	Food: restaurants	9
KFC (Yum Restaurants)	USA	Food: restaurants	10

Source: Franchise Europe (2010). Reproduced with the kind permission of Franchise Europe (www.franchiseeurope.com), a leading portal for the franchise industry worldwide.

A growing type of intermediary is infomediaries, internet-based intermediaries whose core role is the provision of information to channel members throughout the supply chain. See Market Insight 12.4 for an example.

▶ Market Insight 12.4

The Rise of the Infomediary

With the development of the internet, has come the emergence of a new intermediary—the infomediary—which allows online consumers to search for, and provide comparisons among, many online retailers. Comparison Shopping Engines (CSE) such as Kelkoo, Shopping.com, and MoneySupermarket, reached an estimated 17m consumers, 51% of shoppers in the UK every month. Their role cannot be underestimated, especially as the economic downturn sees massive demand for people getting the best price online. Research reports that about half of online consumers use CSEs before choosing a retailer. Infomediaries such as CSEs provide powerful search capabilities to online shoppers to give them a list of potential retailers and the information needed to select the best one. This offers consumers two major types of utilitarian

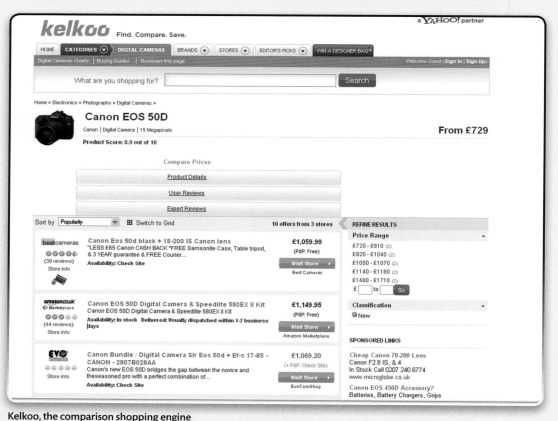

Kelkoo, the comparison shopping engine
Source: Courtesy of Kelkoo.

▶ Market Insight 12.4

benefits: namely, perceived efficiency and effectiveness. Originally retailers were cautious of CSEs, but, with effective use of site traffic metrics from CSEs to retailers sites (e.g. cost-per-click and cost-per-action), the sector aim is to add value and drive traffic to retail sites. Consumers visit CSEs for a number of reasons:

▶ CSEs are experts at driving traffic from individual product searches through both paid and natural search.

▶ CSEs allow consumers to compare retailers' products, prices, availability, and delivery cost quickly and easily.

▶ Many CSEs have evolved from basic price comparison sites to true online shopping portals offering consumer reviews, editorial advice, and special promotions.

(See Market Insight 10.5 for more on comparethemarket.com's advertising campaign.)

Sources: Jai-Yeol, Sung, and Riggins (2006); Papatla and Feng (2009); Cooper (2008).

1 What type of intermediary is an infomediary?

2 What benefits do CSEs offer online shoppers?

3 What impact do you think CSEs could have on the distribution channel structure in the retailing sector?

Intensity of Channel Coverage

With intermediaries, we further need to consider how many we may need to use. This is called the **intensity of channel coverage** and involves choosing between three basic types: intensive, exclusive, or selective distribution (see Figure 12.5).

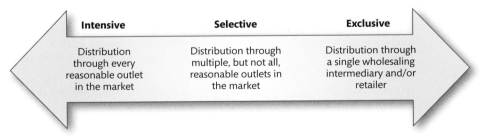

Intensive	Selective	Exclusive
Distribution through every reasonable outlet in the market	Distribution through multiple, but not all, reasonable outlets in the market	Distribution through a single wholesaling intermediary and/or retailer

Figure 12.5
Intensity of distribution continuum

Intensive distribution is about placing a product in as many outlets or locations as possible, and is used most commonly for goods that consumers are unlikely to search for and which they purchase on the basis of convenience or impulse. Magazines and fast-moving consumer goods, such as soft drinks or confectionery, are all examples. Retailers have increased control over the extent to which distribution is intensive. A manufacturer of a new brand of yoghurt, for example, might want its new brand put on the shelves of all supermarkets;

however, owing to limited shelf space, the retailers might limit their assortment to the leading brands of yoghurt.

Selective distribution is where some, but not all, available outlets are used. Typically, this is an attempt to balance a wider reach to the target audience at a lower cost than intensive distribution. Consumer shopping speciality goods and industrial equipment for which customers have a brand preference (e.g. furniture or small appliance brands) are product categories that adopt this type of distribution. Sometimes, an organization might first use intensive distribution to increase awareness of its brand when entering a new market, but then move to a more selective strategy to improve control over product quality and manage costs and product price.

Exclusive distribution is where intermediaries are given exclusive rights to market the product within a defined 'territory', using a very limited number of intermediaries. This is more useful for products where significant support is required from the intermediary and, therefore, the exclusivity is 'payback' for their investment and support. For example, high-prestige goods like Ferrari sports cars and designer fashion apparel like Chanel and Gucci adopt this type of distribution intensity.

The decision about the number of intermediaries is often driven by cost considerations. The costs of intensive distribution are higher because of the number of outlets that must be served. The implications of these three strategies for distribution are summarized in Table 12.2.

Through the internet, nearly all distribution is intensive because of the massive reach of the web. Even the smallest manufacturer can advertise and sell worldwide, using the same courier services to deliver its products as do major firms.

▶ **Table 12.2** Intensity of channel coverage

Characteristics	Exclusive	Selective	Intensive
Objectives	Strong image, channel control and loyalty, price stability	Moderate market coverage, solid image, some channel control and loyalty	Widespread market coverage, channel acceptance, volume sales
Channel members	Few in number, well-established, reputable stores	Moderate in number, well-established, better stores	Many in number, all types of outlets
Customers	Few in number, trendsetters, willing to travel to store, brand loyal	Moderate in number, brand-conscious, somewhat willing to travel to store	Many in number, convenience-oriented
Marketing emphasis	Personal selling, pleasant shopping conditions, good service	Promotional mix, pleasant shopping conditions, good service	Mass advertising, nearby location, items in stock
Examples	Automobiles, designer clothes, caviar	Furniture, clothing, watches	Groceries, household products, magazines

Disintermediation and Reintermediation

An issue that has been hotly debated is the growth in disintermediation, a reduction in the number or strength of intermediaries required in a distribution channel (Atkinson, 2001; Mills and Camek, 2004). Is the number of intermediaries being used decreasing or increasing because of the internet and digital technologies (e.g. extranets)? The assumption is that if producers could reach their customers directly they would no longer need intermediaries, or at least they would not need so many of them. Imagine that a music publisher like Sony could reach and sell to every potential customer directly through its website (www.sony. com). Given the state of technology such as PC sound systems, CD burners, or MP3 players, customers could purchase their music directly from Sony and it could be 'distributed' electronically straight to their PC. In such a scenario, Sony would no longer need to deal with music stores like Virgin and HMV—leading to the disintermediation of the distribution channel. Or would this, in fact, result in growth in electronic intermediaries such as iTunes for music distribution?

The technical possibility of reducing the number of intermediaries doesn't just affect 'bricks-and-mortar' intermediaries, but also electronic intermediaries. In Amazon's case, for example, more consumers could skip the intermediary and buy books online directly from publishers. Even publishers and printers might be disintermediated if authors were to sell 'ebooks' directly to the consumer, as mystery writer Stephen King attempted to do in early 2000 (Kane, 2000). This is becoming increasingly popular as the growth in sales of ebooks continues. The International Digital Publishing Forum (IDPF) reported year-on-year growth in US sales of 339% in February 2010. The evidence to date is that where disintermediation does occur, it is very much dependent on the nature of the products being distributed. Although there are significant numbers of customers who like buying certain products directly, many customers value and prefer the role of traditional intermediaries like bricks-and-mortar retailers for the purchase of certain goods. In fact, such is the value of some intermediaries to both customers and producers that there has been a trend towards reintermediation, the introduction of additional intermediaries into the distribution channel.

▶ Research Insight 12.1

To take your learning further, you might wish to read this influential paper.

Mills, J. F., and Camek, V. (2004), 'The risks, threats and opportunities of disintermediation: a distributor's view', *International Journal of Physical Distribution and Logistics Management*, 34, 9, 714–27.

This paper discusses the trend in disintermediation observed in many industries. Where many recent papers see disintermediation as a phenomenon related to online transactions, this paper defines it more broadly as the removal or a weakening of an intermediary within a supply chain.

Visit the **Online Resource Centre** to read the abstract and access the full paper.

Managing Relationships in the Channel

An important aspect in any channel strategy is managing relationships throughout the distribution channel. However, by their very nature there is often a continuous struggle between channel members. Trust and channel conflict are the key issues here. **Channel conflict** is where one channel member perceives another channel member to be acting in a way that prevents the first member from achieving its distribution activities. Conflict in channels of distribution may involve intermediaries on the same level (tier), such as between retailers (**horizontal conflict**) or between members on different levels (tiers), thus between the producer, wholesaler, and the retailer (**vertical conflict**). These types of channel conflict are presented in Table 12.3.

▶ **Table 12.3** Channel conflict

Types	Occurs between	Causes of conflict
Horizontal conflict	▶ Intermediaries on the same level of the same type (e.g. large grocery retailers like Tesco, Sainsbury's, and ASDA Wal-Mart) ▶ Different types of intermediaries on the same level (e.g. a high street fashion retailer such as Miss Selfridge, a large department store like Marks and Spencer)	Channel members impinge on the market territory of other intermediaries at the same level
Vertical conflict	Most frequently occurs between producer and wholesaler or producer and retailer (e.g. Unilever and Sainsbury's)	▶ Intense price competition ▶ Disagreement about promotion activities ▶ Cost of services rendered ▶ Differing expectations as to channel or intermediary performance ▶ Attempts to bypass intermediary and distribute direct ▶ Tough economic times ▶ Differing policies ▶ Allocation of slotting allowances for premium shelf space
Hybrid channel conflict	Producers compete with retailers by selling through their producer-owned stores (e.g. Esprit and Levi-Strauss stores compete with department stores who also carry their stock)	▶ Grey marketing

Member Incentives

Channel conflict can be reduced if manufacturers provide incentives to channel members, and if the risks, costs, and rewards of doing business are distributed fairly across the channel. Misaligned incentives are often the cause of channel conflict and also excess inventory, stock-outs, incorrect forecasts, inadequate sales efforts, and even poor customer service (Narayanan and Raman, 2004). A historical example is that of Campbell's Soup. In the late 1980s, Campbell's Soup offered distributors discounts several times every year, hoping that the savings would be passed on to retailers. However, distributors bought more units than they sold to retailers, so Campbell's sales fluctuated wildly. The organization sold 40% of its chicken noodle soup each year during the six-week promotional periods. This put a lot of pressure on the organization's distribution channel. Campbell invested in a system to not just track purchases of distributors, but also their sales, and with this system provided distributors with discounts on their sales as opposed to purchases. This helped to improve the performance of the distribution channel.

Grey Marketing

Another area of channel conflict is **grey marketing**, the unauthorized sale of new, branded products diverted from authorized distribution channels or imported into a country for sale without the consent or knowledge of the manufacturer. What occurs is that the prices of authorized dealers in a market are undercut through unauthorized sales. This activity is not necessarily illegal, but could fall foul of licensing agreements or trade regulations (Myers and Griffith, 1999), as Tesco discovered when it attempted to stock and sell Levi's brand jeans, which it had purchased through an unauthorized supplier.

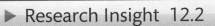

▶ Research Insight 12.2

To take your learning further, your might wish to read this influential paper.

Webb, K. L., and Hogan, J. E. (2002), 'Hybrid channel conflict: causes and effects on channel performance', *Journal of Business and Industrial Marketing*, 17, 5, 338–57.

This paper discusses the role of hybrid channel conflict in not only reducing channel performance but also serving as a mechanism for forcing internal channel coalitions to work harder and smarter to serve their market. The findings indicate that hybrid channel conflict is an important determinant of both channel performance and satisfaction.

 Visit the **Online Resource Centre** to read the abstract and access the full paper.

Logistics Management

Organizations must decide on the best way to store, handle, and move their product so that it is available to customers in the right quantity, at the right time, and in the right place. Logistics includes the activities that relate to the flow of products from the manufacturer to the customer or end consumer. Although these are not traditionally marketing decisions or activities, they require marketing insight. The production schedule may mean that customers are asked to wait too long for products to arrive: this will affect product promotion. Inventory management may mean that there is not enough stock to meet urgent customer needs or unforeseen peaks in demand: this will affect customer satisfaction. So, although these areas are typically managed outside the marketing function, the need for everyone in the organization to share data and information about how a product is delivered is very important.

Importance of Logistics

Logistics management is the coordination of activities of the entire distribution channel. It addresses not just activities of moving products from the factory to customers (outbound distribution), but also moving products and materials from suppliers to the factory (inbound

Flat-packing allows Ikea to sell furniture cheaper than its competitors
Source: Courtesy of IKEA Ltd.

distribution). An example of an efficient inbound logistics system is provided by ASDA Wal-Mart, who use computerized scanning to inform manufacturers very quickly of which products need delivery and in what quantities. More recent developments in electronic technologies, such as RFID tags, are further improving the efficiency and effectiveness with which the logistical activities are managed and implemented.

A core motivation for the growth in the management of logistics is an attempt to lower costs, given that about 15% of an average product's price is accounted for in shipping and transport costs alone. Ikea can sell its furniture 20% cheaper than competitors as it buys furniture ready for assembly, thereby saving on transport and inventory costs. The Benetton distribution centre in Italy is run largely by robots, delivering numerous goods to 120 countries within 12 days. Benetton also uses just-in-time (JIT) manufacturing, with some garments manufactured in neutral colours and then dyed to order, with very fast turnaround to suit customer requirements. However, beyond lowering costs, many organizations are increasing their focus on managing logistical activities due to demands for improved customer service, the explosion in product variety, and improvements in information and communication technologies.

Logistical Functions

Logistical activities or functions include order processing, inventory control, warehousing, and transportation (see Figure 12.6).

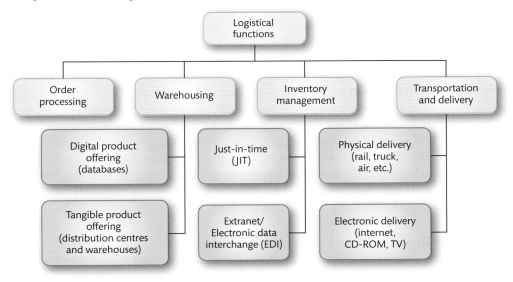

Figure 12.6

Key logistics functions

Order Processing

Accuracy and speed of billing and invoicing customers is vitally important, especially for customer relationships. Increasingly, we are seeing the use of information technology to help manage order-processing activities. Automated emails are sent out to customers following online purchase of, for example, music from iTunes, a book from Amazon, or a train ticket.

In the retailing sector, order-processing technologies provide quick-response programmes to help manage a retailer's inventory replenishment of products from suppliers. Kmart uses this kind of system, with EDI/extranets to transmit daily records of product sales to suppliers, who analyse the information, create an order, and send it back to Kmart. Once in Kmart's system, the order is treated as though Kmart created it itself. Many technologies also speed up the billing cycle. For example, General Electric operates a computer-based system that, on receipt of a customer order, checks the customer's credit rating as well as whether and where the items are in stock. The computer then issues an order to ship, bills the customer, updates the inventory records, sends a production order for new stock, and sends a message back to the salesperson that the customer's order is on the way—all in less than 15 seconds. The hospitality industry also uses order-processing technology to improve service delivery efficiency. Fast food outlets like McDonald's and KFC have for years recorded food orders through telecommunications systems, transmitting them to food preparation areas, with orders fulfilled within a matter of minutes, improving customer satisfaction in service delivery.

Warehousing and Materials Handling

Many organizations exchange tangible goods that require storage while they are waiting to be sold, largely due to the mismatch between when the product is produced and when it is sold and consumed. Books, for example, dry goods such as sugar and canned goods, and even clothing require some degree of storage between the time they leave the manufacturer and when they need delivery to customers. An organization must decide on how many and what types of 'warehouses' it needs, and where they should be located. The type of warehouse is dependent on the type of product: tangible or digital, perishable or not.

Warehousing Tangible Goods

For the storage of tangible goods, such as FMCGs, an organization can use either **storage warehouses** or **distribution centres**. Storage warehouses store goods for moderate to long periods (they have a long shelf life), whereas distribution centres are designed to move goods, rather than just store them. For products that are highly perishable with a short shelf life, such as fruit and vegetables, distribution centres are more appropriate. Grocery chains like Woolworths in Australia and Tesco in the UK use large cold-store distribution centres to move perishable items such as fruit and vegetables to their various retail outlets. For products with a long shelf life, or that might require stockpiling to meet seasonal demands, storage centres are more appropriate.

Warehousing Digital 'Products'

Electronic warehousing systems, or database systems, are being used more and more for the storage of products (or product components) that can be digitized. These systems can be searched or browsed electronically, providing the user with immediate electronic delivery options. For example, emerald-library.com, ABI-Inform, or ScienceDirect are electronic databases accessible through the web that store a vast array of documents electronically in order to facilitate customers' search for information. In addition, many organizations use data warehousing facilities where product information, or even actual products, are stored in digital form awaiting distribution. Apple iTunes is the largest music retailer in the world accounting for over 70% of total world online music sales in 2009. In February 2010, the online store had categorized over 12 million songs, 55,000 TV episodes, 8,500 movies, and 2,500 high-definition videos. This does not include the thousands of games and podcasts electronically stored. Customers can find, download, play, and sync in a fraction of the time it takes to drive to any store.

Inventory Management

Inventory management is an issue that arises from trying to balance responsiveness to customer needs with the resources required to store inventory. Zero-inventory or JIT production is ideal for many organizations as this minimizes the use of resources that are often tied up in stock that doesn't sell. This must be balanced against the risk of not having the products available when customers want them.

Do we store the product so that it is available when customers need it or do we produce the product when it is ordered or stock is low? A balance must be maintained between carrying too little inventory and carrying too much, as carrying larger than needed inventories can be expensive. Imagine the cost of storing all the books Amazon has listed for sale, or the storage of fashion items in the spring ready for summer demand. With JIT systems, producers and retailers carry only small inventories of merchandise, often only enough for a few days' operations. New stock arrives exactly when it is needed, rather than being stored. ASDA Wal-Mart and even Burger King use these systems to track sales to service their outlets worldwide, automatically replenishing their ingredients according to product sales.

Transportation and Delivery

Transportation is considered to be the most important activity in logistics. Transportation is the physical movement of the product using truck, rail, air, pipeline, shipping, and so on. Often, transportation is just seen as concern for supplying tangible goods, but it is just as relevant to many service organizations and delivery of electronic (or digital) products. Consultants, IT companies, and health organizations have to move staff around, incurring transport and accommodation costs. Management of transport usually involves making decisions between usage of one or more transportation methods and ensuring vehicle capacity. Transportation methods include physical transport modes such as rail, truck, water, pipeline, and air; and electronic delivery modes such as electronic vending machines, the telephone, the internet, or electronic data interchange (EDI).

Physical Delivery

Information and communication technologies have improved physical product delivery. For example, where freight moves, the size of typical shipments and the time periods within which goods must be delivered has changed with significant economic benefits to all transportation activities. The top of the list of 'must have' systems for transportation are in-vehicle navigation and route guidance solutions to help manage transport fleets, track shipments, and optimize transportation (Dreier, 2003). Amazon's tracking system assigns a tracking number and, using proprietary software, provides information to customers in real time about where the package or shipment is located, thereby managing customer satisfaction.

Electronic Delivery

As early as the introduction of the TV, radio, or even the telephone, electronic technologies have been used to deliver products electronically. Producers of music, games, video, or software are typically unconstrained by the needs of physical distribution due to product digitization; this has been increased with the development of the internet. For example, Wall Street seemed at first to smirk at the E*Trade group's invitation to investors to make their own trades on the internet. Then the Charles Schwab Corporation jumped at the challenge, and by the late 1990s other brokerages, such as Merrill Lynch and Bank of America Investment Services Inc., were scrambling to catch up. Organizations like travel agents, banks, and insurance companies that traditionally relied on customers coming to a branch or agency have quickly moved to using telecommunications, ATMs, and the internet to reach more customers. The internet has clearly added to the capacity of these electronic distribution channels. In developed economies around the world, large numbers of customers now bank, trade stocks, and arrange insurance and travel.

We will now look more closely at one type of intermediary used in B2C markets, that of the retailer and the activity of retailing.

Retailing

Retailing encompasses all the activities directly related to the sale of products to the ultimate end consumer for personal and non-business use. These differ from wholesalers, who distribute the product to businesses, not end consumers. For every successful large retailer, like Carrefour, or Tesco plc, there are thousands of small retailers, with all having two key features in common: they link producers and end consumers and they perform an invaluable service for both.

Customer Value

In order to purchase a product, consumers must have access to it. The purpose of a retailer is to provide this access. As such it is very important to find out what consumers actually want from a retailer in order to deliver value. Convenience is the primary concern for most consumers, with people increasingly being 'leisure time poor' and keen to trade-off shopping time for leisure time (Seiders, Berry, and Gresham, 2000). Consequently, convenience has driven just about every innovation in retailing, such as supermarkets, department stores, shopping malls, the web, and self-scanning kiosks in pursuit of providing customer convenience. As noted by Seiders, Berry, and Gresham (2000), from a customer's perspective, convenience means speed and ease in acquiring a product and consists of the following four key elements:

▶ access—being easy to reach;

▶ search—enabling customers to be easily able to identify what they want;

▶ possession—ease of obtaining products; and

▶ transaction—ease of purchase and return of products.

These are outlined in more detail in Table 12.4.

▶ **Table 12.4** Retailing convenience: a customer's perspective

Element	Description
Access convenience	▶ Accessibility factors include location, availability, hours of operation, parking, proximity to other outlets, as well as telephone, mail, and internet
	▶ Convenience does not exist without access
	▶ Increasingly, customers want access to products and services to be as fast and direct as possible with very little hassle
	▶ Global trend, e.g. rise of convenience stores in Japan
	▶ Direct shopping driven by time and place utility
Search convenience	▶ Identifying and selecting the products wanted is connected to product focus, intelligence outlet design and layout (servicescape), knowledgeable staff, interactive systems, product displays, package and signage, etc.
	▶ Solutions can be provided in the form of in-store kiosks, clearly posted prices, and mobile phones for sales staff linked to knowledge centres
	▶ One example of good practice is German discount chain Adler Mode Market GmbH, which uses colour-coded tags to help customers quickly spot the sizes
Possession convenience	▶ Is about having merchandise in stock and available on a timely basis. For example, Nordstrom clothing store guarantees that advertised products will be in stock
	▶ However, possession convenience has limitations for certain channels (e.g. highly customized products)
	▶ The internet scores highly for search convenience, yet is generally low in terms of possession convenience
Transaction convenience	▶ The speed and ease with which consumers can effect and amend transaction before and after the purchase
	▶ A number of innovations exist here—self-scanning in Carrefour, Tesco, and Metro. Well-designed service systems can mitigate the peaks and troughs in store traffic as with the use of in-store traffic counters as in Sainsbury's to monitor store traffic
	▶ Even with queue design, single queues in post offices and banks differ from supermarkets due to space and servicescape design
	▶ Transaction convenience is a significant issue on the internet, with pure internet retailers having problems with returns and customers not prepared to pay for shipping and handling costs

> ▶ **Research Insight 12.3**
>
> **To take your learning further, your might wish to read this influential paper.**
>
> **Seiders, K., Berry, L. L., and Gresham, L. G. (2000), 'Attention retailers! How convenient is your convenience strategy?', *Sloan Management Review*, Spring, 79–89.**
>
> In this paper, the authors discuss the key value and benefits consumers derived from retailing. The authors particularly discuss the key benefit of convenience in retailing strategy from a customer's perspective. From this perspective, convenience means speed and ease, and consists of four key elements—access, search, possession, and transaction.
>
>   Visit the **Online Resource Centre** to read the abstract and access the full paper.

Retailer Types

There are numerous types of retailers. These can be classified according to the marketing strategy employed (i.e. product, price, and service) and the store presence (i.e. store or non-store retailing).

Marketing Strategy

Major types of retailers can be classified according to the marketing strategies employed, paying particular attention to three specific elements:

▶ product assortment;

▶ price level; and

▶ customer service.

Table 12.5, although not exhaustive, provides a useful summary of these elements across the differing types of retailing channels.

These retailing establishments can be further distinguished as follows:

▶ **Department stores**—these are large-scale retailing institutions that offer a very broad and deep assortment of products (both hard and soft goods), and provide a wide array of customer service facilities for store customers. Debenhams has a wide array of products including home furnishings, foods, cosmetics, clothing, books, and furniture, and further provides variety within each product category (e.g. brand, feature variety). Debenhams, like many department stores, provide a wide array of customer service facilities to rationalize higher prices and minimize price competition. Value-added services include wedding registries, clothing alterations, shoe repairs, lay-by facilities, home delivery, and installation.

▶ **Table 12.5** Marketing strategy and retail store classification

Retail store	Product assortment	Pricing	Customer service	Example
Department	Very broad, deep, with layout and presentation of products critical	Minimize price competition	Wide array and good quality	David Jones, Debenhams, Harrods
Discount	Broad and shallow	Low-price positioning	Few customer service options	Pound Stretcher, Dollar Dazzlers, Poundland
Convenience	Narrow and shallow	High prices	Avoids price competition	Co-op, 7-Eleven
Limited line	Narrow and deep	Traditional = avoids price competition; new kinds = low prices	Vary by type	Bicycle stores, sports stores, ladies fashion
Speciality	Very narrow and deep	Avoids price competition	Standard; extensive in some	Running shops, bridal boutiques
Category killer	Narrow, very deep	Low prices	Few to moderate	Staples and Office Works, Ikea
Supermarket	Broad and deep	Some = low price; others avoid price disadvantages	Few and self-service	Tesco plc (UK), Woolworths Ltd. (Australia), Carrefour (Europe)
Superstores	Very broad and very deep	Low prices	Few and self-service	Tesco Extra, ASDA Wal-Mart

▶ **Discount retailers**—this type of retailer is positioned based on low prices combined with the reduced costs of doing business. The key characteristics here involve a broad but shallow assortment of products, low prices, and very few customer services. Matalan in the UK, for example, Kmart in Australia, and Target in the USA all carry a broad array of soft goods (e.g. apparel) combined with hard goods such as appliances and home furnishings. To keep prices down, the retailers negotiate extensively with suppliers to ensure low merchandise costs.

▶ **Limited line retailers**—this type of retailer has a narrow but deep product assortment and customer services that vary from store to store. Clothing retailers, butchers, baked goods, and furniture stores that specialize in a small number of related product categories are all examples. The breadth of product variety differs across limited line stores, and a store may choose to concentrate on: several related product lines (e.g. shoes and clothing accessories), a single product line (e.g. shoes), or a specific part of one product line (e.g. sports shoes). Examples include bookstores, jewellers, athletic footwear stores, dress shops, newsagents, etc.

▶ **Category killer** stores—as the name suggests these retailers are designed to kill off the competition and are characterized by a narrow but very deep assortment of products, low prices, and few to moderate customer services. Successful examples include Ikea in home furnishings, Staples in office supplies, and B&Q in hardware.

▶ **Supermarkets**—founded in the 1930s, large self-service retailing environments offer a wide variety of differing merchandise to a large consumer base. Tesco Extra in the UK stocks products from clothing, hardware, music, groceries, and dairy products to soft furnishings. Operating largely on a self-service basis with minimum customer service and centralized register and transactional terminals, supermarkets provide the benefits of a wide product assortment in a single location, offering convenience and variety. Today, supermarkets are the dominant institution for food retailing.

▶ **Convenience stores**, or corner shops—offer a range of grocery and household items that cater for convenience and last-minute purchase needs of consumers. Key characteristics include: long opening times (e.g. 24/7), being family run, and belonging to a trading group. The 7-Eleven, Spar, and Co-op are all examples. Increasingly, we are seeing smaller convenience stores threatened by large supermarket chains such as ASDA Wal-Mart and Tesco, especially as laws for longer open times for larger stores are being relaxed (e.g. Sunday trading hours in the UK).

Store Presence

We can further categorize retailers according to their presence, store or non-store retailing. Most retailing occurs through fixed stores, with existing operators having 'sunk' investments in physical building. The physical location of a store is seen as a source of competitive advantage, providing crucial entry barriers to competitors. Several characteristics make store retailing unique from the customer viewpoint. The retail environment provides the sensation of touch, feel, and smell, which is very important for many product categories, such as clothing, books, or perfumes. Furthermore, the customer might interact with in-store staff, who provide purchase advice. Once the product is selected and the purchase decision made, the customer can walk out of the store with the merchandise in hand. (For more on the importance of sensory marketing, see the BRAND sense agency's approach in Case Insight 3.1.)

In contrast, retailing can also involve **non-store retailers**, retailing activities resulting in transactions that occur away from a fixed store location. Examples include automatic vending machines, **direct selling**, and the rise of internet retailing (Bennet, 1988). Direct selling is one of the oldest forms of retailing methods and is the personal contact between a salesperson and a consumer away from the retailing environment. Activities such as door-to-door canvassing and party plans where a sales presentation is made within the home to a party of guests are examples. Examples include cosmetics companies like Avon, Nutri-Metics skincare, and Amway household products. **Telemarketing** or telesales is another form of non-store retailing where purchase occurs over the telephone. During the 1990s, this form of non-store retailing grew extensively due to rapid developments in computer-assisted and TV shopping networks.

A more recent development of non-store retailing is the **electronic kiosk**, which is being placed in shopping malls to assist the retailing experience. These computer-based retailing environments offer increased self-service opportunities, a wide array of products, and a large amount of data and information to help decision-making. Somewhat different from the electronic kiosk is the automatic vending machine, providing product access 24 hours a day, seven days a week. From cigarettes, soft drinks, hot beverages, to newspapers and magazines, products distributed through vending machines are typical of low-priced products and convenience products. However, we also see the wide adoption of automatic teller machines (ATMs) to facilitate the delivery of financial retailing services.

Another form of non-store retailing is internet retailing. In 2009, UK sales totalled £38bn compared with £127.7bn for Europe. UK consumers also topped the online retail spending tables in 2009, with an average annual spend of £1,102, compared to a European average of £774 on 20 items with an average cost per item of £39. The UK was followed by Denmark (£1,079) and Norway (£979). It is further estimated that online retail sales in Western countries will rise from €68bn in 2009 to €114bn in 2014—or an 11% compounded annual growth rate (Freeman, 2010). The winning purchase categories on the internet are travel, clothes, groceries, and consumer electronics.

go online

Visit the **Online Resource Centre** and complete Internet Activity 12.2 to learn more about the variety of internet retailing sites and importance of delivery information for this sector.

Market Insight 12.5 provides a specific snapshot of the impact the leading online music retailer, iTunes, is having on the retail purchase of music.

▶ Market Insight 12.5

Tuning into iTunes

Online shopping is set to account for nearly 40% of all UK retail sales by 2020, with online sales reaching £38bn in 2009 and set to quadruple to £162bn by 2020. According to uSwitch, 8m UK households spend, on average, two hours a day shopping online. The most popular online purchases are holidays, films, and music.

iPod and iTunes have revolutionised music distribution

▶ Market Insight 12.5   (continued)

One organization playing a key role in the facilitation of this growth of digital music sales is Apples iTunes Music Store (iTMS). The iTunes Store is an online business run by Apple Inc., which sells media files that are accessed through its iTunes application. Opened as the iTunes Music Store on 28 April 2003, it proved the viability of online music sales. The virtual record shop sells music videos, TV shows, movies, and video games in addition to music. iTunes now has several personalization options, and one of them is 'Just For You'. Apple thoroughly dominates the market controlling more than 70% of the worldwide online digital music sales.

Apple's iTunes store allows the users to purchase songs and transfer them easily to the iPod through iTunes. The store began after Apple signed deals with the five major record labels at the time, EMI, Universal, Warner Bros., Sony Music Entertainment, and BMG (the latter two would later merge to form Sony BMG). Music by more than 600 independent label artists was added later, the first being Moby on 29 July 2003. The store now has more than 12 m songs, including exclusive tracks from numerous popular artists, and, in early 2010, Apple celebrated the downloading of the 10 billionth song from Apple

iTunes—the Johnny Cash song aptly titled: 'Guess Things Happen That Way'.

New songs are added to the iTunes catalogue every day, and the iTunes Store is updated each Tuesday. Apple also releases a 'Single of the Week' and usually a 'Discovery Download' on Tuesdays, which are available free for one week. In the words of Apple's CEO, Steve Jobs, 'In 1984 we introduced the Macintosh. It didn't just change Apple, it changed the whole computer industry. In 2001, we introduced the first iPod and it didn't just change the way we all listen to music, it changed the entire music industry' (Allison and Palmer, 2007).

Sources: Apple (2007); Wingfield and Smith (2007); Benson (2007); Tabini (2010).

1 **Why do you think the offline retail sale of music is declining?**

2 **Why do you think iTunes has been such a success as an online music retailer?**

3 **Consider your own recent purchases of music. What retail channel did you use to purchase the music and why?**

▶ Research Insight 12.4

To take your learning further, you might wish to read this influential paper.

O'Cass, A., and French, T. (2003), 'Web retailing adoption: exploring the nature of internet users' web retailing behaviour', *Journal of Retailing and Consumer Services*, **10, 81–94.**

In this paper, the authors provide a discussion of the nature of internet retailing, its growth and importance. The authors further discuss the key elements that influence web retailing adoption and profile online users' web retailing behaviour.

@ Visit the **Online Resource Centre** to read the abstract and access the full paper.

Skills for Employment

▶▶ It is important for graduates to focus on what they know that is different or unique. I get lots of enquiries from people asking for work experience and unfortunately cannot give everyone an opportunity. If students can think about developing a more specialist skill, and offering the company something different, then that's what will make them stand out. ◀◀

Gennaro Castaldo, Head of Press & PR, HMV & Fopp

 Visit the **Online Resource Centre** to discover more tips and advice on skills for the workplace.

Chapter Summary

To consolidate your learning, the key points from this chapter are summarized below:

■ **Define what a channel of distribution is and key considerations in managing a channel strategy.**

Distribution channels can be defined as an organized network of organizations, which, in combination, perform all the activities required to link producers and manufacturers with consumers, purchasers, and users. Distribution channel decisions are about managing which channel best suits the organization's objectives. The key consideration that reveals itself here is the importance of optimizing the balance between the three elements of economics, coverage, and control.

■ **Define and discuss the differing types of intermediaries and their roles in the distribution channel.**

An intermediary is an independent business concern that operates as a link between producers and ultimate consumers or end-industrial users. If using an indirect or hybrid channel structure, the next strategic decision is what type of intermediaries to use. The key difference between the various types is that not all intermediaries take legal title of the product offering or physical possession of it. There are several different types of intermediaries. These include: agents, merchants, distributors, franchise, wholesalers, and retailers.

■ **Differentiate between differing distribution channel structures and selection criteria.**

The relationship between producers, intermediaries, and customers will form a 'direct', 'indirect', or 'hybrid' channel structure. A direct structure involves selling directly to customers; an indirect structure involves using intermediaries; and a hybrid structure will involve both. The degree of efficiency that an intermediary can introduce to the performance of distribution tasks determines what form a channel structure will take. At the simplest level, direct channels offer maximum control but sometimes at the expense of reaching a target market. Indirect channels can maximize coverage, but often at the expense of control as the intermediaries start 'playing' with the marketing mix strategies and demand a share of the profits in return for their involvement. Hybrid strategies often result in greater channel conflict as the intermediaries feel the organization that is supplying them is also the competitor.

■ **Discuss the factors influencing channel design, structure, and strategy.**

In setting down a distribution channel strategy, most organizations make key decisions in order to serve their customers and establish and maintain buyer–seller relationships. The first decision is the selection of the structure of the channel. If it is decided that intermediaries will be required, management then need to consider the type of market coverage that will be required; the number and type of intermediaries to use; and how to manage the relationships between channel members. These choices are important as they can affect the value that is ultimately provided to customers.

- **Distinguish between the logistical functions for effective management.**

Logistics management concerns all the activities that, when added together, relate to the flow of products from the organization to the customer or end consumer. It includes decision areas such as production scheduling, plant location, and purchasing, which are traditionally the domain of production management. It also covers decision areas that are the province of physical distribution management such as transportation, inventory management, and order processing. Although these are not traditionally marketing management decisions, it is important to understand that they require a marketing focus and marketing insight.

- **Discuss the role, function, and importance of retailers in the distribution channel.**

Distributing consumer products begins with the producer and ends with the end consumer. However, between the two there is usually an intermediary called a retailer. Retailing is all the activities directly related to the sale of goods and services to the ultimate end consumer for personal and non-business use. This is also called the retail trade. A retailer or retail store is a business enterprise the primary function of which is to sell to ultimate consumers for non-business use. However, they all have two key features in common: they link producers and end consumers and they perform an invaluable service for both.

- **Compare and contrast the differing types of retailers.**

Types of retailing establishments can be classified as being differentiated by two key characteristics: marketing strategy employed (i.e. product, price, and service) and the store presence (i.e. store or non-store retailing). Examples include: department stores, discount stores, convenience stores, limited line retailers, speciality retailers, category killer stores, supermarkets, and superstores. In addition to the underlying marketing strategy, retailing establishments can be further characterized according to store or non-store presence.

Review Questions

1 Define what we mean by distribution channel management.
2 What are the differing benefits of using intermediaries?
3 Why are economics, coverage, and control important when making distribution channel decisions?
4 What are the key elements of a distribution channel strategy?
5 What are the advantages and disadvantages of the three differing channel structures?
6 What are the benefits of an exclusive distribution strategy over an intensive strategy?
7 Why is logistics management of increasing importance to marketers?
8 What are some of the reasons for channel conflict?
9 What are the differing types of retailers?
10 What do we mean by non-store retailing and what are the main types?

Worksheet Summary

Visit the and complete Worksheet 12.1. This will aid in learning about the differing types of channel structures and different types of intermediaries that could be used to distribute a technology product to a consumer market.

Discussion Questions

1   Having read Case Insight 12.1, how would you advise HMV on the management of its multiple delivery channels to strengthen the repositioning of its offering as a multichannel entertainment hub?

2   Discuss the importance of intermediaries. In your discussion, outline the benefits and limitations of the following types of intermediaries:

   A Avon sales representative;   **D** advertising agency;
   B electrical wholesaler;   **E** grocery retailer;
   C airline;   **F** bank.

3   From your reading and experience, identify the types of product that use the following channels to distribute direct to customers. Discuss the benefits of this channel strategy.

   A telephone;   **E** interactive digital and/or satellite TV;
   B internet;   **F** automated teller machines;
   C mobile technology;   **G** electronic kiosks.
   D catalogues;

4   Convenience has come to the fore as one of the key elements on which to base distribution channel decisions. Assess the arguments for and against focusing on convenience from a customer's perspective.

5   What sort of marketing or distribution channels would you imagine might be most relevant in the following markets in the year 2015? List what you think would be the three most relevant distribution channels for each product offering, and why.

   A music and video;
   B home entertainment software (e.g. video games);
   C business application software;
   D engineering consulting advice (say on mining or construction applications);
   E financial services;
   F shampoo;
   G personal services (e.g. hairdressing, beauty therapies).

6   Some claim that electronic technologies in the distribution channel are creating what is called 'infomediaries'. Discuss what we mean by infomediaries and the changed roles of intermediaries in the channel strategy.

Visit the **Online Resource Centre** and complete the Multiple Choice Questions to assess your knowledge of Chapter 12.

go online

References

Allison, K., and Palmer, M. (2007), 'Into the pack: Apple takes risks in its bid to shake up the mobile market', *Financial Times* (London), 26 June, 11.

Anon. (2005), 'The future of fast fashion', *The Economist*, 18 June.

—— (2010), 'Red Bull has its wings clipped in difficult 2009', *Austrian Times*, 24 February retrieve from: www.austriantimes.at/news/Business/2010-02-24/20990/

Red_Bull_has_wings_clipped_in_difficult_2009, accessed 11 April 2010.

Apple (2007), 'iTunes store tops two billion songs', press release, retrieve from Apple.com, accessed 11 January 2010.

Atkinson, R. D. (2001), 'The revenge of the disintermediated: how the middleman is fighting e-commerce and hurting consumers', retrieve from www.ppionline.org/ppi_ci.cfm?contentid=2941andknlg

AreaID=140andsubsecid=900055, accessed December 2007.

Bennet, P. D. (1988), *Dictionary of Marketing Terms*, Chicago: American Marketing Association.

Benson, C. (2007), 'Retail recovery', *Billboard*, 9 June, 119.

Cooper, W. (2008), 'Price-comparison sector attracts big names', *New Media Age*, 21 August 2008, 12.

Douglas, M. L., James, R. S., and Ellram, L. M. (1998), *Fundamentals of Logistics Management*, New York: Irwin/McGraw-Hill.

Datamonitor (2009), 'Mobile phones industry profile: China', *Datamonitor Report*, December, 1–34.

Dreier, G. (2003), 'Technology that drives transportation', *Transport Technology Today*, July, 9.

Ferdows, K., Lewis, M. A., and Machuca, J. A. D. (2004), 'Rapid-fire fulfillment', *Harvard Business Review*, 82, 11 (November), 104–10.

Franchise Europe (2010), *Top 500 Franchises in Europe*, retrieve from www.franchiseeurope.com/top500/ accessed 29 April 2010.

Freeman, P., and Evans, L. (2010), Western European Online Retail Forecast, 2009 to 2014, *Forrester [Report]*, retrieve from www.forrester.com/rb/Research/western_european_online_retail_forecast%2C_2009_to/q/id/56543/t/2 accessed 27 April 2010.

Gandhi (1979), 'Marketing channels', *American Journal of Small Business*, 3, 3 (January), 50–3.

Hamilton, A. (2007), 'Fast fashion, the remix', *Time* (11 June), 54.

Handfield, R. B., and Nichols, E. L. (1999), *Introduction to Supply Chain Management*, Upper Saddle River, NJ: Prentice-Hall.

Hein, K. (2001), 'A bull's market: the marketing of Red Bull energy drink', *Brandweek*, 28 May.

— (2004), 'Odds against the little guys', *Brandweek*, 23–30 August, 20–5.

Jai-Yeol S., Sung S. K., and Riggins, F. J. (2006), 'Consumer adoption of net-enabled informediaries: theoretical explanations and an empirical test', *Journal of the Association for Information Systems*, 7 (,7), 473–508.

Kane, M. (2000), 'Stephen King rewrites e-book biz', retrieve from http://zdnet.com.com/2100-11-519243.html?legacy=zdnn, accessed December 2007.

Michman, R. D. (1990), 'Managing structural changes in marketing channels', *Journal of Business and Industrial Marketing*, Summer/Fall, 5–14.

Mills, J. F., and Camek, V. (2004), 'The risks, threats and opportunities of disintermediation: a distributor's view',

International Journal of Physical Distribution and Logistics Management, 34, 9, 714–27.

Myers, M. B., and Griffith, D. A. (1999), 'Strategies for combating grey market activity', *Business Horizons*, 42, 6, 71–5.

Narayanan, V. G., and Raman, A. (2004), 'Aligning incentives in supply chains', *Harvard Business Review*, 82, 11 (November), 94–102.

O'Cass, A., and French, T. (2003), 'Web retailing adoption: exploring the nature of internet users' web retailing behaviour', *Journal of Retailing and Consumer Services*, 10, 81–94.

Page, P. (2005), 'Finding the energy for logistics flexibility', *Traffic World*, 1.

Papatla, P., and Feng L., (2009), 'Google or BizRate? How search engines and comparison sites affect unplanned choices of online retailers', *Journal of Business Research*, 62 (, 11), 1039–1045.

Park, S. Y., and Keh, H. T. (2003), 'Modelling hybrid distribution channels: a game theory analysis', *Journal of Retailing and Consumer Services*, 10, 155–67.

Parker, M., Bridson, K., and Evans, J. (2006), 'Motivations for developing direct trade relationships', *International Journal of Retail and Distribution Management*, 34, 2, 121–34.

Russell, S. W. (2000), *Marketing Management*, Englewood Cliffs, NJ: Prentice Hall.

Seiders, K., Berry, L. L., and Gresham, L. G. (2000), 'Attention retailers! How convenient is your convenience strategy?', *Sloan Management Review*, Spring, 79–89.

Tabini, M. (2010), 'iTunes Store: More than 10 billion songs served', *Macworld*, 27 (, 5), 63.

Vitzthum, C. (2001), 'Zara's success lies in low-cost lines and a rapid turnover of collections', *The Wall Street Journal*, 18 May.

Wai-yin Kwok, V. (2008), 'Nokia strengthens position in China cell phone market', *Forbes*, 7 March retrieved from www.forbes.com/2008/03/07/nokia-china-postel-markets-equity-cx_vk_0307markets05.html, accessed 11 April 2010.

Webb, K. L., and Hogan, J. E. (2002), 'Hybrid channel conflict: causes and effects on channel performance', *Journal of Business and Industrial Marketing*, 17, 5, 338–57.

Wingfield, N., and Smith, E. (2007), 'Jobs's new tune raises pressure on music firms: Apple chief now favors making downloads of songs freely tradable', *Wall Street Journal* (Eastern edition), A.1.

Principles of relational marketing

▶ Case Insight 13.1

MOLLY MAID provides a professional and personalized home cleaning service, undertaken by a team of two people. MOLLY MAID is one of the world's largest professional domestic maid cleaning services carrying out 2m home cleans every year worldwide. We speak to Pam Bader to find out more.

Pam Bader for MOLLY MAID

MOLLY MAID is a franchise operation, where franchise owners are awarded an exclusive area of business drawn up using postcodes and lifestyle data. This is used to estimate the number of households in an area, and to then determine the number of households likely to use a professional domestic cleaning service. When there are approximately 12,000 target households in a cluster, we know we can maintain a successful MOLLY MAID franchise, providing the franchisee can maintain at least a 2% penetration of these types of household.

There are several distinctive characteristics of the MOLLY MAID service. The first is the rigorous adherence to providing a quality cleaning service. Such is the strength of our belief in our service that we do not ask customers to sign a contract. The MOLLY MAID service is bespoke and tailored exactly to the requirements of each customer. Once the scope of the service is understood, and terms are agreed, MOLLY MAID begins to deliver the service. The no contract approach means that we rely on our Franchise Owners and their Maids to continue to deliver to the highest possible standard, in order to retain the business. The very fact that we have continued to expand, enjoy success, and ride over the various economic challenges of the last 25 years, is testament to the strength of our business model.

Another distinctive characteristic concerns our strong belief in the power of branding. All of our teams arrive at the customer's home in distinctive MOLLY MAID identified cars, with both of the operatives wearing professional, branded uniforms. They bring with them all of the necessary (branded) cleaning equipment and supplies required to complete the agreed service.

The branding element also helps us provide an element of tangibility to the inherent intangibility of the service provided. A cleaning service cannot be touched or stored for future use, so it is critical that we enable customers to see and remember the name of the company that meets and exceeds their service expectations. We believe our iconic logo and our recognized blue and pink colours help the recognition of our brand. Within the UK, we have over 340 MOLLY MAID liveried blue and pink cars driving up and down our roads every day. Indeed, beyond our direct marketing activity within the network (where over 11m flyers were distributed in the UK in 2009), our cars account for the next most frequently referred to medium, which prompts a customer service enquiry. All this has helped shape the brand, which is now positioned alongside many blue-chip companies. With over 72 Franchise Owners nationwide and with overseas operations in Canada, the USA, Portugal, and Japan, MOLLY MAID is a global brand.

As such, MOLLY MAID has worked hard to increase exposure and presence while also maintaining brand consistency across a variety of marketing outlets such as the internet, as well as the more traditional means such as direct mail.

A third characteristic is our determination to empower our staff and enable them to be proud to be part of the MOLLY MAID organization. Staff are rewarded

▶ Case Insight 13.1

The MOLLY MAID branded cars and uniforms are a distinctive characteristic of the service

through work-related pay, where wages are based on a percentage of the revenue each generates. Benefits accrue through use of the MOLLY MAID car, company uniforms, as well standard employee benefits within an organization, for example holiday pay. This model works effectively with Maids who are keen to maximize their earning potential and who regard the equipment as vital to their job, as it helps them maintain the quality of their work, keep the customer happy and therefore treat them with due respect.

The MOLLY MAID service is centred on delivering high-quality, reliable and professional services, while managing and completing the work to the client's requirements. One of the key tasks faced by MOLLY MAID is ensuring that the quality of service delivered is consistently high. This is so important when delivering a service across a number of different customer contact points. All service providers are vulnerable to variations in service delivery.

So, managing the customer experience is as vital today as it has always been and MOLLY MAID is actively reviewing the processes we use to manage this aspect of our business. So, how would you suggest MOLLY MAID manage the customer experience?

Introduction

Have you ever been frustrated trying to get through to **customer services** to sort out a mobile phone issue, or to the administrators at a university or college to get answers to important questions about your course or exam results? Well, if you have then you understand just how much better it would be if the provider delivered a better service. Services are important because they impact immediately on people and their perception of an organization. It is important, therefore, to understand how marketing activities can enhance the performance of service providers.

In this chapter we consider the nature, characteristics, and issues associated with the marketing of services. Time is spent first considering the distinguishing characteristics and then how the service marketing mix needs to reflect and deliver realistic marketing activities.

One of the critical aspects of services is the **service encounter**, the point at which a service is provided and simultaneously consumed. Getting the service performance right, and getting it right each time the service is delivered, for example each time you phone customer services at your mobile phone operator, is probably one of the most difficult aspects of service marketing management. Therefore, consideration is given to branding, **internal marketing**, and how to measure **service quality**, as these are key dimensions of services marketing.

What is a Service?

Services are different from products. One of the distinguishing dimensions of products is that they have a physical presence. Services do not have a physical presence and they cannot be touched. This is because their distinguishing characteristic is that they are an act or a performance (Berry, 1980). A service cannot be put in a bag, taken home, stored in a cupboard, and used at a later date. A service is consumed at the point where it is produced. For example, watching a play at a theatre, learning maths at school, or taking a holiday all involve the simultaneous production and consumption of the play, new knowledge, and leisure and relaxation. (See Market Insight 13.1.)

▶ Market Insight 13.1

Purity in Products and Services

Sweden's Tetra Pak revolutionized the food packaging industry, Finland's Huhtamäki Oyj is one of the world's leading manufacturers of paper cups and plates, Danish company Schur Technology is a leading North European total supplier of packaging solutions, and the Norwegian company Elopak, is a leading global supplier of cartons for liquid food products. Rexam is one of the world's leading consumer packaging groups supporting the beverage, beauty, pharmaceuticals, and food markets.

What is common to all these organizations? Their skill and core competence in packaging. They make tangible products to which traditionally, there are few service additions.

Alternatively, Bain, McKinsey, Towers Perrin, and PwC are some of the leading management consulting organizations. Owned by IBM, PwC offer a huge range of services across many industries and sectors. Their approach to work is stated to be through 'connectedthinking'. All of these organizations do not make or sell any products, they provide knowledge and skills, i.e. pure services.

Sources: www.schur.com/skabeloner/; www.tetrapak.com/; www.huhtamaki.com/; www.elopak.com/; www.rexam.com/; www.pwc.com/.

▶ Market Insight 13.1

Packaging firms like Tetra Pak manufacture a 'pure' product

Source: Courtesy of Tetra Pak packaging portfolio.

1 Identify ways in which packaging might shape consumer experiences.

2 Think about the role of a marketing consultant and make a list of the different types of knowledge that might constitute 'connectedthinking'.

3 Draw the product/service spectrum and place on it various product/service combinations.

The service industry sector forms a substantial part of most developed economies. Not surprisingly, the range of services is enormous and we consume services in nearly all areas of our work, business, home, and leisure activities. Table 13.1 indicates the variety of sectors and some of the areas in which we consume different types of services.

▶ **Table 13.1** Service sectors

Sector	Examples
Business	Financial, airlines, hotels, solicitors, and lawyers
Manufacturing	Finance and accountants, computer operators, administrators, trainers
Retail	Sales personnel, cashiers, customer support advisers
Institutions	Hospitals, education, museums, charities, churches
Government	Legal system, prisons, military, customs and excise, police

The sheer number of services that are available has grown, partly because it is not always easy to differentiate products just on features, benefits, quality or price. Competition can be very intense and most product innovations or developments are copied quickly. Services provide an opportunity to add value yet not be copied, as each service is a unique experience.

Most products contain an element of service: there is a product/service combination designed to provide a means of adding value, differentiation, and earning a higher return. The extent to which a service envelops a product varies according to a number of factors. These concern the level of tangibility associated with the type of product, the way in which the service is delivered, variations in supply and demand, the level of customization, the type of relationship between service providers and customers, and the degree of involvement people experience in the service (Lovelock, Vandermerwe, and Lewis, 1999).

The product/service spectrum, explored at the beginning of Chapter 8 identifies that there are some products that have very few services and some services that have little product tangibility. Many grocery products have few supporting services, just shelf stocking and checkout operators. The purchase of new fitted bedroom furniture involves the cupboards, dressers, and wardrobes plus the professional installation service necessary to make the furniture usable. At the other end of the spectrum a visit to the dentist or an evening class entails little physical product-based support as the personal service is delivered by the service deliverer in the form of the dentist or tutor.

go online

Visit the **Online Resource Centre** and complete Internet Activity 13.1 to learn more about Professional Services Marketing Group (PSMG) and the marketing of professional services.

The Nature of Services

In view of these comments about the range and variety of services and before moving on, it is necessary to define what a service is. As with any topic there is no firm agreement, but for our purposes the following definition, derived from a number of authors, will be used.

> A service is any act or performance offered by one party to another that is essentially intangible. Consumption of the service does not result in any transfer of ownership even though the service process may be attached to a physical product.

Much of this definition is derived from the work of Grönroos (1990), who considered a range of definitions and interpretations. What this definition provides is an indication of the various characteristics and properties that set services apart from products. The two sections that follow examine the key characteristics of services and the way in which the service mix, as opposed to the product mix, is configured.

Distinguishing Characteristics

Services are characterized by five distinct characteristics, as depicted in Figure 13.1. These are **intangibility**, **perishability**, **variability**, **inseparability**, and a lack of **ownership**. These are important aspects that shape the way in which marketers design, deliver, and evaluate the marketing of services.

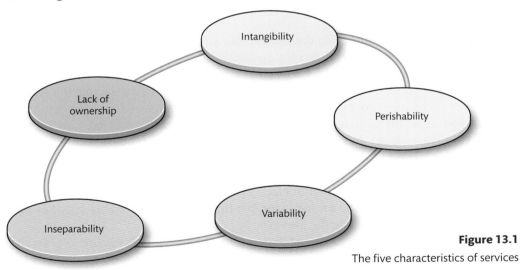

Figure 13.1
The five characteristics of services

Intangibility

The purchase of products involves the use of most of our senses. We can touch, see, smell, hear, or even taste products before we buy them let alone use them. Think of a trip to buy an MP3 player. It is possible to see the physical product and its various attributes such as size and colour, to feel the weight and touch it. These are important purchasing decision cues and even if the equipment fails to work properly it is possible to take it back for a replacement.

However, if a decision is made to buy additional insurance/support, this will be itemized on the receipt but it is not possible to touch, taste, see, hear, or smell the insurance bought. Services are intangible and they are only delivered and experienced post purchase.

Intangibility does not mean that customers buy services without using their senses. What it does mean is that they use substitute cues to help make these purchasing decisions and to reduce the uncertainty because they cannot touch, see, smell, or hear the service. People make judgments based on a range of quality-related cues. These cues serve to make tangible the intangible service. Two types of cue can be identified: intrinsic and extrinsic cues (Olson and Jacoby, 1972). Intrinsic cues are drawn directly from the 'service product' itself, and are regarded as difficult to change. Extrinsic cues on the other hand are said to surround the 'service product' and can be changed relatively easily. Brady, Bourdeau, and Heskel (2005) found that different types of service brands need different types of cue. Financial and invest-ment-based brands prosper from the use of intrinsic cues, which stress objective information sources, such as a strong reputation, industry rankings, and favourable media reviews. The reverse is true for services that have a more tangible element, such as hotels and transport services. In these circumstances, more subjective communication, such as advertising and referrals through word-of-mouth are more influential.

The use of cues is important because they often involve an assessment about the people delivering the service, the location, equipment used, the messages and tone of the communi-cations and associated branding devices, and, of course, price. Carbone and Haeckel (1994) refer to this process of 'tangibilizing the intangible' as 'customer service engineering'. This requires that the service organization first decides on what the customer experience should be like, in other words designs a service blueprint, and then designs a set of facilities and cues that lead customers to the required experience.

Service Blueprints

Service blueprints are used during the early stages of the design process, to help specify the various components of a desired service. Developed by Shostack (1982, 1984, 1987), blue-prints are used to sequentially and visually identify all the activities necessary for designing and managing services effectively. Service blueprinting is a tool for depicting the service pro-cess, points of customer contact, and the evidence of the service as seen by a customer. This perspective reveals the overlapping layers that can be found in a service, ranging from the layer of physical evidence and customer interaction to the layer of internal interaction within the service production process (Zeithaml, Bitner, and Gremler, 2006).

According to Hara, Arai, and Shimomura (2009: 372), service activities are arranged with respect to two lines. The first line of interaction concerns the point at which a customer and a service provider interact. The second is the line that separates the visible activities from the invisible activities performed by the provider.

However, as cited by Hara, Arai, and Shimomura (2009), various researchers (Brooks and Lings, 1996; Pires and Stanton, 2004) suggest that service blueprints are little more than operating manuals depicting how a service should be delivered, rather than representing what customers require. Service blueprints are a managerial representation of the desired level of service as they only set out the required tasks and the order in which they are to be performed. One of the outcomes, therefore, is that an assessment of the quality of the service provided, from a customer's perspective, is problematic.

According to Bitner, Ostrom, and Morgan (2008), there are five components that make up a typical service blueprint. These are customer actions, onstage/visible contact employee actions, backstage/invisible contact employee actions, support processes, and physical evidence. So, a five-star hotel will determine what constitutes a five-star hotel experience and then provide a series of context cues to be delivered by people (humanics) and things (mechanics). These will include appropriate communication devices such as brochures and a website designed to position the hotel as a five-star brand and as a desirable place to stay. Staff will be trained and reservation systems installed such that the humanics and mechanics of customer handling are seamless and consistently high.

go online

Visit the **Online Resource Centre** and follow the weblink to the Hotel Marketing Association (HMA) to learn more about marketing hotel services. See Figure 13.2 for an example of a service blueprint for an overnight stay at a hotel.

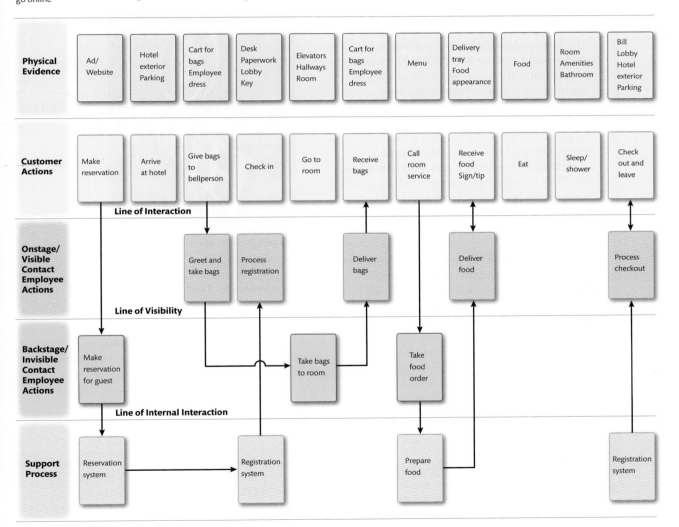

Figure 13.2

Blueprint for an overnight stay at a hotel

Source: From Bitner, Ostrom, and Morgan (2008). Used with permission.

The next step is to decorate and furnish the premises to a standard that reflects the desired positioning before finally providing additional services. At all stages there should be a consistent level of service performance standards, all of which are designed to shape a customer's experiences to meet the original blueprint (see Market Insight 13.2).

▶ Market Insight 13.2

Blueprints for Service Success

The National Endowment for Science, Technology and the Arts (NESTA) wanted to transform their five-week entrepreneur's training programme 'Insight Out' into a service capable of being delivered by approved independent partner organizations. To achieve this, it was important that the consultancy Engine differentiate the service and make it easy to use. This involved designing, producing, and supporting operational processes, including learning and marketing materials required to make it work, so developing a blueprint.

Hilton take pride in delivering an exceptional service
Source: Hilton Hotels.

This was accomplished by developing a user-centred approach, using three project phases Identify, Build and Measure, with the five service design fundamentals in mind: value, systems, people, journeys, and propositions. Engine's approach was to start by trying to understand what the users and providers of the service value. In addition it was important to appreciate how the components and relationships of the programme worked as a system. By working with the different delivery partners, a series of user journeys, highlighting touchpoints and activities, enabled various service opportunities to be identified.

They then produced knowledge and materials describing how to deliver the service, plus a 'shopping list' of service components, job descriptions, process diagrams, web information architecture, and design **briefs** to external designers.

In a different context, hotel group Hilton International focus on the need to deliver exceptional service. Their vice president of marketing comments, 'Delivering the

brand experience is the principal marketing tool we have, and is the beginning and end of what we do'.

Hilton have specified the ideal guest experience (established the service blueprint) and strive to deliver it consistently at all their hotels. It is the Hilton marketing department who set out the requirements for recruitment, training, and development. They also monitor and evaluate the extent to which the desired service level is achieved and take action to correct service delivery when standards are not met.

Sources: McLuhan (2006); www.enginegroup.co.uk/projects/pcs_page/getting_into_business_made_easy.

1 **Identify three different hotels and list three main service differences.**

2 **Write notes explaining your interpretation of the phrase 'delivering the brand experience'.**

3 **Prepare an outline blueprint for a service that you experienced recently.**

Perishability

A bottle of shampoo on a supermarket shelf attracts a number of opportunities to be sold and consumed. When the store closes and opens again the following day, the bottle is still available to be sold and it remains available until purchased or the expiry date is reached. This is not the case with services. Once a train pulls out of a station, or an aeroplane takes off or a film starts, those seats are lost and can never be sold. This is referred to as perishability and is an important aspect of services marketing. Services are manufactured and consumed simultaneously; they cannot be stored either prior to or after the service encounter.

The reason why these seats remain empty reflects variations in demand. This may be due to changes in the wider environment and may follow easily predictable patterns of behaviour, for example family holiday travel. One of the tasks of service marketers is to ensure the number of empty seats and lost-forever revenue is minimized. In cases of predictable demand, service managers can vary the level of service capacity; a longer train, a bigger aircraft, or extra screenings of a film (multiplex facilities). However, demand may vary unpredictably, in which case service managers are challenged to provide varying levels of service capacity at short notice.

One of the main ways in which demand patterns can be influenced is through differential pricing. By lowering prices to attract custom during quieter times and raising prices when demand is at its highest, demand can be levelled and marginal revenues increased. Hotel and transport reservation systems have become very sophisticated, making it easier to manage demand and improve efficiency, and, of course, customer service. Some football clubs categorize matches according to the prestige or ranking of the opposition, and adjust prices in order to fill the stadium. In addition to differential pricing, extra services can be introduced to divert demand. Hotels offer specialist weekend breaks such as golfing or fishing and mini vacations to attract retired people outside of the holiday season. Leisure parks offer family discounts and bundle free rides into prices to stimulate demand.

Variability

As already stated, an important characteristic of services is that they are produced and consumed by people, simultaneously, as a single event. One of the outcomes of this unique process is that it is exceedingly difficult to standardize the delivery of services around the blueprint model mentioned earlier. It is also difficult to deliver services so that they always meet the brand promise, especially as these promises often serve to frame customer service expectations. If demand increases unexpectedly and there is insufficient capacity to deal with the excess number of customers, service breakdown may occur. A flood of customers at a restaurant may extend the arrival of meals for customers already seated and who have ordered their meals. Too many train passengers may mean that there are not enough seats. In both these cases it is not possible to provide a service level that can be consistently reproduced. (See Market Insight 13.3.)

▶ Market Insight 13.3

Variable Recovery Services

Service quality can vary because people get tired, their workload might become too heavy, they might be stressed, lack sufficient experience, or have a poor attitude due to inadequate recruitment, selection, or training.

Companies such as Cisco, Dell, and IBM provide IT service and maintenance contracts each of which may contain a range of service packages. These might be 'the regular package', which guarantees a response in six to eight hours, a 'gold service', which brings response in four to six hours, or a 'platinum service', which provides immediate, on-call support.

Car recovery and breakdown organizations such as the RAC, AA, and Green Flag do not offer different response times but offer a range of types of services. Typically, these are roadside, recovery, at home, and European. These help to shape customer expectations about the type of service they can expect to receive.

Whether the service is IT- or car-related, customer concern about service consistency can be addressed by providing positive third-party referrals, word-of-mouth and written testimonials, and case studies of satisfied customers. In some situations, such as accountancy, consulting, and IT services, many organizations provide qualified teams designated to work with the client in an attempt to generate trust and reduce uncertainty.

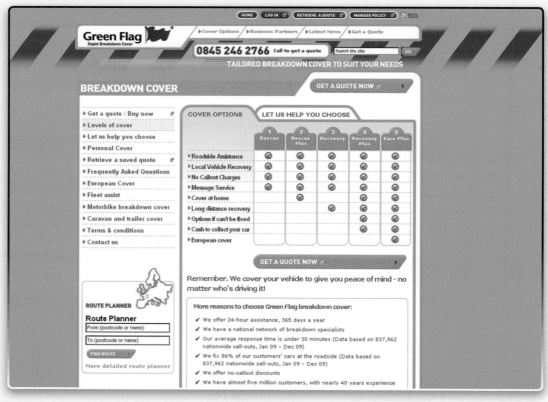

Green Flag, the breakdown service offers a variety of service levels

▶ Market Insight 13.3

1 Think of four reasons why service quality might vary in the car recovery market.

2 Why do organizations such as Cisco, Dell, and IBM offer different maintenance contracts?

3 Visit the following websites and make notes about the different services offered by these competitors: www.greenflag.co.uk and www.theaa.com.

A different way of looking at variability is to consider a theatre. The show may be doing well and the lead actors performing to critical acclaim. However, the actual performance that each actor delivers each night will be slightly different. This change may be subtle, such as a change in the tone of voice or an inflexion, and will pass by relatively unnoticed. At the other extreme, some actors go out of their way to make their performance very different. It is alleged that the actor Jane Horrocks once remarked that during the performance of a certain theatre play she deliberately changed each evening's show in order to relieve the boredom.

There has been substantial criticism of some organizations that, in an effort to lower costs, have relocated some or all of their call centre operations offshore. These strategies sometimes fail as the new provider has insufficient training, local or product knowledge, or in some cases simply cannot be understood. This type of service experience will vary among customers and by each customer. The resulting fall in customer satisfaction can lead to increased numbers of customers defecting to competitors.

The variability of services does not mean that planning is a worthless activity. By anticipating situations when service breakdown might occur, service managers can provide facilities. For example, entertainment can be provided for queues at cinemas or theme parks, in order to change the perception of the length of the time it takes to experience the service (film or ride).

Inseparability

As established previously, products can be built, distributed, stored, and eventually consumed at a time specified by the ultimate end user customer. Services, on the other hand, are consumed at the point they are produced. In other words, service delivery cannot be separated or split out of service provision or service consumption.

This event where delivery coincides with consumption means that not only do customers come into contact with the service providers, but also there must be interaction between the two parties. This interaction is of particular importance, not just to the quality of service production but also to the experience enjoyed by the customer. So, following the earlier example of a theatre play, the show itself may provide suitable entertainment but the experience may be considerably enhanced if the leading lady, Jane Horrocks, Judi Dench, or Scarlett Johansson, actually performs rather than has the night off because she is unwell. Alternatively, private doctors may develop a strong reputation and should there be an increase in demand beyond manageable levels, pricing can be used to reduce or reschedule demand for their services.

The service experiences described in the preceding paragraph highlight service delivery as a mass service experience (the play) and as a solo experience (the doctor). The differences impact on the nature of the interaction process. In the mass service experience, the other members of the audience have the opportunity to influence the perceived quality of the experience. Audiences create atmosphere and this may be positively or negatively charged. A good production can involve audiences in a play and keep them focused for the entire performance. However, a poor performance can frustrate audiences leading to some members walking out and hence influencing the perception others have of the performance and experience of the play.

Interaction within the solo experience (doctor–patient) allows for greater control by the service provider, if only because they can manage the immediate context within which the interaction occurs and not be unduly influenced by wider environmental issues. Opportunities exist for flexibility and adaptation as the service delivery unfolds. For example, a check-in operator for an airline operates within a particular context, is not influenced by other major events during the interaction, and can adapt tone of voice, body language, and overall approach to meet the needs of particular travellers.

One final aspect of variability concerns the influence arising from the mixture of customers present during the service delivery. If there is a broad mix of customers, service delivery may be affected as the needs of different groups have to be attended to by the service provider. Such a mixture may dilute the impact of the service actually delivered.

Lack of Ownership

The final characteristic associated with services marketing arises naturally from the other features. Services cannot be owned as nothing is transferred during the interaction or delivery experience. Although a legal transaction often occurs with a service, there is no physical transfer of ownership as there is when a product is purchased. The seat in a theatre, train, plane, or ferry is rented on a temporary basis in exchange for a fee. The terms associated with the rental of the seat determine the time and use or experience to which the seat can be put. However, the seat remains the property of the theatre owner, rail operator, airline, and ferry company, respectively, as it needs to be available for renting to other people for further experiences.

One last point concerns loyalty schemes such as frequent flyer programmes and membership clubs, where the service provider actively promotes a sense of ownership. By creating customer involvement and participation, even though there is nothing to actually own, customers can develop an attitude based around their perceived right to be a part of the service provider.

The Service Mix

Previously, in Chapter 8, we looked at the product/service spectrum and identified that there are a range of services. These range from services attached directly to a product to some that consist of a pure stand-alone service. From this, and an understanding of the various characteristics of services, it is possible to identify a **services mix**.

▶ Pure product—here there are no services, the offering is purely a product. Examples include salt, sugar, foot cream, and shower gel.

▶ Product with some services—here the product is supported with a range of one or more services. The more technologically sophisticated the product, the more likely that it needs to be supported by services (Levitt, 1972). For example, cars require showrooms, delivery, warranties, and repair facilities, as without them, 'sales will shrivel'.

▶ Combination—here products and services are used in equal proportion in order for customers' expectations to be met. So, in restaurants, service is expected as a complement to the food.

▶ Service with some products—here the emphasis is on the service but some products are a necessary part of the mix. For example, hotel guests rent a room, use leisure facilities, and seek relaxation, but in order for these to be experienced, some products, such as food, drink, internet connections, and perhaps complimentary stationery, are necessary to complete the experience.

▶ Pure service—here no products are involved in the service experience. Examples include dog walking, tax advice, and counselling.

This interpretation of the service mix has been developed from Kotler (1997) and is useful because it demonstrates the wide range of services that are available, their complexity in terms of their variability, and the difficulty of defining and categorizing them.

Services can also be understood in terms of other variables. One important variable concerns the significance and intensity of the equipment that is required to provide the service, as opposed to the intensity of people's contribution to the delivery of a service. So, at one extreme, vending machines are examples of equipment-intensive services and window cleaning an example of people-intensive services.

Other variables include the degree to which customers need to be present at the time a service is delivered, for example a haircut against a car repair. Is the service directed at consumers (personal service) or businesses (business services)?

Service Processes

Services are considered to be processes, and, indeed, a substantial part of the academic literature on services is based on a process perspective. A process is a series of sequential actions that leads to pre-determined outcomes. So, a simple process might be the steps necessary to visit a dentist, whereas a complex process might be the actions necessary to manage passengers on a two-week luxury cruise.

If processes are an integral part of the operations performed by service organizations, in the general sense, what are they processing? Lovelock, Vandermerwe, and Lewis (1999) argue that these processes are directly related to the equipment/people dimension referred to above. On the one hand, a haircut is people-intensive but the failure of a network server is intensely equipment-oriented. Lovelock, Vandermerwe, and Lewis present a four-cell categorization of services based on tangible and intangible actions on people's bodies, minds, and physical assets. The categories involve four different processes: people processing, possession processing, mental stimulus processing, and information processing.

People Processing
In this type of processing people have to physically present themselves so that they become immersed within the service process. This involves them spending varying amounts of time actively cooperating with the service operation. So, people taking a train have to physically go to the station and get on a train and spend time getting to their destination. People undergoing dentistry work will have made an appointment prior to attending the dentist's surgery, will sit in the chair and open their mouths and cooperate with the dentist's various requests. They have physically become involved in the service process offered by their dentist.

From a marketing perspective, consideration of the process and the outcomes arising from participation in the service process can lead to ideas about what benefits are being created and what non-financial costs are incurred as a result of the service operation. For the dentistry example, a comfortable chair, background music, non-threatening or neutral to warm décor, and a pleasant manner can be of help.

Possession Processing

Just as people have to go to the service operation for people processing, so objects have to become involved in possession processing. Possessions such as kitchen gadgets, gardens, cars, and computers are liable to breakdown or need maintenance. Cleaning, storing, repairing, plus couriering, installation, and removal services are typical possession-processing activities.

In these situations, people will either take an item to the service provider, or invite someone in to undertake the necessary work. In possession processing the level of customer involvement is limited, as compared to people processing. In most cases the sequence of activities is as follows. In order for an object to be attended to a telephone call is often required to fix an appointment. Then the item either needs to be taken to the service provider or the customer must wait for an attendant to visit. A brief to explain the problem/task/solution is given before returning at an agreed time/location to pay and take away the renewed item. This detachment from the service process enables people to focus on other tasks. The key difference here is that the quality of the service is not dependent on the owner or representative of the possession being present while the service operation takes place.

Mental Stimulus Processing

These types of services try to shape attitudes or behaviour. In order to achieve this, these services have to be oriented to people's minds, hence the expression mental stimulus processing. So, examples of these types of services include education, entertainment, professional advice, and news. In all of these people have to become involved mentally in the service interaction and give time in order to experience the benefits of this type of service.

Service delivery can be through one of two locations. First, services can be created in a location that is distant to the receiver. In this case media channels are used to deliver the service. Alternatively, services can be delivered and consumed at the point at which they originate, that is, in a studio, theatre, or hall. One of the key differences here is the form and nature of the audience experience. The theatre experience is likely to be much richer than the distant format. Digital technology has enabled opportunities for increased amounts of interactive communication, even though the experience will be different from the original. In the same way, online or e-learning in its purest form, has not yet become an established format, due perhaps to learners' needing to spend some of their learning time in interaction with their co-learners and in the presence of a tutor. For example, the use of summer schools operated by the Open University, and the increasing success of blended learning programmes.

Information Processing

The final type of service concerns the huge arena of information processing, the most intangible of all the services. Transformed by advances in technology, and computers in particular, information processing has become quicker, more accurate, and more frequent. The use of technology is important but we should not exclude people, as individuals have a huge capacity to process information.

One key question that arises concerns the degree to which people should become involved in information processing. Some organizations deliberately route customers away from people processing and into information processing. EasyJet reduces costs to save by making it difficult for customers to telephone the company and seek advice from expensive staff. Their approach is to drive people to their website and use the FAQs to answer customer queries.

The Service Marketing Mix

As explained in Chapter 1, the traditional 4Ps marketing mix was developed at a time when product marketing was prevalent and the role of services was insignificant. As services marketing has become increasingly important, certain limitations regarding the utility of the 4Ps approach have become apparent. For example, the intangibility of services is normally ignored and promotion fails to accommodate the inseparability issue between the production and consumption of services.

As a result of these and other shortcomings, an extended marketing mix of 7Ps has emerged. The three additional Ps have been included in order to meet the express needs of the service context. These are people, physical evidence, and processes. The 7Ps mix can also be applied to business-to-business and relationship marketing, the subjects of the next two chapters.

Product

Products are used to meet and satisfy customer needs and today this can incorporate anything tangible or intangible. Services are now commonly referred to as products in the widest sense. So, holidays, insurance policies, and bank accounts are referred to as products and they can all be categorized within a product mix.

Price

Because of the intangibility of services, price often becomes a means by which customers make a judgment about the quality of service. As there is nothing to touch or feel, making considered opinions about the costs and benefits arising from a service interaction can be problematic.

Price can be an important instrument in managing demand. By varying price across different time periods it is easier to spread demand and ease pressure at the busiest of times. This also enables service providers to reach those customer segments who are willing and able to pay full price, and in doing so deliver a service that meets the expectations of this type of customer.

Place

Place, in a traditional product-only context, refers to the way in which products are distributed in order for customers to be able to access them at a time and place that is most convenient to them. In terms of services, place refers to two issues. The first concerns the reservation and information systems necessary to support the service proposition. Increasingly, this is undertaken remote from the service delivery point. The second refers to the simultaneous nature of the production/consumption interaction. Here, the service should be regarded as a function of direct supply and suggests that place has little relevance in a service context. These interactions can occur at a customer's house or business location, or at the provider's location, such as a beautician's salon, an accountant's office, or a cinema.

Other interactions take place remotely over the internet or telephone. One problem that arises for the provider is that this limits them in terms of their geographic coverage and the number of customers they can manage without suffering a decline in service performance.

Promotion

Promotion is concerned with the presentation of the marketing offer (products and services) to target audiences. However, the promotion of services is essentially more challenging than that for products, simply because of the intangibility issue. So, promotion cannot convey size or volume, and images of the packaging or in-use pictures are also ruled out. In its favour, it is possible to depict or explain the benefits arising from the purchase of a service and it is also possible to show physical evidence of people enjoying the service.

Perhaps the main goal of services-based promotional activity is to reduce the perceived uncertainty associated with the intangibility of a service. This can be achieved by providing tangible clues concerning the nature and quality of the service. First, make the service easy to recognize by providing a logo or brand identifier consistently in all communications. Lloyds Bank used the Black Horse for many years, whereas Scottish Widows use an iconic black-caped young widow to represent their brand. From this point it should be possible to develop a reputation for trust, reliability, and quality that, hopefully, will spur positive word-of-mouth communication.

People

In the production of goods and manufactured items, the people element is removed from the customer at the point when the product is purchased. It does not matter what the engineers look like, how they speak to one another in the factory, or how they dress. In service industries this is an extremely important factor, as people representing the service provider have a direct impact on the perceived quality of the service itself.

Staff represent the service and should deliver the service consistently to a level that matches the desired positioning and service blueprint. The recruitment, training, and rewarding of staff is an imperative if the required standards and expectations associated with customer interaction are to be achieved.

One final aspect concerning people in the services mix is the management of the atmosphere and interaction among customers. For example, in a pub ensuring that the right physical environment is in place, for example, comfortable seats, warmth, low beams, open fireplace, etc., plus making sure that the right segments are attracted, is an important part of service marketing.

Physical Evidence

As mentioned previously, the intangibility of a service means that it is important to provide tangible cues for potential customers to deduce the product quality. One of the more common approaches is to use sales literature and brochures to give signs about the quality and positioning of the service. Staff deportment and dress also provide clues about a service provider's attitude and attention to tidiness, routines, safety, and customer orientation.

Shostack (1977) suggests that physical evidence can take one of two forms: essential evidence and peripheral evidence. Essential evidence refers to those few, key elements that are important criteria when customers make purchasing decisions. For example, the quality of cars used by a car rental company, the newness of planes, or the location and architecture of cinemas provide essential information. Peripheral evidence is, by definition, less important to a customer's evaluation of the overall quality of the service provision. Very often these items, such as sales literature, can be taken away by the customer and used as a reminder of the service brand.

Processes

Understanding service-related processes is important because customers are an integral part of service production. Processes include all the tasks, schedules, activities, and routines that enable a service to be delivered to a customer. If the marketing of services is to be successful, then it is crucial that the processes customers use work effectively and appropriately.

The processes involved in getting a haircut involve making an appointment by phone, arriving at the salon, waiting for attention once booked in, being shampooed by the junior, discussing style and requirements, drinking tea/coffee, having hair cut and styled, drying, paying and tipping, collecting belongings, and leaving. This is a relatively straightforward process; others, as mentioned earlier, can be complex. Knowing these steps means that marketers can build benefits into key steps to avoid boredom or enhance the experience. It is also an opportunity to provide differentiation and reposition service brands.

Service-Dominant Logic

There is an emerging concept based around a group of researchers who believe that products alone are not capable of meeting all of a customer's needs (Grönroos, 2009), particularly in business markets. For customers to derive value from a product they need to consume it and that often requires a level of integration or coordination with a supplier's processes and systems. This it is argued, resembles more of the characteristics of a service than a core product offering. Marketing should, therefore, be considered as a customer management process. This entails not only proposing how an offering might be of value to customers, but it also requires enabling and supporting them to create the value they require through their use of the product.

This is referred to as the **service-dominant logic** (SDL) approach, and was first proposed by Vargo and Lusch (2004). The traditional marketing management approach can be considered as product-dominant logic. So, if products alone are insufficient to meet customer needs, it is better to consider services as a more realistic means of understanding how marketing works. This idea is developed in Chapter 15 and for those interested to know more about this approach refer to Research Insight 13.2.

▶ Research Insight 13.2

To take your learning further, you might wish to read this influential paper.

Vargo, S.L. and Lusch, R.F. (2004), 'Evolving to a new dominant logic for marketing', *Journal of Marketing*, 68, 1 (January) 1–17.

This paper introduces the ideas concerning service-dominant logic. It sets out the conceptual underpinning for the approach by tracking back and considering previous major marketing approaches. It is likely that this paper will become increasingly significant as the concept becomes appreciated by an ever-increasing array of academics and marketing practitioners.

 Visit the **Online Resource Centre** to read the abstract and access the full paper.

Service Encounters

The development of service marketing strategies involves understanding the frequency and the ways in which customers contact service providers. Once this is understood, strategies can be developed that maintain required levels of service, but the processes and linkages that bring the elements of the services marketing mix and associated systems together can be reformulated. Service marketing strategy, therefore, should be based on insight into the ways in which customers interact or contact a service. The form and nature of the customer encounter is of fundamental importance.

A **service encounter** is best understood as a period of time during which a customer interacts directly with a service (Shostack, 1985). These interactions may be short and encompass all the actions necessary to complete the service experience. Alternatively, they may be protracted, involve several encounters, several representatives of the service provider, and indeed several locations, in order for the service experience to be completed. Whatever their length, the quality of a service encounter impacts on perceived service value, which, in turn, influences customer satisfaction (Gil, Berenguer, and Cervera, 2008).

Originally the term 'encounter' was used to describe the personal interaction between a service provider and customers. A more contemporary interpretation needs to include all those interactions that occur through people and their equipment and machines with the people and equipment belonging to the service provider (Glyn and Lehtinen, 1995). As a result, three levels of customer contact can be observed: high-contact services, medium-contact services, and low-contact services (see Table 13.2).

One of the interesting developments in recent years is the decision by some organizations to move their customers from high-contact services to low-contact services. Clear examples of this are to be found in the banking sector, with first ATMs, then telephone, and now internet banking, all of which either lower or remove personal contact with bank employees. Further

▶ **Table 13.2** Levels of customer contact

Contact level	Explanation
High-contact services	Customers visit the service facility so that they are personally involved throughout the service delivery process. For example, retail branch banking and higher education
Medium-contact services	Customers visit the service facility but do not remain for the duration of the service delivery. For example, consulting services and delivering and collecting items to be repaired
Low-contact services	Little or no personal contact between customer and service provider. Service is delivered from a remote location often through electronic means. For example, software repairs and television and radio entertainment

examples include vending machines, self or rapid checkout facilities in hotels, and online ticket purchases (see Market Insight 13.4).

This demarcation of customer contact levels is necessary because it provides a sound base on which to develop services marketing.

go online

Visit the **Online Resource Centre** and follow the weblink to the British Bankers Association (BBA) to learn more about financial services.

▶ **Market Insight 13.4**

Waving Goodbye to Queues

The growth in the number of people choosing to travel by train, bus, trams, the London Docklands Light Railway, and the tube brings service problems not only in terms of seating capacity and general comfort but also in terms of the time and queues associated with purchasing travel tickets and enabling people to keep moving. At peak times, queuing for tickets can be frustrating and cause enormous delays.

Ticket offices provide people with an opportunity to discuss their requirements on an interpersonal basis with a member of staff. However, this is an expensive and, at times, a time-poor use of resources. There are

many people who know what (ticket) they need, and self-service ticket machines are a way of providing a service for people who do not want or need a personal service encounter. There are an enormous number of people who make the same journey each day. In much the same way, airlines use e-ticketing and on-airport self-check-in solutions, such as kiosks, and off-airport self-check-in through kiosk, web, and mobile check-in applications.

The Oyster Card is a pay-as-you-go card used throughout London's public transport system. The card has a radio transmitter embedded in the card's chip and retains up to £90 worth of credit. Used on a pay-as-you-go principle, travellers simply wave the card a few centimetres from a point-of-sale terminal on entry and exit from the tube and the system debits the amount for the journey from the card.

▶ Market Insight 13.4   (continued)

Oyster makes paying for travel easier and more convenient

Source: Courtesy of Transport for London. The Oyster brand and logo are registered trademarks of Transport for London.

More recently, credit facilities have been doing away with the need to top the credit up in each card. This secure method of payment opens up opportunities for 'Wave & Pay' in areas other than travel. For example, for retailers who handle large numbers of low-value payments it is a quick and easy process that speeds up service, increases customer flow, and reduces queues. Convenience stores, cafes, supermarkets, newsagents, and fast food restaurants are all able to use this technology and make life easier for their customers. These cards can also be used for vending machines, road tolls or parking meters, or other remote or unattended payment situations. The technology is even being used to protect fine wines. For cardholders, the benefits include not having to carry cash, a simple wave of a card means a transaction is processed, minimizing travel time, and reducing time spent queuing.

Sources: Oates (2009); Harris (2008); Nugent (2006); Brignall (2006); www.wave-and-pay.co.uk/index.php.

1   How would you classify Wave & Pay as a form of service encounter with Transport for London?

2   How might B2B marketers make use of Wave & Pay?

3   This symbol 〰 on a card indicates that the card uses contactless technology. How might this assist in the marketing of this service?

Key Dimensions of Services Marketing

Many of the strategies appropriate to the marketing of services relate to the particular characteristics that are relevant to each service context and specific target customers. The management processes relating to strategy and planning in service environments are similar to those undertaken by manufacturing and product-based organizations. These are set out in Chapter 5.

However, the marketing of services can be improved if we understand how customers evaluate service performance. This is potentially very difficult as complex services such as surgery or stockbroking have few tangible clues upon which to make a judgment about whether the service was extremely good, good, satisfactory, poor, or a disgrace. Customers purchasing physical goods can make judgments about the features, style, and colour, prior to purchase, during purchase, and even return faulty goods post consumption. This is not possible with some types of services, especially people-processing services.

Zeithaml (1981) determined a framework that categorizes different services, which, in turn, influence the degree to which market offerings can be evaluated. Three main properties were identified.

Search properties are those elements that help customers to evaluate an offering prior to purchase. As mentioned above, physical products tend to have high search attributes that serve to reduce customer risk and increase purchase confidence.

Experience properties do not enable evaluation prior to purchase. Sporting events, holidays, and live entertainment can be imagined, they can be explained, and they can be illustrated, but only through the experience of the performance or feel of sitting in an audience 100,000 people can an evaluation of the service experience be made.

Credence properties relate to those service characteristics that even after purchase and consumption customers find difficult to evaluate. Zeithaml (1981) refers to complex surgery and legal services to demonstrate the point.

As demonstrated earlier, most physical goods are high in search properties. Services, however, reflect the strength of experience and credence characteristics that, in turn, highlight their intangibility and their variability.

However, this classification has been challenged on the basis that it does not entirely reflect contemporary service markets (Garry and Broderick, 2007). Whereas the original classification vested expertise in the service provider, emerging research recognizes customer expertise and sophistication. With more information, customers have increasing skills and abilities to make judgments about the quality of service offerings, prior to purchase. According to Garry and Broderick, this increased focus on customer attributes should also be matched with a consideration of the attributes we associate with service encounters. Here, they consider issues relating to information accessibility, time and interactivity, and finally the level of customer centricity present within a customer experience.

Many organizations recognize the importance and complexities associated with the marketing of services. As a result they often develop and plan their marketing activities in such a way that they help and reassure their customers prior, during, and after purchase. This is achieved through the provision of varying levels of information to reduce perceived risk and to enhance the service experience. Two techniques, branding and internal marketing, are instrumental in delivering these goals in services marketing.

Branding in a Services Context

The development of brand strategies for services is important simply because the intangibility of services requires that customers be helped to understand the value associated with the service offering. Readers unfamiliar with the principles of branding are advised to read Chapter 8 before proceeding.

Essentially, a brand provides a snapshot of the value and position offered by a service. Brands convey information about the standard of service and, in doing so, seek to achieve two main goals. First, brands can reduce the uncertainty associated with the purchase of services, especially when there are no tangible elements on which to base purchase decisions. Consider the complexity and risk associated with buying financial services, such as insurance, pensions, and savings products. Developing strong brands enables these risks to be rolled up into a single identity, one that is familiar and trusted. Just think of Virgin, a relative newcomer to the financial service market but already well established and still growing quickly. The use of sampling and free trials is a popular approach to reducing risk in service-based purchases.

The second goal is to reduce the amount of time people spend searching for a particular service, especially when they are unfamiliar with a particular market or category. When travelling, many visitors to a city will stay at hotels such as Marriott, Travelodge, Holiday Inn, or Hilton because the brands say something about the standard of service that can be expected. Branding shapes customer expectations and can provide a quick answer to a purchase decision. Advertising can also be used to help tangibilize the benefits of a service rather than the features that can be limited or boring, or both. Credit cards often promote the feature of a 0% balance transfer, but they also demonstrate the benefits by showing holidays, electrical goods, or fashion items bought as a result of using the credit card.

Good branding involves the use of logos and symbols plus straplines and slogans. These can also help make the intangible more tangible by relating to some of the core benefits a brand offers. However, care is required as a strapline or term of identification might be perceived as generic to a category. For example, Sony lost a court case in Austria when the supreme court ruled that the word 'Walkman' had become a generic term and the common trade name for portable cassette players. The result of this was that Sony lost its right to use the name 'Walkman', which it had invented, invested in, and developed over many years (Meikle, 2002).

Many service providers use their physical facilities to shape the environment so that customers feel at ease and are attracted into the service process. Booms and Bitner (1981) termed this the **servicescape** and refer to the need to consider customer expectations and their emotional states. Branding the environment using signs, colours, clothing, and other

The servicescape is important at McDonald's

Source: © 2010 McDonald's. All references marked with a ™ or ® are trade marks of McDonald's Corporation and its affiliates. All rights reserved.

physical items can provide recall of previous use of the service provider and also influence customer expectations. Consider the environment and overall design of fast food restaurants such as McDonald's and Burger King. These servicescapes are designed and replicated in high streets across the globe, are easily recognized, and convey immediately information about the type of food offered and the standard of service delivery. Empirical research by Harris and Ezeh (2008) reinforces the view that restaurant managers should actively manage their servicescapes.

The role of marketing communications in the development of these brands is important. Customers use information provided by the organization to learn about the service provider either prior to a service encounter or to reinforce actual brand experience. Marketing communication is used to convey messages not just about product functionality but also the emotional aspects of brands, often referred to as brand personality. Communications help frame customer expectations and so impact on customer satisfaction.

The emotional dimension of service brands has grown in significance as it becomes increasingly difficult to establish and maintain functional differentiation. Through the use of marketing communications, brands seek to develop trust and a positive attachment and identification with a brand's values. This can lead to an emotional preference for a brand and so establish a form of competitive advantage that is difficult to copy. Just as the ownership of prestige brands such as designer fashion brands, trainers, cars, and watches can be used to convey status, so ownership (and display) of many prestige service brands can convey similar status and position. For example, travelling first class, use of platinum credit cards, and being a member of certain clubs or societies.

Finally, not all services are able to develop strong brands; they simply do not have the resources, or inclination. Communications, however, should still be an important part of their marketing. Those delivering services where the credence properties are dominant and customers are unable to distinguish the quality of service can emphasize their professionalism. This can be achieved by displaying certificates and diplomas, having a long list of professional qualifications on their business cards, and referring in their sales literature and websites to the number and types of client they have worked with.

Internal Marketing

Branding is an important aspect in the marketing of services. Its overall role is to manage, by shaping and reinforcing customer expectations about the overall quality of the service itself and to indicate what the service encounter will be like. It is important, however, that services, particularly those that are delivered through face-to-face encounters with customers, are delivered by people who have been trained with respect to delivering both brand values and the functional aspects of the service provision. The variability of service performance is a distinguishing characteristic and every effort needs to be made to ensuring that each time the service is performed it is of a consistent high quality.

Some employees deliver the performance through interaction with customers. Other employees provide support facilities, equipment, or information to enable the service interaction. Therefore, it makes sense to train, support, and motivate employees so that they deliver high-quality service performances each time they meet a customer.

Employees constitute an internal market in which paid labour is exchanged for designated outputs. For some, they are seen as a discrete group of customers with whom management, in order to develop and or maintain exchanges with external stakeholders, interact (Piercy and Morgan, 1991). Although employees have the potential to add considerable value to manufactured goods, they are vitally important to the delivery of services. Indeed, the quality and perception of the way in which service-oriented employees interact with customers can be the crucial determinant concerning whether a customer will return at some point and whether they will speak positively about the service provider. This view about the central contribution of employees in services marketing was first termed 'internal marketing' by Berry (1980).

The role of the employee has changed. At one time they were regarded as just a part of an organization, and they were not required to have external orientation at all. Now their role sees them as brand ambassadors (Freeman and Liedtke, 1997; Hemsley, 1998). This is particularly important in service environments, where employees represent the interface between an organization's internal and external environments and where their actions can have a powerful effect in creating images among customers (Schneider and Bowen, 1985; Balmer and Wilkinson, 1991). Employees are important to external stakeholders not only because of the tangible aspects of service and production that they provide but also because of the intangible aspects, such as attitude and the way in which service is provided: 'how much do they really care?'. Images are often based more on the intangible than the tangible aspects of employee communications.

The values transmitted to customers, suppliers, and distributors through external marketing communications need to be reinforced through the values expressed by employees, especially those who interact with these external groups. Internal marketing is necessary in order to motivate and involve employees with the brand, such that they are able to present a consistent and uniform message to stakeholders. This process, whereby employees are encouraged to communicate with stakeholders in order for an organization to ensure that what is promised is realized by customers, is referred to as 'living the brand'. Hiscock (2002) found that employees can be segmented according to the level and type of support they give a brand. He claims that in the UK 30% of employees are brand neutral, 22% are brand saboteurs and 48% are brand champions, of whom 33% would talk about the brand positively if asked and 15% spontaneously.

Employees are required to deliver both the functional aspects of an organization's offering and the emotional dimensions, particularly in service environments. In order to engage customers in this way, attention needs to be given to the intellectual and emotional elements in internal communications. The intellectual element is concerned with employees buying in and aligning themselves with the organization's strategy, issues, and overall direction. The emotional element is concerned with employees taking ownership of their contribution and becoming committed to the achievement of stated goals. Marketing communications should reflect a suitable balance between the need for rational information to meet intellectual needs and expressive types of communication to meet emotional needs of the workforce.

The level of interaction that customers are prepared to enter into can hamper the degree to which employees can deliver the service promise. For example, a customer who doesn't tell the dentist where the pain is restricts the quality of performance the dentist is likely to give. Therefore, employees need to be trained to communicate with customers in such a way that they provide sufficient information to avoid service failure.

▶ Research Insight 13.3

To take your learning further, you might wish to read this influential paper.

Gummesson, E. (1991), 'Marketing-orientation revisited: the crucial role of the part-time marketer', *European Journal of Marketing*, 25, 2, 60–75.

Gummesson's paper is important because he identified the critical role played by the many part-time marketers (PTMs), inside and outside an organization, rather than the full-time marketers within. He argues in favour of the need for a marketing orientation to be built around these PTMs.

 Visit the **Online Resource Centre** to read the abstract and access the full paper.

Service Quality and Performance

Measuring the quality of a service encounter has become a major factor in the management of service-based organizations. **Service quality** is based on the idea that customer expectations of the service they will receive shape their perception of the actual service encounter. In essence, therefore, customers compare perceived service with expected service.

So, if the perceived service meets or even exceeds expectations then customers are deemed to be satisfied and are much more likely to return at some point in the future. However, if the perceived service falls below what was expected then they are more likely to feel disappointed and unlikely to return.

In order to help organizations manage and provide a consistent level of service, various models have been proposed. Primarily these have been based on performance measures, disconfirmation (the gap between expected and perceived service encounter), and importance-performance ideas (Palmer, 2005) (see Table 13.3).

Each of these approaches has strengths and weaknesses but the one approach that has received most attention is **SERVQUAL** developed by Parasuraman, Zeithaml, and Berry (1988). For some it represents the benchmark approach to managing service quality.

SERVQUAL is a disconfirmation model and is based on the difference between the expected services and the actual perceived service. Inherently, this approach assumes that there is a gap between these variables, and five particular types of GAP have been established across service industries. These are:

▶ GAP 1—the gap between the customer's expectations and management perception.
By not understanding customer needs correctly, management direct resources into inappropriate areas. For example, train service operators may think that customers want places to store bags, whereas they actually want a seat in a comfortable, safe environment.

▶ **Table 13.3** Three approaches to service quality measurement

Contact level	Explanation
Performance measures	Derived from the manufacturing sector, this approach simply asks customers to rate the performance of a service encounter. SERVPERF is the standard measurement technique
Disconfirmation	This approach is based on the difference between what is expected from a service and what is delivered, as perceived by the customer. SERVQUAL is the standard measurement technique
Importance-performance	Seeks to compare the performance of the different elements that make up a service with the customer's perception of the relative importance of these elements. IPA (importance-performance analysis) is the standard measurement technique

▶ GAP 2—the gap between management perception and service-quality specification.
In this case, management perceive customer wants correctly but fail to set a performance standard, fail to clarify it, or set one that is not realistic and hence unachievable. For example, the train operator understands customer desire for a comfortable seat but fails to specify how many should be provided relative to the anticipated number of travellers on each route.

▶ GAP 3—the gap between service-quality specifications and service delivery.
In this situation the service delivery does not match the specification for the service. This may be due to human error, poor training, or a failure in the technology necessary to delivery parts of a service. For example, the trolley-buffet service on a train may be perceived as poor because the trolley operator was impolite because they had not received suitable training or because the supplier had not delivered the sandwiches on time.

▶ GAP 4—the gap between service delivery and external communications.
The service promise presented in advertisements, on the website, and in sales literature helps set customer expectations. If these promises are not realized in service delivery practice, customers become dissatisfied. For example, if an advertisement shows the interior of a train with comfortable seats and plenty of space yet a customer boards a train only to find a lack of space and hard seating, the external communications have misled customers and distorted their view of what might be realistically expected.

▶ GAP 5—the gap between perceived service and expected service.
This gap arises because customers misunderstand the service quality relative to what they expect. This may be due to one or more of the previous gaps. For example, a customer might assume that the lack of information when a train comes to a standstill for an unexpectedly long period of time is due to ignorance or a 'they never tell us anything' attitude. In reality, this silence may be due to a failure of the internal communication system.

Using this GAPS approach five different dimensions of service quality have been established. These are:

1 Reliability—the accuracy and dependability of repeated performances of service delivery.

2 Responsiveness—the helpfulness and willingness of staff to provide prompt service.

3 Assurance—the courtesy, confidence, and competence of employees.

4 Empathy—the ease and individualized care shown towards customers.

5 Tangibles—the appearance of employees, the physical location and any facilities and equipment, and the communication materials.

The SERVQUAL model consists of a questionnaire containing 22 items, based on these five dimensions. When completed by customers it provides management with opportunities to correct areas where service performance is perceived to be less than satisfactory and learn from and congratulate people about the successful components.

Although SERVQUAL has been used extensively, there are some problems associated with its use. These difficulties concern the different dimensions customers use to assess quality, which varies according to each situation. In addition there are statistical inconsistencies associated with measuring differences and the scoring techniques plus reliability issues associated with asking customers about their expectations after they have consumed a service (Gabbott and Hogg, 1998).

▶ Research Insight 13.4

To take your learning further, you might wish to read this influential paper.

Parasuraman, A., Zeithaml, V., and Berry, L. (1988), 'SERVQUAL: a multiple item scale measuring consumer perceptions of service quality', *Journal of Retailing*, 64, 1, 12–40.

This paper is seminal. It established the criteria and methodology that have been used by many academics and practitioners to measure service quality and performance.

 Visit the **Online Resource Centre** to read the abstract and access the full paper.

Service Failure and Recovery

All organizations have times when things go wrong. There is an inevitability that where there is intangibility, inseparability, and variability then service performance may sometimes fall short of the required standard. Where a customer's expectations are not met then the result is service failure (Bell and Zemke, 1987).

Service failures, according to Bitner, Booms, and Tetreault (1990), arise from one of three main areas. These are failure in the delivery system, failure in response to customer requests, and failure through employee actions. Table 13.4 provides a brief explanation of these three types of service failure.

▶ **Table 13.4** Sources of service failure

Type of service failure	Explanation
Failures in the delivery system	Here, links between service personnel and service process break down. This is due to service unavailability (e.g. swimming pool closed), slow service (e.g. airport queues and delays), and core service failure (e.g. undercooked food)
Failure in response to customer requests	Explicit customer requests (e.g. a room with a sea view) or implicit customer requests (e.g. that children be excluded from quiet areas). Alternatively customers make errors (e.g. forgotten PIN number)
Failure through employee actions	Unexpected, non-standard employee actions where delivery of the service is perceived to be rude, dismissive, or unfair

Source: Adapted from Bitner, Booms, and Tetreault (1990).

The problem with service failure is not the failure itself but how managers and customers react. Whereas some customers will tell a few people about exceptionally good service performance, service failure can result in a disproportionate number of people hearing about the lost bag, the slow service, or the cold food. Negative word-of-mouth increases the more dissatisfied customers become (Rananweera and Prabhu, 2003). Dissatisfied customers are unlikely to come back so it is really important to ensure that service performance is correct in the first place. Should a failure occur, steps have to be taken immediately to correct the situation and turn a potentially negative situation into one that leads to positive outcomes for all involved. This is known as service recovery.

Service recovery is concerned with an organization's systematic attempt to correct a problem following service failure (Grönroos, 1988) and to retain a customer's goodwill (Lovelock, 2001). By acting quickly, demonstrating empathy with the customer's perception of the failure, and enabling employees to instigate corrective actions and award appropriate compensation, well-managed organizations are able to overcome service failure and develop positive reputations. Indeed, it has been found that successful service recovery, where customer satisfaction was maximized and negative word of mouth minimized, only occurred when the service recovery process was handled by employees who reacted quickly, courteously, and in a caring way (Hocutt, Bowers, and Donavan, 2006).

Managers should take an active role in service recovery. A survey of 540 travellers found that the most successful recovery strategies involved senior personnel. A fast response by a senior manager, a fast response with a full refund plus some compensation, and a large amount of compensation delivered by a high-ranking manager were considered the best forms of recovery. What was not acceptable was an apology, unless accompanied by some form of tangible compensation (Boshoff, 1997).

▶ Market Insight 13.5

Airline's Service Nose Dives

During a four-year period the number of complaints received by an international airline increased by nearly 60%. The percentage of complainants offered compensation increased dramatically by 147% during this period.

The majority of complaints concerned technical delays, service interruptions, e.g. through frequent strikes, and complaints regarding the attitudes of ground staff. Eighty-nine per cent of customer complaints resulted from 25% of the problem areas. Evidence suggests that the service recovery plan of the airline was not addressing these priority areas according to their significance.

Some of the causes of the delays, diversions, and cancellations are predictable but cannot be controlled and little can be done to avoid their consequences.

For example, 70% of delays in the commercial airline service are caused by weather. Furthermore, external factors such as flight diversions or cancellations due to air-traffic congestion, or a failure in another airport where the airline's aircraft are engaged, can cause service failure, yet are all beyond the immediate control of the airline.

The perceived 'bad attitude' of ground staff was a major area of service failure. The airline's senior management team agreed that for employees to be competent it was necessary to have rigorous selection procedures and appropriate training. However, training was an issue within the airline. Ground staff were not sufficiently trained for the highly 'customer-centred' aspects of their jobs, and therefore lacked appropriate key skills and diplomacy for handling the demands of customers.

It was clear that management had failed to identify and resolve the issues triggering employee dissatisfaction. Furthermore, the senior management

An airline's ground staff can make all the difference to service quality

> ▶ Market Insight 13.5   (continued)

team had been unsuccessful in attempts to improve internal company communications. A comparison of the service recovery elements employed by the focus airline with that of Singapore Airlines (SIA), an airline with a high reputation for service excellence, indicated that the focus airline only pursued one out of the ten service excellence approaches followed by SIA. It was concluded that as the two companies have similar systems in place, the key difference was the level of senior management commitment.

The airline had planned the purchase of new aircraft and, together with a scheduled upgrade of the existing fleet, this was expected to reduce the problems caused by purely technical failure. Service quality was expected to improve and expenditure on compensation to reduce.

Bitner, Booms, and Tetreault (1990) in a study of 700 critical incidents found that most customers do accept that things can go wrong. The real issue is the organization's response/lack of response to a failure that causes resentment and dissatisfaction.

Source: Adapted from Bamford and Xystouri (2005).

1 If you were in charge of the airline, what actions would you take to improve service quality?

2 To what extent should service recovery be based around a number of elements rather than just a letter and a refund?

3 Is it necessary for staff who have no contact with customers to have customer training? Why?

One of the ways in which organizations manage service failure, especially those failures that are not reported formally to the service provider but informally to family and friends, is to actively encourage customers to provide written feedback through questionnaires. By reacting promptly to the feedback and offering additional services free of charge, or financial compensation against the current or future service opportunities, organizations are more likely to retain customers, prevent negative word-of-mouth, and may even enhance their reputations.

However, Johnston and Michel (2008) believe there is an emerging view that service recovery is not just about recovering a dissatisfied customer in order to regain their satisfaction, loyalty, and future patronage. The primary purpose of service recovery is to help drive improvement throughout an organization. As a result of their research, Johnston and Michel suggest that organizations are far from optimizing service recovery outcomes.

Most organizations focus on customer recovery but this appears to have a relatively low impact on financial performance. In terms of employee recovery, organizations with 'good' complaint procedures appear to generate positive employee attitudes and high levels of retention, which lead to a positive impact on financial performance. From a process perspective, those organizations with the better recovery procedures experienced process improvements, which, in turn, led to the highest impact on financial performance. It appears that organizations should manage service recovery by attending to customer, employee, and process outcomes.

Skills for Employment

▶▶ For any graduates wanting to enter the world of marketing, be it on- or offline, attention to detail is key, as is the ability to question everything and put yourself in your customers' or users' shoes. Don't just trust your instinct though; in this social media generation, the power of peer-to-peer recommendation should be harnessed to get the right answers. ◀◀

Helen Guyver, Marketing Manager, World Challenge Expeditions

 Visit the **Online Resource Centre** to discover more tips and advice on skills for the workplace.

Chapter Summary

To consolidate your learning, the key points from this chapter are summarized below:

- **Explain what a service is and describe the relationship between products and services.**

   A service is any act or performance offered by one party to another that is essentially intangible. Consumption of the service does not result in any transfer of ownership even though the service process may be attached to a physical product. There is a spectrum of product/service combinations. At one extreme there are pure products with no services, such as grocery products. At the other end of the spectrum are pure services where there is no tangible product support, such as education and dentistry. In between, there is a mixture of product/service arrangements.

- **Explain the main characteristics of a service.**

   Unlike products, services are considered to be processes, and products and services have different distinguishing characteristics. These are based around their intangibility (you can touch a product but not a service), perishability (products can be stored but you cannot store a service), variability (each time a service is delivered it is different but products can be identical), inseparability (services are produced and consumed simultaneously), and a lack of ownership (you cannot take legal possession of a service). These are important because they shape the way in which marketers design, develop, deliver, and evaluate the marketing of services.

- **Understand the different service processes and outline each element of the services marketing mix.**

   A process is a series of sequential actions that leads to pre-determined outcomes. Four main service process categories can be identified: people processing, possession processing, mental stimulus processing, and information processing. As a result of various shortcomings of the traditional marketing mix, an extended version has been developed in order to account for the particular characteristics associated with services. The three additional Ps are people, physical evidence, and processes.

- **Explain the term service encounters and describe how service management should seek to maintain service performance.**

   A service encounter is best understood as a period of time during which a customer interacts directly with a service (Shostack, 1985). There are three levels of customer contact: high-contact services, medium-contact services, and low-contact services. As more services are introduced so opportunities for service variability and service failure also develop. One response to this problem has been the 'industrialization' of services. Other methods of maintaining service performance include branding, the way a service is identified and understood, and internal marketing, the processes and communications used to develop employees as part of the brand.

- **Explain the principles associated with measuring service quality.**

    Service quality is based on the idea that a customer's expectations of the service they will receive shapes their perception of the actual service encounter. In essence, therefore, customers compare perceived service with expected service. SERVQUAL is a major model used to measure service quality. It is a disconfirmation model and is based on the difference between the expected service and the actual perceived service.

Review Questions

1 Using the product/service spectrum, explain how a service is different from a product.
2 Set out in your own words the essential characteristics of services and find examples of each of them.
3 Now that you have identified these key characteristics, make brief notes explaining how they affect the marketing of services.
4 Explain the term, service encounter.
5 Name the five dimensions of service quality and explain their key characteristics.
6 Identify the four types of service processes and then find two examples to illustrate each of them.
7 Distinguish clearly between the three main methods used to measure service quality.
8 Describe how internal marketing can assist service performance, and then, using your own experience to make examples, explain the dimensions of a service encounter.
9 Explain the three levels of service classification. Why might these not be so appropriate today?
10 What are the elements that make up the services marketing mix?

Worksheet Summary

Visit the **Online Resource Centre** and complete Worksheet 13.1. This will aid in learning about the five gaps between actual and expected service quality: reliability, responsiveness, assurance, empathy, and tangibles.

Discussion Questions

1 Having read Case Insight 13.1, how would you advise MOLLY MAID to manage their customer experience?

2 To what extent is the traditional marketing mix a useful basis to develop marketing strategies for service organizations?

3 IslandAir Services provide airline services for a group of islands in the Pacific Ocean. The organization is severely restrained by fixed capacity and variable demand. Consider what might be the pattern of demand and ways in which IslandAir might adapt their marketing to manage the pattern of demand.

Make brief notes advising IslandAir's marketing manager about the key issues their marketing mix needs to take into account.

4 Working in small groups, select three service organizations and consider the extent to which they overcome the marketing problems associated with intangibility and variability.

5 Using PowerPoint, prepare a short presentation in which you explain the meaning of service interaction.

Visit the **Online Resource Centre** and complete the Multiple Choice Questions to assess your knowledge of Chapter 13.

go online

References

Balmer, J. M. T., and Wilkinson, A. (1991), 'Building societies: change, strategy and corporate identity', *Journal of General Management*, 17, 2, 20–33.

Bamford, D., and Xystouri, T. (2005), 'A case study of service failure and recovery within an international airline', *Managing Service Quality*, 15, 3, 306–22.

Bell, C.R., and Zemke, E. (1987), 'Service breakdown: the road to recovery', *Management Review*, October, 32–5.

Berry, L. L. (1980), 'Services marketing is different', *Business*, May–June, 24–30.

Bitner, M. J., Booms, B. H., and Tetreault, M. S. (1990), 'The service encounter: diagnosing favorable and unfavorable incidents', *Journal of Marketing*, 54 (January), 71–84.

Bitner, M.L., Ostrom, A.L. and Morgan, F.N. (2008), 'Service Blueprinting: a practical technique for service innovation', *California Management Review*, 50, 3, 66–94.

Booms, B. H., and Bitner, M. J. (1981), 'Marketing strategies and organization structure for service firms', in J. H. Donnelly and W. R. George (eds), *The Marketing of Services*, Chicago: American Marketing Association.

Boshoff, C. (1997), 'An experimental study of service recovery options', *International Journal of Service Industry Management*, 8, 3, 110–30.

Brady, M.K., Bourdeau, B.L. and Heskel, J. (2005), 'The importance of brand cues in intangible service industries: an application to investment services', *Journal of Services Marketing*, 19, 6, 401–10.

Brignall, M. (2006), 'Wave and pay cards set to put an end to queues', *The Guardian*, 16 December, retrieve from www.guardian.co.uk/money/2006/dec/16/creditcards. debt; accessed 27 April 2010.

Brooks, R., and Lings, I. (1996), 'A hierarchy of customer satisfaction, the inadequacies of service blueprinting', in: J. Beraçs and J. Simon (eds). *Marketing for an expanding Europe*. Vol. 2. *Proceedings of the 25th annual conference of the European Marketing Academy*, April 1996, Budapest, Hungary, Brussels, Belgium: European Marketing Academy, 147–64.

Carbone, L. P., and Haeckel, S. H. (1994), 'Engineering customer experiences', *Marketing Management*, 3, 3, 8–19.

Freeman, R. E., and Liedtke, J. (1997), 'Stakeholder capitalism and the value chain', *European Management Journal*, 15, 3, 286–96.

Gabbott, M., and Hogg, G. (1998), *Consumers and Services*, Chichester: Wiley.

Garry, T., and Broderick, A. (2007), 'Customer attributes or service attributes? – rethinking the search, experience and credence classification basis of services'. In *Proceedings of the 21st Service Workshop of the Academy of Marketing*, 15–17 November, University of Westminster : Academy of Marketing, 24–39.

Gil, I., Berenguer, G. and Cervera, A. (2008), 'The roles of service encounters, service value, and job satisfaction in business relationships', *Industrial Marketing Management*, 37, 8, 921–39.

Glyn, W. J., and Lehtinen, U. (1995), 'The concept of exchange: interactive approaches in services marketing', in W. J. Glyn and J. G. Barnes (eds), *Understanding Services Management*, Chichester: John Wiley, 89–118.

Grönroos, C. (1988), 'Service Quality: the six criteria of good perceived perceived service quality', *Review of Business*, 9, Winter, 10–13.

— (1990), *Service Management and Marketing: Managing the Moment of Truth in Service Competition*, Lexington, Mass.: Lexington Books.

— (2009), 'Marketing as Promise Management: regaining customer management for marketing', *Journal of Business and Industrial Marketing*, 24, 5/6, 351–59.

Gummesson, E. (1991), 'Marketing-orientation revisited: the crucial role of the part-time marketer', *European Journal of Marketing*, 25, 2, 60–75.

Hara, T., Arai, T., and Shimomura, Y. (2009), 'A CAD system for service innovation: integrated representation of function, service activity, and product behaviour', *Journal of Engineering Design*, 20, 4, August, 367–388.

Harris, L.C. and Ezeh, C. (2008), Servicescape and loyalty intentions: an empirical investigation, *European Journal of Marketing*, 42, 3/4, 390–422.

Harris, M. (2008), 'Leaving the wine cheats high and dry', *The Sunday Times*, 4 April, retrieve from http://technology.timesonline.co.uk/tol/news/tech_and_web/article3683812.ece, accessed 27 April 2010.

Hemsley, S. (1998), 'Internal affairs', *Marketing Week*, 49–50.

Hiscock, J. (2002), 'The brand insiders', *Marketing*, 23 May, 24–5.

Hocutt, M.A., Bowers, M.R. and Donavan, D. T. (2006), 'The art of service recovery: fact or fiction?', *Journal of Services Marketing*, 20, 3, 199–207.

Johnston, R., and Michel, S. (2008), 'Three outcomes of service recovery: customer recovery, process recovery and employee recovery', *International Journal of Operations & Production Management*, 28, 1, 79–99.

Kotler, P. (1997), *Marketing Management*, 9th (international), edn, Upper Saddle River, NJ: Pearson Education.

Levitt, T. (1972), 'Production-line approach to service', *Harvard Business Review*, 50, 5, 20–31.

Lovelock, C. (2001), *Services Marketing: People, Technology, Strategy*, 4th edn, Upper Saddle River, NJ: Prentice Hall.

— Vandermerwe, S., and Lewis, B. (1999), *Services Marketing: A European Perspective*, Harlow: FT/Prentice Hall.

McLuhan, R. (2006), 'How trusted are you?', *Marketing*, 18 October, 33–4.

Meikle, E. (2002), 'Lawless branding: recent developments in trademark law', retrieve from www.brandchannel.com/features_effect.asp?pf_id=103#more, accessed 25 March 2007.

Nugent, H. (2006), 'Customers to wave payments', *The Times*, 23 November, retrieve from www.timesonline.co.uk/tol/news/uk/article646577.ece, accessed 27 April 2010.

Oates, J. (2009), Westminster readies 'wave and pay' parking meters, *The Register*, 29 October, retrieve from www.theregister.co.uk/2009/10/29/westminster_parking_scheme/, accessed 27 April 2010.

Olson, J.C., and Jacoby, J. (1972), 'Cue Utilization in the quality perception process', in the *Proceedings of the Third Annual Conference of the Association for Consumer Research*, M. Venkatesan ed., Association for Consumer Research, 167–79.

Palmer, A. (2005), *Services Marketing*, Maidenhead: McGraw Hill.

Parasuraman, A., Zeithaml, V., and Berry, L. L. (1988), 'SERVQUAL: a multiple-item scale for measuring consumer perceptions of service quality', *Journal of Retailing*, 64, 1, 5–37.

Piercy, N. F., and Morgan, N. A. (1991), 'Internal marketing: the missing half of the marketing programme', *Long Range Planning*, 24, 2, 82–93.

Pires, G., and Stanton, P. (2004), 'The role of customer experiences in the development of service blueprints' [CD-ROM]. *Proceedings of the ANZMAC 2004 conference*, 29 November–1 December, Wellington, New Zealand.

Rananweera, C., and Prabhu, J. (2003), 'On the relative importance of customer satisfaction and trust as determinants of customer retention and positive word of mouth', *Journal of Targeting, Measurement and Analysis for Marketing*, 12, September, 82–91.

Schneider, B., and Bowen, D. E. (1985), 'Employee and customer perceptions of service in banks: perception and extension', *Journal of Applied Psychology*, 70, 423–33.

Shostack, G. L. (1977), 'Breaking free from product marketing', *Journal of Marketing*, 41 (April), 73–80.

— (1982), 'How to design a service'. *European Journal of Marketing*, 16 (1), 49–63.

— (1984), 'Design services that deliver'. *Harvard Business Review*, 84115, 133–139.

— (1985), 'Planning the service encounter', in J. A. Czepiel, M. R. Solomon, and C. F. Surprenant (eds), *The Service Encounter*, Lexington, Mass.: Lexington Books, 243–54.

— (1987), 'Service positioning through structural change'. *Journal of Marketing*, 51, 34–43.

Vargo, S.L., and Lusch, R.F. (2004), 'Evolving to a new dominant logic for marketing', *Journal of Marketing*, 68, 1 (January) 1–17.

Zeithaml, V. A. (1981), 'How consumer evaluation processes differ between goods and services', reprinted in C. Lovelock (ed.), *Services Marketing*, 2nd edn, Upper Saddle River, NJ: Prentice Hall, 1991.

— , Bitner, M. J., and Gremler, D. D. (2006). *Services marketing: integrating customer focus across the firm*. Boston, McGraw-Hill/Irwin.

14 | Business-to-Business Marketing

● Learning Outcomes

After studying this chapter you should be able to:

▶ Explain the main characteristics of business markets

▶ Understand the different types of organizational customers

▶ Describe the different types of goods and services that are sold and bought in business markets

▶ Explain the main processes and stages associated with organizational buying and purchasing

▶ Understand the principles of key account management

▶ Explain what business-to-business marketing is

▶ Be able to compare business and consumer marketing

▶ Case Insight 14.1

Reed Smith is a major global law firm, which represents many of the world's leading companies in high-stakes disputes, strategic transactions, and crucial regulatory matters. We speak to Victoria Gregory to find out more.

Victoria Gregory for Reed Smith

ReedSmith
The business of relationships.

Logo of the global law firm, Reed Smith

With lawyers from coast to coast in the USA, as well as in the United Kingdom, continental Europe, and the Middle East, our firm is known for its experience across a broad array of industry sectors. We counsel 28 of the top 30 US banks and nine of the world's ten largest pharmaceutical companies. Our shipping practice has been designated among the most pre-eminent in the world, and our advertising law practice is regarded as among the legal industry's finest.

We know that successful business-to-business marketing is founded on many dimensions, not just technical competence. Key for us is an understanding of the needs of our customers and the development of relationships that are of mutual benefit. This is important as the market for legal services is becoming increasingly commoditized and competitive. Technical expertise, although critical, is no longer seen as the sole differentiator of legal services. Business clients are ever more demanding of their advisers as they expect more 'added value' services and want lawyers to demonstrate greater commercial understanding of their business. Some of the added-value services we provide clients are

seminars on relevant industry topics, in-house training, direct mail, corporate hospitality, extranets, and secondments.

We have grown partly because of our uncommon commitment to delivering high-quality service and developing long-term client relationships. Our approach to service begins by understanding our clients' business goals. We then work to develop the resources necessary to help achieve them. This commitment to client service is communicated through our branding: 'The Business of Relationships'.

Reed Smith's Marketing Department is split into four teams: Clients and Markets, Business Development, Branding and Communications, and Events. Clients and Markets, a recently formed unit, is devoted to strengthening and expanding Reed Smith's most important client relationships. This is achieved by assisting the legal client teams to:

▶ develop simple, achievable plans for building their client relationships;

▶ gain a deeper understanding of the clients' cultures, strategies, challenges, and legal needs;

▶ use secondment opportunities as the means for further developing client ties;

▶ Spot new cross-selling opportunities.

Business development personnel are based within practice groups in each of our offices and offer

▶ Case Insight 14.1

support to the lawyers within those practice groups on preparing pitches and responses to 'invitation to tender' requests, arranging events and corporate hospitality, maintaining lawyer biographies and other practice-specific literature and practice-specific marketing communications. Branding and Communications deal with all internal and external communications including public relations.

As a global law firm, with over 1,500 lawyers, in 21 offices throughout the USA, Europe, and the Middle East, one of the most important commercial challenges we face is how to share information across the firm so that we can ensure consistency of service to our clients.

How would you share information across a firm such as Reed Smith?

Introduction

For many of us marketing is concerned with consumer products, those that we buy and consume on a fairly regular basis. However, there is also a colossal market that is often hidden from our daily view of the world. This is referred to as the **business market** and business-to-business marketing is concerned with the marketing of products and services that are bought and sold between organizations.

Some of the characteristics of business-to-business (B2B) marketing are very different from those associated with **consumer marketing**. There are numerous reasons for these differences and the way they impact varies among organizations. In this chapter, we explore the nature and impact of these characteristics. We highlight the main types of business-to-business organizations, learn about the different types of goods and services, and develop an understanding about the way organizations make buying decisions, who makes them and what purchasing strategies can be used.

A traditional perception of business marketing activity is that it concerns salespeople selling products with services attached (Leigh and Marshall, 2001). In many ways this was true, but now that the answers to most prior-to-purchase questions and much customer order taking is now an online activity, the sales department has shifted its role. Now salespeople are intent on increasing customer productivity, with a focus on managing relationships. Previously, its thrust was tactical but now it is more strategic (Piercy, 2006).

Citing Vargo and Lusch (2004), Storbacka *et al*. (2009: 892) state, there 'has been a significant shift from product to service (or solution) selling ("servitisation") in many business-to-business interactions'. Research by Storbacka *et al*. (2009) shows that sales is increasingly about process, rather than a series of separate transactions carried out by a specific function. They claim that the sales process is much more relational than it used to be. Second, the sales function now involves close working links between sales and operations, especially as sales becomes linked increasingly with information gathering, processing and interpretation, resource mobilization, and delivery. This then makes sales much more cross-functional than it used to be. Finally, they observe the increasing emphasis on customer issues and also on sales metrics, suggesting that the sales function has shifted from an operational to a strategic activity. These three changes should be considered when reading the rest of this chapter, and indeed the next chapter on Relationship Marketing.

A key part of B2B marketing is associated with managing the relationships that can develop between organizations and the people who represent them. Managing customers, therefore, is vitally important, and one task is to identify and manage those customers that are important to the success of the organization. This is referred to as **key account** management, and we examine this topic because it is becoming an important aspect of B2B marketing. Although the chapter focuses on the differences and characteristics of business marketing, we conclude the chapter with a reflection of the similarities that exist between business and consumer marketing.

What is Business-to-Business Marketing?

Just imagine the complexity associated with the design and construction of a car, a new aeroplane such as Boeing's 787 Dreamliner, the Olympic Park in London, the Millau bridge in France, or the Civil Hospital in Ahmedabad. The huge number of organizations, large and small, all involved with specifying, negotiating, buying and selling, building, delivering and storing, and then replacing parts and materials as they become used, can involve a vast

The spectacular Millau Bridge in France

network of organizations. The operational difficulty alone is enormous and the value of the materials, components, labour, and energy involved far exceeds consumer spending in either the soap, beauty, or confectionery markets. The market for goods and services bought and sold between businesses is simply huge.

In order to make a car, a manufacturer must try to create value: they do this by buying a range of finished and part-finished items, assembling them, and distributing the completed cars to dealers, who sell them to consumers or businesses (fleet-buyers). The array of parts and finished items that the manufacturer buys involves a huge number of suppliers. This is the business market. The actions undertaken by a supplier of a brake system in order to influence the car manufacturer to select their system rather than a competitor's constitute business-to-business marketing.

In a number of ways, B2B marketing is fundamentally different from consumer goods or services marketing because organizational buyers do not consume the products or services themselves. Unlike consumer markets, where goods and services are consumed individually, by the people who buy them, the essence of business markets is that organizations, not individual people, undertake the act of purchase.

Far larger than the consumer market, the business market comprises many types and sizes of organization. Each organization interacts with a selection of others and forms relationships of varying significance and duration. This web of interaction is referred to as a network. Although organizations are often structurally and legally independent entities, a key characteristic is that they are also interdependent. That is, they have to work with other organizations, to varying degrees, in order to achieve their goals.

Characteristics of Business Markets

Business markets are characterized by a number of factors but the main ones are: the nature of demand, the buying processes, international dimensions, and, perhaps most importantly, the relationships that develop between organizations in the process of buying and selling. These are shown in Figure 14.1 and are examined in turn.

Figure 14.1

Key characteristics of business markets

The Nature of Demand

There are three key aspects of demand in business markets: derivation, variance, and elasticity. Demand in business markets is ultimately derived from consumers (Gummesson and Polese, 2009). This may seem a little odd, but consider the demand for building trains. When Banverket, the Swedish Railway Administration and Bombardier Transportation, considered developing a 'Green Train', the goal was to develop a new generation of high-speed, super-efficient trains that meet the special technical and traffic requirements in the Nordic Countries. Part of the project team's calculation was to estimate the number of people prepared to make train journeys and what they are prepared to pay. Even though each train is the result of hundreds of organizations interacting with one another, it is train passengers (consumers) who actually stimulate demand for the construction of trains.

Demand is variable because consumer preferences and behaviour fluctuate. The demand for rail journeys, for example, invariably declines following a major train accident or a significant increase in fares. It also increases in response to petrol price rises and calls for consumers to be more environmentally aware. The subsequent impact could be felt on rail operators, support services, train manufacturers, and the whole array of suppliers and sub-contractors in the market. All of this suggests that organizations should monitor and anticipate demand as cycles unfold. See Market Insight 14.1 for an example.

▶ **Market Insight 14.1**

Fluctuating Demand for Computers

Multinational personal computer companies are typical original equipment manufacturers (OEMs). Companies such as IBM, Dell, and Hewlett Packard assemble their own equipment from components that are largely bought from other manufacturers. However, the computer business is intensely competitive and dynamic mainly because demand is influenced by three main factors.

▶ Falling prices—the price of computers has fallen dramatically. In addition to aggressive price-cutting strategies, all the major companies operate 'just-in-time' stocking systems designed to keep only a few days' supplies of components in their warehouses. This has cut their working capital and allowed them to cut prices.

▶ Rapid technological change—the pace of technological change has been enormous. As chip capacity doubles every 18–24 months, so computer-processing power has increased by a factor of 100 over the past decade. One result of this is that many consumers want the latest designs and often reject technology that is just six months old. Consumers, therefore, can create huge fluctuations in demand.

▶ Volatility—fast technological development and fluctuating market demand often combine to cause great instability in the computer supply chain. Frequent variation in product demand can cause these companies to swing between having no stock to periods of over-production and surplus capacity. This, in turn, can impact on the rate and size of investment made by organizations as they flex themselves in anticipation of 'foreseeable' demand. For

▶ Market Insight 14.1

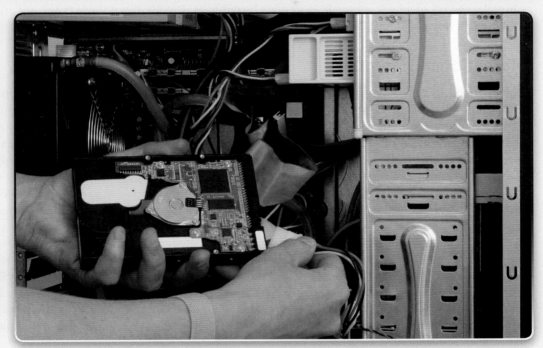

Computer companies assemble products from components bought from OEMs

example, Dell hit a crisis in 1989 when chip capacity went from 256K to 1Mb virtually overnight and the company was left with millions of dollars' worth of unsaleable stock.

Source: Adapted from www.cafod.org.uk/policy_and_analysis/public_policy_papers.

1 From where is the demand for PCs derived?

2 Is demand in the personal computer market elastic or inelastic?

3 How could a marketing manager overcome the volatility of this market?

Demand is essentially inelastic. If suppliers raise their prices, most manufacturers will try to absorb the increases into their own cost structures to prevent letting their customers down in the short term, or because they are tied into fixed price contracts. Incorporating these price increases, at least over the short to medium term, means that there is price inelasticity. In the medium term, manufacturers can either eliminate the original parts, redesign the product, or search for new suppliers.

The Buying Processes

The buying processes undertaken by organizations differ in a number of ways to those used by consumers. These differences are a reflection of the potential high financial value associated with these transactions, product complexity, the relatively large value of individual orders, and the nature of the risk and uncertainty. As a result, organizations have developed particular processes and procedures, which often involve a large number of people. What is central, however, is that the group of people involved in organizational purchasing processes are referred to as a decision-making unit, that the types of purchases they make are classified as **buyclasses**, all of which are made in various **buyphases**. Details about these processes are given later in this chapter.

International Dimensions

In comparison to consumer markets, B2B marketing is much easier to conduct internationally. This is because the needs of businesses around the world are far more similar to one another than the needs of consumers, whose preferences, tastes, and resources vary. As a result, an increasing number of B2B organizations are moving into international markets. This is often enabled by advances in technology, most notably the internet, which permit organizations enormous geographical coverage.

In comparison to B2C markets, B2B organizations benefit from a lower variety of product functionality and performance. This is partly because the various trading associations across the world have agreed standards relating to content and performance. What this means is that buying and selling of products and services, wherever located, are relatively simple and the trading environment reasonably well regulated and controlled. Many industries, for example, the steel, plastic, chemicals, and paper industries, all have common agreed standards, which facilitate interorganizational exchange processes. In B2C markets there are numerous issues concerning consumer culture and values and the adaptation of products and promotional activities to meet various colour, ingredient, stylistic, buying processes, packaging, and language requirements.

go online

Visit the **Online Resource Centre** and follow the weblink to the ABBA, the Association for B2B Agencies to learn more about B2B organizations.

Relationships

If there is one characteristic that separates business marketing from consumer marketing, it is the importance of relationships. In B2C markets, the low **perceived value** of the products, and the competitive nature of the market, which makes product substitution relatively easy, make relationships between manufacturers and consumers relatively more difficult to establish. In business marketing, the interaction between buyers, sellers, and other stakeholders is of major significance. The development and maintenance of relationships between buying and selling organizations is pivotal to success. Interdependence, collaboration, and in some cases partnership, over the development, supply, and support of products and services, is considered a core element of B2B marketing.

The importance of this aspect of B2B marketing cannot be underestimated and is explored in greater depth in Chapter 15.

▶ Research Insight 14.1

To take your learning further, you might wish to read this influential paper.

Dwyer, R. F., Schurr, P. H., and Oh, S. (1987), 'Developing buyer–seller relationships', *Journal of Marketing*, 51 (April), 11–27.

This paper is one of the most cited by other researchers in the subject area. Its popularity is based on the critical observation that buyer–seller exchanges are not discrete activities or events, but a part of ongoing relationships. The authors present a framework for developing buyer–seller relationships that links into marketing strategy.

 Visit the **Online Resource Centre** to read the abstract and access the full paper.

Types of Organizational Customers

Once referred to as industrial marketing, the term B2B marketing has been adopted because it recognizes the involvement of a range of other, non-industrial suppliers, agents, and participants. The government, the non-profit sector, and charities and institutions in most countries are responsible for a huge level of B2B activity. Consider the transactions necessary to support various government functions. For example, the huge range of products and services necessary to support the pharmaceutical and medical supplies in the health service, and the products and infrastructure necessary to maintain the prison and military services, all represent a major slice of B2B activity.

It is possible to categorize organizations by their size (revenue or number of employees), namely large, medium, and small organizations. Macfarlane (2002) refers to global and national organizations, the public sector, small and medium-sized enterprises (SMEs), and small office/home office (SOHOs). However, this approach is too general and fails to accommodate different buyer needs and purchasing procedures. Here, three broad types of B2B organizations are identified: commercial, government, and institutional organizations. See Table 14.1 for a brief outline of their principal characteristics.

▶ **Table 14.1** Key types of business organizations

Type of organization		Key characteristics
Commercial	Distributors	Wholesalers, value-added resellers, retailers and distributors/dealers. Not only do they smooth the progress of products through the marketing channel but they should also add value to them by providing storage (through distribution centres), services (such as training), or financial support (such as credit facilities). See Market Insight 14.2

▶ **Table 14.1** (continued)

Type of organization		Key characteristics
Commercial	OEMs	**Original equipment manufacturers** (OEMs) refers to one company relabelling a product, incorporating it within a different product, in order to sell it under their own brand name and offering its own warranty, support, and licensing. For example, Toyota may have a contract with a headlight manufacturer to supply them with a certain quantity of headlight assemblies. Toyota is the OEM because it builds these headlight assemblies into its different cars and sells the cars as Toyotas, without identifying the manufacturer of the headlight assembly
	Users	Users are organizations that purchase goods and services that are then consumed as part of their production and manufacturing processes. Users, therefore, consume these parts and materials, and they do not appear in the final product offering but do contribute to its production. Toyota will purchase many support materials, for example, machine tools, electrical manufacturing equipment, vending machines, office furniture, and stationery. None of these can be identified within the cars it produces
	Retailers	Retailers need to purchase goods in order to resell them just as other organizations do. However, the buying processes are not always as complex or as intricate as those normally associated with organizational buying and the group of people who make purchase decisions (the decision-making unit or DMU). Suppliers need to understand their retailers and their markets
Government		The value of the business undertaken by governments is very high. Health, policing, education, transport, environmental protection, and national defence and security are a few of the areas that require public investment. Many of the larger projects that concern governments and associated ministries are large and complex and involve a huge number of stakeholders. Although similar in many ways to commercial purchasing procedures and guidelines, those in the government sector are subject to political objectives, budget policies, accountability, and EC Directives (van Weele, 2002)
Institutions		Institutions include not-for-profit organizations such as churches and charities, community-based organizations such as housing associations, and government-related organizations such as hospitals, schools, museums, libraries, and universities. Characteristically, institutions tend to form large buying groups. Through collaboration, the group is able to negotiate greatly reduced prices and much larger discounts, usually related to bulk purchases

▶ Market Insight 14.2

Dealing in Motorbikes

Honda sells over 12m motorcycles in the Asia Oceania region alone, and the management of its distribution networks is a vital element in maintaining customer access and satisfaction. Honda produces a wide range of motorcycles, ranging from the 50cc class to the 1,800cc class, and is the largest manufacturer of motorcycles in the world, in terms of annual units of production. In the region, Honda's motorcycles are produced at sites in Japan, Indonesia, Philippines, Pakistan, and India.

▶ Market Insight 14.2

Honda works with dealers worldwide providing support for sales, service, spare parts and safety
Source: Honda.

In Japan, sales of Honda motorcycles (and automobiles, and power products) are made through different distribution networks. Honda's products are sold to consumers primarily through independent retail dealers, and motorcycles are distributed through approximately 11,600 outlets, including approximately 1,400 PROS authorized dealerships. PROS dealerships sell all Honda's Japanese motorcycle models, not just selected models.

Most of Honda's overseas sales are made through its main sales subsidiaries, which distribute Honda's products to local wholesalers and retail dealers. In Indonesia, Honda has recently developed its dealer network of 4,000 dealers and service shops to support sales and provide excellent aftersales service. In the USA, Honda's wholly owned subsidiary markets Honda's motorcycle products through a sales network of approximately 1,260 independent local dealers.

Many of these motorcycle dealers also sell other Honda products.

In Europe, subsidiaries of the company in the UK, Germany, France, Belgium, the Netherlands, Spain, Switzerland, Austria, Italy, and other European countries distribute Honda's motorcycles through approximately 1,600 independent local dealers.

One core element of Honda's dealer strategy, worldwide, is its comprehensive 4S support system. This covers Sales, Service, Spare parts, and Safety. For example, in 2006, Honda provided its dealers in Thailand, Indonesia, Vietnam, and India with an easy-to-use riding simulator, called 'Riding Trainer', through which riders can get an opportunity to receive risk awareness training and riding practice and, of course, engagement with the Honda brand.

▶ Market Insight 14.2   (continued)

Recently a fifth S has been added, 'Second-Hand (or used)' business. In Thailand, for example, the second-hand motorcycle business has been deliberately strengthened as a means of developing business. The strategy encourages potential motorcycle owners and those ready for an upgrade to purchase pre-owned Honda models. This draws this segment into the brand.

Sources: www.world.honda.com/; www.findarticles.com/p/articles/; http://sec.edgar-online.com.

1 Why does Honda set up subsidiary organizations in each overseas region or country?

2 What do you think are the benefits of the 5S support system?

3 What might affect Honda's dealer network (marketing channel) in the future?

All of these types of B2B organizations, commercial, government, and institutions, buy goods and services on an interorganizational basis. Consumers are only involved through their interaction with retailers or as end users of health treatments, education, or policing for which no direct financial exchange occurs. The type of marketing activities used in order to encourage repeat exchanges between these various types of organization can be considerable. However, one common strategy has been the more overt approach to developing relationships through cooperation and collaboration. These issues are explored in Chapter 15.

▶ Research Insight 14.2

To take your learning further, you might wish to read this influential paper.

Achrol, R. S. (1997), 'Changes in the theory of interorganizational relations in marketing: toward a network paradigm', *Journal of the Academy of Marketing Science*, 25, 1, 56–71.

Achrol sets out how the then-established vertically integrated, multidivisional type of organization started to be replaced by new forms of network organization consisting of large numbers of functionally specialized firms tied together in cooperative exchange relationships. He considers four main types, the variables involved, the economic rationale, and the types of coordination and control mechanisms necessary for organizations to adapt to the new environment.

 Visit the **Online Resource Centre** to read the abstract and access the full paper.

Types of Business Goods and Services

Just as there are a variety of types of organizations in the business sector, so the products and services offered are equally varied and complex. Table 14.2 sets out the three principal business types of goods and services.

Most organizations, at various points in their development, have to decide whether to make/supply their own products and services or buy them in from outsourced providers. This 'make or buy' decision can have far-reaching effects not only on the strategic and operational aspects of an organization, but also on the purchasing function and its role within an organization.

Outsourcing is an increasingly popular activity practised by a wide range of organizations. As a result, purchasing behaviours have had to adapt accordingly, which, in turn, has impacted on business marketing. The development of 'lean management' techniques have enabled organizations to concentrate on their core processes and to outsource all other activities. As organizations have become 'leaner', they dramatically reduce their use of resources and the importance of purchasing increases (Durham and Ritchey, 2009).

▶ **Table 14.2** Types of business goods and services

Type of goods	Explanation
Input goods Raw materials, semi-manufactured parts, and finished goods	Input goods have been subjected to different levels of processing (*raw materials*, *semi-manufactured parts*, and *finished* goods), and they lose their individual identities and become part of the finished item
Equipment goods Otherwise known as capital or investment goods	These are necessary for manufacturing and operations to take place. Land and buildings, computer systems, and machine tools are all necessary to support the production process, but they cannot be identified in the finished product
Supply goods Otherwise known as maintenance, repair, and operating materials (MRO) items	These goods and services are 'consumables' as they are necessary to keep production processes and the organization running
	For example, lubricants, paints, screws, and cleaning materials may all be necessary to maintain a firm's operations. Computer or IT servicing is necessary to maintain operations and to avoid down time, whereas accounting audits are a legal requirement

go online

Visit the **Online Resource Centre** and complete Internet Activity 14.1 to learn more about how the internet is used to market computing software to business customers.

Organizational Buyer Behaviour

Only by appreciating the particular behaviour, purchasing systems, people, and policies used by an organization can suitable marketing and selling strategies be implemented. This section builds on the introduction to buyer processes made earlier in this chapter and the **organizational buyer behaviour** and segmentation information introduced in Chapter 6. It considers some of the key issues associated with the way organizations purchase the goods and services necessary to achieve their corporate goals.

Two definitions of organizational buyer behaviour reveal important aspects of this subject. First, Webster and Wind (1972) defined organizational buying as 'the decision making process by which formal organisations establish the need for purchased products and services and identify, evaluate and choose among alternative brands and suppliers'. This adopts a buying organization's perspective and highlights the important point that organizational buying behaviour involves processes rather than a single, static, one-off event. There are a number of stages, or phases, associated with product procurement, each one often requiring a key decision to be made. These are considered later.

A second definition, by Parkinson and Baker (1994: 6), cited by Ulkuniemi (2003), states that organizational buying behaviour concerns 'the purchase of a product or service to satisfy organisational rather than individual goals'. This takes a neutral perspective but makes the point that organizational buyer behaviour is about satisfying organization-wide needs, and hence requires marketers to adopt processes that take into account the needs of different people, not a single individual.

Organizational buying behaviour is about three key issues:

▶ The functions and processes buyers move through when purchasing products for use in business markets.

▶ Strategy, where purchasing is designed to assist value creation and competitive advantage, and to influence supply chain activities.

▶ The network of relationships that organizations are part of when purchasing. The placement of orders and contracts between organizations can confirm a current trading relationship, initiate a new set of relationships, or may even signal the demise of a relationship.

What should be clear is that organizational buying behaviour is not just about the purchase of goods and services. In addition to this fundamental task, it is concerned with the strategic development of the organization, creating value, and the management of interorganizational relationships, all key issues in B2B marketing. These issues overlap each other and are not discrete items.

Hollyoake (2009) argues that business marketing is increasingly about managing buyers' experiences and interactions. This involves creating expectations, often referred to as the brand promise, and then delivering products and services against these promises. It is important that a customer's evaluation of their experience be ahead of what was expected. Hollyoake develops these ideas to consider 'ease of doing business' as a measure of the supplier–customer relationship and to discover the key dimensions of the customer experience. He suggests that experiences are founded on four pillars; trust, interdependence, integrity, and communication. These ideas are also explored in the following chapter on Relationship Marketing.

Grönroos (2009) develops the principles about expectations into a new perspective of (business) marketing, referred to as Promise Management. These ideas are rooted in what

Grönroos sees as the purpose of contemporary marketing, namely as a value creation process. Firms are involved in developing and delivering value propositions (promises). These propositions of value can only be realized once an offering is consumed, and that can only be done by customers. Therefore, value creation is experienced only by customers as value fulfilment.

Decision-Making Units: Characteristics

Although organizations usually designate a 'buyer' who is responsible for the purchase of a range of products and services, in reality a range of people are involved in the purchasing process. The purchasing process is a means by which an organization creates value. It is, therefore, an integral part of an organization's value at some point in the future. This group of people is referred to as either the **decision-making unit** (DMU) or the **buying centre**. In many circumstances these are informal groupings of people who come together in varying ways to contribute to the decision-making process. Certain projects, usually of major significance or value, require a group of people to be formally constituted and who have express responsibility to oversee and complete the purchase of a stipulated item or products and services relating to a specific project.

DMUs vary in composition and size according to the nature of each individual purchasing task. Webster and Wind (1972) identified a number of people who undertake different roles within buying centres and these are set out in Figure 14.2.

Figure 14.2

Membership of the decision-making unit

Source: Fill and Fill (2005). Reproduced with the kind permission of Katolisys Ltd

Initiators start the whole process by requesting the purchase of an item. They may also assume other roles within the DMU or wider organization.

Users literally use the product once it has been acquired and they will also evaluate its performance. Users may not only initiate the purchase process but are sometimes involved in the specification process. Their role is continuous, although it may vary from the highly involved to the peripheral.

Influencers very often help set the technical specifications for the proposed purchase and assist the evaluation of alternative offerings by potential suppliers. These may be consultants hired to complete a particular project. For example, an office furniture manufacturer will regard office managers as key decision-makers but understand that specifiers such as office designers and architects influence the office manager's decision about furniture decisions.

▶ **Market Insight 14.3**

Alibaba Connects Global Buyers and Suppliers

The roles of influencers and decision-makers are important in the B2B buying process. When faced with risk, decision-makers buy from familiar companies. By providing appropriate information, opportunities can arise for building credibility and providing a sound platform for a long-term customer relationship.

Alibaba.com is a Chinese marketplace portal with more than 42m members, mainly buyers and suppliers, who can contact and trade with each other. In 2009, Alibaba launched a UK campaign encompassing TV, outdoor, and online, targeting small and medium businesses. Using the proposition 'working for you', it featured potential entrepreneurs, with the strapline, 'Whatever your business, get Alibaba.com working for you'.

One ad featured Minster Giftware, a small family business in Nottingham. The company is a direct importer and supplier of furnishing accessories to companies of all sizes throughout Europe. The ad showed how the owner, through using Alibaba.com, was able to research products, find samples and suppliers in just a single day, and then arrange three factory visits prior to launching a whole new product range at extremely competitive prices. Alibaba.com, therefore, enables suppliers to reach potential decision-makers, as well as buyers and influencers.

Source: www.alibaba.com/others/ibdm/emea_worksforyou/success-stories02.html.

1 **What do you think is the main difference between an influencer and an opinion former?**

2 **Think of an industry or sector with which you are familiar and try to determine possible influencers.**

3 **Visit the Alibaba website (www.alibaba.com) and list the advantages and disadvantages of using the site from a marketing perspective.**

Deciders are those who make purchasing decisions and they are the most difficult to identify. This is because they may not have formal authority to make a purchase decision, yet are sufficiently influential internally that their decision carries the most weight. In repeat buying activities the buyer may also be the decider. However, it is normal practice for a senior manager to authorize expenditure decisions involving sums over a certain financial limit.

Buyers or purchasing managers select suppliers and manage the process whereby the required products are procured. Buyers may not decide which product is to be purchased but they influence the framework within which the decision is made. They will formally undertake the process whereby products and services are purchased once a decision has been made to procure them. For example, they may be formal buyers and kick-start the purchase of a type of lubricant because the stock figures have fallen to a threshold level that indicates that current supplies will be exhausted within three weeks. They will, therefore, assume both the roles of an initiator and a buyer.

Gatekeepers have the potential to control the type and flow of information to the organization and the members of the DMU. These gatekeepers may be assistants, technical personnel, secretaries, or telephone switchboard operators.

The size and form of the buying centre is not static. It can vary according to the complexity of the product being considered and the degree of risk each decision is perceived to carry for the organization. Different roles are required and adopted as the nature of the buying task changes with each new purchase situation (Bonoma, 1982). All of these roles might be subsumed within one individual for certain decisions. It is vital for seller organizations to identify members of the buying centre and to target and refine their messages to meet the needs of each member of the centre.

Membership of the DMU is far from fixed, and this fluidity poses problems for selling organizations simply because it is not always possible to identify key members or shifts in policy or requirements. As Spekman and Gronhaug (1986) point out, the DMU is a 'vague construct that can reach across a number of different functional roles with any number of individuals participating or exerting influence at any one time'. It is worth noting, therefore, that within this context the behaviour of DMU members is also largely determined by the interpersonal relationships of the members of the centre.

▶ Research Insight 14.3

To take your learning further, you might wish to read this influential paper.

Johnson, W. J., and Lewin, J. E. (1996), 'Organizational buying behavior: toward an integrative framework', *Journal of Business Research*, 35 (January), 1–15.

Although written in 1996, this paper is important because it includes critical contributions by the leading researchers including the work of Robinson, Faris, and Wind (1967), Webster and Wind (1972), and Sheth (1973). It concludes by developing a model of buying behaviour drawing on a number of constructs developed since these three leading models were published.

@ Visit the **Online Resource Centre** to read the abstract and access the full paper.

The Decision-Making Unit: Processes

Organizational buying decisions vary in terms of the nature of the product or service, the frequency and the relative value of purchases, their strategic impact (if any), and the type of relationship with suppliers. These, and many other factors, are potentially significant to individual buying organizations. However, there are three main types of buying situations. Referred to by Robinson, Faris, and Wind (1967) as buyclasses these are: **new task**, **modified rebuy**, and **straight rebuy**. These are summarized in Table 14.3.

▶ **Table 14.3** Main characteristics of the buyclasses

Buyclass	Degree of familiarity with the problem	Information requirements	Alternative solutions
New task	The problem is fresh to the decision-makers	A great deal of information is required	Alternative solutions are unknown, all are considered new
Modified rebuy	The requirement is not new but is different from previous situations	More information is required but past experience is of use	Buying decision needs new solutions
Rebuy	The problem is identical to previous experiences	Little or no information is required	Alternative solutions not sought or required

Source: Marketing Communications, C. Fill (2009), Pearson Education Limited. Reproduced with the kind permission of Pearson Education Limited.

Buyclasses

New Task

As the name implies, the organization is faced with a first-time buying situation. Risk is inevitably large at this point as there is little collective experience of the product/service or of the relevant suppliers. As a result of these factors there are normally a large number of decision participants. Each participant requires a lot of information and a relatively long period of time is needed for the information to be assimilated and a decision to be made.

Modified Rebuy

Having purchased a product, uncertainty is reduced but not eliminated, so the organization may request through their buyer(s) that certain modifications be made to future purchases. For example, adjustments to the specification of the product, further negotiation on price levels, or perhaps an arrangement for alternative delivery patterns. Fewer people are involved in the decision-making process than in the new task situation.

Straight Rebuy

In this situation, the purchasing department reorders on a routine basis, very often working from an approved list of suppliers. These may be products that an organization consumes in order to keep operating (e.g. office stationery), or may be low-value materials used within the operational, value-added part of the organization (e.g. the manufacturing processes). No other people are involved with the exercise until different suppliers attempt to change the environment in which the decision is made. For example, a new supplier may interrupt the procedure with a potentially better offer. This may stimulate the emergence of a modified rebuy situation.

Straight rebuy presents classic conditions for the use of automatic reordering systems. Costs can be reduced, managerial time redirected to other projects, and the relationship between buyer and seller embedded within a stronger framework. One possible difficulty is that both parties perceive the system to be a significant exit barrier should conditions change, and this may deter flexibility or restrict opportunities to develop the same or other relationships.

The use of electronic purchasing systems at the straight rebuy stage has enabled organizations to empower employees to make purchases, although control still resides with purchasing managers. Employees can buy direct online, from a catalogue list of authorized suppliers. The benefits are that employees are more involved, the purchasing process is speeded up, costs are reduced, and purchasing managers can spend more time with other higher priority activities.

go online

Visit the **Online Resource Centre** and follow the weblink to Electronic Commerce Europe, the biggest online trade network in the world, for more information on the use of electronic B2B purchasing.

Buyphases

Organizational buyer behaviour (OBB) consists of a series of sequential activities through which organizations proceed when making purchasing decisions. Robinson, Faris, and Wind (1967) referred to these as buying stages or buyphases. The following sequence of buyphases is particular to the new task situation just described. Many of these buyphases are ignored or compressed according to the complexity of the product and when either a modified rebuy or straight rebuy situation is encountered.

Need/Problem Recognition

The need/recognition phase is about the identification of a gap. This is the gap between the benefits an organization is experiencing now and the benefits it would like to have. For example, when a new product is to be produced there is an obvious gap between having the necessary materials and components and being out of stock and unable to build. The first decision, therefore, is about how to close this gap and there are two broad options: outsourcing the whole or parts of the production process, or building or making the objects oneself. The need has been recognized and the gap identified. The rest of this section is based on a build decision being taken.

Product Specification

As a result of identifying a problem and the size of the gap, influencers and users can determine the desired characteristics of the product needed to resolve the problem. This may take the form of either a general functional description or a much more detailed analysis and the creation of a detailed technical specification for a particular product. What sort of photocopier is required? What is it expected to achieve? How many documents should it copy per minute? Is a collator or tray required? This is an important part of the process, because if it is executed properly it will narrow the supplier search and save on the costs associated with evaluation prior to a final decision. The results of the functional and detailed specifications are often combined within a purchase order specification.

Supplier and Product Search

At this stage the buyer actively seeks suppliers who can supply the necessary product(s). There are two main issues at this point. First, will the product match the specification and the required performance standards? Second, will the potential supplier meet the other organizational requirements such as experience, reputation, accreditation, and credit rating? In most circumstances, organizations review the market and their internal sources of information and arrive at a decision that is based on rational criteria.

Organizations work, wherever possible, to reduce uncertainty and risk. By working with others who are known, of whom the organization has direct experience, and who can be trusted, risk and uncertainty can be reduced substantially. This highlights another reason why many organizations prefer to operate within established networks that can provide support and advice when needed.

Evaluation of Proposals

Depending on the complexity and value of the potential order(s), the proposal is a vital part of the process and should be prepared professionally. The proposals from the shortlisted organizations are reviewed in the context of two main criteria: the purchase order specification and the evaluation of the supplying organization. If the potential supplier is already a part of the network, little search and review time is needed. If the proposed supplier is not part of the network, a review may be necessary to establish whether it will be appropriate (in terms of price, delivery, and service) and whether there is the potential for a long-term relationship or whether this is a single purchase that is unlikely to be repeated.

Supplier Selection

The DMU will normally undertake a supplier analysis and use a variety of decision criteria, according to the particular type of item sought. This selection process takes place in the light of the comments made in the previous section. A further useful perspective is to view supplier organizations as a continuum, from reliance on a single source to the use of a wide variety of suppliers for the same product.

Jackson (1985) proposed that organizations might buy a product from a range of different suppliers, in other words maintain a range of multiple sources (a practice of many government departments). She labelled this approach 'always a share', as several suppliers are given the opportunity to share the business available to the buying centre. The major disadvantage is that this approach fails to drive cost as low as possible, as the discounts derived from volume sales are not achieved. The advantage to the buying centre is that a relatively small investment is required and little risk is entailed in following such a strategy.

At the other end of the continuum are organizations that only use a single source supplier. All purchases are made from the single source until circumstances change to such a degree that the buyer's needs are no longer being satisfied. Jackson referred to these organizations as 'lost for good', because once a relationship with a new organization has been developed they are lost for good to the original supplier. An increasing number of organizations are choosing to enter alliances with a limited number or even single source suppliers. The objective is to build a long-term relationship, to work together to build quality and help each other achieve their goals. Outsourcing manufacturing activities for non-core activities has increased considerably.

Evaluation

The order is written against the selected supplier, which is then monitored and evaluated against such diverse criteria as responsiveness to enquiries, modifications to the specification, and timing of delivery. When the product is delivered it may reach the stated specification but fail to satisfy the original need. In this case, the specification needs to be rewritten before any future orders are placed.

Developments in the environment can impact on organizational buyers and change both the nature of decisions and the way they are made. For example, the decision to purchase new plant and machinery requires consideration of the future cash flows generated by the capital item. Many people will be involved in the decision, and the time necessary for consultation may mean that other parts of the decision-making process are completed simultaneously.

Buygrids

When the buyphases are linked to the buyclasses, a buygrid is determined. This grid is shown in Table 14.4.

▶ **Table 14.4** The buygrid framework

Buyphases	Buyclasses		
	New task	Modified rebuy	Straight rebuy
Problem recognition	Yes	Possibly	No
General need description	Yes	Possibly	No
Product specification	Yes	Yes	Yes
Supplier search	Yes	Possibly	No
Supplier selection	Yes	Possibly	No
Order process specification	Yes	Possibly	No
Performance review	Yes	Yes	Yes

The buygrid serves to illustrate the relationships between these two main elements. The buygrid is important because it highlights the need to focus on buying situations or contexts, rather than on products. Even though this approach was developed over 40 years ago, it is still an important foundation for this topic.

According to the buyphase model, buyers make decisions rationally and sequentially, but this does not entirely match with practical experience. For example, such a long and complex process is not evident in every buying situation and differs according to the kind of products and services bought, the experience and resources available to organizations, and the prevailing culture. In other words, there are many variables that can influence organizational buying behaviour.

The Role of Purchasing in Organizations

All organizations have to buy a variety of products and services in order to operate normally and achieve their performance targets. What we have set out so far are the general principles, types, and categories associated with organizational buying. However, the way in which organizations buy products and services varies considerably and does not always fit neatly with the categories presented here. Professional purchasing is not only an important (if not critical) feature, but also for many organizations it is an integral part of their overall operations and strategic orientation (Ryals and Rogers, 2006; Pressey, Tzokas, and Winklhofer, 2007).

In the past, an organization's purchasing activities could have been characterized as an 'order-delivery response function'. Purchasing departments signed orders and the right deliveries were made at the right place, at the right time, and then invoiced correctly. The goal was to play off one supplier against another, and, as a result, reduce costs and improve short-term profits. Purchasing departments used to be regarded as an isolated function within organizations, a necessary but uninteresting aspect of organizational performance.

That perspective changed towards the end of the last century. Now organizations reduce the number of their suppliers, sometimes to just one, and **strategic procurement** (as it is often termed) is used to negotiate with suppliers on a cooperative basis, in order to help build long-term relationships. Purchasing has become an integral part of an organization's operations.

One of the main reasons for this changed approach was research that showed that business performance improves when organizations adopt a collaborative, rather than adversarial, approach to purchasing and account management (Swinder and Seshadri, 2001). However, there are several other related issues that have changed the role of purchasing, namely, customer sophistication, increasing competition, and various strategic issues.

Customer Sophistication

Due to increasing customer sophistication, organizations are trying to differentiate their offerings and become more specialized. Organizational purchasing has to follow this movement and also become more specialized, otherwise the organization will become increasingly ineffective in meeting customer needs.

Increasing Competition

With increasing competition, margins have been eroded. As a result, more attention has been given to internal costs and operations. By influencing purchasing costs and managerial costs associated with dealing with multiple suppliers, the profitability of the organization can be directly impacted. Consequently, the importance of purchasing polices, processes, and procedures within organizations have increased.

Strategic Issues

There are several strategic issues related to the purchasing activities undertaken by organizations. First, there is the 'make or buy' decision. Should organizations make and/or assemble products for resale, or outsource or buy in particular products, parts, services, or sub-assemblies and concentrate on what is referred to as core activities or competences? Second, the benefits that arise through closer cooperation with suppliers and the increasing influence of buyer–seller relationships and 'joint value creation' have inevitably led to a tighter, more professional, and integrated purchasing function. The third strategy-related issue concerns the degree to which the purchasing function is integrated into the organization. New IT systems have raised the level of possible integration of purchasing and operations to the extent that the competitive strength of the organization is enhanced (Laios and Moschuris, 2001; Hemsworth, Sánchez-Rodríguez, and Bidgood, 2008).

As if to highlight the variation in approaches to purchasing behaviour, Svahn and Westerlund (2009) identify six principal purchasing strategies used by organizations. The 'price minimizer' purchasing strategy refers to a buyer's efficiency orientation where the main purchasing goal is to seek the lowest price for the product. To help achieve this, the buyer actively promotes competition among several potential suppliers.

The 'bargainer' purchasing strategy, focuses on a dyadic buyer–seller relationship. Here, the buyer's strategy is to achieve operational efficiency through long-term collaboration with a selected supplier (Anderson and Narus, 1999; Håkansson and Snehota, 1995; Grönroos, 1994). The 'clockwiser' purchasing strategy refers to network relationships that function predictably and precisely, just as a clock works. Again, the goal is strict efficiency, achieved through the vigilant integration of production-based integrated control systems and IT, and the careful coordination of the value activities performed by each supply network partner (Glenn and Wheeler, 2004).

The 'adaptator' purchasing strategies focus on adapting the manufacturing processes between the exchange parties. This can arise during the purchase of one major product or service when the seller is required to accommodate its product to the particular needs of the buyer. The 'projector' purchasing strategy occurs between buyers and sellers who are development partners. This can occur during projects when partners develop their products and

Nokia and Skype join R&D efforts for new VOIP mobile service

Source: Courtesy of Skype.

services in close collaboration, after which the joint-development project is completed and the parties continue the development work independently. As an example of this strategy, we could explore the collaboration between Nokia and Skype. These major players in the information and communication technology industry joined their development efforts in order to develop a radically novel type of mobile phone that utilizes the voice-over-internet service (the free call system created by Skype).

The 'updator' purchasing strategy is based on collaboration in research and development. Here, collaboration between partners is continuous and the nature of the relationship is not a dyad but a supply network. This collaboration is intentional as demonstrated by Intel and various PC manufacturers, who produce updated versions of personal computers due to constant co-development.

Customer Portfolio Matrix

These six core strategies reflect the complexity and the variety of purchasing activities undertaken by buying organizations. Most supplying organizations have a mixture of different types of customers or accounts. Each account varies in terms of frequency of purchase, types of products and services bought, prices paid, delivery cycles, time taken to pay, the level of support required, purchasing strategies, and many other factors. These variables are partly a reflection of the strength of the relationship between buyer and seller and they impact on the profitability each account represents to the seller.

It makes sense, therefore, to categorize customers in order to determine their relative profitability. This, in turn, enables sellers to allocate resources to customers according to their potential to deliver profits in the future. One useful approach, called a **customer (or account) portfolio matrix**, brings together the potential attractiveness and the current strength of the relationship between seller and buyer (see Figure 14.3).

The relationship dimension incorporates the strengths from a customer's perspective relative to competitors. A strong relationship, for example, is indicative of two organizations working closely together, whereas a weak relationship suggests that there is little interest in each other. Customer attractiveness refers to total revenue spend, average rate of growth, and the

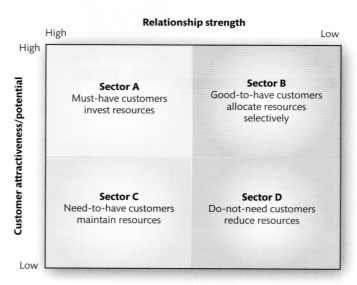

Figure 14.3

Customer portfolio matrix

opportunities a buyer represents to the seller in terms of their profit potential. These calculations can be complicated and involve a measure of management judgment. For reasons of clarity, these scales are presented as either high or low, strong or weak. However, they should be considered as a continuum and accounts can be positioned on the matrix, not just in a sector but at a particular position within a sector. As a result strategies can be formulated to move accounts to different positions, which, in turn, necessitate the use of different resources.

'Must-Have Customers' in Sector A enjoy a close business relationship and are also attractive in terms of their profit potential. Many of these customers are assigned key account status (see next section in this chapter), but all represent investment opportunities and resources should be allocated to develop them all.

'Good-to-Have Customers' in Sector B are essentially prospects because, although they are highly attractive, their relationship with the seller is currently weak. In this situation, marketing resources should be allocated on a selective basis, one that is proportional to the value that each prospect represents: high investment for good prospects and low for the others.

Relationships with customers in Sector C are strong but they do not offer strong potential. Therefore, these 'Need-to-Have Customers' are important because they provide steady background business that is marginally profitable, so resources need to be maintained. Where it is identified that some of these customers are supported by a relatively large sales team, significant cost-savings can be achieved relatively quickly. There is little reason to invest in the 'Do-Not-Need Customers' in Sector D. Relationships with these customers are weak, and, as they are relatively unattractive in terms of profit potential, many of these customers should be 'let go' and released to competitors. They represent a net drain on the selling organization. Therefore, customers in this sector should receive little support and freed-up resources be directed to customers in sectors A and B, as previously established.

One of the benefits of developing a **customer portfolio matrix** is that it becomes easier to allocate sales channels to customers. Multichannel marketing decisions are important and should be rooted within the customer portfolio matrix. A range of channel strategies that relate to the channel needs of business customers and to any end user target consumer segments can be identified (Payne and Frow, 2004). These can be considered to be part of a spectrum. At one end, channels can consist of a dedicated, personal key account manager (highly personalized sales channel), and, at the other end, the channel can be purely electronic with no personal contact at all. In the middle, there will be a range of different combinations of personal and electronic channels (see Figure 14.4).

In reality, most business customers will use a mixture of online and offline resources wherever possible and according to their specific needs. It is important, therefore, for selling organizations to identify and allocate the most appropriate set of channels for their customers, based on the business potential each customer represents. These channels can be changed as the intensity of a customer relationship and their attractiveness develops over time.

Figure 14.4

A spectrum of multi-channel strategies

Key Account Management (KAM)

It should be clear from the previous section that not all customers represent the same potential and profitability. However, it is quite common for a small number of customers to contribute to a disproportionately large part of an organization's income and profitability. As a result, these organizations often become essential to the firm's survival. The term **key accounts** has become the established term to refer to those customers who are considered to be strategically important. A key account might offer the supply side company opportunities to learn about new markets or types of customers. It might provide access to new and valuable resources, offer involvement with other key organizations, or just be symbolically valuable in terms of influence, power, and stature. Size alone is not sufficient for key account status. (See Market Insight 14.4.)

▶ Market Insight 14.4

Castrol Use the World Cup for B2B Campaign

The Castrol lubricants business launched a 12-month B2B campaign in August 2009 based on its official sponsorship of the 2010 FIFA World Cup™. Aimed at decision-makers in its Aviation, Industrial, Marine, and Energy sectors, the 'more than just oil' corporate message was used on the back of the football sponsorship initiative to reinforce the brand via B2B web portals. The challenge was to link technical industries to football, and this was achieved through a performance theme.

Castrol ran print-based ads in the trade media to promote the gaming element of the campaign, including a 'Performance Manager' style game, allowing participants to make their football dream team and offering the chance to win tickets to the 2010 FIFA World Cup™. An internal, employee mini-league and reward programme was also created around the theme of 'winning performance'.

The online media reflected the global scope of the campaign and also provided a functional benefit. As some of Castrol's target customers are based on ships and offshore rigs, access to trade magazines is limited but they can easily get access to the website. Groups

Castrol, BP's lubricants business, sponsors the 2010 FIFA World Cup

Source: Image courtesy of Castrol, photo by Orckid design.

▶ Market Insight 14.4

have even been set up on Facebook and LinkedIn, for people to share knowledge, or just talk about football.

Football-themed customer events were held at B2B trade shows and conferences around the world. For example, the Offshore Europe Exhibition in Aberdeen attracts over 1,500 suppliers of offshore technology and service developments. Castrol used brand ambassadors such as Christiano Ronaldo, Marcel Desailly, and the Arsenal manager Arsène Wenger, all chosen to reflect rigour, passion, and a strategic approach.

Sources: Fisher (2009); Crawley-Boevey (2009); Barda (2010).

1 Why might the World Cup sponsorship have helped or hindered Castrol's B2B campaign?

2 What similarities with consumer marketing can be identified in the Castrol B2B campaign?

3 Identify a major forthcoming sporting event, find one of its premier sponsors, visit their website, and find out if they have partnership arrangements with other organizations.

Establishing key accounts and the supporting infrastructure represents a significant investment for organizations and an opportunity cost.

go online

Visit the **Online Resource Centre** and complete Internet Activity 14.2 to learn more about the use of **salesforce automation** (SFA) applications to aid the management of key client accounts.

So, why have so many organizations established and formalized their key account strategies? There are many reasons, some particular to each organization; however, the main ones relate to changes in the competitive environment and to changes in industry structure.

Changes in the Competitive Environment

In an increasingly complex and competitive environment, where product lifecycles appear to be getting shorter, and differentiation difficult to sustain, the need to find new ways of enhancing business performance has intensified. One of the ways in which this can be achieved is to provide a range of services that are tailored to the needs of each customer.

Many types of service can be customized, for example customized training, advantageous financial arrangements, extranets, customer-driven delivery routes and timings, product support, and advice facilities. However, it is through the provision of added-value services that relationships are often developed and maintained. Establishing key accounts is a natural extension of providing particular services for key customers. Not only does this enhance the profile of these customers, both internally and externally, but it also helps to focus resources on particular customers and their individual needs.

Changes in Industry Structure

Many organizations have centralized their purchasing activities, a move driven by two main factors. First, the amount of industry consolidation, a process by which a few organizations grow larger by merging or acquiring their competitors, so that the industry is concentrated around a small number of large organizations. Industry consolidation has increased substantially in recent years. Second, in industries where consolidation has not been significant, many organizations have moved towards centralizing their purchasing departments, processes, and functions as a means of achieving cost-savings, improving effectiveness and efficiencies, and, in doing so, improving profits. ABB Sweden is a global corporation operating in a variety of industry segments, including power generation, pulp and paper, water, and chemicals. Brehmer and Rehme (2009) evaluate the way in which ABB Sweden used three different approaches to key account programmes, recognizing sales opportunities, customer demands, and a need to be more customer-focused.

The result of both of these actions is that there are a smaller number of purchasing units responsible for a larger proportion of business. For business marketers and suppliers generally, these trends towards industrial concentration and purchasing centralization mean that competition is increased and marketing strategies need to be much more customer-specific. Key account programmes are used with the deliberate intention of building relationships, often achieved by influencing levels of trust and commitment in order to generate more business.

However, in relationships between manufacturers and retailers (e.g. the grocery business), the presence of a key account relationship does not appear to have any significant benefit on the amount of resources allocated to the supplier's products (Verbeke, Bagozzi, and Farris, 2006).

Key Account Relationship Cycles

Key accounts do not just appear and flourish, they are the result of careful management, nurturing, and time. Key accounts represent a particular strength of relationship and, as with good wine, need time to develop to reach full potential. Consequently, each key account will, at any one moment in time, be at a particular stage of relationship development (Millman and Wilson, 1995). Key accounts can be plotted through various stages of a **KAM development cycle**. One such cycle is shown in Table 14.5.

▶ **Table 14.5** Key account management development stages

Development stages within a cycle	Explanation
Exploratory	Suppliers identify and isolate those customer accounts that have key account potential
Basic	In this transactional period, exchanges are used by both parties to test each other as potential long-term partners
Cooperative	An increasing number of people from both parties become involved in the relationship

Development stages within a cycle	Explanation
Interdependent	Mutual recognition of each other's importance. Very often single supplier status is conferred
Integrated	Both parties share sensitive information and undertake joint problem solving. The relationship is regarded as a single entity
Disintegrated	The termination or readjustment of the relationship can occur at any time

The time between stages is not fixed and varies according to the nature and circumstances of the parties involved. The stages can be negotiated quickly in some cases, or may become protracted. The titles to each of the stages reflect the relationship status of both parties rather than of the selling company (e.g. prospective) or buying company (e.g. preferred supplier).

Managing Key Accounts

Key account managers provide the main link between their employer and their key account customers. They provide a route through which information flows, preferably in both directions. They must be capable of dealing with organizations where buying decisions can be both protracted and delayed (Sharma, 1997), and quick and demanding. However, key account managers do not operate alone and are not the sole point of contact between organizations. Normally, there are a number of levels of interaction between the two organizations, to the extent that there could be 'an entire team dedicated to providing services and support to the key account' (Ojasalo, 2001: 109). Therefore, key account managers assume responsibility for all points of contact within the customer organization.

The value that a customer derives from a particular product will have a significant influence on the level of attention given by the buyer to the supplier's programme. Furthermore, the level to which an organization uses centralized buying procedures will also impact on the effectiveness of a KAM programme. Unsurprisingly, key account sales behaviours cannot be the same as those used in field sales roles. So, as the majority of key account managers are drawn internally from the sales force (Hannah, 1998, cited by Abratt and Kelly, 2002), it is necessary to ensure that they have the correct skills mix, or are trained appropriately. Abratt and Kelly found six factors that were of particular importance when establishing a KAM programme. These were the 'suitability of the key account manager, knowledge and understanding of the key account customer's business, commitment to the KAM partnership, delivering value, the importance of trust and the proper implementation and understanding of the KAM concept'.

In addition to the interpersonal relationships that exist between the customer's contact person and the supplier's key account manager, there are also interorganizational relationships that may concern system and policy issues. These will vary in strength and some may not be compatible with the tasks facing the key account manager (Benedapudi and Leone, 2002).

▶ Research Insight 14.4

 To take your learning further, you might wish to read this influential paper.

Millman, T., and Wilson, K. (1995), 'From key account selling to key account management', *Journal of Marketing Practice: Applied Marketing Science*, 1, 1, 9–21.

This paper is interesting because it was one of the first to focus attention on key account management (KAM) systems by taking into consideration the issues faced by buyers, when developing buyer–seller relationships. Previous research had adopted a seller-only perspective. The authors examine the nature of KAM in industrial markets structured around several strategic issues.

Visit the **Online Resource Centre** to read the abstract and access the full paper.

A Comparison of B2B and B2C Buying Characteristics

So far in this chapter, we have considered various characteristics of the business market. These include the different types of products and services, the variety of customers, the processes used to buy business products and services, and the key account management systems used by suppliers to reach and develop relationships with business customers. What do these factors contribute to our understanding of B2B marketing?

Well, overall, the marketing of goods and services between organizations is not the same as consumer goods marketing and, because there are a number of fundamentally different characteristics, diverse marketing strategies and operations need to be implemented to meet the needs of business customers.

Differences

Business marketing can be distinguished from consumer marketing by two main ideas: first the intended customer, which is an organization not an individual; second, the intended use of the product, which is to support organizational objectives. As a result, different marketing programmes are required to reach and influence organizational buyers as opposed to consumers.

In the business sector, organizations buy a range of products and services to either make new products or enable production processes to operate successfully. Defined processes and procedures are used to buy products and services, and the decisions attached to securing the necessary materials, unlike consumer-based decisions, very often involve a large number of people.

Many of the key differences between consumer and business marketing are rooted in the principal characteristics associated with the respective buying behaviours. These are set out in Table 14.6.

One of the main characteristics is that there are far fewer buyers in organizational markets than in consumer markets. Even though there may be several people associated with a buying decision in an organization, the overall number of people involved in buying packaging products or road construction equipment (for example) is very small compared with the millions of people that might potentially buy a chocolate bar.

The financial value of organizational purchase orders is invariably larger and the frequency with which they are placed is much lower. It is quite common for agreements to be made between organizations for the supply of materials over a number of years. Similarly, depending on the complexity of the product (e.g., photocopying paper or a one-off satellite), the negotiation process may also take a long time.

▶ **Table 14.6** A comparison of buying characteristics in organizational and consumer markets

	Consumer buying characteristics	Organizational buying characteristics
No. of buyers	Many	Few
Purchase initiation	Self	Others
Evaluative criteria	Social, ego, and level of utility	Price, value, and level of utility
Information search	Normally short	Normally long
Range of suppliers used	Small number of suppliers considered	Can be extensive
Importance of supplier choice	Normally limited	Can be critical
Size of orders	Small	Large
Frequency of orders	Light	High
Value of orders placed	Light	Heavy
Complexity of decision-making	Light to moderate	Moderate to high
Range of information inputs	Moderate	Moderate to high

Source: Fill and Fill (2005). Used with permission.

Although there are differences, many of the characteristics associated with consumer deci-sion-making processes can still be observed in the organizational context. However, organi-zational buyers make decisions that ultimately contribute to the achievement of corporate objectives. To make the necessary decisions, a high volume of pertinent information is often required. This information needs to be relatively detailed and is normally presented in a rational and logical style. The needs of the buyers are many and complex, and some may be personal. Goals, such as promotion and career advancement within the organization, coupled with ego and employee satisfaction, combine to make organizational buying an important task. It is one that requires professional training and the development of expertise if the role is to be performed optimally.

Similarities

Although there are many differences between the B2C and B2B sectors, there are also an increasing number of areas where the two converge. Two of the most important similari-ties emerge through market orientation, regardless of the sector in which an organization operates.

Both have a customer orientation and work backwards from an understanding of customer needs. Both need the ability to gather, process, and use information about customers and competitors in order to achieve their objectives.

In addition, both types of supplier desire positive relationships with their customers. It does not matter whether they are consumers or organizations, what is wanted is that the relationship is continued for mutual benefit.

The fundamental notion that organizational decision-making is basically rational in nature and that consumer decision-making is more unstructured and emotionally driven is question-able. For example, many personal purchases are of such technical complexity (e.g. financial services) that consumers need to adopt a more rational, factual-based approach to their buy-ing. Some business-oriented decisions are made on the basis of social contacts, consisting mainly of family and friendship networks.

Wilson (2000) explores some of these issues of similarity and observes that consumers use a wide range of inputs from other people and not just those in the immediate fam-ily environment when making product-related purchase decisions. This is similar to group-buying dynamics associated with the DMU. He also suggests that the rationality normally associated with organizational decision-making is misplaced, because in some circumstances the protracted nature of the process is more a reflection of organizational culture and the need to follow bureaucratic procedures and to show due diligence. In addition, issues con-cerning established behaviour patterns, difficulties, and reluctance to break with traditional purchasing practices, intra- and interorganizational politics and relationships, and the costs associated with supplier switching all contribute to a more interpretative understanding of organizational decision-making. Further support for this view is given by Mason and Gray (1999), who refer to the characteristics of decision-making in the air travel market and note some strong similarities between consumers and business passengers.

▶ Research Insight 14.5

To take your learning further, you might wish to read this influential paper.

Gummesson, E. and Polese, F. (2009), 'B2B is not an island!', *Journal of Business & Industrial Marketing*, 24, 5/6, 337–50.

This conceptual paper is based on network theory and case study research. It considers customers as part of value networks and treats B2B and B2C as elements within a larger marketing context, not as independent categories. This represents a new approach to understanding B2B and B2C marketing. A timely contribution.

 Visit the **Online Resource Centre** to read the abstract and access the full paper.

It is also interesting to observe the similarities between the extended problem solving, limited problem solving, and routinized response behaviour phases of consumer buying and the new task, modified rebuy, and rebuy states associated with organizational buying. There is a close match between the two in terms of the purpose, approach, and content. Risk and involvement are relevant to both categories and, although the background to both may vary, the principles used to manage the various phases and conditions are essentially the same, just deployed in different ways.

One further area of similarity concerns branding. In consumer markets, branding is common practice and for a long time was not thought to be of direct concern to business marketers. Now, however, B2B organizations use a variety of branding approaches. Ingredient branding (Intel Inside and Lycra), cause-related branding, cooperative advertising, and dual branding, in addition to joint advertising and sales promotion activities, are all used to raise perceived value (Bengtsson and Servais, 2005). Traditionally, trucking companies have not paid much attention to the way they present themselves. When Eddie Stobart recognized this in the UK trucking market, he used it as a branding opportunity. In addition to the distinctive livery, he ensured his trucks were always clean, that his drivers wore the company's green shirt and tie, and that his operation ran efficiently and always on time. As a result, the Eddie Stobart brand stands out and helps justify a substantial price premium (Hague, 2006).

It is important to recognize that, although there are some substantial differences between consumer and business marketing, there are also several areas where there are distinct

Eddie Stobart, the supply chain company, takes branding seriously
Source: Eddie Stobart Ltd.

similarities. This suggests that the principles of marketing apply equally to the consumer and business markets, and, when planning and implementing marketing programmes, particular care should be given to understanding the nature and characteristics of the buying processes and procedures of the target market.

▶ Market Insight 14.5

Alenia's Networking Flags Some Similarities

As if to demonstrate the similarities rather than the differences, Gummesson and Polese (2009) consider the various B2B, C2B, B2C, C2C combinations that can be identified in different industries. Alenia Aeronautica, a Finmeccanica Company, supplies Boeing, Airbus, and the US Department of Defense among others with various specialized units. The industry is experiencing rapid change, with the number of prime suppliers reduced from seven to eight, to two to three, whereas the number of smaller prime suppliers has

fallen from over 50 to just five to eight. Once there were over 1,000 component suppliers, now there are just 50.

However, all of these organizations are involved in a complex interacting network, all contribute value to the whole chain of suppliers. The Alenia/Boeing relationship is direct B2B, as is Boeing's relationships with the airlines that buy their aircraft. The airlines have close B2C relationships with their customers, essentially passengers. When passengers interact with passengers it is C2C (chat rooms, blogs, communities), but when they interact with the airline with a view to influencing them about food, comfort, entertainment or air-quality issues, this is often through the cabin crew and represents C2B interaction. This information

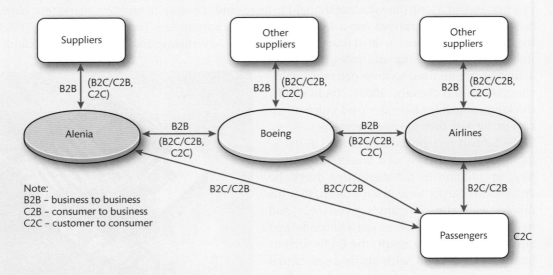

Note:
B2B – business to business
C2B – consumer to business
C2C – customer to consumer

Figure 14.5

Alenia Aeronautica's network of relationships

Source: Gummesson, E. and Polese, F. (2009) 'B2B is not an island!', *Journal of Business & Industrial Marketing*, 24, 5/6 , 337–50 © Emerald Group Publishing Limited all rights reserved.

▶ Market Insight 14.5

Boeing 787 fuselage panel being produced in Grottaglie, Italy

Source: Alenia Aeronautica media gallery.

is then manifest in future orders to Airbus and passed back to Alenia, albeit as indirect interaction, in the form of specifications, updates, and revision. This, in turn, gets passed on by Alenia to its supply network as orders. Alenia is increasingly asking for access to information arising either through the C2C interaction or through Airbus's relationships with the different airlines. Early information means that the development process can be sped up and so add value to the network. See Figure 14.5 for a representation of these various relationships and interactions.

Source: Gummesson and Polese (2009).

1   What are the implications of Alenia's various indirect relationships for its marketing activities?

2   How might Alenia's marketing programmes meet B2B and B2C needs?

3   Think of an industry with which you are familiar and make a list of the different B2B, B2C, C2B, and C2C relationships.

Skills for Employment

> In addition to reviewing applicants' grades we also look for candidates who can demonstrate initiative and are willing to try new things. An ability to get things done and to utilize creative problem skills are key. We also look for a strong ability to listen and, importantly, an understanding of how a task fits into the overall structure. ◀◀
>
> **Sandeep Tiwari, CEO, Zafesoft Inc.**
>
> Visit the **Online Resource Centre** to discover more tips and advice on skills for the workplace.

Chapter Summary

To consolidate your learning, the key points from this chapter are summarized below:

■ **Explain the main characteristics of business markets.**

Business markets are characterized by four main factors: the nature of demand, the buying processes, international dimensions, and the relationships that develop between organizations.

■ **Understand the different types of organizational customers.**

There are a range of organizations that make up business markets and these are classified as commercial, government, and institutional. These organizations buy products and services to make goods for resale to their customers, but they also consume items that are required to keep their offices and manufacturing units functioning.

■ **Describe the different types of goods and services that are sold and bought in business markets.**

Products and services bought and sold through business markets are categorized as input goods, equipment goods, and supply goods.

■ **Explain the main processes and stages associated with organizational buying and purchasing.**

Organizational buying behaviour can be understood to be a group buying activity in which a number of people with differing roles make purchasing decisions that affect the organization and the achievement of its objectives. Buying decisions can be understood in terms of different types of decisions (buyclasses) and different stages (buyphases).

■ **Understand the principles of key account management.**

Some suppliers refer to some of their strategically important customers as key accounts. Relationships with these customers move through various stages, called key account management development cycles. Each stage is marked by particular characteristics and part of the role of the key account manager is to ensure that all contact between the supplier and the customer builds on strengthening the interorganizational relationship.

■ **Explain what business-to-business marketing is.**

B2B marketing is concerned with the identification and satisfaction of business customers' needs. This requires that all stakeholders benefit from the business relationship and associated transactions.

Customers derive satisfaction by purchasing goods and services that are perceived to provide them and/or their organizations with particular value.

■ **Compare business and consumer marketing.**

Both have a customer orientation and work backwards from an understanding of customer needs. In addition, both require information about customers and competitors in order to achieve their objectives. There is a close match in terms of the purpose, approach, and content between the extended problem solving, limited problem solving, and routinized response behaviour phases of consumer buying and the new task, modified rebuy, and rebuy states associated with organizational buying.

 # Review Questions

1 In note format and in your own words set out the essential purpose of B2B marketing.
2 Explain the key characteristics associated with B2B markets.
3 Explain the different types of organizations that make up the business market.
4 Name four of the different types of people that make up a DMU.
5 Distinguish clearly between buyphases and buyclasses.
6 Draw and explain the customer portfolio matrix.
7 Explain how key accounts are different from house or major accounts.
8 Describe the different phases associated with key account development cycles.
9 What are the key differences and similarities between B2B and B2C marketing?
10 What are the main characteristics of the B2B marketing mix?

 # Worksheet Summary

Visit the **Online Resource Centre** and complete Worksheet 14.1. This will aid in learning about the seven buying phases that organizations go through when purchasing industrial goods and services.

 # Discussion Questions

1 Having read Case Insight 14.1, how would you advise Reed Smith to share information across its firm?

2 Discuss the main characteristics of business marketing and consider whether there is really any major difference when compared with consumer marketing.

3 AstraVera Ltd has been developing a conveyor belt designed to meet new government-driven hygiene standards. The problem in many manufacturing, packaging, and assembly plants is that floors underneath conveyor belts can become wet and hence present a danger to people working around the equipment. The new belt has a trough incorporated into it, which runs along its entire length. Spillages feed into the trough where collection sumps and filters remove the excess liquids before they overflow to the floor (developed from Spear, 2006).

   Make brief notes advising AstraVera's marketing manager about marketing the new conveyor.

4 Working in small groups, select three B2B organizations and identify the main influences on their marketing activities. To what extent is it possible to prioritize these influences and does it matter?

5 Using PowerPoint, prepare a short presentation in which you explain the meaning of buyclasses, buyphases, and buygrids.

go online

Visit the **Online Resource Centre** and complete the Multiple Choice Questions to assess your knowledge of Chapter 14.

References

Abratt, R., and Kelly, P. M. (2002), 'Perceptions of a successful key account management program', *Industrial Marketing Management*, 31, 5 (August), 467–76.

Achrol, R. S. (1997), 'Changes in the theory of interorganisational relations in marketing: toward a network paradigm', *Journal of the Academy of Marketing Science*, 25, 1, 56–71.

Anderson, J., and Narus, J.A. (1999), *Business Market Management: Understanding, Creating, and Delivering Value*, Upper Saddle River, NJ, Prentice-Hall.

Barda, T. (2010), 'Slick business', *The Marketer*, March, 24–8.

Benedapudi, N., and Leone, R. P. (2002), 'Managing business-to-business customer relationships following key contact employee turnover in a vendor firm', *Journal of Marketing*, 66 (April), 83–101.

Bengtsson, A., and Servais, P. (2005), 'Co-branding in industrial markets', *Industrial Marketing Management*, 34, 7 (October), 706–13.

Bonoma, T. V. (1982), 'Major sales: who really does the buying?', *Harvard Business Review*, 60, 3 (May–June), 111–18.

Brehmer, P-O. and Rehme, J. (2009), 'Proactive and reactive: drivers for key account management programmes', *European Journal of Marketing*, 43, 7/8, 961–84.

Crawley-Boevey, S. (2009), 'Castrol kicks off football-themed B2B campaign', retrieve from www.brandrepublic.com/News/926057/Castrol-kicks-off-football-themed-B2B-campaign/?DCMP=ILC-SEARCH, accessed 8 February 2010.

Durham, J. and Ritchey, T. (2009), 'Leaning forward; removing design inefficiencies and improving quality', retrieve from www.hfmmagazine.com, 1 July 2009, accessed 5 October 2009.

Dwyer, R. F., Schurr, P. H., and Oh, S. (1987), 'Developing buyer–seller relationships', *Journal of Marketing*, 51 (April), 11–27.

Fill, C. (2009), *Marketing Communications: interactivity, communities and content*, 5th edn, Harlow: FT/Prentice Hall.

— , and Fill, K. E. (2005), *Business to Business Marketing*, Harlow: FT/Prentice Hall.

Fisher, L. (2009), 'Castrol kicks off football-themed campaign in time for World Cup', 5 October, retrieve from www.b2bm.biz/Features/CAMPAIGN-NEWS-Castrol-kicks-off-football-themed-campaign-in-time-for-World-Cup/, accessed 13 October 2009.

Glenn, R.R. and Wheeler, A.R. (2004), 'A new framework for supply chain manager selection: three hurdles to competitive advantage', *Journal of Marketing Channels*, 11, 4, 89–103.

Grönroos, C. (1994), 'Quo vadis, marketing? Toward a relationship marketing paradigm', *Journal of Marketing Management*, 10, 5, 347–60.

— (2009), 'Marketing as promise management: regaining customer management for marketing', *Journal of Business & Industrial Marketing*, 24/5/6, 351–59.

Gummesson, E., and Polese, F. (2009), 'B2B is not an island!', *Journal of Business & Industrial Marketing*, 24, 5/6 , 337–50.

Hague, P. (2006), 'Branding in business to business markets', White Paper, retrieve from www. b2binternational.com/library/whitepapers, accessed 30 December 2006.

Håkansson, H., and Snehota, I. (1995), *Developing Relationships in Business Networks*, London: Routledge.

Hannah, G. (1998), 'From transactions to relationships: challenges for the national account manager', *Journal of Marketing and Sales* (SA) 4, 1, 30–3.

Hemsworth, D., Sánchez-Rodríguez, C., Bidgood, B. (2008), *Total Quality Management & Business Excellence*, 19, 1/2, (January/February) 151–64.

Hollyoake, M. (2009), 'The four pillars: developing a bonded business-to-business customer experience', *Database Marketing & Customer Strategy Management*, 16, 2, 132–58.

Jackson, B. (1985), 'Build customer relationships that last', *Harvard Business Review*, 63, 6, 120–8.

Johnson, W. J., and Lewin, J. E. (1996), 'Organizational buying behavior: toward an integrative framework', *Journal of Business Research*, 35 (January), 1–15.

Laios, L. G., and Moschuris, S. J. (2001), 'The influence of enterprise type on the purchasing decision process', *International Journal of Operations & Production Management*, 21, 3, 351–72.

Leigh, T.W., and Marshall, G.W. (2001), 'Research priorities in sales strategy and performance', *Journal of Personal Selling and Sales Management*, 21, 2, 83–93.

Macfarlane, P. (2002), 'Structuring and measuring the size of business markets', *International Journal of Market Research*, 44, 1 (Winter), 7–31.

Mason, K. J., and Gray, R. (1999), 'Stakeholders in a hybrid market: the example of air business passenger travel', *European Journal of Marketing*, 33, 9–10, 844–58.

Millman, T., and Wilson, K. (1995), 'From key account selling to key account management', *Journal of Marketing Practice: Applied Marketing Science*, 1, 1, 9–21.

Ojasalo, J. (2001), 'Key account management at company and individual levels in business-to-business relationships', *Journal of Business and Industrial Marketing*, 16, 3, 199–220.

Parkinson, S. T., and Baker, M. J. (1994), *Organizational Buying Behavior: Purchasing and Marketing Management Implications*, London: Macmillan Press Ltd.

Payne, A., and Frow, P. (2004), 'The role of multi-channel integration in customer relationship management', *Industrial Marketing Management*, 33, 527–38.

Piercy, N.F. (2006), 'The strategic sales organization', *The Marketing Review*, 6, 3–28.

Pressey, A., Tzokas, N., and Winklhofer, H. (2007), 'Strategic purchasing and the evaluation of 'problem' key supply relationships: what do key suppliers need to know?', *Journal of Business & Industrial Marketing*, 22, 5, 282–94.

Robinson, P. J., Faris, C. W., and Wind, Y. (1967), *Industrial Buying and Creative Marketing*, Boston: Allyn & Bacon.

Ryals, L. J., and Rogers, B. (2006), 'Holding up the mirror: the impact of strategic procurement practices on account management', *Business Horizons*, 49, 41–50.

Sharma, A. (1997), 'Who prefers key account management program? An investigation of business buying behaviour and buying firm characteristics', *Journal of Personal Selling and Sales Management*, 17, 4, 27–39.

Sheth, J. N. (1973), 'A model of industrial buyer behavior', *Journal of Marketing*, 37 (October) 50–6.

Spear, M. (2006), *Smooth Movers*, retrieve from www.foodmanufacture.co.uk/news/fullstory.php/aid/3445/Smooth_movers.html, accessed 30 August 2006.

Spekman, R. E., and Gronhaug, K. (1986), 'Conceptual and methodological issues in buying centre research', *European Journal of Marketing*, 20, 7, 50–63.

Storbacka, K., Ryals, L., Davies, I.A., and Nenonen, S. (2009), 'The changing role of sales: viewing sales as a strategic, cross-functional process', *European Journal of Marketing* 43, 7/8, 890–906.

Svahn, S., and Westerlund, M. (2009), 'Purchasing strategies in supply relationships', *Journal of Business & Industrial Marketing*, 24, 3/4, 173–181.

Swinder, J., and Seshadri, S. (2001), 'The influence of purchasing strategies on performance', *Journal of Business and Industrial Marketing*, 16, 4, 294–306.

Ulkuniemi, P. (2003), *Purchasing Software Components at the Dawn of Market*, retrieve from http://herkules.oulu.fi/isbn9514272188/, accessed 5 September 2006.

van Weele, A. J. (2002), *Purchasing and Supply Chain Management*, 3rd edn, London: Thomson.

Vargo, S.L., and Lusch, R.F. (2004), 'Evolving to a new dominant logic for marketing', *Journal of Marketing*, 68, 1, 1–17.

Verbeke, W., Bagozzi, R. P., and Farris, P. (2006), 'The role of key account programs, trust, and brand strength on resource allocation in the channel of distribution', *European Journal of Marketing*, 40, 5/6, 520–32.

Webster, F. E., and Wind, Y. (1972), *Organizational Buying Behaviour*, Englewood Cliffs, NJ: Prentice Hall.

Wilson, D. F. (2000), 'Why divide consumer and organisational buyer behaviour?', *European Journal of Marketing*, 34, 7, 780–96.

15 Relationship Marketing

● Learning Outcomes

After studying this chapter you should be able to:

▶ Explain the concept of perceived value and the main characteristics of the value chain

▶ Understand the differences between the transactional and the relationship approach to marketing

▶ Describe the different stages of the customer relationship lifecycle

▶ Explain the principles and economics of customer retention and consider the merits of loyalty programmes

▶ Understand the principles of trust, commitment, and customer satisfaction, and explain how they are interlinked

▶ Describe ways in which organizations try to provide customer service and support

▶ Case Insight 15.1

RAKBANK is the highly successful National Bank of Ras Al-Khaimah, in the United Arab Emirates. We speak to Banali Malhotra, Head of Marketing, to find out how they sought to improve relationships with their customers.

Banali Malhotra for RAK BANK

It is very difficult these days to get by without a credit card. Hotel bookings, car rentals, holidays, entertainment, and internet purchases are nearly impossible to make without these pieces of plastic. At RAKBANK, our strategy involved entering the fiercely competitive credit card market. This market was dominated by our competitors' use of Gold and Platinum credit cards. These were positioned on a prestige platform, supported by a range of associated privileges, but they all required an annual fee and various extra charges.

The problem we faced was that customers resented paying these fees and were disenchanted with the financial services community. This dissatisfaction was rooted in the hidden charges and the service fees that were nearly always glossed over in the marketing communications used by our competitors. Their messages centred on financial freedom and desirable lifestyles, but there is no mention of their gratuitous annual fees, extortionate interest rates, complicated cancellation procedures and poor customer service.

RAKBANK was a late entrant into this overcrowded and disgruntled market and we needed to find a strong point of differentiation, something that would resonate with our customers and encourage them to value and maintain their relationship with RAKBANK.

Our research indicated that there was a need for a premium product, one that offered the prestige perception and privileges, but at a cost advantage to customers. This suggested something between the Gold and Platinum cards that currently dominated the market, might be successful. We also needed customers to evaluate the RAKBANK offering by comparing products on the basis of their features and benefits, and service, but not price.

RAKBANK identified four main segments. These are credit card customers, business entrepreneurs, high-net-worth individuals and local people who need personal loans. We developed our strategy on the well-established principle that the delivery of high product quality and above average service levels, leads to improved customer satisfaction levels. This, in turn, promotes higher levels of customer perceived value. We believed that once customers experienced our superior customer service, they would be more likely to take up other product offerings from RAKBANK. However, we needed to find a range of incentives to first attract and then retain customers, and so realize higher revenues from the life time value generated by these customers.

Suggest a name for a credit card that RAKBANK could use to enter the market. What might be the key product incentives necessary to attract and retain customers?

Introduction

If you have read the previous two chapters on services and B2B marketing, can you think of something that ties them both together? Well, if you thought of 'relationships' then you are right. This chapter is about relationship marketing and is a natural extension to the previous two chapters. In this book, the basic marketing approach has been presented around the 4Ps concept or what is regarded as the Marketing Management approach. However, this interpretation has been challenged and is now regarded by many as both an outdated and insufficient explanation of how marketing works. This is partly because business marketing is considered to be about people and the interaction between individuals representing their respective organizations. The 4Ps on the other hand are about managing segmented mass markets. The 'interactional' approach has been interpreted in different ways, but there is common agreement that this new approach should be referred to as relationship marketing.

There are some fundamental differences between the two approaches. The focus of the traditional 4Ps approach is on products and prices, where there is a short-term orientation between the buyer and the seller. Relationship marketing is different because the focus of the exchange is on the relationship and the interaction between buyers and sellers (largely in interorganizational contexts), not products and prices. The more frequent and intense these exchanges become, the more the strength of the relationships between buyers and sellers increases. It is this fundamental relational perspective that has provided the infrastructure for understanding and developing this different approach to marketing. This chapter considers the nature, dynamics, and issues related to relationship marketing.

From this more theoretical position, ideas about **customer relationship lifecycles**, loyalty, and retention programmes are introduced. This is followed by a consideration of various relationship-oriented concepts, such as **trust**, commitment, and **customer satisfaction**. The chapter concludes with an explanation about ways in which organizations try to provide customer service, namely through **customer relationship management** (CRM) and customer contact centres.

However, in order to appreciate the ideas underpinning relationship marketing, and its development, it is important to first understand the principles of perceived value.

Understanding Perceived Value

Customers buy products and services for the benefits that arise from using them. Customers do not buy products and services just for their features. They buy products that enable them to do what they want to achieve. Consumers do not buy toothpaste just because it has a red stripe or a minty taste. What they do buy is a clean mouth, fresh breath, or white gleaming teeth, depending on their segment characteristics. In the same way, business customers buy solutions to business problems not just stand-alone products. These benefits and solutions constitute value-for-customers, and represent the main reasons why one offering is selected in preference to another. For both consumers and business customers, **value** is determined by the net satisfaction derived from consuming and using a product, not the costs involved in obtaining it.

Another way of viewing these solutions and benefits is to consider them as (customer) needs. Customers seek to satisfy their needs through their purchase of products and services. Therefore, by satisfying these needs it becomes possible to deliver value for customers.

Kothandaraman and Wilson (2001) argue that the creation of value is dependent on an organization's ability to deliver high performance on the benefits that are important to the customer, and this, in turn, is rooted in their competency in technology and business processes, or core competences. Doyle (2000) suggests that customer value should be developed on three principles. These are:

1 Customers will choose between alternative offerings and select the one that (they perceive) will offer them the best value.

2 Customers do not want product or service features, they want their needs met.

3 It is more profitable to have a long-term relationship between a customer and a company rather than a one-off transaction.

Value is the customer's estimate of the extent to which a product or service can satisfy their needs. Customers determine the value of a product/service by considering alternative solutions and the costs associated with satisfying their need. Therefore, value is relative to a customer's needs, expectations, and experience of competitive offerings. Value can be derived from sources other than products and prices. For example, value can be generated through the provision of additional services, such as:

▶ training or support facilities, for example those normally provided by Carphone Warehouse for their customers;

▶ through association with a highly regarded brand, for example the co-branding arrangements between Adidas and Porsche and between Disney and Mattel;

▶ legal or insurance provision, for example the financial support provided by government and some regional councils for start-up entrepreneurs and small businesses;

▶ joint working relationships between government and building/finance schemes such as those associated with the Private Finance Initiative.

Menon, Homburg, and Beutin (2005) refer to these as add-on benefits and suggest that they may be more important than the core benefit arising from product and price attributes. However, above all else it is the relationships between buyers and sellers that are considered to represent real value (Simpson, Sigauw, and Baker, 2001), if only because they are longer lasting and difficult for competitors to copy or destroy. Indeed, the creation and the sharing of value are regarded as critical aspects of buyer–seller relationships (Anderson, 1995).

Lefaix-Durand *et al*. (2009) point out that that the customer value concept should be considered from two complementary perspectives. These are *value-to-customers* and *value-of-customers*. *Value-to-customers* focuses on the net-value customers realize from using the products/services provided by suppliers. *Value-of-customers* assumes a supplier's perspective of the net value they derive from their customers (Ulaga and Eggert, 2005). This distinction will be developed later in this chapter.

Value Chain

Customers choose among competitive offerings on the basis of their perceptions of the relative value they will derive from each supplier or product/service. When choosing a new pair of trainers, customers consider various criteria. These may involve the style, durability, comfort, price, and self-image, and the importance of each criterion will vary according to each individual and purchase context. Together, these elements help each customer to assign a value to each pair of trainers, music system, filtration plant, or supply of timber, based on their relative worth. Unsurprisingly, selling organizations compete for business by trying to offer enhanced value. This can be referred to as value propositions, or promises. These propositions are supported through a variety of internal processes, which when combined form a coordinated chain of activities. These activities include product design, production, marketing, delivery, and support. Porter (1985) referred to these activities as the **value chain**. This is shown in Figure 15.1.

The value chain was devised as a tool to appraise an organization's ability to create what Porter terms differential advantage, or in terms of our trainers, a pair that stands out as exactly what an individual wants. The value chain consists of nine activities, five primary activities and four support activities, all of which incur costs but together can (and should) lead to the creation of value.

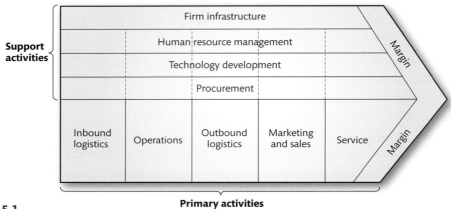

Figure 15.1

The value chain

Source: Reproduced with the kind permission of The Free Press, a division of Simon & Schuster, from COMPETITIVE ADVANTAGE: Creating and Sustaining Superior Performance by Michael E. Porter. © 1985, 1998 by Michael E. Porter. All rights reserved.

The **primary activities** are those direct actions necessary to bring materials into an organization, to convert them into final products or services, to ship them out to customers, and to provide marketing and servicing facilities.

Support activities facilitate the primary activities. For example, the purchase of parts and materials, the recruitment of suitably trained personnel, and the provision and maintenance of suitable technology are important support activities. Management should attempt to create value by reducing costs or improving the performance of each of the activities. However, real value is generated by linking these activities together, using processes and in such a way that customers perceive they are getting superior value. Doyle (2000) refers to three processes:

1 Innovation processes to generate a constant stream of new products and hence ability to maintain margins.

2 Operations processes to deliver first-class performance and costs.

3 Customer creation and support processes to provide a consistent and positive cash flow.

The processes used by an organization become a critical part of the way in which they can add value. Customers, however, lie at the heart of the value chain. Only by understanding particular customer needs and focusing value chain activities on satisfying these needs can superior value be generated.

This idea of a chain of value development activities provides a further, critical point about marketing and relationship management. The development of customer value is a function of various organizational departments working as an integrated whole, not just that of the marketing department working in isolation.

Supply Chains

So far, the value chain has been considered as an internal aspect of an organization's activities. However, organizations do not exist in isolation but work interdependently in order to provide a consistent stream of resources. Therefore, organizations join their value chains together and form **supply chains** (see Figure 15.2). The operation of the overall supply chain helps generate sustainable value for each business.

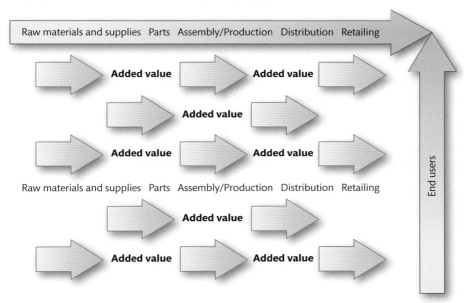

Raw materials and supplies Parts Assembly/Production Distribution Retailing

Added value   Added value

Added value

Added value   Added value

Raw materials and supplies Parts Assembly/Production Distribution Retailing

Added value

Added value   Added value

End users

Figure 15.2
The supply chain concept

The concepts of value and the value chain are important because they provide a reminder of basic principles. First, customers buy superior value, which means that the creation of profits can only be through the delivery and consumption of value that customers want. Trimming costs to save money and to improve the bottom line, but removing the value that customers actually desire, and which represents their reason to buy, may be a wrong decision.

Second, value can be perceived in many ways, for example by providing associations with prestige (exclusivity or membership), reliability, modular formats, ease and speed of servicing, stock and delivery flexibility, ease of customization, and access to new markets. Therefore, the whole of an organization's activities must be considered and their contribution to the generation of superior value appraised. Among other things, this means looking at pre-purchase and post-purchase customer support, pricing, communications, distribution and logistics, and positioning.

The development of new technology and the increasing breadth and depth of business applications has provided new value creation opportunities for organizations. Advances in information, communications, and technology (ICT) can lead to new forms of value being created. Apart from the obvious impact on speed and accuracy of information transfer between organizations, value can be enhanced through product development and customization, production and manufacturing, supply chain management, marketing communications, and, of course, closer interorganizational understanding and relationships (Sharma, Krishman, and Grewal, 2001). For example, commercial photographers can add value by offering particular types of shots, locations, digital libraries, on-demand printing, and presentation services.

Visit the **Online Resource Centre** and complete Internet Activity 15.1 to learn more about how the AA uses its interactive website to provide added-value services and information to AA members.

go online

Principles of Marketing Exchange

Following on from the introduction to value and value chains, the supply chain concept raises interesting points about the nature and scope of the relationships that exist between suppliers and buyers. Organizations interact with other organizations in order to provide superior value for customers. However, it should come as no surprise to read that the quality, duration, and level of interdependence between organizations in the supply chain can vary considerably. The reasons for this variance are many and wide-ranging, and can be considered in terms of the types of exchange that buyers and sellers choose to use.

The different types of exchange should be considered as a continuum, as depicted in Figure 15.3. At one end of the continuum are **transactional exchanges**, characterized by

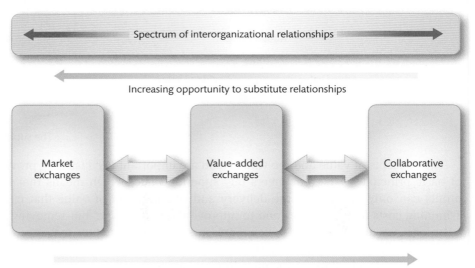

Figure 15.3

Continuum of value based exchanges

Source: Fill and Fill (2005). Reproduced with the kind permission of Katalisys Ltd.

short-term, product- or price-oriented interactions, between buyers and sellers. These are one-off exchanges independent of any other or subsequent exchanges. Both parties are motivated mainly by self-interest. In transactional marketing, value is perceived to be embedded in the product's attributes and its price.

At the other end of the continuum are **collaborative exchanges** (Day, 2000). These are characterized by a long-term orientation, where there is a complete integration of systems and processes and the relationship is motivated by partnership and mutual support. Trust and commitment underpin these relationships, and these variables become increasingly important as stronger relational exchanges become established.

▶ Market Insight 15.1

Electrical Exchanges

Philips, Hotpoint, and Samsung are manufacturers of electrical equipment such as toasters and kettles. They do not sell their products to individual consumers because individual consumers are relatively infrequent buyers of these products, and when they do buy from a retailer, online or offline, it is normally a one-off or market exchange.

Electrical equipment manufacturers normally develop collaborative exchanges with their key distributors and retailers. These organizations tend to buy large quantities of kettles on a regular basis, and sell them through their various offline (shops and catalogues) and online retail channels. Communications and interaction between the parties tend to be continuous and designed to support the relationship over the longer term.

Electrical equipment manufacturers sell batches of each type of product to their appointed retailers at pre-agreed dates. However, it would be incorrect to assume that all of these exchanges are collaborative. Some are transactional exchanges where the goal of the manufacturer is to 'turn' stock and their decisions are not always based on the financial or marketing situation facing each of their distributors or retailers. The element of collaboration and mutual self-help characteristic of collaborative exchanges may be missing within these relationships.

1 How might electrical goods manufacturers develop more collaborative relationships with all of their retailers? Should they even try to do so?

2 Name one electrical manufacturer you consider to be successful. Justify your decision.

3 How might environmental issues be part of a manufacturer's selection of parts and items for their kettles?

Futuristic-looking kitchen appliances from Philips Electronics BV

Source: © Philips Electronics B.V.

The continuum of exchanges provides a visual expression of the diversity of organizational transactions, from the one-off, short-term exchange where value is perceived in the product or service, to those that are long term and based on value rooted in collaboration and partnership.

▶ Research Insight 15.1

To take your learning further, you might wish to read this influential paper.

Day, G. (2000), 'Managing market relationships', *Journal of the Academy of Marketing Science*, 28, 1 (Winter), 24–30.

Day considers that the basis of competitive advantage rests with an organization's ability to create and maintain relationships with their most valuable customers. Part of this advantage rests with the value generated and he presents a continuum of exchanges to express the possible range of values.

 Visit the **Online Resource Centre** to read the abstract and access the full paper.

It is important to put these ideas in the context of what organizations do in practice. Pels, Möller, and Saren (2009: 323) report a series of independent research studies that 'provide clear evidence' that 30% of B2B companies practice transactional marketing, as advocated by the Marketing Management school of thought. A further 30% practice a combination of transactional and relational marketing. The numbers practicing pure collaborative or relational marketing are not itemized but they would clearly be a minority.

Foundations of Relationship Marketing

Founding ideas about industrial (now termed business) marketing were based on market exchanges between organizations, where there was no prior history of exchange and no future exchanges expected. These paired organizations were considered to enter into transactions where products were the main focus and price was the key mechanism to exchange completion. Organizations were perceived to be adversarial and competition was paramount. These undertakings are referred to as market (or discrete) exchanges and often termed 'transactional marketing'.

In contrast, **relationship marketing** is based on the principle that there is a history of exchanges and an expectation that there will be exchanges in the future. Furthermore, the perspective is on the long term, envisioning a form of loyalty or continued attachment by the buyer to the seller. Price, as the key controlling mechanism is replaced by customer service and quality of interaction between the two organizations. The exchange is termed collaborative because the focus is on both organizations seeking to achieve their goals in a mutually rewarding way and not at the expense of one another. See Table 15.1 for a more comprehensive list of fundamental differences between transactional and collaborative-based marketing.

> ▶ **Table 15.1** Characteristics of market and collaborative exchanges

Attribute	Market exchange	Collaborative exchange
Length of relationship	Short term Abrupt end	Long term A continuous process
Relational expectations	Conflicts of goals Immediate payment No future problems (there is no future)	Conflicts of interest Deferred payment Future problems expected to be overcome by joint commitment
Communication	Low frequency of communication Formal communication predominates	Frequent communication Informal communication predominates
Cooperation	No joint cooperation	Joint cooperative projects
Responsibilities	Distinct responsibilities Defined obligations	Shared responsibilities Shared obligations

Although market exchanges focus on products and prices, there is still a relational component, if only because interaction requires a basic relationship between parties for the transaction to be completed (Macneil, 1980).

Dwyer, Schurr, and Oh (1987) refer to relationship marketing as an approach that encompasses a wide range of relationships, not just with customers, but also those that organizations develop with suppliers, regulators, government, competitors, employees, and others. From this, relationship marketing might be regarded as all marketing activities associated with the management of successful relational exchanges.

Gummesson (2002) has suggested that the marketing mix should consist of 30 different types of relationships, or 30Rs as he referred to them, as organizations have potentially 30 different types of relationships. These are grouped under two headings, market and non-market relationships. Market relationships are those between suppliers, customers, competitors, and all those who contribute to a market's operations. Non-market relationships involve all the other organizations that indirectly influence market relationships.

Another approach has been proposed by Christopher, Payne, and Ballantyne (2002). They refer to a six markets model of relationship marketing, where relationships should be deliberately developed with recruitment, supplier, influence, internal, referral, and customer markets. They identify these markets on the grounds that these represent groups that contribute to an organization's performance and marketplace contribution.

This approach encompasses a range of influential types of organization, but at the heart of this model is the customer market. This raises a key question about whether an organization should develop relationships with customers rather than a range of stakeholders: who is the more important? This implies that relationship marketing is about what is done *to* customers rather than *with* them (Worthington and Horne, 1998), a common criticism of early approaches to relationship marketing.

The role of collaboration in relationship marketing is important. However, many organizations maintain a variety of relationships with their different customers and suppliers, some highly collaborative and some market-oriented or, as Spekman and Carroway (2005: 1) suggest, 'where they make sense'.

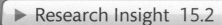

> ▶ Research Insight 15.2

To take your learning further, you might wish to read this influential paper.

Grönroos, C. (1994), 'From marketing mix to relationship marketing', *Management Decision*, 32, 2, 4–20.

This paper is important because it was one of the first to challenge the managerial marketing mix approach. Grönroos cites evolving business trends such as strategic partnerships, alliances, and networks, and suggested that relationship marketing, based on relationship building and management, was an emerging marketing paradigm.

 Visit the **Online Resource Centre** to read the abstract and access the full paper.

The Development of Relationship Marketing

Originally, business marketing theory focused on the actions of individual organizations. This evolved into the recognition of interorganizational interaction with varying degrees of cooperation and dependency. Initially, attention concentrated on dyads (or pairs) of organizations interacting, with market exchange principles guiding their relationship. At first, consideration was given to pairings of individual people, but this changed to a group orientation with the 'introduction of buying centre and selling centre concepts' (Borders, Johnston, and Rigdon, 2001).

Business marketing in the 1960s, 1970s, and early 1980s focused on the units of exchange, namely the products that were transacted between two organizations. The 4Ps approach to the marketing mix variables (the Marketing Management school of thought), was used to guide and construct transaction behaviour. These transactions represented market exchanges between a single-buying and a single-selling organization. The centre of attention was the transaction between these two parties. Buyers were considered to be passive and sellers active in these short-term exchanges. According to Johanson and Mattsson (1994), cited by McLoughlin and Horan (2002), this early work assumed that passive buyers reacted to the offers of sellers in a more or less subservient and unquestioning manner. Consequently, researchers, assuming a purchasing manager's perspective, sought to understand the processes that buyers used when making buying decisions. Work by Webster and Wind (1972) and Sheth (1973) typified this period. The goal was to develop marketing plans that made better use of resources and which targeted appropriate members of the buying centre. Business marketing was based on the premise that marketing and purchasing were separate activities and that the purchase activity involved just a single, one-off purchase event.

The strength and duration of a pairing was determined by the application of an optimal marketing mix. However, Grönroos (1994) argued that the marketing mix concept, as a general theory of marketing, represents a production-oriented approach to marketing where the ingredients are mixed together, according to an organization's perception of their customer's needs. The use of the 4Ps concept encouraged a market exchange orientation. Sellers sought to attract buyers, negotiate, and complete a transaction, and then both parties left the pairing, suitably satisfied. However, with price as the market mechanism and little integration between the ingredients, the 4Ps approach began to be perceived as lacking substance and sufficient rigour to continue as the main general theory of marketing.

However, the assumption that buyers were passive was soon challenged by the notion that, in reality, business customers (organizations) are active problem solvers and seek solutions that were both efficient and effective. It was then accepted that buyers actually practised cooperative behaviours in order to find suitable suppliers. For the first time, the study of interorganizational behaviour became prevalent and focused on the relationship between a pair of organizations, rather than products traded. Thus, research moved to encompass buying-centre and selling-centre characteristics, with one of the goals to better align both parties to achieve greater efficiencies through improved cooperation. For example, the high profile given to 'just-in-time systems' was a manifestation of the prevailing orientation. So, although research remained fixed on the buyer–seller dyad, interaction had now replaced reaction.

In essence, this was a move away from looking at purchasing as a single discrete event, to considering it as a stream of activities between two organizations. These activities are sometimes referred to as episodes. Typically, these may be price negotiations, meetings at exhibitions, or a buying decision, but these all take place within the overall context of a relationship. This framed the Relationship Marketing school of thought, one in which the supplier–buyer relationship was the central element of analysis. Any one episode may be crucial to the relationship but analysing individual episodes is usually insufficient if the context, the overall relationship, is not understood. So, when an advertising agency meets a potential client for a **pitch** (to make a presentation to get their contract) an episode within the overall relationship is said to have occurred. However, understanding the relationship alone does not produce a complete picture either so, as Ford (1980) argues, 'it is important to analyse both individual episodes and the overall relationship, as well as to understand the interaction between the two'. Therefore, buyers and sellers were considered to behave (or interact) within the context of their own dyadic or one-to-one relationship. The focus was no longer the product, or even the individual buying or selling firm, but the relationship and its particular characteristics and over time. See Market Insight 15.2 for a view of how this might work.

Around the same time, attention moved away from vertical integration as the preferred structural business model, to recognition of the significance and relevance of networks and loose alliances among organizations. In terms of understanding business interaction, this brought into consideration the potential influence of the indirect relationships that organizations have with one another. Relationship research (and marketing) needed to focus not just on buyers and sellers but on a wide range of other organizations all interacting with one another in a network of relationships. Understanding about the role and nature of relationships, within an interorganizational context, has therefore evolved over several decades, typified by the **Industrial Marketing and Purchasing** (IMP) group school of thought.

go online

Visit the **Online Resource Centre** and follow the weblink to Association for the Advancement of Relationship Marketing (AARM) to learn more about continuing professional development into relationship marketing.

Relationships Expressed as Value Creation

Just as ideas about relationships have evolved, so have those associated with value. Rather than consider relationships as a function of exchange, an emerging view, driven largely by the **service-dominant** logic (SDL) group, is to consider relationships as a function of value, or what is known as, value-in-use. See also Chapter 13 for more about the SDL approach.

Grönroos (2009) argues that value cannot be created by suppliers but can only be realized by customers when utilized through the use of their own processes, resources, and capabilities. Grönroos considers that value should be considered to consist of two fundamental elements; **value propositions** and **value creation**. Suppliers develop *value propositions* and these are essentially suggestions or promises of value embedded in their offerings. Customers fulfil *value creation* when incorporating products and services into their processes. For example, the benefits (value) arising from the use of a manufacturing software system only occur once the system is installed and operationalized by a manufacturer. So, a software developer might offer (the value proposition) to tailor their software to meet the needs of a particular buyer and install it for them. This means that the system can be installed faster, more accurately, and be of great(er) benefit to the buyer, than a system that is not tailored to their needs. The manufacturer only derives value when the software system is running and supporting their manufacturing processes.

Suppliers can assist customers by creating opportunities to engage with their value-generating processes. The level of interaction between the parties might vary from zero to the full participation that is co-creation. So, an alternative to the spectrum of exchange relationships presented earlier would be a spectrum of different value propositions, leading to various forms of value creation.

Movement along the relationship continuum can be interpreted as a change in the way value is created. Ribeiro *et al.* (2009) identify four core value strategies. These are exchange (or commodity) value, added value, performance value, and value co-creation strategies.

▶ commodity-value—transactional exchange relationships are characterized by an exchange of basic resources. Sellers provide a core offering but it is buyers who assume full responsibility and the resources to create the value they require out of the resources transacted;

▶ added-value—suppliers can choose to provide buyers with resources necessary to help them create the required value. This approach is referred to as an 'added value' strategy and examples include providing training, financial assistance, or installation support. As a result of these interactions, parties become closer and stronger, so that the original value perceived in the exchange of products and prices gradually gives way to a focus on the relationship, which itself becomes of value;

▶ performance-value—further along the continuum organizations provide 'performance value' strategies. Here, value is created by the activities of buyers and sellers working together for mutual benefit, but value is still passed from one to another. Also known as value-in-use, examples include joint product development and projects to enhance the buyer's software systems, and processes and initiatives designed to improve manufacturing efficiencies.

▶ Market Insight 15.2

Cisco Bring Performance Value

Cisco, said to be the world's largest manufacturer and supplier of networking equipment, has created a virtual organization designed to provide added value and efficiencies in the value chain, for all business partners, suppliers, and customers. Part of this strategy has been accomplished through its use of web-based applications that focus on internet, intranet, and extranet applications, designed to link all aspects of its value network.

For example, the company openly encourages its customers' engineers to solve their technical problems through use of Cisco's self-help web-based technical support pages and network configurator.

By making these facilities easy to use, not only is Cisco better placed to manage staffing (time and costs) required for technical support, but also it encourages customers to become more involved in Cisco applications, allowing them to reduce their own organization's systems difficulties. As a result, customer organizations are able to share technical knowledge, and through their satisfaction provide positive word-of-mouth referrals.

Source: www.cisco.com/web/learning/le3/ccie/index.html.

1 Identify the key elements that support the relationship between Cisco and its customers' engineers.

2 How might Cisco communicate with its customers' engineers?

3 Think of ways in which Cisco might co-create value with a major cable manufacturer.

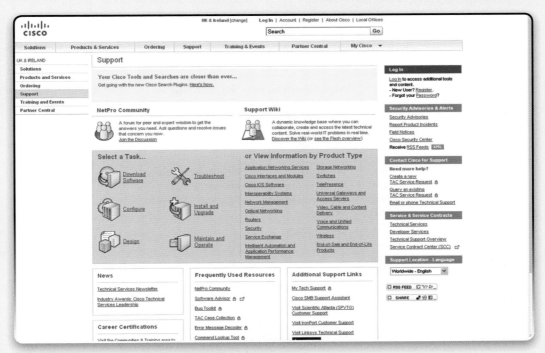

The website of Cisco, the world's largest manufacturer and supplier of networking equipment
Source: Courtesy of Cisco.

▶ co-creation-value—collaborative relationships are characterized by value that is created by both parties as a form of co-production or through 'value co-creation' (Sheth and Uslay, 2007). This occurs where both organizations work together for mutual benefit, and value is generated together, not traded by a supplier to a buyer, as in performance value. More information about these different value strategies can be seen in Table 15.2.

▶ **Table 15.2** Characteristics of value strategies

	Value Strategies			
Defining characteristics	Commodity	Value added	Performance	Value co-creation
Value-generating drivers	Product quality Delivery performance Market price	Services support Personal interactions Product and service quality	The know-how of others Time to market Performance from both (costs, revenues, productivity)	Joint and radical innovation Leveraging new competencies
Management intention	Attract and satisfy	Customer retention (implicit: profit, satisfaction, loyalty, risk, reduction, etc.)	Interactions to establish, develop and facilitate cooperative relationship and mutual benefit	Coordinating relationships among companies in a network to seek new resources and value networks
Duration Adaptation	Discrete Little or no adaptation	Continuous, but discrete hiring Process adaptations	Continuous and long-term contracts Process adaptations	Continuous, mutual cooperation contracts Adaptations and business creation
Description of value offering	'We offer good products and competitive prices'	'We offer excellence'	'We customize, we build on order for the customer'	'Our customers, suppliers and other partners got us here and will take us wherever it need be to generate value'
Management structure	Functional hierarchial: marketing, sales, R&D, etc.	Process and functions like: customer service manager. CRM manager	Customer and market managers/cross-functions and levels	Business managers
Capabilities	Production Delivery Promoting-communicating Process leverage Relationship Mastery and integration into the customer's business model Radical innovation Setting up networks			

Source: Ribeiro *et al.* (2009).

The Economics of Relationship Marketing

Early ideas about marketing considered the subject to be a social anathema because of the perception that it persuaded and manipulated people into purchasing goods and services they did not really want (Packard, 1958). These particular fears and misgivings have generally been overcome only for a further myth to emerge, namely that all customers are good customers. This is patently not true as it is now clear that some customers are far more attractive and of greater value than other customers.

This view has been substantiated through our understanding of the economic and financial issues associated with customer management. From an understanding of transaction economics emerged ideas about how customer relationships might be advantageous. Relationship cost theory identified benefits associated with stable and mutually rewarding relationships. Such customers avoided costly switching costs associated with finding new suppliers, whereas suppliers experienced reduced quality costs, incurred when adapting to the needs of new customers.

Reichheld and Sasser (1990) identified an important association between a small (e.g. 5%) increase in **customer retention** and a large (e.g. 60%) improvement in profitability. So, a long-term relationship leads to lower relationship costs and higher profits. It is on this simple, yet crucial principle that many organizations develop and run loyalty programmes. Many of the major airlines find it difficult to keep their high-mileage business customers, so they develop loyalty schemes, referred to as frequent flyer programmes (FFP), in which they reward travellers with free air miles for paid mileage undertaken with them. A typical FFP scheme, such as the one offered by British Airways, includes not only a mileage scheme, but also offers a range of added-value services, such as graded membership status (and privileges), worldwide lounge access, seating preference records, meal preferences, and priority on busy flights.

Since this early work there has been general acceptance that customers who are loyal not only improve an organization's profits but also strengthen its competitive position (Day, 2000), because competitors have to work harder to dislodge or destabilize their loyalty. It should be noted that some authors suggest that the link between loyalty and profitability is not that simple (Dowling and Uncles, 1997), whereas others argue that much more information and understanding is required about the association between profitability and loyalty, especially when there may be high costs associated with **customer acquisition** (Reinartz and Kumar, 2002). However, the relationship marketing concept was considered to consist of two main elements, namely customer attraction and customer retention.

By undertaking a customer profitability analysis it is possible to identify those segments that are worth developing. This, in turn, enables the construction of a portfolio of relationships, from which it is possible to identify relationships that have the potential to provide mutually rewarding benefits. This then provides a third dimension of the customer dynamic, namely customer development.

▶ Research Insight 15.3

To take your learning further, you might wish to read this influential paper.

Reichheld, F. F., and Sasser, E. W. (1990), 'Zero defects: quality comes to services', *Harvard Business Review*, September, 105–11.

Often quoted by other authors and researchers, this paper by Reichheld and Sasser finds that a small increase in the number of retained customers can have a disproportionately large increase in profitability, and has helped propel a wealth of research and interest in relationship marketing. By definition, loyal customers are less likely to switch and therefore incur lower sales and service costs. They also help, through word-of-mouth, to recruit new customers, so the net result is that they all contribute to higher profits.

@   Visit the **Online Resource Centre** to read the abstract and access the full paper.

The Customer Relationship Lifecycle

Understanding the economics associated with relationship stability and profitability uncovers three main stages within customer relationships. These are customer acquisition, development, and retention. This suggests similarities to the phases or stages of development associated with the **product lifecycle** concept.

Taking this idea one step further allows us to develop a **customer relationship lifecycle**. This consists of four main stages, namely customer acquisition, development, retention, and finally decline or termination. Just as different strategies can be applied to different phases of the product lifecycle, so it is possible to observe that customers have different requirements as a relationship evolves. These requirements are reflected in the intensity of the relationship held and of course the level of intensity will vary through time. See Figure 15.4 for a visual depiction of the **customer relationship lifecycle**.

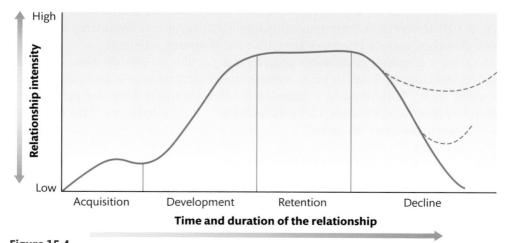

Figure 15.4

The customer relationship lifecycle

Key to this concept is the differing level of **relationship intensity** that determines each stage. Bruhn (2003) suggests that there are three primary elements, or indicators (as he refers to them), that make up this intensity dimension. These are the psychological, behavioural, and economic indicators, and are depicted in Figure 15.5.

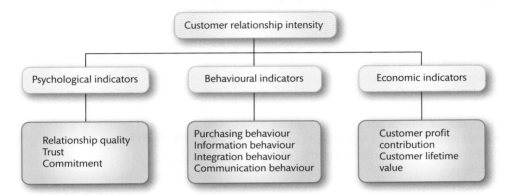

Figure 15.5

Elements of customer relationship intensity

Source: Bruhn (2003).

The psychological intensity indicators are based on a customer's judgment about the quality of the relationship, and the amount of trust in, and commitment to, the seller or supplying organization. These are important foundations for establishing and maintaining ongoing, mutually rewarding two-way relationships. These are explored in more detail later in this chapter. Behavioural intensity indicators refer to the manner and scope of a customer's search for information, including word-of-mouth communication as well as their purchasing behaviour. Economic intensity indicators refer to both the profit contribution and the lifetime value a customer represents.

These three indicators signal the intensity of a relationship. They vary through time and help explain the characteristics associated with each of the relationship stages.

Customer Acquisition

The customer acquisition stage is marked by three main events. First, both buyers and sellers search for a suitable match. Second, once a suitable partner has been found there is a period of initiation or 'settling in', during which both organizations seek out information about the other before any transaction occurs. The duration of this initiation period will depend partly on the strategic importance and complexity of the products and partly on the nature of the introduction. If introduced to each other by an established and trusted organization, certain initiation rights will be shortened.

The third phase is characterized by socialization, whereby once a transaction occurs the buyer and seller start to become more familiar with each other and gradually begin to reveal more information about themselves. The seller is able to collect payment, delivery, and handling information about the buyer and as a result is able to prepare customized outputs.

The buyer is able to review the seller's products and experience the service quality of the seller. Market Insight 15.3 discusses customer acquisition.

▶ Market Insight 15.3

Barclays Profit from Relationships

Banks need to find new small business customers if only because up to 50% of new businesses cease trading in three years. Barclays ran an acquisition campaign designed not only to position the bank as market leader for SMEs, but to also recruit 17,000 new business accounts and 5,500 switchers.

New businesses often need support and advice, whereas established SMEs may switch banks due to their dissatisfaction with the level of service received. In both cases, relationships are key, and, as many financial institutions demonstrate in their communications, campaigns that stress the role of the manager are often the most successful.

Following a period of intensive local branch business manager training, the campaign used branch advertising, radio advertising, internal and external newsletters plus editorials and public relations. The campaign, which cost just £250k made extensive use of their local branch business managers during the campaign, meeting businesses and playing prominent roles in the local community. The campaign achieved all its targets and post-campaign research revealed that the local bank business managers were seen as significant success factor.

(See Market Insight 6.3 for more information on how Barclays profiles and targets banking segments.)

Source: Anon. (2008).

1　What direct marketing activities might have Barclays used to attract business customers?

2　Determine the type of exchange relationship that SMEs might want with their bank, and the type of value offered by Barclays.

3　Why were the local managers given intensive training prior to the campaign?

Barclays' local business bank managers, a key success factor in the bid to win business customers

Source: Courtesy of Barclays Bank plc.

Customer Development

During the development phase sellers encourages buyers to purchase increased quantities, to try other products, to engage with other added value services, and to vary delivery times and quantities. The degree to which buyers respond to the supplier's overtures depends on a variety of factors. Some of these concern their economic and production needs; others will reflect their competitive environment, their purchasing strategies, and their overall drive to become more involved with the supplier.

This stage is critical, as not only do the number and value of transactions increase but also the socialization processes started during acquisition continue as both buyer and seller begin to understand each other's requirements and goals in greater detail. It is also during this stage that sellers develop a better understanding of the wider array of their buyer's stakeholder relationships. This can have a significant influence on the nature of the supplier's relationship with the buyer, often indicating the depth to which the relationship aspires.

Customer Retention

The retention phase is characterized by greater relationship stability and certainty. As a result the relationship becomes stabilized, displaying greater levels of trust and commitment between the partners. This, in turn, allows for increased cross-buying and product experimentation, joint projects, and product development. More commonly, suppliers provide customer loyalty schemes in order to increase the volume and value of products and services bought, and to lock in their customers by creating relationship exit barriers. Customer loyalty schemes are explored in more detail later in this chapter.

Customer Decline

In many cases, relationships become destabilized and higher levels of uncertainty emerge. This might occur after a long period of relationship stability or after a short period immediately after acquisition. The reasons for this are many and varied and range from purchasing agreements and loyalty programmes that are not sufficiently attractive to lock in the customer to changes in the wider environment such as legislative, climatic, or economic developments. As a result, this period is concerned with the demise of the relationship and termination becomes a serious problem or episode for the parties to manage.

The likely process is that the buying organization decides to reduce its reliance on the seller and either notifies them formally or begins to reduce the frequency and duration of contact and moves business to other, competitive organizations. Customer recovery strategies are required at the first sign that the relationship is waning. These are examined later.

Loyalty, Retention, and Customer Satisfaction

The customer relationship cycle implies that customers who keep coming back to buy from a particular supplier are loyal. One problem with this suggestion is that what is understood to be 'loyalty' may actually be nothing more than pure convenience or habit. A person who regularly attends the same supermarket is not necessarily consciously loyal to the supermarket brand, but happy with the convenience of the location and the overall quality and value of the products and services offered. Loyalty might be better appreciated in the context of a football supporter who travels to all away and home fixtures (regardless of domestic commitments), is a member of the club, buys into the merchandise and credit card offerings, and defends their club, even when they are relegated at the end of the season.

Various writers have used a ladder to depict ascending levels of loyalty. One of the better known is entitled the relationship marketing ladder of loyalty (Christopher, Payne, and Ballantyne, 2002) and is shown in Figure 15.6. Following an initial transaction, a prospect becomes a purchaser. These purchasers or customers are designated as clients following several completed transactions, but are still ambivalent towards the selling organization. Customers who enter into regular purchases may still be passive about the organization but are said to be supporters. Advocates are an important group because not only do they support an organization and/or its products but they actively recommend it to others through positive word-of-mouth communications. At the top of this ladder are partners. Their key characteristic is the complete trust and support for an organization. This strength of feeling is reciprocated by the organization and this provides partnership status. Partnership is the essence of relational exchanges and interorganizational collaboration.

Partner: someone who a strong independent relationship with you

Advocate: someone who actively recommends you to others, who does your marketing for you

Supporter: someone who likes your organization, but only supports you passively

Client: someone who has done business with you on a repeat basis but may be negative, or at best neutral, towards your organization

Purchaser: someone who has done business just once with your organization

Prospect: someone whom you believe may be persuaded to do business with you

Figure 15.6
The relationship marketing ladder of loyalty
Source: Christopher, Payne, and Ballantyne (2002).

The simplicity of the loyalty ladder concept illustrates the important point that customers represent different values to other organizations. That perceived value (or worth) may or may not be reciprocated, thus establishing the basis for a variety and complexity of different relationships.

This cycle of customer attraction (acquisition), development, retention, and eventual decline represents a major difference from the 4Ps approach. The relationship approach is customer-centred, and therefore complements marketing values more effectively than the 4Ps model. However, although the focus has moved from product and prices to relationships, questions remain about whose relationship it is that is being managed. Early interpretations of relationship marketing focused on suppliers' attempts to develop relationships with customers. In other words they were 'customer relationships' and this meant there was an imbalance or one-sidedness within the relationship. Today, relationship marketing recognizes the need for balanced customer–supplier relationships in which participants share the same level of interest, goodwill, and commitment towards each other.

Types and Levels of Loyalty

The concept of loyalty has attracted much research attention, if only because of the recent and current popularity of this approach. Table 15.3 represents some of the more general types of loyalty that can be observed.

These hierarchical schemes suggest that consumers are capable of varying degrees of loyalty. This type of categorization has been questioned by a number of researchers. Fournier and Yao (1997) doubt the validity of such approaches, and Baldinger and Rubinson (1996) support the idea that consumers work within an evoked set and switch between brands. This view is supported on the grounds that many consumers display elements of curiosity in their purchase habits, enjoy variety, and are happy to switch brands as a result of marketing communication activities and product experiences.

Loyalty at one level can be seen to be about increasing sales volume, that is, fostering loyal purchase behaviour. High levels of repeat purchase, however, are not necessarily an adequate measure of loyalty, as there may be a number of situational factors determining purchase behaviour, such as brand availability (Dick and Basu, 1994). At whichever level of loyalty, customer retention is paramount and neither behavioural nor attitudinal measures alone are

▶ **Table 15.3** Types of loyalty

Type of loyalty	Explanation
Emotional loyalty	This is a true form of loyalty and is driven by personal identification with real or perceived values and benefits
Price loyalty	This type of loyalty is driven by rational economic behaviour and the main motivations are cautious management of money or financial necessity
Incentivized loyalty	This refers to promiscuous buyers: those with no one favourite brand who demonstrate through repeat experience the value of becoming loyal
Monopoly loyalty	This class of loyalty arises where a consumer has no purchase choice owing to a national monopoly. This, therefore, is not a true form of loyalty

adequate indicators of true loyalty. O'Malley (1998) suggests that a combination of the two is of greater use and that the twin parameters of relative attitudes (to alternatives) and patronage behaviour (the recency, frequency, and monetary model), as suggested by Dick and Basu, offer more accurate indicators of loyalty when used together.

Loyalty and Retention Programmes

The number of loyalty programmes offered by organizations has grown significantly in recent years. These range from supermarket-based points schemes and frequent flyer reward programmes offered by airlines to attract and retain high-margin business customers to discounts and loyalty bonus formats designed to retain contract-based customers such as those associated with mobile phones and financial services, for example, car insurance. One of the more visible schemes has been the Clubcard offered by Tesco, which has been partly responsible for Tesco's market dominance.

The increasing use of loyalty schemes has been propelled by technological developments, one of which was the swipe card. Users are rewarded with points each time a purchase is made. This is referred to as a 'points accrual programme', whereby loyal users are able to build up the necessary points, which are stored (often) on a card, and 'cashed in' at a later date for gifts or merchandise. The benefit for the company supporting the scheme is that the promised rewards motivate customers to accrue more points, and, in doing so, increase their switching costs, effectively locking them into the loyalty programme and preventing them from moving to a competitor brand.

Swipe cards, although still prevalent, have been superseded by smart cards. These cards contain a small microprocessor and can record massive amounts of information, which is updated each time a purchase is made. Smart cards can be used to update database records in order to provide improved product availability and stocking plus improved marketing communications messages and timely offers and incentives. They are also used as a payment facility for use in transportation systems, such as the Octopus card in Hong Kong, the Easyrider card in Nottingham, and the Tcard in Sydney.

The potential number of applications for smart cards is remarkable. However, just like swipe cards, the targeting of specific groups of buyers can be expected to become more precise and efficient, and it is also easier to track and target individuals for future promotional activities.

Nottingham's Easyrider and Hong Kong's Octopus smart cards make travel easier

These schemes are important not only because they help retain customers, but also because they allow for the collection of up-to-date customer information. These data can then be used to target marketing communication campaigns and to make product purchase decisions, volumes, and scheduling, in order to make savings in the supply chain.

There has been a proliferation of loyalty cards, reflecting the increased emphasis on keeping customers rather than constantly finding new ones, and there is some evidence that sales lift by about 2–3% when a loyalty scheme is launched. Yet there is little evidence to support the notion that sales promotions are capable of encouraging loyalty. Schemes do enable organizations to monitor and manage stock, use direct marketing to cross and up-sell customers, and manage their portfolio in order to increase a customer's spending. However, questions still exist about whether 'loyalty' is developed by encouraging buyers to make repeat purchases or whether these schemes are merely sales promotion techniques that encourage short-term retention purchasing patterns.

▶ **Table 15.4** Five loyalty trends

Trend	Explanation
Ubiquity	The proliferation of loyalty programmes in most mature markets Many members have little interest in them other than the functionality of points collection
Coalition	Schemes are run by a number of different organizations in order to share costs, information, and branding (e.g. Nectar) and appear to be the dominant structure industry model
Imagination	Opportunities to exploit technologies and niche markets will depend on creativity and imagination in order to get customer data to feed into the loyalty system
Wow	To overcome consumer lethargy and boredom with loyalty schemes, many rewards in future will be experiential, emotional, and unique in an attempt to appeal to lifestage and aspirational lifestyle goals—wow them
Analysis	To be competitive, the use of customer data analytics and business intelligence is becoming critical, if only to feed CRM programmes. Collect and analyse customer information effectively

Source: Adapted from Capizzi, Ferguson, and Cuthbertson (2004).

This expansion in the number of loyalty programmes leads Capizzi, Ferguson, and Cuthbertson (2004) to suggest that the market is mature. They also argue that five clear trends within the loyalty market can be identified. These are set out in Table 15.4. These trends suggest that successful sales promotions schemes will be those that enable members to perceive significant value linked to their continued association with a scheme (see Market Insight 15.4). That value will be driven by schemes run by groups of complementary brands, which use technology to understand customer dynamics and communications that complement their preferred values. The medium-term goal might be that these schemes should reflect customers' different relationship needs and recognize the different loyalty levels desired by different people.

go online

Visit the **Online Resource Centre** and complete Internet Activity 15.2 to learn more about how to increase customer loyalty.

▶ Market Insight 15.4

Defending Loyal Customers

In response to a slump in the number of business travellers during the recession, British Airways announced that it was to offer membership of its Executive Club to all customers, including all those travelling on economy class tickets. Less than 50% of the scheme's 1.7m UK members have Gold or Silver status, previously the necessary requirement to join the Executive Club. The majority are Blue level members, for whom the key, and perhaps only, benefit is that members can earn frequent flier miles, which can be redeemed for free tickets.

Before the change in economic conditions, access to the Executive Club was dependent on elite passengers

Tesco relaunched their clubcard scheme in 2009, doubling shoppers' points in the process

Source: Courtesy of Tesco Stores Limited.

buying expensive seats and earning the points needed for Gold or Silver membership. This entitled these passengers to a range of world class facilities. The change in policy is not about opening up the facilities to economy passengers but is a defensive strategy designed principally to prevent it losing its Gold and Silver cardholders. These are important customers but many are travelling on cheaper tickets or less often as their employers seek to cut travel costs. The offer might have been made just to create traffic for its business lounges and to ensure the expensive facilities were used.

This defensive posture can be seen to be mirrored by Tesco. When they relaunched their Clubcard scheme in 2009 they doubled the number of points awarded to shoppers. This cost the supermarket group about £5m a week, but was seen by some commentators as a move designed to arrest falling market share following the defection of some Tesco shoppers to other stores and discounters such as Aldi and Lidl. The move proved to be successful as market share had increased by the end of the year.

Sources: Finch (2009); Jamieson (2009).

1 Do you think that extending the benefits in a loyalty scheme is a good idea in the long run? Justify your view.

2 How else might an organization retain customers, particularly in a recession?

3 ASDA have refused to offer a loyalty scheme, preferring to offer low prices. Does this offer customers better value?

Managing Relationships

The next sections of this chapter concern issues associated with the management of relationships. The first section considers ideas about trust and commitment and is followed by related issues concerning **customer satisfaction**. The next section deals with ways in which these important relationships can be managed and, in particular, considers customer service systems and processes such as CRM and customer recovery issues.

Trust, Commitment, and Satisfaction

Many writers contend that one of the crucial factors associated with the development and maintenance of interorganizational relationships is trust (Morgan and Hunt, 1994; Doney and Cannon, 1997). However, this concept, although important, is difficult to define and many authors fail to specify clearly what they mean when using it (Cousins and Stanwix, 2001). A review of the literature indicates that trust is an element associated with personal, intraorganizational, and interorganizational relationships, and is necessary for their continuation. As Gambetta (1988) argues, trust is a means of reducing uncertainty in order for effective relationships to develop.

Cousins and Stanwix also suggest that, although trust is a term used to explain how relationships work, often it actually refers to ideas concerning risk, power, and dependency, and these propositions are used interchangeably. From their research of vehicle manufacturers, it emerges that B2B relationships are about the creation of mutual business advantage and the degree of confidence that one organization has in another.

Trust involves judgments about reliability and integrity and is concerned with the degree of confidence that one party to a relationship has that another will fulfil their obligations and responsibilities. The presence of trust in a relationship is important because it reduces both the threat of opportunism and the possibility of conflict, which, in turn, increases the probability of buyer satisfaction. It has been claimed that the three major outcomes from the development of relationship trust are satisfaction, reduced **perceived risk**, and continuity (Pavlou, 2002).

▶ Perceived risk is concerned with the expectation of loss and is, therefore, tied closely with organizational performance.

▶ Trust that a seller will not take advantage of the imbalance of information between buyer and seller effectively reduces risk.

▶ Continuity is related to business volumes, necessary in online B2B marketplaces, and the development of both on- and offline enduring relationships. Trust is associated with continuity and when present is, therefore, indicative of long-term relationships.

Trust within a consumer context is important as it can reduce uncertainty. For example, brands are an important means of instilling trust mainly because they are a means of condensing and conveying information. Strong brands provide sufficient information for consumers to make calculated purchase decisions in the absence of full knowledge. In a sense, consumers transfer their responsibility for brand decision-making, and hence brand performance, to the brand itself. Through regular brand purchases, habits or 'routinized response behaviour' develop. This is important not just because complex decision-making is simplified but because the amount of communication necessary to assist and provoke purchase is considerably reduced.

One particular aspect of this topic is called institutional trust, that is, trust in organizations rather than individual people or product/service brands. This is important, not only in B2B markets where the overall reputation of the organization is important when dealing with other organizations, but it can also be critical in B2C markets. In these markets the development of trust to encourage safe purchasing can be vital. Airlines and financial services organizations use corporate branding to instil trust, whereas online consumer purchasing requires that risk of credit card fraud and deception be minimized. To achieve this, organizations use a variety of techniques to lower perceived risk.

Pavlou (2002) argues that there are six means by which institutional trust can be encouraged. These are reproduced in Table 15.5.

▶ **Table 15.5** Elements of institutional trust

Element of institutional trust	Key aspect
Perceived monitoring	Refers to the supervision of transactions by, for example, regulatory authorities or owners of B2B market exchanges. This can mitigate uncertainty through a perception that sellers or buyers who fail to conform with established rules and regulations will be penalized
Perceived accreditation	Refers to badges or symbols that denote membership of externally recognized bodies that bestow credibility, authority, security, and privacy on a selling organization
Perceived legal bonds	Refers to contracts between buyers, sellers, and independent third parties, so that the costs of breaking a contract are perceived to be greater than the benefits of such an action. Trust in the selling organization is, therefore, enhanced when bonds are present
Perceived feedback	Refers to signals about the quality of an organization's reputation, and such feedback from other buyers about sellers, perhaps through word-of-mouth communication; can deter sellers from undertaking opportunistic behaviour
Perceived cooperative norms	Refers to the values, standards, and principles adopted by those party to a series of exchanges. Cooperative norms and values signal good faith and behavioural intent, through which trust is developed

Source: Reprinted from Pavlou (2002), with permission from Elsevier.

The presence of trust within a relationship is influenced by four main factors (Young and Wilkinson, 1989). These include the duration of the relationship; the relative power of the participants; the presence of cooperation; and various environmental factors that may be present at any one moment. Although pertinent, these are quite general factors and it is Morgan and Hunt (1994) who established what are regarded today as the key underlying dimensions of relationship marketing. In their seminal paper, they argued that it is the presence of both commitment and trust that leads to cooperative behaviour, customer satisfaction, and ultimately successful relationship marketing.

Commitment is important because it implies a desire that a relationship continues and is strengthened because it is of value. Morgan and Hunt proposed that commitment and trust are the **key mediating variables** (KMV) between five antecedents and five outcomes (see Figure 15.7).

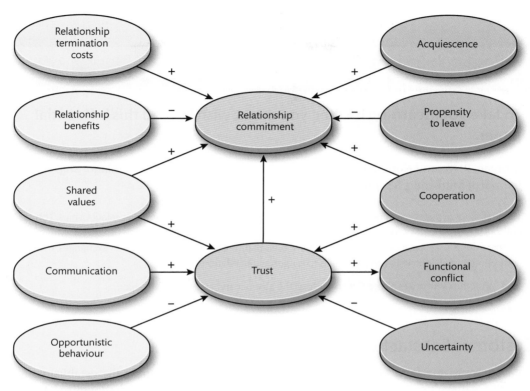

Figure 15.7

The KMV model of relationship marketing

Source: Morgan and Hunt (1994).

According to the KMV model, the greater the losses anticipated through the termination of a relationship, the greater the commitment expressed by the exchange partners. When relationship partners share similar values, commitment increases. Morgan and Hunt proposed that building a relationship based on trust and commitment can give rise to a number of benefits. Some of these include developing a set of shared values, reducing costs when the relationship finishes, and increasing profitability as a greater number of end user customers are retained because of the inherent value and satisfaction they experience. Cooperation arises from a relationship driven by high levels of both trust and commitment (Morgan and Hunt, 1994).

Ryssel, Ritter, and Gemunden (2004: 203) recognize that trust (and commitment) has a 'significant impact on the creation of value and conclude that value creation is a function of the atmosphere of a relationship rather than the technology employed'. Trust and commitment are concepts that are central to relationship marketing.

▶ Research Insight 15.4

To take your learning further, you might wish to read this influential paper.

Morgan, R. M., and Hunt, S. D. (1994), 'The commitment–trust theory of relationship marketing', *Journal of Marketing*, 58 (July), 20–38.

This well-known paper examines the role of trust and commitment in buyer–supplier relationships. The authors present the KMV model to explain various behavioural and cognitive aspects associated with exchange partnerships. Using social exchange theory, it is argued that through mutually beneficial exchanges, trust and commitment develop, which, in turn, leads to longer lasting relationships.

 Visit the **Online Resource Centre** to read the abstract and access the full paper.

Customer Satisfaction

A natural outcome from building trust and developing commitment is the establishment of customer satisfaction. This is seen as important because satisfaction is thought to be positively related to customer retention, which, in turn, leads to an improved return on investment and hence profitability. Unsurprisingly, many organizations seek to improve levels of customer satisfaction, with the intention of strengthening customer relationships and driving higher levels of retention and loyalty (Ravald and Grönroos, 1996). So, the simple equation is build trust, drive satisfaction, improve retention, and increase profits.

However, customer satisfaction is not driven by trust alone. Customer expectations play an important role and help shape a customer's perception of product/service performance. Customers compare performance against their expectations and through this process feel a sense of customer satisfaction or dissatisfaction. More recent ideas suggest that the perceived value of a relationship can be more important than trust when building customer satisfaction (Ulaga and Eggert, 2006).

So, if expectations are met then customer satisfaction is achieved. If expectations are exceeded then customers are delighted, but if expectations are not met then customers are said to be dissatisfied. This simplistic interpretation can be misleading because satisfaction does not always imply loyalty (Mittal and Lassar, 1998). As noted earlier, what may be seen as loyalty may be nothing more than convenience or even inertia, and dissatisfaction need not result in brand desertion (O'Malley, 1998).

Cumby and Barnes (1998) provide a useful insight into what contributes to customer satisfaction:

▶ Core product/service—the bundle of attributes, features, and benefits that must reach competitive levels if a relationship is to develop.

▶ Support services and systems—the quality of services and systems used to support the core product/service.

▶ Technical performance—the synchronization of the core product/services with the support infrastructure to deliver on the promise.

▶ Elements of customer interaction—the quality of customer care demonstrated through face-to-face and technology-mediated communications.

▶ Affective dimensions of services—the subtle and non-core interactions that say something about the way the organization feels about the customer.

This is a more useful insight into what it is that drives customer satisfaction, because it incorporates a wide range of factors and recognizes the importance of personal contact. Customer satisfaction and the quality of customer relationships are related, in differing ways, among differing people and contexts. However, one factor that is common to both is the perceived value of the interaction between parties. This suggests that it is important for marketing communications to deliver messages that reinforce positive beliefs about a brand and provide reassurance.

Customer Service and Relationship Management

The idea that providing a superior customer service might help in the (repeat) purchase decision process is something that some organizations are only just beginning to understand. For a long time it was assumed that product quality and pricing were sufficient differentiators. However, product quality is no longer a viable means of establishing competitive advantage, simply because of shortening lifecycles and improved technologies. Service, although difficult to deliver in a consistent way, is very difficult to replicate and is becoming an important aspect of customer management.

The management of relationships has for a long time been regarded as the responsibility of the sales force. However, this perspective has also changed and it is now expected that a range of employees have a responsibility for satisfying customer needs. Managing trust and reputation, reducing risk, and providing high levels of customer satisfaction are now regarded as an expectation that all suppliers need to meet.

Two elements of customer management are considered here. The first are customer contact centres, and, second, customer relationship management systems (CRM). More detailed information about these systems, other new technologies, and customer services can be found in Chapter 17.

Customer Contact Centres

Many organizations try to help their customers contact them. This can be achieved via a call centre or customer contact centre as they are now known. Instead of customers contacting a variety of people in different offices and perhaps receiving assorted messages, all of which require training and support, it makes sense to have a single point of contact. Very often, this task is outsourced to a specialist company, which is trained in product support and company policy. Specialist organizations can reduce costs, improve efficiency, and enhance a client's reputation through the quality of interaction with customers. Using digital technology to manage voice, web, interactive TV, email, mobile, and fax-originated messages, contact centres enable customers to complain about a product performance and related experience, seek product-related advice, make suggestions regarding product or packaging development, and comment about an action or development concerning the brand as a whole. Very often, this access is referred to as a 'careline': a dedicated telephone and email connection. In addition, organizations can use contact centres to provide outbound calls, often to generate sales leads or to provide market information.

Carelines and contact centres have enormous potential to support brands. The majority of calls to carelines are not about complaints, but are from people seeking advice or help about products. Food manufacturers provide cooking and recipe advice; cosmetic and toiletries companies provide healthcare advice and application guidelines; whereas white goods and service-based organizations can provide technical and operational support. By dealing with complaints in a prompt, courteous, and efficient manner, people are more likely to repurchase a brand than if the service was not available. Carelines are essentially a post-purchase support mechanism, which facilitates feedback and intelligence gathering. They can warn of imminent problems (product defects), provide ideas for new products or variants, and, of course, provide a valuable method to reassure customers and improve customer retention levels.

CRM Systems

The development of customer relationship management (CRM) systems has been a significant development in the way organizations have attempted to manage their customers. CRM applications were originally developed as salesforce support systems (mainly salesforce automation) and later applications were designed for supplier organizations to enable them to manage their end user customers. They have subsequently evolved as a more sophisticated means of managing direct customers and are an integral part of customer contact centres, discussed in the previous section.

The principal aim of CRM systems is to provide superior value by enabling suppliers' access to real-time customer information. This helps suppliers to anticipate and satisfy customers' needs effectively, efficiently, and in a timely manner. To make this happen, a complete history of each customer needs to be available to all staff who interact with customers. This is necessary in order to answer two types of questions. First, there are questions prompted by customers about orders, quotations, or products, and, second, questions prompted by internal managers concerning, for example, strategy, segmentation, relationship potential, sales forecasts, and salesforce management. Market Insight 15.5 discusses the Carphone Warehouse's use of CRM systems.

▶ Market Insight 15.5

First Direct's multichannel marketing strategy

Launched as a 24/7 telephone bank in 1989, First Direct was targeted at people who didn't have time to visit a bank branch or didn't enjoy the experience. Using information to feed the bank's value proposition, First Direct very quickly established itself as the number one provider in terms of customer satisfaction and the number of recommendations offered by customers.

Today, the target market is referred to as the 'Mass Affluent' and interaction with their 1.2m customers is facilitated through a variety of channels, although over 80% of transactions are now conducted online.

First Direct's CRM system is regarded as central and paramount to the coordination of the variety of communication, consumer insight, and service

First Direct pioneered telephone banking in 1989
Source: Courtesy of First Direct.

support activities that the bank undertakes. Customer communications through phone, SMS, written correspondence, and the internet require service representatives to have a single view of all relevant interactions. They also need a view of customer preferences, products, and enquiries. The CRM system is required to integrate all the channel activities and provide real-time information at any time. It is possible for a First Direct agent to engage online customers through text chat and then switch to co-browsing whereby both are looking at the same screen, and so they are enabled to resolve any misunderstanding or difficulties.
Source: Garrett *et al.* (2007).

1 Do you think CRM systems provide customers with added value or are they just a means by which organizations can achieve their business goals?

2 Search the web, identify two online banks and compare their offers.

3 Is the outsourcing of customer contact centres to a different country in the customers' best interests?

Flint, Woodruff, and Gardial (2002) recognize that the customer value concept provides the grounding for customer relationship management (CRM). Acceptance of the notion that different customers represent differing levels of importance to a firm, suggests that different customer segments represent different profit potential and hence different value. So, if different groups of customers represent different levels of profit potential, it is important to manage this variability in order to maximize the use of a firm's resources.

CRM applications typically consist of call management, lead management, customer record, and sales support and payment systems. Ideally, they should be incorporated as part of an overall strategic approach (Wightman, 2000). However, such systems are invariably treated as add-on applications that are expected to resolve customer interface difficulties. Unsurprisingly, many clients have voiced their dissatisfaction with CRM as many of the promises and expectations have not been fulfilled.

Sood (2002) suggests that problems have arisen with CRM implementation because technology vendors have not properly understood the need to manage all relationships with all major stakeholders. Disappointment with CRM systems can also be regarded as a failure to understand the central tenets of a customer-focused philosophy and the need to adopt a strategic business approach to managing customer relationships. If the centrality of concepts such as trust and commitment are not understood, nor a willingness displayed to share information and achieve a balanced relationship, the installation of databases and data warehouses will not, and to date has not, changed the quality of an organization's relationships with its customers.

O'Malley and Mitussi (2002) also refer to the failure of CRM systems in terms of internal political power struggles and associated issues about who owns particular systems and data. Where an organization has not established a customer-oriented culture nor begun to implement enterprise-wide systems and procedures, it is probable that access to certain data might be impeded or at least made problematic.

Referring to customer management systems in the public sector, Stone (2002) draws on experience of CRM in the private sector. He argues that good customer management is never achieved just by changing the interface, for example introducing a call centre or developing a website or portal. Good customer management requires attention to an organization's culture, training, strategy, and propositions and processes. Regretfully, too many organizations focus on the interface or fail to understand the broader picture.

It is important to understand that even the most sophisticated CRM systems are based on data about an organization's contacts and transactions with them. Although these can be processed to supply one-touch, real-time multidimensional views of any relationship, they do not manage it. That, as ever, is the challenge for the people involved.

go online

Visit the **Online Resource Centre** and follow the weblink to CRM Today, to learn more about CRM systems, applications, news, and research.

Skills for Employment

▶▶ It's vital that anyone looking to work in a communications or marketing department shares that company's vision and values. Whilst it can be a strong advantage to have work experience in the field of marketing, experience in other fields can be equally as important so long as you can demonstrate why the experience and skills you have are beneficial to that company. Often work experience in another industry can actually provide you with a fresh perspective on marketing challenges, allowing you to draw on new ideas and approaches utilized in other fields. ◀◀

Fredrik Thor, Brand and marketing manager, Systembolaget

 Visit the **Online Resource Centre** to discover more tips and advice on skills for the workplace.

Chapter Summary

To consolidate your learning, the key points from this chapter are summarized below:

■ **Explain the concept of perceived value, and the main characteristics of the value chain.**

Value is a customer's estimate of the extent to which an offering can satisfy their needs. Value can be generated in many ways, not just through products and prices. One important source of value is the relationship generated through buyer–seller interaction. Organizations interact with other organizations in order to provide superior value for their customers. The quality, duration, and level of interdependence between organizations can vary considerably, and this can be visualized as a continuum. At one end are transactional exchanges, characterized by short-term product-, or price-oriented exchanges. At the other end of the continuum are collaborative exchanges characterized by a long-term orientation, where there is complete integration of systems and processes and the relationship is motivated by partnership and mutual support.

■ **Understand the differences between the transactional and the relationship approaches to marketing.**

Relationship marketing is a more contemporary marketing theory than the 4Ps or transactional marketing. Rather than focusing on products and prices and customer attraction, it is the retention of customers and the relationship between buyers, sellers, and other stakeholders that is at the heart of this approach.

■ **Describe the different stages of the customer relationship lifecycle.**

The customer relationship lifecycle consists of four main stages, namely customer acquisition, development, retention, and finally decline or termination.

■ **Explain the principles and economics of customer retention and consider the merits of loyalty programmes.**

Relationship marketing is based on the premise that retained customers are more profitable than transactional marketing-based customers. Loyalty is an important concept within relationship marketing and the loyalty ladder model illustrates the critical point that different customers represent different value to organizations. This suggests that there are many different forms of loyalty and that different marketing strategies are required to reach each of them.

■ **Understand the principles of trust, commitment, and customer satisfaction and explain how they are interlinked.**

There are several key concepts associated with the management of customer relationships. The main ones are trust, commitment, and satisfaction. These are interrelated and the management of customer relationships should be based on the principles of reducing the influence of both power and the incidence of conflict in order to build customer trust, gain customer commitment, and, through loyalty and retention, generate customer satisfaction. This approach should increase the perceived value of the relationship for all parties.

■ **Describe ways in which organizations try to provide customer service and support.**

The principal aim of customer contact centres and CRM systems is to provide both buyers and sellers with superior value by enabling suppliers to gain access to real-time customer information, in order to satisfy their customers' needs appropriately.

Review Questions

1 In your own words explain the terms 'customer value', value-to-customers, and value-for-customers.

2 The value chain consists of four support activities and five primary activities. Name them.

3 Draw the continuum of value exchanges.

4 Describe the key differences between transaction marketing and relationship marketing.

5 Explain the key aspects of the four phases of the customer relationship lifecycle.

6 Why is customer retention an important aspect of modern marketing?

7 What is a loyalty ladder?

8 Write brief notes explaining why trust is an important aspect of relationship marketing.

9 Describe how customer satisfaction might be achieved.

10 Explain how CRM systems should help organizations. Why do so many fail to live up to expectations?

Worksheet Summary

Visit the **Online Resource Centre** and complete Worksheet 15.1. This will aid in learning about the four general types of loyalty—emotional loyalty, price loyalty, incentivized loyalty, and monopoly loyalty—and how these four types of loyalty can exist for one offering across different customers and situations.

Discussion Questions

1 Having read Case Insight 15.1, how would you advise RAKBANK as to the key product attributes necessary to attract and retain customers?

2 Discuss reasons why organizations should invest in developing customer relationships. Use an organization of your own choice to illustrate your response.

3 Westcliffe and Sons make a range of fruit juice drinks. Their business falls into two main segments, consumers and business users, for example local councils and catering companies. Recent sales figures suggest that orders from some catering companies are down on previous years and some have stopped buying from them altogether. The marketing director of Westcliffe has reported that he cannot understand the reason for the decline in business as product quality and prices are very competitive. Advise the marketing director about the key issues he should consider and discuss how the company should re-establish itself with the catering companies.

4 Using loyalty schemes with which you are familiar, or select any two from the web, make brief notes that compare and contrast their characteristics.

5 Working in small groups devise ways in which a online retailer (e.g. Amazon) might try to improve customer trust and commitment. How might this be different for a high street retailer?

Visit the **Online Resource Centre** and complete the Multiple Choice Questions to assess your knowledge of Chapter 15.

go online

References

Anderson, J. (1995), 'Relationships in business markets: exchange episodes, value creation and their empirical assessment', *Journal of the Academy of Marketing Science*, 23, 4, 346–50.

Anon. (2008), Case Study: Barclays, *The Marketer*, February, 21–5.

Baldinger, A., and Rubinson, J. (1996), 'Brand loyalty: the link between attitude and behaviour', *Journal of Advertising Research*, 36, 6 (November–December), 22–34.

Borders, A. L., Johnston, W. J., and Rigdon, E. E. (2001), 'Electronic commerce and network perspectives in industrial marketing management', *Industrial Marketing Management*, 30, 2 (February), 199–205.

Bruhn, M. (2003), *Relationship Marketing: Management of Customer Relationships*, Harlow: FT/Prentice Hall.

Capizzi, M., Ferguson, R., and Cuthbertson, R. (2004), 'Loyalty trends for the 21st century', *Journal of Targeting Measurement and Analysis for Marketing*, 12, 3, 199–212.

Christopher, M., Payne, A., and Ballantyne, D. (2002), *Relationship Marketing: Creating Stakeholder Value*, Oxford: Butterworth-Heinemann.

Cousins, P.D. and Stanwix, E. (2001), 'It's only a matter of confidence! A comparison of relationship management between Japanese and UK non-owned vehicle manufacturers', *International Journal of Operations and Production Management*, 21, 9 (October), 1160–80.

Cumby, J. A., and Barnes, J. (1998), 'How customers are made to feel: the role of affective reactions in driving customer satisfaction', *Customer Relationship Management*, 1, 1, 54–63.

Day, G. (2000), 'Managing market relationships', *Journal of the Academy of Marketing Science*, 28, 1 (Winter), 24–30.

Dick, A. S., and Basu, K. (1994), 'Customer loyalty: toward an integrated framework', *Journal of the Academy of Marketing Science*, 22, 2, 99–113.

Doney, P. M., and Cannon, J. P. (1997), 'An examination of the nature of trust in buyer–seller relationships', *Journal of Marketing*, 62, 2, 1–13.

Dowling, G. R., and Uncles, M. (1997), 'Do customer loyalty programs work?' *Sloan Management Review*, 38, 4 (Summer), 71–82.

Doyle, P. (2000), *Value Based Marketing*, Chichester: Wiley.

Dwyer, R. F., Schurr, P. H., and Oh, S. (1987), 'Developing buyer–seller relationships', *Journal of Marketing*, 51 (April), 11–27.

Finch, J. (2009), 'Tesco increases market share', *The Guardian*, 10 November. Retrieve from www.guardian.co.uk/business/2009/nov/10/tesco-waitrose-win-market-share, accessed 9 January 2010.

Flint, D.J., Woodruff, R.B., and Gardial, S.F. (2002), 'Exploring the phenomenon of customers' desired value change in a business-to-business context', *Journal of Marketing*, 66, 4, 102–17.

Ford, D. (1980), 'The development of buyer–seller relationships in industrial markets', *European Journal of Marketing*, 14, 5–6, 339–54.

Fournier, S., and Yao, J. L. (1997), 'Reviving brand loyalty: a reconceptualisation within the framework of consumer–brand relationships', *International Journal of Research in Marketing*, 14, 5, 451–72.

Gambetta, D. (1988), *Trust: Making and Breaking Co-operative Relations*, New York: Blackwell.

Garrett, A., Roopalee, D., Wilson, H., and Clark, M. (2007), *First Direct Comes of Age*, Cranfield Customer Management Forum.

Grönroos, C. (1994), 'From marketing mix to relationship marketing', *Management Decision*, 32, 2, 4–20.

— (2009), 'Marketing as promise management: regaining customer management for marketing', *Journal of Business and Industrial Marketing*, 24, 5/6, 351–59.

Gummesson, E. (2002), *Total Relationship Marketing; Rethinking Marketing Management: From 4Ps to 30Rs*, Oxford: Butterworth-Heinemann.

Jamieson, A., (2009), 'British Airways extends loyalty scheme to passengers on cheapest fares', *The Telegraph*, 22 August 2009. Retrieve from www.telegraph.co.uk/finance/newsbysector/epic/bay/6073303/British-Airways-extends-loyalty-scheme-to-passengers-on-cheapest-fares.html, accessed 9 January 2010.

Johanson, J., and Mattsson, L.-G. (1994), 'The markets as networks tradition in Sweden', in G. Laurent, G. L. Lilien, and B. Pras (eds), *Research Traditions in Marketing*, Boston: Kluwer Academic Publishing, 321–42.

Kothandaraman, P., and Wilson, D. (2001), 'The future of competition: value creating networks', *Industrial Marketing Management*, 30, 4 (May), 379–89.

Lefaix-Durand, A., Kozak, R., Beauregard, R., and Poulin, D. (2009), 'Extending relationship value: observations from a case study of the Canadian structural wood products industry', *Journal of Business & Industrial Marketing*, 24, 5/6, 389–407.

Macneil, I.R. (1980), *The New Social Contract*. New Haven, CT: Yale University Press.

McLoughlin, D., and Horan, C. (2002), 'Perspectives from the markets-as-networks approach', *Industrial Marketing Management*, 29, 4, 285–92.

Menon, A., Homburg, C., and Beutin, N. (2005), 'Understanding customer value in business-to-business relationships', *Journal of Business to Business Marketing*, 12, 2, 1–38.

Mittal, B., and Lassar, W. M. (1998), 'Why do consumers switch? The dynamics of satisfaction versus loyalty', *Journal of Services Marketing*, 12, 3, 177–94.

Morgan, R. M., and Hunt, S. D. (1994), 'The commitment–trust theory of relationship marketing', *Journal of Marketing*, 58 (July), 20–38.

O'Malley, L. (1998), 'Can loyalty schemes really build loyalty?' *Marketing Intelligence and Planning*, 16, 1, 47–55.

——, and Mitussi, D. (2002), 'Relationships and technology: strategic implications', *Journal of Strategic Marketing*, 10, 225–38.

Packard, V. (1958), *The Hidden Persuaders*, London: Penguin.

Pavlou, P. A. (2002), 'Institution-based trust in interorganisational exchange relationships: the role of online B2B marketplaces on trust formation', *Journal of Strategic Information Systems*, 11, 3–4 (December), 215–43.

Pels, J., Möller, K., and Saren, M. (2009), 'Do we really understand business marketing? Getting beyond the RM and BM matrimony', *Journal of Business and Industrial Marketing*, 24, 5/6, 322–36.

Porter, M. E. (1985), *Competitive Advantage: Creating and Sustaining Superior Performance*, New York: The Free Press.

Ravald, A., and Grönroos, C. (1996), 'The value concept and relationship marketing', *European Journal of Marketing*, 30, 2, 19–33.

Reichheld, F. F., and Sasser, E. W. (1990), 'Zero defections: quality comes to services', *Harvard Business Review*, September, 105–11.

Reinartz, W. J., and Kumar, V. (2002), 'The mismanagement of customer loyalty', *Harvard Business Review*, July, 86–94.

Ribeiro, A.H.P., Brashear, T.G., Monteiro, P.R.R., and Damzaio, L.F. (2009), 'Marketing relationships in Brazil trends in value strategies and capabilities', *Journal of Business and Industrial Marketing*, 24, 5/6, 449–59.

Ryssel, R., Ritter, T., and Gemunden, H. G. (2004), 'The impact of information technology deployment on trust, commitment and value creation in business relationships', *Journal of Business and Industrial Marketing*, 19, 3, 197–207.

Sharma, A., Krishman, R., and Grewal, D. (2001), 'Value creation in markets: a critical area of focus for business-to-business markets', *Industrial Marketing Management*, 30, 4 (May), 341–402.

Sheth, J. (1973), 'A model of industrial buyer behaviour', *Journal of Marketing*, 37 (October), 50–6.

Sheth, J.N. and Uslay, C. (2007), 'Implications of the revised definition of marketing: from exchange to value creation', *Journal of Public Policy & Marketing*, 26, 2, 302–7.

Simpson, P. M., Sigauw, J. A., and Baker, T. L. (2001), 'A model of value creation: supplier behaviors and their impact on reseller-perceived value', *Industrial Marketing Management*, 30, 2 (February), 119–34.

Sood, B. (2002), *CRM in B2B: Developing Customer-centric Practices for Partner and Supplier Relationships*, retrieve from www.intelligentcrm.com/020509/508feat2_2.shtml, accessed December 2007.

Spekman, R. E., and Carroway, R. (2005), 'Making the transition to collaborative buyer–seller relationships: an emerging framework', *Industrial Marketing Management*, 35, 1 (January), 10–19.

Stone, M. (2002), 'Managing public sector customers', *What's New in Marketing*, October, retrieve from www.wnim.com/, accessed December 2007.

Ulaga, W., and Eggert, A. (2005), 'Relationship value in business markets: the construct and its dimensions', *Journal of Business-to-Business Marketing*, 12, 1, 73–99.

——and—— (2006), 'Relationship value and relationship quality', *European Journal of Marketing*, 40, 3–4, 311–27.

Webster, F. E., and Wind, Y. (1972), 'A general model for understanding organisational buying behaviour', *Journal of Marketing*, 36 (April), 12–14.

Wightman, T. (2000), 'e-CRM: the critical dot.com discipline', *Admap*, April, 46–8.

Worthington, S., and Horne, S. (1998), 'A new relationship marketing model and its application in the affinity credit card market', *International Journal of Bank Marketing*, 16, 1 (February), 39–44.

Young, L. C., and Wilkinson, I. F. (1989), 'The role of trust and co-operation in marketing channels: a preliminary study', *European Journal of Marketing*, 23, 2, 109–22.

16 Not-For-Profit Marketing

● Learning Outcomes

After reading this chapter, you will be able to:

▶ Describe the key characteristics of not-for-profit organizations

▶ Explain why not-for-profit organizations do not always value their customers

▶ Analyse stakeholders and develop appropriate engagement strategies

▶ Describe and assess cause-related marketing campaigns

▶ Understand how marketing can be, and is being, used to achieve social and political change in society

▶ Explain how marketing is used to raise funds for charitable organizations

> ▶ Case Insight 16.1

Founded in 1942, as the Oxfam Committee for Famine Relief, Oxfam opened one of the world's first charity shop chains in Oxford in 1948. But given major changes in the world since, particularly in relation to climate change and the advance of information and communication technologies, how has this world-renowned charity kept pace? We speak to Nick Futcher to find out more.

Nick Futcher for Oxfam

Oxfam GB is an independent development, relief, and campaigning organization that works with others to overcome poverty and suffering, employing around 1,070 people in the UK. When it launched its first shop, it attracted donations ranging from false teeth, and stuffed animals, to a houseboat! Today our shop network, stretching from the High Street to cyberspace, forms an integral part of Oxfam's Trading Division. Oxfam GB is part of Oxfam International,

set up in 1995—a worldwide family of organizations sharing common values and working together for change and development. Oxfam GB's global programme works through eight regions worldwide, offering strategic funding, supporting long-term development programmes, delivering emergency relief in times of crisis and campaigning for a fairer world. Currently, Oxfam's primary organizational focus is combating climate change and mitigating its effects on the poorest people in the world.

Basic marketing techniques employed by Oxfam include TV and outdoor advertising, online advertising, mailings, and face-to-face recruitment. Such techniques have been developed and refined over time. Fundamentally, it pays to be innovative. Oxfam were the first to introduce regular giving with our £2 a month initiative, and started the first online charity 'shop' through a combination of auctions of donated goods in 1996.

Oxfam's supporters range from individuals, institutional donors, trusts and corporations, all the way through to community fundraising groups. There are a variety of individual supporter types that are all pivotal to Oxfam's work, such supporters include: regular donors, one-off donors, legacy leavers, fundraisers, campaigners, volunteers, those that donate goods, those that buy from Oxfam shops, and those that attend Oxfam events.

In developing our marketing activities, all our advertising must adhere to the rules and regulations set

Oxfam's fundraising helps overcome poverty and suffering throughout the world

Source: © iStockphoto LP

▶ Case Insight 16.1

out by the Advertising Standards Agency (ASA) and the Fundraising Standards Board (FRSB), who oversee an independent and transparent scheme for fundraising. This is important because we aim to ensure public confidence in charitable giving is increased.

Oxfam, as a charity, uses marketing for a variety of overarching objectives. The first is to facilitate fundraising—the cornerstone of charitable organizations. This transmits into a variety of marketing strategies within different teams to promote how easy, fun, and ultimately rewarding, supporting Oxfam is. These can range from our events team producing targeted communications to advertise Oxjam, Oxfam's month-long music festival spread across venues all over the UK, to direct mailing for emergency cash appeals and development projects. Oxfam shops represent a more traditional and recognizable touchpoint for engaging supporters, and remain a key mechanism for our Trading Division to raise funds. Oxfam is also a campaigning organization, and marketing is a tool that allows us to inform people of upcoming activities and ways to get involved, such

as petitioning and demonstrating, to raise awareness and help effect lasting change.

Our organizational priority for the short to medium term will remain mitigating the effects of climate change on the world's poorest people. However, the troubled economic climate of recent times has made planning for the future in marketing terms more difficult. Because giving to a charitable cause is largely dependent on engagement with the issues a charity works on, maintaining and consolidating existing support is vital, particularly in a difficult economic climate. However, research was indicating that Oxfam was becoming more distant in the minds of the UK public. Although people respected and trusted us (over 99% of the UK public knew who we are), they had a limited understanding of what we do and didn't feel close to us as a brand. There was considerable potential to improve knowledge and involvement of Oxfam's aims and values.

The key question was, how should we go about repositioning ourselves?

Introduction

Over the last 40 years, the role of marketing in not-for-profit organizations has grown substantially as these organizations have realized the value of marketing in developing a strong understanding of customers and other stakeholders. But have you ever wondered what would happen if a charity ever fully met its strategic objectives? Would it, and should it, cease to exist? Are the techniques and tools we use in commercial marketing equally relevant in a not-for-profit environment, where the remit is not to make shareholders rich? Is there any difference in how we use marketing techniques in a social environment, for example, when governments use marketing to reduce binge drinking among young people, or increase fruit and vegetable consumption to five or six portions a day, or increase voter registration? In this chapter, we seek to answer some of these questions and outline how marketing operates in not-for-profit environments.

Until now in the book, our attention has been centred on commercial organizations, those intent on making profits. However, there are many other organizations that operate in what is referred to as the not-for-profit sector. Kotler and Levy (1969) were the first marketing academics to realize the potential of broadening the application of marketing to not-for-profit enterprises, a suggestion which was ground-breaking at the time. So, for example, marketing is now readily used by local government, churches, museums, charities, universities, political parties, zoos, and public hospitals, all of which operate without profit as their central goal.

Despite the similarities between not-for-profit and commercial marketing highlighted by Kotler and Levy, there are some key differences in how marketing is used in the not-for-profit and for-profit environments, particularly in relation to marketing communications. Rothschild (1979) indicates that these key differences include the following:

▶ Product—with not-for profit 'products', there is typically a weaker unique selling proposition, i.e. weaker direct benefits making it more difficult to direct customer or target audience behaviour in the way desired. For example, giving to charity provides us with a sense of 'doing good' but this feeling may not be sufficient to induce many people to give.

▶ Price—this important component of the marketing mix has different connotations in not-for-profit situations. For example, in a political marketing context, what is the price when marketing a political party? Is it the effort needed to go out and vote, or the economic costs of voting for one party versus another? In relation to charities, the amount donated is often left to the discretion of the donor and is in fact largely determined by the donor, rather than being specified by the seller as in a commercial transaction.

▶ Involvement—whereas we speak of high and low involvement in commercial situations in relation to the extent to which consumers become involved with a product or service in order to learn more about it during the purchasing process, the involvement in non-business situations displays more extreme tendencies. People often either really engage with a charity or political party or cause, for example, or show strong reactions against them.

▶ Segmentation—in the not-for-profit environment, it may be necessary to develop a campaign to drive behaviour in all targets rather than a specific audience, as in commercial markets. For example, a road safety campaign might seek to encourage all adults, rather than a specific audience, to drive at the speed limit. Nevertheless, there may well be a sub-group that needs a specific targeted message, for example, young male drivers who may persistently break the speed limit. But the point is that the general message is applicable to all.

Another key difference in the strategic marketing of not-for-profit organizations is the need to continually check the marketing strategy against the environment, available resources, and the organization's values (Hatten, 1982). In the latter case, the values of the organization have an impact not only on why the organization exists but also how it goes about its marketing activities, including fundraising, promotional programmes, and operational programme developments. Table 16.1 outlines the mission statements for a variety of national and international not-for-profit organizations.

For commercial organizations, the mission statement usually revolves around being the best in a particular marketplace and consequently achieving high levels of profit as a result. In the not-for-profit sector, mission statements revolve instead around causes. The raison d'être of a charity is to solve a particular societal problem, in effect, to extinguish the need for its own existence. Of course in truth, if a charity did indeed help to remove the problem it was designed to create (e.g. a tuberculosis charity ceasing to operate because there were no more cases of tuberculosis in the world), it would simply amend its mission. Like any other organization, a charity interacts with its environment and must stay relevant within the context that it operates in order to attract funding.

▶ Research Insight 16.1

To take your learning further, you might wish to read this influential paper.

Kotler, P. and Levy, S.J. (1969), 'Broadening the concept of marketing', *Journal of Marketing*, 33, 1 (January), 10–15.

In this seminal article, the authors proposed that marketing techniques and concepts, as typified by the 4Ps, could be applied to non-business organizations and therefore could be applied to the marketing of organizations, persons, and ideas. It provoked a considerable debate at the time with some writers suggesting that the concept of marketing had been broadened too far.

Visit the **Online Resource Centre** to read the abstract and access the full paper.

▶ **Table 16.1** A selection of mission statements from not-for-profit organizations

Organization	Mission statement
WWF—World Wildlife Fund (International)	To stop the degradation of our planet's natural environment, and build a future in which humans live in harmony with nature
International Committee of the Red Cross—ICRC (International)	To protect the lives and dignity of victims of war and internal violence and to provide them with assistance. It directs and coordinates the international relief activities conducted by the Movement in situations of conflict. It also endeavours to prevent suffering by promoting and strengthening humanitarian law and universal humanitarian principles
The Democratic Party (USA)	To keep our nation safe and expand opportunity for every American. That commitment is reflected in an agenda that emphasizes the strong economic growth, affordable healthcare for all Americans, retirement security, open, honest, and accountable government, and securing our nation while protecting our civil rights and liberties
China Charity Federation (China)	To deliver much needed assistance at the scene of natural disasters To equip the handicapped to better cope with their limitations To care for orphans and the aged that would otherwise be neglected To provide medical equipment and supplies to relieve and prevent illness To aid education so that everyone can be well educated To generally alleviate suffering and helping people to help themselves

▶ **Table 16.1** (continued)

Organization	Mission statement
The Big Issue (United Kingdom)	To offer homeless and vulnerably housed people the opportunity to earn a legitimate income by selling a magazine to the general public. We believe in offering 'a hand up, not a hand out' and in enabling individuals to take control of their lives
Great Ormond Street Hospital (GOSH) charity (United Kingdom)	To enable Great Ormond Street Hospital to provide world class care for its young patients and their families and to pioneer new treatments and cures for childhood illness by: ▶ contributing to the rebuilding and refurbishment of the hospital ▶ funding the most up-to-date equipment ▶ supporting research into, and development of, breakthrough treatments ▶ providing accommodation and other support services for children and their families

Source: Organizations' websites.

Key Characteristics of Not-for-Profit Organizations

The key characteristics that impact on marketing include: the presence of multiple stake-holders, transparency in the organization's mission and finances, the presence of multiple objectives in business and social terms, a different orientation compared with commercial organizations, and, finally, different customer perceptions (see Figure 16.1). We consider each of these characteristics in more detail below.

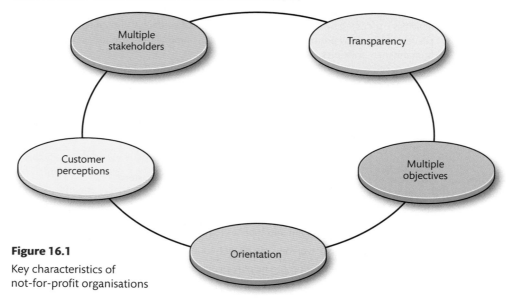

Figure 16.1

Key characteristics of not-for-profit organisations

Multiple Stakeholders

Although profit or private sector organizations need to interact with a range of stakeholders to achieve their business goals, their focus is on target market customers and shareholders. What is different about not-for-profit organizations, as the above mission statements indicate, is that they are concerned with a wider group of interested parties, which we term stakeholders. **Stakeholders** are those groups with whom the organization has a relationship, and which impact on the operations of the organization, including shareholders (or trustees), regulatory bodies, other charity or not-for-profit partners, supply chain partners, employees, and customers. In private companies, revenue is distributed from customers to shareholders, initially converted into profits by the organization, and shareholders are rewarded with a dividend, as a share of the profits earned. Companies have stakeholders also, but those stakeholders are less likely to have an influence on how the organization's profits are distributed.

Not-for-profit organizations also provide products and services but their customers or users do not always pay the full costs incurred by the organization to provide them. Many not-for-profit organizations rely on a range of stakeholders to provide the finance to support the organization. Instead of revenue from customers being used to reward shareholders, there are often no profits to be redistributed as those who help fund the organization do not require a return on their resource provision. For example, central government, local council taxpayers, lottery funding for special projects, and business rate taxes, to name but four sources of income, fund city councils in the UK. Charities are supported by individual and corporate donations. Museums may rely on a mixture of grants, lottery allocations, entrance fees, and individual donations and bequests. Zoos may also rely on a mixture of grants, entrance fees, and individual donations.

Because they serve a range of stakeholders, not-for-profit organizations do not always value their beneficiary customers (i.e. those who receive their charitable services) perhaps as much as they should, and they sometimes do not explain sufficiently to donors (i.e. supporter customers) how those donations are being used. The difficulties that arise in trying to satisfy multiple stakeholder groups are outlined in Table 16.2, which considers beneficiary and supporter customers and explains why charities do not always satisfy, and sometimes undervalue, these groups of customers (see Bruce, 1995).

It is important for not-for-profit organizations to determine which among different stakeholders have the most interest in their activities and the most power to affect their organization's performance. A common method used to distinguish between the interests and power of stakeholders is the stakeholder mapping matrix, outlined in Figure 16.2.

The matrix can be used to identify four types of stakeholder, based on high/low levels of interest that they have in an organization and the level of power they exert over it. Those with high levels of interest and power, group A, are key stakeholders that need to be continuously engaged. They might be funding bodies or powerful regulators, for example. Those with high interest but low levels of power, group B, for example, individual donors to charities, should be informed about that charity's activities in order to maintain their interest. Group C represent those organizations with high power but low interest. For the not-for-profit, it is important to either increase information flow to these organizations to increase their interest so that they can exert their power in the not-for-profit's favour (as a funding body might), or alternatively keep them satisfied if they intend to exert their power against the not-for-profit (as a regulator might, for instance). Finally, an organization's relationships with those stakeholders who have little power or interest should either be disregarded or revived.

▶ **Table 16.2** Why not-for-profit organizations do not always seem to value their customers

Reasons for not valuing beneficiaries	Reasons for not valuing supporters	Interactive reasons for undervaluing customers
Many not-for-profits exist in a monopolistic situation, which potentially creates an arrogant culture towards beneficiaries	Donors claim to be approached too often for donations and do not feel sufficiently appreciated	Dealing with multiple stakeholders can cause intergroup tension as one group's call on resources takes precedence over others. For example, a high-value donor for a university might want his donation to be used in a way that is different from the management of the university
Demand far outstrips supply creating problems in delivering a consistent quality of service	Volunteer service workers can often feel undervalued and undersupported	
Lack of market segmentation for beneficiaries undertaken		
Research into beneficiary customers' needs is not common because funds available are seen as better used for funding operations		

go online

Visit the **Online Resource Centre** and complete Internet Activity 16.2 to learn more about the stakeholders that are relevant to not-for-profit organizations and how to create a stakeholder mapping matrix.

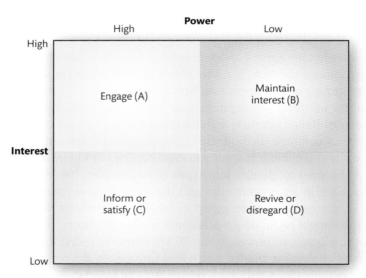

Figure 16.2

The stakeholder power/interest matrix

Source: Adapted from Scholes (2001).

▶ Market Insight 16.1

How The 'Gu' Saved Bilbao

Until 1997, Bilbao had been a decaying former steel and shipbuilding city, the capital of the Basque country in Spain, with little prospect of improvement, and an unemployment rate of 25%. When city planners decided they needed to revive the city, they came up with a brave plan. Why not build an art gallery? But what kind of art gallery and how would it succeed in regenerating the area? If it really was to revitalize the area, it had to have a strong architectural presence, be a spectacular tourist attraction in its own right, and house attractive art collections, which would bring leisure and tourist customers. Tourism can provide a powerful motor for economic investment. Spain had seen this before when the Mayor of Torremolinos transformed the city from a small seaside town into a leisure metropolis complete with skyscrapers in the 1960s, through a unified combination of city planning, tourism, and private investment.

If an art gallery was to be the key draw in Bilbao, what kind of art gallery would it be and who might partner with the Basque government to develop the concept? Then city officials had a brainwave. Why not ask the Solomon R Guggenheim Foundation if they were interested in developing a museum in Bilbao? After all, the Guggenheim Foundation had developed the Peggy Guggenheim Collection in Venice. The Foundation's Board of Trustees received the proposal

The Guggenheim Bilbao Museum's unusual and arresting design

▶ Market Insight 16.1 (continued)

warmly, not least because they had developed a long-term plan to develop Guggenheim museums in a number of international locations. In 1991, after long negotiations, the Basque Government Minister for Culture, the Deputy General of the Provincial Council of Bizkaia, and a member of the board of trustees of the Solomon R Guggenheim Foundation signed the Development and Programming Services Agreement for the Guggenheim Museum Bilbao. Nearly, six years later, the museum finally opened its doors to visitors, becoming an instant overnight sensation. Within a year, it had received 1.3m visitors.

The mission of the Guggenheim Museum Bilbao is 'to collect, conserve, and study modern and contemporary art, to exhibit the art of our times from a variety of perspectives in the context of art history, and to reach a broad and diverse audience. As one of the cornerstones of the Guggenheim Museum Network, and a symbol of the Basque Country's vitality, we hope to promote an understanding, appreciation, and enjoyment of art and its values in an iconic architectural setting'. From the mission statement, it is easy to see the importance of the museum in maintaining the Basque country's cultural heritage.

In 1997, the Deutsche Guggenheim opened in Berlin, to complete the Guggenheims in New York, Venice, and Bilbao. To celebrate contemporary Middle Eastern art, the Foundation is planning the new Guggenheim Museum, Abu Dhabi, to be located in the cultural district of Saadiyat Island, Abu Dhabi, United Arab Emirates. As China and India develop their tourist markets, perhaps it's only a matter of time before a Guggenheim Museum is located there too.

Sources: Marling (2003); www.guggenheim-bilbao.es; www.guggenheim.org/abu-dhabi.

1 **Who do you think were the key stakeholders in the process of developing the Guggenheim Museum Bilbao?**

2 **Who do you think the key stakeholders are now in developing the audiences for the collections that are shown to attract the visitors?**

3 **What are the risks in marketing terms in opening new Guggenheim Museums in different parts of the world?**

Transparency

The use of public money and donations in not-for-profit organizations requires that their source and allocation be easily understood, audited, and tracked. Such public scrutiny or transparency of funding is a feature that distinguishes these organizations from their private sector counterparts. In order for donations to continue to flow, not-for-profit organizations must be able to demonstrate trust, integrity, and honesty. In the case of charities, for example in the UK, they are governed by a different set of regulatory requirements, which require them to provide considerably greater information on how they are governed compared with their commercial counterparts. Charities' executive teams tend to be overseen by boards of trustees; often unpaid volunteers who are senior and experienced people who have some interest in the running of the organization. In parallel, the executive teams of private or public limited companies are overseen by paid executive and non-executive directors respectively.

Private sector organizations very often declare the minimum financial information required; just enough to comply with customs and excise requirements. Sometimes not-for-profit organizations overcompensate, providing considerable details of their internal procedures and processes. This is because they do not want to be judged as financially incompetent, and they want to avoid adverse media coverage and the negative perceptions that can follow. However, a serious outcome might be that future funding streams are curtailed or even terminated because a charity is seen to have sufficient funds to cover its activities. Equally, providing detailed outlines of organizational structures and plans can also provide competitors with valuable competitive intelligence, which could be detrimental to the organization. (See Chapter 4 for more on competitive intelligence).

Multiple Objectives

In the manufacturing, and other sectors, profit is a central overriding goal. Investment decisions are often based on the likely rate of return and resources are allocated according to the contribution (to profit) they will make. Profit provides a relatively easy measure of success. As the name would suggest, in the not-for-profit sector, profit is not the central overriding goal. Not-for-profit organizations have a range of goals, a multiple set of tasks that they seek to achieve. These include generating awareness, motivating people to be volunteers, distributing information, contacting customers, raising funds, allocating grants, and **lobbying** members of parliament for a change in regulations or legislation. Other goals include increasing their geographical spread to reach new people who might benefit from the organization's activities and campaigning to get media attention about a particular issue. In the non-profit sector performance measurement is more challenging, simply because there is the use of a wider set of objectives.

Orientation

Rather than manufacturing, distributing, and selling a physical product, as a general rule, organizations in the not-for-profit sector are oriented to delivering a service. Developing a market orientation (see Chapter 1) is important for a not-for-profit, because the stronger the market orientation, the stronger the organization's market performance, particularly for smaller charities (Seymour, Gilbert, and Kolsaker, 2006). How the not-for-profit raises its funding has an impact on the organization's market orientation. In a study of Portuguese not-for-profits, those organizations relying on private funding, as opposed to state funding, were found to be more market-oriented (Macedo and Pinho, 2006) and therefore more likely to be successful in fundraising.

Not-for-profit organizations need to create positive awareness about the organization's cause or activities. The principal focus of the organization is therefore to motivate and encourage people to become involved and identify with the aims of the organization, which may then lead to either financial contributions and/or volunteering support (e.g. by working in a charity's shop, or by contributing financial, marketing, or other professional services expertise).

In the not-for-profit sector, raising funds is an ongoing critical activity. The payment handed over by a customer to a charity does not operate in the same way that a customer might pay for a banking service at the point of receiving the service. Raising funds for a charity requires people or donors to contribute money, so the expectations of not-for-profit customers are different from those of commercial firms. This leads to a greater focus on engaging supporters to become part of, and identify with, the ethos of the not-for-profit organization rather than simply being a customer.

Customers' Perceptions

Customers of private sector organizations realize that in exchange for products (and services) they are contributing to the profits of the organization they are dealing with. Customers have a choice and organizations compete to get their attention and money. In the not-for-profit sector, customers do not always have a choice. Donors are free to give to one charity rather than another or not to give anything at all. In the public sector, choice is often limited, although governments do try to provide some choice (e.g. in school provision). In reality, however, there is little practical opportunity for the public to choose among different public services in the same way that there is the private sector. Services, for example, provided by local councils such as dinner services (called meals-on-wheels) for the elderly and infirm, magistrate's courts, or building regulations and planning are effectively single source; there is no choice or alternative supplier. In these cases, pressure to deliver a superior level of service interaction can often be based on an individual's own sense of duty and integrity rather than any formal organizational service policy and training.

go online

Visit the **Online Resource Centre** and follow the weblink to the National Council of Non-profit Associations (NCNA) to learn more about the challenges and developments facing non-profit organizations.

Types of Not-for-Profit Organization

We can classify four main types of not-for-profit organizations, including 1) charities, 2) the newly emerging **social enterprise** sector, 3) the public sector, and 4) political parties and campaigning organizations. How marketing is used in each of these organizations is considered further below.

Charities

The increasing success experienced by many charities has resulted partly from improved commercial professionalism and the adoption of many ideas from the private sector, together with greater collaboration with the private sector through **cause-related marketing** activities. However, there has also been a simultaneous increase in the number of charities in the marketplace. This means that there is greater competition as more charities chase a finite number of donor contributions.

The act of making a donation to a charitable organization is the culmination of a decision-making process involving a wide range of variables. Attitude to the cause, personal involvement or related experience, and trust in the charity to use the funds appropriately are critical to encouraging donations to be made. Consequently, charities seek to develop empathy with potential donors and build trust from which an initial transaction or donation can be made. The acquisition of a new donor is relatively expensive compared to the low costs associated with collection of monthly standing orders and direct debits. Costs are minimized when repeat donations occur, so charities, just like private sector organizations, try to practise relationship marketing principles (see Chapter 15).

The process of giving to a charitable cause is often based on a strong emotional involvement with the objectives of the charity. This means that charities try to communicate through messages that invoke an emotional response in their target donors. A powerful example of a British charity that has used an emotional appeal in its fundraising to good effect is the National Society for the Prevention of Cruelty to Children (NSPCC). Its Full Stop! Campaign launched in 1999 to stop cruelty to children, had the objective of bringing in £250m of donations; an objective the organization achieved in just eight years. Charities need to provide people with a rationale, a reason to give money, and this can also be achieved through the provision of factual information and relevant background information.

Charities are also trying to raise funds by working in partnerships with commercial organizations in cause-related marketing campaigns. According to Kotler (2000), companies will increasingly differentiate themselves by sponsoring popular social causes in a bid to win the public's favour. Such an approach, known as cause-related marketing, is generally recognized to be a useful way to build a positive brand image for the private companies as it builds not only customer loyalty, but also employee respect. From the partnership, the charity gains vital income streams.

Business in the Community, a UK membership organization for responsible businesses, defines **cause-related marketing** as: 'a commercial activity in which companies and non-profit organizations form an alliance to market an image, product or service for mutual benefit. In an era of increasing competition and heightened public scrutiny of corporate activities, cause-related marketing can provide the means to use the power of the brand to publicly demonstrate a company's commitment to addressing key social issues through providing resources and funding whilst addressing business marketing objectives' (BITC, 2009). This type of campaign frequently associates a company's sales of products/services with the mission or campaign of a not-for-profit organization and includes a promise to make a donation for each product/service bought. Cooperation between the two organizations, however, can take many forms. Traditionally, these schemes are based on sales promotions whereby a donation to the charity is made as a percentage of sales. This is an increasingly attractive proposition for organizations as several reports have found that a very large proportion of consumers (85% +) agree that when price and quality are equal, they are more likely to buy a product associated with a 'cause' or good deed. Companies are, therefore, likely to increasingly differentiate themselves by coopting social causes (Kotler, 2000). Other relationships, for example the one between Microsoft and NSPCC (the British children's charity), are based on the company providing financial support and technical knowledge. The former uses the relationship to fulfil some of its corporate social responsibility (CSR) goals and to help develop softer, more caring perceptions (of Microsoft). NSPCC gets financial support to help with its increased level of marketing communications. (See Chapter 19 for more on CSR.)

In numerous markets including Britain, Ireland, and Poland, supermarket retailer Tesco has run an initiative called Tesco for schools and clubs where customers save vouchers that can be redeemed for computers for their local schools. The scheme worked on the basis that during the ten-week promotional period each year, customers received one voucher to donate to a school or club of their choice for every £10 spent in a Tesco store. Schools or clubs then collected these vouchers to redeem them for computers and other equipment from a catalogue. The scheme rewarded Tesco in many ways, including increased customer loyalty, stronger community relationships, new shoppers were attracted into their stores, and it also helped to ensure the computer literacy of school leavers and potential employees. Walkers Crisps have also targeted schools, by running a Books for Schools initiative, helping to improve computer and reading literacy, respectively, with around 98% of schools participating (Adkins, 2000).

Another good example of a global cause-related marketing campaign is the Mont Blanc Unicef 'Signature for Good' campaign, where the German luxury goods maker donated 10% of the retail price of every Meisterstück special edition pen sold between June 2009 and May 2010 to Unicef. Mont Blanc guaranteed a minimum US$1.5m donation to support the global children's charity's literacy projects. The campaign also featured 12 beautiful female film and TV stars, including Eva Longoria, Sienna Miller, and Andie MacDowell, who agreed to act as ambassadors. In addition, they also agreed to having a series of iconic portrait photographs taken and sold off at auction, with the proceeds going to Unicef.

Cause-related marketing can affect consumers' overall attitude toward the sponsoring company or brand. It can also affect consumer's cognitive knowledge of the brand (i.e. what they know). Cause-related marketing campaigns tend to be more effective when they are used over a longer period of time and when there is a strong fit between the brand and the cause (Till and Nowak, 2000). The perceived fit between the company and the cause is important to the effectiveness of the campaign. Nevertheless, there are risks to the not-for-profit organization. According to Gifford (1999), the charitable organization's most important asset is its name and as cause-related marketing is a business transaction, it is subject to contract, and so there

The Tesco for Schools and Clubs initiative helps to build stronger relationships within the community

The press conference for Mont Blanc's Signature campaign with UNICEF

is a risk that the charity will suffer reputational damage. To reduce the risk, charities should not sell their association at less than that association is really worth. They should also obtain the fee up front, and control all uses of their name (Gifford, 1999).

The socially responsible company has now become the model for major corporations because of concerns about the impacts of globalization and poor corporate governance, e.g. BCCI—Bank of Credit and Commerce International—in the UK, and Enron and WorldCom in the USA at the beginning of the 2000s, and the impact of the **credit crunch** in the late 2000s. There is an increased awareness of the reputational damage that can occur when companies do not act responsibly.

▶ Research Insight 16.2

To take your learning further, you might wish to read this influential paper.

Varadarajan, P.R., and Menon, A. (1988), 'Cause-related marketing: a coalignment of marketing strategy and corporate philanthropy', *Journal of Marketing,* 52, 3 (July), 58–74.

The authors of this article detailed programmes undertaken by organizations that mixed corporate philanthropic objectives with marketing strategy, sparking decades of discussion around whether or not business should work with charities or leave charity to charities, and how to measure the effectiveness of cause-related marketing programmes. The article outlines how cause-related marketing can be conducted at the strategic, quasi-strategic, and tactical levels within a company and warns of the differences between cause-related and cause-exploitative marketing.

 Visit the **Online Resource Centre** to read the abstract and access the full paper.

Social Enterprises

A new form of organization has emerged in recent years, one with format and purpose that has captured the imagination of many different people, including people in commercial business, people working in the social sector, volunteers, academics, and leading political parties. In the UK, the government considers a **social enterprise** to be one that: 'is a business with primarily social objectives whose surpluses are principally reinvested for that purpose in the business or in the community, rather than being driven by the need to maximise profit for shareholders and owners'. Social enterprises blend social objectives with commercial reality. There is a drive to make a profit, but any surplus is reinvested into the enterprise and not redistributed as a reward to owners. Fairtrade schemes, the Eden Project, Welsh Water (Glas Cymru), Cafédirect, Jamie Oliver's Fifteen, the Co-operative Group, charities such as Age Concern and Shelter, plus various organizations in transport, childcare, many recycling companies, and even farmers' markets are all examples of social enterprise organizations.

Social enterprises are not restricted in format. The sector is very diverse and includes public limited companies (PLCs), community enterprises, cooperatives, housing associations, charities, and leisure and development trusts, among others. All of these can adopt social enterprise values.

Public Sector

The term public sector covers a very wide range of activities based around the provision of local and central government services, and services provided by government agencies. These services are essentially concerned with satisfying social needs, and, in doing so, are designed to benefit society as a whole. The public sector in many countries has grown on the back of the ideas embedded within the welfare state, although many countries have privatized their telecommunication, water, gas, and electricity provision. Now the different types of services provided are founded on the principle of improving the social context in which individuals and groups live their lives. The services seek to provide social equity.

Public sector organizations operate in industrial, governmental, consumer, and societal markets, and their marketing activities are very much driven by a complex web of stakeholder relationships. Marketing in the public sector is governed by three main forces: 1) social, 2) economic, and 3) political. The interaction of these forces within an increasingly uncertain and unstable environment makes the provision of customer choice of service problematic, although not impossible.

Internal marketing is crucial in these organizations, although at times rather unsophisticated in comparison with private sector counterparts. Rather than refer to buyers and sellers, the public sector approach is often based more on official terms such as providers and users, where resources and not investment comprise the primary criterion, although this approach is changing. One distinguishing characteristic of the public sector concerns the political tensions that arise between the various stakeholder groups. For example, the conflict between central and local government is crucial and perceptions of who is responsible for taxation, and why tax rates rise faster than inflation, reflect the power imbalance between the participants. (See Market Insight 16.2 for an example of how different stakeholders were brought together to improve the service the Drivers' Vehicle Licensing Agency in the UK offered to its customers.)

▶ Market Insight 16.2

DVLA: When Customer Service Needn't Be Taxing

The Drivers' Vehicle Licensing Agency (DVLA) is an executive agency of the UK Department for Transport. The agency has a major role in crime prevention and reduction through enforcement, prosecution, and intelligence gathering. Its customers include the general public, vehicle dealers, traders in personalized number plates, and vehicle importers, and its stakeholders include police forces, magistrates' and civil courts, and motor trade associations. In

2008, it licensed 34,390,302 motor vehicles and maintained a register of 43,450,575 full and provisional licence-holders. DVLA collected around £5.5bn in vehicle excise duty in 2008/09 (from tax disc provision), and £80m from selling private car registration plates, and, by 2009, employed 5,690 full-time equivalent staff, most based at its Swansea headquarters in Wales. During the same year, the agency handled 17m calls from customers, issued 8.6m new drivers' licences, 16.2m car registration certificates, handled 45m vehicle licensing (and off-road notification) transactions, and dealt with

▶ Market Insight 16.2

The UK Drivers' Vehicle Licensing Agency, based in Swansea, Wales
Source: Courtesy of DVLA.

over 42,000 police enquiries. What's more, DVLA managed to achieve 92.3% customer satisfaction for private motorists and 84.7% for commercial customers, increased customer take-up of electronic transaction channels to over 47%, as well as achieving 18 out of 18 customer service measures including:

- Delivering ordinary driving licences within ten days.

- Concluding simple medical investigations for driver licensing within 15 days.

- Delivering vehicle excise duty refunds within 30 days.

- Answering emails within three days and ensuring queuing time for 98% of customers takes no more than 15 minutes.

- Acknowledging a complaint within one day.

- Providing a substantive response to correspondence from members of parliament within seven working days.

But to achieve such high levels of customer orientation took a major business transformation project, not least because historically the DVLA had been official in the language it used, as many government services were, and had been more focused on meeting existing and forecasted growth demands than transforming its customer service and channel usage. To do that, DVLA selected IBM's Global Business Services division to develop systems to make car tax compliance easier for customers by shifting channel emphasis from post offices to online and automated telephone renewal. This required a sophisticated back office integration project combining databases from the Passport

▶ Market Insight 16.2 (continued)

Office (to provide digitized driver photographs and signatures), the Vehicle and Operator Standards Agency (which itself collected electronic MOT car safety test certificates from garages), the motor insurers' database, and the Department of Work and Pensions database of disabled drivers (who are not required to pay for vehicle relicensing). By pulling together the necessary information to allow the decision about whether or not to relicense a vehicle, the DVLA were then able to offer relicensing through its website, automated telephone call centre, the post office, and by postal application. The DVLA has achieved excellence in customer service standards by being awarded the Charter Mark Standard, the Customer Service Excellence Standard, and Investors in People status. Its challenge for the next few years ahead is to continue to improve customer service excellence, increase back office integration with other government departments (particularly to service Northern Ireland), and to maintain high customer

service standards despite the economic downturn in the economy and the likely significant impact that will have on new vehicle registrations and agency revenues.

Sources: www.dft.gov.uk/dvla; DVLA (2009); Mouncey (2007).

1   **What differences do you think might exist between being a customer of a government agency like the DVLA and a car insurance company, for example, in terms of how customers are treated?**

2   **The economic downturn is likely to reduce revenues for the DVLA with an obvious impact on staffing costs. How do you think the DVLA might increase their efficiency by maintaining service standards at lower cost?**

3   **In your opinion, why don't more public sector organizations adopt such ambitious customer service standards?**

▶ Research Insight 16.3

To take your learning further, you might wish to read this influential paper.

Walsh, K. (1994), 'Marketing and public sector management', *European Journal of Marketing*, **28, 3, 63–71.**

In this excellent article, the author examines the development of marketing in the public sector over the previous 20 years, arguing that if marketing is to be applied more to the public service, it needs to be adapted to the context of the public sector service in question, and, in particular, needs to take account of the political nature of the service.

@   Visit the **Online Resource Centre** to read the abstract and access the full paper.

But governments frequently also use marketing to bring about societal change. The idea that marketing techniques could be used in this way was first discussed by Kotler and Zaltman (1971). There is debate over the extent to which advertising, for example, can really change people's views and behaviour on social issues. For example, during the 1995 Divorce Referendum in Ireland, the Irish people narrowly voted for divorce (50.3%) to be made legal. Given that there was no precedent to overturn a referendum in Irish history, the 'No' lobby challenged the result in court arguing that the Irish government had behaved unconstitutionally by spending around 500,000 Irish Punts ($750,000) on advertising the referendum, and, in particular, supporting the 'Yes' campaign. The judge in the High Court case cast doubt on the idea that advertising could affect the way people voted on such an important issue but analysis by Harris, Lock, and O'Shaughnessy (1999) indicates that the advertising may indeed have had an effect on the result. In other words, advertising can change peoples' attitudes, even on important value-based issues such as on divorce and religion. Nevertheless, most social marketing campaigns are clear cut, designed to advance social causes to the benefit of a particular audience. Social marketing campaigns are typically, but not exclusively, run by public sector organizations. Some examples include:

▶ Government health departments encouraging healthy eating (i.e. the Danish six-a-day campaign to encourage people to eat more fruit and vegetables), exercising, cessation of smoking and other behaviours, or government departments of transport encouraging road safety (see Market Insight 16.3).

▶ The British Heart Foundation campaign to educate the general public around the symptoms of a person suffering a heart attack so that they can call for emergency services more quickly and provide the emergency operator with important information on the patient's condition.

go online

Visit the **Online Resource Centre** and follow the weblink to the Healthcare Communication and Marketing Association Inc. (HCMA) to learn more about marketing communications and healthcare service profession.

▶ The police or other emergency services using social marketing campaigns to reduce undesirable behaviours, either as an alternative to law enforcement or as a complement (e.g., the London Metropolitan Police unit, Trident, have used hard-hitting billboard and PR campaigns to get across the message that carrying guns can result in long prison sentences or death).

▶ Market Insight 16.3

THINK! Scaring Some Sense into Drivers

Watch the mobile phone advert at the Think Media Centre: www.think.dft.gov.uk/think/mediacentre.

Imagine you are a marketing executive in a government transport department. How would you design a campaign to stop people from drink-driving, or from using their mobile while driving? The difficulty in designing a suitable message for the target audience arises from several concerns. People might know they are breaking the law, but they often

▶ Market Insight 16.3   (continued)

Stills from the Think! broadcast TV campaign (2009)
Source: Courtesy of Department for Transport of the UK (DfT).

think they won't get caught by the police, or are more in control than they really are (so an accident won't happen to them), or simply act habitually without thinking. And that's the point. THINK! is the road safety campaign created by the UK Department of Transport. Launched in 2000, the campaign aims to reduce in-car behaviours that contribute to road casualties and fatalities, including the use of mobile phones to speak or text while driving, driving when too tired, not wearing a seatbelt, driving after taking legal or illegal drugs, and anti-social driving such as tailgating. The campaigns use different tactics to engage the audience from softer, more positive messages to hard-hitting campaigns, which remind people of the consequences of their risky driving behaviour.

One advert based around the second-most important road safety issue, according to drivers, involves the use of a mobile phone while driving. The advert plays out a scenario in which a 'husband' is talking to his 'wife' (presumably) on his mobile while in his car driving home. She tells him that 'the kids are in bed, dinner's on', the scene is set for a perfect representation of family order, until we hear him

crash, see the driving 'husband' hit the windscreen, see blood leak from his nose, and hear the 'wife' sob into the phone, desperately calling his name to get an answer. The narrator comments: 'You don't have to be in a car to cause a crash, think!, the moment you know they're driving, kill the conversation'. The advert aims at stopping drivers from using mobile phones while driving by reminding them of the consequences to themselves and their significant others (e.g. wives, children). But it also aims to stop significant others talking to their husbands or wives while they are driving. The hard-hitting message is, therefore, designed to make us Think!

Source: DfT (2009).

1   Watch the advert. Do you think this advert will be effective? How is it effective?

2   Why do you think the campaign uses the fear appeal? Could another less hard-hitting approach have been used effectively?

3   Can you think of other adverts and products/services where the fear appeal was used? How was it used?

> ## ▶ Research Insight 16.4

To take your learning further, you might wish to read this influential paper.

Kotler, P. and Zaltman, G. (1971), 'Social marketing: an approach to planned social change', *Journal of Marketing*, 35, 3 (July), 3–12.

In this seminal article, the authors asked a question, which almost seems obvious now, but which no one had asked previously: can marketing concepts and techniques be effectively applied to the promotion of social objectives such as safe driving and family planning? It is worth noting that, previously, marketing thought had been preoccupied with the marketing of goods, and, in fact, it took another ten years before scholars even considered that services should be marketed differently (see Chapter 15), so this article was in advance of its time.

@ Visit the **Online Resource Centre** to read the abstract and access the full paper.

However, the application of marketing to encouraging societal change has ethical implications. Marketing does have the potential to improve mass communication, in terms of ensuring the receipt of the message and the positive processing of that message. However, some argue that 'a wholesale application of social marketing could release ethical and social problems of large dimensions', and that, as a result, public oversight bodies should be developed to regulate social marketing techniques (Laczniak, Lusch, and Murphy, 1979). One example of a campaign that caused public concern was when the US State Department, in the wake of the September 11 bombing, spent $5m purchasing airtime on Middle Eastern and Asian TV stations to broadcast a series of adverts designed to convince the Muslim world that America was not waging war on Islam in a campaign called the 'Shared Values Initiative'. In the end, the US State Department pulled the ads after serious criticism in the media, and Al Jazeera and other channels in certain countries refused to air the ads (Fullerton and Kendrick, 2006). The problem was that many people viewed the broadcasts as **propaganda** rather than advertising.

But when is social marketing propagandist? O'Shaughnessy (1996) has argued that social marketing and social propaganda are distinctly different, but admits they are related fields. Social marketing is usually based on a 'research defined concept of audience wants', whereas propaganda is one-way communication and evangelical (i.e. the propagandist is convinced of the message's own rightness). Propaganda also typically uses language aimed at uniting or instilling minority grievances.

However, that idea that marketing can also be used to counter negative social ideas, or grievances, has a long pedigree. Edward Bernays, the grandfather of the public relations industry and nephew of psychoanalyst, Sigmund Freud, wrote a far-sighted article for his time on how America should use marketing and public relations techniques to help people 'see' the true alternative between democracy and fascism, and democracy and Nazism during the Second World War (Bernays, 1942).

Political Parties and Campaigning Organizations

The of use of marketing by political parties and third-party interest groups has risen significantly over the course of the last 50 years since the development of TV and mass media broadcasting, particularly in America and Europe, and elsewhere in Africa and Asia. Scientific methods of assessing market and public opinion have transformed how political campaigns are run in modern times. In addition, charities and other campaigning organizations are increasingly using marketing techniques to influence legislation and public opinion and so use the techniques of political marketing. With the development of globalized industries, the interplay between marketing and politics has increased further and, so, marketing methods associated with political campaigning are increasingly used by companies to influence legislators and regulators (e.g. in the European Parliament, on Capitol Hill in Washington DC, and at World Trade talks). Regulators go on to influence the legislation associated with those commercial markets.

Marketing is used by political parties to bring about an exchange of political support (e.g. votes, petitions, donations, volunteering) for political influence (e.g. legislative change/amendments). Political and electoral campaigns have existed for thousands of years, but the uptake of marketing techniques in these campaigns has increased with the advent of broadcasting, particularly since the TV became commonplace in people's households from the 1950s. Political marketing has been likened to a marketing–propaganda hybrid, mixing marketing and propaganda. This is particularly the case in America, where negative campaigning is rife (O'Shaughnessy, 1990), using 30-second and 15-second advertising spots to pour out malicious attacks on political opponents. A well-known example of such an advertising campaign is former US President, Lyndon B. Johnson's 'daisy spot' TV campaign against Barry Goldwater in the 1964 American Presidential, where a young girl picks leaves off a flower to a narrative of Goldwater's nuclear countdown. Broadcast TV adverts (known in America as 'spots') can be particularly emotive, and the image of the young girl creates mental associations around the future of our children and potential threat of nuclear Armageddon. This powerful image created fear in its audience and the audience automatically associated that fear with voting for the opposition candidate, Barry Goldwater. George Bush Senior also used a highly effective negative spot against Michael Dukakis showing him to be soft on sentencing criminals with a spot that talked graphically about how recent rapes and other vicious attacks were committed as a result of a policy of letting criminals out of jail early. The British Conservative Party also tried to use a similar approach against the Labour Party in the 1990s but the spot was controversial and unsuccessful.

Marketing is used by political parties in representative democracies to provide citizens and voters with information on current and potential political programmes for running the country. In the process, parties aim to improve social cohesion, democratic participation and citizen belongingness. Unfortunately, the recent use of political marketing in post-war democracies around the world also seems to have occurred in parallel with a decline in political participation. Whether or not there is a correlation is difficult to determine. What is clear is that citizens seem to be increasingly disengaged from political parties. Some argue that marketing has been overused, thereby damaging public trust; however, the truth is more likely to be that marketing techniques can be used to market a poor party or candidate just as much as they can be used to market an excellent party or candidate. In politics, it is difficult to determine which is which until the party comes into power. The disaffection and disappointment that citizens and voters then feel can fuel later disengagement. In that sense, politics is a credence service (see Chapter 13). In many countries around the world, there are different legal requirements for political advertising compared with commercial advertising. In Britain, for example, political advertising regulations allow comparison of political parties and adverts must be 'decent' and in good 'taste', although it is more difficult to determine that a political advert must be truthful, as politics is often a matter of opinion and judgment. By contrast, advertising claims for commercial products must always adhere to the guidelines on taste, decency, and truthfulness (for more on the ethics of political advertising, see Chapter 19).

The political marketing 'product' could be said to include political representation. Considering political representation to be a political service provided to companies or voters gives us a better understanding of the political party's reason for existence in relation to its target markets. As marketing techniques, such as advertising and market research, are used increasingly in political campaigns (and have been since the 1930s in Britain) there is increasing use of strategic marketing techniques such as market positioning and market segmentation (see Chapter 6).

Most marketing campaigns for political campaigns (corporate or party political) have historically been undertaken (in Britain) by specialized marketing and PR agencies on an ad hoc basis, although, increasingly, political parties and multinational corporations are conducting their political marketing activity in-house. In America, political consultants are more specialized, undertaking work in such areas as polling, petition management, fundraising, strategy, media buying, advertising, public affairs, grassroots lobbying, law, donor list maintenance, online campaigning, and campaign software consulting. More recently, the internet has become a particularly important tool in generating campaign finance and grassroots support. The internet looks set to become the future battleground of political campaigning in elections around the world (see Market Insight 16.4).

As with the use of marketing for social campaigning, marketing's input to politics strikes concern into many who think that politics should not adopt techniques associated with increasing commercial profitability. Some have recently argued that marketing played a strong role in bringing about revolution against Soviet-allied governments in Serbia, Georgia, and the Ukraine, where American political consultants were advising opposition parties, which deployed 'revolutionary symbols and slogans' to encourage activists to take to the streets (Sussman and Krader, 2008). Given marketing's ability to influence the general public, the question does arise as to what is and is not a legitimate use of marketing in the political sphere.

▶ Market Insight 16.4

Obama and the Rise of the Netizens

The 2008 US Presidential Election was arguably an election like no other, being the longest, most expensive contest in living memory. Bringing in the first African-American President in US history brought new hope in America and the rest of the world, particularly after eight years of the Republican, George W. Bush, who had become deeply unpopular due to foreign policy hitches in Iraq and Afghanistan. Barack Obama, an inexperienced senator

▶ Market Insight 16.4   (continued)

Obama nets the crowds, in the 2008 US Presidential Election

from Illinois, was elected President of the United States of America with 365 electoral college votes (52.9% of popular votes) to the Republican challenger John McCain's 173 electorate college votes (45.7% of the popular vote).

You might ask: how much does it cost to become President of the United States of America? Barack Obama's campaign raised $246.1m to get him elected as the democratic nominee for President alone during the primaries between 1 January and 30 June 2008. Separately, he raised $453.9m up to 31 August for his Presidential campaign. In total, Obama raised around $744.9m by 31 December 2008 to ensure his path into the Oval Office in the White House. But the 2008 Presidential elections were different for another reason; in this election, the main candidates' campaign committees substantially

invested in social networking strategies as a means to both increase voter support and increase online fundraising. Obama's team, which included Facebook founder Chris Hughes, developed MyBarackObama.com, a social networking site, to target voters, and to organize its get-out-the-vote effort allowing members to meet, attend, and organize local meetings and events. More than 1m online members had been recruited by August 2008, organizing nearly 75,000 events offline. The viral marketing undertaken by Obama's team was a particular strength, with the campaign uploading 104,454 videos, viewed 889m times, according to Rajeev Kadam CEO of divinity Metrics. The 'Yes We Can' video by will.i.am and MoveOn.org's CNNBC video drew views of over 13m and over 20m respectively. With unprecedented numbers of young people voting in the 2008 election compared with 2004, particularly after a strong voter registration campaign by Rock the Vote and other

▶ Market Insight 16.4

voter registration campaigns, future elections look set to be fought and won on the internet as parties vie for the support of internet citizens (netizens).

Sources: Aun (2008); Corrado and Corbett (2009): 135; Faucheux (2009: 57); FEC (2009); Fenn (2009); Germany (2009); Johnson (2009: 1).

1 Why do you think the internet has become so important in US political campaigning?

2 How important is the internet in election campaigns in other countries, for example, in Europe, in Asia, in Africa?

3 Do you think social networking is here to stay or is it simply a passing fad?

Under certain circumstances, it is possible to influence the political environment, and therefore the political agenda (see Chapter 2), in favour of an organization's strategy. Charities and not-for-profit organizations frequently focus on campaigning to change legislation or government policy agendas **lobbying**. Such campaigns often use stunts to obtain media publicity to influence public opinion, and, in turn, influence parliamentary opinion in the countries concerned. For example, Greenpeace the global environmental organization has long campaigned against nuclear policy in many countries around the world. It is probably best known in this regard for staging a protest against France's nuclear testing in the Pacific in 1985, when its ship, the Rainbow Warrior was bombed in Auckland Harbour, New Zealand, by French secret service agents (BBC, 2006).

In Britain, the **pressure group** Fathers for Justice has frequently courted media publicity in an attempt to change the law over a father's right to gain access to his children after divorce proceedings (which in Britain have tended to award custody to the mother). The strategy of the group was to effect social change by changing the nature of (child) custody arrangements, and it became infamous for a series of political stunts, which included trying to flour-bomb Tony Blair in the British House of Commons, and staging a protest at Buckingham Palace when one of its operatives scaled the wall and attached himself to a balcony while wearing a batman costume. On another occasion, Fathers for Justice campaigners scaled the walls of the house of Women's Minister Harriet Harman.

We can see from the above examples that publicity is important in pressure group campaigning. Typically, pressure groups try to advance policy change despite government opposition. The publicity, therefore, serves to highlight the cause and to bring supporters from the general public who can then volunteer their time or provide donations, in the same way that they would do with a charity. Marketing activity more generally has a strong role to play in this regard (as we can see from Market Insight 16.5).

▶ Market Insight 16.5

Amnesty Campaigns for Gitmo Closure

Amnesty International (AI) began in 1961 when a British lawyer called Peter Benenson wrote an article in *The Observer* calling for people to speak up for the rights of prisoners who were physically restrained from speaking up for themselves. What was surprising at the time was that so many of these so-called prisoners of conscience were held in the West. Over the years, AI has worked tirelessly to protect human rights in all corners of the world. It encourages its members to write letters and send emails to parliamentarians, to sign petitions, write blogs, and so on.

On 11 September 2001, after the attacks by Al Qaeda suicide bombers using four aeroplanes on the World Trade Center and the Pentagon, causing the deaths of around 2,981 people, US forces picked up hundreds of suspected terrorists in Pakistan and Afghanistan who were secretly taken to Guantanamo Bay, a US maximum security stockade based in Cuba.

In order to campaign for their release or for formal charges to be brought against these prisoners in independent courts, AI organized a series of protests around the world in Dublin, Belfast, Washington DC, London, Madrid, Copenhagen, and Istanbul, with protesters wearing orange 'Gitmo' jumpsuits and white facemasks to gain press attention. As part of

AI's Irish campaign, 35 TDs (parliamentarians from the Irish parliament) and 33 Stormont Assembly members (from Northern Ireland) signed the petition for Guantanamo to be closed down.

President Obama agreed to shut down Guantanamo as soon as he took office and AI's campaign has shifted to calling for the immediate release of prisoners or a fair and independent trial on the US mainland. In addition, they demand a full and independent enquiry into torture both in the USA and in the UK. In the meantime, the US administration is trying to work out what to do with the remaining suspects it still holds. Should it prosecute them in a US court (where secret intelligence obtained through interrogation would be inadmissible as evidence), should it try to send the detainees back to their home countries even though many of these have refused to take their citizens back), set up a special terrorism court, or find some other course of action?

Sources: www.amnesty.org.uk; Cochrane (2008); MacCormaic (2008); National Commission on Terrorist Attacks Upon the United States (2004).

1   How effective do you think the letter-writing campaign was in achieving the shutdown of Guantanamo?

2   What do you think the key aim was of organizing the protests in different cities around the world?

3   What other social marketing methods could Amnesty International have used?

Fundraising

An important role for marketing in charitable organizations is the generation of funds from donors and donor organizations. Whereas commercial organizations are typically funded by their customers (and invested in by shareholders), charitable organizations may generate funds from a variety of sources including government departments, non-governmental organizations (NGOs), foundations (e.g. The Bill and Melinda Gates Foundation), and international agencies (e.g. the UN, WHO, World Bank), in addition to individual donors and customers. In some countries, e.g. China, there may be restrictions on whether or not international charitable organizations can solicit funds from the general public. The marketing role in such countries is then used more to generate supporters and volunteers rather than for fundraising. In most countries, marketing has a key role to play in generating awareness of the need for funding, to stimulate giving, and in profiling supporters (Mindak and Bybee, 1971). Marketing's role in fundraising is important. Common techniques used to solicit funds include the following promotional approaches:

▶ Door drops—where unaddressed mail is posted to an address often within specific targeted locations.

▶ Press/magazine inserts—where details of the charity and its appeal are printed as a looseleaf insert in a particular publication.

▶ Direct mail—targeted, addressed mail delivered to an address either online or offline.

▶ Direct response TV (DRTV)—where advertisements for specific charities encourage viewers to make donations online or by ringing specific telephone numbers.

▶ Face-to-face donor recruitment—where volunteers attend shopping malls or other areas of high potential donor footfall and solicit donations directly, usually for frequent giving through direct debit schemes (i.e. automatic monthly cash transfers from one's bank account).

▶ Face-to-face donation solicitation—where volunteers attend shopping malls, as above, but with the aim of obtaining cash donations, often by rattling their donation tins.

▶ Corporate donations—where a company makes a donation to a particular cause, although some companies donate a fixed proportion of their income (e.g. Ben and Jerry's, the American ice cream company, or Innocent, the British smoothie maker), sometimes to their own foundations, which they set up specifically to deal with associated good causes.

▶ Major gifts—these are typically solicited from wealthy philanthropists, sometimes given as a legacy (i.e. when the philanthropist dies they make a sizeable gift in their will to a particular charitable organization or social enterprise).

go online

Visit the **Online Resource Centre** and complete Internet Activity 16.1 to learn more about how the internet is improving the effectiveness and efficiency of fundraising activities for charitable organizations.

Many charities work on the principle that donors increase in loyalty over a period of time and shift from being non-supporters to infrequent donors. Infrequent donors are then more likely to shift to becoming more regular donors, a proportion then move onto giving major gifts, and finally an even smaller proportion of donors leave legacies in their wills to enable charities to inherit their financial resources. Figure 16.3 shows how as donors increase in loyalty, and therefore giving, the proportion of each group drops in size.

Most charitable organizations and social enterprises recognize that some marketing techniques are more effective than others in raising income. Of the methods outlined above, direct marketing methods tend to be a relatively ineffective and expensive approach to fundraising compared with major gift, trust, and corporate donation solicitation, although charities have been successfully using face-to-face donor recruitment tactics widely in the last ten years or so (Sargeant, Jay, and Lee, 2006). Roughly half of the UK population donate to charity, donating on average £31 per year per person, although the average hides a much lower median donation (i.e. most common amount) of £10 per person (CAF/NCVO, 2009).

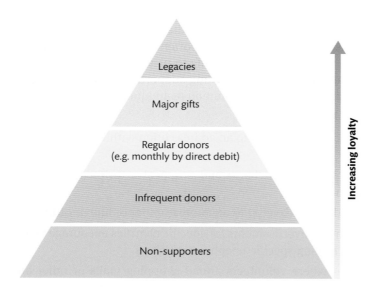

Figure 16.3
The fundraising loyalty ladder

Unfortunately, in the UK, charities tend not to present performance metrics such as market share (i.e. in relation to competition for donations), donor loyalty, retention, and satisfaction to top management, which indicates that marketing is still not used to its full potential in many not-for-profit organizations (Bennett, 2007).

Given the importance of corporate donations, it is interested to note that the top ten corporate givers in Britain in 2007, according to the Directory for Social Change, were mainly banks, demonstrating their commitment to their local communities (see Table 16.3). Interestingly, this list of companies has changed substantially since 1999, when the top ten corporate givers

▶ **Table 16.3** Top ten corporate givers in the UK

Rank	Company	Total community contributions (2007/08)	% pre-tax profit	Region
1	Tesco plc	£77,198,086	2.75	Worldwide
2	The Royal Bank of Scotland Group plc	£57,700,000	0.56	Worldwide
3	Barclays PLC	£38,932,000	0.55	UK
4	Lloyds Banking Group plc	£37,463,000	0.94	UK
5	AstraZeneca PLC	£35,000,000[a]	0.88	Worldwide
6	BT Group plc	£22,300,000	1.13	Worldwide
7	HBOS plc	£18,610.660	0.34	UK
8	HSBC Holdings plc	£18,400,000	0.15	UK
9	Allen & Overy LLP	£16,600,000	3.71	Worldwide
10	WPP Group plc	£16,300,000	2.27	Worldwide

[a]The figure for AstraZeneca does not include £259m of product donations valued at wholesale prices

Source: Directory of Social Change, www.dsc.org.uk. Reproduced with kind permission © DSC.

included Diageo, the drink and food conglomerate; Reuters Group, the information and news company; Marks and Spencer, the clothing and food retailer; BAT, the tobacco company; Cable and Wireless, the telco; and Rio Tinto, the mining group. It is likely that the recession of the late 2000s will have affected corporate giving overall and particularly corporate giving among banks in the UK.

Skills for Employment

▶▶ We look for people who really try to understand the customers' needs and then use these insights to deliver effective new products or services. ◀◀

Claire Lawlor, Oxfam Unwrapped Category Manager, Oxfam

 Visit the **Online Resource Centre** to discover more tips and advice on skills for the workplace.

Chapter Summary

To consolidate your learning, the key points from this chapter are summarized below:

■ **Describe the key characteristics of not-for-profit organizations.**

Not-for-profit organizations are differentiated from their commercial counterparts in numerous ways. Not-for-profit organizations tend to have multiple stakeholders, and, because there are no shareholders, any profit earned is often reinvested in the organization. Because not-for-profit organizations do not distribute funds to shareholders, and are either social enterprises, public sector organizations, or charities, there is a need for transparency in determining how these organizations operate as they are claiming to act in the common good. Accordingly, they have multiple objectives, rather than a simple profit motivation. They have historically not been strongly market-oriented, but this is changing as not-for-profit organizations become more experienced in marketing. Customers' perceptions of the not-for-profit organization differ from their commercial counterparts because the not-for-profit typically has a unique mission and set of values and a non-financial organizational purpose.

■ **Explain why not-for-profit organizations do not always value their customers.**

Not-for-profit organizations frequently do not value their beneficiary customers because they exist in a monopolistic situation, demand far outstrips supply, a lack of market segmentation activity exists, and research into customer needs is not seen as a priority for expenditure and investment. Not-for-profit organizations frequently also undervalue supporter customers because they typically approach them to solicit funds too often and do not sufficiently appreciate them when they do give. Volunteer service workers who generously give of their time can often feel undervalued. Because not-for-profit organizations have multiple stakeholders, there can be problems caused between these groups, which need resolution, but which can often lead to customers feeling undervalued as those tensions are resolved.

■ **Analyse stakeholders and develop appropriate engagement strategies.**

A common way of analysing stakeholders is by mapping them on a power/interest matrix to identify four types of stakeholder, based on the level of interest they display to an organization and the level of power they exert. Those with high levels of interest and power, group A, are key stakeholders in need of continuous engagement. Those with high interest but low levels of power, group B, should be informed about the organization's activities to maintain their interest. Group C represents those organizations with high power but low interest. Here, it is important to either increase information flow to these organizations to increase their interest so that they can exert their power in the not-for-profit's favour, or alternatively keep them satisfied if they intend to exert their power against the not-for-profit. Finally, an organization's relationships with those stakeholders who have little power or interest, Group D, should either be disregarded or revived.

- **Describe and assess cause-related marketing campaigns.**

  A cause-related marketing campaign occurs when companies and non-profit organizations form marketing alliances. Often, these marketing campaigns are focused on sales promotions developed for mutual benefit where the purchase of a commercial product/service is linked to donations to a charitable third-party organization. Such campaigns tend to work best where there is a strong strategic fit between the commercial organization and the not-for-profit organization, particularly in relation to audiences targeted, and when the campaign runs over the longer term.

- **Understand how marketing can be, and is, used to achieve social and political change in society.**

  It is only in the last 50 years that we have embraced the use of marketing for social and political causes. Marketing is now commonly used in government information campaigns to drive positive behavioural change and improve citizens' well-being; however, there is some question as to whether or not government should have this role and over the ethics of using marketing in social and political campaigning at all. The use of marketing techniques in election campaigns has a longer pedigree and is now very common in most democracies around the world. In this scenario, marketing is used to understand the electorate's wants/needs and then to provide them with a set of party policies and leaders, which suits those needs. In addition to the use of marketing by government to influence society, and by political parties to gain support and votes, marketing is often used by third-party organizations (e.g. pressure groups) to drive legislative change in lobbying campaigns designed to achieve grassroots support among the general public, particularly by courting publicity and the media's support more generally.

- **Explain how marketing is used to raise funds for charitable organizations.**

  Funds can be raised from donors using a variety of techniques including: door drops, where unaddressed mail is posted to addresses in targeted locations; press/magazine inserts; direct mail, online or offline; direct response TV (DRTV) advertisements encouraging viewers to make donations online or by ringing specific telephone numbers; face-to-face donor recruitment; face-to-face donation solicitation; corporate donations; and major gifts. Of all of these methods, corporate donations and major gifts (from individuals or trusts) tend to bring in the most funding.

Review Questions

1 What key differences exist in marketing communications for not-for-profit versus for-profit organizations?

2 Can you name the main types of not-for-profit organization reviewed?

3 What are the key characteristics of not-for-profit organizations?

4 Why do not-for-profit organizations sometimes not value their beneficiaries?

5 Why do not-for-profit organizations sometimes not value their donors?

6 What axes are used on a stakeholder analysis matrix?

7 How is marketing used to raise funds for charitable organizations?

8 What is cause-related marketing?

9 How do we assess cause-related marketing programmes?

10 What is the difference between social marketing and social propaganda?

11 How is marketing used in political campaigning?

Worksheet Summary

Visit the **Online Resource Centre** and complete Worksheet 16.1. This will help you learn about some of the unique challenges that are faced by not-for-profit organizations when deciding which stakeholders they should engage, maintain interest, inform or satisfy, or revive or disregard.

Discussion Questions

1 Having read Case Insight 16.1 on Oxfam, how would you use marketing and PR techniques in future campaigns to:

   A Further improve the positive brand associations people have of Oxfam and its mission?

   B Recruit more supporters to the charity, particularly those who give on a monthly basis by direct debit?

   C Raise awareness of how Oxfam is distributing funding to its supporters?

2 Working in small groups, select three different not-for-profit organizations and consider the following:

   A How do their 'products' differ from each other?

   B What is the nature of price in each case?

   C What is the nature of customer involvement for each product?

   D How can the audiences for these 'products' be segmented, if at all?

3 Read the section on stakeholder mapping and draw up maps for the following organizations:

   A An international medical charity undertaking work to alleviate the suffering of people living with HIV/AIDS in sub-Saharan Africa.

   B The US Republican Party, as it develops its campaign plan for the 2012 presidential election.

   C A government department developing a campaign to increase citizens' consumption of fruit and vegetables.

   D The UK social enterprise, *The Big Issue* magazine company.

4 Discuss reasons why charitable organizations should, or should not, communicate with donors on details of what the charity has achieved with their donations.

5 Visit the marketing sections of websites for the following organizations for ideas on how they engage with their audiences:

   A The police service in the country in which you were born.

   B The largest charity in Europe (hint: Google this first).

   C The European Parliament.

   D A social enterprise with which you are familiar (if you are not, visit the website of Prince Charles' company, Duchy Originals).

go online

Visit the **Online Resource Centre** and complete the Multiple Choice Questions to assess your knowledge of Chapter 16.

References

Adkins, S. (2000), 'Why cause-related marketing is a winning business formula', *Marketing*, 20 July, 18.

Aun, F. (2008), 'Over long campaign, Obama videos drew nearly a billion views', ClickZ, 7th November, retrieve from www.clickz.com/3631604, accessed 17 April 2010.

BBC (2006), 'NZ rules out new Greenpeace probe', 2 October 2006, retrieve from http://news.bbc.co.uk/1/hi/world/asia-pacific/5398170.stm, accessed 17 April 2010.

Bennett, R. (2007), 'The use of marketing metrics by British fundraising charities: a survey of current practice', *Journal of Marketing Management*, 23, 9/10, 959–989.

Bernays. E. (1942), 'The marketing of national policies: a study of war propaganda', Journal of Marketing, 6, 3, 236–245.

BITC (2009), 'Cause Related Marketing', retrieve from www.bitc.org.uk/northern_ireland/what_we_do/in_the_economy/sustaining_the_third_sector/crm.html, accessed 17 April 2010.

Bone, J. (2008), 'He was proud of his salad dressing – it meant more than his movies', *The Times*, 29 September, 14.

Bruce, I. (1995), 'Do not-for-profits value their customers and their needs?', *International Marketing Review*, 12, 4, 77–84.

CAF/NCVO (2009), *UK Giving 2009: An Overview of Charitable Giving in the UK 2008/09*, Charities Aid Foundation/National Council for Voluntary Organisations, September 2009, retrieve from www.cafonline.org/ukgiving, accessed 17 April 2010.

Cochrane, K. (2008), 'G2: Anything for an unquiet life: even before she was out of her teens, Irene Khan had seen enough hate and cruelty for several lifetimes. The head of Amnesty International talks to Kira Cochrane', The Guardian, 12 March, 10.

Corrado I., and Corbett, M. (2009), 'Rewriting the playbook on presidential campaign financing', in: Johnson, D.W. (ed.), *Campaigning for President 2008*, New York: Routledge, 126–146.

DfT (2009), 'Adult Road Safety Marketing Strategy and Plan', retrieve from http://think.dft.gov.uk/pdf/389540/0910strategy-adult.pdf, accessed 17 April 2010.

DVLA (2009), DVLA Business Plan 2009/10, retrieve from http://www.dft.gov.uk/dvla/publications.aspx, accessed 17 April 2010.

Faucheux, R.A. (2009), 'Why Clinton Lost'. In: Johnson, D.W. (ed.) *Campaigning for President 2008*, New York: Routledge, 44–59.

FEC (2009), Federal Election Commission – Presidential Campaign Finance, retrieve from www.fec.gov/DisclosureSearch/mapApp.do?cand_id=P80003338&searchType=&searchSQLType=&searchKeyword=, accessed 17 April 2010.

Fenn (2009), 'Communication Wars: Television and New Media', In: Johnson, D.W. (ed.) *Campaigning for President 2008*, New York: Routledge, 210–21.

Fullerton, J., and Kendrick, A. (2006), *Advertising's War on Terrorism: The Story of the US State Department's Shared Values Initiative, Spokane*, WA: Marquette Books.

Germany, J.B. (2009), 'The online revolution'. In: Johnson, D.W. (ed.) *Campaigning for President 2008*, New York: Routledge, 147–59.

Gifford, G. (1999), 'Cause-related marketing: ten rules to protect your non-profit assets', *Nonprofit World*, 17, 6, 11–13.

Harris, P., Lock, A., and O'Shaughnessy, N. (1999), 'Measuring the effect of political advertising and the case of the 1995 Irish Divorce Referendum', *Marketing Intelligence and Planning*, 17, 6, 272–80.

Hatten, M.L. (1982), 'Strategic Management in not-for-profit organisations', *Strategic Management Journal*, 3, 89–104.

Johnson, D.W. (ed.) (2009), *Campaigning for President 2008*, New York: Routledge.

Kotler, P. (2000), 'Future markets', *Executive Excellence*, 17, 2, 6.

— and Levy, S.J. (1969), 'Broadening the concept of marketing', *Journal of Marketing*, 33, 1 (January), 10–15.

— and Zaltman, G. (1971), 'Social marketing: an approach to planned social change', *Journal of Marketing*, 35, 3 (July), 3–12.

Laczniak, G. R., Lusch, R. F., and Murphy, P. E. (1979), 'Social marketing: its ethical dimensions', *Journal of Marketing*, 43, Spring, 29–36.

MacCormaic, R. (2008), 'Protesters seek freedom for Guantanamo detainees', *Irish Times*, 12 January, 5.

Macedo, I.M. and Pinho, J.C. (2006), 'The relationship between resource dependence and market orientation: the case of non-profit organisations', *European Journal of Marketing*, 40, 5/6, 533–63.

Marling, S. (2003), 'Back from the brink: how one building gave a community a new lease of life—Reviving an industrial city with an art gallery sounds unlikely, but Bilbao did so in spectacular style', *The Daily Telegraph*, 11 January, 12.

Mindak, W.A., and Bybee, H.M. (1971), 'Marketing's application to fundraising', *Journal of Marketing, 35 (July 1971), 13–18.*

Mouncey (2007), 'CRM transformation using new technology in the public sector: DVLA case study', Cranfield Customer Management Forum/IBM Global Business Services, retrieve from www.som.cranfield.ac.uk/som/ccmf

National Commission on Terrorist Attacks Upon the United States (2004), The 9/11 Commission Report, retrieve from www.9-11commission.gov/, accessed 17 April 2010.

O'Shaughnessy, N. (1990), *The Phenomenon of Political Marketing*, London: Macmillan Press.

— (1996), 'Social propaganda and social marketing: a critical difference?', *European Journal of Marketing*, 30, 10/11, 62–75.

Rothschild, M.L. (1979), 'Marketing communications in non-business situations or why it's so hard to sell brotherhood like soap', *Journal of Marketing*, 43 (Spring 1979), 11–20.

Scholes, K. (2001), 'Stakeholder mapping: a practical tool for public sector managers', in: Johnson, G. and Scholes, K. (eds) *Exploring Public Sector Strategy*, London: FT Prentice Hall, 165–184.

Sargeant, A., Jay, E., and Lee, S. (2006), 'Benchmarking charity performance: returns from direct marketing in fundraising', *Journal of Nonprofit and Public Sector Marketing*, 16, 1/2, 77–94.

Seymour, T., Gilbert, D., and Kolsaker, A. (2006), 'Aspects of market orientation of English and Welsh charities', *Journal of Nonprofit and Public Sector Marketing*, 16, 1/2, 151–69.

Sussman, G., and Krader, S. (2008), 'Template revolutions: marketing US regime change in Eastern Europe', *Westminster Papers in Communication and Culture*, 5, 3, 91–112.

Till, B.D. and Nowak, L.I. (2000), 'Toward effective use of cause-related marketing alliances', *Journal of Product and Brand Management*, 9, 7, 472–84.

Contemporary marketing practice

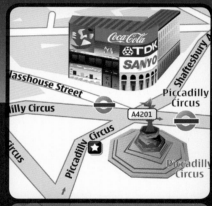

▶ **Part 5: Contemporary marketing practice**

17 | Digital Marketing

 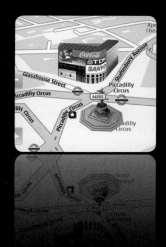 

Learning Outcomes

After studying this chapter you should be able to:

▶ Consider the impact of digital resources on marketing

▶ Describe the key structural characteristics across which digital resources differ

▶ Describe the evolution in the focus of electronic and digital marketing from 'channel push' to 'market pull'.

▶ Discuss key trends in digital marketing: internet advertising, email marketing, search marketing, social web, gaming, and mobile marketing

▶ Outline the wider considerations that influence the effectiveness of a digital marketing strategy

▶ Case Insight 17.1

How important is online word-of-mouth? How could an online community use social networks to oppose an international music franchise and make British music history? We talk to Jon and Tracey Morter from Essex who have shown Simon Cowell they have much more than the X-Factor.

Jon Morter from Essex, UK

The UK Christmas No. 1 best selling single is Britain's most hotly contested music chart of the year and for the past four years Simon Cowell's X-Factor winners, Shayne Ward, Leona Lewis, Leon Jackson and Alexandra Burke, have dominated the Christmas charts. The X-Factor is a franchise originating in the UK in 2004, produced by executive producer Simon Cowell and his company Syco TV. Today, it spans over 24 European countries with aspiring pop artists drawn from public auditions to compete and be voted for by the viewing public for a recording contract and publicity. Although it has been a hugely popular reality TV show, with the 2009 final watched by over 9m viewers, it is also highly criticized as exploiting aspiring music artists and for its lack of artistic integrity.

Fed up with the possibility of yet another X-Factor Christmas No. 1, Tracey and I, started a protest campaign through a Facebook Group. We felt we and the British public were sick of the manufactured artists so promoted a social web campaign to 'Rage Against the X-Factor' and promote a different single for Christmas No. 1. It became one of the most exciting and anticipated music chart battles ever in the UK. We promoted the sale of our favourite single 'Killing in the Name' by artists Rage Against the Machine (RATM) as a possible contender for the 2009 No. 1 Christmas chart position.

Through over 1m Facebook fans, over 50,000 YouTube search results and endless Twitter chatter, everyone encouraged their friends, followers and fans to buy a download of the single by rock band, RATM by the end of Saturday 19 December (23:59 p.m.). The aim: to firmly overthrow conventional marketing techniques by publicly bringing down a major player's mass media campaign through online social networks and word-of-mouth (WOM). We wanted to stop the domination of the Christmas music charts by X-Factor manufactured artists and in that make a statement about the power of online WOM and marketing ethics.

'Killing in the Name', the single by RATM released over 15 years ago, spent nothing on its marketing yet in December 2009, in one week, sold over 502,672 copies, beating X Factor winner Joe McElderry by approximately 50,000, making it the 2009 Christmas No. 1. In taking the title for 2009, 'Killing In The Name' also set two new landmarks, becoming the UK's first download-only Christmas No. 1 and notching up the biggest one-week download sales total in British chart history. HMV's Gennaro Castaldo said 'This is a truly remarkable outcome and possibly the greatest chart upset ever'. The campaign also raised over £101,517 for the charity, Shelter.

So what do you think marketers (and Simon Cowell) can learn from this social web campaign and the power of online word-of-mouth?

Introduction

Consider for a moment the last week of your life and your personal use of digital technologies. How many times did you login to your Facebook or MySpace profile? When logged in did you update your status? Did you comment on someone else's status? Did you receive a private message? Or perhaps you downloaded an application or completed a quiz? Did you use Skype or MSN to chat with your friends? Did you watch or share any YouTube videos? Did you post comments, rate them, or share them with your friends? How did you find information on the web—was it through search engines like Google, video sites like YouTube or perhaps from a link a friend shared with you on Facebook? How often did you use your mobile phone? How many text messages did you send? Did you receive any reminders or promotional offers to your mobile phone? Many of the social interactions and information exchanges we engage in today are facilitated by digital technologies. However, it is not just consumers who use these digital resources to communicate and share information, increasingly the marketing profession are turning to digital resources to complement, and, in some instances, replace traditional channels and marketing activities.

In the developed economies of North America, Western Europe, and Oceania/Australia, internet penetration and adoption stands at approximately 63%, reflecting increasing usage and demand for networked information and connectivity (Internet World Stats, 2009). These three geographical areas were also ranked the top three regions, respectively, in terms of e-readiness, a measure of a country's e-business environment and how amenable its market is to internet-based opportunities (EIU, 2008). With this penetration has come the development and adoption of digital resources, from mobile technologies to internet and social web resources such as **blogs**, social networking sites, wikis and similar multimedia sharing services (Farrar, 2008; de Valck, van Bruggen, and Wierenga, 2009). These digital trends are not only altering consumer expectations of their interaction with the web or an organization, but they are also changing how we market in the digital space.

In this chapter, we discuss digital marketing. First, we provide clarity on the definition of digital marketing, describe the structural properties across which digital and electronic resources can differ, and discuss how the approach to digital marketing has evolved from channel push to market pull. We then provide a review of some key areas of digital marketing investment: internet advertising, email marketing, search marketing, social web, gaming, and mobile marketing. Finally, we review some wider considerations in the development of digital marketing strategy.

Electronic and Digital Marketing

Electronic marketing is an established field brought about by advancements in electronic mass media channels such as cinema, radio, and TV for advertising in the early 1900s. Since its inception in media, many developments in electronic resources have been adopted in marketing. As such, it does not exist in a silo, independent of other marketing principles (e.g. in pricing, distribution, or customer service), but is interdependent as more electronic resources are used to improve the efficiency and effectiveness of marketing activities. Although it does have major implications for the area of integrated marketing communications (see Chapters

10 and 11), electronic resources and their implications for marketing can be considered more widely. Scanning back through the chapters in this book, there are examples of how electronic resources are used to improve price decision-making (see Chapter 9), build customer relationships and loyalty (see Chapter 15), collect customer data for research (see Chapter 4), deliver goods (see Chapter 12), and improve the provision of customer services (see Chapter 13). Electronic marketing can, therefore, be considered quite a broad area of marketing.

As presented in Table 17.1, we define electronic marketing as 'the process of marketing accomplished or facilitated through the use of electronic devices, applications, tools, technologies, platforms and or systems'. In this, we consider a wide array of electronic resources, both older analogue devices (e.g. TV, radio) and newer digital resources (e.g. digital TV, internet, social web) in marketing activities. We have also defined a number of other concepts that are often used interchangeably when discussing this area.

▶ **Table 17.1** Defining electronic and digital marketing	
Electronic marketing	Process of marketing accomplished or facilitated through the use of electronic devices, applications, tools, technologies, platforms, and/or systems. It is not limited to one specific type or category of electronic technology (e.g. internet, TV), but includes both older analogue and developing digital electronic technologies
Digital marketing	Management and execution of marketing using specifically digital electronic technologies and channels (e.g. web, email, digital TV, wireless media, and digital data about user/customer characteristics and behaviour) to reach markets in a timely, relevant, personal, interactive and cost-effective manner
Direct marketing	Type of marketing that attempts to send its messages directly to customers without the use of intervening media and involves commercial communication (e.g. direct mail, email, telemarketing) with consumers or businesses focused on driving a specific call-to-action. Not all direct marketing is electronic or uses digital technologies (e.g. direct mail)
Interactive marketing	Refers to marketing that moves away from a transaction-based effort to a conversation (i.e. two-way dialogue) and can be described as a situation or mechanism through which marketers and a customer (e.g. stakeholders) interact usually in real time. Not all interactive marketing is electronic (e.g. face-to-face sales)

If we narrow the field to digital marketing, we are referring to just the use of digital resources (e.g. web, email, digital TV, wireless media, and digital data about users). Internet marketing is even narrower, in being one form of digital marketing specific to the use of only digital internetworked technologies (e.g. web, email, intranet, extranets). This excludes the use of some digital broadcast media and marketing information systems (MkIS). However, it includes a wide array of resources used for internet marketing activities, such as internet advertising, direct email, online advergaming and social web marketing (see Table 17.2). In this chapter, we focus on digital marketing.

▶ **Table 17.2** Types of digital marketing activities

Internet marketing	A form of digital marketing also referred to as i-marketing, web marketing, and online marketing, specific to the use of only internetworked (i.e. internet) based technologies (e.g. web, email, intranet, extranets) for the marketing of a product offering (includes internet advertising, email marketing, social web marketing.)
Internet advertising	A form of marketing communications that uses the internet for the purpose of 'advertising'—delivering marketing messages to increase website traffic (i.e. click-through) and encourage product trial, purchase, and repeat purchase activity (i.e. conversion). Examples include display advertising, classified listings, rich media ads, search marketing.)
Search marketing	A form of internet marketing that seeks to increase the visibility of websites in search engine results pages (SERPs) through the use of website search engine optimization (SEO) tactics and **search engine marketing** (SEM) activities (e.g. paid placement, contextual advertising, and paid inclusion)
Email marketing	A digital form of direct marketing that uses electronic mail as a means to directly communicate commercial messages, increase loyalty, and build relationships with an audience the individuals of which have given permission (e.g. opt-in) to receive formal messages through email (e.g. email newsletter). Spam, in contrast, consists of unsolicited or undesired email messages
Mobile marketing	A form of digital marketing that enables organizations to communicate and engage with their audience in an interactive and relevant manner through any mobile device or wireless network (e.g. mobile/cell phone, SMS/MMS, PDA)
Viral marketing	Also called electronic word-of-mouth (eWOM) or word-of-mouse, where word-of-mouth, facilitated by communication (e.g. email, SMS) and social networking technologies (e.g. Share), is used to disseminate messages through self-replicating viral processes that have an impact on marketing activities
Online retailing	A type of electronic commerce used for business-to-consumer (B2C) transactions and mail order
Advergaming	The use of video and online games to advertise a product, organization, or an idea. Advergames encourage repeat website traffic and reinforce brand loyalty
Social web marketing	A form of internet marketing that describes the use of social web channels and technologies (e.g. social networks, online communities, blogs, wikis) or any online collaborative media for marketing, sales, public relations, and customer service

Structural Properties of Digital Resources

To aid the use of digital resources for marketing activities, it is important to firstly understand how the many and varied digital resources differ across key structural properties. This helps to make a more informed decision about which resources are most suitable for the achievement of marketing objectives. Be it a digital technology, channel, platform, application, or system, each resource has a unique combination of structural properties that influence how they can be used and also their impact on the user experience. These properties can also be used to compare analogue electronic and non-electronic marketing channels and resources. These are depicted in Figure 17.1 and include: **vividness**, **synchronicity**, **pacing**, **interactivity**, and **mode of transfer**.

Figure 17.1
Structural properties of digital resources

As an example, with social networks like Facebook, LinkedIn, or MySpace, or digital interactive TV like Sky + HD or Virgin Media, users are able to interact in real time and have more control over the form and content of the experience in which they are participating. This is in contrast to traditional mass media channels such as analogue TV and radio. Even some corporate websites in their design enable very little interactivity or user control, and, therefore, the user experience is inherently passive and one-way. These properties, therefore, can have a significant impact on the user experience. More information about the various structural properties across which digital resources may differ and the marketing implications of each are provided in Table 17.3.

▶ **Table 17.3** Structural properties of electronic resources

Property	Definition	Example	Marketing implication
Vividness	The ability of the technology to produce a sensually rich experience	Instant chat has low vividness as only evokes one sense (visual) and quality is poor	Aids the efficiency and effectiveness of information transfer and processing
	Is based on sensory breadth (i.e. no. of senses evoked) and sensory depth (e.g. quality of sensory exchange)	An interactive computer game can have high vividness as the visual, auditory and haptic or touch systems can be stimulated, and the quality can be quite high	The higher the vividness, the more 'realistic' the environment or experience

▶ **Table 17.3** (continued)

Property	Definition	Example	Marketing implication
Synchronicity	The degree to which a user's input into a system/channel and the speed of response he/she receives from the system/channel are simultaneous	**Asynchronous** technologies have delays ranging from a few seconds (email) to a few days (postal mail)	Immediacy of feedback important in improving understanding of the message/information exchanged as it allows for clarification
	The speed of interaction of various media	**Synchronous** technologies with 'real-time' information exchange include chat services like Facebook chat or updating a Facebook status	Can improve the quality of the experience of using the technology
Pacing	Control over the speed and sequence of the information transfer	TV and radio are externally paced as speed and sequence are controlled by the broadcaster	Indicates the control marketers have over the form and content of the information transferred, ensuring message and image consistency
	May be controlled by the sender such as the marketer (i.e. external pacing) or by the receiver such as the customer (i.e. internal pacing)	Social networks like MySpace; publishing platforms like Blogger and Wordpress and Wikipedia allow high levels of internal pacing through user customization	Higher user customization, however, can have a positive impact on learning, involvement, and user satisfaction
Interactivity	Interaction between parties, an exchange of some kind, the speed of that exchange and the degree of control differing parties have during the exchange	Person interactivity is interaction between people mediated by technologies (e.g. Skype, MSN Instant messenger, Twitter or Facebook chat)	Level of interactivity positively related to adoption of technology, user attention and cognitive processing (if desired level), and improving customer satisfaction
	Is influenced by the degree of vividness, synchronicity, and pacing that a technology facilitates	Machine interactivity is interaction between people and machines (e.g. Status updates on Facebook; uploading pictures to Flickr)	
Mode of transfer	A transmissive process by which something travels from source or sender to a receiver	One-to-many (impersonal): involves the flow of information from the source (e.g. marketer) directly to the consumer with no interaction or feedback supported (e.g. TV, radio, website)	One-to-one and many-to-many is potentially more engaging (active) than one-to-many (passive)

▶ **Table 17.3** (continued)

Property	Definition	Example	Marketing implication
	Three transmissive models are presented: one-to-many, one-to-one, and many-to-many modes of transfer	One-to-one: is interpersonal communication between two people and incorporates feedback. It can be face-to-face or mediated (e.g. chat)	Communication with feedback can result in the user feeling like an active participant resulting in higher satisfaction, less frustration with feeling ignored or message not suitable
		Many-to-many: incorporates both impersonal and interpersonal modes (e.g. social networks like Facebook, MySpace)	More attention to message, higher involvement in one-to-one and many-to-many communication modes

These properties are largely evident in developments in the web from Web 1.0 to Web 2.0. Online search technologies such as Google enable both internal and **external pacing** and machine interactivity, with social platforms like Facebook and YouTube in addition to supporting not just one-to-many, but also one-to-one and many-to-many modes of communication transfer and interaction. This has resulted in transfer of power and influence from the marketer to the consumer and their community. Web technologies today increasingly resemble what Tim Berners-Lee's original personal vision was when he invented the web in the 1990s. His vision was the 'Web as a powerful force for social change and individual creativity' (Berners-Lee, 2000). Marketing Insight 17.1 provides a famous example of this, describing how two creative science students were a powerful force in redefining the brand values of Mentos mints and increasing the top-of-mind brand awareness and sales for Mentos and the leading soft drink brand, Coca-Cola.

▶ Market Insight 17.1

Mentos and Coke Go Viral!

In June 2006, two science students conducted a backyard experiment, videoed it and uploaded it to YouTube, starting a cultural phenomenon: the Mentos Geyser Viral campaign. Fritz Grobe and Stephen Voltz filmed themselves dropping various quantities of Mentos into 101 Diet Coke bottles, resulting in mini explosions, from which they created a great ad. This involved neither client nor agency, but was uploaded to their website and YouTube.

To date, this activity has resulted in over 726,000 Google search results for the keywords Mentos + Coke; 105 Facebook groups have been created; and the initial student video, inspired the creation and uploading of over 9,770 similar videos to YouTube by other users. The video won the Webby Award for best viral video and was nominated for an Emmy Award for outstanding broadband content. The creators also

▶ Market Insight 17.1

appeared on the *Late Show with David Letterman*, the *Ellen Degeneres Show*, the *Today Show*, and performed live around the world, from Istanbul to Paris, and even in Las Vegas

In short, the content was fun, user-generated, participatory, but most importantly NOT marketer-generated or controlled. Although it has been of great benefit to both Coca-Cola and Mentos in terms of brand awareness and engagement, it helped to redefine the brand values and key marketing message for Mentos. As a result of this user-generated activity, Mentos evolved from having a brand value of 'fresh

breath' and 'minty taste', to fun, quirky, and different, values that inspired the brand's follow-up campaign, *Trevor the Mentos Intern*.

1 Why do you think control (pacing) was such an important factor in this initiative?

2 What was the impact of this initiative on the values of the brand Mentos?

3 Describe the other elements in this initiative that you think made it such a success?

▶ Research Insight 17.1

To take your learning further, you might wish to read this influential paper.

Hoffman, D. L., and Novak, T. P. (1996), 'Marketing in hypermedia computer-mediated environments: conceptual foundations', *Journal of Marketing*, **60 (July), 50–68.**

This article addresses the role of marketing in hypermedia computer-mediated environments (HCMEs), of which the world wide web on the internet is the first and current global implementation. The authors introduce marketers to various unique characteristics of this medium and propose a structural model of consumer behaviour in a HCME.

 Visit the **Online Resource Centre** to read the abstract and access the full paper.

Marketing's Digital Evolution

Few people in the developed economies of the world today are unaffected by the spectacular development and growth of electronic technologies. From the invention of the telegraph and telephone in the nineteenth century, the way the world worked, communicated, and shared information began to change. Since the Second World War these changes have been even more evident in both proliferation and speed of change; however, in the last quarter of the twentieth century changes became even more significant. With the widespread adoption of the facsimile machine in the 1970s and 1980s, then fibre-optic cables and the proliferation of the micro-chip, the pace of change started to accelerate. Add to these the rapid adoption of the internet because of the world wide web in the early 1990s (e.g. Web 1.0), the proliferation of mobile handsets, the emergence of interactive digital TV, and we start to see the socio-technical environment of marketing changing significantly. Then came the popularity of short-message-services (SMS) or text messaging, the introduction of 3G mobile phone technology, and the rapid development and adoption of digital social media resources (e.g. Web 2.0). The pace of change has accelerated and the impact has changed marketing forever. We now look specifically at the change in marketing focus over the last 15 years, because of the evolution in the web.

The first ten years of the web were characterized by what we call Web 1.0, wherein the web was heavily used as a static publishing and/or retailing (transactional) channel. In many ways it was revolutionary; in the machine interactivity it facilitated and the form, content, and amount of information that could be disseminated compared to earlier electronic channels such as TV and radio. However, it was still mainly used as a one-way asymmetrical medium or retailing channel, with the focus being on the technology and its content, the website, for information dissemination facilitating online and offline transactions, and the electronic delivery (e.g. digital music). De Chernatony and Christodoulides (2004) argued that the concept of brands and marketing in this online environment was enacted through website factors, such as physical delivery and fulfilment options; locating the brand through: search portals; the speed of site content download; the site's visual appearance and brand synergy; ease of site navigation; offline personal support; and the offering of different rewards through online rather than offline channels.

In those days of internet marketing, marketers would often replicate offline marketing and publishing efforts through their use of static brochureware sites. These were lacking in dynamic content and interactivity, particularly person interactivity. They followed a traditional approach of marketing 'push' for communicating to a passive audience through a monologue. There was also an information asymmetry traditionally in favour of the marketer, where communication was controlled (and/or suppressed) by the organization. However, the development of digital resources and the rise in Web 2.0 technologies over the last five years has seen evolution in marketing away from this hierarchical one-sided mass communication model.

The evolution of Web 2.0 (also called the social web) has today classified internet-based digital resources as more participatory technologies or social channels, rather than just information or transactional channels. In functionality and design they facilitate the practice of user-generated, co-created, and user-shared content through both machine and person interactivity. The focus is on the user/participant (not the website or marketer); as active (not passive) participants and co-creators of content in a community of information connections and human conversations. So the focus is more on dialogue not just monologue. This change in focus (from website content to user/participant) is reflective of how digital technologies are changing not only how consumers use and interact with digital technologies, and how they interact with each other and the organization, but also the role of marketers and marketing. In short, we are seeing a move away from a one-way model of passive communication in which information is 'pushed' to its markets, to a multimode (channel) and multiuser approach in which everyone is empowered to not only 'pull' down information, and/or interact with the organization and content, but also with each other. The website factors we mentioned earlier (e.g. download time, site appearance) are now hygiene factors, with an entirely new host of human and social factors to consider, many of these being outside the brand or marketers' control.

In summary, online search, social web, gaming, and mobile resources differ considerably from earlier forms of internet marketing in terms of the external and internal pacing, synchronicity, and the interactivity they enable, and the differing modes of transfer they facilitate. As summarized in Table 17.4, they are about pull (not just push), enabling participation (not just passivity), co-creation of a product offering (not just mass production), engaging in a dialogue (not just a monologue), and shared control over the form and content of a brand's messages, marketing activities, and product offering.

▶ **Table 17.4** The digital evolution of marketing

	Web 1.0	Web 2.0
Marketing focus	Website or content	User/participant
Approach	Push	Push and pull
Market role	Audience	Participants
Market behaviour	Passive	Passive and active
Interactivity	Machine interactivity	Person and machine interactivity
Product offering	Production	Co-production
Communication model	Monologue (one-to-many)	Dialogue (one-to-one, many-to-many)
Control	External pacing	External and internal pacing

This changing socio-technical environment has resulted in marketing and corporate executives considering that how to manage brands and conduct marketing activities in the digital space is considerably different from other channels. As such, we are seeing a change in focus toward, and an increase in marketing spend on, digital channels. In December 2009, Pepsi, the biggest advertiser during the 2009 Super Bowl, spending over $US33m on ads for brands such as Pepsi, Gatorade, and Cheetos, announced that it would no longer be advertising during the US Super Bowl. This ended a 23-year history with the event. Instead, Pepsi moved its marketing efforts mostly online to digital resources (Schwartz, 2010). Table 17.5 provides some quotes from senior executives with respect to how they see the role and evolution of marketing in light of digital resources. Digital marketing is a very important and significantly changing area of marketing theory and practice.

go online

Visit the **Online Resource Centre** and follow the weblink eMarketer.com, to learn more about the adoption, use, and evolution of electronic technology for marketing practice.

▶ **Table 17.5** Quotes from leading advertisers	
Proctor & Gamble (P&G)	'The traditional marketing model we all grew up with is obsolete.' James R. Stengel, CMO, P&G (Stengel, 2004)
McDonald's	'Mass marketing no longer works. It's the end of brand positioning as we know it.' Larry Light, CMO, McDonald's (Light, 2004)
American Express	'To me, the challenge is not awareness, the challenge is engagement.' John Hayes, CMO, American Express (Vranica, 2004)
Ford	'JWT client Ford now spends only 30–40% of its ad budget on traditional advertising, compared with as much as 80% five years ago.' Bob Jeffrey, CEO, JWT (Anon., 2004)

Digital Marketing Activities

Digital marketing encompasses a number of activities (Figure 17.2), and these are increasingly changing as digital resources develop and evolve in both functionality and marketing applicability. Today, we see growth in search marketing, social web marketing, advergaming and mobile marketing, as the market penetration and global reach of these digital resources

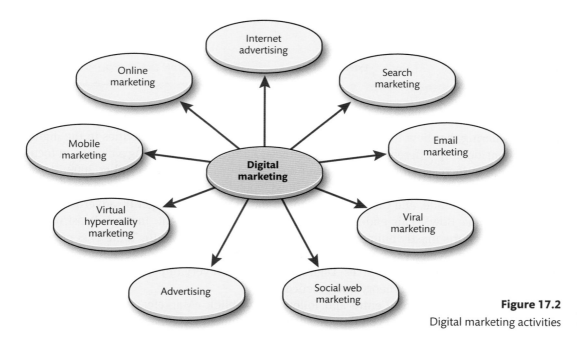

Figure 17.2

Digital marketing activities

grows. According to Nielsen (2009a), search activities online have the highest global active reach (86%), with rapid growth also in member communities (social networks). In 2009, the use of social networking sites at 68% global reach, overtook personal email at 64% for online user activity. Coupled with this is growth in mobile subscriber connections to 4.7bn globally in 2009, making mobile technologies and associated wireless digital services very attractive for marketing activities. Market and user adoption of digital resources, and their management cost, execution speed, and user experience are driving the marketing profession's interest in these differing areas of digital marketing activities.

Internet Advertising

Internet advertising is a very important source of online consumer information, especially as the number of internet users continues to increase. It is a form of marketing communications that uses internet-based resources for the purpose of advertising, delivering messages to drive traffic to a website (**click-through rate**) and also encourage trial, purchase, or repeat-purchase activity (**conversion rate**) (Cheng *et al.*, 2009). Specific online advertising formats include display advertising (e.g. banner ads), rich media ads (e.g. embedded multimedia ads, pop-up ads, **interstitials**), online video-streamed ads, search engine marketing, email advertising, and classified listings.

In 2009, online advertising spend was £3.5bn in the UK, a 4.2% rise from 2008, exceeding TV advertising spend for the first time (Kimberley, 2010). Growth was evident in search engine marketing (up 9.5% to £2.15bn) and video advertising (up increasing 140%, generating £28.3m). This rise in video advertising is attributed to faster broadband and an increase in on-demand platforms such as YouTube and SeeSaw. Display advertising saw a decline (down 4.4% in 2009), as did classified advertising showing investment falling (down 5.3% to £677.4m down from £715.2m in 2008).

Used to achieve brand awareness and encourage click-through to a target site, the major considerations for internet advertising include:

▶ Cost—internet adverts are relatively cheaper than those in other media.

▶ Timeliness—internet adverts can be updated at any time with minimal cost.

▶ Format—internet adverts are richer and can effectively use the convergence of text, audio, graphics, and animation. In addition, games, entertainment, and promotions can be easily combined in online advertisements.

▶ Personalization—internet adverts can be interactive and targeted to specific interest groups and/or individuals.

▶ Location-based—using wireless technology and GPS, internet advertising can be location-based and targeted to consumers whenever they are at a specific time and location (e.g. near a restaurant or a theatre).

▶ Intrusive—some internet advertising formats (e.g. pop-ups) are seen as intrusive and suffer more consumer complaints than other formats.

go online

Visit the **Online Resource Centre** and follow the weblink to the Interactive Advertising Bureau (IAB) to learn more about developments and standards for internet advertising activities.

Search Marketing

The growth in digital content available through the web, has given rise to the number of interactive decision aids used to help webusers locate data, information, and/or an organization's digital objects (e.g. pictures, videos). The main two types of decision aids include a search directory (web directory) and/or a search engine.

A **search directory** is a database of information maintained by human editors. It lists websites by category and subcategory, with categorization usually based on the whole website rather than one page or a set of keywords. Search directories often allow site-owners to directly submit their site for inclusion, and have editors review submissions for fitness. The first directory of websites (webservers) was categorized by Tim Berners-Lee in 1992, during the early development of the web. Today, popular examples include Yahoo! Directory, and the Netscape-owned Open Directory Project (ODP). ODP has categorized over 3,885,506 sites, in 59,000 categories, and has been constructed and maintained by a community of over 85,274 volunteer editors.

In contrast, a **search engine** operates algorithmically or using a mixture of algorithmic and human input to collect, index, store, and retrieve information on the web (e.g. webpages, images, information, and other types of files), making this information available to users in a manageable and meaningful way in response to a search query. Information is retrieved by a webcrawler (also known as a spider), which is an automated web-browser that follows every link on the site, analysing how it should be indexed, using words extracted from page and file titles, headings, or special fields called meta tags. These indexed data are then stored in an index database for use in later queries. When a user enters a query into a search engine (typically using keywords), the engine examines its index and provides a listing of best-matching webpages according to its criteria on search engine result pages (SERPs). There are only a few dominant search engines in the market, with Google leading the global market share rankings with 86%, followed by Yahoo! Search at 6% (see Table 17.6).

The webpage of the world's leading search engine

▶ **Table 17.6** Search engine global market share rankings

Search engine	Domain	Market share (%)
Google–Global	www.google.com	85.78
Yahoo–Global	http://uk.search.yahoo.com	6.16
Bing	www.bing.com	3.17
Baidu	www.baidu.com	2.56
Ask–Global	www.ask.com	0.62
AOL–Global	www.aol.com	0.47
MSN–Global	www.msn.com	0.08
AltaVista–Global	www.altavista.com	0.07
Excite–Global	www.excite.com	0.02
All the Web–Global	www.alltheweb.com	0.01

Source: Net Market Share (2010).

Search Marketing Methods

Search engine marketing (SEM) is one of the main forms of internet advertising, with a UK spend of £2.15bn accounting for 60% of total UK online ad spend. Its aim is to promote websites by increasing their visibility in search engine result pages (SERPs). SEM methods include: search engine optimization (SEO), paid placement, contextual advertising, digital asset optimization, and paid inclusion (SEMPO, 2010). These are outlined in further detail below.

▶ **Search engine optimization** (SEO) is where a website's structure and content is improved to maximize its listing in the organic search engine results pages according to relevant keywords or search phrases. Research reports that, on average, organizations are expect to spend 43% more on SEO in 2010 than they did in 2009 (Econsultancy, 2010).

▶ **Paid placement** or **Pay Per Click** (PPC) is an advertising model used in which advertisers pay their host only when their sponsored ad or link is clicked. Advertisers typically bid on keywords or phrases relevant to their target market, with sponsored/paid search engine listings to drive traffic to a website. The search engine ranks ads based on a competitive auction and other related criteria (e.g. popularity, quality). Google AdWords, Yahoo! Search Marketing, and Microsoft adCenter are the three largest ad-network operators with all three operating under a bid-based model.

▶ **Contextual advertising** is a form of targeted advertising, with advertisements (e.g. banner, pop-ups) appearing on websites, with the advertisements themselves selected and served by automated systems based on the content displayed to the user. A contextual advertising system scans the text of a website for keywords and returns advertisements to the webpage based on what the user is viewing. Google AdSense was the first major contextual advertising programme.

▶ **Digital asset optimization** (DAO) or SEO 2.0 is the optimization of all an organization's digital assets (e.g. .doc, .pdf, video, podcasts, music files, images, and other digital media) for search, retrieval, and indexing.

▶ **Paid inclusion** is where a search engine company charges fees related to inclusion of websites in their search index. Some organizations mix paid inclusion with organic listings (e.g. Yahoo!), whereas others do not allow for paid inclusion to be listed with organic lists (e.g. Google and Ask.com).

All these search marketing methods allow marketers to match specific users with specific content according to their interest. Despite differing search engines and directories taking a different approach, one thing unites them—search marketing is one of the most important and cost-effective methods of digital marketing. From a global online survey of nearly 1,500 client-side marketers and agency respondents, it is estimated that the North American search engine marketing industry will grow 14% from $14.6bn in 2009 to $16.6bn by the end of 2010. Around half the organizations (49%) surveyed are reallocating budgets to search marketing from print advertising. Engagement in SEO activities (90%) has remained steady since 2007, and the proportion of organizations carrying out paid search marketing (now 81%) has increased from 78% in 2009 and 70% in 2008. The research also highlights Google's dominance, with 97% of companies paying to advertise on Google AdWords, nearly three-quarters of companies (71%) paying to advertise on the Google search network, and 56% using the Google content network (keyword targeted) (Econsultancy, 2010).

SEM is of increasing importance to digital marketers, as, in addition to being highly effective in matching content to user needs, the results are measurable, increasing its accountability. Also, search marketing methods (e.g. SEO, DAO, and PPC) are not perceived as being as invasive as other forms of online advertising, such as display and rich-media contextual advertising, heavily disliked by consumers (e.g. pop-up ads) (Nail, Charron, and Cohen, 2005). See Market Insight 17.2 for a review of the UK flight sector's search marketing activities and easyJet's search performance.

▶ Market Insight 17.2

easyJet Pays to Take Off!

An analysis of key search terms used by UK consumers when searching online for flights was conducted for the third quarter of the year in 2009. This independent research,

conducted by Greenlight, identified 3,200 of the most commonly used search terms by UK webusers, which cumulatively deliver 28.1m searches for flight-related terms. The term 'Flight' accounted for 59% of all flight-related searches. Short-haul destinations, largely

▶ Market Insight 17.2

easyJet, clearly visible in the skies and on the internet

within Europe, accounted for almost 5.3m searches in December 2009, with queries for flights to Palma and Rome cumulatively accounting for 16%. The analysis also reported the most visible websites using these keywords, which topped the lists for organic and paid search listings.

▶ Organic listings—in natural search, with 89% visibility, SkyScanner.net ranked at position one on page one of Google for 445 of the 3,200 keywords analysed. TravelSupermarket.com followed with 72% visibility, followed closely by expedia.co.uk (57%), easyJet.com (52%), and lastminute.com (48%).

▶ Paid placement—in paid search it was a very different picture, with easyJet attaining a 65%

share of voice. This was achieved through bidding on 29 of the 30 keywords analysed. BMI Baby followed with 51%, then British Airways (43%), Aer Lingus (43%), and TravelSupermarket (36%, losing 44% share of voice in December, which saw it feature at position five of the top 20 advertisers for short-haul flights.

Sources: Greenlight (2009); Cowen (2009); www.easyjet.com.

1 **What is the difference between natural and paid placement in search engine marketing?**

2 **What factors do you think influence how a website is ranked in a search engine's natural (organic) search listings?**

3 **Why do you think easyJet.com was ranked higher in paid placement compared to organic listings?**

Email Marketing

Permission-based email marketing is another highly cost-effective form of digital marketing (Strategies, 1999; Waring and Martinez, 2002, Cheng *et al.*, 2009). It is a method of marketing by electronic mail, which the recipient of the message has consented to receive. As a marketing tool it is easy to use, costs little to produce, costs next to nothing to send, and has the potential to reach millions of willing prospects in a matter of minutes. Email marketing is regarded as one of the most powerful and cost-effective tools for digital marketers, with the Direct Marketing Association (DMA) recently projecting that email marketing will generate a return on investment of US$43.52 for every US$1 spent on the channel in 2009, twice the return earned by other marketing channels. It includes 'opt-in' and 'opt-out' mailing lists, email newsletters, and discussion list subscriptions, and, used effectively, email goes far beyond sending a sales message. This can help build a brand's relationship with a consumer, create a sense of trust, retain loyal customers, and generate revenue as well as referrals.

The most important element of this form of marketing is that the sender sends the message only to those who have agreed to receive messages. This is the opposite to **spam**: unsolicited email, the junk mail of the twenty-first century, which clogs email servers and uses up much-needed bandwidth on the internet. Spam accounts for 14.5bn messages globally per day, McAfee (2009) reported that spam email accounted for 92% of all email sent in the second quarter of 2009, with an estimated total cost of $130bn worldwide (Ferris, 2009). The USA (25.5%), Brazil (9.8%), Turkey (5.8%), and India (5.6%) lead the generation of spam (McAfee, 2009).

Because of its cheapness and ease of use, the potential for abuse of email is greater than for other communication systems. Table 17.7 provides a list of the fundamentals for delivering successful permission-based email marketing campaigns.

▶ **Table 17.7** Fundamentals of email marketing

Make the campaign targeted—80/20 rule	Think carefully about target audience; exclude those not relevant and design campaign to communicate key benefits
	Pay most attention to the 20% who are most actively engaged with your brand and responsive to email offers
Gain and confirm permissions	Provide a mechanism for list members to opt in or opt out of the relationship
	Confirm this opt-in when a consumer joins
	Allow members to choose different email offerings such as newsletter, discount offers, and product-specific updates
	Include options in the unsubscribe process to retain members
Personalize	First-name personalization has become standard. Studies show personalization can increase response rate by 64%

▶ **Table 17.7** (continued)

Message and copy	Email is often read in the preview screen so ensure key message is contained with this frame
	Keep your message simple—copy that is short and to the point works better
	Design that draws the reader to the call-to-action will increase response rate
	Thank the purchaser and use consumer preferences to guide copy and offers
Subject line	There is more chance the message will be opened if the subject conveys the email's value/benefits
	Limit subject line to 35 characters
	Test subject lines to determine effectiveness
Source address: 'From'	Ensure the from address is consistent with who the recipient opted-in to
	Ensure you comply with privacy regulations and recipient can recognize this
	Ensure the brand name (B2C) or salesperson's (B2B) name appears in the 'from' field
Test, test, and retest	Where possible, test subject line, call-to-action, time-of-day, frequency, incentive, etc., on a statistically valid sample
	Send emails at the right time
Track, report, and mine results	Use an email system that allows tracking and reporting on all elements of the campaign, including opens, clicks, pass-along, unsubscribe, and bounce-backs
	Mine customer data for insights and analyse message frequency coupled with response rate
Collect and follow-up responses	Ensure responses come through to you and dictate how often they are received
	Follow-up responses more likely to warrant higher value or interested prospect
Spam blocking	Check if the system can allow a domain delegation to lower the risk of being blocked by spam filters

Sources: IMT (1999); Glass (2006); Westlund (2009).

Social Web Marketing

According to a report by Nielsen (2009b), two-thirds of the world's internet population regularly visit a social network, blogging, or social media site, and these technologies now account for almost 10% of all time spent on the internet. Social networking has overtaken personal email to become the fourth-most popular online sector after search, portals, and PC software applications. As a result, we are seeing the increased allocation in marketing spend to social web channels, platforms, and technologies. According to a 2009 Chief Marketing Officer (CMO) survey, currently 3.5% of marketing budgets are spent on social web marketing, with that figure predicted to grow to 6.1% within 12 months and 13.7% within five years (CMO, 2009). Further research has identified the movement of marketing spend away from traditional areas. January 2010 saw FMCG giants Coca-Cola and Unilever announce that they were moving away from campaign-led micro websites (microsites) in favour of investments in existing community channels such as Facebook and YouTube (Cooper, 2010). These brands join Dell, Starbucks, Ford, Wrigley-Skittles, and American Express in using the social web to converse, connect, and learn from the communities within which their organizations co-exist. This what we call social web marketing.

Social web marketing (SWM) is a form of digital marketing that describes the use of the social web and social media (e.g. social networks, online

Facebook, the leading social web community © THIERRY ROGE/ Reuters/Corbis

communities, blogs, wikis) or any online collaborative technology for marketing activities—be it sales, public relations, research, distribution, or customer service. The CMO survey (CMO, 2009) found that social networks (Facebook, LinkedIn) are the most favoured by marketers, followed by video-sharing sites (YouTube), image-sharing sites (Flickr), blogging platforms (WordPress), and microblogs (Twitter and Seesmic). Marketers are investing in these to increase their brands' social equity or **social capital**.

Growing a Brand's Social Capital

Whereas human capital can be defined as embodied in the skills and knowledge acquired by an individual, social capital is in the relations among individuals (Coleman, 1988), the social structures and networks within which we live and work. Existent in this is the social web online, with early exploratory research attesting to strong connections between social network usage (Facebook) and an individual's social capital (Ellison, Steinfield, and Lampe, 2007). An analysis of the 100 most valuable brands in the USA (according to BusinessWeek/Interbrand) and how they use 11 different social media channels, ranked the following brands as the most effective in terms of social web engagement: Starbucks, Dell, and eBay based on their breadth and depth of engagement. Following these came Google, Microsoft, Thomson Reuters, Nike, Amazon, SAP, and Yahoo/Intell (a tie), to round out the top ten brands that are deeply engaged with consumers through the social web (Li, 2009). The study also found a positive correlation between the use of the social web and a firm's financial performance. Social web engagement is seen as a good indicator of an innovative risk-taking culture and eagerness to engage with consumers. However, it should also be noted that social capital was particularly gained by those organizations who innovated early, often, and incrementally. Table 17.8 provides a few examples of the early social web activities of these leading brands.

Brand	Early social web activity
Microsoft	Was the first to let employees openly blog. Microsofties began blogging in the late 1990s
Microsoft	Quick to build online communities, launching its inventive Channel 9 platform for developers in 2004
Yahoo and Google	Following the success of Microsofties, Yahoo and Google debut corporate and product blogs in 2004 and Direct2Dell in 2006
Dell and Starbucks	Earliest adopters of crowdsourcing, launching the ambitious sites 'My Starbucks Idea' and 'Dell Idea Storm' in 2007 and 2008 respectively
Amazon	Amazon started offering deals on Twitter back in 2007
eBay	The first ever live-tweet earnings calls in 2008

▶ **Table 17.8** Early social web activity

Social Web Marketing Principles

The social media development of digital marketing is not only having an impact on where we spend our marketing budget, but more fundamentally it is challenging the way we communicate, share information, interact, and create (or produce) a product offering. When anybody who has access can create, comment on, or share information about what we do, what we represent and how we do it—be it a person, organization, or brand—then we no longer have the power or control we thought we had over the way we or our brand is perceived in the marketplace. This is evidenced by Case Insight 17.1, describing Simon Cowell's myopia in terms of community and consumer activism. Changing media habits and growth in digital and social web resources mean that CMOs can foresee a day when many traditional marketing and communication models and principles will no longer work (Court, Gordon, and Perrey, 2005). To cope with this change, many organizations are now hiring social media specialists to complement their marketing skills (PRSA, 2009), with leaders in social web marketing having dedicated in-house social webteams. As a direct result, we are seeing the evolution of marketing principles as driven by the growing number and type of digital and social web channels, technologies, and platforms (Ozuem, Howell, and Lancaster, 2008; Molenaar, 2002). Next, we discuss four key areas in which social web marketing is different from other digital marketing activities.

Sharing Control

Sharing **control** refers to the ability of users in a computer-mediated environment, be they consumers, marketers or competitors, to access content at will, create and modify content to pertain to their needs, and share this content with other consumers, companies, or third-parties. This occurs directly as a result of social media technologies enabling both internal and external pacing. Consider what happened when a frustrated customer filmed a video of a digital cable technician from Comcast Cable Communications Inc. (USA) who fell asleep while repairing the customer's cable TV. The customer uploaded the video to YouTube and the clip became a hit with more than 1m viewings, undermining Comcast's attempts to improve its reputation for customer services (Bernoff and Li, 2008). This is an example of how social digital technologies have changed the role of who controls (or thinks they control) organization-branded communications and the changing mindset regarding the role and purpose of marking and the marketer/brand manager (Christodoulides, 2009). The brand manager who used to be the 'custodian' of the brand, has now become a 'host' whose main role is not to control, but to facilitate sharing, participation, connectivity and the co-creation of a product offering—be it good or bad (Mitchell, 2001).

User-Generated and Co-Created Content

The social web enables users to generate, share, and comment on content (Van den Bulte and Wuyts, 2007). The OECD definition of **user-generated content** (UGC) is: a) content made publicly available over the internet; b) which reflects a certain amount of creative effort; and c) is created outside of professional routine and practices (Wunsch-Vincent and Vickery, 2007). That is, content that is created by general users (not producers). The contribution of user videos to YouTube is an example of UGC. UGC created with a marketing benefit is also called vigilante marketing, 'unpaid advertising and marketing efforts, including one-to-one, one-to-many, and many-to-many commercially orientated communications, undertaken by brand loyalists on behalf of the brand' (Muniz and Jensen Schau, 2007: 35). With cheaper desktop audio, video and animation software, consumers can easily create promotional content to rival professionally produced content. Well-known examples of UGC have been created by fans for Apple iPod, Coca-Cola, Firefox, Nike, and Volkswagen, among other brands. Adcandy.com provides an online space where consumers can create, upload, and comment on user-generated advertising.

In contrast, **co-created content** is more social. It is the act of interacting, creating content or applications by at least two people (Trogemann and Pelt, 2006). Contributions to Wikipedia are a typical example of co-creation.

UGC and co-creation are important in that they provide evidence of consumer perceptions of the brand and brand attributes, are vivid examples of the most compelling marketing messages from the perspective of brand loyalists, and are only going to increase in frequency and prominence as social web channels and technologies develop (Muniz and Jensen Schau, 2007).

Community and Social Networks

The social web is facilitating the development of social connectivity through online networks that arise from informal relations between people, enhancing a 'small world' phenomenon (Morlacchi, Wilkinson, and Young, 2005). Social media enables individuals and organizations to connect to each other individually and communally—it is social, it is about community and the social graph within which we live, work, and study, not just the technologies we use to connect (Simmons, 2008). As such, for marketers the challenge lies in deciding our level of engagement in online social communities, and how can we really participate in the dialogue and add value?

These borderless virtual communities offer individuals the promise of community with large numbers of like-minded individuals who share specialized or similar interests (Burnett, 2000), and are growing exponentially. If we look at technologies specifically for social networking, 2009 saw massive growth. Twitter grew over 1,382%, year over year with a user base of over 14m. This was somewhat overshadowed by Facebook, which still outpaced MySpace with over 350m users globally (Mintel, 2009). China presents a very different social networking graph. Unlike the USA, Europe, and Australasia, Facebook does not even rank in the top 15 social networks in the country, and MySpace has only 6m Chinese users. Tencent QQ (QQ), which runs Qzone, a Facebook rival, is the global leader currently, with over 300m users (Jin, 2009; Godula, Li, and Yu, 2009).

Twitter is just one of the online social communities which marketers can choose to participate in.

Social networking is a huge cultural shift for marketing and has differing levels of engagement. New communities come together and disperse quickly and are often led by different people at different moments for differing reasons. Table 17.9 provides a list of the major reasons why individuals use social networks, with the main reason being to keep in touch with current friends or reconnect with old friends and work colleagues. It's not to click on advertising, receive promotional information, or purchase a product that motivates consumers to connect.

▶ **Table 17.9** Reasons for social network use—September 2009

Reason	%
Keeping in touch with my current set of friends	66
To find old friends and work colleagues	58
To store and share photos, e.g. holiday snaps	37
To see what others in my family are up to	37
To play games, e.g. Scrabble®, quizzes	20
To make new friends	17
To listen to music/watch videos	12
To discuss hobbies with like-minded people, e.g. join/create groups	11
To keep up with current news and online trends	11
To use utilities, e.g. birthday cards, calendar	10
To network for business opportunities	7
To meet members of the opposite sex, e.g. dating/relationship	4
Other	5

Source: Mintel (2009). Base: 1,563 internet users aged 16+ who use social networks.

Conversations and Dialogue

Social web marketing is not about mass marketing, but is focused on facilitating real conversations around the organization, the brand, or an individual. Markets incorporate conversations, and conversations are a fundamental part of being human. As such, commerce is reliant on human conversation and the interaction between people; however, traditionally, business has been divorced from real conversations. Instead marketing has been heavily focused on a traditional one-way monologue or sales pitch. To engage in these digital conversations requires trust and transparency, and involves authentic engagement in a real two-way dialogue. However, it is not the social web that makes these conversations happen, they just support it. By understanding how the social web supports the human desire for conversation, businesses can open up interactions with individuals and communities. But the important point is real conversation, i.e. authenticity, as discovered by Ernst and Young. When Ernst and Young hired an agency to manage its university/college-recruiting presence on Facebook, the results were poor. Only when the organization enlisted a group of interns who were active facebookers to contribute did the conversation become more authentic and draw more traffic, contributing to the company's rapid rise in *Business Week* magazine's ranking of top firms that college students want to work for (Kane *et al.*, 2009).

go online

Visit the **Online Resource Centre** and complete Internet Activity 17.2 to learn more about how Ernst and Young use Twitter to maintain an ongoing real dialogue with their followers.

Market Insight 17.3 shows how a national theatre organization engaged online with its community to develop the brand's social capital.

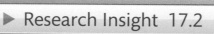

▶ Research Insight 17.2

To take your learning further, you might wish to read this influential paper.

Kane, G. C., Fichman, R. G., Gallaugher, J., and Glaser, J. (2009) 'Community relations 2.0', *Harvard Business Review*, 87 (11 Nov), 45–50.

This paper draws on the study of more than two dozen firms, describing the changes wrought by social media and showing managers how to take advantage of these changes.

 Visit the **Online Resource Centre** to read the abstract and access the full paper.

▶ Market Insight 17.3

National Theatre Wales Takes Centre Stage

Commissioned in January 2009, the National Theatre Wales (NTW) is a dynamic new flexible non-building-based theatre organization supported by the Arts Council Wales and Welsh Assembly Government. NTW is charged with developing and enriching English language theatre in Wales with an international reach. Its aim is to engage and involve the community in surprising ways and unexpected places

through relationships with theatre makers, creative talents, participants, and audiences in and beyond Wales. The key tenants of NTW are to be engaging, innovative, and international.

In the early development of the NTW offering, digital and social web resources were highlighted as essential for NTW's marketing and community development initiatives. NTW wanted to reach new and differing theatre audiences and wanted to engage in an ongoing dialogue with the theatre community before its programme launch in November 2009. As

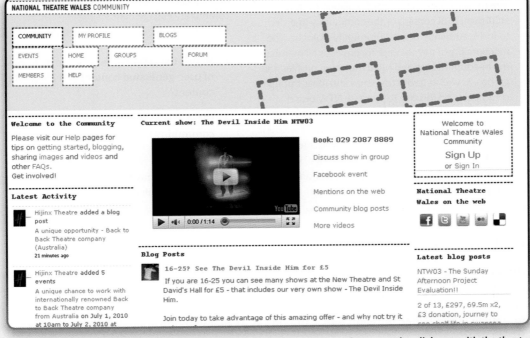

The National Theatre Wales has developed a social web strategy to engage in an ongoing dialogue with the theatre community

▶ Market Insight 17.3   (continued)

such, NTW developed an innovative and engaging social web strategy grounded in online community development to give everyone a stage (a platform) to 'Create, Debate and Respond' about theatre. Specifically, NTW developed an online community based on a Ning platform so everyone could: interact, collaborate on projects; be creative in visual, auditory and written expression; develop deep rich community involvement; provide feedback; promote events; showcase their work; develop social bonds in/across the community; and be more environmentally friendly in their communication activities.

NTW took a very active but careful role in participating in the community, with NTW staff and theatre partners as participants creating content NOT owners of content or the community in order to foster authenticity and community dialogue. The functionality of the community provides all members the freedom to blog and build their own profiles and groups, as well as to discuss issues and ideas through comments and forums. To increase NTW brand awareness and drive online community traffic, social web technologies such as a company Twitter account (@NTWTweets) and individual staff Twitter feeds (@cpaskall, @john_ntw), a Facebook fan page, YouTube channel, NetVibes site, Flickr albums, RSS, and numerous widgets were used.

Within 12 months from its launch in May 2009, the NTW community had over 1,900 members, which has generated over 700 member blog posts (averaging 60 posts a month), 48 community groups (e.g. creatives, writers, theatre companies, each averaging at least 50 members), and 58 discussion forums on issues from how to market theatre, to the role of language and debate in theatre. These have been invaluable as sources of deep rich community insights for the NTW team. With the official launch of the programme of NTW productions on 5 November 2009, for a March 2010 opening night, the NTW community has taken centre stage not only in building the social currency of the NTW brand, but also in co-creating the NTW offering and value proposition through online community engagement.

Sources: Moss (2010); www.nationaltheatrewales.org

1 **How is the NTW community an example of user-generated content and co-created content?**

2 **What impact do you think the online community has on the values of the NTW brand?**

3 **What are some of the challenges NTW might face as a result of the online community?**

Online and Advergaming

Advergaming or in-game advertising (IGA) is another form of digital marketing, often coupled with sales promotions that provide rewards in terms of incentives, novel and fun entertainment. Advergaming is the use of computer and video games as a medium in which to deliver advertising. Advergames can consist of membership models of multiplayers (e.g. *World of Warcraft*), applications downloaded to a mobile device or added to an online social network, or viral games in which the game is passed on from user to user on the web. Most advergames require users to register, allowing for the collection of data for marketing research and other marketing initiatives, and mix interactivity, gaming, and advertising in a novel and innovative way.

Research has identified that the UK has more online and console gamers than anywhere else in Europe, with 73% of those surveyed playing games and many ranking gaming as their favourite pastime ahead of surfing the internet and watching TV (TNS, 2009). Males between the ages of 13 and 19 spend on average 11 hours per week playing games, with increases in use by girls (86%) and people over 50 (42%) spending more time playing games than reading magazines. The research also revealed that mobile phones and social networks such as MySpace and Facebook are the game platforms of the future, beyond PC, console, and portal game platforms (TNS, 2009). Given these statistics in game adoption, and the effectiveness of in-game advertising on brand recognition, recall, and revenue, in-game advertising is an important digital marketing activity.

Creativity and enjoyment (or fun) are normal and essential functions of humanity. Although, since its development, much focus has been on the utilitarian purpose of the web, digital technologies today extend commonly available creative and entertainment spaces. With the rise in apps or apis (i.e. application programming interfaces) on social networking sites and smartphones, hyperreality virtual worlds (e.g. *Second Life*), and advergaming, the level of perceived playfulness and enjoyment from digital resources has increased in importance. Perceived playfulness is the degree to which a current or potential user believes that the technology will bring him or her a sense of enjoyment and/or pleasure (Sledgianowski and Kulviwat, 2009). It is an intrinsic motivator, influenced by the user's experience with the digital environment. Individuals with a more positive playfulness belief in the specific technology view their interactions with technology more positively and are more inclined to use the technology more often and transfer this feeling to associated brands (e.g. advertisers).

Two rising trends in digital gaming platforms are social networks and mobile phones. In May 2007, Facebook opened up its platform allowing outside web developers to create free software programs that members of the social networking site could use to entertain and inform each other. Gaming examples include applications such as *FarmVille* or *Bejeweled*, which induce users to play games with their friends. Facebook now has more than 52,000 applications, allowing Facebook users to send each other virtual hugs, share movie picks, and play games. Every month, more than 70% of Facebook users engage with platform applications, with more than 9,000 applications having over 10,000 + monthly active users (Facebook, 2010).

Gaming applications are not just about online social networking sites, smartphones like the Apple iPhone and the Blackberry Bold 9700 are also playing the game. As at January 2010, Apple's App Store was serving over 100,000 downloadable iPhone apps, with iPhone owners worldwide having downloaded over 2bn apps. Games appear to be the hottest items in the Apple App Store. Of the 100,000 apps, only 16,000 titles are games, yet 65% of the 2bn apps downloaded are games, many of which are fee-based.

Market Insight 17.4 shows how Renault has used gaming to increase awareness of its new line of electric cars to potential markets of avid digital gamers.

▶ Market Insight 17.4

Renault on Virtual Launch

In the first global partnership with the virtual reality game, *The Sims 3*, Renault is set to launch its Zero Emission (ZE) electric vehicle through the virtual reality game. *The Sims 3* is the third in a series of strategic life simulation videogames in *The Sims* franchise. As a virtual reality game, players create and control their Sims (characters) in various

---

▶ Market Insight 17.4 (continued)

---

activities and form relationships and life in neighbourhoods in a manner similar to real life. *The Sims 3* was an instant success, selling 1.4m copies in its first week of release in 2009, making the game very attractive to potential advertisers.

Renault will launch four models of its electric car through the game. The tie-up with *The Sims* will offer consumers their first opportunity to interact with the vehicles before they roll onto the streets. Renault hopes to target digitally savvy consumers and early adopters, as it looks to position itself at the forefront of sustainable technology in the automotive industry.

Gamers across Europe, the Middle East, Africa, Latin America, and Asia will be able to download a free *Sims 3* 'Electric Vehicle Pack', which comprises various environmentally friendly items, including the ZE vehicle and solar panels for their simulated homes.

Users will be encouraged to download the update with the offer of reduced weekly virtual household bills. Given that the electric vehicles are designed to appeal to younger, more socially conscious customers, and especially early adopters, Renault's partnership is based on this group being the heartland of *The Sims 3* community.

(See Market Insight 1.4 for more on electric cars entering the marketplace.)

1 What are the benefits of a virtual reality game opening its platform to potential advertisers?

2 Why do you think Renault chose a virtual reality game to launch the concept of its electric car before the car hits the streets?

3 Why did Renault specifically partner with *The Sims 3* virtual reality game?

Mobile Marketing

Increasingly, we are accessing digital technologies, sharing information, socializing online, and playing games away from the desktop computer. Over the last few years we have seen the number of mobile internet users grow exponentially as the wireless infrastructure and mobile devices required to support mobile internet are rapidly evolving. The global mobile market reached 4.7bn by year-end 2009, and, as shown in Table 17.10, the Asia-Pacific remained the world's largest region, accounting for over 45% (2.1bn) of global mobile connections, mainly due to strong growth in India and China. Leading analysts note that the market for portable electronics is growing unabated (eMarketer, 2009), with Morgan Stanley (2009) further expecting high-speed wireless internet-enabled device shipments to more than double worldwide from 2009 to 2013. Netbooks (i.e. notebooks), e-readers (e.g. kindle), smartphones (iPhone, Blackberry), media players (e.g. iTouch), gaming devices (e.g. Wii), and tablet PCs (e.g. iPad) are all part of the fast-changing world of portable content and communication.

Mobile marketing is the set of practices that enables organizations to communicate and engage with their audience in an interactive and relevant manner through any mobile device or network (MMA, 2009). With the added benefits of store-and-send technology giving the option of message storage, mobile marketing is quick, inexpensive, and reaches markets wherever they are, despite limitations in message content. Mobile marketing differs from traditional mass marketing across four elements: 1) scope of audience—mobile marketing audiences are restricted to owners of mobile devices who opt-in to receive communications; 2)

▶ **Table 17.10** Worldwide mobile subscriber connections

Region	Connections	% of global market
Asia-Pacific	2.1bn	45
Western Europe	519m	11
Americas	504m	11
Eastern Europe	480m	10
Africa	464m	10
USA/Canada	309m	7
Middle East	261m	6

Source: Wireless Intelligence (2009).

type and format of messages—bandwidth capacity and tight screen size constraints restrict the format and type of message possible; 3) location-based targeting—location-based and time-based targeting of messages are facilitated through mobile devices; 4) response tracking—marketers can better track and measure audience responses to mobile messages (Shankar and Balasubramanian, 2009). See Table 17.11 for the many differing types of mobile marketing.

▶ **Table 17.11** Types of mobile advertising methods

Type	Description
Text message	Mobile version of direct marketing can be used for sweepstakes, voting in contents, instant wins, offering consumer statistics, and other data
Games	Branded offerings can range from simple puzzles to custom multiplayer, multilevel advergames that can take months to develop depending on complexity
Interactive voice response (IVR)	Opt-in consumers receive mobile phone calls from star endorsers, celebrity endorsers, or customer service personnel
WAP sites	Existing websites translated for wireless devices to access and download content
Ringtones	Giveaways of brand-related tones and screensavers or wallpaper
Viral	Promotions and UGC designed to spread peer-to-peer about brands and branded messages
Geotargeting	Use of GPS and location-based tracking software to target consumers with products or store-based offers at the point of purchase
Sponsorships/ subsidizing call costs	Consumers offset the cost of a mobile service, programme, and content with advertising
Applications (apps)	Branded software applications for mobile devices, consumers to pull added-value information, customer service, and/or entertainment where and when they want it

With multiple devices, numerous access modes, and shifting consumer preference, for marketers, multimode and multidevice support and content provision is of increasing importance (Shankar and Balasubramanian, 2009). Kodak, for example, began developing iPhone apps in 2008 to support its imaging services. The first was a connection to the Kodak online photosharing gallery that allows customers to upload pictures and share their online album direct from their iPhone. This was soon followed by the Kodak Pic Flick, an app that allows people with certain wi-fi-enabled Kodak products (e.g. digital frame or printer) to simply 'flick' a photo from their iPhone direct to their frame or printer. Social web marketing is also about mobile consumption. There were an estimated 141.1m mobile social network users worldwide by the end of 2009. That number is expected to skyrocket by 2014 to approximately 760.1m (eMarketer, 2010). This is creating both a challenge and an opportunity for marketers today, in matching services and content to the market through the most suitable mobile portable device.

Market Insight 17.5 shows how McDonald's targeted consumers across Finland with location-based promotional offers direct to their mobile phone.

▶ Research Insight 17.3

To take your learning further, you might wish to read this influential paper.

Shankar, V., and Balasubramanian, S. (2009) 'Mobile marketing: a synthesis and prognosis', *Journal of Interactive Marketing*, **23, 118–29.**

This article presents the conceptual underpinnings of mobile marketing and a synopsis of relevant literature, herein the authors discuss four key issues: drivers of mobile device adoption, the influence of mobile marketing on customer decision-making, formulation of mobile marketing strategy, and mobile marketing in a global context.

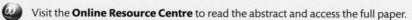 Visit the **Online Resource Centre** to read the abstract and access the full paper.

▶ Market Insight 17.5

McDonald's Maps Finland!

In 2009, leading global advertiser McDonald's conducted a location-targeted campaign in Finland. Powered by NAVTEQ LocationPoint Advertising, a subsidiary of Nokia,

McDonald's trialled the delivery of location-relevant mobile ads to users of Nokia Ovi Maps when they were within a certain distance of one of McDonald's 82 restaurants in Finland. NAVTEQ is the leading global provider of maps, traffic, and location

---

▶ Market Insight 17.5

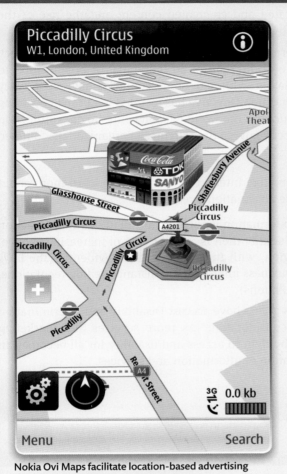

Nokia Ovi Maps facilitate location-based advertising in a variety of locations, including London

Source: Copyright © Nokia 2010.

data (digital location content) enabling navigation, location-based services, and mobile advertising around the world.

The ad campaign promoted a McDonald's cheeseburger for €1. Consumers who clicked on the ads saw the details of the promotion, and could receive driving or walking directions to the nearest store location. The campaign delivered a 7% click-through rate (CTR), and of those who clicked through, 39% selected the click-to-navigate option, which offered 'drive to' or 'walk to' navigation to the nearest McDonald's location, using Nokia's Ovi Maps navigation.

The campaign showed McDonald's that location-targeted mobile advertising does indeed drive foot traffic into their many restaurants. In brief, mobile as a marketing channel brings to advertising personalization and location, and if these are involved in an ad campaign, they provide high relevance to the consumer.

Sources: Anon. (2010); www.navteqmedia.com.

1　What does mobile as a marketing channel give to advertisers?

2　What was the key content and service strategy of the McDonald's mobile campaign?

3　Why do you think this campaign is seen as a good example of effective location-targeting?

Digital Marketing Considerations

With the rise in digital resources, and their increasing use for marketing activities, come complications and changes to legislation and regulated business practices. The sorts of legal and regulatory issues that marketers need to increasingly consider include the following:

▶ Jurisdiction—where does digital marketing activity actually take place? Commercial law is based on transactions within national boundaries, but digital marketing exposes both individual organizations and the community to information, transactions, and social activity outside these boundaries, e.g. EU legislation and Microsoft.

▶ Ownership—who owns the content we create and share? Copyright law is a national issue, and the copyright laws (what can and cannot be used without the originator's permission) differ from one country to the next. Some countries don't have copyright or intellectual property protection, and so ideas, designs, etc., sent to those countries can be taken and used without the agreement of the copyright holder. The value of copyright is also being questioned with the rise in user-generated and co-created content and the rise of the Creative Commons (CC) free licence system.

▶ Permissions—do we have the right permissions to upload and share content? Privacy legislation is also national or regional, and the right of an individual or organization to use information is subject to this legislation. Although some countries have no privacy legislation, the European Union Data Protection Directive has resulted in Europe becoming one of the most highly regulated jurisdictions in the world when it comes to data protection requirements. However, that doesn't directly govern the activities of organizations founded in the USA (e.g. Microsoft, Facebook).

go online

Visit the **Online Resource Centre** and complete Internet Activity 17.1 to learn more about privacy and the use of **cookies** for online observational research.

▶ Security—how secure are the data and information we share? Information and transaction security and protection from fraud and identity theft is another area of increasing change. Legislation varies from country and region, with further differences evident in the laws that govern and protect consumer and business interests (e.g. distance selling regulations, consumer protection (e-Commerce) regulations).

▶ Accessibility—does everyone who wants access have access? Disability and discrimination legislation also requires organization consideration. As more services and marketing information are being shared digitally, the right to access and usability for all becomes an important agenda item for the dissemination of information and services.

▶ Research Insight 17.4

To take your learning further, you might wish to read this influential paper.

Winter, R. (2009) 'New communications approaches in marketing: issues and research directions', *Journal of Interactive Marketing*, 23, 2, May, 108–17.

This article addresses the wider current context within which developing digital channels are influencing how organizations engage and participate in a dialogue with customers and their marketing activities. It reviews the challenges that these present from the perspective of the marketing manager.

@   Visit the **Online Resource Centre** to read the abstract and access the full paper.

Skills for Employment

▶▶ Those people who can truly call themselves digital natives will always have an advantage over others. We need people who already inhabit online digital communities, people who can be as much a part of the business as one of its consumers. ◀◀

Daniel Neville, Brand Co-ordinator & Captain, Idea Bounty

 Visit the **Online Resource Centre** to discover more tips and advice on skills for the workplace.

Chapter Summary

To consolidate your learning, the key points made throughout this chapter are summarized below:

■ **Consider the impact of digital resources on marketing.**

Electronic technologies have been used in marketing activities since the development of early mass media channels such as radio and TV. Since this time, electronic marketing has evolved to encompass a wide range of electronic and digital technologies and types of electronic marketing activity in the areas of integrated marketing communications, pricing, distribution, and customer service. These include: digital marketing, mobile marketing and internet marketing. Internet marketing further encompasses: internet advertising, search marketing, email marketing, viral marketing, advergaming, and social web marketing. These are not mutually exclusive.

■ **Describe the key structural characteristics across which electronic and digital technologies differ.**

The characteristics of technology that marketing practitioners increasingly need to take into consideration when planning the adoption and use of electronic resources include vividness, synchronicity, pacing, interactivity, and mode of transfer. These structural properties across which electronic resources may differ and can be compared have an impact on the nature of the user experience, and the achievement of marketing objectives. As such, marketers need to be increasingly aware of the effect and the marketing implications of electronic and digital technologies.

■ **Describe the evolution in the focus of electronic and digital marketing from 'channel push' to 'market pull'.**

The evolution in digital technologies is resulting in an evolution in the focus of digital marketing activities. This is reflective of how digital technologies are changing not only how consumers use and interact with digital technologies, and how they interact with each other and the organization, but also the role of marketers and marketing. In short, we are seeing the move away from a one-way model of passive communication in which information is 'pushed' to its markets, to a multimode (channel) and multiuser approach in which everyone is empowered to not only 'pull' down information, and/or interact with the organization and content, but also with each other. Earlier applications of the web seen as a publishing 'push' medium, are still valued internet marketing activities (e.g. internet advertising, direct email). However, online search, social web, gaming, and mobile resources differ in that they are about pull (not just push), enabling participation (not just passivity), co-creation of a product offering (not just mass production), engaging in a dialogue (not just a monologue), and sharing control over the form and content of the brand's messages, marketing activities, and product offering.

■ **Discuss key trends in digital marketing: internet advertising, email marketing, search marketing, social web, gaming, and mobile marketing.**

Digital marketing encompasses a number of activities and these are increasingly changing as digital resources develop and evolve in both functionality and marketing applicability. With some digital marketing activities maturing and still of value, e.g. internet advertising and email marketing, today we also see growth in search marketing, social web marketing, advergaming, and mobile marketing, as market penetration and global reach of these digital resources grows. Market and user adoption of digital resources, and their differences in management cost, execution speed, and user experience is what is driving the marketing profession's interest in these differing areas of digital marketing activities.

■ **Outline the wider considerations that influence the effectiveness of a digital marketing strategy.**

With the rise in digital resources, and their increasing use for marketing activities, come complications and changes to legislation and regulated business practices. The sorts of legal and regulatory issues that marketers need to consider include: Jurisdiction—where does digital marketing activity actually take place and which laws govern it? Ownership—who owns the content we create and share? Permissions—who has the right to upload and share our personal information, and what are organizations doing with it? Security—how secure are the data and information you share? How is it governed? Accessibility—does everyone who wants access have access? As more services and marketing information are being shared digitally, the right to access and usability for all becomes an important agenda item for the dissemination of information and services.

Review Questions

1 In your own words, define how digital marketing differs from interactive and internet marketing.

2 What do vividness, synchronicity, pacing, and interactivity entail, and why are they important technology characteristics that marketers should be aware of?

3 What is Web 2.0 and why is it of growing importance to marketing?

4 Compare and contrast the difference between the 'pull' and 'push' approaches to digital marketing?

5 What are the benefits of internet advertising and email marketing?

6 What do we mean by social web marketing and what are its four main characteristics?

7 What is the difference between user-generated and co-created contents?

8 Why is gaming of increasing importance to marketing?

9 What impact is the growth of mobile wireless devices having on digital marketing?

10 Explain, in your own words, the key considerations marketers should be aware of in the development of digital marketing activities?

Worksheet Summary

Visit the **Online Resource Centre** and complete Worksheet 17.1. This will aid in learning about the importance of digital media and electronic word-of-mouth (eWOM) advertising as influencing online behaviour.

Discussion Questions

1 Having read Case Insight 17.1 at the beginning of this chapter, what do you think marketers could learn from 'Rage Against the X-Factor' when it comes to using the social web in their marketing activities?

2 Do you think digital resources are redefining the concept of marketing?

3 Why is the principle of sharing control of a brand and organizational information so difficult for the marketing profession to adopt?

4 Children and men have been playing games for years, making them obvious targets for advertising. What changes in the channels for gaming do you think have increased the wider appeal and reach of advergaming to other target audiences?

5 Privacy and ownership of information are increasingly being challenged because of developments in digital resources. When I participate on Facebook I believe I have control over the data and information, but do I? Discuss.

Visit the **Online Resource Centre** and complete the Multiple Choice Questions to assess your knowledge of Chapter 17.

go online

References

Anon. (2004), 'J. Walter Thompson CEO sees TV spending decline', *USA-Today*, 25 June retrieve from www.usatoday.com/money/advertising/2004-06-25-tv-decline_x.htm.

—(2010), 'McDonald's scores with Cheesy-Location-based Campaign', *Mobile Marketing Magazine*, retrieve from www.mobilemarketingmagazine.co.uk/2010/04/mcdonalds-scores-with-cheesy-mobile-campaign-.html, accessed, April 2010.

Berners-Lee, T. (2000), *Weaving the Web*. Harpers: New York.

Bernoff, J., and Li., C. (2008), 'Harnessing the power of the oh-so-social web', *MIT Sloan Management Review*, 49, 3, 36–42.

Burnett, G. (2000), 'Information exchange in virtual communities: A typology' [Online]; *Information Research: An International Electronic Journal* 5 (4), July 2000, retrieve from http://informationr.net/ir/5-4/paper82.html, accessed 3 April 2010.

Cheng, J.M.-S., Blankson, C., Wang, E.S.-T., and Chen, L.S.-L. (2009), 'Consumer attitudes and interactive digital advertising', *International Journal of Advertising* 28, 3, 501–25.

Christodoulides, G. (2009), 'Branding in the Post-Internet Era', *Marketing Theory*, 9, 1, 141–4.

CMO (2009), *CMO Survey* [Report], sponsored by The Fuqua School of Business at Duke University and the American Marketing Association (AMA), August retrieve from: http://faculty.fuqua.duke.edu/cmosurvey/survey_

results/august_2009_reports/cmo_survey_highlights_and_insights_8-2009.pdf. http://www.cmo.org, accessed 2 October 2009.

Coleman, J. S., (1988), 'Social capital in the creation of human capital', *The American Journal of Sociology*, 94, 95–120.

Cooper, W. (2010), 'Coke drops campaign in favour of social media', *New Media Age*, 14 January, retrieve from www.nma.co.uk, accessed 15 January 2010.

Court, D. C., Gordon, J. W., and Perrey, J. (2005), 'Boosting returns on marketing investment', *The McKinsey Quarterly*, 2, 37–47.

Cowen, M (2009), 'EasyJet tops table for paid-search terms', *Travel Weekly (UK)*, 4 September.

de Chernatony, L., and Christodoulides, G. (2004), 'Taking the brand promise online: challenges & opportunities', *Interactive Marketing*, 593, 238–51.

de Valck, K., van Bruggen, G. H., and Wierenga, B. (2009), 'Virtual communities: a marketing perspective', *Decision Support Systems*, 47, 185–203.

Econsultancy (2010), 'State of search engine marketing report 2010', *Econsultancy* [Report], March retrieve from http://econsultancy.com/reports/state-of-search, accessed 4 April 2010.

EIU (2008), The 2008 e-Readiness Rankings, *Economics Intelligence Unit (EIU)*, [Report]; London, retrieve from http://a330.g.akamai.net/7/330/25828/20080331202303/graphics.eiu.com/

upload/ibm_ereadiness_2008.pdf, accessed 11 May 2009.

Ellison, N., Steinfield, C. and Lampe, C. (2007), 'The benefits of Facebook friends: exploring the relationship between college students use of online social networks and social capital', *Journal of Computer-Mediated Communications*, 12, 4, 1143–68.

eMarketer (2009), 'Online Advertising Pushes Through,' retrieve from www.emarketer.com/Article.aspx?R=1 007024&Ntt=online+ad&No=20&xsrc=article_head_ sitesearchx&N=0&Ntk=basic, accessed 8 April 2009.

—(2010), *Always-On mobile Devices and Networks, New Opportunities to Reach Consumers*, editor: Noah Elkin, eMarketer, retrieve from http://www.emarketer.com/ Report.aspx?code=emarketer_2000639, accessed 29 January 2010.

Facebook (2010), *Facebook Application Directory*, retrieve from www.facebook.com/apps/directory.php, accessed 14 January 2010.

Farrar, J. (2008, 3rd Quarter). 'Stakeholder face-off in the Facebook age', *Directors & Boards*, 32, 22–63.

Ferris (2009), The cost of spam, 2009, *Ferris Spam Cost Report* [Report], retrieve from www.ferris.com/research-library/industry-statistics/, accessed 4 April 2010.

Glass, K. (2006), 'Top 10 tips for targeted email marketing', *B&T Weekly*, 3 November, 21.

Godula, G., Li, D., and Yu, R. (2009), 'Chinese social networks 'virtually' out-earn Facebook and MySpace: a market analysis', *TechCrunch*, 5 April 2009, retrieve from http://www.techcrunch.com/2009/04/05/chinese-social-networks-virtually-out-earn-facebook-and-myspace-a-market-analysis, accessed 3 January 2010.

Greenlight (2009), 'Market share benchmarks in Google search', *Flight Sector Report* [Report], Q2 2009, retrieve from: www.greenlightsearch.com/sectorreports/flights. html, accessed 4 April 2010.

IMT (1999). *Permission Email: The Future of Direct Marketing*, retrieve from www.imtstrategies.com, accessed 9 September 2001.

Internet World Stats (2009), 'Internet usage statistics: the big picture'. *Internet World Stats.*, retrieve from www. internetworldstats.com/stats.htm, accessed 11 May 2009.

Jin, T. (2009), 'Tencent Budgets up to $17m for TV ads', *The Chinese Perspective*, 17 December, retrieve from http://thechinaperspective.com/articles/ tencentbudgetsupto17mfortvads6728/index.html, accessed 3 January 2010.

Kane, G. C., Fichman, R. G., Gallaugher, J., and Glaser, J. (2009), 'Community relations 2.0', *Harvard Business Review*, 87 (11), Nov 1, 132–42.

Kimberley, S. (2010), 'Online display ads fall for the first time in nine years', *Marketing Magazine*, 31 March, retrieve from www.marketingmagazine.co.uk/ news/993983/Online-display-ads-fall-first-time-nine-years/?DCMP=ILC-SEARCH, accessed 4 April, 2010.

Li, C. (2009), 'The Worlds Most Valuable Brand. Who's most engaged'. ENGAGEMENTdb Report: By Altimeter and Wetpaint, retrieve from www.altimetergroup. com/2009/07/engagementdb.html, accessed 20 July 2010.

Light, L. (2004), 'Brand journalism.' *AdWatch: Outlook 2004 Conference Speech*. New York. 16 June.

McAfee (2009), 'McAfee threats report: second quarter 2009', [Report], retrieve from www.mcafee.com/us/ local_content/reports/6623rpt_avert_threat_0709.pdf, accessed 4 April 2010.

Mintel (2009), 'Social networking UK: leading social networks and their users'. *Mintel Report*, retrieve from www.mintel.com, accessed 27 March 2010.

Mitchell, A. (2001), *Right Side Up: Building Brands in the Age of the Organised Consumer*, London: HarperCollinsBusiness.

MMA (2009),'Buy Mobile Marketing', *Mobile Marketing Association*, retrieve from http://mmaglobal.com/about/ content_category/research/10/341.

Molenaar, C. N. A. (2002), *The Future of Marketing*, London: Pearson.

Morgan Stanley (2009), *Mobile Internet Report* [Report], Morgan Stanley, retrieve from www.morganstanley. com/institutional/techresearch/mobile_internet_ report122009.html, accessed 15 December.

Morlacchi, P., Wilkinson, I.F., and Young, L. (2005), 'A network analysis of the evolution of personal research networks among IMP researchers', *Journal of Business to Business Marketing*, 12, 1, 3–34.

Moss, S. (2010), 'National Theatre Wales's roving revolution', *Guardian*, 1 March, retrieve from www. guardian.co.uk/stage/2010/mar/01/national-theatre-wales, accessed 4 April 2010.

Muniz, A. M., and Jensen Schau, H. (2007), 'Vigilante marketing and consumer-created communications', *Journal of Advertising*, 36 (3, Fall), 35–50.

Nail, J., Charron, C., and Cohen, S. M. (2005), *The Consumer Advertising Backlash Worsens*, Report, Forrester Research, retrieve from www.forrester.com/rb/ Research/consumer_advertising_backlash_worsens/q/ id/35123/t/2.

Net Market Share (2010), 'Global search engine market share', *Net Market Share* [Report], March 2010, retrieve from www.netmarketshare.com/search-engine-market-share.aspx?qprid=4, accessed 4 April 2010.

Nielsen (2009a), 'The future is bright for online media in the global online media landscape' (Report), April. retrieve from http://www.nielsen.com, accessed 15 January 2010.

—(2009b). 'Global face and network places: a Nielsen report on social networks new global footprint', March, retrieve from http://blog.nielsen.com/nielsenwire/wp-content/uploads/2009/03/nielsen_globalfaces_mar09. pdf, accessed 11th May 2009.

Ozuem, W., Howell, K. E., and Lancaster, G. (2008), 'Communicating in the new interactive marketspace', *European Journal of Marketing*, 42, 9/10, 1059–83.

PRSA (2009), 'Essential Online Public Relations and Marketing Skills', *2009 Digital Readiness Report*, sponsored by iPressroom, Trend Stream, Korn/Ferry International, and PRSA (Public Relations Society of America), retrieve from www.ipressroom.com/pr/corporate/social-media-communications-skills-survey.aspx, accessed 4 November 2009.

Schwartz, A. (2010), *Pepsi Ditches the Super Bowl, Embraces Crowdsourced Philanthropy Instead, Fast Company* [Blog], retrieve from www.fastcompany.com/blog/ariel-schwartz/, accessed 15 January 2010.

SEMPO (2010), *State of Search Engine Marketing Report* (The Search Engine Marketing Professional Organization), 25 March, retrieve from www.sempo.org/news/03-25-10, accessed May 2010.

Shankar, V. and Balasubramanian, S. (2009), 'Mobile Marketing: Synthesis and Prognosis', *Journal of Interactive Marketing, Tenth Anniversary Special Issue*, 23, 2, 118–29.

Simmons, G. (2008), 'Marketing to Postmodern Consumers: Introducing the Internet Chameleon', *European Journal of Marketing*, 42, 3/4, 299–310.

Sledgianowski, D., and Kulviwat, S. (2009), 'Using social network sites: the effects of playfulness, critical mass and trust in a hedonic context', *Journal of Computer Information Systems*, 49, 4, 74–83.

Stengel, J. (2004), 'The Future of Marketing.' *AAAA Media Conference Presentation*. 12 February.

Strategies, I. (1999), 'Permission email: the future of direct marketing', retrieve from http://whitepapers.zdnet.co.uk/0,1000000651,260013385p,00.htm, accessed December 2007.

TNS (2009), 'UK/Europe National Gamers Survey', *Todays Gamers*, 29 September, retrieve from www.gamesindustry.com/company/542/service/1762, accessed 4 April 2010.

Trogemann, G., and Pelt, M. (2006), 'Citizen Media – Technological and Social Challenges of User-Driven Media', in *Proceedings of the Broadband Europe*, 2006, Geneva, Switzerland.

Van den Bulte, C., and Wuyts, S. (2007), 'Social Networks and Marketing', *Relevant Knowledge Series*, Boston: MA: Marketing Science Institute.

Vranica, S. (2004), 'For Big Marketers Like AmEx, TV Ads Lose Starring Role', *The Wall Street Journal*, 17 May.

Waring, T., and Martinez, A. (2002), 'Ethical customer relationships: a comparative analysis of US and French organisations using permission-based email marketing', *Journal of Database Marketing*, 10, 1, 53–70.

Westlund, R. (2009), 'Best Practices for Email Marketing', *AdWeek*, 31 August, 50, 31, E2–E6.

Wireless Intelligence (2009), 'Wireless Intelligence Report Quarterly World Review', *Wireless Intelligence* [Report]: Q4 2009, December, retrieve from www.wirelessintelligence.com/, accessed 5 April 2010.

Wunsch-Vincent, S., and Vickery, G. (2007), *Participative Web: User-created Content*, retrieve from www.oecd.org/dataoecd/57/14/38393115.

18 Postmodern Marketing

Learning Outcomes

After reading this chapter, you will be able to:

▶ Explain possible meanings of the term postmodern

▶ Explain the key features of postmodern marketing

▶ Explain how markets are becoming increasingly fragmented

▶ Recognize that in the postmodern context, production and consumption are reversed

▶ Explain the role of semiotics in consumption

▶ Deconstruct marketing 'texts'

▶ Debate whether marketing is based more on science or art

▶ Case Insight 18.1

Livity is a youth marketing agency set up with the core aim to be socially responsible. It communicates sensitive messages to hard-to-reach audiences. We speak to Michelle Clothier and Sam Conniff to find out more.

Michelle Clothier and Sam Conniff for Livity

How should a marketing agency work with a government client communicate sensitive sexual health messages (e.g. promoting condom use and safer sex) to a typically disaffected and hard-to-reach youth audience? This was the challenge facing Livity, set up in 2001 by co-founders Michelle Clothier and Sam Conniff.

We wanted the agency to harness the awesome power of marketing to good effect rather than just ruthless profit-making, and early briefs from O2 and Lambeth Council allowed us to grow and develop expertise in this area.

Part of the difficulty for us at Livity is that kids—particularly those in the target audience—don't generally read magazines, listen to commercial radio, or access media in the ways that people are used to. Our challenge was to determine how the sexual health message could be brought to life in their worlds.

Government attempts at getting teenagers to comply with societal rules, including drinking and driving, speeding, the 'Just Say No' drug campaigns of the 1980s and 1990s, and sexual health

campaigns, for example, tended to use a hard-hitting fear appeal outlining the consequences of these activities, and therefore had limited effect as the audience switched off. We don't believe in scaring teenagers, who believe themselves to be impervious to all danger and that they are going to live forever anyway. They are used to being bombarded with

Rhyme 4 Respect gets across a co-created sexual health message
Source: Livity.

> ▶ Case Insight 18.1   (continued)

messages telling them what to do and what not to do, and it's in every way natural and right for a teenager to do the opposite of what they are told, especially if it's being told to them by an institution or organization like the government. We say no to 'Just Say No' campaigns!

The difficulty is in getting across what is a very serious message, to respect yourself by engaging in safer sex when the time is right and to make an informed choice about sexual partners. We needed something symbolic, as symbolism plays an important part in young people's lives. We chose lyrics because lyrics symbolize an everyday phenomenon to young people, a truly democratic medium; something everyone understands; something that everyone can be part of. Lyrics allowed us to benefit from the association with major pop artists to cut through possible cultural and literary barriers and overcome typical teenage

resistance to 'broadcast' messages regarding sexual health. Essentially, music is the symbol of success and empowerment for our target audience.

We wanted to develop a campaign that was fun at the same time as being serious, to make it easier to deal with taboos like sexual health. Nevertheless, developing an advertising campaign that used lyrics to convey the message isn't enough in itself either. We needed something else. An approach that really engaged the audience, an audience with a developing appetite for X-Factor type talent shows, competitions, and a desire to rate their peers.

Given the fragmented nature of the youth group, their disengagement with mainstream media and marketing vehicles, their age, and their roots in popular culture, how would you design the campaign?

Introduction

How many times have you seen an advertisement and wondered what it was trying to tell you? How often have you seen an advertisement that you were convinced was saying something very deep but you couldn't work out quite what? Have you ever enjoyed the actual process of purchasing something more than the use of it, without being disappointed? Why do some brands manage to build up a cult following and others not? We discuss some of the answers to these questions and more in this chapter on postmodern marketing.

This chapter is written in a very different style and tone from the other chapters in the book, principally because **postmodernism** is a very different topic from other mainstream marketing topics and does not lend itself to orthodox, conventional treatment. In fact, not only is it an unconventional topic but also it adopts an unconventional tone. For that reason, to explain postmodernist concepts we use a postmodern tone (otherwise we would be explaining postmodernism in a **modernist** style, which would be entirely against what postmodernism stands for). We explain as many of the words that we use as possible within the text to make the text flow better, and as these may not be familiar to you because they originate mainly from French cultural philosophy. Consequently, you should visit the glossary at the end of the book as often as is necessary to understand the concepts better.

But do not let the need to refer to the glossary deter you! Postmodern marketing is an excitingly different, yet demanding, subject. In a subtle way, it pokes fun at the received ideas of major foundational thinkers. What postmodernist thinkers do is remind us of the cultural context in which marketing operates, particularly associated with advertising and marketing communication, because mediated images are dominant in these contexts. Nevertheless, because postmodernist thinkers regard any work projected to an audience as a statement (not just communications but buildings, art, etc.), postmodern marketing concepts are not exclusively linked with advertising and marketing communications, but with any marketing **artefact**.

We begin by defining first modernism, then its antithesis, its opposite, postmodernism, because postmodernism is really a rejection of modernist thought. We extend our understanding by applying postmodernism and its cultural implications to marketing, discussing ideas such as **fragmentation**, **hyperreality**, the self, and **inverted production**/distribution mechanisms, which may seem strange now but will become clearer later once they are described. To culturally ground the marketing discipline, we look at the changing nature of values within society, to provide evidence of movement in values among citizen-consumers in Western markets from materialist to post-materialist societies and so indicate the usefulness of postmodern concepts in marketing. In addition, we consider how **semiotics**—the so-called science of signs—can be used to help marketers understand the cultural grounding employed in adverts. We consider whether marketing is a **science** or an **art**, concluding in postmodern style that it is both but that the science component has for too long been overemphasized. Finally, we take a brief look at green marketing and sustainability, providing further evidence of the paradoxical shift towards branded anti-consumption among consumers in the postmodern world.

Modernism and Postmodernism

Many writers do not bother defining postmodernism per se, or define it in relation to its exact opposite, modernism. Or they go on to describe it in such detail, and with such a diverse range of other terms, to render it almost indecipherable and meaningless to the common reader. For some, postmodernism is 'impervious to definition' (Heartney, 2001). The postmodern movement has gained popularity in the latter part of the twentieth century in a diverse range of areas including contemporary philosophy, art, critical theory, literature, architecture and design, marketing, business, history, cultural studies, and no doubt many others. The term postmodern is said to have first gained currency in architecture, where it denotes 'a rejection of the functionalism and brutalism of modern architecture (high-rise slums, impersonal box-like office blocks)' (Mautner, 1999). So postmodernism is first and foremost reactionary. As a movement, it disputes the way things are, and should be, and strives to be different in its approach. But this is not all that it is.

'Whereas modernism assumes that there is hidden meaning and truth and is engaged in a search for it, post-modernism, able to recognise absurdity when it sees it, has recourse to **pastiche**, many-layered **irony**, **flippancy**' (Mautner, 1999). So, postmodernism is essentially **anti-foundational** and certainly irreverent. In other words, it aims to show up, and poke fun at, our established beliefs. In typical obscure explanation, postmodernism has been defined as 'an **incredulity** towards **metanarratives**' (Lyotard, 1984), which means that postmodernists are critical and disbelieving of the overarching belief systems—metanarratives—often taken for granted and inherent in any discipline. Such metanarratives in Western society include beliefs in capitalist economic progress, the importance of scientific advancement, the idea of an objective reality, and the independent subject (or man as an unbiased rational observer).

However, we should understand that in order for something to be postmodern, something must first have been modern. Consequently, postmodernism can be regarded as both the end of the evolution of one form of concept and the beginning of the evolution of another concept, with both in constant flux (Lyotard, 1984). As a result of this shifting between old and new, postmodernism represents a crisis of representation (i.e. is it old or is it new?), by which we mean that postmodernism indicates a break with the old ways of thinking and the re-enchantment, or resurrection, of new ways of thinking. We say resurrection here because postmodernism typically conjures up old associations and re-places them in a new light, providing us with new insights into old ideas. In art, for example, French artist Michel Duchamp's urinal, a piece of work he entitled Fountain, complete with his signature, rocked the art world in 1917. In suggesting that the signed urinal was a work of art, Duchamp was making a statement about the quality of existing art while at the same time questioning why urination was such a taboo in French society. His work was voted the most influential modern artwork of the twentieth century by a survey of 500 art experts in 2004 (BBC, 2004), ahead of Picasso's Guernica and Andy Warhol's Marilyn Diptych. Duchamp's work inspired that of influential English artist Tracy Emin, whose unmade bed 'work of art' created a media furore when it was shortlisted for the Turner Prize in 1999.

go online

Visit the **Online Resource Centre** and follow the weblink to the websites of Andy Warhol, Marcel Duchamp, and Tracey Emin, to learn more about these inspiring artists.

Postmodern Marketing

But how does the concept of postmodernism manifest itself in the way consumers consume? Whereas modern marketing is concerned with marketing to individual consumers, postmodern marketing is concerned with marketing to 'tribes' (building customers into communities of consumers). Whereas modern marketing is concerned with building the image of the company and the brand, postmodern marketers are concerned with building customer experiences. Postmodern marketing emphasizes the value of linking with a product/service rather than simply using it, focusing on co-creation of meaning in its use, rather than simply a transference of meaning from the producer to the consumer. For the postmodern marketer, the consumer actively participates in the brand experience, not simply acting as a passive recipient of advertising messages (see Cova, 1996).

There is increasingly a belief among consumer researchers that postmodern consumers are incapable of being grouped and segmented according to their needs (see Chapter 6). The postmodern consumption era is defined by the celebrated late French cultural critic and philosopher Jean Baudrillard (1995) as characterized by the fragmentation and trivialization of our values, images, and symbols. Fragmentation occurs in everyday life experiences and results in a loss of commitment to a single lifestyle (Firat and Shultz, 1997). In these circumstances, the consumer consumes (rather than just purchases), becoming both a customizer and producer of (self-) images in each consumptive experience (Dittmar, 1992; Firat, Dholakia, and Ventakesh, 1995; Gabriel and Lang, 1995).

Modern, as opposed to postmodern, marketing suggests that value for the consumer is materialized in the prescribed benefits of the bundle of product attributes offered to the consumer, and from value inherent in this bundle, customer satisfaction is obtained. But in postmodern markets, production and consumption are reversed. By this, we mean that there is emphasis on the consumption experience, as opposed to what it is that is actually being consumed or purchased (see Market Insight 18.1). In service-based markets, this linkage between production and consumption is further pronounced as production and consumption are considered to be inseparable (see Chapter 13). In postmodern service markets, the emphasis leads to an exaggeration of the importance of process in some cases: of the importance of form over content. For example, in both American and British political campaigns, the increasing use of marketing has led to a perceived slickness of the electoral machinery, a development of the form of citizen politics but not a corresponding development in the substance, the policy, of politics. But politics is just one example.

▶ Market Insight 18.1

Reality Bites: How Co-creation Drives Engagement

An obvious example of the phenomenon of the reversal of production and consumption is the movement in TV generally towards reality ('living soap') TV shows, where the audience is actually taking part both in voting for the outcomes of the show, and quite often in actually appearing on the show itself as contestants or stars. Examples of such shows have included *Big Brother*, first developed by producer John de Mol, and his production company Endemol, in the Netherlands in September 1999, copied quickly in the UK, and exported to many countries around the world including Australia, Russia, countries of the Middle and Far East, and many more. Since then, other examples have included *Pop Idol*, developed in the UK but successfully exported to the USA as *American Idol* and elsewhere, albeit with slightly different formats. *X-Factor* has been particularly successful in the UK, and *Britain's Got Talent* was also exported to the USA and Australia.

Another innovative soap, *Dubplate Drama*, based on the life of a music industry wannabe invites viewers to determine how the soap's plot should develop by voting on a multiple choice, cliff-hanging moral dilemma at the end of each 15-minute show focusing on hard-hitting issues like bullying, gang violence, and teenage pregnancy. It also features cameos by celebrity musicians and DJs. Sponsored by Childline, the National Society for the Prevention of Cruelty to Children's (NSPCC) telephone helpline, the series aired simultaneously on multiple platforms including Channel 4, E4, 4 On Demand, MTV One, MTV Base, and was made available on MySpace and mobile phone networks. Fans of the show can even win a cameo part.

But companies are now beginning to muscle in on the act. Pepsi launched a reality TV 'battle of the bands' style music show in China in 2009 as a major component of its China marketing strategy. Viewers can vote for their favourite bands online and by mobile phone, and the winning bands in the contest will then begin a Pepsi-sponsored concert tour. The competition saw 6,000 bands compete across 122 cities. It seems the desire to be famous is universal.

Sources: Clark (2007); Lim (2009); Tiltman (2009); www.bigbrother.com; www.dubplatedrama.tv.

1 **In what ways are production and consumption reversed in these examples, from the perspective of the TV audience?**

2 **Why do you think the format of these shows has been so successful? What, in particular, has been the secret of their marketing success?**

3 **How could the concept of co-creation by taken even further?**

As a distinct area of thought in marketing, postmodernism has a set of central conditions and key features, which focus on the following concepts (Firat and Shultz, 1997):

▶ Hyperreality—postmodern markets are hyperreal, where illusory and fantastical experiential components of brands are represented to us instead of the functional concrete attributes of brands. Reality is constituted through hype and simulation.

▶ Fragmentation of markets—in postmodernity, there is recognition that we are individuals with multiple or **multiphrenic** (from 'multi' meaning many and 'phrenia' meaning mind) personalities without commitment to a single lifestyle, acting in different ways in different circumstances, at different times, with different people, in different cultures. Experiences with products and services are disjointed and disconnected as a result.

▶ Reversal of production and consumption—in postmodern times, when produce is plentiful, we no longer satisfy our needs but our desires. This change in emphasis requires a complete change in focus on production and consumption. Instead of producing what we need, manufacturers have shifted marketing emphasis to produce what we desire, a level of product and particularly service development more focused on experiential phenomena. Instead of simply passively accepting a product or service, consumers have shifted to actively interpreting brands and how they are used.

▶ Decentred subject—consumers are becoming dominated by the things they consume and the experiences they have. Instead of simply having one self operating in different purchase situations, consumers have many selves operating in different consumption experiences.

▶ **Juxtaposition** of opposites—whereas the modern world can be described in extremes using unipolar and black and white differentials, such as good or evil, for example, or nice *or* nasty, in the postmodern world, we use bipolar dimensions, known as **dialectics**, such as good *and* evil, nice *and* nasty, to explain events, things, places, or other phenomena.

Elliot (1997) argues that consumption in the postmodern era has changed over the latter part of the twentieth century across five such dialectics, which he states include the following:

1 the material versus the symbolic;
2 the social versus the self;
3 desire versus the satisfaction;
4 rationality versus irrationality; and
5 creativity versus constraint.

We consider each of these in the following sections.

 Research Insight 18.1

 To take your learning further, you might wish to read this influential paper.

Elliot, R. (1997), 'Existential consumption and irrational desire', *European Journal of Marketing*, 31, 3/4, 285–96.

▶ Research Insight 18.1

To take your learning further, you might wish to read this influential paper.

Elliot, R. (1997), 'Existential consumption and irrational desire', *European Journal of Marketing*, 31, 3/4, 285–96.

This article considers marketing in the contemporary world from the perspective of five dialectics—material/symbolic, social/self, desire/satisfaction, rationality/irrationality, and creativity/constraint—to provide insights into

The Material versus the Symbolic

Consumption experiences have moved from the satisfaction of mere needs to the realms of the symbolic. Consumers are consuming not only the material components of the products but also the actual meaning that they represent to them. We shift as consumers, not merely as purchasers of petrol from, say, a Shell petrol station, but as purchasers of petrol from a company that we may, or may not, believe is a worldwide environmental leader. As postmodern consumers, we are (not) buying corporate image and activism, just as much as we are consuming their products.

Luxury goods, for example, Louis Vuitton handbags, Omega watches, and Rolls-Royce cars, are products that sell at very high retail price points. They are sold not purely on their functionality but on their **aesthetic**—visual and sensory—value. The Louis Vuitton handbag is the epitome of style, the Omega watch the epitome of sophistication, and Rolls-Royce of arrival and distinction. But although we might expect luxury goods to be sold on the basis of their symbolism, there is an increasing shift towards marketing any product on its symbolism. Witness the movement by some companies towards ethical branding, e.g. the US ice cream maker Ben & Jerry's, Marks and Spencer in Britain, and the Italian retailer Benetton. These companies are not simply selling their products, but also their stance on particular issues. For instance, Ben & Jerry's are famous for their positive stance towards the alleviation of world social and environmental problems. Marks and Spencer aims to become the world's most sustainable major retailer by 2015, implementing a programme they call Plan A, by cutting their own, their customers' and their suppliers' carbon emissions, by reducing waste, by reducing their use of natural resources, through fair partnerships and employment practices, and by working to improve their customers' health and well-being (M&S, 2010). Benetton is perhaps the most famous and controversial example, having pioneered ethical branding for more than 20 years (see Borgerson *et al.*, 2009).

A key feature of postmodern marketing is the development of products and services that feature a new theme on an old product. Brown (2001) defines this as retromarketing or 'the revival or relaunch of a product or service brand from a prior historical period, which is usually but not always updated to contemporary standards of performance, functioning, or taste'.

Visit the **Online Resource Centre** and follow the weblink to the website of Stephen Brown, to learn more about his writings on postmodern marketing and retromarketing.

go online

Such examples include the iconic Volkswagen (VW) Beetle relaunched in 1998 and the New Mini, which attempt to recreate and conjure up associations associated with the past for a new set of consumers. Michelin, the French tyre maker, travel assistance, and lifestyle product manufacturer, recast Bibendum, also known as 'the Michelin man', back in its adverts. First created in 1898, Bibendum has gone from being rather overweight in form to being spritely and dynamic in his modern incarnation. Go to bibendum-in-museums online to see more on how he has evolved over the twentieth century (see also Market Insight 18.2).

An advert for Michelin, featuring Bibendum, now over 100 years old!

Source: Courtesy of Michelin Tyre Public Limited Company.

▶ Market Insight 18.2

Retrotastic: the Trabant Returns?

The Trabant car was the laughing stock of Europe. The national car of the Communist German Democratic Republic in the days before the fall of the Berlin War in 1989 and the reunification of Germany, it could barely muster 88 kph (55 mph), was powered by a 37 cc two-stroke engine, cost less than £1,000 and measured about 3.4 metres long by 1.5 metres wide. Because of the old communist system of central planning, it could take years after ordering to finally take delivery of the car. So it's a bit of a surprise that the new electric model, the nT, unveiled as a concept car at the Frankfurt Motor Show in 2009 will reach up to 120 kph (75 mph), uses an electric powertrain, will cost somewhere between £7,000 and £9,000 and will be about 15 centimetres longer and wider. The new model, however, is also rather better equipped than the old: in true capitalist style it comes with all the **mod cons** including a satellite navigation system and an iPod player. Herpa, the German company behind the new car, will soon put the car into production. The question is will German drivers buy it? Will the memory of the old Trabant be too painful or too comic? Or will drivers love it as a symbol of how far East Germany has come and where it came from?

Sources: Hall (2009); Korzeniewski (2009).

1 What, if anything do you think could prevent the Electric Trabant nT being made? Why do you say this?

2 To what extent might the Trabant's old communist associations impact on consumer update?

3 What other retro products have you come across recently? Did you feel any degree of nostalgia for these brands?

A Concept Electric Trabant nT unveiled at the Frankfurt Motor Show (2009)

Retromarketing attempts to induce feelings of pseudo-nostalgia. We say pseudo-nostalgia because many consumers may not have experienced the original brand. So postmodern marketers try to reproduce an 'authentic' version of the previous model but enhance it in some way to bring it into the present. Retro brands are reminiscent of historical periods, temporal connections, and their attendant national, regional, and political associations (Brown, Kozinets, and Sherry, 2003).

Visit the **Online Resource Centre** and complete Internet Activity 18.1 to learn more about retromarketing and the revival of a brand from a historical period.

go online

That the retro brand is really a copy, however, makes it inauthentic. The fact that some consumers will not have encountered the original version makes the new version, to that group of consumers at least, a copy without an original. This is what Baudrillard (1995) refers to as a **simulacrum**. A simulacrum is a copy without an original. A simulacrum develops through successive evolutionary image-phase-changes comprising different stages of (mis)representation:

1 an image that reflects a profound reality (a *good* likeness);

2 an image that masks and denatures a profound reality (a *bad* likeness);

3 an image that masks the absence of a profound reality (something that plays at being an appearance); and

4 an image that has no relation to any reality whatsoever (a simulacrum, a copy without an original or a simulation).

The concept of the simulacrum helps us to understand how images are produced, and reproduced, in postmodern times, particularly through our electronic media culture. When numerous simulacra come together, we encounter a play of illusion and phantasm (i.e. ghost-like, fleeting appearance), effectively a theme park. One example of such inauthenticity and simulation is the inauthentic 'authentic' Irish theme pubs, supposedly made to resemble original Irish drinking dens, and deliberately made to look as if they have heritage by appearing older in décor than they really are. For Baudrillard, Disneyland and Las Vegas are the perfect examples of places incorporating simulacra. Using fake fantastic worlds, with no reference to any myth or children's folklore (unlike in Europe, for example, where some theme parks conveyed the fantastical worlds of celebrated Danish author Hans-Christian Andersen), Disney quite literally created a Mickey Mouse world, complete with its own fantastical themes. This use of fantasy and illusion, with no real basis in reality, produces a hyperreality.

▶ Research Insight 18.2

To take your learning further, you might wish to read this influential paper.

Firat, A. F., and Shultz II, C. J. (1997), 'From segmentation to fragmentation: markets and modern marketing strategy in the postmodern era', *European Journal of Marketing*, 31, 3–4, 183–207.

▶ Research Insight 18.2

Firat and Shultz's article provides a definitive understanding of how postmodern conditions in the market environment, what the authors call a 'social phenomenon', affect marketing strategy. Particular focus is devoted to the concept of fragmentation, in terms of images, identity, and customer commitment, demonstrating the increasing need consumers have to be, rather than to have, to experience rather than to acquire, to co-produce goods and services rather than to simply receive goods.

Visit the **Online Resource Centre** to read the abstract and access the full paper.

The Social versus the Self

Consumer goods have always meant more to us as consumers than for what they can do, functionally. But in the postmodern environment, goods and services not only affirm who we are to ourselves but also who we are to others. There is social status in owning particular kinds of goods or using particular kinds of services. Our possession of these goods and services projects meaning about us to others within a cultural context. What is particularly different in postmodern environments, is how easy it is to change ourselves, to be someone different. For example, in cyberspace, our anonymity—consuming unknown from behind a computer screen—means that we behave differently because we can operate as multiple selves, consuming in different patterns on different sites than we might otherwise if we were to buy the same things in person (see Market Insight 18.3). But this pattern of buying is increasingly transgressing the real as well as the virtual world, as consumers' individual identities become fragmented, as they become isolated from existing communities, knowing fewer people in the area where they live, but more people across the world, and across cyberspace.

▶ Market Insight 18.3

Marketing in the Community: YouTube.com

First set up in 2005, YouTube—an innovative online video file-sharing service— sells advertising off the back of its huge base of viewers, particularly through content partnership deals with CBS, Warner Music Group, and the National Basketball Association. In 2006, YouTube was acquired by internet supremo, Google, for $1.6bn, as part of the company's strategy to dominate internet TV. According to Pace (2008),

'YouTube represents a sophisticated and visual form of "public intimacy" that one can find in some internet-personal spaces, where people let others see their own lives'. The service allows users to upload user-generated content, thereby living up to the company's tagline of 'broadcast yourself'. According to YouTube, 'marketers have embraced YouTube as a marketing platform and as an innovative and engaging vehicle for connecting with their target audiences. They are increasing sales and exposure for their companies and brands in many different ways.

▶ Market Insight 18.3 (continued)

In some cases, they run video advertising, like InVideo Ads or YouTube video ads, but they are also sponsoring contests, creating brand channels and adding their own original content to the site'. But these are not idle words, large number of companies have signed up to run their own official channels on YouTube. In Britain, terrestrial broadcaster Channel 4 has signed a deal with YouTube to host its programme content on its own official channel on YouTube, sharing advertising revenue for its existing adverts in between programmes when those adverts are shown online. Part of the problem is that broadcasters are increasingly faced with fragmenting audiences and are doing all they can to retain audience loyalty. HSBC bank scored a first in Hong Kong when it used a YouTube branded talent show to boost e-statement take-up by submitting homemade videos on how paperless banking contributes positively to the environment and climate change agendas. After only two weeks, an online banner counted over 23m impressions and 17,545 clicks, and 32,677 visitors watched the clips.

Sources: Anon. (2009a); Hoovers (2009); Pace (2008); Ramsay (2009).

1 Why do you think consumers want to become part of an online video file-sharing service like YouTube?

2 How will becoming an official channel partner of YouTube affect a company's brand? Do you think it depends on what the company is marketing?

3 What are other examples of strong corporate communities? Have you joined any of these? Why did you do so?

Whereas marketers in the past may well have focused on rational consumer buying motives, there is an increasing acceptance and movement towards the idea that consumers purchase things not because of what they want, but what they do not want. Cova (1997) talks of deconsumption, where consumers reject virtual satisfaction through purchasing and repurchasing activity because the acquisition of material possessions is no longer a new or exciting phenomenon for them. Whereas families in the 1800s may have had 150–200 possessions in their home, a typical family at the beginning of the twenty-first century may have many thousands of possessions. As the postmodern consumer loses contact with the community in the traditional sense, time-starved as he or she is, they increasingly crave satisfaction through **emotion** shared with others, and particularly through experiences.

Cova (1997) refers to the process of like-minded (de)consumers gathering together as tribalism. Its effects in the postmodern world are clear for all to see and result in the kind of mass demonstrations, organized by anti-consumer activists, that we saw in Seattle, USA, at the beginning of the millennium. These kinds of events tend to occur on a much more frequent basis in today's world.

Table 18.1 provides some interesting data from the World Values Survey, giving an insight into the shift in Western Europe and the USA towards consumer activism, or what is often termed **consumerism**, in the last quarter of the twentieth century. Consumer activism, a key component of the anti-globalization movement, has particularly risen in the Netherlands and Finland but in Britain as well, although, in general, consumerism remains highest in the USA over the period 1974–2000.

▶ **Table 18.1** Percentage of population who have taken part in a consumer boycott

Country	1974 (%)	1981 (%)	1990 (%)	1995 (%)	2000 (%)	Net shift 1974–2000 (%)
Britain	6	7	14	n/a	17	+11
West Germany	5	8	10	18	10	+5
Italy	2	6	11	n/a	10	+8
The Netherlands	6	7	9	n/a	22	+16
United States	16	15	18	19	25	+9
Finland	1	9	14	12	15	+14
Switzerland	5	n/a	n/a	11	n/a	+6
Austria	3	n/a	5	n/a	10	+7
Mean	6	8	11	12	15	+9

Source: Inglehart and Welzel (2005): 122.

Consumer boycotts are, therefore, becoming more prevalent. Klein, Smith, and John (2004) propose four factors that are found to predict boycott participation:

1 the desire to make a difference;

2 the scope for self-enhancement (e.g. by a reduction, or a feeling of solidarity with others);

3 counter-arguments that inhibit boycotting (e.g. don't use the product enough, boycotting it will cause other problems);

4 the cost to the boycotter of constrained consumption (e.g. the cost of purchasing competing brands).

Shaw, Newholm, and Dickinson (2006) outline how consumers in Britain are increasingly consuming from an ethical/political standpoint, and are therefore quite prepared to boycott brands they think do not deserve their custom, a trend that they argue is not simply a passing middle class fad. One pertinent example of a consumer boycott on political grounds was the animosity Australian consumers showed towards French products as a result of French nuclear testing in the South Pacific initially during the testing in 1996 and even one year later (Ettenson and Klein, 2005). The difficulty for the managers of French companies in this example of course is that there is not a lot they can do about their government's policy. One approach might be, however, to undertake corporate responsibility programmes highlighting environmental causes to offset some of the negative associations consumers might have about their government's stance, or even to advertise more during a boycott to try to rebut some of the negative associations that NGOs or consumer groups are trying to attach to the brand.

We could argue that although there are a few examples of such tribes of consumers, Harley-Davidson, such examples are actually few and far between, and in the main where they do exist, they exist not because they have subverted the product aimed at them but are actually responding to the marketing (Firat, 2005).

Desire versus Satisfaction

Whereas in the modern era, the focus was on satisfying the consumer, particularly through functional appeals, in the postmodern era, the focus shifts to consumer desire. Not so much satisfying desire, because desire can never be satisfied, but simply allowing the consumer to recognize that desire exists and to experience its effects. Much post-war American advertising has tended to focus on functional appeals, particularly in print advertising, where wordy adverts outline how a particular product satisfies a particular consumer need.

For Baudrillard ([1968] 2005: 195), such rational appeal to consumer choice (see Chapter 3) fails to explain why particular brands and commodities are so in demand. For him, economic concepts of consumer decision-making needed to be replaced with a theory of the value of signs, which recognizes the importance of symbolism, and desire, as opposed to need (Cherrier and Murray, 2004). Postmodern marketers recognize the consumer shift away from simple satisfaction of functional needs. Although advertising has long fed our desires as consumers, in postmodern environments, as consumers, we want others to see our desires met also.

In postmodern markets such desire, for its own sake even, is both accepted and acceptable. The consumer is left with the message that it is good to desire something just for the sake of experiencing it, and not because one actually needs it. Consequently, appeals to consumer desire as opposed to consumer rationality are persuasive because they appeal to the subconscious, often through sexual appeal and the satisfaction of previously taboo desires (Elliot, 1999). For some marketing commentators, this shift towards satisfying consumer desire is a step too far. For them, marketing is increasingly being used to increase consumption to the benefits of capitalist exploitation 'by creating a logic of signs and codes that has no other virtue but to serve a system of competitive power where consumer needs are purely dominated' (Cherrier and Murray, 2004).

Rationality versus Irrationality

Consumers buy and consume products and services because they have fun with them, enjoy their use, and gain pleasure from them. These are outcomes of our consumption experience. Although this might seem like common sense, for many years consumer behaviourists have stressed that consumers consider functionality, the results of the use of the product/service, as primary customer considerations.

But our evaluative criteria for brand selection are also psychosocial (e.g. aestheticism, play) rather than simply economic. Inputs to the purchasing decision are based on considerations of time, as well as money, hedonism as opposed to problem solving, right-brain thinking as opposed to left-brain thinking, exploratory behaviour as opposed to information-acquisitive behaviour, and personality type rather than customer characteristics such as lifestyle or social class. Environmental inputs into this experiential consideration of consumer decision-making stress the following:

▶ syntactic forms of communication—how something is said—as opposed to semantic forms—what is actually said;

▶ non-verbal as opposed to verbal stimuli; and

▶ subjective features, as opposed to objective functions, of a product or service.

The experiential consumer decision-making process is particularly appropriate to buying situations involving consumer experiences of entertainment, arts, and leisure products, for example, visits to museums (Goulding, 1999). Other such experiences might include visits to dry ski slopes, travel and leisure generally, and so on.

In making decisions about what we consume, we may use different frames of reference at different points in time to evaluate our experiences. Postmodernists suggest that we are 'multiphrenic', a kind of consumer multiple personality (dis)order where we may simultaneously want something and not want it at the same time, or want very different things at the same time, or want very different things at different times for the same purpose, and so on.

The multiphrenic consumer

Source: Reproduced with the kind permission of Mark Silver, www.marksilver.co.uk.

▶ Research Insight 18.3

To take your learning further, you might wish to read this influential paper.

Holbrook, M. B., and Hirschmann, E. C. (1982), 'The experiential aspects of consumption: consumer fantasies, feelings and fun', *Journal of Consumer Research*, **9 (September), 132–40.**

This definitive article was the first to really challenge the received impression that consumers buy goods purely on a rational basis. Holbrook and Hirschmann have suggested that existing consumer behaviour models do not take account of irrational and experiential considerations. They stress the experiential process of consumer purchasing. Our cognitions of, thoughts about, the brand may not only encompass our current memories but also information from our subconscious, imagery rather than simply knowledge and structure, and fantasies and daydreams.

 Visit the **Online Resource Centre** to read the abstract and access the full paper.

Creativity versus Constraint

In the postmodern world, opposing social forces exist. By this we can question whether advertising reflects reality or reality reflects advertising. In other words, are our needs reflected in the advertising or is the advertising reflected in our needs? There is, to some extent, a backlash by many citizen-consumers against the kind of materialism that advertising has long implicitly put forward. Constant advertising of a good or service leads to the development of the idea that materialism in society is a good thing, that the feeding of our materialistic desires is something worthy of our attention and action. In many, this creates a kind of **psychological reactance** (see Chapter 3), and a desire to adopt a different and opposing frame of reference. Consumption from this new frame of reference, in a creative way, is a way of restoring the freedom those postmodern consumers feel that they are in danger of losing. This leads to the development of a new form of tribal behaviour (Cova, 1997), where consumers develop entire communities around the symbolic consumption of goods and services. Examples of such communities include the Harley Owners Group, and owners of the Volkswagen Beetle.

People's values are defined in marketing as 'consensual views about the kind of life individuals should follow, formal and informal rules specifying the goals they should pursue and how they should pursue them' (Foxall, Goldsmith, and Brown, 1998). Values tend to change and differ from one country to another. In the World Values Survey (Inglehart and Welzel, 2005), numerous countries around the world were organized into eight distinct socio-cultural zones as follows:

1 Protestant Zone (excluding English-speaking countries)—Denmark, Estonia, Finland, Germany, Iceland, Latvia, the Netherlands, Norway, Sweden, Switzerland.

2 English-Speaking Zone—Australia, Canada, Great Britain, Ireland, New Zealand, USA.

3 European Catholic Zone—Austria, Belgium, Croatia, Czech Republic, France, Hungary, Italy, Lithuania, Luxembourg, Malta, Poland, Portugal, Slovakia, Slovenia, Spain.

4 European Orthodox and Islamic Zone—Albania, Armenia, Belarus, Bosnia-Herzegovina, Bulgaria, Georgia, Macedonia, Moldova, Romania, Russia, Turkey, Ukraine, Yugoslavia.

5 Confucian Zone—China, Japan, South Korea, Taiwan, Vietnam.

6 Latin American Zone (plus the Philippines) —Argentina, Brazil, Chile, Colombia, Dominican Republic, El Salvador, Mexico, Peru, Philippines, Uruguay, Venezuela.

7 Islamic Zone (plus India, excluding European Islamic societies) —Algeria, Azerbaijan, Bangladesh, Egypt, India, Indonesia, Iran, Jordan, Morocco, Pakistan.

8 Sub-Saharan African Zone—Nigeria, Tanzania, Uganda, Zimbabwe.

The survey is highly useful to marketers, as it provides an indication of how different countries have similar socio-cultural approaches and their relative differences in values, which helps marketers in developing international marketing strategies and understanding further their own cultures. Generally, throughout the world, people's values are shifting from **materialist** goals to **postmaterialist** goals, emphasizing self-expression and quality of life, similar to what Maslow (1943) called self-actualization needs (see Chapter 3), as opposed to economic and physical security, or what Maslow called safety needs.

As we see increasing conflict between the Middle East and the West, there is a rise in Muslim brands aimed specifically at the Muslim **diaspora** around the world. Al-Jazeera, the pan-Arab Qatari-based TV broadcaster, set its sights on Western markets, targeting non-Arab

Muslims and covering more than just issues of Islamic interest (Mutel, 2004) with considerable success. HSBC, Citigroup, and Union Bank of Switzerland (UBS) all now offer Islamic banking products, not just to their Muslim customers wanting a Sharia compliant mortgage, for example, but to non-Muslims interested in ethical banking practices.

Researching Fragmented Markets

Because of the experiential components of consumption behaviour, the analysis of postmodern consumer buyer behaviour requires the use of research approaches from **cultural anthropology** and **ethnography**. Whereas modern consumer research has used experiments and surveys, postmodern consumer research uses ethnographies, studies of the behaviour of specific groups from within the group. It adopts qualitative forms of research as opposed to quantitative research (see Chapter 4) and is focused on developing theories of consumer behaviour using the emerging data, rather than on testing theories developed prior to the data collection.

▶ **Table 18.2** Modern and postmodern research approaches

Modern	Postmodern
Focused on discovering truth and laws of nature	Focused on creating meaning and generation of understanding
Aims to predict the future by extrapolating from the past	Aims to explain the possible present
Factual emphasis	Subjective orientation
Use of single methodologies in research design	Use of multiple approaches in research design
Quantitative	Qualitative
Experiments/surveys	Ethnographies
Economic/psychological	Sociological/anthropological
Micro/managerial	Macrocultural
Emphasis on cognitions	Emphasis on emotions
Focus on buying	Focus on consuming

Sources: Adapted from Belk (1995) and Brown (1996).

Although modern consumer research tends to be economic/psychological and micro/managerially focused, postmodern research focuses much more on sociological/anthropological paradigms. Postmodern researchers are concerned with understanding consumers from their own perspectives, focusing on consumption behaviour, whereas modern researchers focus on observed, or anticipated, buying behaviour. Postmodern researchers are particularly concerned with the consumers' emotions, the irrational reasons for purchasing and consuming, whereas modern researchers focus on cognitions, the rational reasons for buying (see Table 18.2 for a full list of differences between the two forms of research in marketing). Increasingly, the research community is interested in 'listening' as opposed to asking consumers what they think. Partly, this means mining online conversations in social media forums such as Facebook and Twitter. Partly, it means analysing transcripts of customer relations calls and consumer emails. Wiesenfeld and Bush (2009) suggest that it is important to conduct a listening audit first, asking such questions as: What are consumers saying about our brand? Where are they saying it? How has this changed over time? How does our brand compare to competitors in terms of the volume and content of conversation? A key question for future market researchers, however, will be: are existing approaches to market research valid in postmodern markets? Moisander, Valtonen, and Hirsto (2009) argue that they are not for consumer research, which is too heavily reliant on individual consumer interviews, failing to take account of the sociological and cultural nature of buying.

Semiotics and Deconstruction

Semiotics can be defined as 'a discipline that provides a structure for studying and analysing how signs function within a particular environment' (Zakia and Nadin, 1987). Its defining feature 'is that it takes the culture and not the consumer as the object of study' (Lawes, 2002). In undertaking semiotic analysis, we are particularly concerned with the analysis of signs. A sign can be anything that represents meaning and includes sensory information such as visuals/pictures, sound/music, taste, smell, touch/pain, and cultural forms such as film, dance, gesture, mime, architecture, and more. We might use the term 'symbols' interchangeably here with 'sign', as the sign symbolizes something to the viewer. Semiotics has the power to allow us, as marketers or social analysts, to embed the macroanalysis of consumer decision-making into a theory of cultural interaction. As a result, we can link the consumer to his or her purchasing environment to determine how the two mutually reinforce each other.

To understand semiotics further, we need to understand the concept of sign. For the celebrated Swiss linguist Ferdinand de Saussure, the linguistic sign is a dyadic relationship between the **signified** (e.g. French sparkling wine from the Champagne region) and sound images known as the **signifier** (e.g. the spoken word 'Champagne'). For Saussure, the meaning conveyed by language was formed not only from the words used but also from the way that the words interacted with each other. The idea is that, for example, two words when put together mean more than the sum of their parts. This concept had not been explicitly recognized in linguistics until Saussure's work. To get some idea of the power of combining concepts with apparently different meanings consider the fashion designer Dolce & Gabbana's Spring 10 advertising campaign (see Market Insight 18.4).

> ▶ Market Insight 18.4

Juxtaposing Opposites: Dolce & Gabbana

The leading Italian fashion company Dolce & Gabbana used an unusual advert to launch their Summer 2010 range of clothing. In true postmodern style, making use of the concept of the juxtaposition of opposites, the advert uses the scene of Madonna washing up filthy pots in a kitchen sink, her face a picture of angst, to signify the mundaneness of a typical woman's existence. Yet her dress, her blonde hair flowing beautifully and her demure, vampish pose connote the opposite, of glamour, femininity, and beauty. It's as if she is in the wrong place at the wrong time. Bringing the two concepts together, Dolce & Gabbana mean to say something about modern women, reflecting postfeminist considerations that women can be simultaneously 'glamourous' and 'not glamourous', or that they can be sexy in the most dreary of circumstances. The advert promotes the idea of the self-gift, lending legitimacy

to the idea of a lady buying a haute couture dress as a means to make herself feel good, in order to escape the straightjacket of her everyday life.

Sources: Anon. (2009b,c).

To view the advert, see: www.fabsugar.co.uk/Madonna-Dolce-Gabbana-Spring-2010-6690724 or type dolce+gabbana+madonna+advert into your favourite search engine.

1 **What is the danger of using concepts with opposite meanings when advertising or branding products?**

2 **Regardless of your gender, do you think the advert works? What does the advert convey to you?**

3 **Consider other brands that make use of this concept of the juxtaposition of opposites. What do you think the advertisers are trying to convey, to whom, for what purpose?**

Saussure's concept of signs was built on further by C. S. Peirce (1931–58), who felt that rather than being dyadic, sign processes (or symbolism) are in fact a function of a triadic process. Peirce argued that a sign was anything that gives us an impression of something (its object (or 'item' as it may not be physical)), projected at somebody (its interpreter), in some respect (its context) (Mick, 1986). What results from this triadic interrelationship is some sort of understanding projected from the object, which holds some sort of interpretation in our minds. Peirce calls this understanding that we have as a result the 'interpretant', which is neither the interpreter nor the interpretation, but which is in fact a concept shared within the culture in which it is disseminated. To make this concept easier to understand, we have relabelled the 'interpretant' as 'meaning'.

Figure 18.1 illustrates what we've called the Positioning Triad, demonstrating the three-way relationship between the Item (that which we are communicating something about), the Symbol (what we intend to communicate about the item), and the Meaning (the interpretation of the symbol within a cultural context). What is useful about this concept is that it provides us with a clearer understanding of how the **positioning** process—the way that an offering is perceived in the minds of the customer—in marketing communications works (see Chapters 6 and 10). In the figure, the intended meaning of the item is conveyed as a symbol through the marketing communication process. This meaning, once received by the audience, develops in a concept through shared understanding of its meaning. On the basis of how a

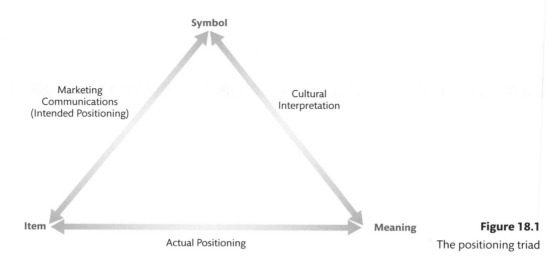

Figure 18.1
The positioning triad

culture perceives the item, its symbolism is either reinforced or altered, and it is correspond-ingly positioned or repositioned as part of the ongoing marketing communications process.

Visit the **Online Resource Centre** and complete Internet Activity 18.2 to learn more about symbolism and the marketing and consumption experience.

In analysing semiotics, we take an outside-in approach, looking at how an audience inter-prets communications, in the sense of the meanings that these communications convey. But how do we analyse those meanings? Semioticians often talk of 'texts' and anything that con-veys meaning can be regarded as a 'text'. Semiotic analysis of competitor advertising can be particularly useful in understanding what messages the advertiser is trying to convey, and how they convey these messages within the cultural context of the consumer. It can be used as an alternative to undertaking positioning studies (see Chapter 6), as it provides us with an insight into how the advertiser wants the audience to see their product or service. If we can decode the signs that the advertiser is intending to present, we can understand their position-ing strategies. With positioning studies, we do not necessarily see how the company is trying to position itself (intended positioning), what we see instead is how the company actually ends up positioned in the minds of customers ('the Meaning'). There is a clear difference between the two. In Market Insight 18.5, Guinness used semiotics to understand how they should advertise their well-known stout beer brand.

▶ Market Insight 18.5

Guinness: Deconstructing the Black Stuff

When international beer brand Guinness, maker of the black stuff, wanted to determine how consumers perceived competitor brands of beer in different markets, it realized that to conduct positioning studies in every market would be a very expensive proposition indeed. Instead, it decided to opt for a much cheaper approach, one that would pay substantial

go online

▶ Market Insight 18.5

dividends. Using an initial process of semiotic analysis, with semiologists in Cameroon, Germany, Malaysia, Spain, UK, and USA, Guinness developed what they called the Competitor Advertising Decoding Kit from an analysis of TV and print advertisements, looking specifically into what the adverts were conveying, to who, and why. The initial findings from this stage of research were then fed into a second stage of analysis undertaken by cross-departmental teams of brand planners, marketers, and non-marketers using the Competitor Advertising Decoding Kit, who sought to propose specific advertising propositions for each competitive brand. What was particularly useful about the semiotic approach was that by using external parties to assess the consumer 'take-outs' of the research, Guinness obtained a strong idea of what impact competitors' advertising was having on the consumer, allowing them to understand how the brands were ultimately positioning themselves in the minds of beer consumers.

Guinness: what does it mean to you?

In the UK portion of the research, it became clear that Carling Black Label advertising was conveying heritage, enjoyment of beer, irreverent masculinity, and sporting achievement, whereas Stella Artois was conveying parody, humour, heritage, and beer enjoyment. Whereas Carling was conveying 'belongingness' and 'strength' to the 'lad user', Stella Artois was conveying impressions of beer superiority to the 'discerning drinker' motivated by drinking for personal indulgence. As a consequence, Carling's

'the ultimate reward'. (See Market Insight 4.4 for how Guinness uses ethnographic research.)

Source: Harvey and Evans (2001).

1 What are the advantages of using the semiotic analysis approach in your view?

2 What might be the disadvantages of using the semiotic approach in your view?

3 Consider a brand of beer or soft drink that you consume. What do you think the advertisers are trying to convey, to whom, for what purpose?

In the postmodern world, pictures interact with words to show some sort of meaningful interaction, as the example above illustrates. There is a free playing between image and word (Scott, 1992). Such works might be interpreted in different ways. Approaches to analysis include the use of the deconstruction linguistic technique, most commonly associated with French philosopher Jacques Derrida. In **deconstruction**, the aim is to revisit what the 'text' is trying to convey. The reader looks at gaps, inconsistencies, and underlying 'absences' in the text (Derrida, 1967). The textual analysis breaks the text down into privileged themes, then determines the 'binary opposites' (e.g. man/woman, white/black, right/wrong) of those privileged themes as the hidden or absent meaning of the work, and essentially proposes that this is what that work was really trying to say.

Postmodern advertisements tend to possess distinctive features in that they use an irrational appeal (to emotion rather than reason), adopt 'feminist' stances (appealing to anti-masculine sentiment), and destroy metanarratives (widely held received ideas about how things should be perceived) (Proctor, Papasolomou, and Proctor 2001). Egg.com, the British internet bank formerly owned by the Prudential, ran a humorous TV advert throughout 2000. In the advert, two male characters, Rob and Stuart, are romping in the shower, one washing the other, a scene that instantly makes us laugh, especially when Rob puts his fingers in Rob's ear and indicates he has found some dirt. In the background to the advert, children's voices are chanting, 'Egg and You, Sitting in a Tree, K-I-S-S-I-N-G'. The scene is clearly surreal (see Proctor, Papasolomou, and Proctor, 2001, for a full discussion of this advertisement). The inference is that Rob is Egg.com and we, the customers, are Stuart and that if we want, Egg.com are more than happy to develop a full relationship with us.

To deconstruct this advertisement, we look for the presence of certain categories and define their opposites. In this advertisement, we can detect such 'binary opposites' as masculine/feminine, lazy/active, friendly/hostile on a brief, surface analysis. Overall, the online bank is indicating to us that traditional banks are hostile, do not try to develop strong relationships with their customers, and that customers are too lazy and accepting of this to bother switching. By 'loving' us as customers in the way they indicate, they hope to get us to switch to their bank, which has a new way of 'doing things'. The irreverence in the execution of the advertisement adds further to our contempt for traditional banks and banking and to our liking of Egg.com. The metanarrative that the advertisement is seeking to destroy through parody is that banks should not develop strong relationships with their customers, which had been the typical approach in marketing financial services until the mid-2000s; a theme taken up by other banks and building societies in subsequent advertising (e.g. Nationwide in the UK).

Marketing: Art or Science?

In marketing, we seem to hold on to certain ideas, regarding their logic as indisputable in their ability to provide us with understanding of marketing phenomena. Many of these ideas are repeated ad nauseum in various chapters in this very text! They include the idea that SWOT and PESTLE analysis can provide us with a solid understanding of the changing environment (see Chapter 2), that the consumer decision-making process is rational (see Chapter 3), that market strategy development can be easily predetermined (see Chapter 5), that market segments can be formed and clearly positioned (see Chapter 6), that the marketing mix principle is still relevant in a consumption-, rather than production-, oriented society (see Chapters 1 and 8–12), that the awareness–interest–desire–action (AIDA) principle still describes best the process of consumer involvement in advertising (see Chapter 10), that what we should be aiming for in the marketing of services is an improvement in service quality (see Chapter 13), and even that marketing practitioners should seek to be more ethical (Chapter 19). Although many of the insights and models with which we are familiar in marketing, including those listed above, have come from thorough and detailed investigation in marketing, through a scientific approach to research, many others have not. Gaining an understanding of customers and consumers (see Chapter 4) is as much about subjective interpretation as it is about objective scientific investigation. Both approaches can lead to marketing understanding.

Postmodern marketers seek to put culture back into marketing. As a sub-discipline of marketing, postmodern marketing aims to critique the current content of marketing by reminding us of the importance of the context (i.e. culture) in which marketing operates. We are reminded that we live in a highly nuanced, multifaceted world, which can be described in many, many ways. Creativity and artistic endeavour is perhaps clearest in advertising and PR (see Chapter 11), but these are not the only areas of marketing where an artistic approach can succeed. At the same time as marketing has been imitating art, art has also been imitating marketing. The cultural surroundings in which we live interact with the marketing world, and the marketing world interacts with, and is itself part of, our cultural world. Indeed, one of the key points of this chapter is that the world is increasingly seeing itself through the consumer lens. Whether marketing in its many and various forms is an art or a science is probably a debatable point. In truth, it contains elements of both. How very postmodern!

A good example of the juxtaposition of art and marketing in popular culture is that of the work of Chinese artist Wang Guangyi, who, in a piece produced shortly after the Tiananmen Square incident, mixes Chinese communist propaganda with Western advertising in *The Great Criticism Series—Coca-Cola*. The question that arises from this work of art is whether or not the propaganda of communist China fits with the propaganda of Western advertising. The answer, at some levels at least, seems to be surprisingly well.

Wang Guangyi, 'Great Criticism Series—Coca-Cola', Oil on Canvas, 80 x 80 inches (1993)
Source: The Farber Collection Courtesy of China Avant-Garde.

▶ Research Insight 18.4

To take your learning further, you might wish to read this influential paper.

Brown, S. (1996), 'Art or science: fifty years of marketing debate', *Journal of Marketing Management*, **12, 243–67.**

Brown's article discusses how the intellectual development of marketing has been hindered over the course of the latter half of the twentieth century as the discipline has remained wedded to modernist concepts of scientific application. Brown suggests that marketing research would benefit from a concentration on a subjective, rather than an objective, orientation, from a focus on experience and imaginative self-expression, and the use of multiple approaches to research methodology, as opposed to rigid scientific (i.e. empirical) approaches only.

 Visit the **Online Resource Centre** to read the abstract and access the full paper.

Skills for Employment

▶▶ After attitude, we of course look for evidence of relevant experience and skills. This includes degrees, activities outside of university, part-time work, personal websites, activities online, and volunteer work. If there are two candidates with excellent attitudes, we would take the one that can demonstrate they have been proactive in gaining relevant experience outwith their university education. ◀◀

Sarah Ronald, Managing Director, Bunnyfoot Ltd

 Visit the **Online Resource Centre** to discover more tips and advice on skills for the workplace.

Chapter Summary

To consolidate your learning, the key points from this chapter are summarized below:

- **Explain possible meanings of the term postmodern.**

  Postmodernism can be described as the artform of society (Scott, 1992). It is first and foremost a reactionary movement. It disputes the way things are, and should be, and strives to be different in its approach. The postmodern movement gained popularity in the latter part of the twentieth century in a diverse range of areas including contemporary philosophy, art, critical theory, literature, architecture and design, marketing, business, history, and cultural studies. The concept first gained currency in architecture. As a philosophical concept, it indicates a break with past ideas regarded as received wisdom (what Lyotard calls metanarratives) and the development of new ideas based on a rejection of the old ones.

■ **Explain the key features of postmodern marketing.**

In the marketing context, a postmodernist application would indicate that marketers need to think more about how we go about segmenting our markets, as markets are fragmenting, about how our consumers choose goods and services, because they are irrational as well as rational beings, being careful not to characterize them as being of one type as we display different selves in purchasing and consumption. Postmodernism in marketing is an orientation, a way of thinking and rethinking, about how we experience the marketing world around us. It denotes a break with the past, with the old concepts of marketing described above, towards a new theory of how marketing should interact with customers in the future. To do this, postmodern marketers will accept the multiphrenic nature of the consumer, experiencing and co-creating the brand, rather than simply consuming it, as the modernist marketers might assert. Postmodern markets are hyperreal, or simulated environments, which are increasingly fragmented in terms of their customer bases and the identities of those customers. Increasingly, customers are more involved with the process of production and consumption and co-produce those consumer products and experiences in a situation where product/service development begins from the perspective of consumption first with production second. The customer becomes dominated or owned by his or her experiences rather than the reverse where in the past customers might have been more likely to have dominated and owned their products. Marketing in the postmodern world has dialectical features with seemingly opposite characteristics existing simultaneously, focusing on the material/symbolic, social/self, desire/satisfaction, rational/irrational, and creativity/constraint dimensions.

■ **Explain how markets are becoming increasingly fragmented.**

In contemporary society, there has been a fragmentation and trivialization of our existing values over the course of the late twentieth century as we have moved from a materialist to a postmaterialist society. This fragmentation has also taken place in markets, as consumers as individuals develop apparently multiple personalities in consumption contexts and weak commitment to a single lifestyle. We act in different ways in different circumstances, at different times, with different people, in different cultures, defying market segmentation and positioning programmes, which seek to categorize us within groups of consumers.

■ **Recognize that in the postmodern context, production and consumption are reversed.**

In postmodern times, when produce is plentiful, we no longer simply satisfy our needs but also our desires. The change in emphasis has required a complete shift in focus from production to consumption. Instead of producing what consumers need, manufacturers have shifted marketing emphasis to producing what they desire, a level of product and particularly service development more focused on experiential phenomena. Instead of simply passively accepting a product or service, consumers have shifted to actively interpreting brands and how they are used, and are increasingly involved in the co-creation of the products/services in a metaphorical and symbolic, as well as a literal sense.

■ **Explain the role of semiotics in consumption.**

Semiotics is the science of signs. A sign can be anything that represents meaning and includes sensory information such as visuals/pictures, sound/music, taste, smell, touch/pain, and cultural forms such as film, dance, gesture, mime, and architecture. In analysing signs, we use linguistic concepts developed by Saussure to determine what is signified by a signifier. Peirce took the concept a stage further by identifying a concept that he called the 'interpretant', which indicates the shared cultural meaning that derives as a result of the image projected from the object. Semiotics is used by marketers to understand such image-meanings, to embed the macroanalysis of consumer decision-making into a theory of cultural interaction. As a result, we can link the consumer to his or her purchasing context to determine how the two interact with each other. Semiotic analysis is particularly useful as a technique to analyse the intended strategy behind competitors' advertising approaches as an alternative to positioning studies.

■ **Deconstruct marketing 'texts'.**

Semioticians often talk of 'texts' and anything that conveys meaning as a 'text'. Approaches to analysis of 'texts' include use of the deconstruction linguistic technique, most commonly associated with French philosopher Jacques Derrida. In deconstruction, the aim is to determine what the 'text' is trying to convey by revisiting its meanings. The reader searches for gaps, inconsistencies, and underlying 'absences' in the text (Derrida, 1967). The textual analysis breaks the text down into privileged themes, and then determines a series of 'binary opposites' (e.g. man/woman, white/black, right/wrong) of those privileged themes as the hidden or absent meaning of the work. Once these binary opposites have been determined, the deconstruction technique proposes that the lesser non-privileged binary opposite is often what the focus of the work was *really* about.

■ **Debate whether marketing is based more on science or art.**

According to Brown (1996), the intellectual development of marketing has been hindered over the course of the latter half of the twentieth century because the discipline has remained wedded to modernist concepts of scientific application. Marketing would benefit from greater concentration on the subjective, rather than the objective, from a focus on experience and imaginative self-expression, and the use of multiple approaches to research methodology, as opposed to rigid scientific (i.e. empirical) approaches only. Marketing research should aim to create meaning and generate understanding of marketing phenomena, by listening rather than asking, to alter managers' and consumers' perceptions, rather than to discover 'truth'.

Review Questions

1 Try to define postmodernism in your own words.

2 Explain the contexts in which postmodern marketing operates.

3 What are the key features of postmodernism in marketing according to Elliot?

4 What is a simulacrum?

5 How are postmodern markets becoming increasingly fragmented?

6 When postmodernists say that production and consumption are reversed, what do they mean?

7 What is the juxtaposition of opposites?

8 What is the discipline of semiotics?

9 What are the three components of the positioning triad?

10 Is marketing more of a science or an art discipline?

Worksheet Summary

Visit the **Online Resource Centre** and complete Worksheet 18.1. This aids in learning about 'postmodern' marketing, and, using the example of a car, outlines the differences between 'postmodern' marketing and 'modern' marketing.

Discussion Questions

1 Having read Case Insight 18.1, how would you advise Livity to devise its next sexual health campaign to teenagers? Given the fragmented nature of youth, their disengagement with mainstream media and marketing vehicles, their age, and their roots in popular culture, how would you design the campaign?

2 Explain how each of the following dialectic postmodern concepts is relevant in marketing the following four product offerings: 1) material versus symbolic, 2) social versus self, 3) desire versus satisfaction, 4) rationality versus irrationality, and 5) creativity versus constraint.

A The Volkswagen Beetle.

B The Star Trek conventions (see www.startrek.com).

C A L'Oréal designer perfume, such as Viktor and Rolf's new fragrance Eau Mega.

D The 'slanket' blanket (see www.theslanket.com).

3 Identify another retro brand not outlined in the chapter (e.g. from your own country or somewhere else). What social, political, and historic connections is the brand trying to conjure up? Do you think it will be successful? Why do you say this?

4 Re-read the section on semiotics and deconstruction. Then have a look at the 'Grand Theft Coke' advert on YouTube. Do you think this is a postmodern ad? Why? What 'binary opposites' can you identify in this ad?

Visit the **Online Resource Centre** and complete the Multiple Choice Questions to assess your knowledge of Chapter 18.

go online

References

Anon. (2009a), 'Case study: HSBC', *Media: Asia's Media and Marketing Newspaper*, 10 August, p. 36.

—(2009b), 'Madonna in Dolce and Gabbana ads!', 17 December, *Grazia*, retrieve from www.graziadaily.co.uk/fashion/archive/2009/12/17/madonna-in-d-g-ads.htm, accessed 16 May 2010.

—(2009c), 'Madonna for Dolce and Gabbana', 17 December, *RTE Fashion*, retrieve from www.rte.ie/fashion/2009/1217/madonna.html, accessed 16 May 2010.

Baudrillard, J. ([1968] 2005), *The System of Objects*, trans. James Benedict, London: Verso Books.

—(1995), *Simulacra and Simulation*, trans. Sheila Faria Glaser, Ann Arbor: University of Michigan Press.

BBC (2004), 'Duchamp's urinal tops art survey', 1 December, retrieve from http://news.bbc.co.uk/1/hi/entertainment/arts/4059997.stm, accessed 22 November 2009.

Belk, R. W. (1995), 'Studies in the new consumer behaviour', in D. Miller (ed.) *Acknowledging Consumption*, London: Routledge, 58–95.

Borgerson J.L., Schroeder, J.E., Magnusson, M.E., and Magnusson, F. (2009), 'Corporate communication, ethics, and operational identity: a case study of Benetton', *Business Ethics: European Review*, 18, 3, 209–33.

Brown, S. (1996), 'Art or science: fifty years of marketing debate', *Journal of Marketing Management*, 12, 243–67.

—(2001), *Marketing: The Retro Revolution*, London: Sage Publications.

—, Kozinets, R.V., and Sherry, J.F. (2003), 'Teaching old brands new tricks: retro branding and the revival of brand meaning', *Journal of Marketing*, 67 (July), 19–33.

Cherrier, H., and Murray, J. B. (2004), 'The sociology of consumption: the hidden facet of marketing', *Journal of Marketing Management*, 20, 509–25.

Clark, N. (2007), 'Childline ties up with urban drama series', *Marketing*, 9 May, 6.

Cova, B. (1996), 'The postmodern explained to managers: implications for marketing', *Business Horizons*, November–December, 15–23.

—(1997), 'Community and consumption: toward a definition of the "linking value" of products or services', *European Journal of Marketing*, 31, 3–4, 297–316.

Derrida, J. (1967), *Of Grammatology*, trans. Gayatri Chakravorty Spivak, Baltimore: Johns Hopkins University Press.

Dittmar, H. (1992), *The Social Psychology of Material Possessions*, Hemel Hempstead: Harvester Wheatsheaf.

Elliot, R. (1997), 'Existential consumption and irrational desire', *European Journal of Marketing*, 31, 3–4, 285–96.

—(1999), 'Symbolic meaning and postmodern consumer culture', in Browlie, M. Ettenson, R., and Klein, J.G. (2005), 'The fallout from French nuclear testing in the South Pacific—a longitudinal study of consumer boycotts', *International Marketing Review*, 22, 2, 199–224.

Firat, A. F. (2005), 'Meridian thinking in marketing: a comment on Cova', *Marketing Theory*, 5, 2, 215–19.

—, Dholakia, N., and Ventakesh, A. (1995), 'Marketing in a postmodern world', *European Journal of Marketing*, 29, 1, 239–67.

—(and Shultz II, C. J. (1997), 'From segmentation to fragmentation: markets and modern marketing strategy in the postmodern era', *European Journal of Marketing*, 31, 3–4, 183–207.

Foxall, G., Goldsmith, R., and Brown, S. (1998), *Consumer Psychology for Marketing*, 2nd edn, London: International Thomson Business.

Gabriel, I., and Lang, T. (1995), *The Unmanageable Consumer: Contemporary Consumption and its Fragmentations*, London: Sage Publications.

Goulding, C. (1999), 'Contemporary museum culture and consumer behaviour', *Journal of Marketing Management*, 15, 647–71.

Hall, A. (2009), 'Trabant is back but this time without the smoke', *The Daily Telegraph*, 14 August, p. 12.

Harvey, M., and Evans, E. (2001), 'Decoding competitive propositions: a semiotic alternative to traditional advertising research', *International Journal of Market Research*, 43, 2, 171–87.

Heartney, E. (2001), *Movements in Modern Art: Postmodernism*, London: Tate Publishing.

Holbrook, M. B., and Hirschmann, E. C. (1982), 'The experiential aspects of consumption: consumer fantasies, feelings and fun', *Journal of Consumer Research*, 9 (September), 132–40.

Hoovers (2009), YouTube LLC, *Hoover's Company Records*. Austin: 15 Nov 2009. p. 148460.

Inglehart, R., and Welzel, C. (2005), *Modernisation, Cultural Change and Democracy: The Human Development Sequence*, Cambridge: Cambridge University Press.

Klein, J.G., Smith, N.C., and John, A. (2004), 'Why we boycott: consumer motivations for boycott participation', *Journal of Marketing*, 68 (July), 92–109.

Korzeniewski, J. (2009), 'Electric Trabant revival slated to debut at Frankfurt', 14 August, *Autobloggreen*, retrieve from http://green.autoblog.com/2009/08/14/electric-trabant-revival-slated-to-debut-at-frankfurt/, accessed 21 November 2009.

Lawes, R. (2002), 'Demystifying semiotics: some key questions answered', *International Journal of Market Research*, 44, 3, 251–64.

Lim, K. (2009), 'Pepsi launches music business initiative with QMusic', *Media*, 6 August, retrieve from www.media.asia/Newsarticle/2009_08/Pepsi-launches-music-business-initiative-with-QMusic/36537, accessed 23 November 2009.

Lyotard, J.-F. (1984), *The Postmodern Condition*, Paris: Les Éditions de Minuit.

M&S (2010), 'Our Plan A Commitments 2010-2015', retrieve from http://plana.marksandspencer.com/media/pdf/planA-2010.pdf, accessed 10 April 2010.

Maslow, A. H. (1943), 'A theory of motivation', *Psychological Review*, 50, 370–96.

Mautner, T. (1999), *Dictionary of Philosophy*, London: Penguin.

Mick, D. G. (1986), 'Consumer research and semiotics: exploring the morphology of signs, symbols and significance', *Journal of Consumer Research*, 13, 196–213.

Moisander, J.; Valtonen, A. and Hirsto, H. (2009), 'Personal interviews in cultural consumer research—post structuralist challenges', *Consumption Markets and Culture*, 12, 4, 329–48.

Mutel, G. (2004), 'Al-Jazeera to go global and broadcast in English', *Campaign* (UK) 41 (8 October).

Pace, S. (2008), 'YouTube: an opportunity for consumer narrative analysis?', *Qualitative Market Research: An International Journal*, 11, 2, 213–26.

Peirce, C. S. (1931–58), *Collected Papers*, ed. Charles Hartshorne, Paul Weiss, and Arthur W. Burks, Cambridge, Mass: Harvard University Press.

Proctor, S., Papasolomou-Doukakis, I., and Proctor, T. (2001), 'What are television advertisements really trying to tell us? A postmodern perspective', *Journal of Consumer Behaviour*, 1, 3, 246–55.

Ramsay, F. (2009), 'C4 set to air full-form content on YouTube', *Marketing*, 14 October, 8.

Scott, L. M. (1992), 'Playing with pictures: postmodernism, poststructuralism, and advertising visuals', *Advances in Consumer Research*, 19, 596–611.

Shaw, D. Newholm, T. and Dickinson, R. (2006), 'Consumption as voting: an exploration of consumer empowerment', *European Journal of Marketing*, 40, 9/10, 1049–67.

Tiltman, D. (2009), 'Pepsi ties strategy to reality TV show', *Media*, 26 March, 1.

Wiesenfeld, D. and Bush, K. (2009), 'Blanket coverage', *Research*, Magazine of the UK Market Research Society, September, 30–3.

Zakia, R. D., and Nadin, M. (1987), 'Semiotics, advertising and marketing', *Journal of Consumer Marketing*, 4, 2 (Spring), 5–12.

19 Marketing, Sustainability, and Ethics

Learning Outcomes

After reading this chapter, you will be able to:

▶ Define sustainable marketing and its implications for marketing practice

▶ Define the term ethics and apply the discipline to marketing

▶ Explain the common ethical norms applied in marketing

▶ Describe the role of ethics in marketing decision-making

▶ Analyse situations to determine the kind of ethical approaches that might be adopted

▶ Recognize how to apply an understanding of ethics to a company's marketing programmes

▶ Case Insight 19.1

The Co-operative Bank was the first, and remains the only, UK high street bank with a customer-led Ethical Policy, which gives customers a say in how their money is used. We speak to Kelvin Collins to find out more.

Kelvin Collins for the Co-operative Bank

make a tiny difference to the world. every day.

I made a choice to be with a bank that stands up for the issues I care about – such as global climate change. It means I never have to worry how my money is invested. It's why they're the right bank for me – they're good with money.

good with money

are you with us?
www.co-operativebank.co.uk

A Cooperative Bank poster demonstrates its ethical principles
Source: Co-operative Bank.

In a recent customer panel over 60% of customers said, 'Well of course we expect you to offer a green mortgage!' Our customers have high expectations from us.

Whatever industry we're in, I believe we should seek out ways to deliver what we all need, then make it better with environmental benefits. I call this Bright Green.

▶ *I believe that 'Green' shouldn't be dull, or a sacrifice*

Yet look at our industry—we're rate crazy. A quick scan of the newspapers would leave anyone thinking the whole country buys on rate alone. However, a recent *Guardian* survey indicates that less than 40% of us are with our financial services provider just because of price. Ethics—in all its varied forms—recruits our customers and keeps them with us.

The origins of our parent company, The Co-operative Group, lie in social banking: in other words, concern for our customers. We have our roots in The Co-operative Movement of the late eighteenth century, which was based on a philosophy that businesses should be run for the benefit of customers, the people who work in them, their families, and the wider community—not a privileged few. In our long life, we have introduced many innovations into the banking sector, including such headline-grabbing moves as being the first high street bank to introduce free banking and internet banking.

The year 1992 was a particularly exciting one for us: we built on our achievements by introducing a customer-led Ethical Policy. What's unique about our policy is that it is based on the issues that matter most

▶ Case Insight 19.1

to our customers. It covers issues as diverse as the arms trade, the environment, genetic modification, and much more. And it's not just hot air—since we launched the policy we've turned away over £700m of loans that have conflicted with our policy.

We also offer different levels of engagement to suit our customers. They all contribute to our Customers Who Care campaign through spending on their credit or debit cards. But they can also join our campaigning activity and lobbying of government, if that's what they want. One of the first campaigns called for a ban on landmines—now outlawed in 144 countries—since then we've campaigned on a wide range of issues from third world debt to human rights, biodiversity to safer chemicals, and trade justice. We are passionate about

ethical banking; our commitment is genuine and we have to convey this to our customers. They expect us to deliver. Every time.

But marketing can sometimes be more about perceptions than substance. Although we were one of the pioneers of ethical business in the UK, the broader marketplace has now finally recognized that consumers do care about social responsibility, and the environmental impact on business, and so other brands have started to adopt ethics and green issues as part of their brand values.

The question is how do we continue to differentiate ourselves from these newcomers in the marketplace, remain true to our history, and take our business forward at the same time?

Introduction

What is sustainable marketing and why is everyone in business talking about it? Why do banks charge penalty fees if you go above your overdraft limit and how fair is it? Do you have to pay more for a coffee on campus than at the local Starbucks? What is an acceptable level of profit for a company to make? When is advertising and marketing communications coercive? When should companies give back to their communities? What is 'good' marketing behaviour and what is 'bad' marketing behaviour? Are corporate social responsibility initiatives a good idea, or are they cynically used by organizations to further their own ends or to suck up to consumers? Why should we care about our company's impact on the environment? These are some of the questions we consider in this chapter.

We begin by discussing a movement in marketing towards sustainable economic development. We also discuss what ethics are, before applying ethics to the marketing context. We outline how ethical situations impact on the marketing decision-making process. Four main ethical approaches to marketing decision-making are outlined. Ethical situations arising in product, promotion, price, and distribution programmes are also explained. We consider ethical issues in international marketing, i.e. whether or not different cultures should have different moral rules. Finally, we go on to define sustainability in marketing and its implications for practice.

Understanding **marketing ethics** is important because we need to understand ethical, legal, and social dimensions of marketing decision-making and develop analytical skills for considering ethical marketing problems. There has been an increased interest in business ethics and the ethically responsible company worldwide. But this is not the only driver for increased interest; other drivers include:

- ▶ An increasing belief that business performance should be sustainable by not negatively impacting on the environment and society in which it operates.

- ▶ Government legislation, e.g. the American Sarbanes–Oxley Act 2002 set up an oversight board for the US accounting profession, enhancing the timeliness and quality of finance reports of public companies, and placed restrictions on the selling of shares in certain situations.

- ▶ The increase in global trade and the rise of the multinational corporation with multicountry interests, particularly in developing countries.

- ▶ The rise of global media companies, operating on a continual 24 hour/seven days a week basis, such as the BBC World Service, CNN, and Asia News, with the potential to damage corporate reputations among large sections of the public around the world.

- ▶ Increasing recognition and belief that climate change (i.e. global warming) is affected by industrial activity, and modern consumer lifestyle choices, which has profound implications for future generations of marketers.

Sustainable Marketing

Sustainable marketing is a movement to accept the limitations of marketing philosophy and acknowledge that there is a need to impose regulatory constraints on the market mechanism in economic development (van Dam and Apeldoorn, 1996), particularly in relation to the impacts of marketing activity on the environment. The concept of sustainable economic development was outlined at the United Nations Conference on the Human Environment in Stockholm in 1972, where sustainable economic development was regarded as development that met the needs of current generations without imposing constraints on the needs of future generations (WCED, 1987). Some examples of how companies have negatively impacted on their market environments are outlined in Market Insight 19.1.

Sustainable marketing is an attempt to broaden the concept of marketing beyond simple economic development. It introduces the concepts of the three Es of sustainability as outlined below:

1 ecological—marketing should not negatively impact upon the environment;

2 equitable—marketing should not allow or promote inequitable social practices; and

3 economic—marketing should encourage long-term economic development as opposed to short-term economic development (as we have seen in the late 2000s with the global credit crunch arising as a result of poor financial regulation in world financial services markets).

Sustainable marketing can also be characterized as the 'third age' of green marketing (Peattie, 2001). In the first age, ecological green marketing, around the 1960s/70s, green marketing was concerned with automobile, oil, and agri-chemical companies, which encountered specific environmental problems in the production process. In the second age, environmental green marketing, in the 1980s, there was the development of the green consumer (i.e. someone who purchased goods usually to avoid negative environmental impacts, e.g. cosmetic products that had not been tested on animals) and companies therefore did try to develop a reputation for being green by offering green products. On occasion this failed, for example, when cosmetic suppliers to The Body Shop were found to have tested some of their products on animals, although The Body Shop later ensured all its suppliers complied with a strict code of practice. Some companies faced a backlash from consumers because their green products failed to live up to customer expectations (Crane, 2000).

The third age of green marketing is sustainable green marketing. In the third age, to successfully pursue sustainable marketing policies, companies will need to lengthen the time horizons under which they achieve returns on their investments. They will emphasize the full costs of purchase rather than simply the price paid. Product development activities will need to fully consider, equitably, inputs and cooperation from members of the supply chain. Companies will need to adopt environmental auditing methods (which include costs for disposal as well as development, delivery, and consumption, for example), and companies/organizations may need to actually discourage consumption in some cases or promote a shift from purchasing products to purchasing services, e.g. emphasizing taking the bus rather than buying a car or in a business-to-business situation, leasing a component and the servicing rather than purchasing it outright with a warranty (Peattie, 2001; Bridges and Wilhelm, 2008). An example of how companies might discourage consumption could include alcohol manufacturers actively demarketing alcohol to those under the legal drinking age. Other companies will work hard to remove potentially negative environmental attributes from their products and services (e.g. food companies removing preservatives and fats from foods and petrol refiners removing lead and sulphur).

Although companies are increasingly recognizing the negative impacts they are having on society (what economists call '**externalities**'), many are also increasingly trying to positively contribute to societal development through corporate social responsibility programmes. We turn to this topic in the next section.

▶ Market Insight 19.1

Unsustainable Marketing in Practice

Over the last 30 years, there have been some spectacular corporate disasters, which have had major effects on human life and society. In many cases, the negative societal effects of these companies' actions are still felt today, with legal action continuing in some cases:

- ▶ 1984: Union Carbide and Bhopal—tonnes of toxic chemical gas, methyl isocyanate (MIC) were leaked from a Union Carbide plant at Bhopal, Madhya Pradesh, India, causing 5,800 deaths and hundreds of thousands of injuries. In 1989, Union Carbide and Union Carbide India Limited (UCIL) eventually settled all claims arising

from the incident with the Indian government for US$470m, although many victims are still seeking compensation from the Indian government.

- ▶ 1989: The Exxon *Valdez* affair—Exxon's *Valdez* oil tanker accidentally dumped 10.8m gallons (approximately 41m litres) of crude oil in the waters around the Alaskan coastline, killing hundreds of thousands of seabirds, many other forms of local wildlife, and ruining the livelihoods of thousands of people in fishing and related industries. Exxon is still appealing against a $4.5bn punitive fine placed on it in a federal court trial in 1994.

- ▶ 1997: Nike's alleged tolerance of the use of sweatshops by its suppliers in Asia, often with the use of child labour in hazardous conditions, for

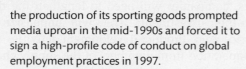

Market Insight 19.1 (continued)

the production of its sporting goods prompted media uproar in the mid-1990s and forced it to sign a high-profile code of conduct on global employment practices in 1997.

▶ 2001: Enron—one of the world's largest energy companies—improper financial accounting, including inflated turnover claims filed to the Securities and Exchange Commission, and fraudulent practices, which resulted in convictions for insider trading and securities fraud against senior employees, led to the collapse of a Fortune 500 company and its auditor, Arthur Andersen, at the time one of the world's largest accountancy firms.

▶ 2008: Sanlu (and other Chinese milk producers)—a major scandal occurred in China when its largest milk producer, and many others in the industry, were found to have added melamine to milk, a banned substance in food

worldwide, in order to falsely improve protein test readings. Around 300,000 infants were made sick as a result and approximately six died.

Sources: Sen and Egelhoff (1991); Kumar (2004); AOSC, 1990; Bayne (2005); Schwarz (1991); Spencer (2008); Swartz and Watkins (2003); Usborne (1997).

1 **What do you think the effect of the crises is on each of the companies in terms of their corporate image? Consider particularly those companies that are still in existence today.**

2 **In Nike's case, the actions of the company led to a boycott of their products by selected consumers. How important is it to take account of your customers' views on matters of public policy such as these?**

3 **How important do you think it is for a company to act responsibly? Why is it so important?**

Research Insight 19.1

To take your learning further, you might wish to read this influential paper.

Van Dam, Y.K., and Apeldoorn, P.A.C. (1996), 'Sustainable marketing', *Journal of Macromarketing*, 16, 45–56.

The authors' intention was to build and develop on the concepts first put forward in articles on societal marketing in the 1970s and green marketing in the 1980s, both of which only partially dealt with the problem of marketing's impact on its environment. However, they argue that, from both micro- and macromarketing perspectives, marketing has an inherent drive towards unsustainable economic development. The authors argue that there is a need for greater regulation, although not necessarily legislation, to encourage marketers towards more sustainable practices.

 Visit the **Online Resource Centre** to read the abstract and access the full paper.

Corporate Social Responsibility

Corporate social responsibility (CSR) initiatives have become increasingly common. Many companies publish annual CSR or sustainability reports, e.g. BAT, GSK, and SSL International. Increasingly, governments and supranational organizations actively encourage CSR initiatives, e.g. the UN Global Compact project. CSR practitioners and academics continue to try to demonstrate the commercial effectiveness of CSR programmes to determine whether or not being a 'good' company translates to being a profitable company.

Despite any obvious return, businesspersons have given to charity for centuries. Famous cases include the John Paul Getty foundation in the USA, which has funded art and social projects around the world based on profits from the oil industry, and Ratan Tata, the Indian businessman who provided welfare services for his employees and worked to stop the spread of HIV/AIDS in India, based on profits from the Tata conglomerate (see Market Insight 19.2). The rationale for developing CSR initiatives irrespective of their financial contribution is based on the following ideas (Buchholz, 1991: 19):

▶ Corporations have responsibilities that go beyond the production of goods and services at a profit.

▶ These responsibilities involve helping to solve important social problems, especially those that they have helped to create.

▶ Corporations have a broader constituency than shareholders alone.

▶ Corporations have impacts that go beyond simple marketplace transactions.

▶ Corporations serve a wider range of human values than can be captured by a sole focus on economic values.

▶ Research Insight 19.2

To take your learning further, you might wish to read this influential paper.

Maignan, I., and Ferrell, O. C. (2004), 'Corporate social responsibility and marketing: an integrative framework', *Journal of the Academy of Marketing Science*, 32, 1, 3–19.

A recent article outlining how marketing contributes to corporate social responsibility and demonstrating the conceptual fit between marketing and corporate social responsibility. CSR is seen principally as action used to conform to stakeholder and organizational requirements. The article concludes by asking a number of important questions such as 'how do stakeholder norms influence business practices?', 'which organizational processes can stimulate socially responsible corporate behaviours?', 'how do different stakeholders react to CSR practices?', and 'how should companies communicate their CSR practices?'.

@ Visit the **Online Resource Centre** to read the abstract and access the full paper.

▶ Market Insight 19.2

CSR at Tata: Are Community Initiatives Good for Business?

The Tata Group is one of India's largest business conglomerates, with revenues in 2008–9 of US$70.9bn (Rs crore 325, 334), contributing 3.6% of India's total corporation tax intake, and a market capitalization of US$59bn in October 2009. As a conglomerate, its principal business interests lie in tea, steel, consultancy services, and the automotive sector, among others. Its separate businesses have always had an interest in the communities in which the group operates. Tata Steel, for example, established an eight-hour work day in 1912, free medical aid in 1915, a welfare department in 1917, leave with pay and a provident and compensation fund in 1920, and maternity benefit for women in 1928—all before these rights became statutory.

Its steel division, Tata Steel, was presented with the Golden Peacock Award for Corporate Social Responsibility for 2009 by Portugal's Deputy Minister of Economy and Innovation at the opening ceremony of the 4th Global Conference on CSR (Corus, 2009). The company has a long history of efforts to improve its employees' welfare, particularly around the steel works at the company's base in Jamshedpur, and its corporate leadership in working to prevent the spread of HIV/AIDS. As a result of its pioneering work, Tata Steel is a member of the UN Global Compact.

Tata Steel, headquartered in Jamshedpur win the 2009 Golden Peacock Award for CSR

Source: Courtesy of Tata Steel Limited.

▶ Market Insight 19.2

But with social deprivation all around India, Ratan Tata, the company's CEO, feels his company has more of a duty to be socially responsible than perhaps Western companies might have within their countries, as the effects of deprivation are felt less.

Sources: Corus (2009); Pandit (2005); Tata (2009a,b).

1 Does a company in a less developed country really have more responsibility to pursue a CSR

agenda than a company in a wealthier country with less deprivation in the population?

2 Why do you think a steel company particularly needs to develop good relations with its communities?

3 What impact, if any, do you think CSR programmes have on Tata Steel's revenues?

A central theme of CSR is that corporations have some responsibility to wider society that goes beyond the pursuit of profit (Martin, 2002). However, the determination of that responsibility is not necessarily a simple exercise. Maitland (2002: 454) comments that drug manufacturers are regarded as social outcasts, second only to big oil and defence contractors 'as the villains of contemporary populist folklore', because they do not make drugs available cheaply or freely to needy citizens in developing countries. But it could be argued that if there is a moral argument for making life-saving drugs available at little or no cost to patients who cannot afford them, then the cost of doing this should be shared widely among society, rather than simply falling on the companies that happen to manufacture them. By comparison, we don't expect food manufacturers to work to eradicate world hunger.

go online

Visit the **Online Resource Centre** and complete Internet Activity 19.1 to learn more about some of the ethical debates that have occurred over the years surrounding sports wear manufacturing.

The above example illustrates the ethical difficulties inherent in marketing decision-making, particularly in relation to sustainable economic development. We, therefore, turn to the topic of ethics next.

Ethics and Marketing

Ethics, as a system of thinking within the discipline of philosophy, has been around for over 2,000 years. The *Oxford English Dictionary* defines it as: the science of morals, the department of study concerned with the principles of human duty; the moral principles or system of a particular leader or school of thought; and as the whole field of moral science, including the science of law whether civil, political, or international. Ethics is concerned with morality (from the Latin *moralis*), with doing 'good' in the realms of civil, political, and international life. The word ethics was originally derived from the Greek *ethos*, meaning habit or custom. Ethics can be divided into the following types:

▶ **Normative ethics**—concerned with the rational enquiry into standards of right and wrong (i.e. norms), good or bad, in respect of character and conduct and which *ought to be* accepted by a class of individuals.

▶ **Social or religious ethics**—concerned with what is right and wrong, good and bad, in respect of character and conduct. It does not claim to be established merely on the basis of rational enquiry and makes an implicit claim to general allegiance to something (e.g. God).

▶ **Positive morality**—a body of knowledge that is generally adhered to by a social group of individuals, concerning what is right and wrong, good and bad, in respect of character and conduct.

▶ **Descriptive ethics**—concerned with the study of the system of beliefs and practices of a social group from the perspective of being outside that group.

▶ **Metaethics**—a form of philosophical enquiry that treats ethical concepts and belief systems as objects of philosophical enquiry in themselves.

Earlier, we defined ethics as the study of morality in order to determine how the 'good' person should behave. In order to determine how to apply ethics to marketing, we must first redefine what marketing is. Although there are numerous definitions in Chapter 1, we shall take the Chartered Institute of Marketing's (CIM) definition here as 'the management process responsible for identifying, anticipating and satisfying customer requirements profitably'. So how does ethics relate to marketing? We could perhaps suggest that marketing ethics is concerned with how we go about that management process of identifying, anticipating, and satisfying customer requirements. The application of ethical principles also should consider what meaning is given to the term profitable. Islamic readers may not be entirely happy with the ultimate objective of a firm being to achieve profit. They might well feel that it is more worthy for a firm to aspire to value maximization (Saeed, Ahmed, and Mukhtar, 2001). Because there are both prescriptive and descriptive components of ethics, we define marketing ethics as: 'The analysis and application of moral principles to marketing decision making and the outcomes of these decisions'.

▶ Research Insight 19.3

To take your learning further, you might wish to read this influential paper.

Hunt, S. D., and Vitell, S. (2006), 'The general theory of marketing ethics: a revision and three questions', *Journal of Macromarketing*, 26, 2, 143–53.

Probably the most highly cited paper in marketing ethics, Hunt and Vitell's original article, 'A general theory of marketing ethics' in the *Journal of Macromarketing* in 1986, defined and gave momentum to the study of marketing ethics. This updating paper suggests that the original 1986 theory required revision because the model was applicable in any ethical decision-making situation, not just in business and management contexts, and required empirical testing. The authors argue that ethical judgments lead to intentions and on to behaviour. Our intentions are made on the basis of whether an action is right in itself (i.e. deontological ethics) and whether our intentions are right (i.e. **teleological ethics**).

 Visit the **Online Resource Centre** to read the abstract and access the full paper.

Ethical Norms in Marketing Decision-Making

Norms are suggestions about how we ought to behave. Professional marketing organizations typically have a code of professional practice that requires members to behave and act in a professional manner. The Chartered Institute of Marketing, the world's largest member-based marketing organization, requires its members to (CIM, 2005):

▶ demonstrate integrity, bringing credit to the profession of marketing;

▶ be fair and equitable towards other marketing professionals;

▶ be honest in dealing with customers, clients, employers, and employees;

▶ avoid the dissemination of false or misleading information;

▶ demonstrate current knowledge of the latest developments and show competence in their application;

▶ avoid conflicts of interest and commitment to maintaining impartiality;

▶ treat sensitive information with complete confidence;

▶ negotiate business in a professional and ethical manner;

▶ demonstrate knowledge and observation of the requirements of other (professions') codes of practice;

▶ demonstrate due diligence in using third-party endorsement, which must have prior approval; and

▶ comply with the governing laws of the relevant country concerned.

In ethics more generally, these norms typically include four general approaches: 1) managerial egoism, 2) deontological ethics, 3) utilitarianism, and 4) virtue ethics (see Table 19.1).

▶ **Table 19.1** The main normative approaches to ethical decision-making

Ethical approach	Explanation
Managerial egoism	An ethical approach that recognizes that a manager ought to act in his or her own best interests and that an action is right if it benefits the manager undertaking that action
Utilitarianism	An ethical approach developed by English philosopher and social reformer Jeremy Bentham which suggests that an action is right if, and only if, it conforms to the principle of utility, whereby utility is maximized (i.e. pleasure, happiness, or welfare)—and pain or unhappiness minimized—more than any alternative
Deontological ethics	An ethical approach where the rightness or wrongness of an action or decision is not judged to be based exclusively on the consequences of that action or decision
Virtue ethics	A form of ethical approach associated with Aristotle, which stresses the importance of developing virtuous principles, 'right' character, and the pursuit of a virtuous life

We outline each approach further below. It is not necessary to be concerned with determining the differences between each of these approaches at this stage. Read through each section, and the associated examples, to begin to understand the differences. If necessary, read through this section several times before moving on to the next section.

Managerial Egoism

The rationale for egoism is the pursuit of our own interests, or self-interest. We assume that the interests of marketing managers in an organization are in agreement with the interests of the organization's owners or directors (which they may not be). Under these circumstances, the ethical principle of **managerial egoism** is the maximization of shareholder value or stakeholder value (for a non-profit). If managers aim to maximize their own self-interest within the free market, economic welfare is maximized across the population, according to Adam Smith (1776). If we adopt the managerial egoist principle, then we conclude that companies should set their marketing programmes to maximize shareholder or stakeholder value. The celebrated economist Milton Friedman suggested that managers should only have responsibility to maximize shareholder returns as they 'lack the wisdom and ability to resolve complex social problems' (Friedman, 1979: 90). Economists have long suggested that markets are amoral, i.e. without any particular moral stance. The free market mechanism does not work to promote ethical decisions, but it does work to supply the optimal amount of goods and services in a society.

There is a view that marketers should not concern themselves with ethics, as long as they uphold the law and manage their own self-interest, as unethical behaviour is subject to sanction in the marketplace anyway. Firms will pursue their own self-interest and act ethically anyway (Gaski, 1999). There is some also evidence to suggest that companies offering services rather than goods might require employees to be more ethical as there is a greater opportunity for unethical behaviour due to the greater interaction between company and customer and the trust generated from this interaction (Rao and Singhapakdi, 1997). Nevertheless, although consumer wants exert a powerful control on marketing behaviour, consumers' vetoes or boycott power alone is not enough to properly regulate a market (Clasen, 1967).

If marketers act according to the law or a company's self-interest only, this could be regarded as a moral minimum. Most societies would require companies to go beyond this. The problem with this ethical approach is that it is not always possible to determine whether a company is pursuing a managerial egoist approach (i.e. acting in their own self-interest because ultimately this will benefit others), or a shareholder value maximization approach. The two sometimes seem the same. The cynic will wonder whether a company that goes beyond its legal duties and apparently acts according to higher morals (e.g. Ben & Jerry's, Benetton, the Co-operative Bank) is simply trying to win over public opinion and maximize long-term shareholder value, rather than be ethical.

Utilitarianism

An ethical approach originally developed by English philosopher and social reformer Jeremy Bentham, **utilitarianism** suggests that an action is right if, and only if, its performance will be more productive of pleasure or happiness or welfare, or more preventive of pain or unhappiness, than any alternative (Mautner, 1999). Utilitarian arguments are concerned with the consequences of an action. Most ethical arguments proposed by marketers are utilitarian. Indeed, the very concept of marketing could be argued to be utilitarian as it is typically concerned with satisfying consumer needs and wants at the market level (Nantel and Weeks, 1996).

Utilitarianism is concerned with 'producing the greater good for the greatest number of people'. The problem is that the maximization of one group's utility can sometimes lead to the minimization of another group's utility. To determine the utility associated with a particular decision, it is necessary to determine the 'costs' and 'benefits', which, quite often, are more or less impossible to quantify. Where products may save lives, such as with life-saving drugs or health treatments, the losers may pay with their lives and the gainers survive, particularly where that product is in scarce supply.

To explain this further, let's consider a train operating company determining how to improve its health and safety record, for instance, when deciding how much to spend on safety instrumentation (i.e. signalling and track equipment). In such a situation, the company has to decide exactly how much to spend on protecting passengers' health and safety needs. The costs of purchasing and fitting equipment to reduce what industrial safety engineers call the **fatal accident rate** (FAR) are typically passed on to the customer. A decision over whether or not to fit the equipment, and how much to spend on it, requires a calculation of the likely reduction in risk of accidents against how likely the passengers are to pay the increased prices, or the company alternatively will have to absorb the extra costs. The question arises, however: is this an acceptable approach? Many would argue that it is not, stating that if even one life lost or damaged can be avoided then the company has a duty to improve the health and safety of all passengers regardless. The decision to ration supplies is an extreme example of utilitarianism, as occurred with food and some household goods in many parts of Europe during the Second World War, with electricity in Chile in 1999, and with petrol in Iran and diesel in China in 2007.

Deontological Ethics

Deontological ethics proposes that the rightness of an action is not determined by the consequences of that action (Mautner, 1999). Rather, deontological ethics tends to emphasize the importance of codes of ethics, e.g. those outlined by the Market Research Society (MRS) governing market research in Britain, or by ESOMAR (European Society for Market and Opinion Research) in Europe. Deontological approaches propose that we have not only a moral duty to ensure the satisfaction of our customers and consumers through the finished product or service, but also a duty to ensure integrity in the way that the product or service is manufactured and marketed to them. The Co-operative Bank is proud of its stance against animal testing, fur trading, investment in defence companies, and acts to advance many other social causes. In Rawls' *Theory of Justice* (Rawls, 1972), he argues that in a just society the following two conditions must be met:

1 'Each person is to have an equal right to the most extensive total system of equal basic liberties compatible with a similar system of liberty for all' (Liberty Principle).

2 'Social and economic inequalities are to be arranged so that they are both:

   a) to the greatest benefit of the least advantaged; and

   b) attached to offices and positions open to all under the conditions of fair equality of opportunity' (Difference Principle).

The Difference Principle applied to marketing situations would suggest that vulnerable groups in society should not be disadvantaged further by management and marketing decisions. It is to this principle that the international media implicitly appeal when criticizing international pharmaceutical companies, oil and gas companies, and banks for what they term to be excessive profiteering. This approach to ethical decision-making would suggest that we have a duty to help the disadvantaged, particularly where they are likely to be adversely affected by our actions.

Virtue Ethics

Previous normative ethical theories, i.e. managerial egoist, utilitarian, and deontological, provide the marketer with decision-making approaches that can be used to choose between alternative courses of 'right' action. In direct contrast, **virtue ethics** stresses the importance of developing virtuous principles, with 'right' character, and the pursuit of a virtuous life. This branch of ethics is associated principally with Aristotle (Mautner, 1999). Virtue ethics proposes the development of good character, suggesting that we should aim to develop the virtuous marketing organization within a company. But what virtues should companies strive to develop? The idea is that if we live a virtuous life, virtuous decision-making will develop naturally.

Many companies claim they are virtuous. The values statements of some pharmaceutical and oil and gas companies emphasize the importance of 'integrity'. Enron, the US energy company, which inflated its own earnings and ended in collapse, extolled its own virtues in its mission statement. But exactly what are virtuous principles and how are they operationalized? Aristotle, in *Nicomachean Ethics*, defines virtue as 'a settled disposition of the mind which determines choice' (Mautner, 1999). He goes on to define 11 virtues comprising bravery, self-control, generosity, magnificence, self-respect, balanced ambition, gentleness, friendliness, truthfulness, wittiness, and justice. Although it is more difficult to apply these concepts to a company, as a company does not have a character in the same way that a person does, its employees do. So, it is possible to consider how these virtues *might* relate to a company. For example, generosity might relate to the development of CSR programmes, or incentives given to employees or channel partners. Table 19.2 outlines each virtue and how it might be applied to organizations.

▶ **Table 19.2** Moral virtues applied to companies

Moral virtue	Application in business and marketing
Bravery, valour	In relation to innovation/new product/service development
Self-control in respect of bodily pleasure	Not given to excessive pricing or profit taking
Generosity	Development of CSR/philanthropy, or in terms of discounted products/services or other incentives given to employees/others
Magnificence	Aiming to build a large enterprise with a well-defined mission, which serves its stakeholders well
Self-respect or pride	Openly communicating to stakeholders both the good and bad news associated with a company's operations

Moral virtue	Application in business and marketing
Having some ambition but not in excess	Competitive, but not at all costs, and not combative within an industry
Gentleness or good temper	The use of a balanced approach to dealings with stakeholder relations, e.g. industrial relations, consumer boycotts
Friendliness	The will to join forces with competitors in the same industry where necessary, e.g. for purposes of self-regulation, to develop industry standards, and an exemplary approach to customer service and satisfaction
Truthfulness	In relation to financial integrity and other stakeholder communications
Wittiness	Taken to mean intelligence and a company's ability to redefine the 'rules of the game' without taking itself too seriously
Justice	The audits of one's own ethical approaches and the initiation of reward/punishment when these are disregarded

go online

Visit the **Online Resource Centre** and complete Internet Activity 19.2 to learn more about The Co-operative Bank's 'Customers Who Care' campaign and the organization's ethical values.

The Ethical Decision-Making Process

Having defined four main ways in which we analyse how an organization ought to behave, we consider how organizations actually go about making ethical decisions. A manager first has to perceive that there might be an ethical dilemma before undergoing the ethical decision-making process (Hunt and Vitell, 2006). Critically, if no ethical dilemma is seen to exist, no consideration of alternative sources of action can take place. However, determining if a situation has ethical content is specific to individual cultures. So, people from some cultures are more likely to perceive ethical breaches than others. Nevertheless, there are some universal standards (e.g., the OECD's Guidelines for Multinational Companies). For example, bribery is almost universally condemned around the world and most countries have laws making bribery of public officials illegal. Early attempts to devise frameworks of how to act ethically involved asking ourselves reflective questions as follows (Laczniak and Murphy, 1993):

▶ Does the contemplated action violate the law (legal test)?

▶ Is this action contrary to widely accepted moral obligations (duties test)?

▶ Does the proposed action violate any other special obligations that stem from the type of marketing organization in focus (special obligations test)?

▶ Is the intent of the contemplated action harmful (motives test)?

▶ Is it likely that any major damage to people or organizations will result from the contemplated action (consequences test)?

▶ Is there a satisfactory alternative action that produces equal or greater benefits to the parties affected than the proposed action (utilitarian test)?

▶ Does the contemplated action infringe on property rights, privacy rights, or the inalienable rights of the consumer (rights test)?

▶ Does the proposed action leave another person or group less well off? Is this person or group already a member of a relatively underprivileged class (justice test)?

An elaborate model of ethical decision-making is shown in Figure 19.1 (Ferrell and Gresham, 1985). The authors cite five key issues for ethical consideration including bid rigging, **price collusion**, bribery, falsifying research data, and advertising deception. In **bid rigging**, sub-contractors submit false bids, perhaps offering goods and services that are too expensive in the knowledge that they will form part of the final contract. Sometimes, companies might agree not to submit a bid so that another company can successfully win a contract. **Collusion** occurs when companies collaborate on submitting bids for some competitions but not others. With price collusion, companies either conspire to set prices or limit production, which typically have the same effect.

Determining what to do when a person in an organization encounters such situations depends on their social and cultural environment. Although bribery is illegal in most countries around the world, it is still more likely to take place in some countries than others (see later section on bribery). How an employee makes a decision on an ethical issue is affected by their own knowledge, cultural background, values, and attitudes, as well as whether or not the company has a code of ethics, a corporate ethical policy, and guidelines on rewards/punishment for ethical and unethical behaviour.

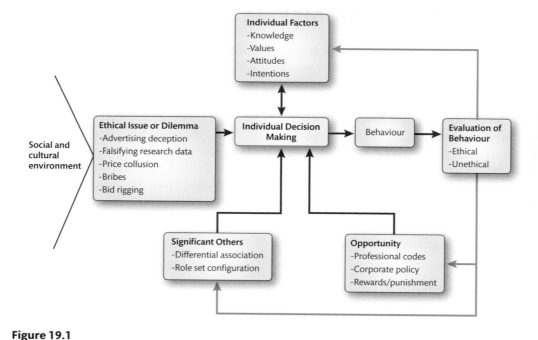

Figure 19.1

A contingency model of ethical decision-making in a marketing organization

Source: Reprinted with permission from *Journal of Marketing*, published by the American Marketing Association. Ferrell and Gresham (1985).

▶ Research Insight 19.4

To take your learning further, you might wish to read this influential paper.

Ferrell, O. C., and Gresham, L. G. (1985), 'A contingency framework for understanding ethical decision making in marketing', *Journal of Marketing*, 49 (Summer), 87–96.

A highly cited, short, highly readable paper outlining how ethical marketing decisions are contingent on the ethical issue itself, the social and cultural environment, individual factors (such as attitudes and values), significant others, and the opportunity (i.e. professional codes with which one operates, corporate policy), focusing academic attention on the fact that ethical marketing decisions are dependent on the circumstances in which the decision-making occurs for the first time.

 Visit the **Online Resource Centre** to read the abstract and access the full paper.

▶ Market Insight 19.3

Ethical Content, In Context

How would you react if you were in the following situations at work? Consider the ethical content of each of the following situations:

▶ You work for a Western defence company (i.e. USA, UK, France) and have just visited an African nation where you are likely to be awarded a multimillion-dollar contract to supply the government with missile technology, which they state that they intend to use only for defence of their nation, rather than aggression against their neighbours. Your African contact within the government asks for a large 'commission' equivalent to about 5% of the contract value for arranging the contract. If you do not arrange the 'commission', you will not get the contract and may lose your job. Do you pay the 'commission'?

▶ You work for a Chinese company exporting a range of fast-selling soft toys to Western Europe. One of your two laboratory test reports—lab tests are required under EU guidelines—indicates that the eye in one of your soft toys easily comes loose and could therefore be swallowed by a child. However, you have already pre-sold 200,000 units to shops in several countries. Do you go through the trouble of destroying or fixing the soft toys, and claiming the costs on your insurance or seeking compensation from your suppliers, or do you do nothing in the hope that there won't be any problems and no one will pick up the error anyway?

▶ An advertising agency devises an awareness-raising campaign for a new perfume aimed at affluent women in Dubai. The campaign uses a slight sexual appeal, which your research indicates does not offend the affluent female target audience and catches their attention. However, it is possible that the campaign could offend others. Would you commission the campaign anyway?

▶ You work for a supplier of electricity, in a Scandinavian country, during an election year.

▶ Market Insight 19.3   (continued)

You think the leading political party in power is in a position once it forms government to allow you to substantially increase the unit price of electricity, but in order to obtain this representation you will need to donate a 'large gift' to the party. Do you make the donation?

1 Go through each one of the above situations and work out what you would do in the given circumstances. Why would you act in this way?

2 Can you think of other marketing situations with ethical content?

3 How important is it for a company to have clear ethical policies? Do you think they can provide guidelines for all situations that employees might find themselves in?

A person's ethical decision-making is determined by how they interact with people who are part of their reference group. Association with others behaving unethically, combined with the opportunity to be involved in such behaviour oneself, is a major predictor of unethical behaviour (Ferrell and Gresham, 1985). Therefore, the behaviour of superiors determines how employees behave and is the most important factor influencing ethical/unethical decisions. Next, we consider how ethics impacts on distribution, promotion, products, and pricing decisions.

Distribution Management and Ethics

Distribution and production policy can have major ethical dimensions. Ethical breaches in distribution management occur when, for example, companies collude over production quotas, when companies abuse their monopoly status, and when companies overcharge or exploit their supply chain partners. The following sections provide examples of companies or situations where ethical breaches have occurred:

▶ Collusion—in the late 1990s, Italian Antitrust authorities (IAA) found its two largest dairy producers Consorzo del Grana Padano (CGP) and Consorzo del Parmigiano Reggiano (CPR) guilty of operating strict production quotas designed to effectively co-manage each other's market share (Braga and Nardella, 2003). A better known and tolerated global example of production collusion is that which takes places in the oil industry, through OPEC (the organization of oil-exporting countries), which co-manages production quotas in countries such as Nigeria, Saudi Arabia, Iran, Venezuela, and elsewhere.

▶ Abuse of monopoly status—in March 2004, the European Union levied a half-billion-euro fine against Microsoft, the American software giant, for abusing its 'near monopoly' status. The EU anti-competition authority called for Microsoft to offer a version of Windows that did not contain its digital media player within three months, and to release a 'complete and accurate' interface code to other software companies to ensure interoperability between competitor companies (Deutsche-Welle, 2004). Microsoft appealed against the ruling but lost its case in 2007. By 2009, Microsoft finally agreed a set of proposals that the European Union was able to accept, which will see Microsoft offer users of its Windows operating system software a choice of 12 different internet browsers (BBC News, 2009).

▶ Exploitation of supply chain partners—a well-known example in Western markets is that taking place between supermarkets and their suppliers, particularly those supplying multinational supermarket groups. European countries have brought in legislation to stop supermarkets from wielding excessive power. For instance, in France the 'Châtel Act' replaced the 'Loi Galland', which forbade supermarkets to charge so-called **listing fees**. The new act strengthens legislation to stop supermarkets selling at below-cost prices and is aimed at increasing competition in the sector. All discounts and services provided by the distributor to the supplier now require stipulation upfront in an annual agreement (see Boutin and Guerrero, 2008). A historic example was the sweatshop suppliers employing child-workers used by Gap and Nike in Cambodia in the production of its footwear (Panorama, 2000), causing both companies to revise their supply chain management policies.

Promotion and Ethics

There are many advertising issues that prompt ethical consideration. Some considerations include when to use shock and sexual appeals in advertising, the labelling of consumer products, the use of propaganda and advertising in political situations, and marketing to children.

The Use of Sexual and Shock Appeals

Advertisers use emotional appeals because they capture our attention. We are persuaded by them because we are less likely to consider objections about why we might not agree with the message. For the celebrated French philosopher Jean Baudrillard (2005: 187), advertising has an erotic element to it as through advertising, 'the product exposes itself to our view and invites us to handle it; it is, in fact, eroticised—not just because of the explicitly sexual themes evoked'. But the ethical question arises because a substantial proportion of adverts do use sexual themes explicitly, e.g. naked or semi-naked attractive models, sometimes male, but more often than not female, to advertise their products. Many critics argue that this exploits women, and much less frequently men, as sex objects. The fashion industry has consequently decided not to use models under the age of 16 years.

Others argue that sexual appeals in advertising might be appropriate for the product in question, i.e. a perfume, as this product is so closely linked with sexuality. The difficulty arises in determining how far to go in the use of sexual appeals. For what products is it appropriate, in what countries, and targeted at people of what ages? Reebok, a shoe manufacturer, uses sex appeal in its adverts, aimed particularly at women in an effort to get them to exercise more to achieve a perfect body shape. Is it ethical to appeal to women in this way? On one hand it is, because Reebok are encouraging women to exercise and be healthy. From another angle, one might argue that the advertising is coercive because it uses a women's sense of inadequacy in body image to drive her behaviour to purchase the training shoes.

Shock advertising appeals have also created furore and controversy. Perhaps the best example of shock appeals used in advertising is that used by governments to reduce tobacco smoking. Under Canadian law, the top 50% of the front and back of each cigarette pack depicts a full-colour, stark graphic warning. The pictures have included depictions of a lung tumour, a brain after a stroke, and a damaged heart. It has, however, been argued that shock appeals are limited in their effectiveness because viewers, when encountering a dismaying image, simply ignore the messages, in a process psychologists call 'emotional forgetting'. This is not forgetting in the usual sense, but simply a form of selective exposure (see Chapter 3). It's a way of ignoring the message to filter out the unwelcome negative state of mind induced by the image. The ethical consideration for an advertiser is to determine what level of shock is appropriate to get the audience's attention about a particular issue or product.

Product Labelling

With product labelling, the key ethical issue is whether or not labels mislead the buying public. Proper labelling is particularly important in the food, pharmaceutical, and cosmetic industries, as we literally consume these products or absorb them into our skin. Increasingly, food products, and particularly meat products in Europe and elsewhere, are required to demonstrate their country of origin. For Europe's Muslims, whether or not food products are correctly labelled halal is important as Muslims believe that animals should be slaughtered according to the custom of cutting the animal's throat while it is alive and then draining its blood. Some animal rights groups now condemn the practice, and Sweden, Norway, Iceland and Switzerland condemn the practice outright (Economist, 2009).

Unscrupulous companies can, and do, circumvent product labelling rules by importing food products from one country, processing them in another, and claiming that they come from the country where they are processed. In most countries of the European Union, regulations were created after the EU passed the EC Packaging and Packaging Waste Directive 94/62/EC to govern the composition of packaging and its recycling. Guidelines on advertising claims, however, are not contained in this act and are covered in Britain by the Trading Standards Service, which investigates misleading packaging and labelling on behalf of the consumer through officers attached to local authorities.

Propaganda and Political Advertising

In many countries, political advertising is exempt from the rules and regulations associated with traditional advertising. In America, for instance, freedom of speech, enshrined in the Fifth Amendment, allows a vitriolic and negative approach to political advertising based on 15- and 30-second advertising spots used to assassinate the character of political opponents. In Britain, political advertising on billboards, in cinemas and magazines is exempt from the advertising rules set by the Advertising Standards Authority (ASA). Political parties are not expected to be truthful, i.e. to validate their claims, unlike their commercial counterparts. Broadcast political advertising is illegal; instead, a system of party political broadcasts operates. There are examples of political advertising that have bordered on the propagandist as, for example, when the British Conservative Party depicted Blair as the devil in the 1997 British General Election campaign. The ethical question is should our politicians, seasoned users of marketing tools and techniques, be exempt from the rules and regulations associated with traditional marketing activity?

 Visit the **Online Resource Centre** and follow the weblink to the Advertising Standards Authority (ASA) to learn more about advertising rules and regulations.

go online

The Conservative Party's campaign depicting the then-leader of the Opposition, Tony Blair, as the devil

Source: The Conservative Party (UK).

A much more difficult ethical question surrounds the use of marketing tools and techniques by terrorist groups and governments in wartime. O'Shaughnessy and Baines (2009) explain how terrorist groups use propaganda videos to market the cause of suicide bombing, through the use of visual rhetoric—distributed through Qatari TV station Al Jazeera, and on the internet. By contrast, the American and British military both used propaganda methods in their bid to justify the Iraq War, particularly the practice of **embedding** journalists in allied combat units, but also through press censorship and event staging (see Baines and Worcester, 2005). An understanding of marketing and public relations provides its user with the means to persuade mass groups of people. The question arises as to whether or not it is legitimate for governments to use these means to persuade electorates about the legitimacy of war before, during, and after the event. Equally, just as marketing/propaganda methods can be used by legitimate governments so they can be used by illegitimate governments and terrorist groups.

Marketing to Children

Scholars have frequently commented on whether or not children should be targeted for advertising, given their immature views of time, money, and identity. In a research study on marketing to children in Britain, undertaken on Business in the Community's (BITC) behalf by Research International and Lightspeed Research, researchers found evidence that children are increasingly targeted in promotional campaigns and that parents are increasingly concerned by this. A summary of the report outlines:

▶ Children are more exposed to marketing than before and parents increasingly feel that they are losing control of the marketing directed at their children.

▶ Parents are particularly concerned about the marketing channels such as the internet and mobile phones, which can target their children directly.

▶ Inappropriate marketing to children damages the brand, making it less likely that you will get past the parent as gatekeeper.

▶ More appropriate marketing methods are those that are informative and help parents to feel more in control.

Children are more exposed to marketing than ever before

▶ Consumers are willing to support companies that communicate with children in a responsible way.

▶ It is up to marketers, especially advertisers, to use the means of communication appropriately and to educate parents and children alike on newer and less traditional communication mediums. Ensuring the responsible use of these less traditional mediums is paramount (Daniels and Holmes, 2005).

One company that has come under pressure in relation to its promotion to children is McDonald's, as its products particularly appeal to children, through the use of licensed characters and celebrity endorsement. Child obesity is regarded as a problem in many countries (e.g. Australasia, Britain, EU generally, America). One view sees the problem as being at least partly caused by food advertising to children, although the evidence is unclear as it could also be linked to inactive lifestyles and a lack of exercise. Fast food retailers such as McDonald's, KFC, and Burger King are coming under increasing pressure to make their menus healthier around the world. Mars is now starting to advertise the fact that its chocolate bars are free from artificial colours, flavourings, and preservatives, an increasing trend in the grocery market and of particular relevance to children given the amount of confectionery they consume, often on a daily basis.

Mars removes the e-numbers from its renowned chocolate bar

Source: Reproduced by kind permission of Mars. MARS, SNICKERS, TWIX, MILKY WAY and RAISING THE BAR are trademarks. © Mars 2009.

▶ Market Insight 19.4

Durex and STIs—A Sensitive Topic

The UK retail condom market is projected to reach a value of £65m (€71m) by 2013 at 2008 prices, an 8% decline over five years. Market leader SSL International distributes condoms under the brand name Durex, and takes about 84% market share, by value. The nearest competitor is Ansell Health Care, who distribute the brand Mates. Condoms are designed to reduce the incidence of sexually transmitted infections (STIs) and to be a form of birth control, so sales are dependent on trends in sexual activity. The manufacturers of condoms have a strong role to play in discouraging sexually promiscuous behaviour and teenage pregnancy. The UK has the highest rate of teenage pregnancies in Europe. Operating in such a sensitive market, there is a need to have clearly defined ethical marketing standards, which SSL International (2009) outline as follows:

'As part of its ongoing commitment to excellence, SSL International plc (SSL) is committed to producing the highest quality products across all the company's business areas. By consistently providing products that please customers and meet or exceed international standards, we will develop user loyalty and so achieve strong business performance. All employees are expected to help the company attain high quality standards. It is company policy to:

▶ 'maintain and keep records of a quality management system in accordance with international standards, regulations and directives;

▶ ensure all staff are fully trained and understand their role providing quality products and good customer service;

▶ provide products which fully meet customer requirements;

▶ develop or acquire products which are effective, safe and reliable;

▶ make sure the services and materials from suppliers are of consistent and sufficient quality;

▶ strive for continual improvement in performance, underpinned by the necessary financial resources, and highlight objectives and progress through internal and external communications.'

Durex's product range includes the Durex Play range of lubricants and personal sexual devices, in addition to its range of condoms including Fetherlite, Extra Safe, Avanti, Performa, Sensation, Select Flavours, and others.

Yet, according to consumer research, although nearly 70% of respondents felt at risk of contracting a STI, only 13% of consumers always use a condom and only a third of consumers use a condom with a new partner and so, not surprisingly, STIs are on the rise. Advertising campaigns do not seem to have made an impact on consumer behaviour. Part of the problem is that the advertising of condoms is restricted on British TV before 9 p.m. (except on Channel 4 where they must advertise after 7 p.m., and images of unwrapped condoms cannot be shown before 10.30 p.m.).

Given the high standard of product quality (condoms remain one of the safest forms of contraception), and the increasing incidence of STIs, how can SSL International promote greater condom use and stay within the regulations?

Source: SSL International (2009); Mintel (2008).

1 **The Fetherlite and Extra Safe products of the Durex range are reportedly the company's bestsellers. Why is it so important that product quality standards are of the highest levels possible in this product market?**

2 **Read the above company policy relating to product quality. How different is this policy from say that of a toy manufacturer?**

3 **What other products require strict adherence to product quality guidelines? Why?**

Products and Ethics

In marketing, we should consider whether or not goods/services comply with industry health and safety standards. Most multinational companies must follow guidelines on the quality of their offerings. Where consumers have concerns about a particular company's product quality, they can inform a government body that will then be charged with looking into the case on the consumer/customer's behalf. For instance, the US Consumer Product Safety Commission, the UK's Office of Fair Trading, Sweden's National Consumer Agency, Dubai Municipality's Central Laboratory Department (DCLD), and the EU's Health and Consumer Protection Directorate-General all perform this role. Most countries have organizations charged with ensuring product quality; however, the same degree of protection for ensuring service quality does not exist, probably because it is more difficult to monitor service quality, decide on minimum service standards, and determine whether or not breaches have been made. Agencies often provide consumer information. For instance, the UK's Office of Fair Trading provides information on such services as buying warranties for electrical goods, funerals, buying and selling your home, holidays, pawnbroking, ticket agents, and private dentistry—often industries where sharp practice occurs.

go online

Visit the **Online Resource Centre** and follow the weblinks to the various consumer agencies and government fair trading bodies to learn more about regulations and guidelines organizations must follow to ensure the health and safety of consumers and the conduct of fair business practice.

Breaches in product quality can be extremely serious leading to loss of life and grave injury, particularly in the food industry. For this reason, many countries have separate official bodies charged with ensuring food safety guidelines, e.g. the American Food and Drug Administration, Britain's Food Standards Agency, France's Agence Française de Sécurité Sanitaire des Aliments (AFSSA), and the bi-national Food Safety Australia and New Zealand (FSANZ) organization covering both territories. Pertinent examples of defective products causing death, injury, and inconvenience include the following examples:

1　Thalidomide, a tranquillizer administered to pregnant women, sold in the UK, under the brand name Distaval, by Distillers (Biochemicals) Limited. The drug caused limb deformity and death in around 10,000 babies throughout the world. The drug was withdrawn in 1961 but Diageo plc retains the moral responsibility to fund the Thalidomide Trust (until 2022), which makes compensation payments to Thalidomide victims in the UK.

2　Coca-Cola, the American global beverage manufacturer, was forced to recall 2.5m bottles of Coca-Cola, Coca-Cola Light, Fanta, and Sprite in Belgium when bottles of the product were found to be contaminated with defective carbon dioxide and/or pesticide, resulting in the hospitalization of 100 children (Campbell, 1999).

3　Dell was forced to recall 4.1m laptops of its notebook computers because its laptop batteries, manufactured by Sony, posed a fire risk. After other computer manufacturers such as Apple were also forced to recall the batteries, Sony's profits dived 94% in 2006 as they struggled to cope with the recall and the delayed launch of their PS3 console (Simmons, 2006).

Determining when to recall products is a difficult ethical problem. Where a risk of injury is likely, a product should be recalled. This might occur when:

- ▶ a serious consumer illness or injury is caused by the contamination of products;

- ▶ there are similar complaints of illness or injury that apply to a specific product;

- ▶ a design or manufacturing failure could result in potential harm to consumers; or

- ▶ there is defective product labelling that could result in potential harm to consumers; or where a product has been tampered with.

Pricing and Ethics

An important consideration in marketing ethics is whether or not the price of a product or service is set at a 'fair' level. Key considerations concern price gouging, where the price of a good or service is far higher than what is considered reasonable; **price discrimination**, where the price of a good or service is set differently for certain groups of people, and price collusion, where competitors work together to set prices or distribution targets to the detriment of consumers and excluded competitors.

Price gouging occurs when a company charges more than governments perceive is fair for products and/or services. It occurs when companies operate a demand pricing formula (see Chapter 9) that leads to very high prices being charged to customers/consumers. One example was the pricing of anti-retroviral drugs in South Africa prior to 2002, when major global pharmaceutical companies charged very high prices for AIDS/HIV treatments despite

Ayutthaya Historical City operates a discriminatory pricing policy for Thai and non-Thai nationals

Source; Ning Baines.

generic versions being available at far lower prices. Of course, the issue was complicated by these companies holding global patents but the issue raised by the world's media was not the legality of the situation but the morality of it.

Price discrimination involves the setting of different prices for different groups of people. Thus, price discrimination is frequently linked to market segmentation (see Chapter 6). It is not unethical as a practice in itself, where the product is differentiated for different groups. The practice is more questionable though where there is no difference in product or other element of the offer, and the price remains the only difference. Nevertheless, price discrimination is a frequent occurrence. For instance, a sign at Ayutthaya Historical City, Thailand, shows the price to visit the monument for foreigners as 30 baht (about 60p at the time of writing), but (in Thai script) only 10 baht (about 20p) for Thai nationals.

Price discrimination occurs on airlines, e.g. easyJet and Ryanair use so-called **yield management** systems to sell airline tickets based on different prices being charged dependent on the time of booking. Women's haircuts are frequently more expensive than men's, although there is some scope for the argument that the service provided is more attentive and takes longer. Universities frequently offer discriminatory aid and welfare packages and price their undergraduate and postgraduate courses differently depending on whether or not you are a home or overseas student (see Chapter 9). Women are provided with cheaper car insurance than men, e.g. in Britain, Diamond offer female-only car insurance, although they will allow their male partners to go on their female customers' insurance policies as named second drivers! Sheila's wheels, part of e-sure, also offer women-only insurance in the UK (and not Australia, as the name might suggest).

In some markets, this concept goes further, with every customer potentially paying a different price through **haggling**, which is also a form of discriminatory pricing (see Kimes and Wirtz, 2003). Haggling is more common in some markets than in others, e.g. house and car buying in Europe, and in some countries compared with others, e.g. Middle Eastern and South-East Asian countries such as Egypt, Morocco, Thailand, and Indonesia as opposed to West European countries like France, Sweden, and the UK. Do you remember the last time you haggled when buying something? Where were you? What were you buying?

Price Collusion

Amazingly, some of the world's most well-known companies have been fined for price collusion. In 2007, The US Department of Justice and the UK Office of Fair Trading fined British Airways £148m and £121.5m, respectively, after the company held illegal talks on at least six occasions between 2004 and 2006 with rival Virgin Atlantic over the introduction of fuel surcharges, charging customers an extra £5–60 over the period in question. This was the first time in corporate history that the USA and UK had brought simultaneous charges against a company for anti-competitive behaviour. Although Virgin Atlantic was also deemed to have acted anti-competitively, it was not fined because it reported the collusion (BBC News, 2007).

Another example was Japanese computer game and console maker Nintendo, which was fined €149m (£92.1m) by the European Commission for trying to rig the computer game market. The firm and seven distributors were found guilty of attempting to keep prices artificially high in some EU states over a seven-year period between 1991 and 1998. The fine, the fourth-highest ever handed out by the EU for a single offence at that time, was justified by Nintendo's role as 'the driving force behind the illicit behaviour', the Commission said.

Pretty in pink—Sheila's Wheels, the women-only insurance company

Source; © esure Services Limited.

Distributors, including Scotland-based retailer John Menzies, were fined €18m (BBC News, 2002; European Commission, 2002).

Price collusion is regarded as unethical because it results in unfair, and higher, charges to consumers, and it can stifle innovation—as competitors do not need to develop better competing product. Consumers do not, as a result, benefit from improvements in product quality and/or performance.

Universalism/Relativism in Marketing Ethics

Some cultures seem less likely than others to perceive ethical dilemmas. Ethicists say different groups of people see ethical situations from two perspectives. Under one perspective, ethicists suggest that universal ethical codes of practice should exist because there are some things that are simply 'wrong', no matter what the colour or creed of the people concerned (e.g. murder, bribery, extortion). This is termed universalism. The opposite argument, termed cultural relativism, suggests that different groups legitimately consider ethical situations from different viewpoints and that there is nothing wrong with this (e.g. gifts, corporate entertainment). The debate in international marketing ethics concerns itself principally with this dichotomy, i.e. cultural relativism versus ethical universalism.

How should a director of a company based in Western markets react when managers use bribery to ensure access to certain African markets for the company's products, on the basis that if those managers didn't act this way, other companies would, and they would win the business? Looking at the problem from a cultural relativist perspective, we would say such practice was ethically unacceptable, except where bribery might lead to a greater good, say widespread distribution of health-giving pharmaceuticals, whereas the universalist perspective would suggest that bribery is a fundamental ethical breach regardless of the circumstances. In a study outlining American–Thai differences in ethical behaviour, American marketers were found to be more likely to perceive unethical marketing behaviours to be more serious than their Thai counterparts (Marta and Singhapakdi, 2005). In a separate study of how Thai managers made ethical decisions, Singhapakdi *et al.* (2000a) stated that one approach to improve ethical decision-making by Thai marketing managers would be to encourage idealism—the degree to which individuals 'assume that desirable consequences can, with the "right" action, always be obtained', rather than relativism—where 'an individual rejects universal moral rules' (Forsyth, 1980).

Idealism could be encouraged through training programmes and communication of clear company policies on ethical matters. In another study, Singhapakdi *et al.* (2000b) found that there is a very strong positive relationship between a marketer's religiousness and their degree of idealism. In other words, the more religious you are, the more likely you are to hold universal ethical principles. Less religious marketers, according to these authors, tend to reject universal moral principles when evaluating situations with ethical content and the consequences of situations when examining them retrospectively.

A study of marketing ethics in Korea, Kim and Chun (2003) found that Koreans perceived the seriousness of ethical problems in order of importance as follows:

1 bribery;

2 unfair price increases;

3 exaggerated advertising;

4 sexual discrimination.

They found in their research that younger Koreans were less likely to perceive situations as having ethical content generally, whereas the older generation perceived less ethical content in bribery situations. Overall, they felt that such a lack of ethical concern would have a negative impact on Korean business, affecting company performance, if there was no education on marketing ethics.

Microcultural differences do seem to have a big impact on perceived ethical problems, according to a study of the Javenese, Batak, and Indonesian-Chinese managers in Indonesia (Sarwono and Armstrong, 2001). Each sub-culture responded differently to situations with ethical content. As a result, the authors suggested that Indonesian managers and expatriates operating in Indonesia should undergo cultural training including evaluating ethical perceptions held by local managers, together with the establishment of formalized codes of conduct.

Bribery

Transparency International, the international organization with a mission to stamp out bribery and corrupt practices around the world, published a Bribe Payers Index based on survey data to determine the propensity to bribe public officials from 21 leading exporting nations shortly after the OECD Convention on Combating Bribery of Foreign Public Officials in International Business Transactions was introduced. In 2008, the worst perceived offender was Russia, followed closely by China. The top four countries least likely to pay bribes were considered to be Belgium, Canada, The Netherlands, and Switzerland. The worst offending industries from which bribe payers were most likely to originate included public works and construction. Companies in these industries have a greater need to provide ethical training, confidential helplines, and robust whistle-blowing procedures, where employees can highlight ethical breaches to senior managers without fear of penalty. Where bribery occurs, it is used to attempt either to influence potentially adverse legislative programmes, or to obtain favourable contracts at another company's expense. In 1997, the OECD—the USA and 33 other countries—signed the OECD Convention on Combating Bribery of Foreign Public Officials in International Business Transactions.

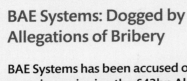

▶ Market Insight 19.5

BAE Systems: Dogged by Allegations of Bribery

BAE Systems has been accused of bribery ever since winning the £43bn Al Yamamah arms deal with Saudi Arabia in the late 1980s. The UK Serious Fraud Office (SFO) brought an action against BAE for corruption, which they were forced to abandon in 2006 after

Lord Goldsmith, the Attorney General, intervened to stop the case from proceeding, citing national security reasons and arguing that Saudi Arabia was threatening to stop intelligence-sharing as a result. In 2009, the company again came under pressure to accept a hefty fine to end other investigations by the SFO into cases of alleged bribery in deals made in South Africa, the Czech

▶ Market Insight 19.5   (continued)

Republic, Austria, and Tanzania in the late 1990s and early 2000s, but BAE has refused to accept the plea bargain. Whereas these cases relate to alleged past practices, BAE set up an independent ethics committee in 2007 chaired by Lord Woolf, a former Lord Chief Justice, to evaluate the company's ethics policies. In 2008, BAE announced a three-year programme to embed all 23 recommendations proposed in the Woolf report to improve the company's ethical conduct and to produce a principle-driven code of business conduct for all of BAE Systems approximately 97,000 staff worldwide. In 2010, BAE was handed over £286m in fines in the UK and the USA in a jointly coordinated UK/US government action to end years of corruption investigations into the company in what has been billed as a final settlement over allegations of corruption in arms deals in Saudi Arabia, Hungary, and the Czech Republic. The company outlines the following statement on bribery to its employees:

'Our Standard
We will not offer, give or receive bribes or inducements for any purpose whether directly or through a third party.

What it means to me (the employee)
Even the suggestion of corruption may damage the reputation of the company and affect its ability to do business. It may also bring the personal integrity of individuals into question. Employees, advisers, consultants, distributors, joint venture partners, or anyone else who may be acting on the company's behalf must not offer, make or receive bribes or corrupt payments. A bribe includes any payment, benefit or gift offered or given with the purpose of influencing a decision or outcome. The payment may not necessarily be of large value. It could be as simple as a lunch or an invitation to a sporting event.

We will not offer, give or receive any payment, benefit or gift which is intended or may be construed as a bribe. We are each responsible for knowing what our business guidance allows and what the law permits in our own country of operation regarding gifts and benefits given to or received from government officials, customers, suppliers or other third parties.

Always seek guidance and approval before accepting or giving any gift or entertainment. Such gifts must be formally recorded in a gift register. This ensures that we are transparent and that neither you, nor the company, can be accused of misconduct.'
Source: BAE Systems (2009a,b); O'Connell (2009); BBC News (2010).

1 Can you think of other companies that have been mired in bribery allegations? Look into the case of AB Bofors in Sweden, for example.

2 Is it *always* unethical to offer bribes when doing business? Might there be a circumstance in which it is ethical to give a bribe?

3 Is a gift always a bribe? What are legitimate entertainment expenses when doing business in the defence industry, especially in gift-giving cultures?

Skills for Employment

> ▶▶ It's not just about academic ability—as a graduate on our development programme you will need to have a unique mix of skills and behaviours. You'll share our values and principles and be passionate about our business. The programme isn't for everyone. The challenges the business will throw at you will mean you have to be confident, tenacious, resilient and flexible. ◀◀
>
> © Rachel Rotherham, Graduate Programme Manager, The Co-operative Group
>
> Visit the **Online Resource Centre** to discover more tips and advice on skills for the workplace.

Chapter Summary

To consolidate your learning, the key points from this chapter are summarized below:

■ **Define sustainable marketing and its implications for marketing practice.**

Sustainable marketing has been termed the third age of green marketing and is concerned with ecological, equitable, and economic impacts of marketing practice. It is concerned with ensuring that marketing activities meet not only existing generations' needs but that in doing so do not compromise meeting the needs of future generations. As a result, companies are reimagining marketing practices, for example, by recovering the costs of investment financing over longer payback periods, by emphasizing the full costs of purchase to customers, by considering all members of the supply chain and ensuring they are paid equitably, and by demarketing consumption to vulnerable groups of consumers or those who are overconsuming.

■ **Define the term ethics and apply the discipline to marketing.**

Marketing ethics is concerned with how marketers *go about* the management process of identifying, anticipating, and satisfying customer requirements profitably. In particular, it is the application of moral principles to decision-making in marketing and the consideration of the outcomes of those decisions.

■ **Explain the common ethical norms applied in marketing.**

Marketing ethics can be divided into normative and descriptive branches, which distinguish between how we *ought* to act in a given marketing decision-making situation and how people *actually behave* when making marketing decisions.

■ **Describe the role of ethics in marketing decision-making.**

Models of marketing decision-making outline the importance of the ethical content of a situation, the importance of 'significant others', employees' values, and the ethical training given by a company in line with its own ethical policy. Hunt and Vitell's model (2006) of marketing decision-making is perhaps the best known as it stresses the importance of considering what is the *right* thing to do (deontological norms) and what are the right intentions for us to follow (teleological norms).

■ **Analyse situations to determine the kind of ethical approaches that might be adopted.**

There are four main normative approaches to marketing decision-making, including managerial egoism (doing the *right* thing because it's the best thing to do), utilitarianism (doing the *right* thing for the largest number of people), deontological ethics (doing the *right* thing because it's the *right* thing to do), and virtue ethics (doing the *right* thing for everyone), each of which can be applied to any given ethical situation.

■ **Recognize how to apply an understanding of ethics to a company's marketing programmes.**

Ethical breaches can occur in all areas of an organization's marketing activity including distribution, pricing, promotion, and product policies. From a service's marketing perspective, the people and process components of the extended marketing mix are particularly appropriate as ethical breaches are often undertaken by employees who may or may not be following company ethical guidelines and codes of conduct appropriately.

Review Questions

1 What is sustainable marketing?

2 How will sustainable marketing impact on marketing practice?

3 How do we define marketing ethics?

4 What are the common ethical norms applied in marketing?

5 What role does ethics in marketing play in the marketing decision-making process?

6 What are key ethical considerations when pricing goods and services?

7 What are key ethical considerations when promoting goods and services?

8 What are key ethical considerations when distributing goods and services?

9 What are key ethical concerns when developing the product offering?

10 What are the problems associated with developing the socially responsible company?

11 What are key examples of company irresponsibility in marketing?

Worksheet Summary

Visit the **Online Resource Centre** and complete Worksheet 19.1. This will help you learn about the three 'E's of marketing sustainability—ecological, equitable, and economic.

Discussion Questions

1 Having read Case Insight 19.1, how would you advise The Co-operative Bank to continue to develop and promote its Ethical Policy? Think about how it could differentiate itself within the marketplace when other banks are increasingly adopting ethical approaches to promoting their businesses.

2 Reread the section of the chapter on normative ethics. Consider SSL International plc's condom product, Durex, designed to reduce the proportion of people sustaining sexually transmitted diseases (STDs) and women having unwanted pregnancies. To what extent might it be appropriate for SSL International to promote condom usage to young children, particularly in 1) Catholic countries and 2) African countries? Discuss this ethical problem using the following normative ethical approaches (check the definitions in the Glossary if necessary):

A managerial egoism—the principle of managerial self-interest;
B utilitarianism—the principle of the greater good for the greater number of people;
C deontological ethics—the principle of duty-based ethics.

3 **Consider whether or not it is unethical to act in the following ways in the following circumstances:**

  A You are a salesperson working for a Chinese construction company trying to secure a natural gas plant building contract in Qatar. You know that if you do not pay a 'commission' to the public official in charge of tendering for the project, you will not win the contract. Should you pay the 'commission' or do you have other choices of action?

  B You are a London-based banker. A potential new client in Dubai insists on taking you to a very exclusive restaurant at the Burj al Arab at her expense to discuss a loan she requires to purchase a new building for her rapidly expanding business. Should you accept?

  C You are a farmer supplying a large chain supermarket in Stockholm with selected prime cuts of meat products. The supermarket requests an upfront 'listing' fee of £20k before they can accept you as a supplier. You can then expect orders of millions of kronor. Should you pay the 'listing fee' to the supermarket? Would the situation be different in France? Why?

4 **Go online to find examples of companies that have a strong stance on sustainable marketing. Are there any common characteristics across these companies?**

Visit the **Online Resource Centre** and complete the Multiple Choice Questions to assess your knowledge of Chapter 19.

go online

References

AOSC (1990), 'Spill, the wreck of the *Exxon Valdez*: implications for safe transportation of oil', *Final Report*, Juneau, Alaska: Alaska Oil Spill Commission.

BAE Systems (2009a), 'Being a responsible company, what it means to us—code of conduct', retrieve from www.baesystems.com/BAEProd/groups/public/documents/bae_publication/bae_pdf_759of003_001.pdf, accessed 12 October 2009.

—(2009b), Woolf Committee Report, retrieve from http://ir.baesystems.com/investors/woolf/, accessed 18 October 2009.

Baines, P., and Worcester, R. (2005), 'When the British Tommy went to war, public opinion followed', *Journal of Public Affairs*, 5, 1, 4–19.

Bayne, K. (2005), 'The *Exxon Valdez* catastrophe', *The Times*, 26 May, 9.

BBC News (2002), 'Nintendo fined for price fixing', 30 October, retrieve from http://news.bbc.co.uk/2/hi/business/2375967.stm , accessed 18 October 2009.

—(2007), 'BA's price fix fine reaches £270m', Wednesday 1 August, retrieve from http://news.bbc.co.uk/1/hi/business/6925397.stm, accessed 18 October 2009.

—(2009), 'EU approves new Microsoft pledges', 7 October, retrieve from http://news.bbc.co.uk/1/hi/business/8294587.stm, accessed 18 October 2009.

—(2010), 'BAE Systems handed £286m fine in UK and US', 5 February, retrieve from http://news.bbc.co.uk/1/hi/business/8500535.stm, accessed 2 May 2010.

Baudrillard, J. (2005), *The System of Objects*, trans. James Benedict, London: Verso Books.

Boutin, X. and Guerrero, G. (2008), 'The "Loi Galland" and French consumer prices', June, retrieve from www.insee.fr/en/indicateurs_conj/archives/june2008_d1.pdf, accessed 18 October 2009.

Braga, F. and Nardella, M. (2003), 'Supply chain management, agricultural policies and anti-trust: the case of Parmagiano Reggiano and Grana Padano', *International Food and Agribusiness Management Review*, 5, 4.

Bridges, C.M. and Wilhelm, W.B. (2008), 'Going beyond green: the "why" and "how" of integrating sustainability into the marketing curriculum', *Journal of Marketing Education*, 30, 1, 33–46.

Buchholz, R. A. (1991), 'Corporate responsibility and the good society: from economics to ecology; factors which influence corporate policy decisions', *Business Horizons*, 34, 4, 19–31.

Campbell, T. (1999), 'Crisis management at Coke', *Sales and Marketing Management*, 151, 9, 14.

Corus (2009), 'Tata Steel wins Golden Peacock award for CSR', 26 February, retrieve from www.corusgroup.com/en/news/news/2009_tata_wins_golden_peacock, accessed 18 October 2009.

CIM (2005), 'Professional marketing standards: a guide for employers', retrieve from www.cim.co.uk/standards, accessed 17 October 2009.

Clasen, E. A. (1967), 'Marketing ethics and the consumer', *Harvard Business Review*, January–February.

Crane, A. (2000), 'Facing the backlash: green marketing and strategic reorientation in the 1990s', *Journal of Strategic Marketing*, 8, 277–96.

Daniels, J., and Holmes, C. (2005), *Responsible Marketing to Children: Exploring the Impact on Adults' Attitudes and Behaviour*, London: Business in the Community.

Deutsche-Welle (2004), 'Microsoft slapped with biggest fine in EU history', 24 March 2004, retrieve from www.dw-world.de/dw/article/0,,1149932,00.html, accessed 18 October 2009.

Economist (2009), 'Cut-throat competition', *The Economist*, September 19, p.83.

European Commission (2002), 'Commission fines Nintendo and seven of its European distributors for colluding to prevent trade in low-priced products', *European Commission Report IP/02/1584*, 30 October, retrieve from http://europa.eu.int/, accessed 3 December 2005.

Ferrell, O. C., and Gresham, L. G. (1985), 'A contingency framework for understanding ethical decision making in marketing', *Journal of Marketing*, 49 (Summer), 87–96.

Forsyth, D. R. (1980), 'A taxonomy of ethical ideologies', *Journal of Personality and Social Psychology*, 39, 1, 175–84.

Friedman, M. (1979), 'The social responsibility of business is to increase profit', in T. Beanchamp and N. Bowie (eds), *Ethical Theory and Business*, Englewood Cliffs, NJ: Prentice Hall.

Gaski, J. E. (1999), 'Does marketing ethics really have anything to say? A critical inventory of the literature', *Journal of Business Ethics*, 18, 315–34.

Hunt, S., and Vitell, S. J. (2006), 'The general theory of marketing ethics: a revision and three questions', *Journal of Macromarketing*, 26, 2, 143–53.

Kim, S. Y., and Chun, S. Y. (2003), 'A study of marketing ethics in Korea: what do Koreans care about?', *International Journal of Management*, 20, 3, 377–83.

Kimes, S. E., and Wirtz, J. (2003), 'Has revenue management become acceptable? Findings from an international study on the perceived fairness of rate fences', *Journal of Service Research*, 6, 2, 125–35.

Kumar, S. (2004), 'Victims of gas leak in Bhopal seek redress on compensation', *British Medical Journal*, 329, 366.

Laczniak, G. R., and Murphy, P. E. (1993), *Ethical Marketing Decisions: The Higher Road*, Englewood Cliffs, NJ: Prentice-Hall.

Maignan, I., and Ferrell, O. C. (2004), 'Corporate social responsibility and marketing: an integrative framework', *Journal of the Academy of Marketing Science*, 32, 1, 3–19.

Maitland, I. (2002), 'Priceless drugs: how should life-saving drugs be priced?', *Business Ethics Quartely*, 12, 4, 451–80.

Marta, J. K. M., and Singhapakdi, A. (2005), 'Comparing Thai and US businesspeople: perceived intensity of unethical marketing practices, corporate ethical values and perceived importance of ethics', *International Marketing Review*, 22, 5, 562–77.

Martin, R. L. (2002), 'The virtue matrix: calculating the return on corporate responsibility', *Harvard Business Review*, 80, 5–11.

Mautner, T. (ed.), (1999), *Penguin Dictionary of Philosophy*, London: Penguin.

Mintel (2008), 'Contraceptives—UK', July, London: Mintel International Group, retrieve from www.mintel.com, accessed 4 October 2009.

Nantel, J., and Weeks, W. A. (1996), 'Marketing ethics: is there more to it than the utilitarian approach?', *European Journal of Marketing*, 30, 5, 9–19.

O'Connell, D. (2009), 'BAE rejected £300m offer to settle "bribery" case', *The Sunday Times*, 4 October, 1.

O'Shaughnessy, N.J. and Baines, P. (2009), 'The selling of terror: the symbolisations and positioning of jihad', *Marketing Theory*, 9, 2, 227–41.

Pandit, R. (2005), 'What's next for Tata Group: an interview with its chairman', *McKinsey Quarterly*, 4.

Panorama (2000), 'Gap and Nike: no sweat?', *Panorama* programme disseminated 15 October, retrieve from http://news.bbc.co.uk/1/hi/programmes/panorama/970385.stm, accessed 18 October 2009.

Peattie, K. (2001), 'Towards sustainability: the third age of green marketing', *The Marketing Review*, 2, 129–46.

Rao, C. P., and Singhapakdi, A. (1997), 'Marketing ethics: a comparison between services and other marketing professionals', *Journal of Services Marketing*, 11, 6, 409–26.

Rawls, J. (1972), *A Theory of Justice*, Cambridge, Mass.: Harvard University Press.

Saeed, M., Ahmed, Z. U., and Mukhtar, S.-M. (2001), 'International marketing ethics from an Islamic perspective: a value-maximisation approach', *Journal of Business Ethics*, 32, 127–42.

Sarwono, S. S., and Armstrong, R. W. (2001), 'Microcultural differences and perceived ethical problems: an international business perspective', *Journal of Business Ethics*, 30, 41–56.

Schwarz, W. (1991), 'Nescafe boycott urged by synod', *The Guardian*, 16 July, 3.

Sen, F., and Egelhoff, W. G. (1991), 'Six years and counting: learning from crisis management at Bhopal', *Public Relations Review*, 17, 1, 68–93.

Simmons, D. (2006), 'Sony's rough ride through 2006', 17 November, retrieve from http://news.bbc.co.uk/1/hi/programmes/click_online/6157430.stm, accessed 18 October 2009.

Singhapakdi, A., Salyachivin, S., Virakul, B., and Veerayangkur, V. (2000a), 'Some important factors underlying ethical decision-making of managers in Thailand', *Journal of Business Ethics*, 27, 271–84.

—, Marta, J. K., Rallapalli, K. C., and Rao, C. P. (2000b), 'Towards an understanding of religiousness and marketing ethics: an empirical study', *Journal of Business Ethics*, 27, 305–19.

Smith, A. (1776), *The Wealth of Nations*, London: Penguin.

Spencer, R. (2008), 'China reveals 300,000 were made ill by tainted milk', 2 December, retrieve from www.telegraph.co.uk/news/worldnews/asia/china/3540917/China-reveals-300000-children-were-made-ill-by-tainted-milk.html, accessed 18 October 2009.

SSL International (2009), retrieve from www.ssl-international.com/copy/about/company/policies/quality.htm, accessed 4 October 2009.

Swartz, M., and Watkins, S. (2003), *Power Failure: The Inside Story of the Collapse of Enron*, London: Aurum Books.

Tata (2009a), *Corporate Social Responsibility*, retrieve from www.tatatiscon.co.in/index.asp, accessed 18 October 2009.

—(2009b), Tata Group Financials, retrieve from http://www.tata.com/htm/Group_Investor_GroupFinancials.htm, accessed 16 July 2010.

Usborne, D. (1997), 'Nike agrees code to ban sweated labour', *The Independent*, 15 April, 3.

van Dam, Y.K. and Apeldoorn, P.A.C. (1996), 'Sustainable marketing', *Journal of Macromarketing*, 16, 45-56.

World Commission on Environment and Development (WCED) (1987), *Our Common Future—The Brundtland Report*, Oxford: University University Press.

Glossary

accessory equipment goods these support the key operational processes and activities of the organization.

adaptation orientation a firm believes that each country should be approached separately as a different market, buying or conducting market research into the particular country and developing specific market strategy for that particular market.

Advergaming (or In-game Advertising IGA) the use of video and online games to advertise a product, organization, or an idea. Advergames encourage repeat website traffic and reinforce brand loyalty.

advertising a form of non-personal communication, by an identified sponsor, that is transmitted through the use of paid-for media.

aesthetic consideration of what is beautiful or in good taste, particularly in art.

affective a psychological term referring to our emotional state of mind. Values are affective because they are linked to our feelings about things.

aggregated demand demand calculated at the population level rather than at the individual level.

AIDA a hierarchy of effects or sequential model used to explain how advertising works. AIDA stands for *awareness*, *interest*, *desire*, and *action* (a sale).

AMA the American Marketing Association is a professional body for marketing professionals and marketing educators based in the USA, operating principally in the USA and Canada.

Ansoff's matrix the product–market matrix provides a useful framework for considering the relationship between strategic direction and market opportunities.

anti-foundational a reaction against the development of something or an idea. An attempt to destroy the foundations of something, someone, or an idea.

anti-globalization a term most commonly ascribed to the political stance of people and groups who oppose certain aspects of globalization. Participants are united in opposition to the political power of large corporations, as exercised in trade agreements and elsewhere, which they say undermines democracy, the environment, labour rights, national sovereignty, the third world, and other concerns.

a priori method segments are pre-determined using the judgment of the researchers beforehand.

art use of imitation, imagination, and creative flair, typically to make, draw, write, build, or develop something.

artefact a term derived from archaeology to denote man-made objects retrieved from dig sites but used in a metaphorical sense in marketing to indicate cultural meanings and brands.

asynchronous delays in interaction or information exchange ranging from a few seconds to even longer such as a few days or weeks.

ATR a framework developed by Ehrenberg to explain how advertising works. ATR stands for awareness–trial–reinforcement.

attitudes refers to mental states of individuals that underlie the structuring of perceptions and guide behavioural response.

audience fragmentation the disintegration of large media audiences into many smaller audiences caused by the development of alternative forms of entertainment that people can experience. This means that to reach large numbers of people in a target market, companies need to use a variety of media, not just rely on a few mass media channels.

backward integration when a company takes over one or more of its suppliers, it is said to be backward integrating. Taking over a buyer is forward integrating.

benefits sought by understanding the motivations customers derive from their purchases it is possible to have an insight into the benefits they seek from product use.

bid rigging when organizations conspire to determine which company or companies should win a particular contract.

blogs frequent web-based publication of personal thoughts and weblinks made accessible to a wider online audience that supports audience feedback.

Boston Box a popular portfolio matrix commonly also referred to as the BCG, developed by the Boston Consulting Group.

brand association a concept relating to the psychosocial meanings people are encouraged to make with some brands.

brand comprehension refers to what we understand the brand to mean to us, both in functional terms, i.e. how it solves a particular problem, and in emotional terms, i.e. whether or not we like it and how we relate to it.

brand equity this is a measure of the value of a brand. It is an assessment of a brand's physical assets plus a sum that represents their reputation or goodwill.

brand extensions a term used to refer to the process when a successful brand is used to launch a new product into a new market.

brand personality the set of human characteristics that some individuals associate with a brand.

brands products and services that have been given added value by marketing managers in an attempt to augment their products with values and associations that are recognized by, and are meaningful to, their customers.

breakdown method the view that the market is considered to consist of customers who are essentially the same, so the task is to identify groups that share particular differences.

briefs written documents used to exchange information between parties involved with the development and implementation of a campaign.

build-up method considers a market to consist of customers that are all different, so here the task is to find similarities.

business markets characterized by organizations that consume products and services for use within the manufacture/production of other products or for use in their daily operations.

business-to-business marketing activities undertaken by one company, which are directed at another.

buyclasses the different types of buying situations faced by organizations.

buyers people who select suppliers and manage the buying process whereby the required products and services are procured. They formally undertake the process whereby products and services are purchased once a decision has been made to procure them.

buying centre *see* decision-making unit.

buyphases a series of sequential activities or stages through which organizations proceed when making purchasing decisions.

call-to-action a part of a marketing communication message that explicitly requests that the receiver act in a particular way.

capital equipment goods buildings, heavy plant, and factory equipment necessary to build or assemble products.

capitalism the political system in which private (as opposed to governmental) capital and wealth is the predominant means of producing and distributing goods.

category killer a large retail outlet typically positioned in out-of-town locations, specializing in selling one area of products with the aim of killing off the competition, e.g. DIY stores such as Homebase in the UK, Toys Я Us in the USA, France, and UK, and other countries. These stores are characterized by a narrow but very deep product assortment, low prices, and few to moderate customer services.

causal research a technique used to investigate the relational link between two or more variables by manipulating the independent variable(s) to see the effect on the dependent variable(s) and comparing effects with a control group where no such manipulation takes place.

cause-related marketing a campaign where a company is linked to a charity or social cause with the express intention of building its own customer goodwill, providing the charity with an increase in resource, and the company with either a concomitant increase in sales of its product/service or a reputational dividend.

celebrity endorsement usually famous or respected members of the public, used by advertisers because they are perceived to be expert or knowledgeable or for their ability to display particular attractive qualities, to market specific goods and services.

channel conflict is where one channel member perceives another channel member to be acting in a way that prevents the first member from achieving its distribution activities.

choice criteria denotes the principal dimensions on which we select a particular product or service. For a hairdresser, this might be price, location, range of services, level of expertise, friendliness, and so on.

CIM the Chartered Institute of Marketing is a professional body for marketing professionals based in the United Kingdom, with study centres and members around the world.

classical conditioning a theory of learning propounded by Russian physiologist Ivan Pavlov, who carried out a series of experiments with his dogs. He realized that if he rang the bell before serving food, the dogs would automatically associate the sound of the bell (conditioned stimulus) with the presentation of the food (unconditioned stimulus), and begin salivating. Classical conditioning occurs when the unconditioned stimulus becomes associated with the conditioned stimulus.

click-through-rate (CTR) the amount of traffic on a website.

client brief a written document developed by clients to provide their appointed agencies with key information about their markets, goals, strategies, resources, and contacts. Client briefs should provide the agency with an insight into the client's task or communication problem that needs to be resolved.

co-branding the process by which two established brands work together, either on one product or service. The principle behind co-branding is that the combined power of the two brands generates increased consumer appeal and attraction.

co-created content (CCC) is the act of interacting, creating content or applications by at least two people.

coding in a survey when answers are assigned numbers in order to allow them to be more easily analysed; they can be either pre-coded (i.e. analysed before the questionnaire is completed, when answers are set) or coded after the questionnaire is filled in (when closed questions are used).

cognition knowing or perceiving something, typically as a result of rational thought.

cognitive a psychological term relating to the action of thinking about something. Our opinions are cognitive. Cognitions are mental structures formed about something in our minds.

cognitive dissonance a psychological theory proposed by Leon Festinger in 1957, which states that we are motivated to re-evaluate our beliefs, attitudes, opinions, or values if the position we hold on them at one point in time does not concur with the position held at an earlier period due to some intervening event, circumstance, or action.

collaborative exchanges a series of economic transactions between parties who have a long-term orientation towards, and are primarily motivated by, concern for each other.

collusion when a group of competitor companies conspire to control the market, often at the expense of the consumer/customer, and typically in relation to price fixing.

communication objectives goals related to the outcome of a marketing communications campaign. Normally set in terms of desired levels of awareness, perception, comprehension/knowledge, attitudes, and overall degree of preference for a brand.

communication the sharing of meaning created through the transmission of information.

competitive advantage achieved when an organization has an edge over its competitors on factors that are important to customers.

competitive intelligence the organized, professional, systematic collection of information, typically through informal mechanisms, used for the achievement of strategic and tactical organizational goals.

computer-assisted personal interviewing (CAPI) an approach to personal interviewing using a hand-held computer or laptop to display questions and record the respondents' answers.

computer-assisted telephone interviewing (CATI) an approach to telephone interviewing using a laptop or desktop computer to display the questions to the interviewer who reads them out and records the respondents' answers.

computer-assisted web interviewing (CAWI) an approach to online interviewing where the respondent uses a laptop or desktop computer to access questions in a set location to which the respondent must go. Questions are automatically set based on the respondents' answers.

conative a psychological term relating to our motivations to do something. Attitudes are conative because they are linked to our motivations to do things.

concentrated or niche marketing strategy recognizes that there are segments in the market;

however, a concentrated strategy is implemented by focusing on just one or two or a few market segments.

conceptual equivalence the degree to which interpretation of behaviour, or objects, is similar across countries.

consumer the user of a product, service, or other form of offering.

consumer durables manufactured consumer products that are relatively long-lasting (e.g., cars or computers) as opposed to non-durables (e.g. foodstuffs).

consumerism a movement concerned with the protection of consumers', as opposed to producers', interests.

consumer juries consist of a collection of target consumers who are asked to rank in order ideas or concepts put to them and to explain their choices.

consumer marketing refers to marketing activities undertaken directly to influence consumers, as opposed to other businesses.

context analysis the first stage of the marketing communications planning process. It involves the analysis of four main contexts (or situations), the customer, business, internal, and external environmental contexts, in order to shape the detail of the plan.

contextual advertising a form of targeted advertising, on websites, with advertisements selected and served by automated systems based on the content displayed to the user.

contracting is where a manufacturer contracts an organization in a foreign market to manufacture or assemble the product in the foreign market.

control (digital media) the ability of users in a computer-mediated environment to access content at will, and create, modify, and share the content.

control (distribution) means achieving the optimum distribution costs without losing decision-making authority over the product offering and the way it is marketed and supported. This is, therefore, about maximizing your capacity to manage all the marketing mix decisions.

control group a sample group used in causal research, which is not subjected to manipulation of some sort. *See* causal research.

convenience products non-durable goods or services, often bought with little pre-purchase thought or consideration.

convenience sampling a method used to select respondents where the criteria for selection are not restricted and the selection of the respondents is left entirely to the judgment of the researcher and the chance of selection beforehand is unknown.

convenience stores or corner shops offer a range of grocery and household items that cater for convenience and last-minute purchase needs of consumers. Key characteristics include: long opening times (e.g. 24/7), usually family run, and often belong to a trading group.

conversion rate a form of marketing communication to encourage, trial, purchase, or repeat purchase activity from a website.

cookie an electronic 'token', a piece of data or record transmitted by a webserver to a client computer. More simply put, a cookie is a small text file found on your hard drive that allows information about your web activity patterns to be stored in the memory of your browser.

corporate objectives the mission and overall business goals that an organization has agreed.

cost leadership a strategy involving the production of goods and services for a broad market segment, at a cost lower than all other competitors.

counter-implementation the behaviour employees exhibit when they resist tasks associated with the implementation of strategic programmes, whether intentionally or unintentionally, which is often motivated by anxiety.

coverage is about maximizing the amount of contact and value (or benefits) for the customer (in terms of product offering availability). This is the marketer's desire to have the product available to the maximum number of customers, in the maximum number of locations, across the widest range of times.

credit crunch a period of economic turbulence during which economies around the world entered recession. The turbulence was caused by lax regulation in banking markets and the improper securitization of sub-prime mortgage debt, which led to very low rates of inter-bank lending and difficulties in obtaining consumer and wholesale credit (hence the term credit crunch).

CRM *see* customer relationship management.

crowdsourcing when an organization outsources a function originally undertaken by its employees to a group ('crowd') of people either as an open call or in a more restricted way.

CSR (corporate social responsibility) typically a programme of social and/or environmental activities undertaken by a company on behalf of one or more of its stakeholders to develop sustainable business operations, foster goodwill, and develop the company's corporate reputation.

cultural anthropology a branch of study concerned with observing and explaining cultural differences in human behaviour.

culture the values, beliefs, ideas, customs, actions, and symbols that are learned and shared by people within particular societies.

customer the person who purchases and pays for (or initially requests and specifies, in the case of a non-financial transaction) a product, service, or other form of offering from a company or organization.

customer acquisition all marketing activities and strategies used by organizations to attract new customers.

customer portfolio matrix a 2 X 2 grid that is used to reflect the strength of the relationships between a buyer and seller and the profitability each account represents to the seller.

customer relationship lifecycle the stages a customer moves through during their relationship with an organization. These stages are customer acquisition, development, retention, and decline or termination.

customer relationship management (CRM) software systems that provide all staff with a complete view of the history and status of each customer.

customer relationship marketing all marketing activities and strategies used to retain customers. This is achieved by providing customers with relationship-enhancing products and/or services that are perceived to be of value and superior to those offered by a competitor.

customer retention all marketing activities and strategies used by organizations to keep current customers.

customer satisfaction a state of mind reached when the provision of goods or services meets or exceeds a customer's pre-purchase expectations of quality and service.

customized targeting strategy in which a marketing strategy is developed for each customer as opposed to each market segment.

cuts adverts are initially produced in cartoon format, complete with dialogue before they are produced, filmed, and edited.

deciders people who make organizational purchasing decisions, often very difficult to identify.

decision-making unit (DMU) a group of people who make purchasing decisions on behalf of an organization.

decision-making unit structure the attitudes, policies, and purchasing strategies used by organizations provide the means by which organizations can be clustered.

decoding that part of the communication process in which receivers unpack the various components of the message, and begin to make sense and give the message meaning.

deconstruction a form of textual analysis, associated with French philosopher Jacques Derrida, used to uncover hidden or 'absent' meanings by breaking the text down into privileged themes, then determining the binary opposites of those privileged themes, as the hidden or absent meaning of the work, and essentially proposing that this is what the work was really trying to say.

demographic key variables concerning age, sex, occupation, level of education, religion, and social class, many of which determine a potential buyer's ability to purchase a product or service.

deontological ethics a form of ethical approach by which the rightness or wrongness of an action or decision is not judged to be exclusively based on the consequences of that action or decision.

department store a large-scale retailing institution that has a very broad and deep product assortment (both hard and soft goods), with the provision of a wide array of customer service facilities for store customers.

descriptive ethics (ethnoethics) concerned with the study of system of beliefs and practices of a social group from the perspective of being outside that group.

descriptive research a research technique used to test, and confirm, hypotheses developed from a management problem.

desk research *see* secondary research.

dialectics the art of investigating the truth of opinions by considering that which is said from opposing perspectives to determine which of the two opposite forces is dominant.

dialogue the development of knowledge that occurs when all parties to a communication event listen, adapt, and reason with one another, about a specific topic.

diaspora peoples dispersed, or those who have emigrated, from their homeland. Often used in relation to the Jewish peoples.

differentiated targeting approach recognizes that there are several market segments to target, each being attractive to the marketing organization. To exploit market segments, a marketing strategy is developed for each segment.

differentiation a strategy through which an organization offers products and services to broad particular customer groups, who perceive the offering to be significantly different from, and superior to, its competitors.

Digital Asset Optimization (DAO) is the optimization of all an organization's digital assets for search, retrieval, and indexing.

digital value the means by which digital processes and systems can be used to provide customers with enhanced product and service value.

direct channel structure where the product goes directly from the producer to the final customer.

direct exporting involves the manufacturing firm itself distributing its product offering to foreign markets, direct to customers.

direct investment or foreign manufacture, some form of manufacture or production in the foreign or host country is sometimes necessary.

direct marketing a marketing communications tool that uses non-personal media to create and sustain a personal and intermediary-free communication with customers, potential customers, and other significant stakeholders. In most cases this is a media-based activity.

direct-response advertising advertisements that contain mechanisms such as telephone numbers, website addresses, email, and snail mail addresses. These are designed to encourage viewers to respond immediately to the ads. Most commonly used on television and known as DRTV.

direct selling is one of the oldest forms of retailing methods. Defined as the personal contact between a salesperson and a consumer away from the retailing environment, this type of retailing may also be called in-home personal selling.

discount retailers this type of retailer involves comparatively low prices as a major selling point combined with the reduced costs of doing business.

distribution *see* place.

distribution centres are designed to move goods, rather than just store them.

distribution channels can be defined as an organized network of agencies and organizations, which, in combination, perform all the activities required to link producers and manufacturers with consumers, purchasers, and users to accomplish the marketing task of product distribution.

distributor brands brands developed by the wholesalers, distributors, dealers, and retailers who make up the distribution channel. Sometimes referred to as own-label brands.

distributors organizations that buy goods and services, often from a limited range of manufacturers, and normally sell them to retailers or resellers.

diversification a strategy that requires organizations to grow outside their current range of activities. This type of growth brings new value chain activities because the firm is operating with new products and in new markets.

divest a strategic objective that involves selling or killing off a product when products continue to incur losses and generate negative cash flows.

DRIP the four primary tasks marketing communications can be expected to accomplish: differentiate, reinforce, inform, and persuade.

dumping some organizations need to get rid of some excess stock and, with limited opportunity for sales in domestic markets, seek overseas markets in which to offload some of this stock.

durable goods goods bought infrequently, which are used repeatedly, and which involve a reasonably high level of consumer risk.

dyadic essentially means two-way. A commercial relationship that is dyadic is an exchange between two people, typically a buyer and a seller.

early adopters a group of people in the process of diffusion who enjoy being at the leading edge of innovation and buy into new products at an early stage.

early majority a group of people in the process of diffusion who require reassurance that a product works and has been proven in the market before they are prepared to buy it.

ego a Freudian psychoanalytical concept, which denotes the part of our psyche that attempts to find outlets for the urges in our id, moderated by the superego.

elasticity an economic concept associated with the extent to which changes in one variable are related to changes in another. If a price increase in a good causes a decline in volume of sales of that good, we say the good is price elastic and specify how much. If it causes no change or very little change, we say it is inelastic.

electronic kiosks are being placed in shopping malls to assist the retailing experience. Mediated by hypermedia web-based interfaces, these computer-based retailing environments offer consumers increased self-service opportunity, wide product assortments, and large amounts of data and information aiding decision-making.

electronic marketing the process of marketing accomplished or facilitated through the application of electronic devices, appliances, tools, techniques, technologies, and or systems.

elicitation techniques a technique of disguising questioning so that information is obtained without the imparter recognizing what they are divulging.

email marketing direct marketing using electronic mail as a means directly to communicate messages, increase loyalty, and build relationships with an audience who have given their permission.

embedded (journalists) refers to the practice of the government inviting selected journalists to report on military activity while based inside units involved in major combat operations. This provides the journalist with some degree of protection, but exposes them to the same risks as the soldiers from enemy combatants. Thus, it could be argued that their journalistic impartiality is compromised as a result.

emotion mental feeling or disturbance arising instinctually.

encoding a part of the communication process when the sender selects a combination of appropriate words, pictures, symbols, and music to represent a message to be transmitted.

engagement refers to the moment of audience captivation, achieved through the delivery of messages that are relevant, meaningful, of interest and or which arouse curiosity.

environmental scanning the management process internal to an organization designed to identify external issues, situations, and threats that may impinge on an organization's future and its strategic decision-making.

ethnocentric approach views the domestic market (home market) as the most important, and overseas markets as inferior with foreign imports not seen as representing a serious threat.

ethnographic studies involve an approach to research that emphasizes the collection of data through participant observation of members of a specific sub-cultural grouping and observation of participation of members of a specific sub-cultural grouping.

ethnography a sub-discipline derived from cultural anthropology as an approach to research, which emphasizes the collection of data through participant observation of members of a specific sub-cultural grouping and observation of participation of members of a specific sub-cultural grouping.

evoked set a group of goods, brands, or services for a specific item brought up in a person's mind in a particular purchasing situation and from which he or she makes a decision of which product, brand, or service to buy.

exclusive distribution is where intermediaries are given exclusive rights to market the good or service within a defined 'territory', and thus a limited number of intermediaries are used.

exhibitions events when groups of sellers meet collectively with the key purpose of attracting buyers.

exploratory research a research technique used to generate ideas to develop hypotheses based around a management problem.

exporting manufacturing goods in one country, but selling them to customers overseas in foreign markets.

extensive problem solving occurs when consumers give a great deal of attention and care to a purchase decision where there is no previous or similar product purchase experience.

externalities negative impacts that arise as a result of economic development, e.g. on the environment, to society, and so on.

external pacing occurs where the speed, sequence, and content are controlled by the sender of the message/information.

face validity the use of the researcher's or an expert's subjective judgment to determine whether an instrument is measuring what it is designed to measure.

fatal accident rate (FAR) a term used in industrial safety engineering to denote how many people would be killed under certain hypothetical conditions. Typically, the FAR is calculated with a view to minimizing the number of fatalities in any given industrial scenario.

feedback a part of the communication process referring to the responses offered by receivers.

field marketing a marketing communications activity concerned with providing support for the sales force and merchandising personnel.

firmographics an approach to segmentation of business-to-business markets using criteria such as company size, geography, standard industrial classification (SIC) codes, and other company-oriented classification data.

fixed capital the cost of plant, equipment, and machinery owned by a business.

fixed costs costs that do not vary according to the number of units of product made or service sold. For instance, fixed costs in the pharmaceutical market would include manufacturing plant costs. In a service business like the airline industry, fixed costs would include the cost of purchasing the plane.

flippancy to be disrespectful by treating something serious with less importance than others expect.

focus a strategy based on finding gaps in broad market segments or in competitors' product ranges.

focus group *see* group discussion.

fragmentation refers to the process of the trivialization of our value systems and corresponding break-up of associated market segments, the break-up of consumer identities, and a weak commitment to a single consumer lifestyle.

franchise where a company offers a complete brand concept, supplies, and logistics to a franchisee that invests an initial lump sum and thereafter pays regular fees to continue the relationship.

franchising a contractual vertical marketing system in which a franchisor licenses a franchisee to produce or market goods or services to certain criteria laid down by the franchisor in return for fees and/or royalties.

full-service agencies refers to advertising agencies that provide their clients with a full range of services, including strategy and planning, designing the advertisements, and buying the media.

functional equivalence relates to whether or not a concept has the same function in different countries.

gatekeepers people who control the type and flow of information into an organization and in particular to members of the DMU.

generic brands brands sold without any promotional materials or any means of identifying the company.

geocentric approach sees the world as a single market—global, with the organization looking for global segments (e.g. ageing market) and global opportunities to rationalize communications, production, and product development.

geodemographic this approach to segmentation presumes that there is a relationship between the type of housing and location that people live in and their purchasing behaviours.

geographic in many situations the needs of potential customers in one geographic area are different from those in another area. This may be due to climate, custom, or tradition.

geographic proximity closeness of the market in physical terms to the domestic market.

global capability the willingness and capability to operate anywhere in the world with a direct result in global brand recognition.

globalization refers to increasing global connectivity, integration, and interdependence in the economic, social, technological, cultural, political, and ecological spheres.

government the system of organization of a nation state.

grey marketing is the unauthorized sale of new, branded products diverted from authorized distribution channels or imported into a country for sale without the consent or knowledge of the manufacturer.

gross domestic product (GDP) a measure of the output of a nation, the size of its economy. It is calculated as the market value of all finished goods and services produced in a country during a specified period, typically available annually or quarterly.

gross national product (GNP) total domestic and foreign added value claimed by residents of a state.

group discussions (or focus group) a group discussion on a pre-selected series of topics among 8–12 people introduced by a moderator where group members are encouraged to express their own views and interact with one another.

habit a repetitive form of behaviour, often undergone without conscious rational thought in a routine way. The processes underlying the routinization process are, however, voluntary (i.e. controllable) rather than reflexive (uncontrollable).

haggling when a customer argues with a supplier, usually a retailer, over the price to be paid for a good or service and is successful in obtaining a discount.

halal a term referring to what is permissible under sharia law and most typically used in Western societies when referring to permissible foodstuffs. For a food to be halal it must not contain alcohol, blood, or its by-products, or the meat of an omnivore or carnivore. In addition, where the food is from an animal, a Muslim must have pronounced the name of Allah before slaughtering the animal.

harvesting a strategic objective based on maximizing short-term profits and stimulating positive cash flow. Often used in mature markets as firms/products enter a decline phase.

hierarchy of effects (HoE) general sequential models used to explain how advertising works. Popular in the 1960s–1980s, these models provided a template that encouraged the development and use of communication objectives.

hold a strategic objective based on defending against attacks from aggressive competitors.

horizontal conflicts may arise between members of a channel on the same level of distribution.

host country a country in which international marketing operations take place.

hybrid channel conflict conflict is bound to occur when producers compete with retailers by selling through their producer-owned stores.

hybrid channel structure where some products go directly from producer to customers and others go through intermediaries.

hyperreality a play of illusions and phantasms, an imaginary world, made up of simulacra.

id a Freudian psychoanalytical concept referring to the part of our psyche that harbours our instinctual drives and urges.

incredulity disbelief of someone, or towards something (e.g. an idea).

in-depth interview a qualitative research method used to identify hidden feelings, memories, attitudes, and motivations of the respondents using a face-to-face interview approach.

indirect channel structure where the product goes from the producer through an intermediary, or series of intermediaries, such as a wholesaler, retailer, franchisee, agent, or broker, to the final customer.

indirect exporting takes place where production and manufacture of the product offering occurs in the domestic market and involves the services of other companies (intermediaries) to sell the product in the foreign market.

industrial marketing and purchasing group (IMP) IMP represents a school of thought about relationship marketing.

industry type (SIC codes) standard industrial classifications (SIC) are codes used to identify and categorize all types of industry and businesses.

inflation when prices rise.

influencers people who help set the technical specifications for a proposed purchase and assist the evaluation of alternative offerings by potential suppliers.

information utility the provision of information about the product offering before and after sales; it can further provide information about those purchasing it.

initiators people who start the organizational buying decision process.

innovators a group of people in the process of diffusion who like new ideas, are most likely to take risks associated with new products.

inseparability a characteristic of a service, one that refers to its instantaneous production and consumption.

intangibility a characteristic of a service, namely that it does not have physical attributes and so cannot be perceived by the senses—cannot be tasted, seen, touched, smelt, or possessed.

integrated marketing communications (IMC) a process associated with the coordinated development and delivery of a consistent marketing communication message(s) with a target audience.

integrative a growth strategy based on working with the same products and the same markets but starting to perform some of the activities in the value chain that were previously undertaken by others.

intensity of channel coverage number of intermediaries to use when they want or need it.

intensive a growth strategy that requires an organization to concentrate its activities on markets or products that are familiar.

intensive distribution means placing your product or service in as many outlets or locations as possible, in order to maximize the opportunity for customers to find the good or service.

intention in the consumer context, this is linked to whether or not we intend, are motivated to, purchase a good or service.

interaction model the flow of communication messages that leads to mutual understanding about a specific topic.

interactive marketing is more accurately described as creating a situation or mechanism through which a marketer and a customer (or stakeholders) interact, usually in real time.

interactivity as such interactivity is about the interchange between two or more parties (i.e. people or machines) and the effect one party has on the other's response.

intermediary an independent business concern that operates as a link between producers and ultimate consumers or end industrial users. It renders services in connection with the purchase and/or sale of the product offering moving from producers to consumers.

internal marketing the application of marketing concepts and principles within an organization. Normally targeted at employees with a view to encouraging them to support and endorse the organization's strategy, goals, and brands.

international marketing marketing activity that crosses national boundaries.

internet advertising a form of marketing communications that uses the internet for the purpose of 'advertising'; delivering marketing messages to increase website traffic.

internet marketing (or online marketing) a form of electronic marketing limited in technical context and thus a tool-based definition denoting the use of internet-based technologies only

(e.g. web, email, intranet, extranets, etc.) for marketing.

interstitials webpages that are displayed before an expected content page, often to display advertisements.

inverted production/consumption a concept indicating that the traditional pattern of consumption following production is changing in postmodern times, to a pattern of production following consumption, e.g. in reality television where the viewer votes on which contestants should enter/leave a particular show.

involvement the greater the personal importance a person attaches to a given communication message, the more involvement they are said to have with that communication.

irony to say one thing and mean the opposite is to be ironic, often as a form of humour. To have something happen to you when the opposite was expected indicates an ironic event.

joint venture when two organizations come together to create a jointly owned third company. This is an example of cooperative as opposed to competitive operations in international marketing.

juxtaposition to place items beside each other, with connotations of contrast.

KAM development cycle the development stages experienced by organizations as relationships with key account customers develop.

key accounts business customers who are strategically significant and with whom a supplier wishes to build long-lasting relationships.

KMV the 'key mediating variables', commitment and trust, used within the Morgan and Hunt model of relationship marketing.

laggards a group of people in the process of diffusion who are suspicious of all new ideas and whose opinions are very hard to change.

late majority a group of people in the process of diffusion who are sceptical of new ideas and only adopt new products because of social or economic factors.

lead generation activities undertaken by a company or organization to develop lists of prospective customers.

licensing a commercial process whereby the trademark of an established brand is used by another organization over a defined period of time, in a defined area, in return for a fee, to develop another brand.

lifestage analysis is based on the principle that people need different products and services at different stages in their lives (e.g. childhood, adulthood, young couples, retired, etc.).

limited line retailers this type of retailer has a narrow but deep product assortment and customer services that vary from store to store.

limited problem solving occurs when consumers have some product and purchase familiarity.

listing fee when a retailer charges a supplier a fee to allow the supplier to supply the supermarket. This fee is not typically related to any discounts already provided to the retailer. Such fees are illegal in France.

lobbying the process, employed by companies, charities, and third-party interest groups to develop and build relationships with regulatory and political bodies in order to influence legislation in their favour or in order to advance a particular cause.

logistics the process of transporting the initial components of goods, services, and other forms of offering, and their finished products, from the producer to the customer and then on to the consumer.

logistics management broadly, the coordination of activities of the entire distribution channel to deliver maximum value to customers: from suppliers of raw materials to the manufacturer of the product, to the wholesalers who deliver the product, to the final customers who purchase it.

maintenance, repair, and operating (MRO) products, other than raw materials, that are necessary to ensure that the organization is able to continue functioning. Often referred to as consumables.

management problem a statement that outlines a situation faced by an organization requiring further investigation and subsequent organizational action.

managerial egoism a form of ethical approach to the effect that a manager ought to act in his or her own best interests and that an action is right if it benefits the manager undertaking that action.

manufacturer brands created and sustained by producers who seek widespread awareness and distribution because there is high demand for these brands.

market development strategy involves increasing sales by selling existing or 'old' products in new markets, either by targeting new

audiences domestically or entering new markets internationally.

marketing communications mix the five key communication tools used by organizations to reach consumers and other organizations with product- and organization-based messages. These tools are advertising, sales promotions, public relations, direct marketing, and personal selling.

marketing communications planning framework (MCPF) a model of the various decisions and actions that are undertaken when preparing, implementing, and evaluating communication strategies and plans. It reflects a deliberate or planned approach to strategic marketing communications.

marketing ethics the analysis and application of moral principles to marketing decision-making and the outcomes of these decisions.

marketing information systems a system incorporating ad hoc and continuous market and marketing research surveys, together with secondary data and internal data sources, for the purpose of decision-making by marketers.

marketing metrics a measure or set of measures that senior marketers use to assess the performance of their marketing strategies and programmes.

marketing mix the list of items a marketing manager should consider when devising plans for marketing products, including product decisions, place (distribution) decisions, pricing decisions, and promotion decisions. Later, the mix was extended to include physical evidence, process, and people decisions to account for the lack of physical nature in service products.

marketing myopia a term coined by Harvard Business School professor Theodore Levitt to denote the mindset that some companies get into, when they completely fail to identify new competitors within their industry, which result from the development of substitute products and services.

marketing objectives marketing goals to be accomplished within a particular period of time. Usually referred to in terms of market share, sales revenues, volumes, ROI (return on investment), and other profitability indicators.

marketing research the design, collection, analysis, and interpretation of data collected for the purpose of aiding marketing decision-making.

market orientation refers to the development of a whole-organization approach to the generation, collection, and dissemination of market intelligence across different departments and the organization's responsiveness to that intelligence.

market segmentation the division of customer markets into groups of customers with distinctly similar needs.

market sensing an organization's ability to gather, interpret, and act on strategic information from customers and competitors.

materialism a tendency to place superior value on physical things rather than spiritual or intellectual values.

measurement equivalence concerns the extent to which the methods by which the researcher collects and categorizes essential data and information from two or more different sources are comparable.

media facilities used by companies to convey or deliver messages to target audiences. Media is the plural of medium.

media fragmentation the splintering of a few mainstream media channels into a multitude of media and channel formats.

media usage data on what media channels are used, by whom, when, where, and for how long provides useful insight into the reach potential for certain market segments through differing media channels, and also insight into their media lifestyle.

media vehicle an individual medium or media vehicle, used to carry advertising messages.

merchant a merchant performs the same functions as an agent, but takes ownership.

Metaethics a form of philosophical enquiry that treats ethical concepts and belief systems as objects of philosophical enquiry in themselves.

metanarrative an overarching belief system, held by the majority. Might also be called the received wisdom. Examples in contemporary Western society are the belief in the need to maintain capitalist economic growth and the need for continual scientific advancement.

metric in a marketing sense, a measure or set of measures used to assess the performance of marketing strategies and programmes.

mission a statement that sets out an organization's long-term intentions, describing its purpose and direction.

mixed price bundling when a product or service is offered together with another typically complementary product or service, which is also available separately, in order to make the original product or service seem more attractive (e.g. a mobile phone package with text messages and international call packages included in the price).

mobile marketing is the set of practices that enable organizations to communicate and engage with their audience in an interactive and relevant manner through any mobile device or network.

mod cons a colloquialism, an abbreviated form of modern conveniences.

mode of transfer a transmissive process is the method by which something travels from source or sender to a receiver.

modernist a style of thought based on logic and associated with the ideals and assumptions of the Enlightenment period advocating capitalist economic growth and the importance of scientific advancement among other ideals.

modified rebuy the organizational processes associated with the infrequent purchase of products and services.

multi-domestic competitive strategy an organization pursues a separate marketing strategy in each of its foreign markets while viewing the competitive challenge independently from market to market.

multiphrenic the many-minded consumer, who can want different kinds of consumer experiences all at the same time or at different times in the same sort of circumstances. A kind of consumer multiple personality disorder.

mystery shopping this form of research is designed to evaluate standards of customer service performance received by customers commissioned either within one's own organization or within a competitor's organization.

neoclassical economics refers to a meta-theory of economics predicated on delineating supply and demand based on rational individuals or agents each seeking to maximize their individual utility by making choices with a given amount of information.

new task the organizational processes associated with buying a product or service for the first time.

niche market a small part of a market segment that has specific and specialized characteristics that make it uneconomic for the leading competitors to enter this segment.

niche marketing strategy *see* concentrated.

noise influences that distort information in the communication process and, which, in turn, make it difficult for the receiver to correctly decode and interpret a message.

non-durable goods low-priced products that are bought frequently, are used just once, and incur low levels of purchase risk.

non-probability sampling a sampling method used where the probability of selection of the sample elements from the population is unknown. Typical examples include quota, snowball, and convenience sampling approaches.

non-staple in the grocery context, grocery products that are not a main or important food.

non-store retailers retailing activities resulting in transactions that occur away from the retail store.

non-tariff barrier obstacle to international markets from a non-fiscal source (e.g. product safety legislation).

normative ethics concerned with the rational enquiry into standards of right and wrong, good or bad, in respect of character and conduct and which ought to be accepted by a class of individuals.

observation a research method that requires a researcher to watch, and record, how consumers or employees behave, typically in relation to either purchasing or selling activities.

observational study a study where behaviours of interest are recorded, e.g. mystery shopping and mass transit studies.

omnibus survey a regular survey made up of questions from several different clients at any one time, each buying one or more questions and spreading the cost of the survey between them.

online marketing *see* internet marketing.

online retailing a type of electronic commerce used for business-to-consumer transactions and mail order forms of non-shop retailing.

operant conditioning a learning theory developed by B. F. Skinner, which suggests that when a subject acts on a stimulus from the environment (antecedents), this is more likely to result in a particular behaviour (behaviour) if that behaviour is reinforced (consequence) through reward or punishment.

opinion followers people who turn to opinion leaders and formers for advice and information about products and services they are interested in purchasing or using.

opinion formers people who exert personal influence because of their profession, authority, education, or status associated with the object of the communication process. They are not part of the same peer group as the people they influence.

opinion leaders people who are predisposed to receiving information and then reprocessing it in order to influence others. They belong to the same peer group as the people they influence, they are not distant or removed.

opinions refer to observable, verbal responses given by individuals to an issue or question and are easily affected by current affairs and discussions with significant others.

opportunity cost the difference between the revenues generated from undertaking one particular activity compared with another feasible revenue-generating activity.

organization or corporate strategy the means by which the resources of the organization are matched with the needs of the environment in which the organization decides to operate.

organizational buyer behaviour the characteristics, issues, and processes associated with the behaviour of producers, resellers, government units, and institutions when purchasing goods and services.

organizational goals the outcomes of the organization's various activities, often expressed as market share, share value, return on investment, or numbers of customers served.

organizational size grouping organizations by their relative size (MNCs, international, large, SMEs) enables the identification of design, delivery, usage rates, or order size and other purchasing characteristics.

organizational values the standards of behaviour expected of an organization's employees.

original equipment manufacturers (OEMs) the process whereby one company purchases and relabels a product and then incorporates it within a different product in order to sell it under a different (their own) brand name.

overt search the point in the buying process when a consumer seeks further information in relation to a product or buying situation, according to the Howard–Sheth model of buyer behaviour.

ownership utility goods are available immediately from the intermediaries' stocks, thus ownership passes to the purchaser.

pacing the control of the speed and sequence of information transfer.

paid inclusion can provide a guarantee that the website is included in the search engine's natural listings.

paid placement *see* pay per click.

panel study a study that uses information collected from a fixed group of respondents over a defined period of time.

pastiche something made up of different parts, especially in relation to music or picture, or a work of art composed in the style of another, often well-known, author.

pay per click (PPC) advertising that uses sponsored search engine listings to drive traffic to a website. The advertiser bids for search terms, and the search engine ranks ads based on a competitive auction as well as other factors.

perceived quality a relative subjective measure; we talk of perceived quality because there is no truly objective absolute measure of product or service quality.

perceived risk the real and imagined risks that customers consider when purchasing products and services.

perceived value a customer's estimate of the extent to which a product or service can satisfy their needs.

perception a mental picture in our heads based on existing attitudes, beliefs, needs, stimulus factors, and factors specific to our situation, which governs the way we see objects, events, or people in the world about us. Our perceptions govern our attitudes and behaviour toward whatever we perceive.

perceptual mapping a diagram, typically two-dimensional, of 'image-space' derived from attitudinal market research data, which display the differences in perceptions that customers, consumers, or the general public have of different products/services or brands in general.

performance environment organizations that directly or indirectly influence an organization's ability to achieve its strategic and operational goals.

perishability a characteristic of a service, one that recognizes that spare or unused capacity cannot be stored for use at some point in the future.

permission-based email marketing (opt-in) opt-in email or permission marketing is a method of advertising by electronic mail wherein the recipient of the advertisement has consented to receive it.

personal selling the use of interpersonal communications with the aim of encouraging people to purchase particular products and services, for personal gain and reward.

personality that aspect of our psyche that determines the way in which we respond to our environment in a relatively stable way over time.

PESTLE an acronym used to identify a framework that examines the external environment. PESTLE stands for the political, economic, socio-cultural, technological, legal, and ecological environments.

picking in the context of consumer behaviour, this word has a different meaning from the same term used in common parlance. It is the process of deliberative selection of a product or service from among a repertoire of acceptable alternatives, even though the consumer believes the alternatives to be essentially identical in their ability to satisfy his or her need.

pitch a presentation, made by competing agencies, in order to win a client's account (or business).

place or distribution is essentially about how you can place the optimum amount of goods and/or services before the maximum number of members of your target market, at times and locations that optimize the marketing outcome, i.e. sales.

political environment that part of the macroenvironment concerned with impending and potential legislation and how it may affect a particular firm.

polycentric approach each overseas market is seen as a separate domestic market, each country seen as a separate entity, and the firm seeks to be seen as a local firm within that country.

positioning the way that an audience of consumers or buyers perceives a product or service, particularly as a result of the marketing communications process aimed at a target audience.

positive morality a body of doctrine that is generally adhered to by a social group of individuals, concerning what is right and wrong, good and bad, in respect of character and conduct.

post hoc method the segments are deduced from research.

postmaterialist emphasizes self-expression and quality of life, as opposed to economic and physical security.

postmodernism a rejection of modernist thought and approach, which at its heart contravenes and pokes fun in an irreverent way at the existing received wisdom as a way to draw attention to itself and challenge the existing order.

pre-code in surveys, in order to speed up data processing, answers to questions are assigned a unique code e.g. male 1, female 2, so that they can be easily analysed.

pressure group an organisation that campaigns to change legislation in a particular area, and frequently seeks publicity to support its cause.

price the amount the customer has to pay to receive a good or service.

price collusion occurs when companies conspire to fix, raise, and maintain prices, and allocate sales volumes in their industries.

price discrimination occurs where the price of a good or service is set differently for certain groups of people.

price elasticity the percentage change in volume demanded as a proportion of the percentage change in price, usually expressed as a negative number. A score close to zero indicates that a product or service price change has little impact on quantity demanded, whereas a score of –1 indicates that a product or service price change effects an equal percentage quantity change. A value above –1 indicates a disproportionately higher change in quantity demanded as a result of a percentage price change.

price gouging occurs when a seller sets the price of a good or service at a level far higher than what is considered reasonable.

price sensitivity the extent to which a company or consumer increases or lowers their purchase volumes in relation to changes in price. Thus, a customer is price insensitive when unit volumes drop proportionally less than increases in prices.

pricing cues proxy measures used by customers to estimate a product or service's reference price. Examples include quality, styling, packaging, sale signs, and odd-number endings.

primary activities the five direct activities within the value chain necessary to bring materials into an organization, to convert them into final products or services, to ship them out to customers, and to provide marketing and servicing facilities.

primary research a technique used to collect data for the first time that has been specifically collected and assembled for the current research problem.

probability sampling a sampling method used where the probability of selection of the sample elements from the population is known. Typical examples include simple random, stratified random, and cluster sampling methods.

process of adoption the process through which individuals accept and use new products. The different stages in the adoption process are sequential and are characterized by the different factors that are involved at each stage.

process of diffusion the rate at which a market adopts an innovation. According to Rogers, there are five categories of adopters: innovators, early adopters, early majority, late majority, and laggards.

procurement the purchasing (buying) process in a firm or organization.

product anything that is capable of satisfying customer needs.

product class a broad category referring to various types of related products. For example, cat food, shampoo, or cars.

product differentiation when companies produce offerings that are different from competing firms.

product lifecycle the pathway a product assumes over its lifetime. There are said to be five main stages: development, introduction, growth, maturity, and decline.

product lines groups of brands that are closely related in terms of their functions and the benefits they provide.

product mix the set of all product lines and items that an organization offers for sale to buyers.

product placement the planned and deliberate use of brands within films, TV, and other entertainment vehicles with a view to developing awareness and brand values.

product usage segments are derived from analysing markets on the basis of their usage of the product offering, brand, or product category. This may be in the form of usage frequency, time of usage, and usage situations.

projective techniques an indirect questioning approach that encourages the subject to reveal their hidden feelings, values, and needs using word association, role playing, pictorial construction, and completion tests, for example.

promotion the use of communications to persuade individuals, groups, or organizations to purchase products and services.

promotional mix the combination of five key communication tools: advertising, sales promotions, public relations, direct marketing, and personal selling.

propaganda a technique used by a communicating party expressing opinions or activities to influence the opinions or activities of a receiving party, to direct them towards a pre-determined agenda drawn up by the communicating party, often using psychological and symbolic manipulations.

psychographic (lifestyles) analysing consumers' activities, interests, and opinions, we can understand individual lifestyles and patterns of behaviour, which in turn affect their buying behaviour and decision-making processes. On this basis, we can also identify similar product and/or media usage patterns.

psychological proximity perceived cultural and societal similarities between countries.

psychological reactance when a consumer perceives their freedom to pursue a particular decision alternative is blocked, wholly or partially, they become more motivated to pursue that decision alternative.

public relations a non-personal form of communication used by companies to build trust, goodwill, interest, and ultimately relationships, with a range of stakeholders.

pull strategies marketing communication strategies used to communicate directly with end user customers. These may be consumers but they might also be other organizations within a business-to-business context.

purchase situation this approach segments organizational buyers on the way in which a buying company structures its purchasing procedures, the type of buying situation, and whether buyers are in an early or late stage in the purchase decision process.

purchase/transaction data about customer purchases and transactions provides scope for analysing who buys what, when, how often, how much they spend, and through what transactional channel they purchase. This provides very rich data for identifiable 'profitable' customer segments.

purchasing power parity exchange rate a measure used to determine relative wealth of the population based on the cost of an identified basket of goods, which allows us to compare the wealth of one population with another.

pure price bundling when a product or service is offered together with another typically complementary product or service, which is not available separately, in order to make the original product or service seem more attractive (e.g. a CD with a music magazine).

push strategies marketing communication strategies used to communicate with channel intermediaries. These may be dealers, wholesalers, distributors, and retailers, otherwise referred to as the 'trade' or channel buyers.

qualitative research a type of exploratory research using small samples and unstructured data collection procedures, designed to identify hypotheses, possibly for later testing in quantitative research. The most popular examples include in-depth interviews, focus groups, and projective techniques.

quantitative research research designed to provide responses to pre-determined, standardized questions from a large number of respondents involving the statistical analysis of the responses.

quota a non-tariff barrier that limits imports to an agreed percentage of the market.

quota sampling a method used to select respondents where the criteria for selection are restricted but the final selection of the respondents is left to the judgment of the researcher and the chance of selection beforehand is unknown.

random digit dialling a procedure used in telephone interviewing to provide a randomized sample of telephone numbers using specialized software programs.

receivers individuals or organizations who have seen, heard, smelt, or read a message.

recession a fall in a country's gross domestic product for two or more successive quarters in any one year.

recognition when new images and words presented are compared with existing images and words in memory and a match is found.

reference group group that an individual uses to form his or her own beliefs and attitudes. A reference group can be positive, in which we align our opinions, attitudes, values, or behaviour with theirs, or negative, in which we are repelled by their behaviour and seek to dissociate our opinions, attitudes, values, and behaviour from theirs.

reference price the price band customers judge the purchase price of goods and services against in their own minds.

regional approach grouping countries together, usually on a geographical basis (e.g. Europe), and providing for the specific needs of consumers within those countries.

relationship intensity the depth of trust and commitment and overall feelings a customer perceives in a relationship.

relationship marketing the development and management of long-term relationships with customers, influencers, referrers, suppliers, recruiters, and employees.

relative price denotes the price of company A's product/service as a proportion of the price of a comparable product/service of typically the market leading company (B), or its nearest competitor (where A is the market leader).

reliability the degree to which the data elicited in a study are replicated in a repeat study.

research and development (R&D) the department within an organization in charge of using basic and applied science to develop new technologies, which are, in turn, used to develop new product, process, and service specifications, which can be leveraged into the development of new or reformulated customer propositions.

research brief a formal document prepared by the client organization and submitted to either an external market research provider (e.g. a market research agency or consultant) or an internal research provider (e.g. in-house research department) outlining a statement of the management problem and the perceived research needs of the organization.

research proposal a formal document prepared by an agency, consultant, or in-house research manager and submitted to the client to outline what procedures will be used to collect the necessary information, including timescales and costs.

resellers organizations that purchase goods and services from wholesalers, distributors, or even direct from producers and manufacturers, and make these available to organizations for consumption.

retail audit panel studies undertaken for retailers providing competitor (pricing) and market information.

retailers organizations that purchase goods and services from wholesalers, distributors, or even direct from producers and manufacturers, and make these available to consumers.

retailing all the activities directly related to the sale of goods and services to the ultimate end consumer for personal and non-business use. This is also called the retail trade.

retromarketing the practice of resurrecting a brand or iconic product from the past and re-marketing it.

reverse engineering the process of developing a product from the finished version (e.g. from a competitor's prototype) to its constituent parts rather than the usual approach from components parts to a finished product.

routinized response behaviour a form of purchase behaviour, which occurs when consumers have suitable product and purchase experience and where they perceive low risk.

sale force automation (SFA) occurs when firms computerize routine tasks or adopt technological tools to improve the efficiency or precision of sales force activities.

sales promotion a communication tool that adds value to a product or service with the intention of encouraging people to buy now rather than at some point in the future.

sampling equivalence concerns the extent to which samples representative of their populations are comparable across countries.

sampling frame a list of population members from which a sample is generated, e.g. telephone directories, membership lists.

scenarios pictures of the future that show how different outcomes may result from different strategic decisions.

science the pursuit of knowledge through a systematic method based particularly on the use of mathematical principles and the collection of empirical data, and in particular relation to studies of the natural world.

search directory is a database of information maintained by human editors. It lists websites by category and subcategory, usually based on the whole website rather than one page or a set of keywords.

search engine operates algorithmically or using a mixture of algorithmic and human input to collect, index, store, and retrieve information on the web and making it available to users in a manageable and meaningful way in response to a search query.

search engine marketing (SEM) a set of marketing methods to increase the visibility of a website in search engine results pages (SERPs).

search engine optimization (SEO) attempts to improve rankings for relevant keywords in search results by improving a website's structure and content.

search marketing a form of internet marketing that seeks to increase the visibility of websites in search engine results pages.

secondary research a technique used to collect data that have been previously collected for a purpose other than the current research situation. The process is often referred to as desk research.

selective contestability the ability to disaggregate generic markets into meaningful sub-markets or segments, select those most attractive, and position the product offering appropriately.

selective distribution where some, but not all, available outlets for the good or service are used.

selective exposure the process associated with how consumers screen out that information that we do not consider meaningful or interesting.

semiotics the science of signs and how they convey meaning in their representation.

service-dominant a core orientation that considers marketing to be a customer logic management process, in which services (not products) are the principal consideration for value creation.

service encounter an event that occurs when a customer interacts directly with a service.

service failure an event that occurs when a customer's expectations of a service encounter are not met.

service processes a series of sequential actions that lead to pre-determined outcomes when a service is performed correctly.

service quality a measure of the extent to which a service experience exceeds customers' expectations.

service recovery an organization's systematic attempt to correct a service failure and to retain a customer's goodwill.

services any acts or performances offered by one party to another that are essentially intangible and where consumption does not result in any transfer of ownership.

servicescape the stimuli impacting on the customer in the service environment. The concept is similar to the atmospherics present in a retail environment.

services mix a combination of different service elements, including products.

servitization an integrated bundle of products and services where the services are an integral part of the core product.

SERVQUAL a disconfirmation model designed to measure service quality. It is based on the difference between the expected service and the actual perceived service.

shopping product a type of consumer product that is bought relatively infrequently and requires consumers to update their knowledge prior to purchase.

signified a term used in linguistics, developed by Ferdinand de Saussure to refer to something being discussed, e.g. French sparkling wine from the Champagne region of France (*see* signifier).

signifier a term used in linguistics, developed by Ferdinand de Saussure to refer to sound images used to represent something, e.g. the spoken word 'champagne' is used to refer to the signified French sparkling wine (*see* signified).

simple random sampling a method used to select respondents from a known population frame using randomly generated numbers assigned to population elements.

simulacrum the concept of a copy without an original, advanced by French philosopher Jean Baudrillard. A simulacrum comes into being through successive image-change phases, and after successive reproduction an end copy is so different from the original that it is no longer a copy but a simulated version only.

SMART an approach used to write effective objectives. SMART stands for 'specific, measurable, achievable, realistic, and timed'.

snowball sampling a method used to select respondents from rare populations where the criteria for selection are based on referral from an initial set of respondents typically generated through newspaper advertisements or some other method and this set of respondents refers another set of respondents and the process repeats.

social anthropology the scientific discipline of observing and recording the way humans behave in their different social groupings.

social capital is the relations among individuals, the social structures, and networks within which we live and work.

social class system of classification of consumers or citizens, based on the socio-economic status of the chief income earner in a household, typically into various sub-groupings of middle- and working-class categories.

social enterprise a business the primary objectives of which are essentially social and the surpluses of which are reinvested for that purpose in the business or in the community, rather than dispersed to the owners.

social grade a system of classification of people based on their socio-economic group, usually based on the household's chief income earner.

social learning social learning theory, advocated by Albert Bandura, suggests that we can learn from observing the experiences of others, and in contrast with operant conditioning we can delay gratification and even administer our own rewards or punishment.

social or religious ethics concerned with what is right and wrong, good and bad, in respect of character and conduct. It does not claim to be established merely on the basis of rational enquiry and makes an implicit claim to general allegiance to something (e.g. God).

social web marketing a form of internet marketing that describes the use of social web channels and technologies or any online collaborative media for marketing, sales, public relations, and customer service.

society the customs, habits, and nature of a nation's social system.

spam unsolicited email, the junk mail of the twenty-first century, which clogs email servers and uses up much-needed bandwidth on the internet.

speciality products these are bought very infrequently, are very expensive, and represent very high risk.

sponsorship a marketing communications activity, whereby one party permits another an opportunity to exploit an association with a target audience in return for funds, services, or resources.

SPSS Statistical Package for the Social Sciences, a software package used for statistical analysis marketed by SPSS, a company owned by IBM.

stakeholders people with an interest, a 'stake', in the levels of profit an organization achieves, its environmental impact, and its ethical conduct in society.

standardization orientation a firm operates as if the world were one large market (global market), ignoring regional and national differences, selling the same products and services the same way throughout the world.

storage warehouses store goods for moderate to long periods.

storyboards before advertisements are made, an outline of the story that the advertisement will follow is produced showing key themes, characters, and messages.

STP process the method by which whole markets are subdivided into different segments, for targeting and positioning.

straight rebuy the organizational processes associated with the routine reordering of good and services, often undertaken from an approved list of suppliers.

strategic business unit an organizational unit, which, for planning purposes, is sufficiently large to exercise control over the principal strategic factors affecting its performance. Typically abbreviated to SBU, these might incorporate an entire brand and/or its sub-components, or a country region, or some other discrete unit of an organization.

strategic market analysis the starting point of the marketing strategy process, involving analysis of three main types of environment, the external environment, the performance environment, and the internal environment.

strategic procurement the long term assignment of a single, or a few suppliers, in order to develop mutually beneficial purchasing relationships.

stratified random sampling a method used to select respondents from known homogeneous sub-groups of the population where sub-groups are determined on the basis of specific criteria.

strong theory a persuasion based theory designed to explain how advertising works.

superego a Freudian psychoanalytical concept, which denotes the part of our psyche that controls how we motivate ourselves to behave to respond to our instincts and urges in a socially acceptable manner.

supermarket a large self-service retailing environment, which can be defined as a large-scale departmental retailing organization that offers a wide variety of differing merchandise to a large consumer base.

supply chains formed when organizations link their individual value chains.

support activities the indirect activities necessary to facilitate the primary activities within the value chain.

sustainable competitive advantage when an organization is able to offer a superior product to competitors, which is not easily imitated and enjoys significant market share as a result.

sustainable marketing marketing activities undertaken to meet the wants/needs of present customers without comprising the wants/needs of future customers, particularly in relation to negative environmental impacts on society.

switching costs the psychological, economic, time, and effort-related costs associated with substituting one product or service for another or changing a supplier from one to another.

SWOT analysis a methodology used by organizations to understand their strategic position. It involves analysis of an organization's strengths, weaknesses, opportunities, and threats.

synchronicity refers to the degree to which a user's input into a system/channel and the response they receive from the system/channel are simultaneous.

synchronous immediate or near so 'real-time' information exchange.

systematic random sampling a method used to select respondents from a known population using an initial random number generated to determine the first sample respondent but where each subsequent sample respondent is selected on the basis of the nth respondent proceeding,

where n is determined by dividing the population size by the sample size and rounding up.

tangibility possessing the characteristics of something that is physical, i.e. it can be touched. As a result, it has form. When products are tangible they have physical presence.

tariff barrier a financial tax on imported goods.

telemarketing or telesales is a form of non-store retailing where purchase occurs over the telephone.

teleological ethics a form of ethical approach by which the rightness or wrongness of an action or decision is judged primarily on the intentions of the decision-maker.

test marketing a stage in the new product development process, undertaken when a new product is tested with a sample of customers, or is launched in a specified geographical area, to judge customers' reactions prior to a national launch.

test markets regions within a country used to test the effects of the launch of a new product or service, typically using regional advertising to promote the service and pre- and post-advertising market research to measure promotional effectiveness.

time utility manufacture, purchase, and consumption might occur at differing points in time; time utility bridges this gap.

transactional exchanges short-term economic transactions between parties who are primarily interested in products and prices. Participants are primarily motivated by self-interest.

transfer pricing typically occurs in large organizations and represents the pricing approach used when one unit of a company sells to another unit within the same company.

translation equivalence the degree to which the meaning of one language is represented in another after translation.

transvections a term proposed by Alderson and Miles to denote the relationships (transactions) that occur in the development of a product or service that cross between company (i.e. product/service) ownership boundaries to produce a finished product or service. We would now consider such cooperation in manufacturing from the perspective of supply chain management as vertical integration or cooperation.

trust the degree of confidence that one person (or organization) has in another to fulfil an obligation or responsibility. Trust is achieved by reducing uncertainty, the threat of opportunism, and the possibility of conflict while at the same time building confidence, the probability of buyer satisfaction, and longer term commitment, necessary for effective relationships to be sustained.

t-test a statistical test of difference used for small randomly selected samples with a size of less than 30.

two-step model a communication model that reflects a receiver's response to a message.

undifferentiated approach there is no delineation between market segments, and instead the market is viewed as one mass market with one marketing strategy for the entire market.

user-generated content (UGC) content made publicly available over the internet which reflects a certain amount of creative effort and is created by users not professionals.

users people or groups who use business products and services once they have been acquired and who then evaluate their performance.

utilitarianism an ethical approach originally developed by English philosopher and social reformer, Jeremy Bentham, it postulates that an action is right if, and only if, it conforms to the principle of utility, whereby utility—pleasure, happiness or welfare—is maximized, or pain or unhappiness minimized, more than any alternative..

utility a measure of satisfaction or happiness obtained from the consumption of a specific good or a service in economic thought, typically measured as an aggregate.

validity the ability of a measurement instrument to measure exactly the construct it is attempting to measure.

value the regard that something is held to be worth, typically, although not always, in financial terms.

value chain a term determined by Michael Porter that refers to the various activities an organization undertakes and links together in order to provide products and services that are perceived by customers to be different and of superior value.

value creation the benefits derived by a customer resulting from the incorporation of particular products and services.

value proposition the benefits promised by a supplier if their products or services are used.

values values are beliefs of a social group or individual, which are held with some conviction, often learned from parents and formed early in life, and tend to change less and less with age, which define how we ought to behave.

variability a characteristic of a service, one that refers to the amount of diversity allowed in each step of service provision.

variable costs costs that vary according to the number of units of product made or service sold. For instance, variable costs in the pharmaceutical market would include plastic bottles in which to place the pills. In a service business like the airline industry, variable costs would include airline meals.

vertical conflict conflict between sequential members in a distribution network such as producers, distributor, and retailers over such matters as carrying a particular range or price increases.

vividness the ability of the technology to produce a sensually rich experience. Based on sensory breadth and depth.

viral marketing the unpaid peer-to-peer communication of often provocative content originating from an identified sponsor using the internet to persuade or influence an audience to pass along the content to others.

virtue ethics principally associated with Aristotle, this branch of ethics stresses the importance of developing virtuous principles, with 'right' character, and the pursuit of a virtuous life.

vision how an organization sees its future and what it wants to become.

weak theory a view that suggests advertising is a weak force and works by reminding people of preferred brands.

wholesalers stock products not services before the next level of distribution.

winner's curse terminology associated with the bidding process in commercial markets where a company ends up submitting a bid at a price that is unprofitable or not very profitable just to win the contract.

word-of-mouth a form of communication founded on interpersonal messages regarding products or services sought or consumed. The receiver regards the communicator as impartial and credible as they are not attempting to sell products or services.

working capital in accounting terms, this represents a company's short-term financial efficiency and is the difference between its current assets (what it owns) and its current liabilities (what it owes).

Wünderkind a German term referring in this context to an exceptionally bright (i.e. intelligent) person.

yield management a system for maximizing the profit generated from activities, which carefully manages price to ensure full utilization of capacity, while balancing supply and demand factors.

z-test a statistical test of difference used for large randomly selected samples with a size of 30 or more.

Index